Capitalism, Democracy, and
Ralph's Pretty Good Grocery

*

Capitalism, Democracy, and and Ralph's Pretty Good Grocery

*

JOHN MUELLER

PRINCETON UNIVERSITY PRESS

PRINCETON, NEW JERSEY

Library of Congress Cataloging-in-Publication Data

Mueller, John E.

Capitalism, democracy, and Ralph's Pretty Good Grocery / John
Mueller.

p.   cm.

Includes bibliographical references and index.

ISBN 0-691-00114-6 (cloth : alk. paper)

1. Capitalism.   2. Democracy.   3. Entrepreneurship.   I. Title.

HB501.M83   1999

330.12′2—dc21   99-17412

This book has been composed in Baskerville

The paper used in this publication meets the minimum
requirements of ANSI/NISO
Z39.48-1992 (R 1997) (*Permanence of Paper*)
http://pup.princeton.edu

Printed in the United States of America

1   3   5   7   9   10   8   6   4   2

To JAM and ESM,

to Karl, Michelle, Karen, Erik, Susan, Kraig,

and now Timothy,

and in memory of

Ernst A. Mueller, capitalist

✳ *Contents* ✳

✳ *Acknowledgments* ✳

For INVALUABLE advice, information, and pointed commentary at every step, I would like to thank Stanley Engerman with his encyclopedic mind and equally encyclopedic library. I also received beneficial comments and suggestions from Zoltan Barany, Edward Bird, William Bluhm, Randall Calvert, Henry Carey, Ian Fried, James Johnson, David Landes, Eric Larson, Christopher Lasch, Michael Mandelbaum, Henry Manne, Mira Marody, Karl Mueller, John Nye, Normand Perreault, Ronald Resnick, Richard Rosecrance, Andrew Rutten, Edward Schleh, Kenneth Shepsle, Randall Stone, and David Weimer.

I also benefited when portions of the argument were presented to conferences and seminars at Skidmore College; Ohio University; Harvard University; the University of California, Los Angeles; the University of California, Irvine; the University of Warsaw; the Hungarian School of Public Administration; the Comenius University; Bratislava, Slovakia; the Civic Education Project Conference at Košice, Slovakia; the Bucharest Social Science Center; the Bratislava Symposium; the Universidad Nacional Autónoma de México; the University of Rochester; the University of South Florida; the Council on Foreign Relations, Washington, D.C.; the University of Alberta; the Brookings Institution; the University of Texas; and the RAND Corporation. I am grateful to Michael Mandelbaum for guidance in publishing an earlier version of parts of the argument. Elements have appeared as well in *American Journal of Political Science* and are recycled here with permission. And thanks as well to Malcolm Litchfield and the crew at Princeton University Press for their wise care and help.

It is customary to excuse others, such as those listed above, from responsibility for the excesses and errors in the text, and I, of course, do so now. However, there is an important sense in which it could be said that the lapses in this book are the fault of William Riker. In the early stages I was able to bounce my ideas off him, but because of his death in 1993 I have had to flail on without his immeasurably valuable counsel. I miss it, and him, greatly, and so, I'm afraid, will the readers of this book.

Capitalism, Democracy, and
Ralph's Pretty Good Grocery

*

INTRODUCTION

*

CHAPTER 1

Capitalism and Democracy

IMAGES AND IMAGE MISMATCHES

Democracy and free-market capitalism seem to suffer from image problems—opposite ones, as it happens. Capitalism is much better than its image, while democracy has turned out to be much worse than its image.

Although capitalism is generally given credit, even by its many detractors, for generating wealth and for stimulating economic growth, it is commonly maligned for the deceit, unfairness, dishonesty, and discourtesy that are widely taken to be the inevitable consequences of its apparent celebration of greed. But capitalism actually tends, all other things being equal, systematically, though not uniformly, to reward business behavior that is honest, fair, civil, and compassionate, and it inspires a form of risk-taking behavior that can often be credibly characterized as heroic. Under capitalism, as it happens, virtue is considerably more than its own reward.

Meanwhile, democracy is often compared to an ideal image which envisions citizens actively participating on an equal basis and entering into a form of enlightened, or at any rate informed, deliberation about the affairs of governance. By contrast, actual democracy, notable chiefly for discord, inequality, apathy, hasty compromise, political and policy ignorance, and manipulative scrambling by "special interests," is found to be disappointingly wanting.

These disconnections can have significant, and often detrimental, consequences. The mismatch of capitalism with its image can damagingly impede economic growth and development, particularly if people in business misguidedly embrace the negative stereotype. The democracy mismatch can enhance cynicism about the process—even to the point of inspiring a yearning to scrap the system entirely—and it can rouse minorities into misguided rebellion, lead to an undue pessimism about the prospects for democracy's growth and acceptance, and facilitate the efforts of tyrants to postpone or avoid political change.

CAPITALISM

The negative image of capitalism has been propagated for centuries—perhaps forever—not only by communists and socialists, but by the church, popular culture (including capitalist Hollywood), intellectuals, aristocrats, and often by capitalists themselves—particularly those who have lost out in the competitive process. Swindlers and moral monsters sometimes do become rich (in both capitalist and noncapitalist systems), but contrary to the popular image, capitalism by its nature rewards many important values that are highly regarded. Of course, capitalism generally inspires business behavior that is industrious, prescient, diligent, and prudent. But modern business has also found that such slogans as "Honesty is the best policy; it's also the most profitable," "A happy employee is a productive employee," and "The customer is always right" are not only sound advice, but are part of a broader set of self-effacing moral principles that are, on average, wealth-enhancing.

This is not to say that capitalists necessarily and always behave virtuously. Many, indeed, have lied, cheated, behaved shabbily, and let themselves be dominated by arrogance and ego. But such behavior is, on balance, on average, in general, and in the long run, economically foolish.

Nor does the existence of the capitalist virtues mean that there is no room for government or that capitalism can be entirely self-regulating. Societies may find it useful, usually for noneconomic reasons, to use tax policy and regulation to redistribute wealth, to aid the unfortunate, to enhance business competition, to provide for public health and safety, and to control undesirable side effects or externalities such as air pollution. They may also consider it desirable to ban or inconvenience the propagation of certain goods and services for which there is profitable demand, like drugs, pornography, prostitution, cigarettes, liquor, and gambling. And it should be emphasized that capitalists do not pursue virtue to the point of stupidity—the virtues do not require one to cut an unfavorable deal, keep open an unproductive factory, trust a swindler, or retain excess workers when business slackens.

But virtue is, on balance and all other things equal, essentially smart business under capitalism: nice guys, in fact, tend to finish first. Not all successful capitalists are necessarily nice people. Some scoundrels become rich even as some heavy smokers escape cancer. But, as nonsmoking is, in general, good for your health, virtuous business behavior is, in general, good for your bottom line.

Capitalism's image mismatch causes problems. In particular, it can hamper economic development because the often unacknowledged capitalist virtues are necessary, or at least extremely helpful, for economic growth: without them, countries can remain mired in poverty. Fortunately, because it generally furnishes a business with a competitive advantage, virtuous behavior can arise from normal competitive pressures and does not need to be artificially imposed by outside authority. For that to happen, however, someone must lead—innovate—by actually behaving virtuously, and sometimes the widely accepted negative image of capitalism keeps this from coming about. Virtuous business practices may be financially beneficial in the long term, but in part because of the traditional image, this reality may not be obvious to the very capitalists who stand to benefit from them.

DEMOCRACY

Democracy suffers from the opposite image problem.

The nature of democracy has been debated for several millennia as philosophers and other thinkers have speculated about what it is, what it might become, and what it ought to be. After democracy actually came into being in large countries some two hundred years ago, however, a remarkable dilemma emerged.

On the one hand, democracy worked rather well by the values

most theorists and idealists have held to be important. When compared to competing forms of government and methods of organizing society, democracy has characteristically produced societies that have been humane, flexible, productive, and vigorous, and under this system leaders somehow emerged who—at least in comparison with your average string of kings or czars or dictators—have generally been responsive, responsible, able, and dedicated.

On the other hand, democracy didn't come out looking the way many theorists and idealists imagined it could or should. It has been characterized by a great deal of unsightly and factionalized squabbling by self-interested, shortsighted people and groups, and its policy outcomes have often been the result of a notably unequal contest over who could most adroitly pressure and manipulate the system. Even more distressingly, the citizenry seems disinclined to display anything remotely resembling the deliberative qualities many theorists have been inclined to see as a central requirement for the system to work properly. Indeed, far from becoming the attentive, if unpolished, policy wonks hoped for in many of the theories and images, real people in real democracies often display an almost monumental lack of political interest and knowledge.

Inspired by their optimal illusion and confounded by grim democratic reality, disappointed theorists, idealists, and reformers have generally taken one of two courses to deal with this mismatch. One is to retreat into the vapor and to conclude that democracy, as it turns out, doesn't really exist at all, but that it is just some sort of attractive, impossible dream. Thus, in February 1990, Czechoslovak president Václav Havel patiently explained to the Congress of the world's oldest democracy that the country it represented still hadn't made it and, actually, never would: "As long as people are people, democracy in the full sense of the word will always be no more than an ideal; one may approach it as one would a horizon, in ways that may be better or worse, but it can never be fully attained. In this sense you are also merely approaching democracy."[1]

The other recourse is to stress dilemma. For example, one analysis first notes that, "in theory, a democracy requires knowledgeable citizens," and then goes on to observe that "for the last two hundred years the United States has survived as a stable democracy, despite continued evidence of an uninformed public." It labels this "the paradox of modern democracy."[2]

Inspired by such thinking, democratic theorists, idealists, and reformers have sought to perfect the system, attempting to refashion democratic institutions and their human constituents to more nearly approximate the qualities called for in the theories, and in the ideals that derive from some of the theories. As part of this effort, reformers have frequently tried to make the process more politically equal and to control the play of "special interests." They have also sought to elevate the human race to match such rarified images as the one projected by John F. Kennedy: "Democracy is a difficult kind of government. It requires the highest qualities of self-discipline, restraint, a willingness to make commitments and sacrifices for the general interest, and it also requires knowledge."[3]

By contrast, I will suggest in this book that the fault in the mismatch between democracy's image and its reality lies more with the ideals than with the facts—more in the stars than in ourselves, as Shakespeare's Cassius didn't put it. After all, if my theory tells me the moon is made of green cheese and then a spacepersonage inconveniently brings home a lunar soil sample composed entirely of dirt and rock, even my closest friends would be disinclined to label the resulting conundrum a "paradox." Most people would be so ungracious as to suggest that my theory has been soundly disconfirmed. And they would probably deride any effort to implant the moon with green cheese in order to make it more closely resemble my theory.

Perfect democracy, in my view, is an oxymoron, and the undisciplined, chaotic, and essentially unequal interplay of "special interests" is democracy's whole *point*. Moreover, the patent and inevitable contrast between the hopelessly ideal images of democracy—such as those so sonorously promulgated by Havel and Kennedy—and its rough-and-ready reality often inspires the very cynicism about the democratic deliberative process that the idealists continually bemoan and profess to want to reduce. Bismarck once observed that "If you like laws and sausages, you should never watch either one being made." It is a fundamental property—and perhaps defect—of democracy that citizens may watch laws being made, and when they do so they often compare democracy to its mystical, Kennedyesque image and then reject the actual process with righteous disdain, even outrage, opaquely dismissing it as bickering and correctly, but uncomprehendingly, labeling it "politics as usual." Effectively, however, politics as usual is the same as democracy in action.

RALPH'S GROCERY

Ralph's Pretty Good Grocery in Lake Wobegon, a Minnesota town invented by humorist Garrison Keillor, operates under a sensible, if rather unexhilarating, slogan: "If you can't get it at Ralph's, you can probably get along without it." (The opposite slogan, hopelessly hyperbolic, promotes Alice's Restaurant—in some other town, presumably—where "you can get anything you want"—excepting Alice.) It is a central perspective of this book that democracy and capitalism, despite their image problems, have triumphed in part because people have essentially been persuaded to accept a version of Ralph's slogan: the systems can't supply everything, but on balance, people have effectively if sometimes rather reluctantly concluded, if you can't get it with democracy and capitalism, you can probably get along without it.

For example, it is possible to create a society in which order reigns supreme, but experience suggests that society in the process loses flexibility, responsiveness, intellectual growth, and individual freedom. Although they complain about it all the time, democrats have basically decided that, even though democracy is distressingly, profoundly, and necessarily messy and disorderly, it's better, on balance, to get along without the blessings an orderly society can bring.

And capitalism revels in—indeed, seems viscerally to require—a considerable amount of insecurity, risk, and uncertainty. It may be possible, at least in principle, to design an economy in which privilege, station, prices, employment, and economic security are comfortably, reassuringly, and authoritatively preserved. Since these approaches tend to stifle the economically invigorating effects of selfish acquisitiveness, however, they lead to slower growth and to less wealth overall. Experience seems to suggest, then, that it is better to learn to get along without total security.

In addition, capitalism and democracy are in important respects viscerally unequal and unfair at the systemic level, if not at the personal level.

This condition stems naturally and inevitably from the related facts that both systems leave individuals free to pursue their interests and that some will simply do better at the pursuit than others. Thus even when everyone is equally free, some people under democracy will be more successful at manipulating the political system in a beneficial way (extracting favors from it, getting it to support their pet policy projects). And under capitalism, some will prosper because they are more successful at providing goods or services other people happen to value at the moment.

This inequality of result will often emerge because people are differently abled: differently skilled, differently capable. For some people, particularly for those who are inclined to overrate their own abilities, this condition is deeply unpleasant, even unbearable, and they can become resentful.

But inequality will sometimes also result not so much because people are differently abled but because they are differently lucky: they succeed because they just happen to know or be related to someone who can help them out at a crucial point, because they just happen to be in the right place at the right time, or because an ill-considered, even foolish, gamble just happens to pay off. In an important sense, then, freedom is notably unfair. Democracy is perhaps worse off than capitalism with regard to the issues of equality and fairness. Capitalism does not profess to make everyone equally wealthy, but the beguiling, ringing notion that "all men are created equal" has often been taken to suggest that some sort of political equality is central to democracy; the system can be seen, then, to be viscerally hypocritical.

But if capitalism and democracy can't supply orderliness, certainty, equality, security, and systemic fairness and are thus (only) pretty good in the Ralph's Grocery sense, their image mismatches make them pretty good in opposite senses. Democracy compared

11

to its image is (merely) *pretty* good, while capitalism compared to its image is (actually) pretty *good*.

The laid-back and markedly unromantic perspective of the folks at Ralph's Pretty Good Grocery—unexhilarating perhaps, but blessedly free of misdirecting hyperbole—is relevant to the development of democracy and capitalism in another sense as well.

It seems to me that an institution is likely to be fundamentally sound if it can function adequately when people are rarely, if ever, asked to rise above the ignorance and selfishness with which they have been so richly endowed by their creator. Or, putting it a bit more gently, since human beings are a flawed bunch, an institution will be more successful if it can work with human imperfections rather than requiring first that the race be reformed into impossible perfection. Therefore, it may well actually be fortunate that democracy does not require people to be good or noble, but merely to calculate what is best for them or what they take to be in the best interest of society, and to seek to further these interests if they happen to be so inclined, while capitalism raises selfishness and acquisitiveness to dominant motivations. And it may be desirable that democracy and capitalism are about as romantic, to apply Charlotte Brontë's phrase, as Monday morning.

THE PLAN OF THE BOOK

This book traces—and celebrates—the ascendancy, the curious and unexhilarating triumph, of the pretty good over the ideal, the certain, the harmonious, the romantic, the orderly, the secure, the divine, the transcendent, and the sublime. It assesses the consequences of the image mismatches, and it also seeks to explain the remarkable growth of the political institution of democracy and the economic institution of free market capitalism over the last two centuries or so.

Fundamentally, it seems to me, capitalism will emerge if people are left free to be acquisitive, and democracy can come about if people are left free to complain and to organize complainants. Neither quality, it seems, is terribly difficult to inspire. The United

States Constitution, for example, nowhere deems it necessary to call upon people to complain or to pursue their selfish interests; rather it simply and wisely restricts the government's ability to abridge those instincts. It follows from this perspective that democracy and capitalism should not be terribly difficult to institute or to maintain, that no elaborate prerequisites are necessary for them to emerge, and that they are not fundamentally fragile.

Capitalism is considered first.

Chapter 2 begins by focusing on the individual behavior the system tends to inspire and reward—honesty, fairness, civility, compassion, and heroism. The motivation for these virtues is essentially insincere under capitalism—virtuous business behavior is inspired not by the virtues' intrinsic value but by the quest for profit. However, in practice it is very difficult for people to fake the virtues over extended periods of time, and therefore people who are genuinely nice guys tend, on balance, to finish first and to flourish. At the same time, in its rapacious desire to supply people with any product or service they happen to think they want at the moment (and can afford to pay for) capitalism can lead to a kind of cultural materialism that many people may consider unpleasant, distasteful, and even debased. It can also generate considerable economic inequality and what may be taken to be an unfairness of result. Government can be used to soften the cultural, fairness, and equality problems somewhat, but to a substantial degree they are built in.

Chapter 3 assesses the many sources of capitalism's negative image over the ages. Socialists, communists, religious leaders, storytellers, intellectuals, and aristocrats have all contributed to that image. But it also seems that the image may have been substantially built on reality because businesspeople, insufficiently unaware of the profitability of the business virtues, may often have behaved in an economically foolish manner—that is, they have behaved as if capitalism's negative image were correct.

Chapter 4 evaluates the consequences of capitalism's negative image on economic development. It argues that for growth to happen people in business need to abandon that image and to behave virtuously. However, since virtuous business behavior turns out actually to be profitable, it is generally not necessary to impose such behavior from above by establishing policing institutions: rather, it can emerge from normal competitive activity. Because the profitability of virtuous business behavior has apparently often not been obvious, however, a business innovator must discover the economic value of virtue and then act upon this important discovery. Others, out of competitive pressures, will then imitate. The chapter also suggests that a rise of business virtue may well have been an important element in the amazing economic development much of the world has experienced over the last two centuries. And it concludes that virtue-enforcing institutions are more nearly the result of the rise of virtue than its cause.

Chapter 5 proposes that the world's economic development in the future is likely to be enhanced even further because of the rise in credibility and effectiveness of the economics profession and because politicians and policymakers are increasingly willing to take the profession's often politically painful advice. Over the last century or two, economists and like-minded idea entrepreneurs seem to have substantially sold four important propositions, the acceptance of which, among other things, suggests the demise of empire as well as major (and perhaps minor) international war. These propositions are: the growth of economic well-being should be a dominant goal; wealth is best achieved through exchange rather than through conquest; international trade should be free; and economies do best when the government leaves them substantially free.

The chapter also observes that, although the rise of capitalism over the last two centuries has coincided with, indeed has importantly helped to cause, a very substantial betterment of the human condition in what we now call the developed world, happiness has failed to soar in tandem there—in fact, people seem simply to have taken the remarkable economic improvement in stride and have deftly found new concerns to get upset about. In an important sense, then, things never get better. However, the seemingly unquenchable quest for economic improvement may be useful—crucial, even—for economic advance.

A similar assessment is then carried out for democracy.

Chapter 6 defines democracy as a form of government which is necessarily and routinely (though not necessarily equally) responsive, and it argues that democracy comes about when the people effectively agree not to use violence to overthrow the leadership and when the leadership leaves them free to try to overthrow it by any other means. Much of the real stuff of what goes on in a democracy comes from petition and pressure, not from elections and legislative voting—indeed, it seems to me that it is possible, though not necessarily desirable, to have an effective, responsive democracy even without elections. Democracy is a form of government in which people are left (equally) free to become politically unequal, and it works because it is characterized not by political equality, active participation by the citizenry, and something resembling majority rule and consensus, but by political inequality and substantial apathy—effectively, by minority rule and majority acquiescence. Because of this characteristic, democracy has been able to survive a potential defect that theoreticians had previously considered terminal: democracy was able to coopt, rather than to alienate, the rich.

The chapter concludes by comparing democracy to its competitors and argues that, for all its scruffiness in practice, democracy seems superior (though, of course, far from perfect) in governmental effectiveness and in choosing leaders. It is also fairly good at protecting minorities: democracy does often persecute minorities but, unlike other forms of government, it routinely allows the persecuted to work to change things, a process that has often been remarkably effective even for tiny minorities which are regarded with disgust and contempt by the majority. There is also strength in that democracy can work quite well with real people and generally does not require a great deal from them.

Chapter 7 seeks to ferret out some of the consequences of the mismatch between democracy's image and its reality. It begins by assessing the quests for equality, for deliberative consensus, for active participation, and for an enlightened citizenry, and it concludes that these quests, while not necessarily undesirable, are substantially hopeless—there is no conceivable way, for example, that the average factory worker can have remotely as much political clout as the average industrial leader or newspaper columnist. Moreover the quest itself can inspire cynicism when citizens are continually asked by reformers to compare grim democratic reality with its idealized image.

The chapter also suggests that the overselling of equality can be profoundly harmful for democracy when that notion is extrapolated to the economic realm, because the only way economic equality can be fully achieved in a democracy is by destroying democracy itself. Another danger is that the image may inspire minorities logically to conclude that, if democracy is truly about equality and majority rule by an active citizenry, they face certain persecution in a democracy and must rebel to protect themselves. The chapter ends with some cautionary comments about the field of transitology which often holds out ideals for new democracies to seek, an approach that is not only often unrealistic, but one that can inspire a damaging short-range perspective.

Chapter 8 traces the rise of democracy. It argues that, contrary to the ideal image—an image which has often inspired a considerable pessimism about its prospects and one which can furnish authoritarian leaders with a convenient excuse for neglecting reform—democracy is really quite a simple and easily graspable form of government. As Americans should surely know by now, any dimwit can do democracy. If this is true, it follows that the chief barrier to democracy's expansion has not been any inherent technical, historical, social, cultural, economic, or anthropological difficulty, but the effective exertions of antidemocrats. Sometimes these people can be, simply, thugs with guns. But at other times they have been people projecting a different vision that can be arrestingly beguiling. Democracy's growth, it appears, has not been the result so much of broader economic, social, or cultural developments; rather, it has been the consequence of a sort of marketing process that has been characterized by product testing, by luck, by fashion leadership, by the convenient self-destruction of competing institutions, and particularly by the effective propaganda endeavors of idea entrepreneurs—politicians, writers, and organized interest groups.

At base, I suggest, democracy is merely an idea (a pretty good one, as it happens), and about the only requirement for its acceptance is that people be persuaded to take it up. Accordingly, the world could just as well have embraced it centuries earlier. Or the world could have missed it entirely, and we'd still be living, like most of the human race for most of its existence, under the capricious rule of queens and kings and eunuchs.

The concluding chapter juxtaposes democracy and capitalism to ferret out connections between them. It argues that, while capitalism can exist without democracy as has often been noted, recent experience in some postcommunist countries demonstrates that democracy can exist without capitalism as well. The chapter also suggests however, that, for better or worse, democracy has been associated of late with capitalist prosperity. This undeserved connection could lead to destructive disillusion in some places, but it might also help democratic development if the world is really in the process of massive economic improvement. There could also be trouble in some areas in the casual and popular, if undeserved, connection of democracy and capitalism with crime.

While democracy may not be necessary for capitalism, democracy probably does benefit capitalist growth. It does so by furnishing property owners some potential remedy against governmental confiscation, by establishing the rule of law, by routinely encouraging an openness and transparency of information, by allowing *all* interest groups (rather than just a privileged subset of them) to attempt to influence government policy, by providing a mechanism for removing defective leaders, and, at least in recent years, by furnishing an atmosphere of stability and predictability. Finally, democracy and capitalism, it seems, are similar in that they can often work pretty well even if people generally do not appreciate their workings very well. As human institutions, in fact, that paradoxical quality may be one of their most important strengths.

17

CAPITALISM

*

Capitalism's Image

CAPITALISM is routinely assumed to inspire in its practitioners behavior that is deceitful, deceptive, cowardly, unfair, boorish, and lacking compassion. I assess this negative image in this chapter and conclude that, however popular, the image is fundamentally misguided. On the contrary, capitalism systematically encourages and rewards business behavior that is honest, fair, civil, and compassionate, and it also encourages, and often rewards, behavior that in many cases should reasonably be considered heroic. Moreover, people who are genuinely honest, fair, civil, and compassionate are more likely to succeed in business than those who simply feign such qualities. Or, more generally, nice guys tend to finish first.

It is important to stress at the outset that I am *not* arguing that all capitalists are always honest, fair, civil, and compassionate. Rather, under capitalism, honest, fair, civil, and compassionate business behavior is, on average, economically advantageous, and those who behave in another way will generally do less well. Indeed, in later chapters I will argue that capitalists have often engaged in economically foolish behavior because they apparently have not understood the advantages of the business virtues, and furthermore, that such behavior has often hampered economic growth.

The chapter includes a consideration of the capitalist culture so many people find objectionable and of the inequality and apparent unfairness of result that competitive capitalism often fosters at the systemic level. It appends a discussion of capitalism's central dependence on the gambling instinct and thus, in effect, on business behavior that is essentially irrational and effectively altruistic.

Capitalism is an economic arrangement in which the government substantially leaves people free to pursue their own economic interests as long as they do so without physical violence (including physical theft). That is, capitalism emerges when it is possible and legal (or effectively legal) to make a profit nonviolently. Nathan Rosenberg and L. E. Birdzell suggest that capitalism can be viewed as an arrangement where economic investment is primarily carried out by individuals who will gain if they are right, will lose if they are wrong, and "lack the economic or political power to prevent at least some others from proving them wrong." Interestingly, with minor modifications, this might also be used as a definition of democracy.[1]

There has been a lively debate over the degree to which the government should intervene in the free market. By the end of the twentieth century, this debate seems substantially to have been won by those who argue that it is best for long-term economic growth if the free market is allowed to prevail and if the government moves toward reducing its hold on the economy—though there remains a wide (and sometimes reluctant) acceptance of the notion that the government will still play a notable role particularly by providing for public safety, furnishing a safety net for losers, establishing an effective legal structure, and regulating undesirable side effects like pollution. Although I will mostly not engage in that debate in this book, an appreciation for its course is a central concern of chapter 5.

THE CAPITALIST VIRTUES

In assessing the capitalist virtues, I will not assume that capitalists are saintly in any sense, but rather that they are essentially impelled as envisioned by their caricaturists: their highest goal and motivation is the acquisition of financial wealth—greed, it is often called. Moreover, although they must eschew violence under capitalism, the system does in principle leave them generally free to lie, cheat, swindle, collude, misrepresent, price-fix, engage in fraud, be discourteous, and attempt to stifle competition. I assume, however, a *long-term acquisitiveness* in all this—the concept of "short-term greed" is really quite oxymoronic after all.

From time to time some individual capitalists may be impelled as well by motivations that are generally more esteemed. But the point to be developed here is that, under capitalism acquisitiveness alone encourages certain kinds—though not necessarily *all* kinds—of behavior that are generally held to be moral, virtuous, and admirable. And, if the community generally values honesty, fairness, civility, and compassion, the sensible capitalist will, inspired by acquisitiveness, seek to furnish them—or at least seem to furnish them—in full, unambiguous measure.

Capitalists often spend a great deal of money on advertising, but as most would readily agree, the most generally effective advertisement is word of mouth. Thus the best way to get ahead (that is, to become rich) in the long term is to establish a good word-of-mouth reputation. Conversely, a wealth-seeking capitalist can be severely punished, often at little cost to the aggrieved, if the word of mouth becomes unfavorable. As a business slogan puts it, "A customer who goes away happy will tell three friends; a customer who goes away unhappy will tell ten." This phenomenon gives individual customers and fellow deal-makers a considerable enforcement mechanism. They can punish behavior they find unsuitable by refusing again to deal with, and by bad-mouthing, someone they have had a bad experience with or have heard unfavorable things about.

But virtuous business dealings often make sense even in cases where repeated dealings are unlikely. A stork clerk who is civil to a one-time customer, for example, is more likely to make a sale than one who is not.

Honesty

It is impossible, or nearly so, to create a perfect written contract, and it would be wildly inefficient to require even an imperfect one for every transaction. It would be even more inefficient to have contracts regularly adjudicated in court. Therefore, in its general day-by-day dealings, business requires, and inspires, integrity, honesty, trustworthiness, and reliability in order to achieve its vaunted efficiency and growth. As the Better Business Bureau puts it, "Honesty is the best policy. It's also the most profitable." That is, although it is certainly possible to make a quick profit by cheating and lying, the best prospects for secure, long-term wealth derive from honest business practices.

Thus, in a classic study of actual business practices Stewart Macaulay found that the strong norm, "One does not welsh on a deal," is enforced because "both business units involved in the exchange desire to continue successfully in business and will avoid conduct which might interfere with attaining this goal." In consequence, each is "concerned with both the reaction of the other party" and "with his own general business reputation." Similarly, George Stigler observes that "A reputation for candor and responsibility is a commercial asset"; Donald McCloskey that "One must establish a relationship of trust with someone in order to persuade him"; and Benjamin Franklin that "Tricks and treachery are the practice of fools that have not wit enough to be honest." Or, as Gregory Kavka puts it crisply, "Time wounds all heels."[2]

The Quakers, a religious group that requires absolute honesty from its members, enjoyed a competitive advantage because of this quality: all other things equal, customers preferred a business run by Quaker because they knew they could trust the Quaker to be honest. They discovered "that if they sent a child to their shops for anything, they were as well used as if they had come themselves," and the shopper's inquiry became, "Where is there a draper or shopkeeper or tailor or shoemaker or an other tradesman that is a Quaker?"[3] Accordingly, Quakers became prosperous. But, because the image of capitalism holds that one can only become wealthy by cheating, Quakers have regularly been accused of being hypocrites: as Balwant Nevaskar observes, "although they established a reputation as reliable merchants, the Quakers were often suspected of being shrewd, conniving, sly, and dishonest."[4]

The experience of the legendary P. T. Barnum furnishes another arresting example. He is best known for supposedly having coined the phrase, "There's a sucker born every minute." Not only did Barnum never make this statement, but it would be out of character.[5] Although a few of his famous "humbugs" early in his career did have a degree of (rather good-natured) fraud about them, he became wealthy in the circus not by bilking "suckers" but by providing a good, honest show that people appreciated and were quite happy to patronize year after year.

Before Barnum, circuses were very often run by fly-by-night cheats: ticket takers would regularly short-change customers; pickpockets, working on a commission, would roam the grounds; "Monday men" would steal the wash from clotheslines or burglarize homes when the citizenry was at the performance or watching the circus parade; shows would be frauds; games would be fixed.[6] Quick profits were made this way, but soon the entire industry was on the verge of extinction because its customers, through experience, no longer were foolish enough to attend.

Barnum was one of the circus innovators who changed all that. He used honest ticket takers, hired private detectives to police pickpockets, and spent a lot of time and money creating what he (with characteristic understatement) labeled "The Greatest Show on Earth." Whether customers always fully agreed with that representation, they did find the show, and the whole experience of attending the circus, enjoyable, and they were happy to come back year after year. Accordingly, Barnum and such like-minded circus managers as the Ringling Brothers, applying their "Sunday School" approach to business, soon became far richer than the cheats who had preceded them. As journalist George Ade observes, they "found the business in the hands of vagabonds and put it into the hands of gentlemen." They "became circus kings of the world by adopting and observing the simple rule that is it better to be straight than crooked."[7]

In his spirited pamphlet and popular lecture, "The Art of Money Getting," Barnum stresses that integrity "is more precious than diamonds or rubies" and argues that "the most difficult thing in life is to make money dishonestly," since "no man can be dishonest without soon being found out" and "when his lack of principle is discovered, nearly every avenue to success is closed against him forever." Therefore, even "as a mere matter of selfishness," he concludes, "honesty is the best policy."[8]

This conclusion holds also for businesses which generally do not service the same customer repeatedly. Since a taxi driver is unlikely ever to see the rider again, it is to the driver's short-term advantage to cheat the rider. However, where this is common, the taxicab system as a whole gets a reputation for fraud, and people take cabs only when they have no other choice. Thus the industry as a whole makes much less money than it would if it had a reputation for honesty and integrity.[9] Consequently, taxi companies have often found it very much in their interest to establish industry regulations which keep their own drivers from cheating. In Mexico City, government-certified taxicabs cost *more* than other ones, and do an excellent business with visitors who are willing to pay extra for the simple favor of assured honesty.

This pressure for honesty even affects that most legendary of fly-by-night operators, the traveling salesman. The lessons of the unusually insightful musical, *The Music Man,* are instructive in this regard. The chief protagonist, Harold Hill, is a skilled con artist who descends on a town to pump up the populace, sell a decrepid line of band uniforms, and then vanish into the night before the townsfolk can discover they have been bilked. But behavior like that gives a bad reputation to traveling salesmen as a group, and another traveling salesman (a heavily laden representative of the Gibraltar Anvil Company) informs on him in an Iowa town out of a feeling that he's "got to protect the good reputation of the traveling fraternity from that swindler" because "he spoiled Illinois for me, but he's not going to spoil Iowa." Perhaps unfortunately, such self-policing, if self-interested, crusaders were insufficient to resuscitate the reputation of the fraternity, and traveling salesmen of his sort, precisely because of their soiled reputation, have largely gone, or been forced by government, out of business—something that almost happened to circuses in the nineteenth century. That is, they have made much less money than they would if they had been able to establish a reputation for honesty.

Something similar may be happening currently to telephone marketing. Because of public complaints about fraud (and also, of course, about nuisance), regulators are coming closer to banning it outright.[10] On the other hand, telephone ordering—where a customer initiates the contact—has expanded enormously. This business overwhelmingly relies on trust and honesty; if it gained any sort of reputation for fraud or unremediable misrepresentation, it could die out quickly.

The quality known as "transparency" is closely related to honesty, and it is also generally good for business sometimes even in single transactions. Suppose that two different people are selling two comparable used cars, but that one seller is evasive about the car and its repair history while the other is very open, supplying repair records and even pointing out defects, like a cigarette burn in the back seat, that the prospective buyer may have overlooked. The transparent seller will have a competitive advantage and will be far more likely to get the sale—in many cases even if the selling price is a bit higher.

Although they are often disparaged as formulaic and lacking in variety and humanity, chain and franchise stores have an even greater incentive for integrity than individual stores: a customer who feels cheated in one store is unlikely to patronize not only that one, but any other in the chain or franchise. Conversely, of course, a pleased customer will tend to venture into any store in the chain. Something similar can be said about brand-name merchandise.[11]

The principle can be writ larger. In general, as the organizers of the Better Business Bureaus strongly suggest, it is harmful to business as a whole for swindlers to be able to flourish since they taint all business, reducing sales in the aggregate. Honest business may be bad for swindlers, but it is good for business generally and therefore, as will be suggested more fully in chapter 4, for economic growth.

Honesty is also important in successfully (that is, profitably) managing a firm and in dealing with employees. For manager James Autry, "Honesty is the single most important attribute in a manager's relationship with employees and fellow workers." Management guru Peter Drucker strongly concurs, and emphasizes that integrity is "the one absolute requirement of a manager." If a manager "lacks in character and integrity—no matter how knowledgeable, how brilliant, how successful—he destroys. He destroys people, the most valuable resource of the enterprise. He destroys spirit. He destroys performance." Fellow workers "may forgive a man a great deal: incompetence, ignorance, insecurity, or bad manners. But they will not forgive his lack of integrity. Nor will they forgive higher management for choosing him."[12]

Fairness

Since people value fairness, a vendor or deal-maker who is perceived to be unfair will do less well in the long run than one who appears to be fair. Unfair treatment can also inspire the feeling in others that they have been cheated, causing the deal-maker to gain the reputation not only for unfairness, but for dishonesty—indeed, the two words are often used interchangeably.

Thus, businesspeople who acquire the reputation of being sharp operators—those who take "unfair" advantage of a situation when the opportunity presents itself—will be approached with a wariness that is not beneficial to them from an economic standpoint. In general, they will become less rich—find it more difficult to make deals—than those who have been able to create a reputation for fairness and for fair dealing.

Hence, it is to one's long-term economic advantage that the other party walk away from the deal feeling that the agreement has been fair even though this might mean cutting a deal that is somewhat less favorable or immediately profitable. Nothing riles people more than the feeling that they have been "taken." It was for this reason that, for example, John D. Rockefeller would not fight for the last dollar in forming mergers and always tried to conclude deals cordially; as he put it, he was not "so short-sighted as to antagonize" the very people he would later seek to have a close and profitable relation with. As Stigler observes, the main asset of the great merchandizing companies has been "their reputation for fair and careful dealing." Or as Barnum puts it succinctly, "Men who drive sharp bargains with their customers, acting as if they never expected to see them again, will not be mistaken."[13]

Similar observations are routine in many of the thousands of books and tracts published by businesspeople about how to achieve success—that is, about how to create and run a profitable business enterprise. For example, in his book, *What They Don't Teach You at Harvard Business School*, Mark McCormack notes that "people do not like to feel they are being conned"; that "sometimes you make the best deal for yourself by driving a soft bargain"; and that "I've often found that by recognizing extenuating circumstance and letting someone off the hook I have accomplished much more for myself and my company in the long run." Or, in his sequel, *What They* Still *Don't Teach You at Harvard Business School:* "People often agree to do things and then for reasons beyond their control are unable to do them. If you let them off the hook, are you being a nice guy or a fool? Obviously, if you intend to do business with them again, the choice is not that tough. . . . Rarely have the long-term benefits from such decisions made me feel foolish."[14]

The economic value of fairness is also seen in the curious phenomenon of price stickiness. There seems to be a nearly universal aversion to what is called price gouging, a practice that is generally considered unfair. Accordingly, even when demand clearly comes to outstrip supply, a smart business will be careful about suddenly charging the higher prices that would be myopically dictated by economic rationality. Ski resorts, for example, do not abruptly boost their prices during peak seasons because they know that "If you gouge them at Christmas time they won't come back in March."[15]

This problem can sometimes be handled by establishing list prices and then discounting from them.[16] Thus airlines may charge $1,000 to fly between Rochester and Los Angeles, discounting to $500 if the traveler buys the ticket well in advance and accepts certain restrictions, rather than announcing a price of $500 that will be increased to $1,000 if the customer waits until the last minute and wants no restrictions. Similarly, a university whose effective tuition is $18,000 might list its price at $25,000 and discount from that amount rather than advertising its price as $18,000 except for people it thinks can afford it who will be charged $25,000. The economic effect, obviously, is the same in either case, but the discounting device is generally accepted as being more fair. And airlines and universities use it even though it carries the disadvantage, to them, of sticker shock.

Relatedly, it is most interesting that in advanced capitalist economies bargaining over prices has been abandoned almost entirely in ordinary retail commerce, a phenomenon that will be considered more fully in chapter 4. This development has presumably been to the short-term disadvantage of retailers who, since they bargain all the time and obviously know the product better, have an advantage, on average, over the casual ordinary customer. Nevertheless, businesses have found they tend to do better in the long run if they handicap themselves by setting (attractive) prices for a commodity, a practice that eliminates the often unpleasant and emotionally unsettling task of haggling over a price, the fear of being unfairly taken, and the possibility, generally held to be unfair, of charging different prices to different customers for the same product.

The chain or franchise store effect shows up on the issue of fairness as it does on the one of honesty. Hotel chains in Super Bowl cities, for example, decline to hike prices on the Big Day out of fear that customers will deem the practice unfair and resentfully bypass other hotels in the chain at other times.[17]

Fairness is also important in a business's relations with its employees. At a time of downturn, it may make the most economic sense to lay off the least productive workers and to retain the most productive, but the usual approach is to fire those with least seniority instead because that policy is more likely to be considered "fair" even by those who have been laid off.

Civility

Although rudeness is hardly unknown among capitalists, the system itself rewards civil behavior: in Barnum's words, "politeness and civility are the best capital ever invested in business."[18] The philosophy that "The customer is always right" is self-effacing, even cravenly self-abnegating perhaps, but it enhances profits.

It seems reasonable to speculate that the reason McDonald's insists its employees treat customers courteously is not simply that Mr. McDonald (or whoever) is an especially nice person. Rather, the company has calculated that when salespeople are pleasant and polite, the customers will likely return to buy more. As Barnum observes, "Large stores, gilt signs, flaming advertisements, will all prove unavailing if you or your employees treat your patrons abruptly. The truth is, the more kind and liberal a man is, the more generous will be the patronage bestowed upon him."[19]

John Wanamaker, the nineteenth-century retailer, reports on an experience he had as a boy that, he says, helped him later to create the foundations of his extremely successful retail business. On a Christmas Eve around 1850 he went into a jewelry store to buy his mother a gift. He spent a long time looking at the goods on display and finally made a choice, but as the jeweler was wrapping it up, the boy changed his mind and said he would like to take another piece instead. The impatient jeweler refused, and Wanamaker recalls that he was "too abashed to protest." But as he left, he said to himself, "When I have a store of my own the people shall have what they want."[20] Wanamaker doesn't mention it, but it seems a reasonable speculation that he never patronized that store again.

Civility even makes sense for panhandlers. Although aggressive panhandling probably is more effective in the short term, it is quite unwise in the long term. Politely saying "Have a nice day" to a potential patron who has turned down a panhandler's entreaty is likely to instill a bit of guilt in the patron who may then mellow the next time. It may also get the panhandler on good—that is to say, profitable—terms with anyone who overhears the exchange. Aggressive panhandling, by contrast, is very bad for public relations because it turns customers off and inspires later avoidance behavior, and because it gives the whole industry a bad name which could ultimately lead to its being entirely outlawed.

In their exuberant, best-selling book, *In Search of Excellence*, published over a century after Wanamaker's valuable, if traumatic, experience with the foolishly boorish jeweler, Thomas Peters and Robert Waterman stress that excellent (that is to say, highly profitable) businesses "love the customers," and they have an "*obsession*" for "a seemingly unjustifiable overcommitment to some form of quality, reliability, or service." A major reason IBM became the world's most profitable company, notes Robert Cringely, was "customer hand holding." And one study found that, when customers were asked why they had stopped shopping at a store, 69 percent gave poor service as their reason whereas only 13 percent mentioned product satisfaction and only 9 percent mentioned high prices. As John Templeton, head of one of the world's most effective—that is, most profit-producing—mutual funds, has put it, "If you are trying to do the most for people, if you are trying to help people the most, you'll be most successful."[21]

Similarly, employers who are considerate and courteous to their employees will tend to find them working harder for less money or doing more work for the same money—a happy employee, as they say, is a productive employee. Contented employees are also likely to be more impervious to the potentially problematic attractions of union organizers and to be less likely to steal from the company. Peters and Waterman stress "productivity through people," and they admonish, "Treat people as adults. Treat them as partners; treat them with dignity; treat them with respect. . . . In other words, if you want productivity and the financial reward that goes with it, you must treat your workers as your most important asset."[22]

For example, McCormack cites the qualities of an executive who, he suggests, "has all the earmarks of a champion CEO," and as evidence cites the testimony of a fellow worker: "No matter who you are, when you're in the room with her, she acts as if you're the only person who matters. She makes you feel like her equal. She defers to you, cares about your opinions, gives you time to present your views. If there are other people present, even if you are a secretary or minor flunkie, she treats you like the chairman of the board." And capitalists who are pleasant to work with tend to find other deal-makers willing to cut special, favorable agreements. As McCormack admonishes, "Be nice to people. . . . All things being equal, courtesy can be most persuasive."[23]

Rudeness was routine—notorious—in communist enterprises, and, more generally, it is commonly found in agencies (such as passport or driver's license offices) where two conditions prevail: supply is outstripped by demand, and the seller is unable to raise the price. Under these conditions customers become supplicants, and there is no economic disincentive to incivility, surliness, and arrogance. One Soviet citizen tells of being kept waiting by a butcher who was chatting with a friend. When she asked for meat, he turned grumpily to her and said, "Next, I suppose you'll want me to cram it in your mouth for you." Another points out the dilemma: "Where else can you go if they have what you want?" And David Landes vividly recalls how, until eventually forced to change by European Community standards, the French post office would often use several stamps on an airmail letter, enhancing its weight and boosting the cost of sending it: "One had to experience these exercises in petty tyranny," he suggests, "to understand the retardative effects of bureaucratic constipation."[24] Since enterprises like these cannot ration by price, they are inclined to ration by rudeness, by creating inconvenience or, where possible, by corruption—demanding side payments to obtain the product.[25]

The point here, of course, is not to suggest that incivility never shows up in a capitalist system, but rather that the system encourages and rewards civility. Sometimes a capitalist may feel there are qualities more important than economic gain: individual executives may like the sense of personal control over underlings and take pleasure in lording it over them, for example. Thus, McCormack relates the tale of a CEO who gathered his 100 employees in a room and then fired an executive in front of them. Such essentially sadistic behavior may have few negative consequences for the perpetrator when he is a drill sergeant terrorizing a group of conscripted recruits, but it is a distortion of sensible acquisitive behavior under capitalism, and people indulging themselves will pay an economic price. As McCormack puts it pointedly, "I leave it to you to judge how this stunt would motivate the ninety-nine survivors."[26]

Compassion

Logically, it might be expected that appropriately acquisitive capitalists would be essentially indifferent to any human suffering or inadequacy that doesn't affect their own enterprises: neither supportive nor opposed. In strict economic principle, capitalism doesn't oppress the unfortunate so much as it simply neglects them.

In practice, however, it is to the capitalist's advantage—that is to say, it is good for business—to show a sense of compassion, of community responsibility, of charity, and of altruism. People who do have money to spend and deals to make like doing business with people like that, and consequently a reputation—image—for decency and community concern is good for profits.

Barnum had something to say on this issue, none too surprisingly: "Of course men should be charitable, because it is a duty and a pleasure. But even as a matter of policy, if you possess no higher incentive, you will find that the liberal man will command patronage, while the sordid, uncharitable miser will be avoided." He carried out his various business ventures with an eye toward what he called "profitable philanthropy." For example, when managing soprano Jenny Lind's spectacularly successful tour he saw advantage in the many charity concerts she gave: bread cast on such waters, he observed, "would return, perhaps buttered; for the larger her reputation for liberality, the more liberal the public would surely be to us and our enterprise."[27]

Or, as another New England businessman, the CEO of a Boston bank, explained over a century later, his company's enthusiastic involvement with "community service" was a "win for the shareholders" in part because of "the pride that's built within our employees and the respect from our customers." As the company founders point out, people buy Ben and Jerry's ice cream in part because they "like what our company stands for," and the more the company manages to "actualize" its "commitment to social change, the more loyal customers we attract and the more profitable we become."[28]

Richard Steckel and Robin Simons begin their book *Doing Best By Doing Good* with the frank contention that "no matter how altruistic a company may look, when push comes to shove what really counts is money." But they then go on to show how putatively altruistic behavior can be managed to enhance a company's image and credibility, target markets, make it stand out from the crowd, reinforce advertising, increase consumer loyalty, create cost-effective promotions, increase retail activity, facilitate product launches and market entry, attract beneficial media coverage, reverse negative publicity, strengthen community relations, entertain clients, develop new products, lower research and development costs, improve employee morale, create inexpensive employee perks, help with employee retention and recruitment, enhance visibility, diversify the company's income base, help it gain experience in managing promotional campaigns, attract future donors and business partners, reinforce business skills, and offer an opportunity for executives to rub shoulders with people they'd like to meet such as potential customers, lobbyists, opinion makers, and policy makers. Another survey of the ways business interests can be serviced by corporate philanthropy includes attracting loyal customers ("we're giving away money, but we're doing it in a way that builds business"—American Express), building a productive workforce ("one more notch on its belt to show why it's a great organization to be affiliated with"—Merchants National Bank), supporting research that can help a firm's general economic interest (as on "innovative uses of computing and engineering applications"—IBM), and promoting probusiness public policy. It would be difficult to measure precisely the benefits that derive from such policies, of course, but the same can be said for advertising.[29]

Of necessity, however, capitalism often requires acts that can be viewed as lacking compassion: the firing or laying off of employees for cause or when business slackens, for example. Even in this case, however, the wise capitalist will seek to be as compassionate as possible—striving to ease the blow because a reputation for casual heartlessness can harm employee morale, foster hostile union relations, and pose difficulties in times of labor shortage.

Hence, the rise of the "golden handshake," a departure payment, very often not required by employment contracts or union agreements, that is generally accepted as wise business. As McCormack observes, "when people feel they have been fired 'fairly'— treated with dignity, respect, and sensitivity in what, by definition, is a demeaning experience—they will be reluctant to bad-mouth their excompany. And they just may—as has happened to us on several occasions—become valued future business associates." Or, in Autry's words, "there's just one way to fire someone: with love and support and deep, deep regret." Applying a concept that is almost oxymoronic, he suggests that as far as possible firing an employee should be a "caring confrontation."[30]

Perhaps the most famous disemployer during the downsizing 1990s in the United States is Albert Dunlap, who specializes in rescuing companies in severe decline and very often finds it necessary to fire substantial portions of their workforces in the process. However, in a book that discusses his adventures in business and is bluntly entitled *Mean Business,* Dunlap points out that he proceeds with great care and consideration. He can justify firing 35 percent because it means secure jobs for the remaining 65 percent (as opposed to zero percent if the company collapses), but "when I fire people, *of course,* I feel for them." He says he is proudest of what happens in labor relations, and he works very hard openly and clearly to explain the situation and to establish trust. And he treats "those who would be let go with respectful separation packages," helping them to "leave with dignity" even though this is often quite expensive.[31]

More generally, managers who are able to show compassion toward their employees—to show they care—will have a more productive workforce and higher profits. As one corporate executive puts it, "take our family-leave policy. It costs us next to nothing. And yet the statement it makes to employees is powerful. It says to them that we care. And when employees know you care about them, they tend to be more productive. It's the same with our day care. To me, it's a no-brainer."[32]

Not all capitalists act in a compassionate manner, of course. But those who fail to do so are generally acting foolishly if their goal is to maximize long-term profits.

Heroism

In her anticapitalist play, *The Little Foxes,* Lillian Hellman wants us to believe that her capitalist characters are essentially parasitic and never actually *do* much of anything even though it is clear that they have been working on a deal for months with great skill and expertise, and that they are willing to risk their fortunes to make it a reality. Hellman undercuts the risk issue by simply positing that the business venture is certain to be a success, when in fact ventures of the sort she depicts stood at best a fifty-fifty chance of survival. The dramatically convenient omission of the crucial element of risk is particularly notable also in the traditional vilification of speculators.

However, to be successful an entrepreneuring capitalist must continually run risks. Bankers, often criticized for stodgy, conservative behavior, in fact take more risks in a single business day than many of their critics do in a lifetime. Indeed, as it is often put, "The greatest rewards are usually not far from the greatest risks." Often, in fact, entrepreneurs risk their financial futures on a venture, a large proportion of which miscarry—the failure rate for new products and services in the United States is 80 to 90 percent—often with consequent harm to the adventurer's long-term (and in some cases short-term) physical health.[33]

As historian Allan Nevins has pointed out, contrary to popular mythology, the rise of John D. Rockefeller's Standard Oil "was not meteor-like, but accomplished over a quarter of a century by courageous venturing in a field so risky that most large capitalists avoided it, by arduous labors, and by more sagacious and far-sighted planning than had been applied to any other American industry." He further suggests that "the best businessmen have been great adventurers. . . . They played it with zest and gusto, they enjoyed it even when it was perilous, and they took its ups and downs with equanimity."[34]

And, of course, such risk-taking behavior will characteristically be successful only if it also benefits others by supplying or helping to supply a product or service people are freely willing to purchase.

In war or in conventional adventuring and exploring, risk-taking behavior is considered to be heroic. However, as George Gilder has pointed out, creative, risk-taking capitalists, successes and failures alike, are never given anything like the same credit.[35]

The Capitalist Virtues and the Monopolist

For the most part, even a monopolist will find it profitable to subscribe to the capitalist virtues. Good employee relations remain important to generate productivity, and deals still need to be made with fellow capitalists. Moreover, monopolists with a reputation for honesty, fairness, civility, and compassion are more likely to be able slide price boosts past a wary public—that is, such moves are less likely to inspire angered customers to use less of the product and/ or to engender embittered protest to governmental agencies.

Hence, it is not surprising, for example, to find cable television monopolies treating their customers with civility and sponsoring public relations projects to show how responsible they are. And taxicab companies which have cleverly managed to gain a monopoly in certain areas—serving an airport, for example—have sometimes come to the dawning realization that they will make more money if they are honest, fair, and courteous, because their customers will then be less inclined to invest time and effort inconveniently arranging for alternative means of transportation. Tips will be higher as well.

The Essential Insincerity of Capitalist Morality

It should be acknowledged that the honesty, fairness, civility, compassion, and heroism that characterize successful capitalism are essentially insincere, or even cynical and hypocritical. Capitalism encourages people in business to be honest, fair, civil, compassionate, and heroic not because those qualities are valued for themselves, but because of acquisitiveness or greed. Thus businesspeople do not seem to pass Wilson's test for a "moral man": "one whose sense of duty is shaped by conscience, that is, by the impartial spectator within our breast who evaluates our own action as others would evaluate it." Similarly, a century ago Archbishop Richard Whately observed that someone who acts on the principle that honesty is the best policy is not honest—meaning, as Stigler parses it, that "he who behaves honestly because it is remunerative is simply an amoral calculator; an honest man is one whose principles of right conduct are adopted independently of their consequences for him."[36]

Accordingly, if one walks into an automobile showroom and says, "I want to buy that car over there but I demand that I be treated dishonestly and with consummate discourtesy," one can reasonably expect the dealer to evince few moral qualms in complying. A true saint, by contrast, would likely undergo a certain angst when trying to service that improbable request.

But essential insincerity can often be found in other moral systems as well. For example, the soldier may be heroic not because he values heroism for itself but because it leads to medals and admiration. Or his heroism is rewarded by the kick of exultation some combatants feel in battle (rather similar, perhaps, to the high that pious masochists received when self-flagellation was a respected and admired activity). And the common moral injunction, "Do unto others as you would have them do unto you," certainly implies that the moralizer is chiefly inspired not so much by conscience as by a cagy calculation of ultimate, if collegial, self-interest.

More importantly, however, most people find it difficult to counterfeit morality. Sam Goldwyn is alleged to have said, "The most important thing about acting is sincerity: once you've learned to fake that, you've got it made." This may well be true for acting, but not for real life: most people cannot consistently and routinely fake sincerity. And using not much more than commonsense, people very often can, at least on substantial exposure, spot pretenders. Indeed, part of the growing-up process involves the development of social skills for sizing up others for the purposes of forming, or avoiding, relationships. As Wilson observes, "A person can be fooled by a chance encounter, but during a continuing relationship he will usually form an accurate assessment of another person's character." Or, in Peter Drucker's words, "The men with whom a man works, and especially his subordinates, know in a few weeks whether he has integrity or not."[37]

As McCormack puts it succinctly, "people don't like phonies."[38] Therefore, the penalties for an act—or even to a vague suspicion—

of phoniness can be severe and immediate: customers stop coming back and bad-mouth the business to friends, fellow deal-makers fail to return telephone calls, employees become resentful and less productive. Ben and Jerry have been financially successful in part because they really do seem to believe in those uplifting causes they so exuberantly advocate; if their double-dipping customers acquired the suspicion that the company had been double-timing them, its competitive advantage, its profitability, and perhaps even its existence could vanish in a heartbeat.

Thus, a clerk or manager who actually hates people is unlikely to be successful because the customers and employees will eventually see through the act. As one manager puts it in a book pointedly entitled *Love and Profit*, "*If you don't care about people, get out of management before it's too late.* I mean it. Save yourself a heart attack and save many other people a lot of daily grief." I have an acquaintance who became a doctor only to discover that he was ill suited to the work because he had great difficulty dealing with people. Accordingly, he went back to school and became a pathologist, and is now quite happy because the only patients he has to deal with come in the form of disembodied fluids and chunks of flesh. This seems to have been an especially wise career decision. A number of studies have shown that the quality of care provided is not a major determinant of malpractice claims: that is, incompetent physicians are not more likely to be sued than competent ones. Rather, complaints tend to be registered against those who, in the view of the patient, devalue the patient, fail to understand the patient's perspectives, communicate poorly, and, in general, do not establish relationships that are personal, caring, and respectful.[39]

And most salespeople find that it is much easier to sell a product if they truly believe in it. The "fundamental selling truths" are laid out by McCormack: "If you don't know your product, people will resent your efforts to sell it; if you don't believe in it, no amount of personality and technique will cover that fact; if you don't sell with enthusiasm, the lack of it will be infectious."[40]

It is likely, then, that, in general, the best way to *seem* honest and fair and civil and compassionate, is actually to *be* honest and fair and civil and compassionate. A visiting management consultant who was interviewing various employees of a firm found that they all very proudly told the same story when asked about the boss: "Elmer Smith? I'll tell you what kind of a guy Elmer Smith is." It seems that an employee had once borrowed Smith's new, expensive automobile and then managed to smash it up. When he called the boss with great and understandable trepidation to report the incident, Smith's immediate reaction was to wave off any concern about the car and urgently to inquire instead whether the employee had been hurt. It is possible, of course, that this was all an act: perhaps Smith really cared much more about his damaged vehicle than about his employee's health, but acted under the crafty realization that putting on a show of concern for the employee would be great coup for employee relations, causing him to be loved by his employees who would then be inspired to work happier and harder for the company and at lower wages, all of which would ultimately increase his profits. I suspect, however, that the interviewees had it right: the story really does tell you what kind of a guy Elmer Smith is. Moreover, if his employees came even to suspect that Smith's humane response had been calculated and manipulative, their reaction would be hugely negative—far worse than if Smith had expressed concern only about the car in the first place.

Therefore, successful capitalists will tend to be naturally honest and fair and civil and compassionate—like, it seems, Elmer Smith. Or perhaps they can acquire the virtues in the course of doing business.

Whether the virtue of honesty can be learned is questioned by Drucker: integrity, his one "absolute requirement" of a manager, "is not something a man can acquire; if he does not bring it to the job, he will never have it." Nonetheless, as will be discussed more fully in chapter 4, it does seem possible to learn to appreciate the economic value of honesty. P. T. Barnum did. He found that all the colorful "humbugs" of his early career "ended in disaster" and reduced him to the "pinching income of $4 per week." The fortune he acquired later "was accumulated almost wholly from enterprises which were undoubtedly legitimate."[41]

WHY NICE GUYS FINISH FIRST

All other things equal, deals among friends are both more secure and more likely to happen than deals among nonfriends. This is partly because the potential punishment for reneging on an agreement is higher than it is for a misfired deal among nonfriends. An injured friend has the usual array of weapons for inflicting punishment on an offending person—such as legal action or reputational retaliation like letting it be widely known that the reneger is a jerk. But an offending person who is a friend will obligingly undergo self-punishment in addition. That is, friends who let friends down punish themselves by feeling bad because, putting it in econospeak, the friend's welfare has entered their utility function (or, returning to English, they feel guilty). In fact, if they don't feel bad when they let the friend down, that condition suggests pretty conclusively that they actually weren't friends to begin with.[42] As McCormack puts it, "All things being equal, people will buy from a friend. All things being not quite so equal, people will *still* buy from a friend."[43]

Nice guys are quite a bit like friends. Again pretty much by definition, a nice guy will feel bad (punish himself) if he causes harm. Consequently, all other things equal, it is sensible to prefer to deal with someone you consider to be a nice guy because a nice guy will be hurt more than a non-nice guy if he lets you down—he will feel your pain. Thus, a deal with a nice guy is effectively more secured (less risky) and therefore more likely to happen.

In addition, cutting a deal with a nice guy will usually generate some pleasure and so one might be quite rationally willing to give in a bit more in a deal with a nice guy than in one with a non-nice guy. The casual business phrase, "It's a pleasure doing business with you," may not always be sincerely felt, but it does suggest an emotional element that can have real economic benefit to those who supply the pleasure.

In result, nice guys, on average, have a competitive advantage over non-nice guys, and accordingly they will tend to prosper. Sometimes, of course, it is darkly suspected that nice guys will, precisely because of their niceness, be incapable of making hard, but necessary, business decisions—cutting back the workforce in bad times, for example. In this case, however, niceness is a problem not for its own sake, but because it is correlated with incompetence or with an economically foolish sentimentality: it hampers a person's ability to do a job effectively. My argument is not that incompetent nice guys will do better than competent non-nice guys, but that nice guys will do better than non-nice guys who are comparably competent.

Extrapolating the Capitalist Virtues

In principle, if a person is virtuous in business, those qualities need not necessarily affect other areas of that person's life because there is no necessary reason why one can't successfully be (or act) virtuous in business and still be a cad and liar in other aspects of life. In practice, however, a schizophrenic life style could be economically dangerous. If people come to see a person as dishonest, unfair, uncivil, and uncompassionate in private life, they may assume the person is a sleaze and cannot be trusted in business either, thus potentially exacting an economic cost. In general, then, it makes sense to carry business virtues over to private life.

McCormack discusses a man who had sold his house to someone who suddenly wanted to back out of the deal because of an unexpected death in the family. The seller agreed, and McCormack observes: "There was no long-term benefit for him, but it was the right thing to do."[44] However, the very fact that McCormack relates this story and undoubtedly has told it to many businesspeople over the years, suggests that there probably *was* long-term benefit. Or, put another way, if the seller had refused to bend under the circumstances, McCormack would still be telling the story, but now the man would be painted as a heartless sleaze, to his long-term detriment.

Moreover, given the difficulty most people find in putting on an act, people who are naturally virtuous will tend to do best in business as I have already argued, so there is likely to be a kind of reinforcement of virtuous behavior. There may also be a process of habituation or spillover. Wilson hopefully suggests, for example, that the civility forced upon a young McDonald's worker might just be carried over to other portions of that person's life. And Adam Smith suggests that merchants bring probity "into fashion," a proposition that will be examined in chapter 4.[45]

It seems to be remarkably easy, however, for different moral standards to prevail when one is dealing with the revenuers. Honesty may be central to ordinary business transactions where both parties gain and where each often has a long-term reputation to maintain, but the acquisitive have a strong incentive to minimize the confiscation of their wealth (e.g., taxes) by any means feasible. Even in societies where honesty is rampant, tax evasion is probably kept in check substantially by the effective threat of detection and coercion.

The tax collectors will, of course, be aided if the people in the society would be likely to distrust a known tax evader—that is, where a reputation of dishonesty toward the government could hurt one's private transactions. The publication of names of tax miscreants could then be a useful method of control. But it seems entirely possible for tax cheats to be lauded, or at least accepted, while still being trusted fully in business or private life. Adam Smith, probably the most important non-fan of tariffs in history, observed that the smuggler, although a patent breaker of laws Smith famously and influentially considered foolish, was often accepted as "an excellent citizen" and an "innocent" nonetheless. Indeed, "to pretend to have any scruple about buying smuggled goods . . . would in most countries be regarded as one of those pedantick pieces of hypocrisy" which would expose the pretender "to the suspicion of being a greater knave than most of his neighbours." Similarly, although, as Richard Tilly observes, business behavior in Britain and Germany became noticeably more honest during the course of the nineteenth century (a phenomenon to be assessed more fully in chapter 4), the "tax morality" of businessmen does not seem to have risen at the same time.[46]

I was once working on a project with a man from Denmark, the country with perhaps the highest marginal tax rates in the world.

He is one of the most decent and honest people I have ever met: if he found an unsealed envelope with five thousand dollars in cash in it and the owner's address on the outside, I fully expect he would deliver it to its owner immediately—in fact, he would probably stuff a few more bills into the envelope out of sympathy. However, when he was told he could be paid for his work on the project in cash, he seemed to be uncommonly delighted. It is possible, of course, that when he got back to Copenhagen he went directly to the revenuers' office to declare his take and to let them hack out their generous slice, but somehow I doubt it. My suspicions on that score, however, do not dampen my trust of him in the slightest.[47]

Capitalist Culture, Capitalist Inequality and Unfairness, Capitalist Competition

I have mostly dealt here with capitalism at the individual level—considering the relations between deal-making businesspeople, between employers and employees, and between retailers and customers. But some criticisms of capitalism stress its unpleasant features more at the cultural level and at the level of relations between competitors.

In this regard, economic historian Stanley Engerman suggests that capitalism has had to contend with three central criticisms in seeking to gain acceptance. One critique points with dismay to the nature of the culture the system generates or seems to generate. Another bemoans the unfairness of the distribution of wealth and income that capitalism fosters. And the third voices alarm at the periodic and apparently uncontrollable economic catastrophes like the Great Depression of the 1930s that have often seemed to be an inevitable component of capitalism's workings. I will argue in chapter 5 that, because of the maturation of the science of economics, the last of these problems may now possibly be subject to some degree of control or at least of understanding.[48] However, there is no way the cultural and inequality problems can be fully finessed.

Culture

The cultural critique is inspired in part by the fact that capitalism is devoted to supplying people uncritically with what they happen to think they may want at the moment, no matter how banal or debased or even lethal, as long as the purchasers are willing and able to pay for it. In defending this result, capitalists can argue that they are simply supplying public tastes and therefore any blame for debased products and services should more properly be placed on the popular tastes themselves; otherwise, as George Stigler puts it, "It is like blaming the waiters in restaurants for obesity." And capitalists can also readily concede, with Stigler, that their system makes no provision for those "whose talents and interest are not oriented to profit-seeking economic activity." He observes, for example, that it does not supply an air force, alms for the poor, or even babies, and thus he simply concludes that "a society needs more than a marketplace."[49]

Critics of capitalism often contend, however, that, in R. H. Tawney's words, "A reasonable estimate of economic organization must allow for the fact that, unless industry is to be paralyzed by recurrent revolts on the part of outraged human nature, it must satisfy criteria which are not purely economic." Moreover, the critics sometimes argue that, rather than merely supplying needs (or wants), capitalists actively create them. That is, people don't actually *need*, for example, flush toilets: after all, Shakespeare, Mozart, Moses, and the rest of the human race survived quite well without them for millennia. Therefore the only reason people have come to consider that item desirable, nay, essential, is that they have been cleverly and insidiously brainwashed by agile and dissembling promoters from the megalopolistic plumbing industry.[50]

Capitalists certainly would dearly love to be able to fabricate demand for whatever they happen to be selling at the moment. But it is probably more accurate to say that, rather than confidently creating demand, capitalists put products and services on display in hopes that a demand for them will materialize, and that they mostly quest after unappreciated market niches that might profitably be serviced. And the results of such efforts are none too predictable: as noted, the vast majority, in fact, fail. The producers of the hula hoop were probably surprised (and elated) by the fact that people actually seemed, for a while at least, to need their nonsense item, just as the producers of the Edsel were surprised (and depressed) by the fact that few consumers seemed to need theirs. The promoters of compact discs found there was a large and ready market (or need) for their product out there, but the promoters of digital audio tape, a product that does everything a CD can do and records as well, did not.

In general, under a growing capitalist economy, desirable (or at any rate desired) goods and services tend to become cheaper, better, more abundant, and more widely dispersed.[51] Nonetheless, there will still be plenty of lamentable (and colorfully lamented) instances when, merely because that is what most people happen to want, the distasteful will drive out the refined, the machine-made the handcrafted, the schlock the subtle, the gross the quaint, the factory-made the artisan-fashioned, the bland the distinguished, the fast the laid-back, the mediocre the splendid, the K-Mart the corner emporium, the engineered McDonald's the homey greasy spoon.

However, if some people—the Amish, for example—happen to want to pursue lifestyles of a different sort—more etherial and less materialistic, perhaps—the system will generally put no barrier in the way. In fact, it may well assist them in their endeavors if a profit can be made by so doing: capitalist Hollywood, for example, is quite happy to make movies that ingratiatingly, and profitably, service the prejudices of those hostile to capitalist culture, often making a pretty buck off movies that show capitalism to be debased, uncaring, deceitful, and brutal. And there are plenty of businesses selling equipment at attractive prices to provide basic comforts—even the occasional guilty luxury—for anyone who wishes to wander into the wilderness to commune with Nature or Whomever else is out there.

Capitalism also fosters, indeed depends on, competition, and this element of its culture is often deemed vulgar and grasping. As

Alfred Marshall observes, "the term 'competition' has gathered about it evil savour, and has come to imply a certain selfishness and indifference to the wellbeing of others."[52]

I have contended in this chapter that some of the criticism of the culture supposedly fostered by capitalism is based more on faulty, ideology-inspired, and cliché-ridden image-making than on reality. As capitalists have gradually discovered, capitalism tends to inspire (that is, systematically to reward) not the deceit and incivility and boorishness so commonly associated with it by detractors, but business behavior that is honest, fair, civil, and compassionate. However, capitalists can often be fiercely competitive, and the public crowing by some of the most self-obsessed and aggressive of them can often be arrogant and distasteful, a quality emphasized in the common disdain for the *nouveau riche*. Even Adam Smith was appalled at the tendency for high profits to "destroy that parsimony which in other circumstances is natural to the character of the merchant." People in business, particularly successful ones, can also become egotistic about their enterprises, not unreasonably seeing them as extensions of their personalities, and they can come to behave like despots in their self-generated and often rather petty domains. They can also become arrogant and superior about their success, attributing it entirely to their own skills and moral excellence: even the mild-mannered and genuinely pious John D. Rockefeller once disparagingly asserted that "the failures that a man makes in his life are due almost always to some defect in his personality, some weakness of body, mind or character, will or temperament."[53]

But there is something of a selection bias here. Those capitalists who remain quiet and unassuming and who fail to engage in such colorful and irritating behavior tend not to be noticed.

Moreover, my point in all this, of course, is not to argue that arrogant and boorish business behavior does not exist, but that such behavior is, on balance and in the long run, economically foolish. Certainly, it is easy to find instances where capitalists have allowed themselves to become entrapped by ego and end up paying the price. An excellent case in point is furnished by John Ringling. He became so outraged at the (sensible) business decision of Madison

Square Garden in 1930 to continue its highly profitable Friday prize fights during the run of the circus that he cascaded into bankruptcy in part because of his futile effort to show the Garden management up.[54]

Behavior like that does not come about because capitalism mandates it, but because, on the contrary, people in business have sometimes allowed themselves to give in to instincts and proclivities that cloud their judgment and that are not a sound expression of sensible, self-effacing acquisitive behavior. And capitalism often punishes them for it.

Inequality and Unfairness

Capitalism must plead guilty as well to the second criticism, that it necessarily leads to economic inequality and that it often is—or seems—fundamentally unfair in its results.

In principle, I suppose it could be argued that capitalism as a system does not necessarily *require* inequality. It is vital to the system that people be given an incentive and opportunity to enrich themselves for otherwise they will scarcely subject themselves to the system's rigors, uncertainties, and sacrifices. But a capitalist determinedly bent on self-enrichment doesn't mind if everyone else becomes equally rich at the same time—in fact, the richer other people are, the easier it will presumably be to sell one's product or service to them.

In practice, however, some people will do better than others at the self-enrichment process. And, in consequence, notable, even glaring, economic inequalities will emerge.[55]

Moreover, capitalism, like life and democracy, is inherently unfair in the sense that, while ambitiousness, hard work, resourcefulness, careful planning, virtuous business behavior, and frugal sobriety may increase one's chances of success, luck and timing (including the capricious whims of the consumer) also play an important role. Indeed, if it is true that the greatest profits (as well as the greatest failures) are accompanied by the greatest risks, people who have become very rich in business must usually have taken large risks and much of their success is very likely to have depended on luck.

Baseball's Branch Rickey famously and eloquently proposed that "luck is the residue of design." If so, Rockefeller was blessed with a huge residuum. He was a highly talented businessman but, as Ron Chernow observes, he also "benefited from a large dollop of luck in his life." In the beginning, Rockefeller poured all his money into petroleum, a speculation most judicious investors considered a "rope of sand" because of two "antithetic nightmares": the oil wells might dry up (as geologists routinely predicted) or vast quantities of oil might suddenly be discovered, creating a glut which would cause prices to fall below overhead costs.[56] Another of what Chernow characterizes as Rockefeller's "colossal gambles" was his heavy investment in some new oil that was almost completely unusable because when burned it smelled repellently— "skunk oil," they called it. Rockefeller couldn't even get his own board at Standard Oil to buy this idea and persuaded them only when he proposed to use his own money on the venture, selling the investment to the company if a way was found to eliminate the smell and taking the loss if it wasn't (it was).[57] Later he aggressively invested in the Mesabi iron range even though experts like Andrew Carnegie considered the ore useless because it clogged furnaces when heated. Rockefeller gambled—correctly, as it turned out— that a way could be found to remedy that defect. And Rockefeller's truly colossal fortune was created only after he had retired, when someone else happened to invent the automobile, causing demand for petroleum to skyrocket.[58]

Someone in business might gain a crucial advantage simply because of information casually picked up at a cocktail party or because a brother-in-law just happens to know someone who knows someone who is in the right position to help. Or because a competitor happens to make an exceptionally foolish decision: at one key point Microsoft was greatly benefited because a competitor was out flying around in his small airplane when IBM came to call. That is, in the classic whimsy, 6-Up could easily fail while 7-Up triumphs. Moreover, as Robert Cringely notes, "In business, as in comedy, timing is everything." Thus a product introduced in March may fail while the same product introduced the next October might succeed. Barnum substantially overstates the case (and not for the first time) when he advises, "Fortune always favors the brave, and never helps a man who does not help himself."[59]

Therefore, although capitalism tends to reward fairness at the level of the individual transaction as discussed above, economic inequality at the systemic level is inevitable, a result that is often considered unfair, unjust, or at least highly undesirable. There is no way capitalism can avoid a dilemma on this score since in an important sense, the system routinely creates not only the deserving poor but some rich people who certainly do not seem to have done much to deserve their wealth.

This can engender resentment, as well as bitterness, often mixed with jealousy perhaps, toward the whole system. Nevins's conclusion that "the best businessmen" take the market's "ups and downs with equanimity"[60] is only true if it is tautological; many losers in the competitive process have been among the most resentful, preferring to blame the system for their fate rather than facing up to their own inadequacies or admitting simply to bad luck, a phenomenon to be discussed more fully in the next chapter.

Often such resentments are focused on "bigness." In almost any commercial competition the successful are likely to develop, almost by definition, larger—often vastly larger—enterprises than the less successful, a disparity that may be further enhanced by the economies of scale big companies often enjoy in the marketplace.

That bigness may not be a necessary or notable evil is suggested by some of the earlier discussion. Big companies must normally take a longer-term perspective and are more likely than the small operator to find value in honest, fair, civil, and compassionate business dealings—indeed, as will be discussed in chapter 4, that discovery may have been one of the reasons for their comparative success. But the conventional bias against bigness can aid the comparatively unsuccessful in their efforts to use public resources to rein in the big and to coddle the small, an effect which sometimes has considerable political appeal however little economic sense it may often make.[61]

The result of capitalistic competition is, on average, economic growth. And in the end the only way to prevent greater inequalities from emerging from this process is to hamper development itself. Thus, the surging disparities in world economic development that have taken place over the last two centuries (see figure 4.1 on p. 74) could only have been curtailed by keeping the developed world from developing. Since most people win in a growing economy, if capitalism generates more growth than other systems, it also creates more winners. But there are always plenty of losers as well, and this inevitable result can seem heartless and unfair.

Mellowing the Equality and Cultural Effects

Nonetheless, government can be used to reduce both the equality and the cultural effects somewhat without destroying the system.

Frequently, the political establishment may seek to supply those commodities and services it believes are insufficiently supplied by the market. Cultural agitators, for example, have often been able to shame politicians into deciding that the sometimes inadequate market for the fine arts should be supported and embellished with public largess.

On the other hand, throughout most of history the very considerable market for such desired commodities as pornography, drugs, prostitution, gambling, and liquor has been suppressed or restricted by the government. More recently there has been a growing consensus that the market for cigarettes should be stamped out or at least severely inconvenienced, no matter how much pleasure smokers derive from their carcinogenic addiction. At the same time, however, the notion of banning one of the most destructive devices ever invented, the private passenger automobile, has never taken hold—or even been substantially advanced.[62]

In dealing with the fairness and equality issues, there is opportunity in the fact that capitalism tends to generate greater wealth than other economic arrangements. Once quite a bit of money is made in this way, some of it can be taxed away from the rich without undue pain, and these revenues can be used to redistribute income or to soften the blows that capitalism inevitably inflicts on some people—cushioning the pain of unemployment or bankruptcy, for example. Governmental redistribution policies have been generally accepted even by some of capitalism's most fervent advocates.

In addition, the wealthy can be goaded, or encouraged by judicious tax policies, into giving some—even lots—of their money away, thereby further easing inequality. Barnum may again overstate the case when he declares, "as a general thing, money getters are the benefactors of our race," but he is not completely off target.[63]

Sometimes those policies may be purchased at a cost in overall growth and efficiency that can make them unwise or even counterproductive, however. In many cases it may be sensible to leave the money in the hands of successful capitalists because it will be used for further development, engendering more jobs and wealth for the society. Although he was justifiably proud of his many philanthropic achievements, Rockefeller may well have been correct when he repeatedly insisted that these were far less important than the good he had accomplished in his business by creating jobs and by furnishing affordable oil products.[64]

Some concerns about capitalism's fairness focus on the fact that prices and supplies are determined by impersonal market forces rather than by specific and perceptible flesh-and-blood human beings. Thus in a 1998 visit to, appropriately enough, communist Cuba, Pope John Paul II may have gained a bit of favor with his superannuated host by denouncing capitalism because "it subordinates the human person to blind market forces."[65] This view is a common one, and it is unlikely ever to go away, as suggested by the outcries that erupt in advanced capitalist countries like the United States whenever cable television companies try to abandon prices that others deem "just" in favor of ones that merely reflect what the traffic will bear. At the extreme, this perspective has led to wage and price controls, a popular, if economically damaging, policy that, as discussed in chapter 5, is only now being overcome.

In spite of their quest to eliminate economic inequality, socialist and communist systems still contained a great deal of it—often even more than under capitalism, according to some studies.[66] Moreover, in the process they generally generated much less wealth and therefore effectively perpetrated more poverty. However, when a new, substantially merit-free aristocracy—the nomenklatura—arose under Communism, those less well off could console themselves in the belief that their humble position in society derived not from any inherent lack of worth, but from their noble refusal to subordinate themselves to the party nonsense—rather like a poor peasant who could blame his condition on the inevitabilities of the class system rather than on his own inadequacies.[67] Under capitalism such excuses are no longer available, and resentments, accordingly, can be given free play.

Although government policy may be able to mellow capitalism's cultural and equality effects somewhat, in the end the problems of culture and of economic inequality simply have to be lived with under capitalism. Therefore to get the system accepted its proponents must convince people to embrace a version of the Ralph's Grocery philosophy in order to cope. The culture, the inequality, and the apparent unfairness of result may seem distasteful and undesirable at times, but they are inevitable: you can't have capitalism without them. If you do not allow the economy to supply people with what they happen to think they want at the moment, if you do not allow people to profit from successful enterprise, and if you want prices to be settled by "justice" rather than by the market, you will not have capitalism. And if you want all people to be rewarded equally for their labors and if you want a system in which everyone all the time will feel that they have been treated fairly, you cannot have capitalism.

THE PROFOUND IRRATIONALITY OF CAPITALISM: INVESTORS AS UNINTENDED ALTRUISTS

A final comment on capitalism and its image may be in order. When one examines the oft-neglected issue of risk, it appears that many capitalists effectively act as altruists—that is, they knowingly and systematically take a financial loss that, as it happens, betters the economic condition of their fellow human beings. And the capitalist system is profoundly irrational because it importantly depends on such economically bizarre behavior.

Two facts are central to this conclusion. First, people who actively speculate on the stock market, even the most seasoned and highly skilled, do worse on average than those who simply and almost randomly buy the market across the board. Some individual investors, of course, may do better than random just as some coin flippers may come up with ten heads in a row. But there is abundant and widely appreciated evidence that those who do better than the stock-market average are actually less numerous than one would expect by chance, and that those who do well in one period are not notably likely to do so in the next one.[68]

Second, for its fundamental workings capitalism requires that speculative investment money be generally transferred from bad enterprises to good ones. That is, investors regularly evaluate their holdings and express their confidence and concerns by moving their money in such a way that, in general and on balance and over the long run, they reward well-managed, productive companies and penalize poorly run, underproductive ones. Indeed, a central argument for reducing the capital gains tax is to encourage such beneficial, even benevolent, economic behavior.

Economic growth would be substantially less coherent and capitalism would develop far less effectively if this vital evaluative behavior were not taking place. On the other hand, those who do speculate in this manner are, on average and on balance and in the long run, making less money than they would if they simply bought the market and stood pat. Consequently, stock-market speculators are effectively unconscious altruists: their activities are an important aid to productive economic growth, but on average they are taking a financial loss in performing their highly useful function. If no one engaged in such activity, the rest of us would be less rich, and therefore we owe a debt of thanks to the speculators who are, indeed, less well off than they would be if they stopped speculating.

Thus at base, capitalism depends on the self-lacerating thrill of the gamble. Speculators, of course, are not principally trying to aid the general economy, but to become rich themselves, prefer-ably quickly. However, in the end and on average, their collec-tive gambles aid the general economy, and the gains they derive from their curious behavior are less than optimal. While this result may not be intentional, its ultimate effect is benevolent and self-sacrificing—and therefore effectively altruistic.

Sources of Capitalism's Negative Image

T HE PREVIOUS CHAPTER developed the suggestion that acquisitive capitalists are well advised, in the punchy, bulleted official philosophy of the highly successful head of Harley-Davidson, to tell the truth, keep your promises, be fair, respect the individual, and encourage curiosity.[1] The standard and well-aged image of capitalism, however, is of course quite the reverse. This negative image has been propagated over history by a wide variety of dectractors: socialists, communists, fiction writers, intellectuals, religious thinkers, and aristocrats. But the advancement of capitalism's negative image has also sometimes been aided by inept capitalist propaganda, by disenchanted capitalists, and by economically foolish behavior by capitalists themselves.

SOCIALISTS AND COMMUNISTS

Some of capitalism's critics, like socialists and communists, champion an alterative economic system—one, they propose, that is more humane and fair and productive than capitalism. Their goal has had a considerable utopian appeal, and over the last couple of centuries, often armed with ingenious and appealing folk songs and stirring promises, they have proved to be extremely adept propagandists—well organized and colorful.

As part of their promotional activities, they have naturally criticized and caricatured the competition and have done so with great, and often highly effective, élan. They have also ably used capitalism's apparent lapses, like the Great Depression, to make their point.

CHAPTER 3

STORYTELLERS

Another impressive source of negativism is storytellers who, quite apart from any leftist leanings, generally have found foolish capitalism to be more dramatic and interesting than its actual, boring sensible self.

Thus, gambling mobsters always seem inexplicably to rub out their debtors rather than cutting deals that might at least give them partial recompense. Employers who unwisely create dissension by brutalizing their charges are more engrossing than ones who maximize profits by cleverly maintaining a contented workforce. Landlords who mindlessly harass their tenants supply more dramatic punch than ones who realize they can charge higher rents if the tenants find the building to be especially desirable and its management especially pleasant. Labor negotiations that break down and lead to pitched battles between strikers and company goons are far more colorful than ones that lead to mutually satisfactory agreements. Wall Street entrepreneurs who cheat are found to be much more fascinating than ones who profit from integrity. Swindling adds grist to a tale even if it requires positing an improbable gullibility to the swindled.

And the factory system has rarely been portrayed by storytellers as the escape it often was from an unbearably grim, starvation-threatened, and highly exploitative rural existence, an escape which advanced the status of a class that "had never owned its own tools—or much of anything else, for that matter," as Rosenberg and Birdzell put it. Rather the factory system is almost invariably portrayed as something that cruelly reduced the status of independent artisans.[2]

Building a business can be an excitingly creative and dramatic experience. It requires quick thinking and improvisation in the face of enormous uncertainty; it is filled with risks and close calls; it frequently comes accompanied with personal, psychological, and family tensions; and it often ends in disaster. A great many people—from corner store owners to Wall Street wheelers and dealers—have been fascinated and excited by such risky, creative, and adventurous activity over the ages, and they have found enormous satisfaction in success and devastating misery in failure. It is impressive, therefore, how very few works of art have been devoted to exploring this process. We have uncountable tales of cops pursuing robbers, cowboys pursuing Indians, private eyes pursuing criminals, scientists pursuing space aliens, soldiers pursuing glory, men pursuing women, women pursuing men, athletes pursuing victory, artists pursuing expression, and courtroom lawyers pursuing what they hope will turn out to be the truth, but virtually none about entrepreneurs pursuing financial success.[3]

Perhaps capitalist risk-taking has been found to be difficult to portray because no one usually gets shot or involved in a car chase and because the costs of failure, the occasional suicide aside, show up in such unphotogenic and comparatively mild conditions as ulcers, insomnia, quiet despair, and reduced life expectancy. Indeed, in most fictional accounts, risk is rarely shown. For example, John D. Rockefeller worked assiduously and zealously to build his business, undergoing in the process emotional stress, nervous strain, physical fatigue, anxiety, indigestion, depression, and broken health, conditions that cumulated to force him into retirement at the age of fifty-two.[4] Then, even as he was retiring, electric and gas light began to destroy the demand for lamp oil which was, at the time, the main source of profit in petroleum. This was followed by fortuitous and nearly simultaneous invention of the internal combustion engine that caused demand for Rockefeller's product to soar.[5] A good story about such factors of risk and luck might be told, but mostly that capitalist is simply represented as effortlessly and ruthlessly successful.

Contrary to myth, in fact, capitalism is not treated sympathetically or realistically even in the Horatio Alger stories where the typical boy hero displays integrity, propriety, and industriousness, but is rewarded not through success in business, but because he stumbles upon an inheritance or because his virtues inspire the charity of an already wealthy patron. "'Money is the root of all evil,' my young friend. It is an old proverb, and, unfortunately, a true one," one of these patrons philosophizes in typically stilted manner in one of Alger's novels.[6]

Moreover, insofar as business activities are dealt with at all, there is a tendency to idolize and idealize lone inventors slaving self-lessly away in musty labs and dusky garrets and to neglect—in fact usually to caricature—deal-making marketers whose creative energies are often at least as important to an invention's eventual acceptance and success. In *Marketing Myths That Are Killing Business* (they come up with 172 of them), Kevin Clancy and Robert Shulman, point out, in fact, that when a product or service fails to sell it is usually the fault of marketing, not of inadequacies in the product or service itself. Similarly, it is the hired director who is generally held up as the central guiding force in the success of a motion picture, when in reality the producer's creative contribution in garnering funding, choosing scripts, and casting the major roles (as well as in marketing the final product) is often at least as important.[7]

It turns out, then, that if you build a better mousetrap, the world is entirely likely to be able to contain its enthusiasm for beating a path to your door, at least until someone, often at great cost and risk, is able to make it conveniently available at an attractive price—and the world may not come visiting even then. Rosenberg and Birdzell note that "innovation is a product of the organized enterprise, not just of the individual with an idea." In other words, as virtually any entrepreneur can attest—but scarcely any story-teller has ever noticed—an idea by itself is simply not enough. As Robert Cringely stresses, "There is an enormous difference between starting a company and running one. Thinking up great ideas, which requires mainly intelligence and knowledge, is much easier than building an organization, which also requires measures of tenacity, discipline, and understanding. Part of the reason that nineteen out of twenty high-tech start-ups end in failure must be the difficulty of making this critical transition from a bunch of guys in a rented office to a larger bunch of guys in a rented office with customers to serve." Apple Computer, he finds, tends to have good products, but poor "follow-through," while Microsoft has had a "terrific implementation of mediocre products." In this contest, Microsoft wins.[8]

As Irving Kristol has rhetorically observed of capitalism, "what poet has ever sung its praises? what novelist was ever truly inspired by the career of a businessman?"[9] Instead, over the centuries writers have persistently disparaged capitalism in broadside and in banner, in polemic and in poem, in tract and in novel, in movie and in folk song, for its supposed heartlessness, cruelty, vulgarity, and casual exaltation of debased human values.

INTELLECTUALS

More generally, there has also been something of a natural, historic antipathy toward capitalists on the part of intellectuals. In George Stigler's understatement, "The intellectual has been contemptuous of commercial activity for several thousand years"— Plato pointedly consigned the trader to the lowest level in his ideal society—and this perspective, Donald McCloskey argues, has escalated to a "sustained sneer" during the last century and a half. Or, as César Graña puts it, the "tradition of intellectual contempt for the bourgeoisie" has become "not only an attitude of dismissal, but a habit of implacable accusation."[10]

Intellectuals, almost by definition, tend to prize flights of fancy, grand generalizing, and cosmic conceptualizing: to Václav Havel, for example, "an intellectual is a person who has devoted his or her life to thinking in general terms about the affairs of this world and the broader context of things."[11] On the other hand, people who are successful in business must be comparatively practical, mundane, materialistic, banal, unreflective, methodical, pedestrian, plodding, unideological, routine, unromantic, patient, tidy, and, ultimately, boring to those who exalt evanescent and often vaporous flights of fancy.

Many intellectuals, like prophets of religion, have an alternative vision of what people ought to want, a vision insufficiently serviced, in their eyes, by rapacious capitalism. Consequently, they are often distressed, even offended, at the drive of capitalists uncritically to service whatever tastes the consumer might happen to have at the moment.[12] Thus, Havel exalts those intellectuals who care "whether a global dictatorship of advertisement, consumerism, and blood-and-thunder stories on TV will ultimately lead the human race to a state of complete idiocy."[13] Reflecting a perspective like this, intellectuals in Europe controlled radio and television for decades and made sure the media only presented programs that people *should* want to experience as opposed to the ones misguiding capitalism was likely to determine they might actually prefer.

Such thinkers as Alexis de Tocqueville, Thomas Jefferson, and Montesquieu professed great concern that rampant commercialism would lead to a timid and indifferent citizenry, leaving a country ripe for despotism. And the scholar-bureaucrats who guided traditional China through most of its history (and, in the process, kept it comparatively poor) emphasized classical learning and cultivated a contempt for material goals and acquisitiveness, though, of course, these value preferences do not appear to have implied that they, themselves, need necessarily pursue an ascetic lifestyle.[14]

In addition, the overly gregarious, glad-handing, hail-fellow-well-met demeanor of many people in business also can seem offensive, vulgar, and phony to many garret-loving, library-haunting, muse-awaiting intellectuals. Much of the uninformed association of capitalism with the novels of Horatio Alger may stem from the satisfaction of being able to ally business with works of fiction that are simplistic, banal, manipulative, and formulaic.

Intellectuals may also be understandably turned off by the often embarrassingly ingenuous and simple-minded prose of business books, most of which have all the wryness and subtlety of cheerleading as they exuberantly assemble lists of business principles that often seem banal, flip, corny, self-contradictory, and perhaps hypocritical, and as they rail on and on about loving the customer and assembling a "winning team."[15] For example, the ultimate "Key No. 9" in Lester R. Bittel's typically exuberant *Nine Master Keys of Management* (if there had been ten of these, the "keys" would no doubt have been labeled "commandments") turns out to be "Know Your True Self" for which the author conveniently supplies a "Self-Knowledge Tree."[16]

Businesspeople have also often been prone to high-minded

rhetoric that could appear disingenuous at best and hypocritical at worst to skeptical intellectuals. For example, a book on the rise of the Better Business Bureau is subtitled, rather too nobly, "A Story of What Business Has Done and Is Doing to Establish and Maintain Accuracy and Fair Play in Advertising and Selling for the Public's Protection." And in the book's introduction, Joseph Appel intones with off-putting self-righteousness: "When advertising . . . becomes . . . untruthful, insincere, fraudulent, and thus misleading and unfair to the consumer, it merely reflects the evils that exist in our social, political, and economic circumstances, all of which are inherent in the nature of man himself. The basic cause of these evils is *selfishness*. Commercial selfishness arises from human selfishness. And human selfishness is the root of all our problems."[17]

From the perspective of the intellectual, then, people in business may appear small-minded, crass, menial, and even stupid— though typically they will understand their business in greater depth and finer nuance than the average intellectual will ever understand anything. That the successful capitalist (intellectuals routinely ignore the many unsuccessful ones) makes far more money than the average intellectual can often inspire a special resentment among intellectuals. And they may be further offended of late by the prominence of successful businesspeople and by the fact that the economic function, as Graña observes eloquently, is "no longer a backstage chore relegated to classes which, since Plato, had been regarded as morally tainted by virtue of their very usefulness and efficiency."[18]

Robert Nozick stresses the role education may play in all this. Schools recognize and routinely reward intellectual achievement, not such business skills as "social grace, strong motivation to please, friendliness, winning ways, and an ability to play by (and to seem to be following) the rules." Thus, he argues, intellectuals, particularly "wordsmith" intellectuals, very often experience a sort of "relative downward mobility" of esteem when they enter real society after graduation, and they tend to focus their resentment at this perceived injustice on the capitalist system itself which, "by its nature, is neutral toward intellectual merit."[19] (However, intellectuals often do seem to pick up their anticapitalist views even while they are still in school and before they have discovered any personal devaluation in the larger society.)

Interestingly, the intellectual's antibusiness mentality often infects the views even of economists and of putative defenders of capitalism. When James Wilson announced that he would teach a course called "The Morality of Capitalism" at the UCLA School of Management, he reports that some of his business school colleagues "looked at me as if I were teaching one on 'Squaring the Circle' or 'Building a Perpetual Motion Machine'." Adam Smith gloomily maintained that the "commercial spirit . . . confines the views of men" with the result that their minds "are contracted, and rendered incapable of elevation." And his theory of the "invisible hand," whereby "natural selfishness and rapacity" and "vain and insatiable desires" have the effect, "without intending it, without knowing it" of advancing the interests of society, does have a rather patronizing tone and, as George Gilder suggests, rather "leaves the entrepreneur as a blind tool of appetite." John Maynard Keynes declared the capitalists' "money-motive" to be "a somewhat disgusting morbidity, one of those semi-criminal, semi-pathological propensities which one hands over with a shudder to the specialists in mental disease." Joseph Schumpeter, somewhat along the lines of Smith, argued (erroneously it seems) that capitalism would, or had, become stiflingly bureaucratized so that "human energy would turn away from business" and "other than economic pursuits would attract the brains and provide the adventure." And Francis Fukuyama, even while recently celebrating the triumph of capitalism, predicts that this success will lead to a "very sad time" notable chiefly for an all-consuming boredom: "The struggle for recognition, the willingness to risk one's life for a purely abstract goal, the worldwide ideological struggle that called forth daring, courage, imagination, and idealism, will be replaced by economic calculation, the endless solving of technical problems, environmental concerns, and the satisfaction of sophisticated consumer demands."[20]

What perspectives like these seem to demonstrate is the intellectual's inability to appreciate, even snobbish contempt for, the endlessly continuing drama, excitement, creativity, and even fun of the capitalist entrepreneurial endeavor.

RELIGION

Another traditional enemy of capitalism and an effective source of anticapitalist propaganda has been the church. St. Augustine denounced money lust as one of the three principle sins (right up there with power lust and sex lust), and Stigler identifies "a dislike for profit seeking" as "one of the few specific attitudes shared by the major religions."[21]

Capitalists can only prosper if they are able to come up with a product or service people genuinely value and (therefore) are willing to pay for. Accordingly, as noted in the preceding chapter, they routinely pander to the capricious whimsy, frivolous self-indulgence, crass materialism, all-consuming selfishness, and flighty narcissism of their customers. Religion, on the other hand, attained prominence in human life in part because it supplies relief from material woes and fates, and because it seeks to give higher meaning to a dreary and difficult life.

Therefore, it is not surprising to see the pope railing in a 1991 encyclical against capitalistic practices he finds distasteful, labeling them "consumerism," which he defines as a condition in which "people are ensnared in a web of false and superficial gratifications rather than being helped to experience their personhood in an authentic and concrete way."[22] Similar rejections of economic well-being and growth in favor of concrete personhood have routinely been advanced by such religious or semireligious leaders as Khomeini and Gandhi.

In the process, the church often seems to display what might be called a contempt for the consumer. For example, joining forces with like-minded socialists and with competition-fearing small businesses, it has often pushed to restrict shop hours in order to inconvenience trade and the general enjoyment of the mere material things in life.

ARISTOCRATS AND THE HONORABLE

The hostility of those who exalt the aristocratic and martial virtues—chivalry, honor, nobility, glory, valor, martial heroism—has also been a problem for capitalism. For these critics, observes McCloskey, "Don Quixote's idiocies in aid of chivalry are uncalculated, but noble," and an "impatience with calculation is the mark of romance."[23]

After quoting Benjamin Franklin on the economic value of hard work, honesty, punctuality, and frugality, Max Weber notes that such sentiments "would both in ancient times and in the Middle Ages have been proscribed as the lowest sort of avarice and as an attitude entirely lacking in self-respect," though, as Graña observes, this belief—or pose—has managed to retain much of its appeal in the nineteenth and twentieth centuries as well.[24]

Appropriately acquisitive capitalists will indeed routinely grovel. They will have no apparent sense of honor or self-respect or dignity as they seek to satisfy the whims of the consumer who, they feign to believe, is "always right" even when patently wrong. As long as they profit financially, they should be quite happy to let others walk all over them. Put positively, Mark McCormack praises an executive whose "greatest virtue is her ability to stifle her ego for the sake of others." Put negatively, novelist Richard Wright disgustedly tells of a man who allowed people to kick him for money, a service which could be considered entirely sensible from a strictly capitalistic standpoint.[25]

From such behavior, Adam Smith concluded that capitalism could render a man "incapable of defending his country in war. The uniformity of his stationary life naturally corrupts the courage of his mind, and makes him regard with abhorrence the irregular, uncertain, and adventurous life of a soldier." Smith did appreciate the bold, risk-taking behavior of merchants. But he put that kind of courage in an entirely different category, and then concluded, just like some of capitalism's most ardent opponents, that commerce "sinks the courage of mankind" with the result that "the heroic spirit is almost utterly extinguished," and the "bulk of the people" grow "effeminate and dastardly" by "having their minds constantly employed on the arts of luxury." By contrast, he held the "art of war" to be "certainly the noblest of all arts."[26]

Tocqueville was so alarmed at the prospect of the decadence of plenty that he advocated the occasional war to wrench people from their lethargy. And Immanuel Kant once argued that "a prolonged peace favors the predominance of a mere commercial spirit, and with it a debasing self-interest, cowardice, and effeminacy, and tends to degrade the character of the nation."[27]

Extollers of the martial virtues like Smith, Tocqueville, and Kant have been joined—or trumped—by such exultant war-glorifiers as the German historian Heinrich von Treitschke who fairly glowed at the turn of the century over the thought that war "brings out the full magnificence of the sacrifice of fellow-countrymen for one another . . . the love, the friendliness, and the strength of that mutual sentiment." By contrast with commerce, Treitschke held, something as sublime as a war should never be waged for mere "material advantage": "modern wars," he urged, "are not fought for the sake of booty." Similarly, German general Friedrich Bernhardi was of the opinion that "all petty and personal interests force their way to the front during a long period of peace. Selfishness and intrigue run riot, and luxury obliterates idealism. Money acquires an excessive and unjustifiable power, and character does not obtain due respect."[28]

Herbert Spencer concluded at about the same time that the destructive militancy of war should now be given over to the constructive competition of commerce, but war proponents like Homer Lea, an American military analyst of the time, while conceding that commercialism is "a form of strife," argued that it is a "debased one—a combat that is without honor or heroism."[29] Similarly, in Japan the code of Bushido held the pursuit of (material) gain to be dishonorable and accordingly held the economic pursuit of profit in contempt.[30]

Chivalry may, as they say, be dead, but chivalric contempt for the "bourgeois values" and for "trade" continues to this day in many quarters.

INEFFECTIVE CAPITALIST PROPAGANDA

Greed has never been an easy sell, and capitalism is, in economist Paul Samuelson's words, an "efficient but unlovable system with no mystique to protect it." Mario Vargas Llosa agrees: "unlike socialism, capitalism has never generated a mystique; capitalism was never preceded by a utopian vision."[31]

But even taking that into account, capitalists, many of whom have been spectacularly effective at selling their own products and services, have not been terribly good—or often, it seems, even very interested—in selling the system as a whole. Perhaps they have simply been too busy making money.

For example, promoters of capitalism sometimes try to pretend, utterly unconvincingly, that acquisitiveness is somehow secondary to its functioning. Or, as Peter Drucker laments, they go to the opposite extreme, and "make it impossible for the public to understand economic reality" as they crow, sometimes boorishly, over profit maximization, leaving risk and the cost of capital unmentioned and failing to explain why "profitability is a crucial *need* of economy and society."[32]

In addition, they generally stress capitalism's efficiency and economic productivity, leaving uncountered those who argue that capitalism is characterized by deceit, dishonesty, and uncaring cruelty. For example, Milton and Rose Friedman's 1980 book, *Free to Choose*, an agile and spirited defense of capitalism, tirelessly stresses the economic value of freedom, but nowhere suggests that capitalism inspires, encourages, or rewards honesty, integrity, compassion, or civility—indeed, those words do not even appear in the index. Meanwhile, Friedman's famous attack on corporate philanthropy may have a certain logic to it, but it plays magnificently into the hands of anticapitalists. And Friedrich Hayek's important and best-selling book, *The Road from Serfdom,* could be taken to assert uncaringly and absurdly that any government efforts to control business excesses or provide welfare for ordinary people will lead inexorably to totalitarianism.[33]

Thus, although the capitalist virtues are continually advocated in modern business books that are meant to be read by fellow acquisitive capitalists, the same virtues are rarely stressed by propagandists for the system as a whole. Rather, when they deal with such issues at all, they tend to emphasize the rather more modest qualities Montesquieu identified over two centuries ago as springing from "the spirit of commerce": frugality, economy, moderation, work, wisdom, tranquility, order, regularity.[34]

Notable politicians who have promoted capitalism have also sometimes been less than fully effective as propagandists. Ronald Reagan could be lovable, but he could also seem unaware and simple-minded, and Margaret Thatcher often came off as a strident, even threatening, schoolmarm. And both sometimes gave the impression that they simply didn't *care* about the poor and the unfortunate, a damaging inference that can also result from the many insufficiently nuanced attacks by braying conservatives on big government and welfare and handouts and high taxes and regulation and pointy-headed bureaucrats. There are welfare cheats, of course, but that doesn't mean no welfare check ever helped anybody in need or that the system is a complete failure. And, while environmental regulation may sometimes be foolish, it nonetheless deserves much of the credit for the enormous improvement in air quality that has taken place in the last decades.[35] At the same time, a remarkably small amount of procapitalist rhetoric has been devoted to showing how capitalism has actually been the greatest—indeed, the only significant—alleviator of poverty in history.

Ironically, two politicians from opposition parties, Bill Clinton and Tony Blair, have presided over what appears to be the final triumph of Reaganomics and Thatcherism in the 1990s (a phenomenon discussed more fully in chapter 5). These adept campaigners have substantially adopted their rivals' economic policies, but they have been able to convince people that they will nonetheless apply them with "compassion" and "inclusiveness" (Blair) because they "feel your pain" (Clinton).[36]

CAPITALISTS

In fact, many capitalists essentially seem to believe much of the anticapitalist caricature. Just as retail customers tend to recall most vividly the occasional instance in which they have been treated rudely or have been short-changed, businesspeople who may live daily in a business environment that is overwhelmingly honest, reliable, civil, and fair, often tend most graphically to remember and to recount the rare instances when they have been cheated, dealt with unfairly, or given painfully unkind treatment. That is, the many fair and honest deals or the general tone of easy and productive geniality do not live in the memory so much as the occasional fraud and the infrequent, if vivid, acts of boorishness and outrageous incivility—like the story McCormack relates of the (economically foolish) boss who berates and then summarily dismisses a worker in the presence of his co-workers.[37]

Moreover, many people in business are not really all that comfortable with competition. "Markets are," as George Shultz stresses, "relentless," and the change competition and development produce, notes David Landes, "is demonic; it creates, but it also destroys."[38] Losers in the process, who tend to have more time on their hands than winners, may, as noted in the previous chapter, spend much of it crying foul. As Alfred Marshall observes, traders or producers who are undersold by a rival often "are angered at his intrusion, and complain of being wronged; even though . . . the energy and resourcefulness of their rival is a social gain." (He also points out that this perspective can lead many to spend less time actually competing than seeking to reduce the risks of competition by guild or government regulation or through collusion and price-fixing.)[39] The alternative, of course, is to admit one's own failings or at least one's own bad luck. Blaming the winner, and positing nefarious motives and tactics, are often much more satisfying.

For example, after losing a dramatic, high-stakes, but essentially honest and straightforward buyout battle of the late 1980s, F. Ross Johnson was inspired loudly to proclaim his crisp and memorable, if newly discovered, "Three Rules of Wall Street": "Never play by the rules. Never pay in cash. And never tell the truth." Similarly, partisans of Apple Computer like to stress that the winning arch-demon, Bill Gates of Microsoft, lifted—or was mightily inspired by—some Apple ideas, rather than admit that Apple made a series of foolish marketing decisions. And although, as Alan Nevins stresses, Rockefeller generally paid a fair price for his rivals' property when he bought them out, he was routinely accused of underpaying, particularly by people who distrusted the future of the petroleum industry even though they had been part of it, and blundered by taking payment in cash rather than in Standard Oil Company stock which was later to appreciate massively in value.[40]

Partly in consequence of all this, the anticapitalist stereotype may historically have inspired capitalists detrimentally to behave, or to think they should behave, in a manner consistent with the negative image of capitalism. And such behavior in turn would, of course, reinforce the stereotype.

Moreover, the notion that it is to one's long-term economic benefit to carry on one's business with honesty, fairness, civility, and compassion may not be all that readily apparent even to the people who stand to profit from such behavior. For virtuous business behavior to take hold, someone must go against the age-old image and conventional wisdom to demonstrate the profitability of such behavior. Business virtue, it appears, comes about not necessarily naturally, but rather as an innovation. This phenomenon, an important one for economic development, is considered in the next chapter.

The Consequences of Capitalism's Image
for Economic Development

I HAVE ARGUED that business behavior that is honest, fair, civil, and compassionate is, on average, wealth-enhancing. It follows that, all other things equal, places where these business virtues flourish will be more prosperous than places where they don't.

And, indeed, that seems to be substantially the case. As Max Weber once pointed out: "The universal reign of absolute unscrupulousness in the pursuit of selfish interests by the making of money has been a specific characteristic of precisely those countries whose bourgeois-capitalistic development . . . has remained backward."[1]

As this suggests, one of the most important causes of economic development seems to have been the gradual acceptance of the business virtues. Policies like price controls or high taxes will cramp free economic activity and hinder economic growth as economists point out all the time. But so will business behavior that is routinely deceitful, unfair, uncivil, and uncaring. Because the cost of doing business in that sort of environment is effectively higher, people will engage in less economic activity, and economic growth, accordingly, will be lower.

This chapter advances five connected propositions. First, for countries to prosper, it is important that they develop the appropriate business virtues. Second, popular acceptance of capitalism's negative image—particularly by capitalists themselves—can hamper this process, often severely. Third, since the business virtues are economically advantageous, they can arise and flourish through normal competitive pressures and for the most part do not need to be superimposed from above by governmental, quasi-governmental, or religious authorities. Fourth, for this to happen, however, a sort of business innovation is required: because the value of virtuous business behavior has not typically been intuitively obvious, someone must actually come to realize that virtuous business behavior is economically beneficial in the long run and act accordingly. And, fifth, it is likely that the rise of business morality has been, and continues to be, a major, not an incidental, contributor to economic development.

THE UNEQUAL RATE OF ECONOMIC DEVELOPMENT

Perhaps the most important single fact about economics, economic history, and economic development—and, indeed, about human material well-being—is tidily conveyed in figure 4.1. In 1750, as can best be determined, all areas of the world were fairly equal economically—actually, equally poor by present-day standards since the vast majority of people everywhere, and at all times up until then, lived in substantial misery, even wretchedness.[2] Economic historian Paul Bairoch, whose data are displayed in the figure, estimates that the ratio of per capita wealth between the richest and poorest countries was no more than 1.6 to 1 in 1750. But, beginning in the nineteenth century, and accelerating over the next two centuries, an enormous gap opened between what we now call the developed world—North America, Europe, and, eventually, Japan—and the rest. By 1977 this disparity had become 7.7 to 1 when all the developed countries are compared to all the underdeveloped ones, or 29.1 to 1 when the most developed countries are compared to the least developed ones.[3]

This remarkable, even astounding, historic change has been dubbed "the European miracle" by Ernest Jones. It has also sometimes referred to as the industrial or the technological revolution, but it might more properly be called the capitalist revolution, for, as David Landes notes, "those economies grew fastest that were freest."[4]

One of the most comprehensive efforts to explain the West's economic growth is *How the West Grew Rich* by Nathan Rosenberg and L. E. Birdzell. Their assessment stresses technological innovation and development, an expansion of knowledge, science,

73

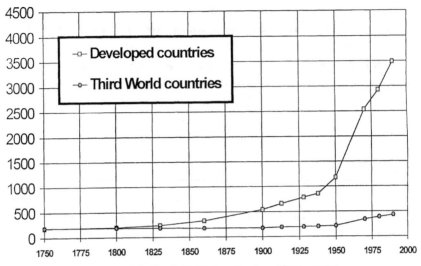

FIGURE 4.1. Real GNP Per Capita, 1750–1982
(1960 U.S. dollars and prices).

and education, and the fact that, government and religion came, advertently or inadvertently, to allow people the freedom to exploit and pursue economic opportunities as they arose or were created. Or, as Donald McCloskey puts it succinctly, growth was caused by "originality backed by commercial courage." As part of their explanation, Rosenberg and Birdzell stress the importance of organizational innovation including a notable rise in business morality.[5]

Of course, virtuous business behavior is not *sufficient* for economic development. Inept government policies, religious prescriptions (like a bias against usury), or detrimental social attitudes (like laziness or endemic distrust or the conventional acceptance of the notion that prices should be set by custom or tradition) will discourage business and entrepreneurship and hamper growth no matter how honest or fair or civil or compassionate the business norms. But norms are important to economic development because when people generally expect to be treated dishonestly, unfairly, or discourteously in business they will tend to avoid making transactions, and hence there will be less wealth and growth because there will be less economic activity.

SUPERIMPOSING THE CAPITALIST VIRTUES

If the capitalist virtues are important for economic development, it becomes equally important for these virtues to become accepted by people doing business. One possible route is for them to be superimposed from above.

Thus, in his important attempt to account for the rise of the business norms appropriate for economic development, Douglass North stresses the role of formal institutions which regulate, police, and enforce contracts and agreements. As a prime example of a place where such institutions do not exist, he points to markets of exchange in the Middle East and North Africa in which there is "a multiplicity of small-scale enterprises," where nearly half the labor force is engaged in the exchange process, where skill in exchange "is the primary determinant of who prospers in the bazaar and who does not," and where haggling "is pervasive, strenuous, and unremitting." He argues that "The key is men seeking gains at the expense of others. In essence, the name of the game is to raise the costs of transacting to the other party to exchange. One makes money by having better information than one's adversary."[6]

But high transaction costs in this system seem not so much to be the "name of the game" as the unintended, detrimental result. And, most importantly, given the sheer difficulty of dealing, and the attendant substantial danger of being treated dishonestly or unfairly, people—particularly insecure and underinformed ones—will tend to avoid engaging in economic exchange when they can. Thus, just about everyone will be poorer.

North finds it difficult to "understand why these inefficient forms of bargaining" should persist. One would expect, he suggests, that "voluntary organizations would evolve to ensure against the hazards and uncertainties of such information asymmetries." But that has not happened, he suggests, because "the fundamental underpinnings of legal institutions and judicial enforcement that would make such voluntary organizations viable and profitable" are missing. "In their absence," he concludes, "there is no incentive to alter the system."[7]

In their discussion of economic development, Rosenberg and Birdzell consider essentially the same puzzle, and they also mostly stress the importance of institutions. "Somehow," they note, "appreciable numbers of people with money . . . must have come to believe that others . . . were honest, diligent, and could be trusted." How this "business morality" came about "we cannot know for sure," but they suggest that it may have emerged from merchant associations, perhaps reinforced by the "appeal of the Reformation and its concomitant morality" or by religion more generally (though presumably not directly from the anticapitalist teachings of the Catholic Church).[8] Similarly, Alexander Gerschenkron, while noting that "a sociology of business honesty still remains to be written," speculates that "over large areas of Europe the historical experience of the craft guilds, with their attempts to increase and to maintain standards of quality and reliability, was of considerable importance in forming the business ethics of the community."[9]

But such reasoning may have gotten the causal flow backward. A mechanical imposition of appropriate legal, moral, social, religious, or judicial mechanisms is not adequate. Religions everywhere routinely prescribe moral behavior, yet the extension of this value to the business sphere is by no means obvious. And as North himself stresses, poor countries often remain that way even when they adopt the laws and formal institutions of developed countries: "Although the rules are the same, the enforcement mechanisms, the way enforcement occurs, the norms of behavior, and the subjective models of the actors are not." Similarly, Gerschenkron observes that the attempt by the Russian government to create guilds by fiat "could not yield the same positive results as did their spontaneous evolution in Western Europe."[10] Furthermore, it is difficult to see how such business-enhancing virtues as civility and compassion and, to a degree, fairness, could be formally enforced by courts, guilds, or regulatory agencies in any case.

In addition, it does not seem that government policy is hampering the development of sensible voluntary organizations at least in the markets North is assessing: as he observes, "governmental controls over marketplace activity are marginal, decentralized, and mostly rhetorical"[11] That is, the economy, perhaps mostly by default, is essentially free—but relatively poor.

VIRTUE AS A BUSINESS INNOVATION

What seems to be required is not so much formal institutions of control or enforced morality, but rather the realization by people doing business that honest, fair, civil, and compassionate dealing will be profitable. What the bazaar mainly needs are innovators with the enlightened business mentality of a Barnum or a Wanamaker. Neither they nor the Quakers needed "the fundamental underpinnings of legal institutions and judicial enforcement" to discover that honest, fair, civil, and compassionate dealing was a smart, profitable way to do business.

The mechanism of economic development, then, would run something like the following. Someone comes to the (apparently non-obvious and difficult) realization that honest, fair, civil, and compassionate dealing will lead to greater profits. Shattering tradition, that person innovates and puts together a business with those qualities. The business enjoys a competitive advantage and accordingly prospers (that is, there is no collective action problem: the innovating business will not place itself at a competitive disadvantage by its virtuous behavior). Other businesses, noticing the success of the innovator, follow suit, and eventually a substantial number of businesses become characterized by such behavior. This process reduces the sheer pain of doing business—effectively it reduces the costs of obtaining products and services by reducing the costs of the transaction itself. As a result, people more and more overcome their traditional, well-founded aversion, and cheerfully do business with such enterprises. Economic activity therefore increases overall and the general economy grows.

After honest, fair, civil, and compassionate businesses come to dominate an area of economic activity, they may become concerned that they are being given a bad name by the relatively few members who still engage in (economically foolish) dishonest, unfair, uncivil, and uncompassionate business practices. Accordingly the dominating honest, fair, civil, compassionate businesses form associations and work with the government to force the dishonest, unfair, uncivil, and uncompassionate businesses to shape up or to leave the industry.[12] People become more and more pleased with the ease and pleasure of doing business, and confidence soars. Growth happens.

When dishonest business practices are common, courts or regulatory systems would be swamped if they tried to eliminate these practices. But when honesty is the norm, the courts and regulators would be capable (strongly encouraged by the many honest businesses) of enforcing the comparatively rare breaches of contract and other infractions, thus keeping business transactions even more honest, and consequently further encouraging economic growth (though at no time will institutions become very important in enforcing norms of civility, compassion, and perhaps fairness). It seems likely, then, that effective institutions are more nearly the result of virtuous norms than the cause of them.

North notes that "we are not yet able to explain precisely the forces that shape cultural evolution," but "the most common explanations lean heavily upon evolutionary theory, although with the additional feature that acquired characteristics are culturally transmitted."[13] And he stresses the importance of "path dependence," the notion that current developments are the result of forces set in motion long ago in the society.

By contrast, the explanation for economic development I am suggesting stresses only the development of a key innovation: the grasping of the idea that honesty, fairness, civility, and compassion furnish a competitive advantage. Economies prosper when that idea is seized and then imitated.

The idea may seem very simple, but that doesn't mean it is obvious. Many ideas which seem in retrospect to be both simple and obvious took centuries, indeed millennia, to become accepted. As Landes points out, "just because something is obvious does not mean that people will see it, or that they will sacrifice belief to reality." For example, Rosenberg and Birdzell note that the factory system, an innovation of major historical significance, was only dreamed up around 1750 even though it could clearly have been invented and developed centuries earlier since it did not depend on the development of machinery and could have been profitably applied to ancient crafts like ceramics.[14] Something similar could be said for such notable innovations as Arabic numerals and the idea of zero, the wheel, the alphabet, separate left-turn lanes on city streets, just-in-time management techniques, and home delivery of pizza. Indeed, a major reason professional magicians protect their secrets so assiduously is that their successful illusions often exploit devices that are very simple but yet, clearly, are not obvious. When the tricks are explained, most of the previously mystified would probably react not with awe at the magicians' cleverness, but with amazement at their own naivete.

Evolution and "path dependence," it seems, are not necessary for economic growth to take place. All that is required is that people be acquisitive and that they understand that virtuous business behavior is profitable. Acquisitiveness seems to be built in: as Rosenberg and Birdzell put it, "it is not so much the urge to advance one's own interests which has varied conspicuously through human experience, as the possibilities of gratification and the way these possibilities have been pursued."[15] And the idea that virtuous behavior in business is profitable appears to be easy to grasp and imitate once its value is demonstrated by an innovator. Accordingly, whatever their historical path, economies can turn around quickly—something that seems to have happened in the last years in Spain and in a number of Latin American countries despite the rather gloomy implication North drew when he applied his path dependency approach to them in 1990.[16]

Wanamaker's Saga

The economic development process I have in mind can be illustrated by the experience of American retailing entrepreneur John Wanamaker. Judging from his recollections, American business practices in the 1860s were quite similar to those discussed by North for the Middle East and North Africa: "The law of trading was then the law of the jungle, take care of number one. The rules of the game were: don't pay the first price asked; look out for yourself in bargaining; haggle and beat the seller as hard as you can. . . . And when a thing was once sold—no returns. . . . Schools in stores for training employees were unknown."

Shattering this ill-tempered tradition with its high transaction costs—a tradition that probably goes back to the origins of commerce—Wanamaker consciously set out to provide "a service exactly opposite to the ancient custom that 'the customer must look out for himself.'" He applied set prices—called "one-price" since the same price was paid by all buyers—and importantly combined this with a money-back offer which essentially guaranteed a low price. Moreover, he carefully trained his employees. They were told to "place yourself in the customer's place and give such service as you would like to have given you were you buying instead of selling," to "give information and show new goods just arriving without allowing an unspoken grumble to appear on your face," and, when customers come back with goods to return, to "be, if possible, more agreeable than if they had come to make other purchases."[17]

The approach proved, in the words of business historian Joseph Appel, "sound not only in morals, but in economics as well."[18] Wanamaker became rich, his success was imitated by his competitors, a retailing revolution took place, customers became much happier to part with their money, and the economy prospered. But the revolution took an innovator—someone had to realize that "ancient custom" was dictating a foolish way to do business, then devise an effective alternative, and finally show that it would work in practice.

Barnum's Fable

The same mechanism can be seen in microcosm in a story related by my favorite capitalist, P. T. Barnum:

> One of the ushers in my Museum once told me he intended to whip a man who was in the lecture room as soon as he came out.
> "What for?" I inquired.
> "Because he said I was no gentleman," replied the usher.
> "Never mind," I replied, "he pays for that, and you will not con-

vince him you are a gentleman by whipping him. I cannot afford to lose a customer. If you whip him, he will never visit the Museum again, and he will induce friends to go with him to other places of amusement instead of this, and thus, you see, I should be a serious loser."

"But he insulted me," muttered the usher.

"Exactly," I replied, "and if he owned the Museum, and you had paid him for the privilege of visiting it, and he had then insulted you, there might be some reason in your resenting it, but in this instance he is the man who pays, while we receive, and you must, therefore, put up with his bad manners."

My usher laughingly remarked, that this was undoubtedly the true policy, but he added that he should not object to an increase of salary if he was expected to be abused in order to promote my interests.[19]

This story neatly illustrates several points. First, it shows the capitalist's acquisitive interest in subordinating classic, and apparently natural, notions of "honor" to ones of profit as discussed in the previous chapter. Second, it demonstrates that the business virtues are not necessarily self-evident: the usher had to have the company's interests explained to him. (It also illustrates what economists call the principal-agent problem or the problem of agency cost or risk: the personal interests of the business owner, the principal, are not identical to those of the employee, the agent, and a wise manager must make special effort to instill in the employees an awareness of, an appreciation for, and, at best, a personal identification with, the interests of the business at large.) And third, it shows that these interests are quickly grasped once they are explained and that they may soon be extrapolated to further logical and self-interestedly useful conclusions.

The Tale of the Saturn

A more contemporary illustration of the development process may come from a recent innovation in the automobile industry, which is just about the only American retail business after the Wanamaker revolution that still haggles with consumers.[20] It seems no coincidence that car salesmen consistently receive the lowest ratings for "honesty and ethical standards" in polls.[21]

Venerable traditions, however, are now being challenged by the Saturn automobile which has a policy of charging set prices. It happens that not only have Saturn sales been brisk, but in *Consumer Reports* questionnaires returned by 120,000 new car buyers in 1995, Saturn placed solidly first in satisfaction with the car-buying experience. Most interestingly, Saturn was most closely followed on the satisfaction list not by other inexpensive cars, but by expensive ones like Infiniti, Saab, Lexus, and Mercedes, whose high ratings are not surprising because, as the magazine notes, "The potential profit in an expensive car is a powerful incentive for such dealers to stroke their customers." Obviously, Saturn is exceptional, and it is clear that "the no-haggle policy followed by Saturn dealers contributes greatly to that make's high standing."

The magazine interestingly compares the process of buying a Saturn with that of buying a Toyota. The staff member who did the comparison actually got a better deal on the Toyota, which is, in addition, a better car. However, his attitude toward the buying experience is expressed this way: "In all, it took me nearly two hours to escape from the showroom" at Toyota while, at Saturn, he found things to be "relaxed" with "no haggling—just a civilized take-it-or-leave-it price." As a result, he paid more money for a worse car and was much more satisfied with the transaction. The magazine concludes, "for many people, the happy experience may be worth a little extra money."[22] Or, put another way, the Saturn effectively costs less because the cost (pain) of transacting business is lower.

There are signs other automobile dealers are beginning to follow Saturn's successful one-price or no-haggle or no-dicker policy. If so, the industry might well enjoy greater overall sales since more people will buy more cars more often—essentially because the transaction costs have been substantially reduced. But the value of this approach, which may come to seem obvious, has clearly not been so until now. It will have taken an effort by one company to show the approach's value, after which other acquisitive retailers will follow suit to the benefit of just about everyone.[23]

Confiscating Autocrats

Martin McGuire and Mancur Olson have argued that autocrats with long-range perspectives ought, out of simple self-interest, to be benevolent to the societies they control since they will do better themselves if these societies are productive. Consequently, to maximize their extractions from the society in the long term, autocrats are best advised to limit their short-term extractions. Or, as Bradford De Long and Andrei Shleifer put it in a related study, governments which set lower and less destructive tax rates allow for faster growth and therefore benefit in the long run.[24]

However, when one looks at the behavior of autocrats in the dynastic systems of preindustrial Europe, short-sighted confiscation rather than enlightened benevolence was clearly the norm. And as a result, growth was generally quite low. In an effort to explain this curious phenomenon, scholars argue that the autocrats must have had short-term planning horizons.[25]

But while the princes and kings in Europe often led challenged regimes, many of them reigned for decades and almost all, probably, wanted very much to believe that they were establishing dynasties which would last for ages. Consequently, it seems more plausible that these autocrats engaged in self-interestedly foolish behavior not because they thought only in short run terms, but because it never occurred to them that benevolence was to their long-term benefit, and accordingly they applied confiscatory and arbitrary taxation policies that were substantially self-destructive. What they lacked was not a long-term perspective, but an enlightened and ingenious innovator like Wanamaker who could show them the advantage of abandoning established custom. This wisdom, so clear to twentieth-century economists, was not so to ancient autocrats—any more than the wheel was to American Indians.

THE RISE OF BUSINESS VIRTUE

It seems to me, then, that Montesquieu is quite correct when he proclaims, "it is almost a general rule that wherever manners are gentle, there is commerce," but that he exaggerates when he adds, "and wherever there is commerce, manners are gentle." Similarly, Adam Smith seems in error to argue that "Whenever commerce is introduced into any country probity and punctuality always accompany it. These virtues in a rude and barbarous country are almost unknown"; or to insist that "when the greater part of people are merchants they always bring probity and punctuality into fashion, and these, therefore, are the principal virtues of a commercial nation." The same problem exists when James Q. Wilson suggests that capitalism fosters "a reasonable concern for the opinions of others," or when Daniel Klein concludes that "commerce elevates manners and probity," or when an eighteenth-century Scottish historian, William Robertson, contends that commerce "softens and polishes the manners of men."[26]

There is clearly plenty of commerce in the bazaar North discusses or in the American business "jungle" Wanamaker grew up with and helped revolutionize, but apparently little in the way of probity, gentleness, or soft and polished manners. These virtues, then, do not follow automatically from commerce; it is quite possible to have commerce that is also rude and barbarous. North's bazaar and Wanamaker's jungle are not "barbarous" or "backward" because they lack commerce or trade. Rather, they are "barbarous" or "backward"—that is, relatively poor—because commerce and trade are being carried out without the capitalist virtues.

An interesting discussion in Adam Smith may help to illustrate this process further. Smith makes three connected observations. First, "mercantile manners" in Spain and Portugal are worse than those in London, and these in turn are worse than in Amsterdam. Second, the merchants of Spain and Portugal are a good deal less rich than those of London who, in turn, are less rich than those of Amsterdam. And third, the rate of profit is highest in Spain and Portugal, lower in London, and lowest in Amsterdam. From this set of observations, Smith concludes that high rates of profit cause one to have bad mercantile matters.[27]

But there is another interpretation. The merchants of Amsterdam are relatively rich *because* they have good mercantile manners. Moreover, the relatively high rates of honesty and fairness among

the merchants of Amsterdam me
when the rate of return is low, while
able Spain and Portugal only make de
because they need to compensate for th
in their uncertain and unreliable (and u.
atmosphere.

It appears, then, that capitalists are not ⋅
honest simply by nature. For them to become ⋅
them that honest, fair, civil, and compassionate ⋅
will increase their long-range profits. And it may
quite a long time for them to grasp the economic b⋅
behavior. Indeed, one of the reasons for capitalis⋅
image may be that for millennia capitalists—like thos⋅
maker's jungle and in North's bazaar—often *were* disho⋅
fair, and uncivil at various levels because, like Europe's a⋅
of old, they were foolishly unaware of their own long-rang⋅
nomic interests. Lacking was *enlightened* self-interest.

Business Virtue Before the Nineteenth Century

It is difficult, but not impossible, to find a clear appreciation for
the economic value of the business virtues before the nineteenth
century. The Quakers did bring virtue to business early on, and
they prospered because of that behavior, but they were virtuous for
religious reasons, and their wealth perhaps therefore could be
seen in a sense to have been accidental or incidental. As early as
1748 Benjamin Franklin stressed the economic value of honesty in
enhancing one's ability to obtain loans,[28] and there have long
been informal reputational mechanisms like guilds and systems of
merchant law for policing honesty among businesspeople.[29] Like
Franklin, Daniel Defoe appreciated the value of business honesty.
He was a businessman for decades before he became a novelist—
indeed, invented the novel—with *Robinson Crusoe* in 1719 at the
age of fifty-nine. In an insightful discussion of business practices of
the time, he does chance to observe that "An honest tradesman is
a jewel indeed, and . . . is valued wherever he is found."[30] And even
if the capitalists of his era were not systematically writing about the

ist virtues, Adam Smith did, as noted above, detect probity
gentleness of manner as common characteristics at least of
ommerce in his neighborhood.[31]

ndoubtedly some capitalists have long understood the value of
ous behavior and did not bother to articulate the practice into
explicit business principle because it was second nature. Thus,
modern businessman, Mark McCormack, contends that keeping
ur word is part of the "unwritten code of business" and that be-
ieving in your product is one of the "self-evident truths of salesmanship."[32] At once, then, he declares such notions to be so obvious that they hardly need to be explicated, and then does exactly
that by writing his book. (However, neither notion, it seems safe to
suggest, has ever been self-evident to any Hollywood scriptwriter.)

The Rise of Business Virtue in the Nineteenth and Twentieth Centuries

However, as an elaborated, self-conscious principle, the notion
that honesty and especially fair dealing, civility, and compassion
bring wealth—a notion commonly found in contemporary books
on business like McCormack's—seems to have been generally discovered, or to have been made clearly explicit, only in the nineteenth century or so. In fact, P. T. Barnum's mid-century tract, *The
Art of Money-Getting*, is the earliest publication I have been able to
find in which the profitability of virtuous business behavior is
specifically and extensively laid out.

This rather remarkable silence suggests that the explicit discovery of the capitalist virtues and their conscious application to actual business behavior may be fairly recent. In fact, the rise of these
virtues seems very much to have coincided with the remarkable
economic rise of the West documented in figure 4.1, and probably
importantly helped cause it.

I was once struck in this regard by a passage in a recent guide-
book to Italy. Travel guides tend to be very upbeat, but when the
author got to Naples he became unhinged: a beautiful spot, he
pointed out, but avoid dealing with Neapolitan merchants because
they are unrelievedly vicious and, given half an opportunity, will

rob you blind. This sort of reputation, one suspects, was none too good for the local tourist industry or for the area's economic development more generally.[33] Similarly, Edward Banfield tells of the labor situation in a southern Italian town he visited in the 1950s: "An employer who can get away with it is almost sure to cheat his employees," and relations with employees are accordingly poisoned by "anxiety, suspicion, and hate." The result of this condition is not only that the employees work less hard and less reliably for their employers, thus reducing profits to the enterprise, but that the economic development of the whole area suffers. Banfield notes that "mutual distrust between landlords and tenants accounts in part for the number of tiny, owner-operated farms," because: "rather than work a larger unit on shares, an arrangement which would be more profitable but which would necessitate getting along with a landlord, the peasant prefers to go it alone on his uneconomic holding." Many peasants simply subsist on their private plots, and since these are too small to keep them occupied much of the time, the result is that a great deal of labor potential is lost to the economy. Banfield notes that in some towns in the area the upper class, out of tradition, "has always been brutal toward the peasants," a phenomenon that would similarly hamper economic development.[34]

This business behavior seems to be a contemporary holdover from the kind that was once quite standard in Europe. For example, a prominent business writer in 1771, declaring what Rosenberg characterizes as the "conventional wisdom" of the time, argued, "Every one but an idiot knows that the lower classes must be kept poor or they will never be industrious. . . . they must (like all mankind) be in poverty or they will not work." Or Sir William Temple, in his severely mistitled *Vindication of Commerce and the Arts*, published in 1758, let it be known that the only way to make laborers "temperate and industrious" was "to lay them under the necessity of labouring all the time they can spare from meals and sleep." And Richard Tilly points to an "employer ideology" that was quite common in the nineteenth century: the belief among industrialists that "workers were naturally lax, undependable, opportunistic, and that only the threat of extreme poverty supplied

adequate motivation to work." In partial response to such employer attitudes, the labor movement grew and demanded that
these attitudes be changed: for example, there were a series of
strikes in Poland in 1905 in which the workers explicitly demanded
not only that certain particularly hated company officials and su-
pervisors be fired but that company officials treat them with respect and dignity, in part by abandoning the use of familiar forms
of address that implied they were children.[35]

To allow a condition to develop in which employee-employer relations are so filled with hate and suspicion that workers feel they
have to *strike* to be treated with dignity and respect and trust is almost mind-bogglingly stupid by the standards of modern business
management—or, more precisely, from the standpoint of the management it is economically foolish.[36]

Gradually, the notion, now accepted as elemental and even sim-
ple-mindedly obvious, that "a happy employee is a productive employee," has taken hold. For example, Tilly traces the dawning
awareness during the nineteenth century by industrial entrepreneurs that "peaceful industrial relations and high labour productivity have generally gone together." This realization made them
"increasingly willing to deal with their workers as economic partners who had the right to fair and honest treatment." By 1996,
when strikes in the United States dropped to a fifty-year low, corporate officials suggested that the phenomenon stemmed from "increased employer-employee team-work and from management's
treating workers with more respect."[37]

Before such now-conventional approaches were discovered,
however, businesses must have frequently, even routinely, been run
with a fair amount of what we would now consider arrant (and foolish) viciousness toward employees because management believed
workers would only produce when threatened with poverty. Accordingly, employer-employee relations must have been filled with
the rancor, distrust, and intense hostility Banfield found more recently in southern Italy. Small wonder unionism and revolutionary
socialism began to grow.

The admonitions of famous and successful capitalists like P. T.
Barnum probably helped businesspeople begin to grasp the busi-

ness virtues. So, perhaps, did the striking revelations of the experiments at the Hawthorne Works of Western Electric in the 1920s which systematically suggested that higher employee morale led to greater and more efficient production.[38]

But the most effective approach in disseminating these essential insights was probably simple competition. Those business which have prominently gone against the once-conventional wisdom and have treated their employees as partners rather than as children and with respect rather than suspicion have benefited economically, and other businesses have either had to follow suit or, on average, to fall behind economically. Management consultants Thomas P. Peters and Robert Waterman supply a litany of modern instances.[39]

Similarly, the setting of prices for retail goods and the sense of fairness the practice induces, which began only in the nineteenth century thanks to such innovators as Wanamaker, is now accepted as standard operating procedure in developed countries. So, more generally, is the concentrated and dedicated effort to make the shopping experience a pleasant one rather than an encounter filled with inefficient—and, for many people, alienating—rancor and dispute as buyer and seller trade wary insults across a counter in a manner neatly caricatured in 1727 by Daniel Defoe:

> *Lady.* I like that colour and the figure well enough, but I don't like the silk, there's no substance in it.
>
> *Mercer.* Indeed, Madam, your Ladyship lies, 'tis a very substantial silk.
>
> *Lady.* No, no, you lie indeed, Sir, 'tis good for nothing, 'twill do no service.
>
> *Mercer.* Pray, Madam, feel how heavy 'tis; you will find 'tis a lie; the very weight of it may satisfy you that you lie, indeed, Madam.
>
> *Lady.* Come, come, show me a better; I am sure you have better.
>
> *Mercer.* Indeed, Madam, your Ladyship lies; I may show you more pieces, but I cannot show you a better; there is not a better piece of silk of that sort in London, Madam.
>
> *Lady.* Let me see that piece of crimson there.
>
> *Mercer.* Here it is, Madam.

Lady. No, that won't do neither; 'tis not a good colour.
Mercer. Indeed Madam, you lie; 'tis as fine a colour as can be died.
Lady. O fie! You lie, indeed, Sir; why it is not in grain.
Mercer. Your ladyship lies, upon my word, Madam; 'tis in grain, indeed, and as fine as can be died.[40]

Despite Defoe's witty mockery, it took the better part of two centuries before retailers came fully to the apparently non-obvious realization that this sort of activity was economically foolish. Those who did so not only prospered (on average), but so did the economies they flourished in. Robert Frank suggests that "the art of bargaining" is "in large part the art of sending misleading messages" about how much one would be willing to buy or sell an item for. The problem is that to the degree people don't like to receive (or send) misleading messages, they will be disinclined to deal at all.[41]

Although it is difficult to chart precisely or to quantify, Tilly argues that honesty in business affairs grew notably during the nineteenth century in Britain and Germany. Entrepreneurs, he finds, increasingly came to view "individual transactions as links in a larger chain of profitable business ventures, as building blocks in a long-run process of capital accumulation" rather than as "one-time opportunities to be exploited to the utmost." He notes, for example, that, even though business activities were expanding greatly, there was no rise in the number of complaints about breaches of contract or fraud. Indeed, the business done by Prussian banks expanded by 563 percent over a forty-year period, while their bad debts accounts declined by 20 percent. At the same time, "'honest' business practices such as the refund of cash or the exchange of bad merchandise to disappointed buyers, the introduction of fixed prices, brand labels and also longer-run credit agreements, would seem to have become more widespread."[42]

Writing in 1890, economist Alfred Marshall could see this happening. He noted that the quickly developing modern economy "has undoubtedly given new openings for dishonesty in trade." New ways "of making things appear other than they are" had been discovered, and "the producer is now far removed from the ultimate consumer" and thus "his wrong doings are not visited with the prompt and sharp punishment which falls on the head of a person who, being bound to live and die in his native village, plays a dishonest trick on one of his neighbours." However, although "the opportunities for knavery are certainly more numerous than they were . . . there is no reason for thinking that men avail themselves of a larger proportion of such opportunities than they used to do. On the contrary, modern methods of trade imply habits of trustfulness on the one side and power of resisting temptation to dishonesty on the other, which to do exist among a backward people."[43] But in my opinion, the modern economy was developing precisely *because* habits of trust had been developed, not, as Marshall suggests, the other way around.

Tilly finds that "established business leaders played a dominant role in the deliberations and negotiations that produced legal codification of business norms" but also that the legalization of behavioral norms took place precisely when the norms had already become widely accepted. For example, fraud and dishonest practices by the larger German merchant houses in wholesale trade had become quite rare because they were "'monitored' (or controlled) by competition, and the problem was to extend these practices to the smaller firms which were often "devoid of any solid mercantile tradition" and had "no reputation to lose." This process can also be seen in the history of the American circus. By 1910, circuses like Barnum and Bailey and Ringling Bros. had profited by clean business practices and had come to dominate the industry. They became concerned, however, that business on the road was being harmed by bad business practices that still persisted. Consequently, the successful circuses, at the instigation of Charles Ringling, met to create agreement that the generally profitable "Sunday School" approach should dominate.[44]

This is all quite recent, it seems. Concentrated efforts by businesses to establish agencies to police industry-embarrassing and therefore profit-harming fraud and misrepresentation began in the United States only about a hundred years ago: Underwriter's Laboratories, for example, was not founded until 1901, the Better Business Bureau not until 1912. But by the time modern economics was coming into its own in the twentieth century, its practitioners were so used to honest business behavior that their economic models, as Stigler observes, "almost invariably postulate transactions free of fraud or coercion," a regularity which suggests to him that the profession has implicitly concluded that fraud and coercion "are not empirically significant elements in the ordinary economic transactions of an enterprise economy."[45]

Spreading Virtue

Rather curiously, then, as the experience with the bazaar cited by North or the American business jungle observed by Wanamaker suggests, capitalism per se doesn't seem necessarily to generate a long-term perspective: although acquisitiveness may be natural, it has apparently often taken an effort for people—like Barnum's usher, many nineteenth-century business leaders, or princes in preindustrial Europe—to grasp the concept of enlightened, long-term economic self-interest. Indeed, in Poland workers were striking to get management to do something that, Peters and Waterman would insist, was overwhelmingly in the business interest of the people they were striking against, who, however, were too boneheaded—or too steeped in erroneous conventional business wisdom—to figure this out on their own.

But, as in the case of Barnum's usher, once the concept is clearly and profitably introduced by an innovator, its economic value can be easy to grasp. This may bode well for the economies of many postcommunist countries in Europe, despite "path dependence" problems arising both from the fact that their peoples lived for decades under a system that was devotedly anticapitalistic and from the fact that these countries were comparatively poor even before that—a condition Gerschenkron attributes in part to "disastrously low" standards of honesty in business.[46] For the most part, people in these countries now seek to achieve the wealth of the West, and many seem quite willing, even eager, to imitate Western business practices to do so. Moreover, they have local role models in the newly established branches of successful Western businesses which routinely and prominently apply established and tested procedures of honesty, fairness (including set prices accompanied by a return policy), civility, and compassion to their business practices.

Thus the invasion of institutions like McDonald's and K-Mart can have a very beneficial impact on the business climate in many places. The new Russkoye Bistros in Moscow provide "fresh ingredients and fast and pleasant service in a clean environment," and the marketing director of the Moscow McDonald's remarks, "I really see it not so much as competition as the acceptance of our way of doing business. They have seen what we can do and I hope they will learn from it." Indeed, local businesses that fail to follow suit, by, for example, continuing to treat their customers with the incivility so familiar in the Soviet era, are likely quickly to find themselves in financial trouble.[47]

The Relative Importance of Business Virtue in Economic Development

The rise of business virtue, then, seems to have been strongly associated with economic development: "business honesty and capital accumulation," observes Tilly, "go hand in hand." Although it would be extremely difficult to determine with precision the degree to which economic development can be attributed to the rise of capitalist virtue, it is quite possible that the rise of such virtue is massively and crucially important. Indeed, as Tilly suggests, "Honesty, in the sense of adherence to generally accepted rules of behavior, would seem to be a fundamental prerequisite for the development of market economies."[48] And so, in my view, would be the associated virtue of fairness, as well as those of civility and compassion, that are so important to effective management.

Per capita income in the United States quadrupled between 1869–78 and 1944–53, and an important study by Moses Abramovitz concludes that changes in capital and labor inputs as conventionally defined and measured can account for only a small fraction of this remarkable increase: in fact, about 90 percent of the economic growth remained to be explained, a portion economists, straining the language almost to the breaking point, came to label "the residual."[49]

In assessing this striking finding, Rosenberg, in an article pointedly entitled, "Neglected Dimensions in the Analysis of Economic Change," suggests that what may be mainly important in economic development are "important qualitative changes in the human agent as a factor of production . . . which typically escape the scrutiny of the economic theorist." As examples he lists "knowledge, technical skills, organizational and managerial abilities, levels of economic aspiration, responsiveness to economic incentives, capacity to undertake and to adapt to innovation, etc." And he concludes that "economic growth is, in many important respects, a learning process whereby the human factor acquires new skills, aptitudes, capabilities, and aspirations."[50]

In this, Rosenberg, an academic economist, comes perilously close to embracing the point of view of a huge number of how-to management books that embody the perspective expressed in the title of one of them: *What They Don't Teach You at the Harvard Business School.* Typical is the harangue by Peters and Waterman in their multiyear bestseller, *In Search of Excellence.* The approach to management typically taught in business schools, they argue, "doesn't tell us what the excellent companies have apparently learned." What they have learned, it seems, are essentially the business virtues: "to love the customers," to appreciate "the rock-bottom importance of making the average Joe a hero and a consistent winner," to "show how strongly workers can identify with the work they do if we give them a little say-so," to understand that "self-generated quality control is so much more effective than inspector-generated quality control," to "overspend on quality, overkill on customer service, and make products that last and work," and to know that "good managers make meanings for people, as well as money."[51]

Tilly observes that "In economically underdeveloped countries of the twentieth century one can observe low standards of business morality reminiscent of Europe's backward areas of the eighteenth and nineteenth centuries."[52] Similarly, Marshall noted in 1890 that among those peoples "who have none of the originating power of the modern business man, there will be found many who show an evil sagacity in driving a hard bargain in a market even with their neighbours."[53]

Although there are many reasons economies grow, developed countries are distinguished from underdeveloped ones, it seems, not so much by differences in natural resources or in native brainpower or in skill levels as by differences in business virtue. And the European experience strongly suggests that a deficit in business virtue is a problem that can be readily overcome.

THE RELEVANCE OF AN EFFECTIVE LEGAL SYSTEM
TO ECONOMIC DEVELOPMENT

"Little else," Adam Smith once said, "is requisite to carry a state to the highest degree of opulence from the lowest barbarism, but peace, easy taxes, and tolerable administration of justice."[54] Following Smith, many have argued that a viable judicial system is important for the development of capitalism, particularly as the ultimate arbiter of contracts and property rights and as final recourse against fraud.

However, an effective court and norm-regulating system, while certainly valuable, may be somewhat less vital to economic development than might first appear. A fair and reliable judicial system facilitates capitalism and may be useful as an accepted ultimate arbitrator, but it is a clumsy and costly expedient. (And, as observed above, it is unlikely to be able to do much to enforce such important business-enhancing qualities as civility, compassion, and often fairness.)

Daniel Klein observes that "the simple explanation for integrity would seem to be that agreements are enforced by court and constable." However, "everyday experience and numerous scholarly studies suggest that official contract enforcement is often costly and impractical, yet promises usually work out nonetheless." For example, in his study of actual business behavior, Stewart Macaulay found that only five of the twelve purchasing agents and only two of the ten sales managers he interviewed "had ever been involved in even a negotiation concerning a contract dispute where both sides were represented by lawyers," and *none* had ever "been involved in a case that went to trial." Instead, he found that "disputes are frequently settled without reference to the contract or potential or actual legal sanctions." Indeed, "there is a hesitancy to speak of legal rights or even to threaten to sue." As one respondent put it, "You don't read legalistic contract clauses at each other if you ever want to do business again. One doesn't run to lawyers if he wants to stay in business because one must behave decently." In this regard, "holding a customer to the letter of a contract is bad for 'customer relations.' Suing a customer who is not bankrupt and might reorder again is poor strategy."[55]

Principally, then, people in American business rely on trust and reputation to make deals happen. For example, the agreements between Standard Oil and the railroads in the nineteenth century, of enormous economic consequence to both parties, were mostly sealed simply with a handshake. Indeed, if there is even a small chance that the courts would be required to make a deal work, the deal will probably not be consummated in the first place. Macaulay, in fact, is able to find remarkably few reasons written contracts exist at all, and many of these are essentially extralegal. He points out that contracts are often mainly put together because they are required by the federal government, or by a lender of money, or for the convenience of outside lawyers who are obsessed with avoiding "any possible legal difficulty" and demand a formal contract because it makes their job easier in the (highly unlikely) event that a future dispute will have to be settled in court or by legal pressure.[56]

Actually, where trust has arduously, and profitably, been built up, efforts to further guarantee honesty by mechanical legalistic devices could actually be counterproductive, even in the consumer field. Suppose, for example, that the successful mail-order merchant, L. L. Bean, were to attempt to enhance its reputation for business integrity by establishing a policing organization in cooperation with a governmental agency guaranteeing that any customer cheated by the company would receive quick and full recompense. It seems likely that this innovation would generate, rather than lower, concern about the company's integrity, and it would almost certainly reduce sales. It is sounder business for Bean to rely simply on its reputation for honesty, even though this is secured by nothing grander than its appreciation for the fact that this reputation is money in the bank.[57]

It is surely desirable to have enforceable antifraud legislation, but it is worth noting that the buyer must still be wary of fraud even in the United States with its highly developed and substantially incorruptible court system. A consumer who has been cheated can report the fraud to the authorities, and the cheater may perhaps eventually be put in jail. But as a practical matter the swindled have very little chance of ever getting their money back, particularly since the courts are already jammed with criminal (especially drug) cases. Moreover, a huge portion of transactions do not involve enough money to make a civil suit a sensible recourse—and, of course, many agile swindlers will wisely keep their fraudulent profit per sucker low enough to make sure of that.[58]

In fact, it appears that an effective court system came relatively *late* in the economic development process. For the most part, European states mainly absorbed preexisting commercial and merchant law into their evolving legal systems. And, as Rosenberg and Birdzell suggest, this did not come about even in advanced England until late in the eighteenth century after a great deal of commercial expansion had already taken place: an effective court system did not *cause* commerce but rather was "a *response* to the expansion of commerce"; as such it (merely) "*added* to the ability to predict the behavior of others." Or, as Adam Smith observes, "commerce and manufactures gradually introduced order and good government," not the other way around.[59] Similarly, as noted above, the codification of economic norms into law and government-enforced regulations generally took place after the norms had already become fairly standardized forms of behavior.

Furthermore, as the experience of contemporary China demonstrates, if other conditions are appropriate, a great deal of economic development and investment is possible even when a commercial legal system can scarcely be said to exist. The process, however, does tend to put a premium on informal contacts with government, and there tends to be an emphasis on shorter-term investments and transactions.[60]

What is mainly needed for the emergence of an effective court system, it appears, is the development of such business norms as honesty, integrity, fairness, and reliability. At that point, the relatively few miscreants will stand out and can perhaps be dealt with by the courts; without the norms, the courts would be utterly overwhelmed. It is the central message of this chapter that, because those adhering to the norms have a competitive advantage in the long run, the norms tend to emerge naturally out of ordinary competition when an innovator grasps the economic benefit of such virtues and demonstrates their advantage by putting them into practice.

Development, Happiness, and the Rise of the Politically Incorrect One-Handed Economist

As NOTED in the previous chapter and as charted in figure 4.1, over the last two centuries or so an enormous and accelerating expansion of economic wealth and well-being has taken place in the developed world. This development has been utterly unprecedented in the history of the human race, and in my view it has been importantly enhanced by the gradual acceptance by people in business of the virtues of honesty, fairness, civility, and compassion as innovative capitalists discovered the economic value of these virtues.

The rather uniform anticipation among economic historians is that this remarkable economic expansion will continue, broaden, and even escalate in the future.[1] This cheery prediction may prove pessimistic, however, because it leaves out the enhancing benefits that will derive from the efforts of the economics profession itself.

The remarkable economic expansion of the past has taken place substantially by accident or default: it was not notably guided by government policy—indeed, it frequently took place *despite* government policy. This is because it occurred when economists often didn't know what they were talking about or fundamentally disagreed, or, when they could agree, were often ignored by decision makers who were pursuing divergent agendas, were mesmerized by faulty economic folk wisdom or ideology, or were paralyzed by political cowardice.

In this chapter I propose that there has been an important change in this condition by the end of the twentieth century. Economists, I suggest, now basically have reached a substantial and probably correct consensus about how economies work, and they are able to prescribe policies that have a good chance of enhancing an economy's ability to grow. And there is another change. In the past, the advice of economists was very often politically unattractive—politically incorrect—because policymakers gave noneconomic values higher priority, or because other advisers seemed to have more intuitively plausible palliatives, or because acceptance of the advice would cause short-term political pain. Now, however, the economists' advice is increasingly being accepted by decision makers.

This chapter explores the rise of economic science, its increasing acceptance, and the consequent prospects for vastly expanded economic growth worldwide. In the process, economists and likeminded idea entrepreneurs seem substantially to have managed to get across four highly consequential and enormously controversial ideas: the growth of economic well-being should be a dominant goal; wealth is best achieved through exchange rather than through conquest; international trade should be free; and economies do best when the government leaves them substantially free.

The chapter also muses over the curious fact that advances in economic well-being do not necessarily cause people to profess that they have become happier. Rather, each improvement seems quickly to be taken in stride, and standards are continually raised to compensate. However, this phenomenon seems to help stimulate further economic development, and it may have a kind of intellectually invigorating quality of its own.

ONE-HANDEDNESS

Lawrence Henderson of Harvard University once suggested that by 1912, for the first time in human history, "a random patient with a random disease consulting a doctor chosen at random stood better than a fifty-fifty chance of benefiting from the encounter." This vivid observation suggests how recent the rise of medical science has been and, further, it points to the fact that not so long ago, physicians, while perhaps generally dedicated and well meaning, often did more harm than good. After all, a doctor who doesn't understand germ theory may innocently carry a disease from one patient to the next, making matters far worse than if the patients had instead consulted a priest, a shaman, or a snake oil salesman, or if they had simply stayed quietly at home in bed. In a similar vein, Sir William Osler of Johns Hopkins observed in 1894 that "we may safely say (reversing the proportion of fifty years ago) that for one damaged by dosing, one hundred are saved."[2] Chanting a thousand "Hail Marys" many not do much good physically (though it might have a beneficial placebo effect), but misguided, if well-intentioned, bleeding or leeching or uninformed dosing could easily make the malady worse—and, by Osler's reckoning, did so almost all the time as late as the mid-nineteenth century.[3]

Economics, it seems to me, is now about where medicine was a century ago. Essentially, economics has probably reached the point where the random government official or business executive consulting the random economist is likely to benefit from the encounter. Fifty years ago, Harry Truman, frustrated with economic advisers who kept telling him on the one hand that a certain consequence could be expected from a particular action, while on the other hand the opposite consequence might come about, frequently expressed a yearning for what he called "a one-handed economist." Increasingly over the twentieth century, economists, through trial and error, experiment and experience, abstraction and empirical test, seem to have developed a substantial consensus about broad economic principles, if not always about nuance and detail. And thus we seem to be approaching the age Truman yearned for—the age of the one-handed economist.

I need to stress that I am applying a standard here that is significant, but not terribly exalted. By present standards, after all, medicine was woefully inadequate at the turn of the century, and physicians were still misguidedly killing a fair number of their patients. But, as figure 5.1 demonstrates, over the course of this century medicine has advanced from a base that has turned out to be essentially sound, and the result has been a spectacular and historically unprecedented increase in life expectancy, first in developed countries, and then more recently in the less-developed world.[4] In like manner, although economics is hardly an exact science, if economists have, at last, essentially gotten the basics correct, this

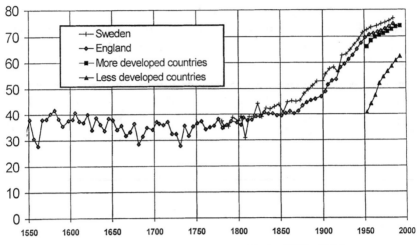

FIGURE 5.1. Life Expectancy at Birth, 1550–1990.

accomplishment is potentially of enormous importance to the advancement of economic well-being.

The "economists" I am referring to might perhaps be better designated "policy economists"—people whose business it is to derive coherent and practical policy prescriptions from what they take to be the central notions of economic science. Included in this group would be not only many academics in economics departments and business schools, but also policy and financial analysts working for or running think tanks, private businesses, and investment firms, as well as those hanging out at policy agencies like the Federal Reserve, the Congressional Budget Office, the International Monetary Fund, and the World Bank. It would also include those seeking to develop technical tools for analyzing and assessing the real world—as, of course, modern medicine has been dependent for much of its success on the development and proliferation of a raft of probing, measuring, and analyzing methods and tools.[5]

I do not propose that these economists now have an all-embracing theory of the economy: after all, physicians were correctly convinced that aspirin relieves pain and that smoking causes cancer before much of an explanation was developed for why these things were so.[6] Nor, certainly, do I mean to suggest that economists never disagree or err. The removal of tonsils has ceased to be routine. And for a very long time physicians ordered parents to warm formula milk before feeding it to their infants, presumably on the plausible assumption that bottled milk should be the same temperature as breast milk; eventually, however, someone determined that babies were generally quite capable of digesting cold milk, and the conventional advice was accordingly abandoned after causing great inconvenience to parents and occasional danger to their babies when sleepy parents inadvertently fed them scalding milk.

But I propose that, in general, economists now are substantially on top of their topic, that they are amassing knowledge in a manner that is generally progressive and cumulative, and that the advice they render is likely—or more likely than not—to be sound.

A impressive indication of this came in the early 1990s when economists were confronted with a new and quite astounding problem. For various reasons, some two dozen countries with highly controlled (and underproductive) economies, including some of the biggest in the world, were suddenly freed of economy-stifling ideological controls and wished to become rich. As Lawrence Summers observes, the death of communism caught the economics profession unprepared: although there had been quite a few studies at that point about the transition of market economies to controlled or command economies, "there was not a single book or article on the problem of transforming an economy from the communist to a market system." Indeed, the word "privatization" had only been recently developed in connection with Margaret Thatcher's relatively modest efforts to denationalize comparatively small portions of the British economy.[7]

Economists were called in to sort out this novel problem. Even though their ideas about how to encourage economic well-being and growth had been principally developed through the analysis of economies that were relatively free, it is impressive testimony to the fundamental soundness of these ideas that the advice so generated proved to be substantially (though not invariably) sound even when applied under these unprecedented and unstudied circumstances. In case after case, countries that generally followed the advice have been able to achieve considerable (though certainly not painless) success in transforming their economies and in achieving meaningful growth, often in an astoundingly short period of time. Similar success, following similar advice, seems to have recently been achieved in many places in southern, eastern, and southeastern Asia and in much of Latin America.[8]

Thus, it appears that George Stigler had it essentially right in his 1964 presidential address to the American Economic Association when he assessed the state of the art and decided to gloat for a minute: "For 200 years our analytical system has been growing in precision, clarity, and generality, although not always in lucidity," he argued, and during the preceding half-century there had been an "immense increase in the power, the care, and the courage of our quantitative researches."[9] Moveover, it seems to me that economics, like medicine, has importantly improved in those respects in the decades since he delivered that address.

POLITICAL INCORRECTNESS

Historically, however, there has been another problem to overcome. Economists may render sound advice, but, as the variable postcommunist experience shows, the politicians and administrators who are their advisees may reject it because they find it politically incorrect.

They may find it so, first, because they disagree with the value or the goal the economists advocate. For the most part, this has not been a problem for medicine: the physician's goal—better health for the patient—is readily accepted. By contrast, the economist's goal of economic growth and well-being has often been rejected— been found to be politically incorrect—because people hold other, often conflicting, values, like honor or class differentiation or traditional justice or piety to be more important. Accordingly, for economic science to triumph, it has been necessary for economic goals to become dominant.

Second, modern economists, like modern physicians, have had

to convince their advisees that they know what they are talking about and that their proposed remedies will function. This has not been an easy task because, as modern economics has advanced, it has developed a perspective that often runs counter to some competing notions about how economies ought to work. Many of these alternative notions are morally appealing and alluringly common-sensical—and hence politically correct—like the still popular views that the best way to protect domestic employment is to restrict competitive imports or that the best way to beat inflation is for the government to dictate prices.

Finally, the advice of economists, even when accepted as valid, may be rejected because politicians and administrators find it to be politically painful to carry out. In this case, the analogy with medicine works quite well. As it has burgeoned, the science of medicine unfortunately did not discover that maladies could be cured by such agreeable remedies as eating chocolate. Rather, it kept coming up with remedies that involved cutting patients open, encasing them with plaster, drilling into their aching teeth, consigning them to passive inactivity, giving them bad-tasting tonics, denying them the tasty foods they most want to eat, mandating boring exercises, and puncturing them with long needles. (Lately, however, beneficial health effects have happily been found in the moderate, but regular, ingestion of red wine, liquor, and pizza.[10] Maybe things are beginning to turn around.) People had to become convinced that physicians and dentists knew what they were doing before they would follow advice like that. And they also had to become willing to swallow the medicine—that is, to suffer short-range pain for the promise of long-term benefit—particularly when priests and palm readers regularly arrived at palliatives that were less painful and more convenient.

In like manner, many—perhaps most—of the remedies modern economics has advanced have turned out to be politically painful, particularly in the short run. As Michael Weinstein puts it, economists "compulsively remind people to eat their spinach."[11] For example, if economists could discover that subsidies to politically active dairy farmers would not only help the farmers but also importantly benefit the economy as a whole, politicians would be hanging on their every word—the advice would be pure political chocolate. Unfortunately, economists have generally prescribed political spinach: cutting the dairy farmers from the public dole— no matter how deserving they may be as people, no matter how bucolic their farms, no matter how well-groomed their cows—and letting them descend quietly into ignominious bankruptcy and then perhaps to seek other, unsubsidized, work. Moreover, there is very often a political dilemma in the fact that the people who will benefit in the long term from the economists' advice don't know who they are while those who will be disadvantaged in the short term know this only too well and are quick to scream.

Four Economic Propositions That Have Become Increasingly Accepted

For the economists' politically incorrect perspectives and prescriptions to prevail, then, populations and policymakers have had to become convinced that economists know what they are talking about and also to accept their dominant goal—achieving a healthy, growing economy—as well as their often painful devices for achieving that goal. It has been a long, uphill struggle, but as the century closes, economists and their allies seem substantially to have been successful in this endeavor.

Four propositions seem central to this process, and each has been mightily contested over the last century or two. In my view, it has been essential for economists and like-minded idea entrepreneurs to get these propositions accepted in order to be effective— in order for economists to become, in Stigler's words, "the ornaments of democratic society whose opinions on economic policy shall prevail."[12]

Moreover, if these four elemental propositions have become substantially accepted, the ancillary consequences are enormous. Not only do they seem to hold the formula for a huge expansion of economic well-being, but in combination they suggest the demise of such central human institutions as empire and war.

106

1. The Growth of Economic Well-Being Should be a Dominant Goal

As central goals, economists often stress, or effectively stress, advances in economic well-being, a concept that usually includes considerations of economic growth as well as assessments of the way the wealth generated by that growth is distributed, particularly insofar as it brings people out of poverty. To develop this perspective, they frequently assume, model, and essentially favor people who are acquisitive: people who are centrally, indeed entirely, occupied with advancing their own long-term economic well-being.

As discussed in chapter 3, this perspective has traditionally rankled with people who treasure such values and goals as honor, heroism, empathy, altruism, sacrifice, selflessness, generosity, piety, patriotism, racism, self-respect, spirituality, nationalism, and compassion. They often condemn the economic motives as crass, materialistic, cowardly, vulgar, debased, hedonistic, uncaring, selfish, immoral, decadent, and self-indulgent.

Many economists are, or at any rate act like, economic determinists and, to be sure, when anything notable takes place there is almost always someone somewhere who is profiting financially. Agile economic determinists (working on the principle, "follow the money") can usually ferret out the profiters (or "profiteers") and triumphantly proclaim them to be the essential cause of the event. (The fact that there are also often many important and influential people *losing* money on the event rarely troubles them very much.)

However, noneconomic values have often been deemed more worthy than economic ones. For example, Simon Kuznets has pointed out that the quest for otherworldly eternity and the quest to maintain inborn differences as expressed in class structure have often been taken to be far superior to economic advancement. And, as Rosenberg and Birdzell observe, a number of business innovations that clearly have been successful economically—such as joint-stock companies, department stores, mail-order houses, chain stores, trusts, branch banks, and multinational corporations—have inspired great efforts to make them unlawful by those who prefer to maintain traditional, even folksy, ways of doing things even if this means slower economic development. At the same time, sentimental, economically dubious preference has often been shown for cooperatives, small farms, and mom-and-pop stores.[13]

An important area in which noneconomic values have usually dominated is war. Like murder, war rarely makes all that much economic sense even though it would be difficult to find a war from which no one has profited financially. For the most part, in fact, economic motivations often seem like a rationale for impulses that are actually more nearly moral, aesthetic, emotional, or psychological. As Quincy Wright observed after a lifetime of study of the matter: "Studies of both the direct and the indirect influence of economic factors on the causation of war indicate that they have been much less important than political ambitions, ideological convictions, technological change, legal claims, irrational psychological complexes, ignorance, and unwillingness to maintain conditions of peace in a changing world." Consider, in this respect, the conclusions of historian Hartmut Pogge von Strandmann about the process by which Germany began World War I:

> The drive to the east and to the west was underpinned by an imperialist culture which spread the virtues of Social Darwinism, the conquest of markets, the penetration of spheres of influence, competition between capitalist partners, the winning of living-space, and the rising power of the state. Buoyed up by an assumed military superiority, general economic strength and particular industrial vigor, widespread optimism and a mood of belligerence, the military and political leaders found, when they made the decision to push for war, that this was an acceptable option to many Germans, possibly even to the majority. . . . Confidence, determination, and the belief in victory were the ingredients of a willingness to fight an expansionist war.[14]

Economics—the "conquest of markets"—is in there, but buried among a fusillade of other, and probably far more important, motivating factors. Moreover, if businessmen had actually been running the combatant nations in World War I, they would likely have found it sound business to cut losses once the war devolved into the inconclusive, pointless, and hugely punishing trench warfare phase.

Similarly, Hitler's invasions a generation later were linked to a sort of crackpot economic theory about "living space," but to see his goals as primarily economic is to give short shrift to his ego-mania and to his much more motivating notions about race and the value of war in nation building.[15] Elsewhere and at the same time, Japan's catastrophic refusal to abandon its hugely—even ab-surdly—costly effort to conquer China when the United States so demanded made little economic sense. And, on the other side, the main reason the United States became involved in Asia in opposi-tion to Japan in the late 1930s was an aesthetic, sentimental, or moral impulse to keep the heroic, persecuted Chinese from being dominated by a vicious foreign regime: as Bruce Russett notes, "by embargoing Japan in 1941 the United States was giving up an ex-port trade at least four times that with China."[16]

The Cold War and its various damaging hot wars in places like Korea and Vietnam were mainly impelled by a communist expan-sionary ideology that stemmed not so much from economics as from an elaborate theory about social class warfare that was pro-foundly romantic and sentimental (and misguided). The Cold War abruptly evaporated not out of economic necessity, but be-cause the communists abandoned their threatening theory.[17]

Likewise, although the Gulf War of 1991 is often considered to have been primarily about petroleum, if economic considerations of that sort had indeed been dominant, Saddam Hussein would have quickly retreated after his economy was destroyed and it be-came clear he would be unable actually to sell the oil he had just conquered in Kuwait. Moreover, George Bush (motivated, it ap-pears, mainly by aesthetic or humanitarian repulsion and by per-sonal pique) would never have invaded because any problem of oil supplies had already been solved by the quite cheerful willingness of Saudi Arabia and other countries to pump additional supplies—indeed, the only thing keeping oil prices high at the time was Bush's threat to start a war.[18]

It seems likely, then, that, if people with business motivations had actually been running the world, its history would have been quite a bit different (and generally better). Economists and their like-minded allies have made an important contribution by helping to teach the world to value economic well-being above passions that are often economically absurd.[19]

As Bush and Hussein demonstrated in 1990, the pursuit of wealth is hardly the only motivating factor today. The desires in China for reintegrating Taiwan or in South Korea for reunification with the impoverished north are essentially romantic and sentimental, and tempestuous and violent disagreement over the fate of Jerusalem scarcely makes much economic sense either. One can even find sober, deliberative Canadians who would rather be less wealthy than open up their trade with the United States because that, they fear, might besmirch the quest for a Canadian national identity. As one former Canadian diplomat, an opponent of expanded trade with the United States, put it, "Canada has never made economic sense, and Canadians have always had to pay an economic price for their political and cultural identity."[20]

However, the single-minded pursuit of wealth has come generally to be unashamedly accepted as behavior that is desirable, beneficial, and even honorable, and we seem now to be reaching the point where business motivations have become much more important than they have been in the past. Thus in formulating his policy toward China in the 1990s, American President Bill Clinton decided that economic considerations should substantially dominate ones about human rights—a conclusion that, however dismaying to some rights groups, generally went down well politically.

In this regard, it may be useful to review the association, noted in chapter 3, once proposed by Immanuel Kant between the "commercial spirit" and "self-interest, cowardice, and effeminacy." Maybe he had it right, and maybe that's not such a bad thing.

After all, under the free systems advocated by economists, people can service their long-term economic self-interest only if they are able to provide a good or a service other people freely find of value. And in the process of producing this good or service, acquisitive providers have generally discovered, as argued in previ-

110

ous chapters, that they can profit better when their business practices are honest, fair, civil, and compassionate.

Moreover, although it may be cowardly by the standards of those who exalt the martial virtues to turn one's back when insulted, it is possible, by other standards (the ones Barnum uses in his fable on p. 80), to suggest that lethal battles fought over the cut of one's coat or over the color of one's sneakers or over "spheres of influence" or over a chunk of land not big enough to bury the slain, are not only economically foolish, but quite childish.[21] Perhaps a world where a form of cowardice is rampant might be better than one where people are routinely running around looking for fights to prove, or test, their manhood—constantly seeking the bubble reputation even in the cannon's mouth, as Shakespeare's Jaques puts it.

And it may be effeminate to avoid unnecessary conflict, to temper anger, and to be guided by the not entirely unreasonable notion that other people do, in fact, sometimes have feelings. But, as I have suggested, such gentle, accommodating behavior is, in general, economically beneficial—that is, it enhances the general prosperity. And a world where that quality is in abundance may not, after all, be all that undesirable even if it sometimes comes laden with a degree of treacly sentimentality.

Thus, a society dominated by "self-interest, cowardice, and effeminacy" might, under some circumstances, prove to be entirely bearable. And, in part through the insidious efforts of generations of economists, societies in the most advanced portions of the world have increasingly moved in that direction.

2. Wealth Is Best Achieved Through Exchange, Not Through Conquest: The Demise of Empire and War

The nineteenth-century British historian Henry Thomas Buckle hailed Adam Smith's *Wealth of Nations* as "probably the most important book that has ever been written" because it convincingly demonstrated that gold and silver are not wealth but are merely its representatives, and because it shows that true wealth comes not from diminishing the wealth of others, but rather that "the benefits of trade are of necessity reciprocal."[22] Smith's insights are elemental and profound, and, as Buckle suggests, they had once been counterintuitive—that is, Smith and others had to discover them and point them out. Thanks in part to the promotional efforts of legions of economists and other like-minded idea entrepreneurs, they have now substantially infused the world.

The gradual acceptance over the course of the twentieth century of propositions 1 and 2 has helped lead to one of the most remarkable changes in world history: the virtual eradication of the ancient and once vital notion of empire. Putting it another way, "the conquest of markets," a notion identified by Pogge von Strandmann in the German thinking of 1914, has declined markedly as even a partial reason, or excuse, for military action.

For millennia, the size of a country's empire was accepted as one of the chief indicators of its greatness. Although the quest for empire was often impelled by noneconomic factors such as the appeal of adventure or the need to "civilize" or convert the unenlightened, it was often partly based—or rationalized—as well on economic or pseudo-economic reasoning. Over the last century, economists and allied idea entrepreneurs like the best-selling English journalist and economic writer, Norman Angell, have successfully undercut the appeal of empire by convincing people more and more that economic well-being, not the vague sense of "owning" distant lands, should be the dominant goal and that trade, not conquest, is the best way to accumulate wealth.[23]

Another combined effect—not necessarily intended—of agreement with propositions 1 and 2 is that war becomes unacceptable.

In 1795, reflecting a view of Montesquieu and others, Immanuel Kant argued that the "spirit of commerce" is "incompatible with war" and that, as commerce inevitably gains the "upper hand," states would seek "to promote honorable peace and by mediation to prevent war." However, this notion is incomplete because, as Buckle pointed out, "the commercial spirit" has often been "warlike."[24] Thus, commerce truly becomes "incompatible with war" only when *both* the second proposition—that wealth is best achieved through exchange rather than conquest—*and* the first one—that wealth-enhancement should be a dominant goal—are accepted.

This was also understood by Angell. His critics, such as the prominent American naval historian Admiral Alfred Thayer Mahan, argued that even if it were true that war is economically unprofitable, nations mainly fight for motives other than economic ones such as "ambition, self-respect, resentment of injustice, sympathy with the oppressed." Angell replied by continuing to stress, reflecting proposition 2, that the inescapable economic chaos of war "makes economic benefit from victory impossible." But he also argued, in line with proposition 1, that nations should come to realize that "bread and a decent livelihood" are of paramount concern, not such vague and elastic goals as honor, power, and influence.[25]

Angell helped to crystallize a line of reasoning that has been gaining in acceptability ever since. It is the central contention of Richard Rosecrance's important book, *The Rise of the Trading State*, for example, that over the course of the last few centuries more and more countries have come to the conclusion that the path to wealth is through trade rather than through conquest, and he cites the striking and important examples of two recent converts: "Today West Germany and Japan use international trade to acquire the very raw materials and oil that they aimed to conquer by military force in the 1930s. They have prospered in peaceful consequence." Among trading states, Rosecrance observes, "the incentive to wage war is absent."[26] Put another way, free trade furnishes the economic advantages of conquest without the unpleasantness of invasion and the sticky responsibility of imperial control.

Thus war is unlikely if countries take prosperity as their chief goal *and* if they come to believe that trade is the best way to achieve that goal. Thanks in part to the success of economists, both propositions have now gained wide currency.

Furthermore, although war has hardly evaporated from the planet, it is worth noting that the advanced nations of the world have avoided war with each other for the longest period of time since the days of the Roman Empire, a remarkable development that is partly (though certainly not entirely) due to the increasing joint acceptance of propositions 1 and 2. Thomas Jefferson once referred to Europe as "an arena of gladiators," and countries like France and Germany once seemed to spend almost all their time either preparing for wars against each other or fighting them. But they have now lived—and prospered—side by side for over half a century without even a glimmer of war talk. Whether this will set the pattern for the rest of the world remains to be seen, but it is certainly of interest and may be of consequence that areas like Latin America and east and southeast Asia, where wars were endemic for decades after World War II, have now opted for peace and, not unrelatedly, for the banal pleasures of economic development.[27]

3. International Trade Should Be Free: From Adam Smith to Bill Clinton

One may accept economic development as a primary motivation and agree that exchange is a better way to prosper than conquest, but one could still conclude that prosperity is best achieved by restricting imports in order to favor and protect local enterprises—the once-dominant mercantilist view. Free trade, in fact, has been a hard sell, but at the end of the twentieth century it seems to have emerged triumphant, and the active proselytizing of the economics profession has probably been especially crucial in this important development.[28]

In 1993, the American president, Bill Clinton, committed one of the greatest acts of political heroism in the nation's history: energetic (and successful) support for approval of the North American Free Trade Agreement. He was well positioned politically to finesse and evade the issue and was urged to do so by many of his political advisers. Nevertheless, he decided to counter not only this recommendation but also the adamant desires of one of his party's most important supporters, organized labor, as well as those of many of his party's major figures including the majority leader in the House of Representatives.[29] (It is not true that "only Nixon could have gone to China"—Democratic presidents before him tried several times to improve relations with that country only to find the door closed—but it does seem likely that no Republican could have amassed the necessary (mainly Democratic) votes in Congress to pass NAFTA.)[30] As far as I can see, Clinton took up this painful and difficult task for only one reason: he had come to the conclusion that NAFTA—and, more generally, free trade—was good for the country in the long term.

From this remarkable achievement Clinton (predictably) gained no notable electoral advantage. Indeed, his advocacy chiefly inspired the (temporary) hostility of labor which seems to have been inclined to sit on its hands in the 1994 elections, something that may have helped bring about the losses Clinton's Democrats sustained in that contest. However, by his actions Clinton strongly put the Democratic imprimatur on the notion of free trade, got the world off its decades-long delay on advancing the General Agreement on Tariffs and Trade, and essentially put a consensual cap on a notion that economists had gradually come to accept over the two centuries since the publication in 1776 of Adam Smith's *Wealth of Nations*.[31]

Thus, by the end of the twentieth century the world has come substantially to embrace the idea, not only that wealth is enhanced by exchange rather than by conquest as in proposition 2, but that unfettered trade between countries is the best way for everyone to prosper. There will, of course, be countless bobbings and weavings, and even some notable setbacks, on this principle in specific application as countries jockey to obtain the best deal in a rapidly changing world. But what is important is that the basic idea seems substantially to have been accepted.

In many ways, the increasing acceptance of free trade is quite remarkable because political logic is notably on the side of protectionists and mercantilists. After all, domestic businesses (and labor organizations) have great clout in a country's politics while foreign businesses generally have little, and the locals should be able to use their advantageous position to keep foreign competition out.[32] In addition, the businesses and workers who will be hurt by cheaper or better foreign products are likely to know who they are, while those who will gain from exports are less likely to be aware of their advantage since the benefits are likely to materialize only in the long term. Moreover, even if a firm does find a market abroad and

115

thus has an incentive to lobby for free trade, the firm is often likely to discover soon that entrepreneurs in the nation to which is it exporting espy its success, set up local competition, and then pressure their government to close out the hapless innovative foreigner. Finally, free traders are up against the sentimental, intuitive appeal of autarky or self-sufficiency, concepts that go back at least to Aristotle and have been dominant for millennia.[33]

Deeply awed by such obstacles, George Stigler suggested gloomily in 1975 that free trade was "unattainable without a fundamental restructuring of the political system." No such restructuring has taken place. Yet, although Clinton was surely well aware that free trade was a politically incorrect venture, he still went ahead with it. It seems to me that the chief reason he and other otherwise sensible politicians have been willing to bear that pain is that they have finally—and understandably, rather reluctantly—bought the free-trade line that has been consensually touted for decades now by economists. As a certifiable policy wonk, Clinton has undoubtedly heard and ingested the arguments economists make about why free trade is a good idea, but he is not an economist himself, has never made a systematic analysis of the idea on his own, and has probably never even read a technical study of the issue. Chiefly, I suspect, he favors free trade (even to the point of risking his political life on the issue) because, like the patient who dutifully swallows the distasteful medicine prescribed by the authoritative physician, he trusts the expert consensus.[34]

Economist Paul Krugman considers free trade to be "as close to a sacred tenet as any idea in economics," and Milton Friedman agrees: "no subject has so united economists since Adam Smith's *Wealth of Nations* was published in 1776 as belief in the virtues of free trade." Unfortunately, Friedman noted in 1984, "that professional consensus has not prevented one country after another from imposing trade barriers."[35] But now, in considerable part because of Clinton's (and Friedman's) efforts, a substantial international consensus by policymakers on this issue does seem finally to have been achieved. Whatever waffling and backsliding there may be on the details of implementation, the general thrust and trend seem clear.

The relation between peace and trade. Although Kant and many others have proposed that trade enhances the prospects for peace, history does not suggest that this notion has much validity: most wars, after all, are civil conflicts, waged between groups which know each other only too well and trade with each other only too much.[36]

But a good case could be made for the opposite causal proposition: peace often leads to, or at any rate facilitates, trade. That is, peace ought to be seen not as a dependent, but rather as an independent, variable in the relationship.

For example, the long and historically unprecedented absence of war among the nations of Western Europe since 1945 has not been caused by their increasing economic harmony. Rather, their economic harmony has been caused, or at least expedited, by the peace they have enjoyed. Similarly, the rise of the multinational corporation and the building of the long-envisioned Channel Tunnel between France and Britain are the consequences of peace, not its cause.

Put the other way, international tensions and the prospect of international war have a strong dampening effect on trade. Each threatened nation has an incentive to cut itself off from the rest of the world economically in order to ensure that it can survive if international exchange is stifled by military conflict, and policies of autarky, self-reliance, and self-sufficiency are likely to be very appealing. In the peaceful modern trading world, however, such once-seductive notions have become to seem quaint.[37]

Similarly, the Cold War could be seen in part, as Edward Yardeni has pointed out, as a huge trade barrier.[38] With the demise of that politically derived and economically foolish construct, trade will be liberated. But it is peace that will have facilitated trade, not the opposite.

4. Economies Do Best When Governments Leave Them Substantially Free

As Japan has shown, one can accept free trade between nations while still maintaining that the domestic economy should still be kept under major governmental control. But, as the notion that international trade should be free and open has become increasingly accepted, so has the proposition that the domestic economy should also be free.

This is a fairly recent development. It has not been that long since Joseph Schumpeter famously and repeatedly declared "centralist socialism" to be the "heir apparent" to capitalism. In 1976, Fred Hirsch published a book about why the twentieth century had "seen a universal predominant trend toward collective provision and state regulation in economic areas," and around the same time Milton Friedman presented a paper (a very depressing one from his point of view) seeking to explain why collectivist beliefs flourish in the world of ideas.[39]

However, things have changed markedly since then. As economist Robert Heilbroner, not usually known as an ardent free-marketeer, noted only a few years ago: "There is today widespread agreement, including among most socialist economists, that whatever form advanced societies may take in the twenty-first century, a market system of some kind will constitute their principal means of coordination. That is a remarkable turnabout from the situation only a generation ago, when the majority of economists believed that the future of economic coordination lay in a diminution of the scope of the market, and an increase in some form of centralized planning." Likewise, in the words of an economist who *has* been a consistent free-marketeer, R. M. Hartwell, "The intellectual agenda about the role of the government has changed from one determined by the desirability of intervention to one determined by the desirability of market economy." The big question, he observes happily, is no longer "Why not more government, more public ownership, and more control and regulation of the market," but rather "Why not less government, more privatization, and less interference with the market?"[40]

These are particularly interesting observations in light of Henderson's assessment of the state of medicine in 1912. Essentially, Heilbroner and Hartwell are saying that, by the present state of economic knowledge, the random politician or governmental official consulting the random economist only a generation ago was likely to get the wrong advice: it would perhaps have been better, on average, to consult a reader of tea leaves or an astrologer.

Much of the most widely accepted economic thinking of the time derived from the work of John Maynard Keynes, whose central theme, according to his biographer, was "the state is wise and the market is stupid." Working from that sort of perspective, India's top economists for a generation supported policies of regulation and central control that failed abysmally—leading one of them to lament recently, "India's misfortune was to have brilliant economists." And Latin American economies were misdirected for decades by antimarket *dependencia* theory as forcefully and confidently advocated by well-regarded economists in the United Nations Economic Commission on Latin America. "I well remember," says Tony Judt, "sitting in the graduate lounge of Cambridge University in 1969 while a tenured member of the economics faculty assured us that the Chinese Cultural Revolution, then at its paroxysmic height, was the last best hope for humankind."[41]

In many respects the economic consensus Heilbroner and Hartwell note has burgeoned only recently, particularly after the abject and pathetic collapse of command and heavily planned economies in the late 1980s and early 1990s. As a top Indian economist put it recently, "Between the fall of the Berlin Wall in 1989 and the collapse of the Soviet Union in 1991, I felt as though I were awakening from a thirty-five-year dream. Everything I had believed about economic systems and tried to implement was wrong."[42]

The economic advice decision makers around the world are hearing, and increasingly are accepting, is to rely on the market rather than forcing upon it externally derived and politically comfortable concepts of fairness and justice. And with this acceptance, a set of alternative propositions about the virtues of revolution and about the justice possible through a command or heavily manipulated economy have effectively been scrapped as romantic, unrealistic, unproductive, and, increasingly, irrelevant.[43] In practice, all capitalist, or market capitalist, states, may not end up looking a great deal like each other, any more than all democracies do. In particular, the degree to which the government intervenes in the economy with tax and welfare policy, regulation, trade restrictions, price supports, and direct control over certain individual enterprises varies considerably. But the trend seems clear.

The new consensual approach can probably be summed up in one short phrase: "trust the market." Like the rise in international trade, this advice has been facilitated by a decline of war fears: as a prominent Italian economist has put it, "A state company has to do with war, national interest, and self-defense," whereas privatization "is driven by the absence of war, and by the opening of the international system that makes raw materials, money, and technology available to everyone."[44]

One of the principles that inform this advice, that international trade should be free, has already been discussed. Among the others seem to be the following:

Wages and prices should be allowed freely to find their own ranges and limits. It would be difficult to overestimate the economically pernicious effects of efforts to determine the "just wage" and the "just price" by nonmarket judgments. Yet for millennia prices were substantially set by custom, government, or the church, and the progressive abandonment of this intuitively appealing and hence politically correct approach has been one of the major achievements of modern economics—it is quite possibly the economic equivalent of the germ theory. And it has been a tough struggle. Rationing has enjoyed quite a bit of political appeal even in peacetime, and many politicians, like Harry Truman, have had a deep and abiding belief in wage and price controls; while a Republican president, Richard Nixon, suddenly reinstituted them as late as the 1970s.[45] The quest for the "just price" is still popular in some areas—over cable television rates, for example, and rent control lingers in a declining number of places—but, substantially, the battle has been won.

Government regulation is often unwise and can be counterproductive. For the most part, the quest for optimal regulation or for full-bore economic planning has been changed to a preference for reducing or even ending regulation and planning in many areas. Government may still sometimes play a helpful economic role by maintaining a viable justice system to enforce contracts and property rights and to police fraud and violent coercion, and it may also usefully seek to regulate matters of health and safety and to control socially undesirable side effects or externalities like air pollution—

though even here regulations designed to shape parameters to allow the market to do the hard work may well prove to be sounder than efforts to plan. But, as Yergin and Stanislaw put it, the idea would be to move the state away from being the "producer, controller, and intervenor" to being the "referee, setting the rules of the game to ensure, among other things, competition."[46]

The government should abandon enterprises that can be handled by the private sector. "Privatization" is a word that came into notable use only in the last decades of the twentieth century, intended to be used in pointed distinction to a much older word, "nationalization." The realization has taken hold that private enterprise simply does much better than the state at providing a whole series of goods and services—from communications to transportation to education to utilities to mail service to shipbuilding—that many once felt could be provided better, and more justly, by the state. Privatization has been a key development in the postcommunist states, and even the highly entrenched welfare states of Western Europe have sold off over a hundred billion dollars in state assets since 1985.[47]

High taxes, especially at the top, can be economically counterproductive, and capricious or discretionary ones almost always are. The campaign against confiscatory and discretionary expropriation, which was once a standard practice by rulers around the world, has been a long and arduous one even though, as noted in the previous chapter, tax restraint has almost always been to the long-term economic disadvantage of the confiscators.[48]

A considerable amount of economic inequality is inevitable and essentially desirable. Government may sometimes play a useful social or safety net role by cushioning pain through the judicious transfer of some degree of wealth from the economically successful to the unsuccessful.[49] But the communist experience suggests that efforts to induce true economic equality are likely to fail and, to the degree they are successful, to exact a cost—often a very considerable one—in economic growth.

Uncompetitive enterprises should not be subsidized and should be allowed to fail. This notion is, of course, extremely painful politically, but the disastrous experiences in the Soviet Union and elsewhere (in India a major state fertilizer company with twelve hundred employees, completed in 1979, had by 1991 yet to produce any fertilizer for sale) have helped economists to underscore its wisdom.[50]

Government spending should be kept reasonably low and government deficits should be kept under control. A form of the welfare state remains in place in all developed countries, but the belief that such spending can very detrimentally get out of hand seems increasingly to be accepted, and some of the most entrenched welfare states are judiciously trimming back.[51]

Principles like these centrally informed the successful advice given to the postcommunist states and to others seeking economic growth, and they have often been considered counterintuitive, immoral, or unjust. But these notions, however politically painful, seem increasingly to be accepted by policymakers and politicians around the world.[52]

Of course, the gathering—indeed, gathered—consensus among economists does not mean there is no room for debate. There may be controversy, for example, over the desirable trade-offs between growth and the distribution of wealth, or over whether it is better to go for maximum growth or to sacrifice some development in order to reduce the amplitude of the boom-and-bust cycles around an upward path, or over how high a government's deficit can rise without stifling the economy, or over the degree to which a regulation will hurt more than it will help, or over what rate of inflation is most desirable. But, substantially and increasingly, the debate is likely to be more nearly a matter of degree than of fundamental principles.

THE PROSPECTS FOR MASSIVE ECONOMIC GROWTH

If it is true that economists now generally know what they are talking about and if it is true that policymakers are now substantially and increasingly willing, however reluctantly, to accept and act upon their often counterintuitive and politically painful advice, the prospects for major economic advances in all—or virtually all—corners of the globe are highly favorable. This expansion would go beyond even the optimistic predictions based essentially on projecting into the future the economic development much of the world has experienced over the last two centuries as seen in figure 4.1 (p. 74). As the state of medical knowledge at the turn of the current century portended major health improvements in the century to come, we may now be on the verge of similar advances in the area of economic growth as we enter the next one.

Of course, there is no way to be sure that economists really know what they are talking about, any more than one could have been certain a century ago that Henderson and Osler were correct about the state of contemporary medical science. It is, I suppose, possible that the economists' current affinity for markets will prove as faddish and unsound as the bias many of them once showed toward planning, regulation, and trade restrictions. If so, we are in big trouble to the extent that their advice is increasingly being accepted by decision makers. However, judging from the depth of the emerging consensus and in particular from the frequent successes of economic analysis and advice in recent years, I find it reasonable to propose that this time, at long last, the economists may very well have gotten it right, and that the consequent benefits to the well-being of the planet's population could be enormous.

Economic Development, Professed Happiness, and the Catastrophe Quota

A considerable expansion of economic well-being does not mean people will feel—or at any rate say they feel—happier, however.

Aristotle once argued that "The happy man is one whose activity accords with perfect virtue and who is adequately furnished with external goods." Or in the words of a Slovak filmmaker, "It is better to be rich and healthy than poor and sick." Or, as Pearl Bailey put it even more succinctly, "I've been rich, and I've been poor, and rich is better."[53]

If people will be furnished with external goods in the next century to a degree scarcely imaginable even by our present standards of affluence, it might seem to follow that, as long as virtue at least

123

holds its own, people will become much happier. The evidence, however, suggests that this will not occur.

Three Conclusions about Happiness

Happiness, or a sense of well-being, is a rather elusive quality, but insofar as it can be specified and measured in public opinion surveys, there seem to be three reasonably clear conclusions.

1. People profess to hold economic considerations important when they assess the degree to which they are happy. When people in various countries are asked about happiness and their personal concerns, economic matters—including such issues as the standard of living and housing—tend to be the most often mentioned. Not surprisingly, health also scores highly as do family and personal relationships.[54]

2. Moreover, wealthier people are more likely to profess being happy than poorer ones in the same society. One survey of the happiness literature describes as "overwhelming" the amount of evidence showing that there is a positive—though sometimes not a very high—correlation between income on the one hand and happiness and other measures of subjective well-being on the other. This relationship holds even when other variables such as education are controlled.[55]

3. However, when a country grows economically, the professions of its people as to their state of happiness do not similarly grow. The very considerable economic growth the United States experienced in the postwar era was not associated with a corresponding increase in professions of happiness in public opinion surveys. Data from Western Europe from the 1970s and 1980s suggest much the same thing.[56]

One study, however, argues that these results are not surprising because they deal with economic improvement in areas that were already comparatively affluent. It contends that a notable rise in happiness in England, France, the Netherlands, and West Germany took place between the terrible immediate postwar years and the 1960s or 1970s. Thus, it is concluded, the wealth-happiness connection is subject "to the law of diminishing returns": once a person is adequately furnished with external goods, in Aristotle's phraseology, further increases in happiness do not take place.[57]

At best, of course, this suggests that happiness will increase only when a country moves from misery to some degree of economic security and that little additional gain is to be expected thereafter. But, as Richard Easterlin notes, even this conclusion is questionable when one looks at data from Japan. By 1958, that country had substantially recovered from the war, but it sported an income level lower than or equal to ones found in many developing countries today. During the next thirty years, Japan experienced a truly spectacular economic resurgence in which real per capita income multiplied fivefold and in which the benefits of economic growth were quite widely spread throughout the population. Yet there was little or no increase in Japanese happiness ratings.[58]

Four Explanations for the Remarkable Inability of Economic Growth to Inspire Professions of Happiness

If economic growth is what it is all about, then, the world is likely soon to experience massive improvement. But if happiness (or at any rate professions thereof) is what it is all about, it won't.

There seem to be several possible explanations for this curiously infelicitous state of affairs about felicity.

1. It is relative wealth, not absolute wealth, that matters. In exploring this explanation, Easterlin has ferreted out a crisp observation by Karl Marx: "A house may be large or small; as long as the surrounding houses are equally small it satisfies all social demands for a dwelling. But if a palace rises beside the little house, the little house shrinks to a hut." Thus, the argument runs, people may use a relative standard, not an absolute one, when assessing their wellbeing. If everybody's wealth increases at more or less the same rate, accordingly, relative incomes remain the same, and so does happiness. There exists a "consumption norm," suggests Easterlin, and one gauges one's happiness relative to this norm, not to the norm's absolute placement.[59]

But this cannot be the full explanation. After all, health is also an important component in happiness self-evaluations, and while people may think of wealth in relative terms, they are unlikely to think of health in the same way. That is, people simply do or do not feel healthy, and the health of others is likely to be quite irrelevant to their judgment on this issue. Since health has been improving at least as impressively as income in places like the United States, happiness should be going up even if people adopt a relative standard with respect to the wealth component of the happiness calculation. But it isn't.

There is a difference, of course, between the two issues in that one can imagine a maximum, satiated condition of health but not necessarily of wealth (moreover, sick people are obviously less likely than poor ones to be interviewed in surveys). However, concerns about one's future must play a role in health considerations, just as they do in ones about wealth. Thus, healthy people in, say, the 1940s should have found their happiness tainted a bit by fears that they or their children could at any moment come down with polio. When medical science cured that problem, people should, to that degree, have become happier; but they didn't.

2. Nonmaterial concerns dominate perceptions of happiness. The observation that happiness does not increase when material well-being increases has logically led to the conclusion that material well-being is not very important to people's sense of happiness. Angus Campbell adopts such a point of view and concludes that happiness is positively related to status and marriage and to having family, friends, and a satisfying job.[60]

But economic and health considerations are clearly of very considerable importance in personal assessments of happiness and well-being, as noted above. And, since there have been enormous improvements in wealth and health in the United States and other surveyed countries, the failure of happiness to rise cannot be due to other factors unless it can be shown that these have greatly deteriorated over the same period of time—something Campbell does not find.[61]

3. Material accumulation leads not to satisfaction, but to boredom and discontent. Tibor Scitovsky argues that prosperity, particularly in the United States, is simply not very satisfying—that it has led not to contentment and pleasure, but to leisure-induced boredom and then to rebellion, drug-taking, violence, and environmental deterioration. People, he suggests, seek "satisfaction in the wrong things, or in the wrong way, and then are dissatisfied with the outcome."[62]

This perspective distrusts prosperity—a process in which people are bountifully and indiscriminately supplied at an attractive price with the things they happen to think they want. The concern is that, in a world that lacks danger and stimulating challenge, people will come to wallow in luxury and to give in to hedonism (some may even be tempted to slouch toward Gomorrah). In the process, not only do their minds rot, but they wallow in malaise, ennui, and Weltschmerz until they become dissatisfied and unhappy.

It is an old fear for successful capitalism, a fear voiced even by some of its champions. Adam Smith anticipated that as workers came to concentrate on repetitive tasks, they would "become as stupid and ignorant as it is possible for a human creature to become" and be rendered incapable of exercising "invention" or "of conceiving any generous, noble, or tender sentiment." Similarly, Alexis de Tocqueville was concerned that when "the love of property" becomes sufficiently "ardent," people will come to regard "every innovation as an irksome toil," "mankind will be stopped and circumscribed," the mind "will swing backwards and forwards forever without begetting fresh ideas," "man will waste his strength in bootless and solitary trifling," and, though in continual motion, "humanity will cease to advance." In this century Joseph Schumpeter opined that managers would lose vigor and initiative as they became embedded in huge bureaucracies.[63]

There may be something to such concerns, but they would lead one to anticipate that happiness should actually decline in affluent areas, something that hasn't happened.[64] In addition, they tend to square rather poorly with indications that the world's economy is becoming increasingly, not decreasingly, competitive and that human capital—drive, intelligence, innovation, and risk-taking initiative—is fast becoming the quality in greatest demand. Intellectuals who consider business to be boring, mindlessly repetitive, unsatisfying, or lacking in daring, courage, and imagination have never tried to run—much less start—one.

4. *Improvements in well-being are effectively unappreciated: the catastrophe quota.* I have yet to run into an American over the age of

forty-seven who regularly observes, "You know, if I had been born in the nineteenth century, I'd very probably be dead by now." Nobody really thinks in such terms, yet the statement is completely true—and, of course, I don't mean in the sense that just about everybody who happened to be born in the last century is no longer with us, but that life expectancy in the United States as late as 1900 was forty-seven years.

It is often observed that people don't appreciate their health until they get sick, their freedom until they lose it, their wealth until it is threatened, their teeth until they ache. In other words, when things get better, we quickly come to take the improvements for granted after a brief period of assimilation: they become ingested and seem part of our due, our place in life.

Occasionally, people in affluent societies might pause to wonder how they, or anyone, ever got along without air conditioning, credit cards, faxes, EKGs, jet transportation, frozen pizza, VCRs, garbage disposals, cable television, automatic money machines, flu shots, Vanna White, laser surgery, thermal underwear, telephone answering machines, or quilted toilet paper, but on those rare occasions, the pause is brief, the observation is generally something of a joke, and few are willing seriously to concede that at least some of these eagerly accepted additions to their lives might somehow have made them happier. As Ludwig von Mises puts it philosophically: "Under capitalism the common man enjoys amenities which in ages past gone by were unknown and therefore inaccessible even to the richest people. But, of course, these motorcars, television sets and refrigerators do not make a man happy. In the instant in which he acquires them, he may feel happier than he did before. But as soon as some of his wishes are satisfied, new wishes spring up. Such is human nature."[65]

Lebergott proposes that if every economically significant good added since 1900 were to disappear, and if the remaining items— like salt pork, lard, and houses without running water—were marked down to 1900 prices, few would judge their economic welfare to have improved. Yet nostalgic images of, say, 1900 American life rarely remember rotten teeth, or note that each day at least three billion flies were created in cities by horse manure. Instead there is a tendency to look back at the past myopically, forgetting its complexities, horrors, and inconveniences, and often bathing it in a golden glow.[66] As part of this, we like to view the past as a simpler time, though the plays of Shakespeare and Aeschylus rather tend to suggest that people in olden times really did have some pretty complicated problems. Similarly, successful people in the postcommunist countries often complain that they now spend so much time accumulating wealth that they are no longer able to spend long evenings with friends drinking cheap vodka and talking and laughing.[67] Complaints like this arise even though economic development generally increases options; it does not close them off. As the Amish have shown, it would still be entirely possible to reject economic change and to wile away evenings unproductively with friends. Opportunities may increase, but that doesn't mean one has necessarily to reject the old ones.

A systematic, if quiet, process of standard raising also takes place. A label poised above an old carpet sweeper on display in an exhibit in the Strong Museum in Rochester, N.Y., observes, "Labor-saving devices like carpet sweepers helped middle-class people satisfy their desire for cleanliness within the home." Lest one conclude that this was an improvement however, the label writer quickly adds, "Unfortunately, each new development raised standards and expectations for cleanliness, making the ideal as hard as ever to achieve."[68]

The media may play something of a role in all this. Good news often doesn't sell well. For example, life expectancy at birth for Americans rose in 1993 to a record 75.5 years, a fact the *New York Times* found so boring that it simply reprinted an Associated Press dispatch on the issue and buried it on the thirteenth page of its September 1 issue. The *Atlantic,* seems addicted to articles like "The Crisis of Public Order," "The Drift Toward Disaster," "The Coming Anarchy," and "The Coming Plague," and the editors will only be truly happy, some suggest, when they come across an authoritative article entitled, "World Ends, Experts Say." Sensitive to such proclivities, a *New Yorker* wag once proposed as the first line of a poem: "Harm's bordello is the op-ed page."[69] In part because of such press proclivities, the remarkable long-term trends documented in Figures 4.1 and 5.1 often surprise people.

The political process is also essentially devoted to bringing out the bad news. Incumbents may often like to stress the positive, but challengers can't—they must work very hard to ferret out things that are wrong and that, at the same time, concern a fair number of voters. If they are successful in this, it would be impolitic for the incumbents simply to dismiss the voters' concern. They must agree, or appear to agree, that the problem is genuine and then propose a solution that seems superior to the one proposed by the challenger. The process leads to nice anomalies: air quality in the United States has improved markedly over the last decades—yet most people think (and many people seem to *want* to think) that the opposite is true.[70]

Moreover, although some advances, like the end of the Cold War, can come about with dazzling speed and drama, many improvements of the human condition are quite gradual and therefore difficult to notice. Rosenberg and Birdzell observe that the remarkable transformation of the West from a condition in which 90 percent lived in poverty to one in which the incidence of poverty was reduced to 20 or 30 percent of the population or less took a very long time: "Over a year, or even over a decade, the economic gains, after allowing for the rise in population, were so little noticeable that it was widely believed that the gains were experienced only by the rich, and not by the poor. Only as the West's compounded growth continued through the twentieth century did its breadth become clear."[71] Clearly, the same can be said for the massive improvements in life expectancy over the last century that have proved to be so easy to ignore.

In result of all this, the catastrophe quota always seems to remain comfortably full. When a major problem is resolved or eliminated or eased substantially or when a major improvement is made, there may be a brief period of reflective comment, but then problems previously considered small are quickly elevated in perceived importance.

Nowhere is this clearer than in international affairs where the Cold War and the threat of nuclear holocaust have evaporated in recent years to the distinct inconvenience of doomsayers everywhere. But with scarcely a pause for breath they have adroitly come up with a list of "new" problems to plague us in our "new world disorder"—for example, "the proliferation of weapons of mass destruction and the ballistic missiles to carry them; ethnic and national hatreds that can metastasize across large portions of the globe; the international narcotics trade; terrorism; the dangers inherent in the West's dependence on mideast oil; new economic and environmental challenges."[72] But wars deriving from ethnic and national hatreds are neither new nor increasing in frequency in the world, and nuclear proliferation is no more a new problem—in fact, may well be less of a problem—than it was in 1960 when John Kennedy repeatedly pointed out with alarm that there might be ten, fifteen, or twenty nations with a nuclear capacity by 1964.[73] And the international drug trade has obviously been around for quite some time, while the West's supposedly dangerous dependence on Mideast oil has been a matter of pointed concern at least since 1973. The impact of terrorism has often been more in the exaggerated hysteria it generates than in its actual physical effects—fewer Americans are killed by international terrorists than are killed by lightning.[74] Economic and environmental challenges are hardly new either, but new alarms can be raised.

And if these concerns don't seem alarming enough, we can always hark back to the time when we could ventilate about the government's budget deficit, a problem chiefly caused by the fact that people were living too long: improved medical care not only generated a wonderful new problem to complain about (for a while at least), but supplied the average American with nearly thirty additional years of lifetime in which to do so.[75]

As prosperity expands, we will also be nicely poised to become concerned that people will become overwhelmed, even paralyzed by the array of choices confronting them in the marketplace. One pundit asserts that "As social scientists, we know that with an increase in choices, people tend to become more anxious"; a sociologist points out that "If you have infinite choice, people are reduced to passivity"; and a futurist ominously worries about "overchoice—the point at which the advantage of diversity and individualization are canceled by the complexity of the buyer's decision-making process." Clearly, if Hamlet was faced by only two alternatives and found himself agonizing over it for five full acts, we must be far, far worse off today. This conundrum seems to be an updated version of the classic philosophic puzzle known as "Buridan's ass" in which the animal is placed at an equal distance from two bundles of hay and eventually starves to death in terminal indecision.[76] There seems to be no evidence any ass ever actually underwent this agony, but the information thus far is merely anecdotal, and this might well be one of those many issues crying out for well-funded systematic research. (Such research, however, might sometimes find that the problem solves itself: if customers in supermarkets become paralyzed with indecision in front of, for example, the corn flakes, they will block the aisles, threatening the profits of the store owner who will then logically be forced to increase the aisle space, reducing in turn the choice angst confronting the customers.)

DEVELOPMENT AND THE QUEST FOR HAPPINESS

In the end, however, there may be benefits to the endless, and endlessly successful, quest to raise standards and to fabricate new desires to satisfy and new issues to worry about. Not only does this quest keep the mind active, but it probably importantly drives, and has driven, economic development as well. Rosenberg and Birdzell find it unlikely that a "self-satisfied people could move from poverty to wealth in the first place," and David Hume observes that commerce "rouses men from their indolence" as it presents them with "objects of luxury, which they never before dreamed of," raising in them a desire for "a more splendid way of life than what their ancestors enjoyed."[77]

By contrast, Richard Easterlin puts a rather negative spin on all this when he applies the phrase, "hedonic treadmill," to the process and concludes that "each step upward on the ladder of economic development merely stimulates new economic desires that lead the chase ever onward." The word "treadmill" suggests an enveloping tedium as well as a lack of substantive progress. However, the "chase" not only enhances economic development, but often has invigorating appeals of its own. As Hume notes, when industry flourishes people "enjoy, as their reward, the occupation itself, as well as those pleasures which are the fruit of their labour." As part of this process, "the mind acquires more vigour" and "enlarges its power and faculties."[78]

Moreover, there is no evidence that economic development exhausts the treaders, lowers their happiness, or inspires many effective efforts to turn back the clock. Professions of happiness may not soar, but, despite the anguished protests of some intellectuals, people do not seem to have much difficulty enduring a condition of ever-increasing life expectancy and ever-expanding material prosperity.

DEMOCRACY

✳

Images and Definitions

THERE IS a famous Norman Rockwell painting that purports to portray democracy in action. It depicts a New England town meeting in which a workingman has risen in a contentious situation to present his point of view. His rustic commonsense, it appears, has cut through the indecisiveness and bickering to provide a consensual solution to the problem at hand, and the others in the picture are looking up at him admiringly.

As it happens, that misty-eyed, idealized snapshot has almost nothing to do with democracy in actual practice. Democracy is not a process in which one shining idea conquers all as erstwhile contenders fall into blissful consensus. Rather, it is an extremely disorderly muddle in which clashing ideas and interests (all of them "special") do unkempt and unequal, if peaceful, battle and in which ideas are often reduced to slogans, data to distorted fragments, evidence to gestures, and arguments to poses. Speculation is rampant, caricature is routine, and posturing is de rigueur. If one idea wins out, it is likely to be severely compromised in the process, and no one goes away entirely reconciled or happy. And there is rarely a sense of completion or finality or permanence: in a democracy, as Tod Lindberg points out, "the fat lady never sings."[1] It's a mess, and the only saving grace is that other methods for reaching decisions are even worse.

In this chapter I develop an approach to democracy that contrasts substantially with the romantic Rockwell ideal. It stresses petition and lobbying—the chaotic and distinctly nonconsensual combat of "special interests"—as the dominant and central characteristic of democracy and it suggests that while elections are useful and often valuable in a democracy, they may not be absolutely necessary. I also argue that democracy in practice is not about equality, but rather about the freedom to become politically unequal, and that it functions not so much by rule by the majority as by minority rule with majority acquiescence, qualities which have productively allowed it to coopt, rather than to alienate, the rich. In the process I explore the possible virtues of apathy.

I also contrast democracy with other governmental forms. Although the advantage is only comparative, democracy seems to do better at generating effective governments, choosing leaders, addressing minority concerns, creating a livable society, and functioning effectively with real, flawed human beings. The following two chapters then assess some of the consequences of the image mismatch between the ideal Rockwellian caricature and grim democratic reality.

DEFINING DEMOCRACY: RESPONSIVE GOVERNMENT

In defining democracy, it is particularly important, I think, to separate the essential institution itself from the operating devices that are commonly associated with it—mechanisms like written constitutions, the separation of powers or "checks and balances" (including an independent judiciary), and even elections. Any definition of democracy is inadequate, I think, if it can logically be taken to suggest that Britain (which has neither a written constitution nor separation of powers) is not a democracy or that Switzerland did not become one until 1971 (when women were finally given the vote).[2]

For example, Samuel Huntington defines "a twentieth-century political system as democratic to the extent that its most powerful collective decision-makers are selected through fair, honest, and periodic elections in which candidates freely compete for votes and in which virtually all the adult population is eligible to vote." This definition, with its entangling focus on elections and mass suffrage, would exclude everything known as a democracy before the twentieth century, as he suggests in his definition, as well as very many putative democracies during it including Switzerland.[3]

By contrast, it seems to me that what is essential to democracy is that the government be routinely and necessarily responsive. The crucial point of democracy is not to have constitutions or a separation of governmental powers or even to hold elections. Rather, it is to create, in Abraham Lincoln's classic phrase, something that resembles "government of the people, by the people, for the people."

This perspective is central to several definitions and approaches. Among political scientists, Robert Dahl says, "I assume that a key characteristic of a democracy is the continued responsiveness of the government to the preferences of its citizens, considered as political equals," and William Riker concludes that "democracy is a form of government in which the rulers are fully responsible to the ruled in order to realize self-respect for everybody." Historian Robert Wiebe finds democracy's "core" in the notion that it "entails some version of popular self-government that assures citizens access to the political process, never bars losers from that process, and keeps officials responsive to their constituents." Or in H. L. Mencken's irreverent pronouncement, democracy is "the theory that the common people know what they want, and deserve to get it good and hard."[4]

In my view, democracy is characterized by government that is necessarily and routinely responsive—although this responsiveness is not always even, fair, or equal. It comes into effect when the people effectively agree not to use violence to replace the leadership, and the leadership effectively leaves them free to criticize, to pressure, to organize, and to try to dislodge it by any other means. This approach can be used to set up a sort of sliding scale of governmental forms. An *authoritarian* government may effectively and sometimes intentionally allow a degree of opposition—a limited amount of press disagreement, for example, or the freedom to complain privately, something sometimes known as the freedom of conversation. But it will not tolerate organized attempts to replace it, even if they are peaceful. A *totalitarian* government does not allow even those limited freedoms. On the other end of the scale is *anarchy:* a condition which holds when a government "allows" the use of violence to try to overthrow it—presumably mainly out of weakness or ineffectiveness.

Authoritarian and even totalitarian governments can sometimes be responsive as well, of course. But their responsiveness depends on the will and the mindset of the leadership. By contrast, democracy is *routinely, necessarily* responsive: because people are free to develop and use peaceful methods to criticize, pressure, and replace the leadership, the leaders must pay attention to their critics and petitioners.

It seems to me that the formal and informal institutional mechanisms variously applied in democracies to facilitate this core consideration are secondary—though this does not mean that all institutions are equally fair or efficient. One can embellish this central democratic relationship with concerns about ethos, way of life, social culture, shared goals, economic correlates, common purposes, customs, preferred policy outcomes, norms, patriotism, shared traditions, and the like. These issues are interesting, but, as will be discussed more fully later, they don't seem to be essential or necessary to the functioning of democracy.[5]

ELECTIONS: USEFUL, BUT NOT ESSENTIAL

Dahl and Riker emphasize elections as a device to make democratic responsiveness happen—indeed, Riker argues that "the essential democratic institution is the ballot box and all that goes with it."[6] But it really does seem that if citizens have the right to complain, to petition, to organize, to protest, to demonstrate, to strike, to threaten to emigrate or secede, to shout, to publish, to export their funds, to express a lack of confidence, and to wheedle in back corridors, government will tend to respond to the sounds of the shouters and the importunings of the wheedlers: that is, it will necessarily become responsive—pay attention—whether there are elections or not.

There are plenty of nonviolent methods for removing officeholders besides elections. Governments often topple or are effectively threatened by scandal, legal challenge, formal petition, letter writing, street protest, pointed behavior at public meetings, embarrassment, strikes, capital flight, mass demonstrations, economic boycott or slowdown, threats to emigrate or secede, stockmarket collapse, or other expressions of loss of confidence by key sections of the population.

The addition of elections to this panoply of devices may sometimes change policy outcomes, and it probably makes the enterprise more efficient in some sense because elections furnish a specific, clearly visible, and direct method for replacing officeholders. Elections—fair and free ones, at any rate—also may make the process more just, at least by some standards, because they extend participation to those who only care enough about what's going on to meander to the polls every few years to pull a few levers or make a few X's (though the weight of an individual's vote on policymaking is so small that the act of voting might be considered to be scarcely a rational use of one's time), and because they give a bit of potential clout to those who don't vote but could do so if sufficiently riled or inspired. Gerald Pomper aptly observes that "the effect of elections is to require government to pay greater attention to unorganized mass groups and comparatively less to elite groups of smaller numbers." But, as he suggests, the difference is simply comparative and, "like any political device, popular elections will tend to protect some interests more than others."[7]

In the end, most of what democratic governments actually do on a day-by-day basis is the result of pressure and petition—lobbying, it's called—and of their own reactions and policy initiatives. As Stephen Bailey observes in a classic study, majority opinion as expressed in elections "can be, and frequently is, almost hopelessly splintered by the power struggles of competing political, administrative, and private interests, and is finally pieced together, if at all, only by the most laborious, complicated, and frequently covert coalition strategies."[8]

As this suggests, the policy message of elections is almost always ambiguous and often utterly undecipherable: "votes," observes one analysis, "communicate little information about the concerns and priorities of the voter." For example, after the 1994 elections in the United States the victorious Republicans claimed they had been given a mandate to carry out the promises outlined in their prominent campaign document, the "Contract with America." Yet a month after the election a national poll found that 72 percent of the public claimed never to have heard or read anything about the highly touted Contract. Four months later, after endless publicity over the varying fortunes of the Contract, that number had not changed at all.[9]

Petitioners can sometimes use the threat of elections, implied or otherwise, to influence officeholders. And in some democracies contributions toward campaign expenses can help petitioners to facilitate access or to affect policy (a phenomenon that many see as a perversion). But the essential interaction between government and citizenry can take place without elections if the right of petition is viable and if people have the right to organize and to devise peaceful methods to pressure and overthrow officials.

Suppose, for example, that a governmental system were formed in which all authority were vested in a single person or group whose tenure in office was at the mercy of a sort of supreme court or council of elders whose duty it was to listen to, and weigh, the complaints and concerns of the citizenry who would be completely free to speak, publish, organize, demonstrate, and complain as long as they did so nonviolently. Even though there would be no elections under that system, it seems to me it would be essentially democratic: the government would be routinely and necessarily responsive to the concerns of the public.

Indeed, people excluded from participation in elections often have nevertheless profoundly affected policy if they had the right to petition and protest. A prime instance is the feminist movement, which achieved many of its goals—including eventually votes for women—even though the vast majority of its members were excluded from the electorate. As this experience demonstrates, it is absurd to suggest that people who are barred from voting can have no impact on public policy.

Moreover, there exist cases of what might be called democracies without elections: Mexico and British Hong Kong. People go to the polls in Mexico, of course, but the ruling party counts the ballots and for decades, curiously enough, never lost an election (though in most cases the ruling party probably would have won even if the ballots had been counted fairly). In Hong Kong, the government was appointed from afar. Yet in both places people have been free to petition and protest and organize, and the governments can be said in a quite meaningful sense to have been responsive to the will and needs of the population. Elections might shade or reshape policy in one way or another, and some democrats would undoubtedly deem the result to be more just, but the essential responsiveness is already there.

Thus, although they are fully aware of Mexico's electoral defects and although they document the fact that Mexicans have been equally aware of these defects, Gabriel Almond and Sidney Verba have no difficulty accepting Mexico as a functioning democracy in a classic study. As one Mexican observer has put it, "we have democracy 364 days a year and lack it only on one day—election day." Not ideal perhaps, but not all that bad as averages go. Mexico's record toward opposition voices is hardly perfect, but for the most part, political leaders are responsive: they "find out what their potential constituents want and establish a reputation for taking care of problems," observes Martin Needler, and, because of "the ideological range embraced by the Mexican ruling class and its ideological inclusiveness," the able dissident is generally coopted, rather than ostracized or suppressed. Similarly, Robert Scott notes that "the extent of accommodation of interest provided by Mexico's political mechanisms is little short of amazing."[10] Although elections may often have been fixed, people have still been substantially free in other ways, and the ruling party has usually responded to notable nonviolent dissent not by (undemocratic) suppression, but by buying off or coopting potential opponents, and it has shown a considerable desire to give people a sense that it cares about their welfare.

In Hong Kong, rulers were traditionally sensitive to vigilant and entrenched business elites who, in turn, helped to keep the rest of the population docile, reasonably content, and politically apathetic. When the government signed a treaty in 1984 promising to hand the colony over to China in 1997, however, this traditional apathy was substantially overcome as treaty opponents screamed loudly, organized pressure groups, signed petitions, staged mass demonstrations, and pointedly threatened to emigrate. An authoritarian government would have responded by suppressing the protest and jailing its leaders, but in Hong Kong the rulers acted like democrats: they listened, and they tried to mollify and coopt

143

the protest movement by giving in to some of its demands and by letting it compete for some previously appointed leadership positions. When the opponents did well in this competition, the government further responded by replacing some of its hardline appointees with apolitical professionals.[11]

Although the government in Hong Kong was responsive, in the end, of course, it did not deliver on the central demand that Hong Kong remain independent of China. Responsiveness means that the government will necessarily and routinely pay attention to notable pressure, not that pressuring groups will inevitably get their way. Like the appealing and enduring yearnings for governments to at once lower taxes and increase expenditures, the demand that Hong Kong should remain independent, while highly attractive politically, was essentially unfulfillable.

Elections are, of course, a standard device in democracy, and they certainly do assist its functioning. But the cases of Mexico and British Hong Kong suggest that democracy can effectively flourish if people are free even if open and competitive elections are not held. On the other hand, if the freedom to speak, publish, protest, and organize is restricted, a country ceases to be a democracy by any definition. Thus, severe restrictions on the rights of speech and petition (as well as the vote) of blacks in the American South for much of its history and in South Africa for almost all of its history, suggest that those areas could not be considered democracies by either standard.

It is vital in a democracy that the right peacefully to speak, petition, publish, and organize be preserved, and the courts obviously can be an important part of that process. However, "judicial independence"—which does not exist, essentially, in democratic Britain where Parliament dominates—is not necessarily required. It is the result that matters, not the institutional devices that are erected to guarantee it.

None of this is to argue that the policies of democratic governments are entirely determined by the efforts of outside pressure groups and other petitioners. Parties, individual politicians, and government officials often have their own agendas and, in addi-

144

tion, often search out, and sometimes even invent, issues which might exercise citizens and citizen groups.[12]

POLITICAL INEQUALITY

Throughout history most democrats have advanced equality as an essential part of their intellectual baggage, and this theme has routinely been burlesqued by antidemocrats. Plato mockingly called democracy "a pleasant condition" which distributes "its peculiar kind of equality to equals and unequals impartially" because democracy seems to require a ridiculous leveling.[13] Similarly, in the Gilbert and Sullivan opera *The Gondoliers,* a couple of democrats, having inherited a kingdom and unwilling to abandon their "Republican fallacies," determine that in their kingdom "all shall equal be," whether they be the Lord High Bishop orthodox, the Lord High Coachman on the box, or the Lord High Vagabond in the stocks. Accordingly they establish "a despotism strict combined with absolute equality," in which as monarchs they spend their day variously making proclamations, polishing the plate, receiving deputations, and running little errands for the ministers of state.

In modern practice, however, democracy has not looked anything like that. It came to be associated with a special, and perhaps rather minimal, form of political equality, the kind usually called equality of opportunity. In a democracy all people are free—that is, equally unfettered as far as the government is concerned—to develop their own potential, to speak their minds, and to organize to promote their interests peacefully. Riker asserts that "equality is simply insistence that liberty be democratic, not the privilege of a class." And when John Locke concludes that "all men by nature are equal," he defines equality as "that equal right that every man hath, to his natural freedom, without being subjected to the will or authority of any other man," and he goes out of his way to point out that such attributes as age, virtue, and merit might give some a "just precedency." Thus political equality is something that seems to evolve without much further ado when people are free—it is subsumed by, dependent upon, and, appears in fact to be indistinguishable from, liberty.[14] If people are free, they are, as far as democracy is concerned, politically equal as well.[15]

Initially, this freedom (and hence equality) of opportunity stood in opposition to class distinction, and it makes democracy subversive of hereditary class as it relates to politics: the pool from which leaders are chosen is widened to include everybody, and all are free to participate if they choose to do so. As the chief author of the American Declaration of Independence, Thomas Jefferson is generally held responsible for the most famous promulgation of the notion that "all men are created equal." But in other writings he made it clear that far from supplanting distinction, democracy merely replaces one form of distinction with another. Rather than having "an artificial aristocracy, founded on wealth and birth," he pointed out, a democracy would be ruled by "a natural aristocracy" based on "virtue and talents." Or as Pericles put it in ancient Athens, in a democracy "advancement in public life falls to reputation for capacity, class considerations not being allowed to interfere with merit."[16]

It is true that each member of the electorate in modern democracies has more or less the same voting strength at the ballot box. (Actually, this is often only approximately true: in the United States, for example, a resident of Wyoming has a substantially greater voting weight in national elections than a resident of a much more populous state like Ohio.)[17] However, the political importance of an individual is not very significantly determined by this circumstance, and therefore political inequality effectively prospers: some people are, in fact, more equal than others. A store clerk may count for as much in an election as does the head of a big corporation or a columnist for the *New York Times*, but, as I will discuss more fully in the next chapter, it would be absurd to suggest that the clerk is, or could readily become, remotely equal to the other two in ability to affect and influence government policy.

Unlike in authoritarian systems, therefore, the political weight of individuals in a democracy is not rigidly predetermined by class, personal loyalties, or ideological tests. One is free to try to increase one's political importance by working in politics or by supplying money in appropriate places, or one can reduce it by succumbing to apathy and neglecting even to vote. In practice, then, *democracy is a form of government in which individuals are left free to become politically unequal.*[18] That is, the actual working out of the process encourages people to explore, develop, and express their differences, not to suppress them. Democratic individualism, in fact, is in many respects the antithesis of the kind of equality that Plato and W. S. Gilbert ridiculed.[19]

The result of all this is that democracy, like life and capitalism, may often be notably unfair. Some people, because of their manipulative skills, social position, or sheer luck will do much better under the system than others. Unlike other systems, however, democracy gives to everyone the opportunity without regard to social status or ideological conviction to seek to manipulate the system in their favor. However, those who make little effort to do so may well be ignored, or maybe even persecuted, by it.

DEMOCRACY IN PRACTICE: COOPTING THE WEALTHY

Opponents have traditionally anticipated that in a democracy demagogues would mesmerize and bribe the masses and then rule as bloody tyrants. For example, Plato surmised that in a democracy all a politician need do is assert "his zeal for the multitude" and they would be "ready to honor him." Therefore, assuming that numbers were all that mattered in a democracy, he expected such demagogues to "plunder the propertied classes, divide the spoil among the people, and yet keep the biggest share for themselves."[20] That this grim scenario was not entirely fanciful was demonstrated in the years after the French revolution of 1789 where democracy soon degenerated disastrously into the sort of tyrannical, murderous mobocracy that Plato had envisioned two millennia earlier. Moreover, it eventually became associated with an expansionary ideology, with war, and, under Napoleon, with aggressive, continent-wide military conquest.

Generally, however, once democracy was put into practice (market-tested, it might be said), it turned out, quite amazingly, that

Plato's persuasively dire prediction did not come about. The result has been that in order *really* to plunder the propertied it has been necessary to abandon democracy—as in China, the Soviet Union, Cuba, Nicaragua, Burma, Iran, Vietnam, revolutionary France, Cambodia. Where the would-be plunderers have remained democratic—as in Sweden—the propertied have generally been able to hang on to many of their assets and have not felt it necessary to flee. A most extreme test of this will be in South Africa where a massive expansion of political freedom has put those who once ran the system very much into the minority. If the system remains democratic, experience suggests they should be able to maintain much of their privilege.

There seem to be at least three reasons for this substantially unanticipated development: political inequality, commonsense, and apathy.

Inequality

While it is true that the rich form a minority of the electorate, their money and status can be parlayed into substantial political influence on issues that they really care about such as confiscation of their property. As I have argued, the simple arithmetic of the ballot box is only a portion of the democratic effect, and perhaps not even a necessary one. Elsewhere, a sort of weighted voting takes place, and the rich, left free to become politically unequal, enjoy influence far out of proportion to their numbers on issues that really matter to them—something, as will be discussed more fully later, that other minorities have also discovered.

Commonsense

In addition, it turns out that in practice, the poor have not shown the shortsighted stupidity that Plato posited. Resentment of the wealthy may have some immediate demagogic appeal, but ordinary people have often shown a resistance to demagogues and a rough appreciation for the fact that a systematic dismemberment of the propertied class is not all that good for the poor either.[21]

Plato anticipated that bloody tyranny would emerge in a democracy because "he who is the president of the people finds a mob more than ready to obey him." In *Coriolanus,* set in at least semi-democratic Rome, Shakespeare vividly depicts such a process. A military leader is at first honored by the great unwashed, but he is unable to bring himself hypocritically to grovel before them, and soon the people, manipulated by wily demagogues, turn and crush him. For Mencken, too, "The most popular man under a democracy is not the most democratic man, but the most despotic man. The common folk delight in the exactions of such a man. They like him to boss them. Their natural gait is the goose-step."[22]

It is noteworthy, however, that once in authority, the tyrants who emerged in revolutionary France, as well as later ones who came into authority more or less democratically, like Hitler and Mussolini, felt it necessary to abandon democracy in order to maintain control. Wiser than Plato, Mencken, and even Shakespeare about mobs, they knew that if they left the field free to rivals, the people might well come to follow a competitor. That is, the notion that masses of people are readily, predictably, and consistently manipulable proved to be naive. Moreover, as will be discussed more fully in the next chapter, a cynicism toward politics and politicians, endemic in democracies it seems, may sometimes enhance popular resistance to the appeals of shallow demagogues and extremists. As such would-be manipulators as advertisers, public relations specialists, and political candidates could assure Plato, Mencken, or Shakespeare, putting out an idea a free public will buy is uncertain at best.

The agile demagogue and would-be tyrant is aware of the essential validity of a famous, and, at base, rather cynical, observation about democracy—perhaps the most profound thing ever said about the institution and a key to why, despite its patent defects, democracy more or less works. The observation concludes first that Plato, Mencken, and Shakespeare were right: people in general can *all* sometimes be faked out: "you can fool all of the people some of the time." Moreover, some people will *never* get it right: you can fool "some of the people all of the time." What makes anything work, however, is that people, in fact, are *not* equal: somewhere there are a few people at least who will eventually figure it out: "you can't fool all of the people all of the time."[23]

Additionally, it turns out that voters have often been inclined, rather surprisingly perhaps, to support rich people for office—something that has routinely driven Marxists crazy. This could be seen in the earliest competitive elections in the American colonies, a hundred years before the Declaration of Independence. As Edmund Morgan observes, the people elected "were generally those whose birth and wealth placed them a little or even a lot above their neighbors." Moreover, even "where most seats were filled by comparatively ordinary men, those who stood highest socially and economically seem to have been deferred to by the other representatives and appointed to the committees that directed legislative action."[24]

Accordingly, while democracy may open up the competition for leadership to people who would have been barred under an authoritarian system for genetic or ideological reasons, changes in leadership have not usually been terribly revolutionary: by and large, the same people, or sorts of people, remain in office. Thus democracy generally did not prove destructive of aristocratic dominance because voters tended to support many (though not all) of the same patricians who would have been in office if unalloyed monarchy had still been the order of the day. Democracies, like monarchies, have largely been run by the well connected and the well born, although democratic myth-builders, particularly in America, have usually chosen to emphasize the occasional political success of upstarts raised in log cabins.[25]

More recently, a similar phenomenon may be taking place in post-communist countries as the (presumably more capable) members of the formerly ruling nomenklatura remain in place, often prosper, and frequently win free elections.[26] And the experience with democracy suggests that Adam Przeworski should not find it so "astonishing" that in Spain "the political system has been transformed without affecting economic relations in any discernable manner" and that "those who were satisfied with the Franco regime are also likely to be satisfied with the new democratic government."[27]

Apathy

Finally, apathy has also played a central role in making democracy function and in helping the rich to retain much of their privilege. Plato, Shakespeare, and Mencken not only exaggerate the ease with which people can be manipulated, but they also ignore the difficulty of gaining their attention in the first place.

In fact, one of the great, neglected aspects of free speech is the freedom not to listen. As Hubert Humphrey reportedly put it, "The right to be heard doesn't automatically include the right to be taken seriously." It is no easy task to persuade free people to agree with one's point of view, but as any experienced demagogue is likely to point out with some exasperation, what is most difficult of all is to get them to pay attention at all. People, particularly those in a free, open society, are regularly barraged by shysters and schemers, by people with new angles and neglected remedies, with purveyors of panaceas and palliatives. Very few are successful—and even those who do succeed, including Adolf Hitler, owe their success as much to luck as to skill.

As will be discussed later, apathy helps importantly with the problem that is usually called the tyranny of the majority. It is not difficult to find a place where the majority harbors a considerable hatred for a minority—indeed, it may be difficult to find one where this is not the case. Polls in the United States regularly have found plenty of people who would cheerfully restrict not only the undeserving rich, but also homosexuals, atheists, accused Communists, Nazi paraders, flag burners, and people who like to shout unpleasant words and perpetrate unconventional messages. But it is not easy to get this majority to do anything about it—after all, that would require a certain amount of work.

Because of apathy, therefore, people, sometimes despite their political predispositions, are effectively tolerant.[28] For democracies the danger is not so much that agile demagogues will play on hatreds and weaknesses to fabricate a vindictive mob-like tyranny of the majority: the perversions of the French Revolution have proved unusual. More to be feared, it seems, is the tyranny of a few

151

who obtain bland acquiescence from the uninterested, and essentially unaffected, many.

MINORITY RULE AND MAJORITY ACQUIESCENCE

Essentially, then, democracy is characterized by minority rule and majority acquiescence. Surely, the history of the oldest large democracy supplies much evidence for this: often against the interests and the desires of the majority, beekeepers gain price supports for honey, selected industries are insulated from competition, gun enthusiasts secure protection from seizure, artists are granted medals and subsidies, and the credit union industry routinely enjoys special tax privileges even though it represents only a few percent of the market and even though its privileges are ardently opposed by the huge banking industry. Similarly, the tiny sugar industry continues to inspire benevolent governmental policies which artificially boost the price of sugar, a policy strongly contested by the huge soft drink industry and one that is clearly opposed to the interests of legions of soft drink guzzlers, many of whom vote quite regularly.[29] (On the other hand, as dieticians and dentists unpleasantly remind us with every health bulletin, sugar is a really terrible food. Therefore making it more expensive may contribute a bit to the public health—perhaps even to that vaporous commodity, the "common good," which so many supple philosophers have so often mused about at great and eloquent length.)

People routinely rail against such developments as the workings of "special interests," a phenomenon assessed in the next chapter. But pressure and petition are crucial and central to democracy, not a distortion of it. James Madison was alarmed at the prospect of what he called "faction," defined as a group of citizens "who are united and actuated by some common impulse of passion, or of interest, adverse to the rights of other citizens, or to the permanent and aggregate interests of the community."[30] But, to a substantial degree, democracy is a system of freely contending factions. That

152

people with common interests should be allowed freely to attempt to sway government policy is, in fact, democracy's whole point.

DEMOCRACY IN COMPARISON

When asked, "How's your wife?" comedian Henny Youngman was given to responding: "Compared to what?" In an essay first published in 1939, E. M. Forster adopted just such an appropriate comparative approach when he observed that democracy "is less hateful than other contemporary forms of government." Or, as it is usually put: democracy is the worst form of government except for all the rest.[31] The ultimate appeal of democracy is, I think, not that it is, or could become, a perfect or ideal form of government, but that, however imperfect, it has distinct advantages when compared to other forms.

Governmental Effectiveness

Some of the competitors to democracy have seemed to offer admirable—even sublime—qualities that are not attainable in a democratic system. They cater to such natural desires as the need for order, security, certainty, and community, and they seductively proclaim the existence of a general will supplied by God, by temporal authority, or by a cosmic populist sense, thus relieving individuals of the burden of determining their own self-interest in matters of governance. They often offer to manage individual idiosyncracies for the greater good and to give security to all by arranging to have the collective or an overseer protect the individual against the traumas of risk and failure. And they sometimes claim to be able to supply authoritative truth through comforting revelation, freeing people from the uncertainties of individual error. One classic if extreme, expression of this perspective is the Grand Inquisitor in Dostoyevsky's *The Brothers Karamazov*. As he sees it, people are terrified of the freedom and individualism of democracy, and they are willing, indeed anxious, to surrender it for bread, security, mira-

cle, mystery, authority, and the warmth of communal unity. "All
that man seeks on earth," he explains, is "some one to worship,
some one to keep his conscience, and some means of uniting all
in one unanimous and harmonious ant-heap."[32]

It would seem that, if the Grand Inquisitor were right, prisons
and slavery would be more popular. But it must be acknowledged
that democracy is, and will always be, distressingly messy, clumsy,
and disorderly, and that in it people are permitted loudly and ir-
ritatingly to voice opinions that are clearly erroneous and even
dangerous. Moreover, decision making in democracies is often
muddled, incoherent, and slow, and the results are sometimes ex-
asperatingly foolish, shortsighted, irrational, and incoherent. As
Tocqueville argued in the 1830s with respect to foreign policy,
democracy "can only with great difficulty regulate the details of
an important undertaking, persevere in a fixed design, and work
out its execution in spite of serious obstacles. It cannot combine
its measures with secrecy or await their consequences with patience."[33] And some, including James Bryce, have lamented that
democracies do not often promote the best people in the society
to political leadership (assuming, presumably, that the society
would be better off with the best in those positions rather than in
science, business, or medicine).[34] But the key question in all this
remains Youngman's: "Compared to what?"

Dictatorships aspire to devise a method for governing that cuts
through all the messiness and gets on with it. They have sought to
come up with a system that sports a strong, wise, and effective
leader—a guardian, a philosopher king, a superman—who can
provide authoritative direction without all the compromise, contention, obstruction, and waffling. But how does one get people
like that into leadership positions?

It is useful in this regard to look at the quality of the people
democracies have generally selected and to compare them to leaders who have emerged in nondemocratic societies. In such a comparison, it seems, democracies do rather well.

The overall record for nondemocracies, after all, is fairly
abysmal. Rebecca West may exaggerate somewhat when she observes that in 645 years of rule the Hapsburg family produced "no

genius, only two rulers of ability . . . , countless dullards, and not a few imbeciles and lunatics," but she is not that far off the mark. Although not an entirely unbiased observer, Thomas Jefferson once had the opportunity to visit the monarchs of Europe and found them to be fools, idiots, hogs, and just plain crazy—except perhaps for Catherine of Russia who stood out only because she "had been too lately picked to have lost her common sense." A more sympathetic observer, Louis XIV of France, the longest-reigning monarch in European history and one of the most ardent exemplars of the monarchical system, was however also fully aware of the system's defects: "I have often wondered how it could be that love for work being a quality so necessary to sovereigns should yet be one that is so rarely found in them."[35]

In general, democracy looks pretty good, then, when one compares the leadership and decision-making qualities of the tsars of Russia or the kaisers of Germany or the kings of Saudi Arabia or the dictators of just about any place with those of the prime ministers of Britain or Canada or the presidents of the United States. As Jefferson plausibly concluded, "there is not a crowned head of Europe, whose talents or merits would entitle him to be elected a vestryman by the people of any parish in America."[36] While democratic governments have made their share of blunders, these, it might well be argued, pale in comparison to the disasters nondemocratic countries have experienced under such leaders as Hitler, Mussolini, Kim Il-Sung, Khomeini, Mao, Stalin, and Saddam Hussein.

Some of the democratic advantage in this comes about because any system of governance will tend to do better if the top leadership is regularly reevaluated whether through elections or some other mechanism. Leaders may be quite capable and effective at the start, but there is no guarantee they will remain so after years or decades in office, and occasional reexamination guards against such decline. If there is competition to replace the leaders, and if the current leaders, with all their advantages, can enter the competition, it seems unlikely that almost any set of judges will do worse than a system where such periodic reevaluations are not held. Even if the reviewers resolve merely to end the tenure of rulers who have patently become monsters or utter incompetents things would be better.[37]

A case in point is the Soviet Union, an authoritarian system which did have provisions on the books for regular review of its leaders as well as for orderly succession. Nonetheless, Josef Stalin gained control and held it without effective challenge or further review for twenty-five years during which time he launched a massive tyranny. Later, leadership devolved into the hands of Leonid Brezhnev whose experience is in its way an even more devastating commentary on the Soviet review process than the Stalin case. Stalin terrorized and murdered his potential reviewers, but Brezhnev's reviewers did not have that to worry about. Nonetheless Brezhnev held on to authority even as his effectiveness dwindled because of illness and even as evidence mounted that his policies were leading the country into economic, political, and social stagnation and ruin.

This problem might be reduced somewhat if dictators responsibly groomed their successors. But the danger is that a designated successor of capacity who is truly able might be inclined to come into office early by overthrowing the reigning tyrant. Therefore it often makes sense to select sycophants, weaklings, and mediocrities for the role.

Only democracies generally have been able to establish effective review and succession arrangements and thereby solve an elemental problem of governance.[38]

In addition, in a democracy those who yearn to become leaders have a peaceful and legal device for fulfilling their ambitions. If they don't like the way the present incumbents are performing, they can work to try to replace them. Thus, democracy furnishes a safety valve for discontent: those with complaints may or may not ever see relief of their grievances, but rather than wallowing in frustration, they are supplied with the opportunity to express themselves and potentially to change things in a direction they prefer.

And it seems that the rigors of the democratic leadership-selection campaign process is a fairly good selector by itself, though some of these qualities can also be required in leadership struggles within an authoritarian government. To succeed, a candidate must be able to work hard, to avoid public blunders, to improvise under adverse conditions, to size up and placate disparate personalities, to communicate well, to exude a sense of purpose and direction, to be able to differentiate the tactical from the strategic, to seize opportunity, to inspire confidence, to make prudent and timely decisions, and to be able to deal with people both individually and in groups. All of these qualities are valuable for leaders as well.

Critics of democracy have argued that the campaign process puts a premium on image, on the toothy grin, on the slick facade. But too many nonmesmerizers—Lyndon Johnson, for example— have handily attained high office to conclude that a seductive television image is a necessary or vital component of success in democracies. And the public's resistance to shallow demagogues has been discussed earlier. There is of course no surefire way to predict how a candidate will perform in office, and to rely on the common-sense of the masses—including those among them who can't be fooled all the time—seems, rather remarkably, to work comparatively well. Interestingly, in an important sense, voters in democracies often do not have a great deal of choice. Parties generally put forward candidates who are ambitious, hardworking, and dedicated—thus, on those dimensions at least, voters can't make a mistake. On the other hand, candidates with those qualities are put forth in the belief that they have what the electorate is looking for.

In the end, William Riker's perspective on all this seems sound: a liberal democracy is characterized not by "popular rule" but by various devices providing for "an intermittent, sometimes random, even perverse, popular veto" which "has at least the potential of preventing tyranny and rendering officials responsive." Riker agrees that this is "a minimal sort of democracy," but he contends that it "is the only kind of democracy actually attainable." If people remain free to use whatever common sense they choose to muster at the moment, and if they are free to generate competing ideas, there's a reasonable chance they'll get it more or less right eventually.[39]

There have been mistakes and exasperations and sometimes

157

even disasters. But it can be plausibly argued that democracies on the whole have done comparatively rather well at managing their affairs, at correcting their inevitable mistakes, and at choosing and evaluating leaders, and that governments so instituted have been responsive to the will, if any, of the people—or at any rate to the apparent will of those who choose to organize and to complain.

The Persecution of Minorities

Carole Pateman, following arguments by Joseph Schumpeter and Peter Bachrach, argues that a country that persecutes groups like Jews, witches, and Christians cannot be considered democratic even if the persecution measures were established by democratic methods.[40] Experience suggests, however, that democracies do frequently persecute minorities. Unlike nondemocracies, however, they allow persecuted groups the freedom to petition and organize to alter or revoke offending laws, regulations, and policies. And, in fact, offended minorities are often able to gain redress even when the majority remains essentially hostile to them.

For generations (actually, for millennia) homosexuals have been persecuted both in democracies and nondemocracies, and their defining sexual activity has been routinely outlawed. This tiny minority is still held in open contempt, even disgust, by many members—probably most—of society.[41] Nevertheless, it has gradually been able to undo a great deal of official persecution in democracies in the space of only a couple of decades.

It is significant that this change took place only after homosexuals came out of the closet and openly organized to advance their interests. Democracy is not very good at inflicting pain on some people in order to supply benefits to other people who don't seem to want them. But once a minority organizes responsibly to put forward its demands, democratic governments are often remarkably responsive. And it is quite possible to imagine that other contemptuously dismissed groups whose principal activity has been outlawed—like drug addicts and prostitutes and, increasingly it seems, cigarette smokers—could obtain similar redress if they organized and worked on it.

Similarly, although all problems between blacks and whites in the United States have hardly been resolved, black people there, although they constitute little more than 10 percent of the population, have been able to get an enormous amount of legislation passed to lift discriminatory laws and practices and to guarantee their rights and position in society—including even some laws which give them preferential treatment. Notably, the vast bulk of this legislation came about only in the last forty years, after blacks themselves began to organize on a really substantial basis. Indeed, a central point of the massive and historic March on Washington, led by Martin Luther King in 1963, was to demonstrate that, contrary to the arguments of many hostile politicians, blacks generally—not just a troublemaking elite—actually wanted reform.[42] Important legislation was passed only a year later.

Often groups can get their way in a democracy even when they are denied the vote. As noted earlier, the American feminist movement achieved many of its goals even though the vast majority of its members were excluded from the electorate. Fairly quickly, and long before women gained the vote, feminists were able to secure passage of important legislation to protect women's rights on marriage, property, employment, and education issues. Gaining the vote was more difficult in large part because the movement was unable to demonstrate that women in general actually wanted it: an advisory referendum in Massachusetts in 1895, for example, went disastrously awry when, inspired by an antisuffrage movement comprised mainly of women, hardly any women even showed up to vote. A truly mass movement for suffrage in the United States was only achieved by 1916, or by 1913 at the earliest, and Congress passed the suffrage amendment in 1919.

Or there is the case of the disabled, a group that historically has not been so much persecuted as simply neglected. A considerable amount of legislation benefiting this minority was passed once the disabled were able to get their act coherently together even though the legislation caused notable inconvenience and expense to the majority.

Like the interests of the wealthy in earlier days, minority interests can be maintained in a democracy, but this comes about not particularly because the majority will embrace the minority with fraternal good will, but because democracy leaves the minority free to organize to pursue its interests—and effectively vastly to increase its political weight—on issues that matter most to it.[43] The majority may not come to have all that much sympathy with members of a minority group, but as long as the minority is reasonably subtle, circumspect, and unthreatening (and persistent) about pursuing its interests, it can expect a fair amount of benign neglect—effectively, tolerance—from the generally distracted and uninterested majority.

Often there are additional benefits to a pressuring group when it organizes for democratic combat: it may gain status and self-respect ("gay pride" activities have been central to the homosexual political movement), and there is a tendency for responsible and effective leaders to arise within the group itself. It will be of great interest to see if the people in central and eastern Europe at the bottom of the status ladder—the gypsies or Romanies—will organize to protect and advance their interests and coherently to chart their destiny.[44] Democracy affords the opportunity.

A Livable Society

Beyond these considerations, democracy also rather automatically comes encumbered with certain values and perspectives that many find congenial in themselves, quite apart from how they may or may not affect the political order. The act of voting or of participating in public discussion carries with it a sense of belonging that some people find quite satisfying psychologically. And among those who believe in the democratic myth, the voting act is taken to bestow a certain sense of legitimacy upon the government so chosen (those who believe that only God can choose leaders, on the other hand, will remain unimpressed).

Riker suggests that democracy gives people a sense of dignity and self-respect, while Robert Dahl plausibly finds that the democratic process "promotes human development, not least in the capacity for exercising self-determination, moral autonomy, and responsibility for one's choices."[45]

In general, democracy also comes accompanied with a permissiveness and effectively a tolerance, an openness, and a comparative absence of cant and mendacity, that are quite appealing to many—and are also qualities that may be very helpful for economic growth, as will be discussed in the concluding chapter. E. M. Forster, for example, likes democracy because it "admits variety" and because it "permits criticism." Those are his "two cheers" for democracy.[46] The folks at Ralph's Grocery would probably deem two cheers to be quite sufficient—pretty good, in fact.

DEMOCRACY AND REAL PEOPLE

It seems, then, that democracy, like God, works in mysterious ways its wonders (such as they are) to perform—ways that call into question many theories, hypotheses, expectations, and images generated both by supporters and by opponents about how the institution really ought to work. Democracy, it seems to me, is built not on political equality, but on political inequality; not on majority rule, but on minority rule and majority acquiescence; not on enlightened consensus, but on apathy and distraction; and not nearly so much on elections as on the frantic and chaotic interweavings and contestings of isolated, self-serving, and often tiny special interest groups and their political and bureaucratic allies.

Democracy is an admirable form of government, in my view, not because it furnishes a guide and goal for people to become ever better in a quixotic quest for atmospheric and unreachable Rockwellian ideals, but because it is a governmental form, generally compatible with a vigorous and productive society, that functions rather well when people manage, on average, to be no better than they actually are or are ever likely to be: flawed, grasping, self-centered, prejudiced, and easily distracted. In fact, democracy does not require a great deal from people: they do not need to be particularly good or noble, but merely to calculate their own best interests or, if they wish, interests they take to reflect those of the collectivity, and, if so moved, to express them.

In 1823, eight years after the end of the Napoleonic Wars, the

British writer and essayist Sydney Smith penned a letter railing exhaustedly against war in all its vigor, absurdity, and "eloquence," and in the process he expressed a yearning for four qualities of a more basic, even mundane, nature: "apathy, selfishness, common sense, arithmetic."[47] In this view, human beings are not incapable of such admirable qualities as eloquence, nobility, grandeur, altruism, self-sacrifice, and unblinkered obedience. But they are a flawed bunch, and it seems wiser, and certainly less tiring, to work with human imperfections rather than to seek zealously to reform the race into impossible perfection.[48]

To begin with, people have in them a strong streak of apathy and are not readily roused to action. In other words, they will tend to pursue concerns that matter to them rather than ones that other people think should matter to them. As it happens, some people will be quite content to spend their time taking naps, watching television, hanging out on street corners, boozing away the evening, or reading trashy novels rather than pursuing high culture, changing the world, or saving souls. (Sir John Falstaff, who might be seen as a sort of quintessential caricature of the Smith liberal, mutters at one point, "I were better to be eaten to death with a rust than to be scour'd to nothing with perpetual motion.") Relatedly, they will be selfish—guided more reliably by their own interests than by perceptions of the general good.

At the same time, however, people do not act randomly but rather apply commonsense and arithmetic. That is, they have a canny, if perhaps not terribly sophisticated, ability to assess reality and their own interests and to relate things in a fairly logical way. If left free, therefore, there's a good chance that a number of them will eventually see through even the most effusive flatteries and the most exquisite fabrications of the most dazzling illusionists.[49] At any rate, cagey illusionists seem to have been aware of the danger: once in political control they have quickly moved to destroy democracy before it destroys them.

An institution is likely to prove particularly effective if it can be fabricated so that it will function properly even when people need exhibit virtues no more exalted than those which emerge in the Smith—or the Ralph's Pretty Good Grocery—perspective.

Democracy has proved to be fundamentally sound—in harmony with human nature—in the sense that it does not routinely require much more from the human spirit than apathy, selfishness, common sense, and arithmetic. Indeed, in some respects it exalts and revels in these qualities.

Consequences of the Democratic Image

In the previous chapter, I developed a perspective about democracy based not on ideal images but rather on how the form actually seems to work, stressing that it is characterized by a chaotic interplay of special interests in a political environment distinguished by inequality, by minority rule, and by a sort of majority acquiescence that substantially derives from inattentiveness and apathy. The chapter concluded with something of a paean to democracy, albeit one that some democratic idealists might well consider a bit perverse.

While many of those exalting the democratic ideal might grudgingly agree that democracy does more or less work the way I have described it, they hold that things would be much better if democracy in practice were more nearly to approach its attractive theoretical ideal. They urge, therefore, that there should be continual efforts to make people more equal politically and to refashion democratic decision making so that it is more nearly a process of deliberative consensus carried out, or watched over, by a citizenry that is active and enlightened—or at least knowledgeable.

Often these reforms seem to be advocated for their own sake. That is, it is held to be important for democracies to more closely approximate the democratic ideal because it is important for democracies to more closely approximate the democratic ideal. Sydney Verba and Norman Nie, for example, declare that "if democracy is interpreted as rule by the people then . . . the more participation there is in decisions, the more democracy there is."[1] They do not maintain that decisions or policies will somehow be objectively better—that is, they do not suggest that there is something wrong, even rotten, in, say, the state of Switzerland, and then argue that higher voter turnout there will likely fix it. Rather, reformers often essentially conclude that participation—or equality or deliberation or knowledge—are important for their own sake.

I do not necessarily oppose the reformers' efforts, but I think it unlikely, realistically, that much progress can be made. And in this chapter I suggest there may actually be some negative consequences to the quest to close the very considerable mismatch between the democratic ideal—its impossible dream—and what I take to be its grim, grimy, and unavoidable reality.

To begin with, it seems to me that constantly stressing the clash between democracy's shining ideal image and its decidedly unlovely reality often induces, or at any rate reinforces, a cynicism about the democratic process that is uncomprehending and mostly (though not entirely) undesirable. Sometimes it becomes common, even fashionable, opaquely to dismiss the whole system as "corrupt." The cynicism about the form so commonly found in democracies, and so often lamented by democratic idealists, in fact, is partly—maybe even substantially—caused by them.

Second, I suggest that the continual overselling of equality by democratic idealists has encouraged the rise of a destructive and profoundly antidemocratic form—I call it hyperdemocracy—when this ideal is transferred to the economic realm. At various times, important activists, like Vladimir Lenin, have come to the (correct) conclusion that democracy allows the rich minority to protect its advantages and thus that democracy cannot deliver anything like strict economic equality. Therefore, they have sensibly, if murderously, concluded that the only way to achieve true economic equality is to crush democracy itself.

I argue, third, that adherence to the democratic image can logically lead some minorities to fear that, if the form is actually about equality, majority rule, and active participation, they stand to be persecuted in a democracy. In fact, as argued in the previous chapter, it happens that democracy has a rather good, if far from perfect, record of dealing with minorities, in large part because selective minority agitation is facilitated by majority apathy or inattentiveness. But minorities can be led to rebel in misguided desperation if they take the democratic ideal too seriously.

Finally, I append a few cautionary comments about the burgeoning field of transitology which sometimes tends to advance a perspective that can inspire a damaging short-term perspective in new democracies, and I also question the usefulness of the concept of "democratic consolidation."

In the following chapter I consider some of the consequences of the image mismatch on democratic development.

CYNICISM ABOUT THE DEMOCRATIC PROCESS

Democratic reformers, theorists, and image-makers often express alarm at the almost palpable cynicism routinely expressed by the public in democracies, both ones which have been around for a while and ones which have only recently emerged. Indeed, cynicism about the form seems to be the quality people most quickly pick up when their country turns democratic.[2]

A number of studies argue that things have gotten worse on this score lately, at least in the United States, where it is held that cynicism, discontent, frustration, and a sense of disempowerment and helplessness have markedly increased since the 1960s. For example, in a provocative recent book Michael Sandel points to polls showing that more people in the 1990s than in the 1960s say they distrust government to do what is right, think it wastes a lot of money, and feel it is run by a few big interests rather than for the benefit of all. He blames this increase on Vietnam, the assassinations of Robert Kennedy and Martin Luther King (but not on the inconveniently early one of John Kennedy), Watergate, the inflation of the 1970s, oil shocks, the Iran hostage crisis, the stagnation of middle-class incomes, the escalating deficit, crime, drugs, urban decay, and various other problems. Others, like Robert Putnam, add that there has also been an alarming decline in interpersonal trust over that period and attribute this to congenital press negativism or to that perennial receiver of brickbats, television.[3]

Interestingly, Sandel and Putnam do not notably allege so much that government has actually *become* less competent or trustworthy

166

or more wasteful or interest-dominated, but only that people have come to *feel* that this is so. Thus, Sandel argues that people feel a "loss of mastery" or a "sense of disempowerment," not that they actually *have* less "mastery" or "empowerment" than in days of old.[4] The problem, therefore, apparently is not so much with reality as with perception.

The implication of these studies is that trust and confidence in the United States have traditionally—that is, until the middle or late 1960s—been high. But quite a bit of data suggest that although expressions of cynicism may have been relatively low in the early 1960s, the seeming increase in cynicism and distrust since that time is more nearly a return to normal levels. Consider, for example, the responses of Americans to two questions asked at various points over the last half century, shown in the accompanying tables.

If you had a son, would you like to see him go into politics as a life's work?

	Yes	No
1945	21	68
1953	20	70
1955	26	60
1962	23	69
1965	36	54
1973	23	64
1991	24	72
1993	22	70
1994	25	71
1995	32	63

Do you think most people can be trusted?

	Yes	No	Don't Know
Mar 1942	66	25	9
Mar 1948	66	30	4
Aug 1952	68	30	2
Nov 1953	57	39	4
Jan 1954	62	34	4
Nov 1954	66	32	2
Apr 1957	75	22	3
Nov 1963	77	21	2
Mar 1983	56	41	3

Similarly, turnout rates reached a sort of peak in the early 1960s and afterwards returned to more normal levels, and confidence in the United States Congress peaked in the mid-1960s before declining again. More broadly, there is good reason to believe that political participation even in the "golden years" of American politics before the Civil War were, contrary to the usual supposition, marked mainly by apathy and political cynicism.[5]

In addition, if one examines the 1945–60 period—when, according to Sandel, a "sense of mastery prevailed"—it is quite easy to generate a list of calamities that rivals the one he delineates for the later one: food and housing shortages, continuous labor unrest, the rise of the Cold War, the fall of China, McCarthyism, Communist victory in Indochina, racial tensions over school integration, the continual humiliations due to Sputnik and the space race, the rise of Castro, various scandals over corruption in the government, incompetence at Suez, U.S. impotence when Soviet tanks crushed Hungarian independence, the arms race, continuing crises over Berlin, the looming threat of thermonuclear war, and, above all, the Korean War.[6]

In fact, during Sandel's age of mastery a huge sociological or pop-sociological literature was spawned about "alienation," "lonely crowds," the sameness of ticky-tacky suburban developments, and conformity and grey-flannel suits, as well as about how terrible it was that American soldiers allowed themselves to be brainwashed in Korea, that the clean-cut Charles Van Doren lied on a prime time television quiz show, and that CIA spy Francis Gary Powers neglected to kill himself when his U-2 spy plane was downed over the Soviet Union.

For example, in 1960 Murray Levin declared that "voters find voting to be meaningless . . . the electoral process to be a sham . . . the average voter feels that politicians are selfish and irresponsible. . . . they indicate a widespread disgust and disillusionment with the political process and politicians in general." And in the same year, Harvard's Kenneth Keniston, while acknowledging that there remained "pockets of enthusiasm," managed to miss any sense of mastery in the age, arguing instead that "there has seldom been as great confusion about what is valid and good as there is now," and found the age characterized by "alienation, estrangement, separation, withdrawal, indifference, disaffection, apathy, noninvolvement, neutralism." Similarly concerned that the country had lost its sense of national purpose (while the surging Communists supposedly knew exactly where they were going), President Eisenhower went so far as to appoint a national commission to find out what the country's goals, after all, were.[7]

Thus, even granting that political cynicism may have risen in recent decades, the quality itself seems more nearly to be a constant than a variable quality in American politics. And while this rise of cynicism may be mostly undesirable, it is hardly terminal: long and extensive experience with democracy suggests that E. J. Dionne is patently wrong when he argues that "a nation that hates politics will not long survive as a democracy" as is Michael Nelson when he asserts that the form "cannot long endure on a foundation of cynicism and indifference."[8]

To counter such lamentable, or at any rate widely lamented, qualities, democratic thinkers have resolved to reform the democracies and the peoples who make them up more nearly to approximate their ideal images of what it, and they, should be like.

Thus, Sandel suggests that democracy "depends" on a "civic life" which we must "restore" (thereby implying that it once really existed). This apparently means we must share in self-rule, which in turn requires "the capacity to deliberate well about the common good," which further implies that "citizens must possess certain excellences—of character, judgment, and concern for the whole." A tall agenda, clearly, but he sees hope for "our impoverished civic life" in campaigns like those in New England against Wal-Mart stores where "civic values" triumph over "consumer values" and people (that is, groups of dedicated, self-interested agitators) array themselves around such uplifting slogans as "I'd rather have a viable community than a cheap pair of underwear."[9]

Putnam also tends to idolize Rockwellian town-meeting decision making—very unlike James Madison, incidentally, who found societies in which a small number of citizens assemble and administer government to be susceptible to mischievous passions and interests, to be "spectacles of turbulence and contention," to be "incompatible with personal security or the rights of property," and in general to be "as short in their lives as they have been violent in their deaths." Putnam urgently calls for the reversal of what he views as "a broad and continuing erosion of civic engagement" and consequently of "social capital."[10] Like Sandel, however, he writes at a time in which the American economy is soaring (in part, as suggested in chapter 4, because of high levels of business trust and honesty). And he fails to indicate that the trend he laments has actually had any tangible negative policy consequences.

In contrast to these perspectives, it seems to me that democratic cynicism stems not as much from the inadequacies of people or of democracy as from the ministrations of the image-makers: people contrast democratic reality with its ideal image, note a huge discrepancy, and logically become cynical about the process. If cynicism about the form is a problem, what may need to be reformed is not so much the system as the theory—and perhaps the theorists.

I should stress again that I do not hold efforts to increase political equality, deliberative consensus, participation, and citizen knowledge necessarily to be undesirable. However, I do think that long experience with democracy suggests that it is hopeless to imagine that things can be changed a great deal. Inequality, disagreement, apathy, and ignorance seem to be normal, not abnormal, in a democracy, and to a considerable degree the beauty of the form is that it works despite these qualities—or, in some important respects, because of them.[11]

The Quest for Political Equality

As noted in the previous chapter, the notion that all men are created equal suggests that people are *born* equal—that is, that none should necessarily be denied political opportunity merely because of their hereditary entrance into the wrong social or economic class or because they do not adhere to the visions or dictates of a particular ideological group. The notion does not, however, suggest that people must necessarily be equal in their impact on the political system, but this damaging extrapolation is often made by reformers, at least as a goal to be quested after.[12]

An extensive study on the issue of equality by a team of political scientists finds, none too surprisingly, that people in a real democracy like the United States differ in the degree to which they affect the political system. Political effectiveness, the study concludes, depends on three varying factors: resources, especially time, money, and skills; psychological engagement with politics; and "access to networks through which individuals can be recruited to political life." The variance of effectiveness, the authors then conclude, poses a "threat to the democratic principle of equal protection of interests." Another analyst, reviewing their findings, makes a similar observation: "liberal democracies fail to live up to the norm of equal responsiveness to the interests of each citizen."[13]

But instead of seeking to reform the system or the people who make it up, we may want instead to abandon, or at least substantially to modify, the principle and the norm. They clearly express a romantic perspective about democracy, a perspective which has now been fully and repeatedly disconfirmed in practice. Democracies are responsive and attentive to the interests of the citizenry—at least when compared to other forms of government—

but they are nowhere near equally responsive to the interests of each citizen.

Related is the perennial clamor against "special interests." As the futile struggle for campaign finance reform in the United States suggests, people who want or need to influence public policy are very likely to find ways to do so no matter how clever the laws that seek to restrict them. As Gil Troy observes, "for all the pious hopes, the goal of the Watergate-era reforms—to remove the influence of money from presidential elections—was, in hard and inescapable fact, ridiculous." (He also notes that the entire cost of the 1996 election campaigns was about 25 percent of what Procter & Gamble routinely spends every year to market its products.) A rare voice of realism amid all the sanctimonious, politically correct bluster from politicians about campaign finance reform in the United States in the 1990s was that of Senator Robert Bennett of Utah: "rich people will always have influence in politics, and the solution is not to create barriers that cause the rich people to spend even more money to hire lawyers and consultants to find ways around the law to get the same results."[14]

In the end, "special interests" can be effectively reined in only by abandoning democracy itself, because their activities are absolutely vital to the form. Indeed, it is quite incredible that two prominent Washington reporters merely deem it "simplistic" to argue that "people with common interests should not attempt to sway government policy." In a democracy the free, competitive play of "special interests" is fundamental. To reform this out of existence would be uncomprehending and profoundly antidemocratic.[15]

Most of the agitation against political inequality is focused on the special privileges business is presumed to enjoy. For example, concern is voiced that the attention of public officials can be differently arrested: "a phone call from the CEO of a major employer in the district may carry considerably more weight than one from an unknown constituent."[16] It is possible, of course, that the unweighty and unknown constituent has just come up with a plan which will achieve permanent worldwide bliss in the course of the next six months, but, since there are only twenty-four hours in a day, public officials (like the rest of us) are forced to ration their time, and they are probably correct to assume, as a first approximation at least, that the concerns of a major employer are likely to be of wider relevance to more people than are those of the hapless lone constituent.

But if the CEO's access advantage to a time-pressured politician is somehow reprehensible and must be reformed, what about other inequalities—that is, why focus only on economic ones? A telephone call from a big-time political columnist like David Broder of the *Washington Post* is likely to get the politician's attention even faster than that of the CEO. Should the influential David Broder hold off on his next column until the rest of us deserving unknowns have had a chance to put in our two cents in the same forum? Inequalities like these are simply and unavoidably endemic to the whole political system as, indeed, they are to life itself. It may be possible to reduce this inequality, but it is difficult to imagine a reform that could possibly raise the political impact of the average factory worker—or even of the average business executive—remotely to equal that enjoyed by Broder.

Robert Dahl aptly notes that "significant inequalities in power have been a universal feature of human relationships throughout recorded history; they exist today in all democratic systems." This, he concludes, "falls short of the criteria of the democratic process" and the result is a "serious problem for democratic theory and practice."[17] But it seems to me that the "serious problem" may lie not so much with the universal fact of inequality, but rather with the theory and with the "criteria of the democratic process" which, as Dahl essentially suggests, have clearly, repeatedly, consistently, and overwhelmingly been demonstrated to be fanciful.

Dahl, on the other hand, seeks a method by which citizens can "possess the political resources they would require in order to participate in political life pretty much as equals." He doesn't suggest that pretty much all of us should have something like a equal crack at the op-ed page of the *Washington Post,* but he does place quite a bit of hope in "telecommunications." These, he suggests, could be used to provide "virtually every citizen" with "information about public issues" and to establish "interactive systems" to "participate in discussions with experts, policymakers, and fellow citizens."[18]

Perhaps because newspapers, magazines, television, libraries, public meetings, telephones, and talk radio already supply much of this, and perhaps because most people freely choose to ignore this mass of readily available information, Dahl then essentially seems to abandon the equality theme by suggesting that what we really need is simply "a critical mass of well-informed citizens large enough and active enough to anchor the process, an 'attentive public,' as Gabriel Almond put it many years ago," favorably citing a book written forty years earlier that concluded that such a helpful elite group already substantially exists.[19]

Finally, Dahl resolves to save elective democracy for the future almost—it seems—by proposing to abandon it. To guarantee that at least part of the attentive public be "representative," he suggests that a group of some thousand citizens be selected by random methods (rather than by elective ones) and that it then be forced or hired to deliberate issues of the day (by telecommunications) and from time to time to "announce its choices." These choices would complement those made by elected bodies that already happen to exist, and would "derive their authority from the legitimacy of democracy." Using methods like this, "citizens in an advanced democratic country would discover others" and "the democratic process could be adapted once again to a world that little resembles the world in which democratic ideas and practices first came to life." Such romantic devices are necessary, Dahl concludes thunderingly, because "the democracy of our successors will not and cannot be the democracy of our predecessors."[20] In my opinion, it clearly will and it just as clearly can.

The Quest for Deliberative Consensus

Rather than accepting democracy for what centuries of experience have shown it to be, many democrats—both in old democracies like the United States and in new ones like those in postcommunist Europe—get angry when democracy allows them to watch the process in all its chaotic, unkempt finery. Instead of accepting Bismarck's wisdom comparing the making of laws to the making of sausages, many people continue to quest for an illusive, and, I think, illusory, ideal, one which suggests that lawmaking under democracy, in contrast to all other sorts, should be characterized by careful deliberation and consensual resolution in which the views of honest and naive little people, like moviemaker Frank Capra's mythical Mr. Smith, should eventually prevail.[21]

Thus Dionne lauds "the belief that self-government is not a drab necessity but a joy to be treasured," in which "politics is not simply a grubby confrontation of competing interests but an area in which citizens can learn from each other and discover an 'enlightened self-interest'."[22] However, in real world decision making grubbiness almost always prevails over joy for the simple, elemental reason that people happen to disagree, often profoundly, about many key issues. (In addition, because of the existence of cyclic preferences in the collective—shifting majorities may prefer A to B and B to C, but also C to A—it is often logically impossible to discover a true majority preference.)[23]

People seem to have an aversion to haggling and in result, as discussed in chapter 2, the practice has been virtually eliminated at the retail level in advanced capitalist countries. A comparable aversion to political contention, however, cannot be serviced because contention is both inevitable and necessary. Nonetheless, people contrast Bismarkian grubbiness with the Rockwellian image projected by Dionne and others, and they often come to dismiss it all as unseemly bickering—"politics as usual"—and become cynical.

Thus, in the United States, Congress and the president often slump in popularity whenever they are caught in the act of trying to solve or resolve a difficult and contentious problem. In October 1990, for example, President George Bush and the Democrats went at each other over the budget: there was a difficult deficit to confront, and this required such painful remedies as spending cuts or tax increases or (as it turned out) both. In due course they worked out a sensible compromise, but people, incensed over all the furor, started screaming—as the cover of the 22 October 1990 issue of *U.S. News and World Report* headlined—to "throw the bums out." The popularity of both Congress and the president reached conspicuous lows.[24]

A bit more recently, it could be argued that the health care debate in the United States in 1993 and 1994 showed democracy at its finest. A problem the voters had sensibly determined to be important was addressed and debated. President Bill Clinton had a solution, others in Congress had theirs, affected interested groups appropriately weighed in with theirs, and months of thoughtful and nuanced (if sometimes confusing and boring) discussion of this difficult topic took place. Admittedly, a solution (apparent or real) to this complicated concern was not smoothly worked out in two years of effort, but the problem did not have to be solved immediately, and there was plenty of time in the next years to come up with judicious remedies with this groundwork laid—something, indeed, that substantially happened. Yet voters, few of whom paid much attention to the substance of the often tedious debate, dismissed it all as "bickering," cried "gridlock," and often became angry and cynical.[25]

Two of Washington's top reporters, David Broder and Haynes Johnson, have written a book on this episode. In tone and substance the book continually suggests that the system failed in the health care debate—indeed, that the public was "duped." Despite the abundant evidence arrayed in their book of the wide-ranging discussion that took place on the issue, they somehow manage to conclude that a "great public debate" about health care never occurred. Yet the authors acknowledge that "Where no strong consensus exists, major change should wait"—which is exactly what happened.[26]

As they note, the experience may have heightened popular cynicism about the process. However, some of that came from books like theirs which suggest that democracy really ought somehow to be different from what history has regularly and consistently shown it to be: a disorderly, manipulative, but often remarkably productive, muddle.

At any rate, after this experience, the popularity both of the president and of Congress predictably plummeted. Exacting revenge in the 1994 elections for the unpleasant untidiness, the voters threw out many of the leading bums, particularly the ones who had started the contentious debate in response to the voters' earlier concerns. Thus, an analysis of exit polls in the election finds "no unifying theme" among the voters except for "an overall distaste for government." It suggests Clinton got the election's message, such as it was, when he concluded that the voters were saying "Look, we just don't like what we see when we watch Washington. And you haven't done much about that. It's too partisan, too interest-group oriented, things don't get done. There's too many people up there playing politics."[27]

Emerging from this experience was a swelling demand for term limits and perhaps for a third party, based on two quite remarkable assumptions: 1) that the people elected under such altered conditions will behave notably different from those elected under the present ones; and 2) that voters are somehow being unfairly manipulated when, despite their vigorously expressed cynicism about politicians, they regularly and overwhelmingly reelect incumbents.[28]

When politicians respond to what they think their constituents want they are routinely accused of "pandering to public opinion" and of "doing anything to be elected." When they go in a direction different from what public opinion seems to dictate, they are accused of "ignoring the will of the people" and "pandering to special interests." If they have sharp differences, they are accused of polarizing the situation, "encouraging an 'either/or' politics based on ideological preconceptions rather than a 'both/and' politics based on ideas that broadly unite us."[29] If they manage to agree, they are accused of selling out principle for a Tweedledum and Tweedledee me-tooism. It's a tough racket.

Related is the concern about "negative campaigning." The implication, apparently, is that if politicians can't say something nice about other politicians, they shouldn't say anything at all. As Riker has observed, however, by any standard of what reasonable discourse should be like, there is nothing wrong or indecent about negative campaigning if it helps to differentiate candidates and issues—as it almost always does. Moreover, it is a commonplace in democratic campaigns, never more so than in the intensely contentious ratification campaign for the since-sanctified United States Constitution.[30]

In an important study of political campaigning, Stephen Ansolabehere and Shanto Iyengar find that campaign advertising—including negative advertising—"informs voters about the candidates' positions and makes it more likely that voters will take their own preferences on the issues into account when choosing between the candidates." Therefore they conclude that political advertising, particularly television advertising, "actually fosters the democratic ideals of an informed and reasoning electorate."

However, at the same time Ansolabehere and Iyengar become greatly concerned because negative campaign advertising increases the voters' cynicism about the electoral process and because it is taken by some voters, particularly nonpartisan ones, to be "a signal of the dysfunctional and unresponsive nature of the political process itself," causing them to lose interest in voting, thereby "eroding the participatory ethos of the American public." To help "short-circuit this cycle of negativity," they consider several remedies. One might be to encourage journalists and media watchers to police the ads, but they find that this approach gives the negative ads even more play and that the negativity of press coverage of negative ads only adds to the problem. More promising, they suggest, is to charge candidates more for negative ads than for positive ones and to strengthen party campaign organizations on the (highly dubious) grounds that "party-centered campaigns remove the incentive to air personal attacks."[31]

Thus, on the one hand this study finds that negative advertising clarifies and informs; on the other that it alienates some members of the voting public who have, despite hundreds of years of disconfirmation, fallen for the mythical notion that democracy is about Rockwellian deliberative consensus. The fault clearly lies with the myth, not with the reality, but instead of seeking to abandon the endlessly attractive, if thoroughly discredited myth, we are urged to mellow reality in hopes that it will somehow come to resemble it. Interestingly, the most famous sustained instance of negative campaigning was probably Harry Truman's colorful and successful give-'em-hell presidential campaign of 1948, but reformers don't seems to be concerned about that one. It may be that the recent popular cynicism about negative campaigning is being caused not so much by the campaigning itself as by the campaign against negative campaigning.

At any rate, like other democratic values and practices, negativity does seem to be something new democracies pick up with considerable ease. A report from Paraguay after a mere two years of experience with the political form observed that "newspaper, television, and radio reports are filled with mud-slinging worthy of the most mature democracy."[32] That, it seems, is the way democracy is. To be deeply offended by it is fundamentally misguided.

The problem in all this, as John Hibbing and Elizabeth Theiss-Morse have aptly put it, is that people lack "an appreciation for the ugliness of democracy." In fact, "true democratic processes in any realistic environment are bound to be slow, to be built on compromise, and to make apparent the absence of clean, certain answers to important questions of the day." Yet, people want "both procedural efficiency and procedural equity," a sort of "stealth democracy."[33]

Actually, as Bismarck's aphorism may suggest, the unpleasantness is not really peculiar to democracy; it applies to law-making more generally. The problem is heightened in a democracy, however, because all interests can participate, because people are allowed freely to speak their minds—thereby perhaps enhancing its natural disorderliness—and also because the decision-making process is comparatively open in all its chaotic, appalling finery.[34] Reformers and idealists who yearn for Rockwellian consensus and closure only enhance the public's unrealistic and uncomprehending misperception, and consequently they heighten cynicism about the process.

There are a number of potential solutions to this problem, if problem it be. One, of course, is for law-makers simply not to appear to do much of anything, and, indeed, in early 1998 when the most visible accomplishment of the American Congress was to rename an airport, the popularity of the institution soared.[35] But this approach is clearly not feasible overall, and it is hardly desirable from the standpoint of decision making. Nor is an effort to make decision making less grubby likely to be either successful or sensible. Even Hibbing and Theiss-Morse toy with the suggestions that "ways must be found to limit the influence of key actors" like interest groups, and that "important steps need to be taken to reassure people that monied interests are not getting preferential treatment."[36] But the interplay of interests (virtually all of them "monied") is at the very heart of the process, and it simply cannot and should not go away. Moreover, some interests will inevitably get "preferential treatment"—that is, what they want—while others will not.

More hopeful, following another suggestion of Hibbing and Theiss-Morse, might be to seek to educate the public to more nearly understand and appreciate democracy's inevitable and congenital ugliness. However, because of the popular and apparently universal belief—tirelessly fostered by democratic theorists and idealists—that democracy really ought to be much different than it has always and everywhere been, this effort, too, is unlikely to be very successful. Nonetheless, it might be refreshing sometime to hear a politician and even the occasional educator rise above sanctimony for a moment and frankly admit that "special interests," far from being a distorting evil, are what the whole thing is all about, and that, in the words of playwright John Mortimer, "freedom is perpetual fussing."[37]

The Quest for Participation

Democratic theorists, idealists, and image-makers maintain that "democratic states require . . . participation in order to flourish," or that "a politically active citizenry is a requisite of any theory of democracy," or that "democracy was built on the principle that political participation was not only the privilege of every man, but a necessity in ensuring the efficiency and prosperity of the democratic system," or that "high levels of electoral participation are essential for guaranteeing that government represents the public as a whole," or that "to make a democracy that works, we need citizens who are engaged."[38]

But we now have over two hundred years of experience with living, breathing, messy democracy, and truly significant participation has almost never been achieved anywhere. Since democracy exists, *it simply can't be true* that wide participation is a notable requirement, requisite, guarantee, need, or necessity for it to prosper or work. Routinely, huge numbers of citizens even—in fact, especially—in "mature" democracies simply decline to participate, and the trend in participation seems to be, if anything, mostly downward. In the United States, nearly half of those eligible fail to vote even in high-visibility elections and only a few percent ever actively participate in politics. The final winner of a recent election for the mayor of Rochester, N.Y., received only about 6 percent of the vote of the total electorate. (However, he is a very popular choice: if everybody had voted, he would almost certainly have achieved the same victory.) Switzerland is Europe's oldest democracy, and it also boasts the continent's lowest voter turnout.[39]

Statistics like these frequently inspire a great deal of concern—after all, it is argued, "political participation" is one of the "basic democratic ideals."[40] But it may be more useful to reshape democratic theories and ideals to take notice of the elemental fact that democracy works even though it often fails to inspire very much in the way of participation from its citizenry.

And it might also be asked, why, exactly, is it so important for citizens to participate? Most analyses suggest that nonvoters do not differ all that much from voters in their policy concerns, though there are some (controversial) suggestions that leftist parties might do a bit better in some countries if everyone were forced to vote.[41] However, once in office, responsible leftist and rightist parties both face the same constraining conditions and, despite their ideologies and campaign promises, often do not differ all that much from each other in their policies—frequently to the disillusionment and disgust of their supporters who may come to feel they have been conned.

Some hold voting to be important because "of the problem of legitimacy." The idea is that "as fewer and fewer citizens participate in elections, the extent to which government truly rests on the consent of the governed may be called into question"; moreover the "quality of the link between elites and citizens" will erode.[42] Actually, such callings into question seem to happen mostly when a candidate, like Bill Clinton in 1992, gets less than half of the recorded *vote*—and these are principally inspired by partisan maneuvering by the losers to undercut any claim that the winner has a mandate. And in local elections, the often exceedingly low turnout and participation levels rarely even cause much notice: I have yet to hear anyone suggest that the mayor of Rochester is illegitimate or "unlinked" because hardly anybody managed to make it to the polls when he was elected.

Moreover, it really seems to strain credulity to suggest that "if people feel distant from the electoral process, they can take no pride in the successes of the government." *No* pride? It seems that even nonvoters celebrated victory in the Gulf War. Or that nonvoters "avoid responsibility for the problems facing the nation."[43] But nonvoters seem to have no more difficulty than voters in routinely (and sometimes even correctly) blaming the politicians for whatever is wrong. And it is simply too glib to conclude that "if you don't vote, you don't count."[44] If that were true, women would never have gotten the vote, slavery would still exist, and there would never have been prison reform or legislation aiding the homeless.

There are also claims that low turnout levels "contribute to the problem of an unrepresentative policy agenda." But it is difficult to understand what this could possibly mean—or, better, what a "representative policy agenda" would look like. Agendas are set by people actively trying to pursue their interests; they are not out there somewhere in the miasma waiting for us objectively to snap them up. As Steven Rosenstone and John Mark Hansen argue, "political participation is the product of strategic interactions of citizens and leaders." People "participate when politicians, political parties, interest groups, and activists persuade them to get involved." Thus, there will not be an "ideal" or even "normal" degree of participation. Rather, participation will increase when "salient issues reach the public agenda . . . when governments approach crucial decisions . . . when competitive election campaigns stimulate, when social movements inspire."[45]

Hundreds of years of experience, then, suggest that the pursuit of participation for the sake of participation is rather quixotic. Instead, applying a philosophical observation attributed to impresario Sol Hurok, perhaps we should accept the fact that "if people don't want to come, nothing will stop them." Moreover, discontent and cynicism about the system itself (and consequently perhaps nonvoting) are increased when alarmists passionately lament that many people, as they have throughout democratic eternity, freely decide to pursue interests they find more pressing than politics, or manage to come up with more interesting things to do on election day than to go through the often inconsequential ritual of voting. (Sometimes, actually, nonvoters, by the very act of not voting, may be indicating their concerns and preferences more eloquently than those who actually do vote.)[46]

The Quest for an Enlightened Citizenry

"If a nation expects to be ignorant and free," Thomas Jefferson once said, "it expects what never was and never will be."[47] Pretty much ever since those memorable words were issued, the United States has managed to be both, and with considerable alacrity.

Fortunately for America, eternal vigilance has not proven to be the price of democracy—it can come quite a bit cheaper. In ideal democracies, James Bryce once suggested, "the average citizen will give close and constant attention to public affairs, recognizing that this is his interest as well as his duty"—but not in real ones. And Horace Mann's ringing prediction that "with universal suffrage, there must be universal elevation of character, intellectual and moral, or there will be universal mismanagement and calamity" has proven untrue.[48]

Nonetheless, democratic idealists continue to insist that "democracies require responsibility." Or they contend that democracy "relies on informed popular judgment and political vigilance." Or they persist in defining democracy "as a political system in which people actively attend to what is significant."[49] One would think it would be obvious by now that democracy works despite the fact that it often fails to inspire or require very much in the way of responsibility and knowledge from its citizenry. Democracy does feed on the bandying about of information, but that is going to happen pretty much automatically when people are free to ferret it out and to exchange it. Democracy clearly does not require that people generally be well informed, responsible, or actively attentive.

Recent surveys find that around half the American people haven't the foggiest idea which party controls the Senate or what the first ten amendments of the Constitution are called or what the Fifth Amendment does or who their congressional representative or senators are. Moreover, this lack of knowledge has generally increased (particularly when education is controlled for) since the 1940s.[50] A month after the Republican victory in the 1994 election that propelled the vocal and energetic Newt Gingrich into the speakership of the House of Representatives and into the media stratosphere, a national poll found that 50 percent hadn't heard enough about Gingrich even to have an opinion about him. Four months later, after endless publicity over Gingrich's varying fortunes and after *Time* magazine had designated him its "Man of the Year," that number had not changed (so much for the power of the press).[51] In a poll conducted two years later, half were still unable to indicate who the speaker was. Meanwhile, less than 20 percent guessed correctly that over the preceding twenty years air pollution and the number of the elderly living in poverty had declined, and most people were of the wildly distorted impression that foreign aid comprised a larger share of the federal budget than Medicare.[52]

One recent analysis observes that "for the last 200 years the United States has survived as a stable democracy, despite continued evidence of an uninformed public."[53] It also notes that "in theory, a democracy requires knowledgeable citizens." Although it then labels the contradictory condition "the paradox of modern democracy," it seems, rather, that it is the theory that should be called into question, not the reality.

Moreover, it may not be entirely clear why one should expect people to spend a lot of time worrying about politics when democratic capitalism not only leaves them free to choose other ways to get their kicks, but in its seemingly infinite quest for variety is constantly developing seductive distractions. Democratic theorists and idealists may be intensely interested in government and its processes, but it verges on the arrogant, even the self-righteous, to suggest that other people are somehow inadequate or derelict unless they share the same curious passion. Many studies have determined that it is the politically interested who are the most politically active. It is also doubtless true that those most interested in unidentified flying objects are the ones most likely to join UFO clubs. UFO enthusiasts, however, get no special credit by political theorists for servicing their particular obsession, while politics junkies are lauded because they seem to be fulfilling a higher, theory-sanctified function.

In the end, the insistence that terrible things will happen unless the citizenry becomes addicted to C-SPAN can inspire cynicism about the process when it is observed that the Beverly Hillbillies (or whatever) enjoy vastly higher ratings.

Cynicism and Resistance to Demagogues

Cynicism about the process may be a standard pose among citizens in democracies, one substantially inspired by the very people who so passionately bemoan it—democratic theorists, idealists, and image-makers questing after their vaporous democratic ideal. This pose, derived in my view from a fundamental incomprehension about how democracy works, is probably undesirable, and it can certainly become tedious. But I do not wish to argue that cynicism is necessarily in all cases a bad thing.

One of the classic objections to democracy, voiced by Plato and many others, is the supposed susceptibility of the masses to the wily seductions of demagogues. Apathy and commonsense have probably helped solve this potential problem as noted in the previous chapter, but so also has a substantial, if often unfair and undeserved, wariness about politicians. Indeed, in many postcommunist countries a healthy distrust of all politicians has probably been important, as Stephen Holmes suggests, in keeping extremists from gaining much political ground there.[54]

HYPERDEMOCRACY

Tocqueville once observed that "democratic institutions awaken and foster a passion for equality which they can never entirely satisfy."[55] At its extreme this passion has proven to be extremely destructive.

I have argued that under democracy people are inevitably and substantially unequal in their impact on the political system, though individuals retain the freedom to alter their political weight on an issue of concern to them and regularly do so. As part of process, people of wealth or "advantage" have generally been quite capable of using their position to guide—or manipulate— the political system to keep it from confiscating their wealth or severely diminishing their advantages. Thus, as Martin McGuire and Mancur Olson point out, no democracy has ever voted to eliminate private property.[56]

Because of this phenomenon, there seems to be no realistic hope of achieving the ideal of true equality that democratic image-makers often seem to revere—particularly as it relates to economic equality—unless democracy is itself destroyed.

Agitators like Vladimir Lenin—hyperdemocrats, they might be called—have followed exactly this logic. He begins by observing, correctly, that under democracy the same people—rich and well-born like him—tend to retain their privileges, and, citing Marx, he caricatures capitalist democracy as a condition in which the "oppressed" are "allowed, once every few years, to decide which particular representatives of the oppressing class should be in parliament to represent and oppress them." To sever this control he proposes a "modification of democracy" characterized by the "suppression by force" of the capitalist class. This process, he assures us, would ultimately lead to a condition of "equality of labour and equality of wages."[57]

Thus the logic of the democrat's idealistic and romantic emphasis on equality can lead to calls for democracy's suppression. (However, the ultimate irony of all this, as noted in chapter 2, is that under the schemes and devices and mechanisms put together by Lenin and his followers, economic equality was not really reduced.)

In fact, of course, Leninism is profoundly antidemocratic not only in its ultimate conclusions, but in its starting assumptions. In the end, democracy trusts the commonsense and reasonableness of ordinary people, and it leaves them free to think and to contribute as they wish even if this sometimes (or even often) leads to results some might consider ill-advised, even foolish. By contrast, the version of communism that took hold in Lenin's Soviet Union and elsewhere was based on the theory that ordinary people actually *don't* know what is good for them, taking as conclusive proof of this the very fact that rich people are able to maintain much of their advantage in democracies. From this they conclude that ordinary people have had their heads filled with all sorts of devious capitalistic propaganda giving them a "false consciousness" about life and about the class conflict. Accordingly, it was necessary for an elite group of revolutionary, conspiratorial intellectuals, styling itself the "vanguard of the proletariat," to think for the naive, manipulated, and unaware masses, and to organize their activities until they come to their senses.[58]

THE REBELLION OF MINORITIES

The problem of convincing minority peoples to accept democratic rule is heightened by democracy's idealistic association with political equality, majority rule, and active political participation by the mass of people. Taking these three notions at face value, a national or other minority—particularly one that knows it inspires considerable hostility in the majority—can quite logically come to fear persecution in a democratic system since it will obviously be outnumbered by its perceived enemies. This perception can lead to despair, desperation, and rebellion. Democratic image-makers characteristically argue that the minority's only hope is that the majority will somehow treat it with respect, tolerance, and good will—an argument that in many cases will never be remotely persuasive.

As discussed in the previous chapter, democracy has actually had a good, if imperfect, record of dealing with minority issues, particularly when compared to other forms of government. But this is not so much because democratic majorities have been notably tolerant of minority concerns. Rather, it stems from the opportunities that democracy affords minorities to increase their effective political weight—to become more equal, more important, than their arithmetical size would imply—on issues that concern them. This holds even for groups held in considerable contempt by the majority, like homosexuals. Moreover, the fact that most people most of the time pay little attention to politics—the phenomenon of political apathy—helps interested minorities to protect their rights and to assert their interests, particularly when they are reasonably persistent and circumspect about it.

The civil wars in Croatia and in Bosnia-Hercegovina in the early 1990s were triggered, in part at least, because Serbs there did not understand this democratic reality and instead reacted—or overreacted—to the conventional democratic image. Believing inaccurately that democracy is centrally built around political equality, active participation, and majority rule, they responded to alarmists and propagandists who claimed that they would mainly face persecution in a democracy in which they were outnumbered.[59] (Something similar might be said for Kosovars in Serbia and for Palestinians in, and in areas occupied by, Israel.)

Experience suggests, by contrast, that the Serbs could well have substantially maintained their interests, identity, and dignity if the system had remained essentially democratic. (Although democracy came under substantial assault in war-racked Croatia and Bosnia-Hercegovina, it is remarkable how much of it survived and persisted even under those conditions, and it is reasonable to expect that it would have remained fairly well-developed—in part because of pressures from the West—if war had been avoided.) In the process the Serbs would probably have found that, to a considerable degree, their numerical inferiority was largely an arithmetical technicality. This seems, for example, substantially to have been the experience since 1989 in Bulgaria for the Turkish minority (which had been severely persecuted under the Communists) and in Lithuania of the Polish minority.[60]

However, it must be conceded that there are no certain guarantees. As observed in the previous chapter, a majority that is sufficiently large and determined can at times indeed persecute the minority in a democracy. Obviously, whites in the American South were able for decades to keep blacks from participating effectively in the political system—although, as also noted there, that condition rather quickly broke down when blacks effectively organized. And, even though the American Constitution has a specific guarantee against unreasonable seizures, the property of Japanese-Americans was often summarily confiscated in the United States during World War II. What is impressive, however, is how unusual such arbitrary seizures have been in democracies.

Democracy routinely and necessarily leaves a minority free to organize peacefully to protect itself, and it provides legal mechanisms for the minority to express its views and to pressure the government for recognition and for relief of grievances. There is no such regular, systematic, or necessary assurance in other systems.

The Trouble with Transitology

A couple of Polish writers were discussing conditions in their country on a street corner in Warsaw fairly recently. At one point, one reflected, "I think we all must now believe that this is it."

In my view most of the postcommunist countries of central and eastern Europe as well as many of the new democracies elsewhere have essentially completed their transition to democracy: they are already full-fledged democracies by the nonideal standards I have proposed in this book. Judging from two hundred years of experience with democracy, what they have now is, pretty much, *it*. It will, in all likelihood, never get much better.

There will, of course, be continued political change in these countries and some of this will be quite important. Politicians will come and go; some parties will fall and others will rise in voter favor (with luck perhaps the beer-drinkers' party will once again capture seats in the Polish parliament); constitutional and legal structures will undergo development; controversial issues will emerge and decline; economic and trade policies will be reshaped and refined; governmental subsidies will be increased and decreased; tax laws will be altered. But barring some sort of violent upheaval, the time of fundamental change is substantially over in many of these countries, and further developments will take place in environments which are essentially democratic. The societies may become more or less efficient, humane, responsible, productive, corrupt, civil, or effective, but these changes will probably have to come about within (or despite) the present political framework, not through further fundamental institutional transformation.[61]

Accordingly, it may now be sensible to decrease the talk of "transition" and to put a quiet, dignified end to the new field of transitology at least as it applies to countries like Poland. Transitological thinking may cause people in the new democracies in Europe and elsewhere to continue to think that things may become substantially different—hopefully better—in the future.[62] Thus, not only are transitologists sometimes spreading visions that will never come to pass, but their perspective can inspire or reinforce a short-term point of view that is undesirable from a political standpoint and even more so from an economic one.[63]

There may be similar misdirecting mischief in the related notion of "consolidation." Democracies do become more or less democratic, a phenomenon traced in various democracy ratings schemes such as those put out regularly by Freedom House. It is certainly appropriate to keep track of the new democracies and to become concerned by any retreat that might take place—if, for example, opposition leaders are harassed or if organized protesters are forcibly stifled, or if newspapers find it difficult to publish facts the government deems inconvenient. (In my approach, such freedoms are more central to democracy than the existence of elections.) Thus, Peru in the 1990s lost some of its democratic character, and Chile in 1973 abandoned democracy almost entirely for several years. It is sensible to be sensitive to such changes.

But to seek to establish a point at which a country becomes "consolidated" may not be terribly helpful since, as with Chile in 1973, this condition can be overthrown at any time by sufficiently dedicated and effective antidemocrats—some of whom might have even have previously been democrats.[64]

Many new democracies, then, have fully completed their transitions and are about as "consolidated" as any country is likely to get. And, like the older democracies that are their model, the new democracies are unlikely ever to achieve orderly deliberation, political equality, or wide and enlightened participation by the mass of the public.[65]

Rather than urging the new democracies on to impossible perfection, it would probably be better to take the laid-back approach adopted by the Polish writer, Adam Michnik. He suggests that we color democracy gray and notes that it frequently "chooses banality over excellence, shrewdness over nobility, empty promise over true competence." At its core, he points out, democracy is "a continuous articulation of particular interests, a diligent search for compromise among them, a marketplace for passions, emotions, hatreds, and hopes." But it is also "eternal imperfection, a mixture of sinfulness, saintliness, and monkey business." Yet only democracy has the "capacity to question itself" and the "capacity to correct its own mistakes," and "only gray democracy, with its human rights, with institutions of civil society, can replace weapons with arguments."[66]

Only pretty good, perhaps, but, as they'll be quick to assure you down at Ralph's Grocery, that's about as good as it gets.

The Rise of Democracy

I HAVE ARGUED that, contrary to the gloomy and sometimes strident claims of many of its well-wishers, democracy can function remarkably well even when its constituents participate only as moved to do so and even when they exhibit little in the way of self-discipline, restraint, commitment, knowledge, or sacrifice for the general interest. For democracy to operate, people do not generally need to be good or noble, nor do they need to be deeply imbued with some sort of democratic spirit or culture. They need merely to muse about how they think things ought to be, relying on their best guesses about what would be in their own best interests or what they think might be in the general society's best interests, and, if they happen to be sufficiently moved by these musings, to express them in nonviolent ways. Maybe someone will listen.

It follows from this perspective that no elaborate prerequisites or cultural preparations are likely to be necessary for democracy to emerge, and that an agonizing process of "democratization" is not required. Indeed, unless democracy is suppressed by thugs with guns, it seems likely that it can come about rather easily, almost by default, if leaders 1) happen to come to the conclusion that democracy is the way to go; and 2) put the institution into effect by allowing people generally the freedoms to complain and to attempt to overthrow the leadership nonviolently.

Accordingly, in this chapter I question the notion, popular among theorists, that, in part, perhaps, because democracy requires a high degree of participation and deliberativeness, the form is a difficult, even delicate, one to put, and to keep, in place. In particular, I question the view that democracy's development is essentially the result of broader intellectual, cultural, educational, social, and economic trends. Among other things, that view has generated a considerable pessimism about the pace at which democracy can develop in the world, a pessimism that persists even though recent history strongly suggests that it is singularly unjustified. And it has also provided autocrats with a convenient excuse for neglecting democratic reforms.

Democratic development, it seems to me, has principally been a matter of convincing leaders to do democracy. That is, democracy is merely an idea and its rise has essentially been the result of a two-hundred-year competition of ideas, not the necessary or incidental consequence of grander changes in social, cultural, economic, or historic patterns. It has triumphed not because it was somehow required by wider forces, but because its ideas, ably executed and skillfully promoted—or marketed—at one point in the world's history, have increasingly managed to catch on. This chapter traces that development, and it muses a bit about democracy's prospects.

A Democratic Dialogue

My perspective on democracy may perhaps be clarified in the following fanciful dialogue between a pair of citizens in a prospective democracy.

"It's been decided: we're going to be a democracy."

"Democracy? What's that?"

"Form of government."

"Mm. What's it about?"

"Well, you're free to say whatever you want."

"You mean, I can complain and stuff?"

"Right. And the government won't do anything to stop you."

"So if I don't like the way things are going, I can scream and holler?"

"Yes. You can organize and publish and petition, too. Form groups, demonstrate, strike. Things like that."

"Sounds fair enough. Can I throw rocks?"

"No. You can't use violence."

"But if I have a gripe I can change things I don't like?"

"Well, you can *try*."

"Try?"

"Just because you have a beef doesn't mean you'll be successful at getting your way."

"You mean I can complain, but nothing will happen?"

"Probably. After all, other people are free too. They can refuse to listen, disagree, call you names—whatever."

"What's the point of complaining if all that happens is that other people call me names?"

"You should have thought about that before you started complaining."

"That's democracy? Anything else?"

"We're going to have elections too. You can decide who you want to run the government."

"You mean, *I* get to decide the whole thing?"

"Well, you and all the other voters. The candidate wins who gets the most votes. You're just one of them."

"How am I supposed to know who to vote for?"

"Up to you. Just choose. Whatever suits your fancy."

"That's it? But what if I don't know anything about the candidates?"

"Doesn't matter. You can vote anyway."

"What about the other voters?"

"Same for them. They can decide however they want."

"How many voters really know what's going on?"

"Beats me. Not many, probably."

"Wouldn't it be better to keep the ignorant and the incompetent from voting?"

"Tried that. Doesn't seem to make all that much difference so they just let everybody vote."

"How do you know you'll get good leaders with all this?"

"Well, actually it seems to work pretty well where it's been tried."

"Amazing. You mean it works even if people don't really know what they're doing?"

"Seems to."

"Can't they be fooled by clever candidates?"

"Sure. But not all of them all of the time."

"That's the hope? That someone somewhere will not be fooled?"

"That's about it."

"Seems pretty slender. You know, this voting stuff seems like it could become a lot of bother, particularly if everybody else gets to vote too. I'm pretty busy a lot of times. Do I have to vote at all?"

"Nope. Fact is, your vote can hardly make any difference to the outcome anyway."

"What's the sense of voting then?"

"Might make you feel good."

"So, with democracy I get to vote for leaders if I want, whether I know what I'm doing or not. And the saving grace is that my vote mostly doesn't matter much anyway?"

"Something like that."

"There seems to be even less here than I thought. What else is democracy about?"

"That's about it. Pretty simple, isn't it?"

"Simple is right. Sounds like any dimwit can do democracy."

"Yeah, that's probably true. Made me think of you somehow."

"Thanks. What else you got?"

The Historical Movement of Ideas

As this dialogue suggests, and as Americans should surely know by now, it doesn't take a population of rocket scientists or moral paragons to pull off a democracy. Therefore, about the only prerequisite for democracy is that people—probably only the ones who happen to be in charge at the moment, actually—become convinced to allow it to come into effect.

In practice, democracy seems to be about as difficult to put on as a new suit of clothes, and it has spread so assiduously in recent years not so much because it has been made cosmically inevitable by various economic or social developments, but because it has come into style: it's what just about everyone who is anyone is wearing this season. And indeed, democracy has lately been taken up most effectively not by countries which are necessarily the most economically, socially, culturally, or historically prepared or advanced, but by those with leaders who identify most with, who most admire, and who most want to join, the fashionable company of democracies.

It seems useful, therefore, to consider what Francis Fukuyama has called "the autonomous power of ideas" or what Robert Dahl terms the "historical movement of ideas." As Dahl warns, however, "One can hardly exaggerate how badly off we are as we move into this terrain. If it is difficult to account satisfactorily for the acquisition of individual beliefs, it is even more difficult to account for historical shifts in beliefs." But it seems important to do so: as Dahl continues, "because of their concern with rigor and their dissatisfaction with the 'softness' of historical description, generalization, and explanation, most social scientists have turned away from the historical movement of ideas. As a result, their own theories, however, 'rigorous' they may be, leave out an important explanatory variable and often lead to naive reductionism."[1]

Ideas in this view are very often forces—independent variables—themselves, not flotsam on the tide of broader social or economic patterns. As Ernest Gellner has pointed out, "a great deal can happen without being necessary," without being "inscribed into any historic plan." In the case of democracy, it seems quite possible that the human race could have discovered and developed democracy quite a bit earlier. Or it could have missed or suppressed it, and remained mired in what Gellner calls "the dreadful regiment of kings and priests" for quite a bit longer.[2] Moreover, since it is (merely) about ideas, the process by which democracy has become widely accepted can perhaps be reversed or superseded without notable social or economic change if other ideas come along which seem, or can be made to seem, superior.

In this regard, consider one of the more interesting developments of the last two centuries: the rise of the notion that the venerable institution of slavery ought to be abolished. Substantial efforts have been made by scholars and analysts to use material factors, particularly economic ones, to explain the origin and the amazing success of this once-novel idea. But, as Stanley Engerman has observed, New World slavery never was in economic decline—indeed, at the same time that the abolition movement was taking flight the Atlantic slave trade was entering an extremely profitable phase. Consequently the success of the movement has to be explained by "political, cultural, and ideological factors."[3] The idea of abolishing slavery was successfully promoted at a propitious time, and it seems to have been not only an idea whose time had come, but one which has proved to have considerable staying power.

I am primarily concerned in all this not with the process by which the democratic idea was developed by intellectuals, but rather with the process by which it came to be broadly accepted. Thinkers are always spinning out ideas (that's why we call them Thinkers), but few of these generate wide appeal, however much they may entrance other Thinkers. Ideas take effect when they are widely espoused and accepted, not when they are being formulated by some guy sitting on a rock someplace. At any given time there are always a huge array of ideas around, and only a few of these catch on. Some may be of lengthy pedigree while others may be quite new and original. People sort through this market of ideas and prove receptive to some while remaining immune to others. Their receptivity may not be easily predictable, but it is surely not random.

THE CORRELATES OF DEMOCRACY

Before developing this approach, however, it would be useful to assess another perspective, one that has dominated much of the literature: the notion that the rise of democracy has been principally caused by social or economic developments. As Dahl has pointed out, democracy has been "strongly associated" with a whole series of social and economic characteristics: "a relatively high level of income and wealth per capita, long-run growth in per capita income and wealth, a high level of urbanization, a rapidly declining or relatively small agricultural population, great occupational diversity, extensive literacy, a comparatively large number of persons who have attended institutions of higher education, an economic order in which production is mainly carried on by relatively autonomous firms whose decisions are strongly oriented toward national and international markets, and relatively high levels of conventional measures of well-being."[4]

That such characteristics are more nearly correlates than causes, Dahl observes, is suggested by the case of India where political leaders were able to establish a viable democracy even though "the population was overwhelmingly agricultural, illiterate ... and highly traditional and rule-bound in behavior and beliefs." Or "even more tellingly" there is the case of the United States which took to democracy when it was still "overwhelmingly rural and agricultural."[5]

So it goes with the other supposed relationships—political culture, for example. Democracy may have been established earlier in Protestant countries than in Catholic ones, but once Catholic countries took a notion to become democratic, their religious tradition did not seem to cramp their style very much.

Moreover, modern methods of transportation and communication do not seem to be required even in large democracies: the United States became democratic before the development of the steamboat, the railroad, and the telegraph—that is, when things and information moved scarcely faster overland than in the days of ancient Athens. And democracy has lately been established in large, underdeveloped countries like Botswana, Mongolia, and Namibia, while it remains neglected in such technologically sophisticated societies as Saudi Arabia.

Some analysts have held that a sizeable middle class is necessary for democracy: as Barrington Moore put it, "No bourgeois, no democracy."[6] The cases of India and quite a few other places call that generalization into question, and the recent experience in eastern Europe seems to shatter it.

Accompanying democracy's rise over the last two centuries have been the industrial revolution, enormous economic growth, the rise of a middle class, a vast improvement in transportation and communication, surging literacy rates, and massive increases in international trade. But if these developments somehow "caused" the growth of democracy, they also stimulated its direct opposites: Nazism, fascism, Bolshevism.[7] Moreover, the process of development was often wildly out of synchronization. Democracy and the industrial revolution may have flowered together in England in the late eighteenth century, but firm democracy did not come to industrial Germany until 1945 (and then it had to be imposed from the outside), and it is only now being developed in industrial Russia.

By the end of the twentieth century it is quite easy to find democracy comfortably accepted in places like Mali, Mongolia, and Namibia that are very poor, have yet to develop much of a middle class, and are still quite backward in industry, literacy, communications, transportation, and trade. Meanwhile, some of the world's richest countries—like the Arab oil states—are also among the least democratic. As Samuel Huntington has pointed out, countries "transit to democracy at widely varying levels of development."[8]

Democracy does indeed correlate with various social and economic characteristics—wealth, capitalism, literacy, and so forth—but these correlations are, in my view, essentially spurious: democracy, after all, is also correlated with the rise of the string quartet. The McDonald hamburger sold first, and continues to sell best, in rich capitalistic, literate, Protestant countries, but it doesn't follow that you have to be rich or capitalistic or literate or Protestant or well-prepared or sophisticated or middle class or industrialized or cosmopolitan or uncontentious to buy one.

The correlation may suggest that certain social and economic developments make democracy more feasible. But this correlation—at best very imperfect—is often extrapolated to the point where the social or economic developments are seen to be *necessary* to democratic development. Thus, Huntington maintains that "economic development makes democracy possible," or that "political leaders cannot through will and skill create democracy where preconditions are absent." Such assertions seem to suggest that, despite the cases of India, Paraguay, Mali, much of the Caribbean, Botswana, Mongolia, and eighteenth-century America, democracy is impossible without economic development. And he suggests that in Haiti in the late 1980s the "obstacles to democracy" would likely "confound even the most skilled and committed democratic leader." But a few years earlier, as Giuseppe Di Palma notes, some might have said (in fact, did say) the same thing about poor, isolated countries like Portugal and Spain.[9] The obstacle to democracy in Haiti seems to have been a group of thugs with guns, not the absence of "preconditions," and it will be interesting to see if the current experiments there take long-term effect as they apparently have in Portugal and Spain.[10]

"General theories correlating democracy with the level of economic development or 'modernization,' or indeed associating it with some particular type of 'political culture,'" Laurence Whitehead observes, "necessarily abstract from" the "unpredictability" of the process. Noting the rise of democracy in southern Europe in the mid-1970s and its decline at the same time in countries where it was well established like Chile and Uruguay, he concludes that "the stock of available theories is of little help in explaining the timing, the longevity, or the geographical incidence of recent experiences of democratization."[11] What good, one might ungratefully be led to ask, are the theories then?

Pessimism about the Pace of Democracy

The notions that various attitudinal, cultural, economic, and atmospheric developments are necessary before democracy can be put in place has regularly led to considerable pessimism about the prospects for the expansion of democracy.

Thus, in a classic article, Dankwart Rustow envisioned the establishment of democracy as a slow, gradual process in which national unity leads to prolonged and inconclusive struggle which leads in turn to a conscious decision to adopt democratic rules followed by habituation to these rules. Applying a similar habituation analysis, Dahl anticipated in 1971 that "In the future as in the past," democracy is "more likely to result from rather slow evolutionary processes" and "the transformation of hegemonic regimes" into democracies is likely to be "measured in generations." In early 1989, on the brink of a major expansion of democracy as the Soviet empire collapsed, he concluded that "it would be surprising" if the proportion of the countries in the world that are democratic "were to change greatly over the next twenty years."[12]

In 1976, specialist Howard Wiarda assessed the possibilities that Portugal might develop a genuinely democratic political system, and, voicing agreement with a study done for the State Department, concluded that this was the "least likely" outcome because of the country's "legacy of authoritarian and autocratic rule," the lack of political experience of centrist parties, and the "absence of a political culture capable of supporting liberal-democratic institutions."[13]

In 1984, in the midst of what he was later to label the "third wave" of democratization, Huntington looked to the future and essentially concluded that democracy could only emerge though economic development or through force: "with a few exceptions, the prospects for the extension of democracy to other societies are not great. These prospects would improve significantly *only* if there were major discontinuities in current trends—such as if, for instance, the economic development of the Third World were to proceed at a much faster rate and to have a far more positive impact on democratic development than it has had so far, or if the United States reestablished a hegemonic position in the world comparable to that which it had in the 1940s and 1950s. In the absence of developments such as these, a significant increase in the number of democratic regimes in the world is unlikely."[14] Neither major discontinuity took place, but democracy surged anyway, and it often did so in countries that quite clearly lacked the supposed requisites.

In 1986, Latin Americanist Robert Kaufman applied a "political-economic perspective" to developments in Argentina, Brazil, Chile, and Uruguay, and found "some room for hope, but little for optimism" that these countries could break "cycles of fragile civilian regimes and prolonged periods of 'exclusionary' military authoritarianism."[15] They were soon to do exactly that.

And, in late 1993, economist Robert Barro, employing an economic model of democratic development on South Africa, came to a confident and decisive conclusion: "Considering the country's

level and distribution of income, the ethnic divisions, and the political and economic experiences of most of the countries of Sub-
Sahara Africa, this event would perhaps be the greatest political accomplishment in human history. To put it another way, it's not
going to happen." When that country unobligingly became a
democracy a few months later, an unbent Barro predicted that
"The political changes in South Africa in 1994 have probably already overshot the mark, and a substantial decline of political freedom is likely after this year."[16] We continue to wait.

Prerequisitism as an Excuse for Neglecting Democratic Rreform

The prerequisite approach has also supplied a convenient excuse
for authoritarian leaders in underdeveloped countries to avoid or
"postpone" democratic reform.

Di Palma, for example, points out with some dismay that "a recent carefully drawn propositional inventory of conditions favoring the development or maintenance of democracy in the Third
World lists forty-nine demanding conditions—mostly, in fact, preconditions." Some cagy authoritarian leaders in Africa justify their
control by sweetly citing theories that democracy can only flourish
when a country develops a middle class and sustains economic
growth. Such evasions can only be bolstered by assertions that
democracy depends on "democratic dispositions," or by authoritative declarations like the one rendered in 1996 by former British
Prime Minister Margaret Thatcher: "Democracy needs the right
kind of carefully nurtured soil to grow in."[17]

THE MARKETING OF DEMOCRACY

Recent experiences in the postcommunist countries and elsewhere (certainly including South Africa) suggest that democracy
is not terribly difficult to institute, that it can come about very
quickly, and that it need not necessarily come accompanied by, or
preceded by, the social, economic, and cultural clutter that some

have found necessary. This in turn suggests that the pessimism of some of democracy's analytic well-wishers may be very substantially overdrawn and that the agile excuses of authoritarian foot-draggers are invalid.

Democracy, in my view, is essentially a governmental gimmick, not a logical or empirical consequence of other factors. As Dahl points out, the role of beliefs is "pivotal" for the rise of democracy: it is difficult to see, he notes, how democracy could exist "if there is a weak commitment to democratic principles among the political activists." By the same token, it seems to me that a country can quite easily become democratic—*fully* democratic—without any special historical preparation and whatever the state of its social or economic development, if elites or political activists generally come to believe that democracy is the way things ought to be done and if they aren't physically intimidated or held in check by authoritarian thugs.[18] For example, it is likely that about the only thing keeping isolated, backward, impoverished, prerequisite-free Burma from being democratic is a group of thugs with guns.

As an alternative to elevating correlates to causes, it seems to me important, in Dahl's words, to "treat the beliefs and ideas of political activists as a major independent variable."[19] The remarkable rise of democracy over the last two centuries appears chiefly to be the result of successful efforts by idea entrepreneurs who have actively sought to promote—or market—the concept to political elites around the world. I use the notion of "marketing" substantially as a metaphor or analogy of course, and its chief advantage is that it may allow one to begin to come to grips with the historical movement of ideas.

In modern times the idea of democracy took hold first primarily in Britain, the United States, and northern Europe, areas that have proved in many respects over the last two centuries to be fashion leaders—watched, admired, and then imitated. The wealth and vigor of these countries have not been irrelevant to the appeal of their ideas: advertisers always picture admirable, attractive people using or modeling their products. But the message is not that you must *be* admirable and attractive in order to buy the product, but rather that you will *become* admirable and attractive *if* you buy it.

At one time Paris was the center of fashion for women's clothes. Designs shown there soon filtered to other areas in the world in a fairly predictable pattern: cities and areas that were with it copied Paris quickly, those less with it took longer or avoided infection entirely. For the most part, Paris was imitated most quickly by people in other large urban areas in the developed world. Paris fashions did well in New York not because New York is a large city like Paris, but because New Yorkers were more anxious to be with it than people in rural areas—or indeed than people in other large cities like Los Angeles or Atlanta. There is a strong, if imperfect, correlation between Paris fashion and urbanization. But the essential determinant, the one that explains the diffusion best, is not city size, but rather the degree to which people are tuned in to fashion cues coming out of Paris.

The diffusion of democracy seems best explained by a similar analysis. After a long marketing process, democracy has been selling well, particularly lately, even in such isolated and backward places as Burma. Like soccer and Shakespeare and fast food and the cotton gin and the airplane and the machine gun and the computer and the Beatles, it caught on first in one corner of the world and is in the process, except where halted by dedicated forces, of spreading worldwide. Eventually, I suppose, it could fall from fashion, but for now things look pretty good.

The process by which a product—or an idea—is successfully marketed can be quite complicated. And, although those who have sought to promote democracy have been successful, it does not follow that their triumph derives simply from their own manipulative cleverness. As any knowledgeable marketeer will admit, no amount of promotion can guarantee that a product will sell: if marketing alone could assure the success of a product, we'd all be driving Edsels. Careful planning and adept promotion are important, but so are happenstance and luck.

A sketch of the tactics and strategies applied by democracy's promoters might include several components.[20]

Undermining the Competition

First, they needed to undermine the competition, to seize upon, and to bring out its defects. When democracy emerged it had first to contend with hereditary monarchy, and later with other forms of authoritarianism.

Some reasons why democracy is superior to, or less inferior than, the competition were arrayed in chapter 6. But, although democrats were able to show as time went by that democracy is inherently a good—or pretty good—product, and also that it is markedly superior in several important respects to the competition, this was not enough to assure success. Inherent superiority has never guaranteed that a product will come to dominate a market. Most objective experts agree that Beta is superior to VHS for home video recording; yet VHS captured an overwhelming share of the market. As noted in chapter 3, Apple fans passionately argue that something comparable is happening, or has happened, in the computer field. To be sure, it is easier to peddle a pretty good product than a pretty bad one, but products rarely sell themselves: they need to become available at the right time and to be pushed in the right way.

Until around 1800 (and even after) the most common form of government was the hereditary monarchy—an authoritarian arrangement in which succession was determined by the fate of birth. Associated with it was a two-tiered class system in which leadership positions were generally reserved for those of appropriate birth: talented people who did not spring from approved loins were artificially excluded. This institution presumably came about because it seemed to be a sort of sensible expansion of the smallest natural social unit, the family. Certainly kings, emperors, czars, sultans, kaisers, and other such potentates have regularly adopted a paternalistic pose and have been hailed as father figures by their subjects. Very often, too, monarchy has been closely allied with religion—the divine right of kings and all that—and this artfully developed connection enhanced its acceptance.

But, as discussed in chapter 6, hereditary monarchy is a remarkably defective form of government, and democracy's chief initial competitor was thus something of a pushover. Monarchy's amazing longevity over the millennia and in all corners of the globe was probably due chiefly to the fact that it simply had no effective competition as a form of government. Once formidable alternatives were fabricated—chiefly highly flawed democracy—monarchy faded out in rather short order—over a century or so—particularly in the developed world.

Creating Demand for Congenial Values

Second, democracy's advocates needed to create demand for values which, if embraced, would rather automatically aid the acceptance of their product. For example, democracy will be helped (but its success will not necessarily be assured) if the notion becomes accepted that the government owes its existence and its perpetuation not to the dictates of God as expressed in the genetic process, but to the general consent and approval of the people at large. Or that political freedom is a natural, supreme right of all. Or that the class system, restricting political office to members of a limited gene pool, is unwise and unjust and that all people are created—that is, born—equal.

While the gradual acceptance of such concepts aided in the growth of democracy, it was quite possible to accept them without necessarily embracing democracy itself—indeed, the concepts have often been promoted by people who were antidemocrats. However, as crusaders for clean air necessarily aid the promoters of nuclear energy, so those who espoused theories about the importance and validity of the consent of the governed, about the injustice of the class system, and about the virtues of freedom and tolerance necessarily assisted the cause of those who wanted to promote democracy.

For example, although the influential Voltaire assiduously propagandized for freedom of thought and for tolerance of diverse opinion, he was not a democrat: he advocated rule by enlightened philosopher kings (preferably witty ones, I suspect), not by the people, whom he dismissed as "stupid and barbarous" and in need of "a yoke, a cattle prod, and hay." Isaiah Berlin has suggested the possibility of a liberal-minded despot—Voltaire's ideal, presumably—and has argued that there is a sense in it which it could be said that liberty is not "logically connected with democracy or self-government." In time, however, democracy's promoters were able to demonstrate that the liberal-minded despot is something of an illusion. In fact, if the individual's liberty includes the freedom to organize to attempt peacefully to replace the leadership, the notion of the liberal despot is a fundamental contradiction in terms. The best, and perhaps ultimately the only, system that actually guarantees individual freedom is democracy, or as Huntington puts it, "liberty is, in a sense, the peculiar virtue of democracy. If one is concerned with liberty as an ultimate social value, one should also be concerned with the fate of democracy."[21] Voltaire, a nondemocrat, was playing into the hands of democracy's promoters by helping to create demand for a commodity that, ultimately, only democracy could fully and reliably supply.[22]

A similar sort of intellectual evolution took place in the 1960s when the Catholic Church adopted the notion that it ought to seek to promote "social change" and to protect "basic personal rights." These conclusions did not particularly stem at the time from a new found love for democracy, but from a need to respond to various then fashionable forms of "liberation theology," some of which were totalitarian (and violent) in nature. By the late 1980s, however, things had importantly evolved: the pope still specifically denied that he had become an "evangelizer of democracy," but he now argued that, since he was "the evangelizer of the Gospel" to which "of course, belong all the problems of human rights," it followed that democracy "belongs to the message of the Church" because, he had now come to believe, "democracy means human rights."[23]

Market-Testing the Product

Third, the product had to be market-tested—put into practice somewhere to show it could actually work. Rather remarkably, and very much contrary to the anticipations of such influential antidemocrats as Plato, it soon became clear, as discussed in chapter 6, that democracy was, comparatively speaking, a rather effective method for choosing and reviewing leaders, and that it does not necessarily lead to a vast social leveling, the persecution of the rich and other minorities, or rule by mobs, incompetents, and demagogues.

The American experiment, as R. R. Palmer observes, demonstrated that ideas of liberty, class equality, responsible citizenship, popular sovereignty, religious freedom, free speech, separation of powers, and deliberately contrived written constitutions "need not remain in the realm of speculation, among the writers of books, but could be made the actual fabric of public life among real people, in this world, now."[24] And, even as the United States showed that one could have a quite respectable country without kings and without a traditional hereditary aristocratic class, the market test in Britain demonstrated that a country could move from monarchy to democracy in an orderly fashion without physical destruction of the aristocratic class.

A key issue in the growth of democracy concerned the size of the electorate. Reasonable questions about the competence of ordinary people to review the policies and activities of their leaders had been raised for thousands of years. Effectively, those market-testing democracy had a simple experimental solution to this problem. Initially they restricted the vote to the best and the brightest (and the richest). When that proved to work out pretty well, they gradually broadened the electorate to see if special problems would emerge as suffrage was expanded. Political and social pressure—particularly by feminists—also enhanced this process. It seems likely that those in authority soon learned that political clout was only imperfectly measured by the strict, simple arithmetic of the ballot box: those in the minority could still usually generate substantial influence through position, money, and organization. Thus suffrage expansion rarely was terribly problematic as long as the system remained democratic.[25]

Luck and Timing

Finally, there is the matter of luck and timing. Good promoters always stand ready to use fortuitous events and circumstances to advance their product, and successful promotion is often less a matter of artful manipulation than of cashing in on the tides of history or of being in the right place at the right time. One must be there when opportunity knocks, and one must be prepared to lurch into productive action while the sound of the knock is still reverberating.

Admirable market tests: fashion leadership. Promoters of democracy were lucky that they first test marketed their product in Britain and America (in the United States it was explicitly called "the American experiment") because, in the process, democracy came to be associated with countries which were held to be admirable—that is, which became fashion leaders or role models—for reasons that were often quite irrelevant to the institution itself.

It was probably the British experiment, not the American one, that was most influential in democracy's competition with monarchy. During the nineteenth century democratic Britain became the strongest and most important country in the world. It ruled the seas, developed the world's dominant economy, established a vast and impressive overseas empire, and was the scene of a substantial intellectual renaissance in philosophy, literature, and science. It was led in these endeavors by democratically selected politicians, such as Benjamin Disraeli and William Gladstone, who would be considered exceptional by the standards of most any age. Even more to the point, it was difficult to imagine that Britain could have attained all this if things were run, as in days of old, by its monarch, in this case the fussy and simple Queen Victoria.

The disastrous French Revolution. Democracy's promoters were also lucky that the French Revolution came after, rather than before, the substantial establishment of democracy in the United States and Britain. As Thomas Jefferson wrote in 1795, "What a tremendous obstacle to the future attempts at liberty will be the atrocities of Robespierre!"[26]

The French experience may have helped to spread democratic ideology across Europe, but its excesses, including expansionary war, probably acted, on balance, to slow democratic progress as conservatives banded together throughout Europe to bar a repetition of the French disaster. For example, Catherine the Great of

Russia, once a liberal reformer, became convinced by the experience that "equality is a monster."[27] In fact, it seems entirely possible that the French experience could have permanently discredited democracy had there not been the more congenial British and American examples to suggest that its excesses were not an inevitable consequence of democracy.

In Germany over a century later, democracy also degenerated into chaos, the rise of a dictatorship, and then aggressive, continent-wide military expansion. In the wake of that war, however, the Western victors blamed chaos (particularly economic chaos) for the phenomenon, not democracy, and they advocated democracy as a remedy.

The disastrous American Civil War. There was also luck for democracy in that the spectacular, if temporary, failure of democracy in America—the Civil War—didn't happen earlier. In the preface to the 1848 edition of his *Democracy in America,* Alexis de Tocqueville proclaimed the United States to be the "most stable of all the nations on earth" because, "while all the nations of Europe have been devastated by war or torn by civil discord, the American people alone in the civilized world have remained at peace."[28] Thirteen years later (and three years after Tocqueville's death), unable democratically to resolve central issues of slavery and the right of states to secede, the United States descended into four years of catastrophic civil war, an event that many saw as a crisis not only for American democracy but for democracy generally. Accordingly, as Abraham Lincoln put it (a bit overdramatically perhaps) in one of history's most famous speeches, it was imperative that after the war the nation should "have a new birth of freedom" in order that democracy—that is, "government of the people, by the people, for the people"—"shall not perish" not only from America, but "from the earth."

The American Civil War showed, soberingly, that democracies, like other governmental forms, were perfectly capable of cascading into the calamity of internal warfare. But the successful reestablishment of democracy after that disastrous interregnum (and perhaps the subsequent absence of any serious possibility of a repetition) could be taken by democrats to be heartening. Riker suggests, perhaps only a bit too rhapsodically, that "the present world-wide ascendancy of democratic theory is in no small part a consequence of the fact that American democracy survived its civil war."[29]

The World Wars. Democracy's ancient competitor, monarchy, was in well-deserved decline in Europe throughout the nineteenth century. World War I proved useful, though perhaps not essential, to the rise of democracy in that it spelled the final demise of the three remaining effective European monarchies. They were taken principally to have been responsible for initiating the catastrophic conflict either through desire (Germany) or through bumbling incompetence (Austria-Hungary, Russia).

The chief winners of World War I were all democracies, and in the war's wake a slew of new, rather imitative, democracies emerged in Europe. But then important governments sprang up that were virulently antidemocratic: Fascist Italy, Falangist Spain, theocratically nationalist Japan, and Nazi Germany and Austria. Moreover, in the 1930s these regimes often seemed to be on the upswing—fashion leaders, even—and their decisiveness and apparent virility made them widely attractive, particularly when compared to the stodgy, meek, economically troubled, indecisive democracies of Britain, France, and the United States.

As it happened, however, the authoritarian leaders of Italy, Japan, and Germany had secretly built international war and conquest into their ideology and agenda. At least in Europe, war was decidedly unpopular among the people, and it seems unlikely that Germany and Italy would have gone to war if a democratic debate had been allowed.[30] Without that constraint, however, the authoritarian masters were able to plunge their countries into cataclysm. As European monarchy had met its demise in World War I, Fascism and Nazism, together with Japanese militarism, died, bloodied and discredited, in World War II.

At the war's end the democracies, once again victorious, set about foisting their form of government upon the portion of Germany they occupied and upon Italy, Austria, and Japan. This, despite the fact that none of the countries would seem to have been very well prepared for it. Japan had had only limited and sporadic experience with democracy—or with liberal thought in general. Democracy in Italy, Germany, and Austria had never been very strong or satisfying, and in each case it had proved powerless to prevent a takeover by vicious and destructive antidemocratic forces. To the people of each country, however, it must have seemed that even democracy at its worst was better than the alternative that had just brought catastrophe upon them, and they took up—or lapsed into—democracy without a great deal of apparent effort.

Examining the Third Wave

In the aftermath of World War II, then, modern democracy had been on the market for less than two centuries. During that time it had been suitably tested, refined, and packaged to increase its appeal; it had rebounded from such potentially discrediting calamities as the Reign of Terror in France and the Civil War in America; and it had seen its comparative appeal and credibility enhanced as it survived two wars in which several of its major competitors had been destroyed. All the countries of West Europe except for Spain, Portugal, and perhaps Greece were now solidly in the democratic camp. And except for some shaky moments in a few of these countries, particularly France, democracy has generally proved quite robust there—and in Japan as well. Together with the United States, Canada, New Zealand, Iceland, and Australia, these countries represented then, and now, the vast majority of the world's wealth, and they had considerable potential for fashion leadership.

It seems unlikely that the rise of democracy was inevitable. If democracy had been badly marketed—if, for example, the British and American democratic experiments had become negative role models by degenerating into the mob violence and expansionary war that characterized France after its putatively democratic revolution of 1789—the world might never have adopted democracy at all, no matter how much economic or social development took place at the same time. On the other hand, since literacy, economic development, and modern communications do not seem to be required for a country to become democratic, the world—or substantial portions of it—could have become democratic centuries earlier if the right people at the right time had gotten the idea, had deftly promoted and market-tested it, and been graced by the right kind of luck.

It may be useful to apply such considerations to what Huntington in an important study has labeled the "third wave" of democratization. By his reckoning, the first two waves took place in 1828–1926 and 1943–64, and the third began around 1975. Since that time, not only has one competitor—hyperdemocratic communism—died out, but a more traditional competitor, the strong-armed dictatorship, has also been very considerably weakened.

It seems to me that about the only requirement for a country to become a democracy in this period, as in earlier ones, is the more or less general desire to do so. That is, for a country to become a democracy it has been a necessary and sufficient condition that the country—or perhaps only its political elite—find the idea attractive, that it catch the bug.

In assessing the rise of democracy during the third wave, Huntington does acknowledge "the beliefs and actions of political elites" as "probably the most immediate and significant explanatory variable." He concludes, however, that, while this may be "a powerful explanatory variable, it is not a satisfying one. Democracy can be created even if people do not want it. So it is not perhaps tautological to say that democracy will be created if people want democracy, but it is close to that. An explanation, someone has observed, is the place at which the mind comes to rest. Why do the relevant political elites want democracy? Inevitably, the mind wants to move further along the causal chain." As his mind moves further along, he clings to the concept of economic preconditions, but his other explanations for the recent democracy wave stress persuasional and promotional elements that fit nicely into a marketing approach: democracy's stylishness and the influence of fashion leaders (or what he calls "demonstration effects" or "snowballing"), changes of doctrine in the Catholic Church, the role of key converts like Gorbachev, the failures of the competition, and patterns of imitation.[31]

In a more recent article, Huntington continues to contend that economic development "has a strong positive effect on democratization." But he ends up concluding that "democratic development occurs when political leaders believe they have an interest in promoting it or a duty to achieve it."[32] In my view, as the democratic dialogue above suggests, this is just about the only requirement.

The View in 1975

Despite the postwar advances, democracy didn't seem to be in good shape in 1975. Many democracies or near-democracies had recently been taken over by authoritarian forces, including Greece in 1967, the Philippines in 1972, and two of Latin America's oldest democracies, Chile and Uruguay, in 1973. Then in 1975 democratic Lebanon descended into virulent civil war, and India, the world's largest democracy, became an authoritarian state (only for a couple of years, as it turned out), while communism, substantially contained since 1949, began to gain market share: it picked up Cambodia, Vietnam, and Laos in 1975, and was to add Angola in 1976, Mozambique and Ethiopia in 1977, South Yemen and Afghanistan in 1978, and Nicaragua and Grenada in 1979.

Many western democrats were plummeted by those developments into deepest gloom. The usually ebullient Daniel Patrick Moynihan, then the American envoy to the United Nations and a former ambassador to India, proclaimed in 1975 that democracy "increasingly tends to the condition of monarchy in the 19th century: a holdover form of government, one which persists in isolated or peculiar places here and there" but "which has simply no relevance to the future." In a similar mood, Germany's Willy Brandt was reported to believe at the time that "Western Europe has only 20 or 30 more years of democracy left in it; after that it will slide, engineless and rudderless, under the surrounding sea of dictatorship."[33]

Actually, even from the perspective of 1975 this gloom was a bit excessive. Democracy may have been clobbered by the competition in many areas of the globe, but it was alive and thriving not merely "in isolated or peculiar places," but in most of the major countries of the world. And then, quite remarkably, as if in conspiracy to embarrass Moynihan and Brandt—or to cheer them up—the world launched itself into something of a democratic binge that has been going on ever since. Democracy became all the rage.

Decolonization

Since 1975 just about every country that has received independence from Western colonizers—mainly small island republics in the Caribbean, but also such unlikely contenders as Papua New Guinea (1982) and Namibia (1989)—has adopted democracy. For many ex-colonies, former British overseership may have aided the democratic process. However, overall, as Huntington pointed out in 1984, most "former British colonies have *not* sustained democracy."[34] That is, it appears that the difference is not so much British preparation as the fact that these countries were decolonized in a period in which democracy was beginning to be the way things were done.

Southern Europe

The real tide of democracy seems to have begun in the three remaining nondemocracies in Europe outside the communist bloc. Even before Moynihan's gloomy prognosis was in print, Greece had moved from military dictatorship to democracy: after a failed venture in Cyprus, the discredited Greek leaders resigned in favor of civilian rule and Greece again became a democracy. Then in 1975 the focus shifted to Portugal where a struggle took place between democratic and communist forces in the wake of the collapse of an authoritarian dictatorship. For months the communists were on top, and they were clearly moving to consolidate their control. When they tried to close the country's last noncommunist newspaper, however, massive street demonstrations erupted, the cabinet shifted direction, and free elections in 1976 put a noncommunist government in control. In short order a similar transformation took place in Europe's last noncommunist nondemocracy, Spain, after the death of its long-time dictator.

The crucial dynamic in all this seems to have been essentially one of imitation, not one of economic or social necessity. By 1975 dictatorial Portugal and Spain had become something of anachronisms in the neighborhood. Released from old-fashioned authoritarianism, they shopped around for role models and found them in solidly, contentedly, and prosperously democratic Western Europe; as Huntington puts it, there was a "pervasive desire to identify their countries with Europe."[35] Portugal, in particular, had little previous experience with democracy and Spain's experiment with it in the 1930s had devolved into a disastrous civil war. Nevertheless both took to democracy well.

Latin America

Democracy's growth in Latin America since 1975 has been particularly impressive—by 1990 almost the entire area had turned democratic. This sweeping change over such a short period of time is difficult to credit to objective forces such as increasing wealth, a rising middle class, or burgeoning literacy rates. Indeed, over the period most countries in Latin America probably became *worse* off in many material ways—the rise of democracy there took place during a very substantial debt crisis.[36]

Nor can the democratic trend be readily credited to American pressure or salesmanship. For a century and a half the United States has repeatedly and often evangelically urged democracy upon its neighbors to the South, and it has often been quite prepared to use money (and sometimes military force) to gild the philosophic pill. These policies seem rarely to have made much lasting difference. For example, in 1913 President Woodrow Wilson dramatically declared the United States to be the "champion" of democracy in the Americas. To show he meant business, he dispatched U.S. troops to Nicaragua, Haiti, and the Dominican Republic to champion the democratic process. All three countries subsequently lapsed into extended dictatorships.[37]

The promoters improved neither the product nor the packaging. What changed was the receptivity of the customers: democracy caught on, at least among political elites, as an idea whose time had come.

The gradual acceptance of democracy by the Roman Catholic Church may have been helpful in this process as discussed above. But probably more important was the fact that each of the converted countries had been run by a military dictatorship—a form of government very familiar in the area—that in many cases had become discredited because of corruption and because of murderous suppression policies, usually against violent leftist insurgencies. The experience showed that military dictatorship, unchecked by public opinion, often led to excessive violence, and that it was generally less effective—or at any rate no more effective—at confronting the rebellions than civilian democracy. In Argentina, in addition, the military had led the nation into a failed, if brief, war against Britain over some nearly barren islands in the South Atlantic.

In olden days, of course, a discredited authoritarian regime would characteristically be replaced not by an effective democracy, but by another military dictatorship. By the 1970s, however, military leaders throughout Latin America appear to have become convinced that the military dictatorship was a thing of the past, and they often seem to have been embarrassed that their countries were so out of fashion. They had once subscribed to an almost "messianic self-image as *the* institution ultimately interpreting and ensuing the highest interests of the nation," in the words of Guillermo O'Donnell and Philippe Schmitter. But, partly because of the destruction the military had wreaked, Latin American societies came to reject that image, and gradually the military came to accept, and to facilitate, transitions to civilian democratic rule. Increasingly, the generals began to realize that they actually might do better under democracy where they "don't have to answer the hardest questions." As a result, a consensus has emerged that constitutional rule is the future of Latin America. When a clumsy coup effort was launched in Argentina in 1990, the country's president reacted not so much with alarm as with contemptuous dismissal. He labeled the effort "ridiculous antics" and, as one observer noted, he "just said no and it was over in a matter of hours."[38]

At the same time, and not unrelated, was the increased willingness of leftist groups to eschew violence and to seek to advance their cause through peaceful democratic means. As one reporter put it in the 1990s, "the Latin American left's 30-year obsession with armed struggle as a means to revolution has come to an end."[39]

Perhaps the most spectacular case of a new, instant democracy created during the third wave is Paraguay, a country that had never known any kind of government except Jesuit theocracy or rigid military dictatorship. In 1989 Paraguay's guiding autocrat, entrenched since 1954, was overthrown by a man who had been one of his chief henchmen and who had become fabulously wealthy in the process. The new leader, however, was sensitive to the fact that democracy is what everyone is wearing nowadays—that "despots have gone out of style," as a reporter from the *Economist* put it. Accordingly he held fair elections and promised that, if elected president, he would guide the country to full democracy in four years. Paraguayans, in the first free election in their grim history, took him at his word, and on schedule in 1993 another election was held and another man became president.[40]

That military leaders still had (and have) the physical ability to maintain themselves in office is suggested by a couple of counterexamples to this trend. In Panama in 1989 General Manuel Noriega, in classic Latin American fashion, calmly stole an election that went against him and was deposed only by an American military invasion. Liberated from this anachronistic tyrant, the country became a democracy. In the 1990s, a somewhat similar process took place in Haiti.

Asia

In 1984, Huntington observed correctly that "democratic regimes that last have seldom, if ever, been instituted by mass popular action."[41] The rise of democracy in Portugal might have been taken to be an exception at the time, but soon such exceptions were to proliferate enough to disprove the rule.

Demonstrations in the Philippines in 1986, together with pressure from the United States, forced a dictator from office, and democracy was established there. And in 1987 demonstrations, with far less American pressure, pushed the government of prospering South Korea toward democracy.

Most remarkably, massive prodemocracy demonstrations erupted in 1988 in Burma, one of the poorest and most isolated places on the globe. Somehow the people there had gotten the message: clearly, neither prosperity, economic growth, a burgeoning middle class, nor frequent and close contact with the West were necessary for the democratic idea to find receptive minds. The democracy movement was put down by force, but some moderately free elections were held in 1990—although the military then refused to let the newly elected government take office.

Meanwhile, the regime in Taiwan, seeing the light, liberalized substantially, and a somewhat rocky democracy was established in Pakistan in 1988. Advances were also made in Thailand and Malaysia and, in the late 1990s, Indonesia.

Of particular interest in this regard was the remarkable absence of military coups during the very considerable economic crises in the area that began in 1997. This is a change that strongly resembles the one that has taken place in Latin America. In Thailand, for example, where the military had ousted civilian leaders no less than seventeen times since 1932, most recently in 1991, the army's commander in chief had come by 1998 to believe that "The coup d'état is outdated. The more time passes, the more it is obsolete. My soldiers must stay completely out of politics." A similar realization seems to be dawning in Pakistan.[42]

Soviet Communism Implodes

Communism, a hyperdemocracy established by Lenin in the Soviet Union, was viscerally devoted to the proposition that democracy, or at any rate Western democratic capitalism, should, and eventually would, perish from the earth through internal revolution and through "wars of national liberation."[43] In result, a virulent and sometimes violent contest between the promoters of democracy and those of communism took place as each group sought to peddle its wares—to win hearts and minds—using agitation, propaganda, demonstration projects, and caustic disparagement of the competition.[44]

Communism's sales efforts were substantially aided by the Soviet Union's apparent economic progress and by its dramatic launch in 1957 of the first artificial space satellite. In America, the hastily assembled, if august and authoritative, President's Commission on National Goals declared the democratic world to be in "grave danger" from communism's "great capacity for political organization and propaganda" and from the "specious appeal of Communist doctrine to peoples eager for rapid escape from poverty." Meanwhile, the Central Intelligence Agency alarmingly calculated that the Soviet gross national product might be triple that of the United States by the year 2000.[45]

By the late 1970s or early 1980s, however, it was becoming clear to a few Soviet officials and intellectuals that the Soviet social and economic system was stagnating under the weight of a stifling and cynical bureaucracy, an irrational and often erratic planning mechanism, and an incompetent and sometimes vicious ideological apparatus.[46] Moreover, it was becoming increasingly clear that many of the problems came about *because* the Soviet Union wasn't democratic, or at any rate, free. The all-encompassing secretiveness and suspiciousness of the ruling elite meant that the flow of information was severely hampered, new ideas were routinely stifled, suggestions for improvement were casually ignored, and attempts at protest were forcibly suppressed. Devices that might weaken the system's control of information, like personal computers, photocopying machines, home videotape recorders, and telephone books were strictly regulated.

Most importantly, blunders went unappreciated, unexamined, and uncriticized. For a decade and probably much more, no one at the top seems to have understood what was going on with the economy. Not only was it increasingly unproductive and uncompetitive, but the leadership was mindlessly straining it by expanding the defense budget and gathering to its embrace a collection of costly overseas dependencies (the ten countries that fell into its orbit between 1975 and 1979) to add to its older ones, like Cuba.

Meanwhile, its colonies in east Europe, particularly Poland, were becoming more of a psychic and economic burden—the empire was striking back.[47] Added to this was war: in 1979, without discussing the decision widely or apparently considering it very carefully, the Brezhnev regime sent tens of thousands of troops into neighboring Afghanistan to prop up a faltering friendly regime there, and costs and casualties mounted.

Meanwhile, communism was failing in the outer reaches as well. For decades it had preached that successful revolution would be followed by social, political, and economic bliss. But successful Communist revolutionaries repeatedly led their countries instead into civil war, economic collapse, and a state of severe social injustice, most horrendously in Cambodia where Communist romantics found that their revolutionary theory required them to commit genocide, killing over a million people.[48]

By contrast with all this, democratic reform began to look pretty good—or at least less bad than the obvious alternatives. Wherever there was a suitable contrast, noncommunist countries were doing comparatively well economically: East Germany versus West Germany, North Korea versus South Korea, Hungary versus Austria, Vietnam versus almost any noncommunist country in Southeast Asia. As in Latin America, it was economic decline, not economic development, that was leading to calls for democracy.

Mikhail Gorbachev was one of those insiders who had begun to see the defects in the system. After assuming leadership in 1985, he quickly garnered an increasing appreciation for the appalling mess he had inherited, and he tried to free up the system. As he did so the democratic idea flared up throughout the Communist empire in east Europe. In country after country demonstrators demanded democracy, the removal of despised leaders, and ultimately the overthrow, through elections, of Communist domination. A key element in the success of this movement in 1989 was the suggestion from Gorbachev that, unlike his predecessors, he would not use force to suppress independent democratic developments in the area.

That the Soviet Union might eventually tire of its troublesome and dependent east European empire and allow it to wriggle free was perhaps predictable.[49] The astounding speed of the transformation was not, however, as Communist authorities gave in, with various degrees of reluctance, to a seemingly unstoppable force. Remarkably, communism yielded to democracy more smoothly, and far more quickly, than had monarchy, first in East Europe, and then in Gorbachev's USSR when peaceful, but massive, street demonstrations helped undercut a coup by Communist hardliners in 1991.

Actually, some of this development might have been at least partly anticipated. In 1956, Hungary declared it planned instantly to become a multiparty democracy, and in 1968 there came a similar glimmer in Czechoslovakia. Both ventures were crushed by Soviet tanks, but the 1989 experience suggests that most of the countries in eastern Europe (and probably those on the Baltic Sea) would have been democratic but for the artificial dictates of the occupying forces of the Soviet Union.[50]

However, it had generally been assumed that Communists, who had heretofore never relaxed their control over any of their acquisitions, were dedicatedly tenacious. Reflecting this perspective, Huntington concluded in pre-Gorbachev 1984 that "The likelihood of democratic development in Eastern Europe is virtually nil" and that democratization could occur there "only if either the Soviet Union were drastically weakened through war, domestic upheaval, or economic collapse (none of which seems likely), or if the Soviet Union came to view Eastern European democratization as not threatening to its interests (which seems equally unlikely)."[51] The Soviet Union did weaken, though not "drastically," but it did come to fear democracy less.

THE FUTURE OF DEMOCRACY

After two hundred years of development—with a considerable burst after 1975—democracy may be ripe for some setbacks. Indeed, as Larry Diamond and Charles Gati point out, democracy has not actually taken—that is, authoritarian rulers have taken over—in some of the postcommunist countries, particularly those in Asia.[52] However, although democracies have often reverted to authoritarian rule historically, this does not mean that democracy is a peculiarly fragile form: any government can be overthrown by a sufficiently large and dedicated group of thugs with guns, and it is not at all clear that authoritarian governments—fraught with histories of coups and countercoups, and with endless battles for succession—are any less fragile. The problem seems to be one of definition. When a democracy gets overthrown we say it has failed, but when one dictator topples another we sometimes see this as persistence of form and a kind of stability.

What will be most likely to foster democracy in countries that do not now have it, and what is most likely to maintain democracy in ones that do, will not be economic or social development, but rather the desire of ruling elites to emulate the established democracies. The leaders of, say, Poland want very much to join the West, and, since democracy is clearly the price of admission, they will willingly pay it. The leaders of, say, Turkmenistan or Afghanistan, on the other hand, may find neither the goal nor the price to be of much interest.

China

One important setback to democratic development took place in China in 1989 when democracy demonstrators with rather mild demands were forcibly put down. This suppression was carried out by aging Communist leaders who concluded, probably correctly, that to give in to the movement could eventually result in the demise of Communist Party control: the freedom to speak and petition implies, and sets into motion, the potential for the replacement of regimes even if the formal mechanism of elections is not in place.

China is still given the lowest possible score on Freedom House's democracy rating scheme, but there clearly has been vast liberalization from the totalitarian days of Mao (when China also received the lowest possible score, of course). In fact, as economist Gale Johnson stresses, "The greatest improvement in civil rights the world has ever seen occurred in China when the communes were abolished. Virtually every day, people living in the communes had no civil rights; the commune controlled the economy, their lives as workers, the political and police powers. That all disappeared overnight, and 700 million people were released from domination by a bunch of bureaucrats."[53]

In a 1996 assessment, Henry Rowen observes that although the Communist Party retains its authoritarian control, there have lately been three notable, if underreported, democratic developments: the emergence of semicompetitive democratic elections at the village level, the growth of a viable legal system, and an increasing liberalization in the media.[54] Rowen, however, remains something of an economic determinist, and he concludes that it will take until around 2015 before China is wealthy enough to become a democracy.

But it seems to me that the key determinant in China and elsewhere is more likely to be the mentality of the leadership. There is a possibility that Chinese rulers are becoming embarrassed by their political backwardness, very much like Latin American military leaders in the 1970s and 1980s. Moreover, the observation that President Jiang Zemin is reportedly given to reciting from the American Declaration of Independence and the Gettysburg Address at public functions (as well as mysteriously singing "Kiss Me Once, Kiss Me Twice, and Kiss Me Once Again") suggests he is being influenced by Western fashion leaders. There is also the potentially subversive acquisition of democratic, liberal Hong Kong in 1997 and the clear desire in Beijing eventually to bring democratic Taiwan into the fold, something that is likely to happen only if the Taiwan Chinese can be persuaded that their interests and life-style will be preserved in a united China. Strands like these suggest Rowen could prove to be a pessimist.

Islam

Democracy has yet to penetrate Islamic countries very deeply. Indeed, of the fifty-three countries rated "not free" by Freedom House in its 1996 ratings, twenty-nine were Muslim.

As Huntington has observed, Islam often associates democracy with the Western influences many in the religion oppose.[55] Thus the elites in many Islamic countries specifically do *not* find the Western democracies to be attractive fashion leaders, even as those in, say, Hungary, do. Consequently, although many Islamic states are far overdue for democracy from an economic determinist's standpoint, even rich Islamic states have adroitly managed to resist the trend.

But this again demonstrates that it is the mindset of the elites that matters, not economic or social preparation. Where Muslim leaders have allowed elections, as in Algeria and Iran in 1997, the voters displayed considerable ability to differentiate and express themselves even though the choice of candidates and the freedom of speech were limited. And some Muslim states, such as Mali, Turkey, Pakistan, and Qatar have certainly been able to move substantially toward democracy.[56] The Islamic countries are kept undemocratic not by the necessary dictates of their culture or by the state of their economic development, but by the will of their leaders.

Africa

In Africa, there has been notable democratic progress in quite a few places. The most spectacular case, of course, is South Africa, but there has also been democratic development in Tanzania, Botswana, Malawi, Namibia, Mozambique, Ghana, Benin, Kenya, Zimbabwe, Zambia, Madagascar, Gambia, Nigeria, and Senegal.

Most impressive is impoverished, isolated Mali—Africa's Paraguay perhaps. By becoming democratic it stands as an embarrassment to those leaders in other African states who self-servingly excuse their authoritarian ways by blandly serving up the notion from classic transitological literature that democracies can only flourish where there is a middle class and sustained economic development.[57]

One-party and dictatorial authoritarian regimes have generally performed as badly in Africa as in Latin America, while many of the continent's democracies or near-democracies are comparatively serene and prosperous. And there appears to be a substantial exhaustion with mindless sloganeering and with aging, ineffectual ideology. Quite a few African dictators began nervously whistling in the dark after the dramatic east European events of 1989. To justify their tenure, they continue to insist that only a one-party system can provide unity against the potentially centrifugal forces of tribalism and ethnicity. But given their failures, a little democratic disunity begins to take on a certain appeal. As a citizen of once-democratic Kenya put it, "Since the multiparty system works elsewhere and has previously worked in Kenya, one would like to know the aspect of our human nature which rendered us incapable of making it work after 1982."[58]

Prospects

Although there may well be some softness in the democratic trend of the last decades of the twentieth century, the prospects seem generally rather favorable for further democratic development. In very substantial portions of the globe democracy has become all the rage, and it could well capture an even greater market share in the future. As Fareed Zakaria puts it, "there are no longer respectable alternatives to democracy; it is part of the fashionable attire of modernity."[59]

Democracy is, of course, entirely capable of making colossal mistakes. But, as Machiavelli observes hopefully, "the people are guilty of fewer excesses than the prince," and their errors "are of less importance, and therefore more easily remedied."[60] The advantage may be merely comparative but, as democracy's competitors become discredited, people increasingly seem to have come to conclude that it is real. And, quite possibly, they are right.

Democracy is an intellectual construct that has been on the market for quite a while, has an intrinsic appeal, has a fairly good track record, has proved in market tests to be notably better (or less bad) than the competition, and, despite some occasional overeager and inflated claims, has been rather well marketed and packaged by its promoters who, after several lucky breaks and after two hundred years of patient, persistent salesmanship and judicious product modification, are now cashing in. In general, economically advanced countries have tended to buy this idea (as well as many other related ones) comparatively earlier, but it is the exertions of idea entrepreneurs that have been more determining of the pace of democratization than the correlated wealth of their customers.

CONCLUSION

*

Democracy and Capitalism

CONNECTIONS AND DISCONNECTIONS

IT HAS been a running theme of this book—its bottom line, in fact—that there is a considerable disconnection between democracy and its image and between capitalism and its image. This chapter includes an assessment of the connections, if any, between democracy and capitalism themselves.

Democracy and capitalism, it seems, are actually quite independent: each can exist without the other. However, democracy may benefit on balance from its (erroneously alleged) association with capitalist prosperity, and both institutions, on the other hand, are often unfairly associated with crime, something that could undermine their acceptance.

Moreover, although capitalism does not require democracy to function effectively, democracy probably does enhance capitalist economic growth by reducing the threat of government confiscation, by helpfully establishing a reasonably coherent rule of law, by maintaining a fundamental bias toward openness and transparency, by allowing *all* interest groups (rather than a privileged subset) to enter the political fray, by providing a process for ousting failed leaders, and, lately at least, by gaining a perhaps undeserved association with stability and predictability.

Finally, there seem to be a number of conceptual connections, or at least similarities, between democracy and capitalism, not the least of which is their ability to function even when their constituents generally do not appreciate them very well.

CAPITALISM WITHOUT DEMOCRACY, DEMOCRACY WITHOUT CAPITALISM

While it is no news to observe that capitalism can exist without democracy—quite a few countries have managed that quite effectively—it is commonly maintained that a country must be capitalist in order to become a democracy. Thus, for Charles Lindblom, "only within market-oriented systems does political democracy arise." And Peter Berger maintains that "capitalism is a necessary but not sufficient condition of democracy under modern conditions," while Milton Friedman finds that "history suggests" that "capitalism is a necessary condition for political freedom." Robert Dahl observes that "it is a historical fact that modern democratic institutions . . . have existed only in countries with predominantly privately owned, market-oriented economies, or capitalism if you prefer," and then extrapolates this historical regularity: "it looks to be the case that market-oriented economies are necessary to democratic institutions."[1]

Both the generality and the logic of such declarations could bear some analysis, however. To begin with, until the rise of real command economies in communist countries in this century, nearly all countries in the modern world have been capitalistic in some reasonable sense of the word—ill-managed, perhaps, or foolishly restrictive, but nonetheless basically capitalistic. That is, outside the communist world all democracies have been capitalistic, but so also have just about all nondemocracies.

In this circumstance, the only way a noncapitalist democracy could have arisen would be for a democracy to abandon capitalism. However, after a capitalist country becomes democratic, successful capitalists and other people of wealth, although a minority of the population, have been able to use democratic opportunities to keep the government from substantially confiscating their wealth, a process discussed in chapter 6. This has been true even in countries controlled by important democratic socialist movements that have been explicitly devoted to creating a command economy. For example, in 1918 Britain's Labour Party pointedly adapted a clause in its constitution (one not removed until the 1990s and then only after a furious internal battle) that called for "common ownership of the means of production, distribution, and exchange."[2] The party was never able to carry out this anticapitalistic stipulation, however, even though it ruled the country with a substantial parliamentary majority for many years.

Thus, democracies have generally been established in capitalist countries and, because of the democratic process itself, they have remained essentially capitalist. Since a capitalist democracy cannot by its nature become noncapitalist, then, a noncapitalist democracy could emerge only if democracy were imposed upon a country that was neither capitalist nor democratic. This became a possibility only after 1989 when many countries with command economies took up democracy in the aftermath of the collapse of communism. And that experience seems to do considerable damage to the commonly accepted and previously unassailable notion that democracy cannot exist in a noncapitalistic economy.

Many of the postcommunist countries, particularly in central Europe, successfully became democracies even though the vast majority of their people continued to work for the government, even though the economy continued to be centrally planned, and even though most property continued to be state-owned. Politicians in these countries have worked (and continue to work) to change that of course, but only because the old economic system has become discredited, not because the process of democracy mandates it.

Bulgaria appears to furnish the clearest case in point. For various political reasons, very little meaningful economic reform took place for several years after 1989—all the important sectors of the economy remained controlled by the government and most everyone remained its employee. Moreover, prices were substantially controlled, peasants were actively dissuaded from farming privately, bankruptcy remained unknown, state-owned enterprises continued to be heavily subsidized, privatization was very limited, and the government stubbornly rejected all the reform conditions proffered by the International Monetary Fund. Yet, although Bulgaria's politics were often tumultuous, they remained free and open—that is to say, fully democratic. People remained free to speak, publish, and organize, and fair elections were held every couple of years. Eventually, fed up with the hugely mismanaged economy, massive, but peaceful, street protests brought down the government at the end of 1996, and a subsequent, duly elected government finally began to institute meaningful economic re-

233

forms.[3] But for the better part of a decade, democracy worked quite well in the effective absence of capitalism.

Analysts who argue that democracy can only flourish in a capitalist economy have generally pointed to the importance of independent money. Thus William Riker argues that "when all economic life is absorbed into government, there is no conceivable financial base for opposition."[4] Friedman follows a similar line of reasoning. If "all jobs are under the direct control of political authorities" it would take "an act of self-denial" for the government "to permit its employees to advocate policies directly contrary to official doctrine." Moreover, he questions whether those in opposition would be able to "finance their cause. . . . How could they raise the funds?" But just that sort of "self-denial" clearly did take place in Bulgaria, and the opposition was able to come up with the necessary means to launch its successful protest. (Indeed, in many countries, protest against government policies has often come from students even though many of them are entirely dependent on government stipends for their livelihood.) Friedman also finds it difficult to imagine that the government might help finance "subversive propaganda."[5] But in many democracies that is exactly what happens as opposition parties are automatically guaranteed, and regularly receive, governmental funds if they can make a plausible case that they represent even 2 or 3 percent of the population.

History no longer suggests, it seems, that capitalism is a necessary or logical condition for democracy.

DEMOCRACY'S CONNECTION WITH CAPITALIST PROSPERITY

I have argued that democracy is merely an idea, one that has been peddled with increasing success by idea entrepreneurs over the last couple of centuries. A potential danger to democratic development is that democracy may have been oversold by these promoters in some important respects. In particular, democracy may have been bought by many people, especially lately, because it seemed to be associated with capitalist prosperity.

While prosperity and democracy seem to have gone hand in hand in the developed Western world, prosperity certainly did not accompany democracy in India or the Philippines, and some may eventually be led to notice that much of the present prosperity of Spain, South Korea, and Taiwan was achieved under authoritarian regimes.[6] Moreover, since, as discussed in chapter 5, successful economic development does not inspire people to acknowledge they have become happy, some disillusionment is likely, and it is possible disappointed democracy-embracers might start shopping around for other forms of government.

There is another prospect, however. As was also suggested in chapter 5, capitalist prosperity has been on a roll in much of the world for quite some time now for various reasons including the rise of wealth-enhancing business virtue. Moreover, this economic expansion will likely not only accelerate but spread much more broadly around the world in the future (particularly in the absence of major war) because of the ascent of the politically incorrect one-handed economist: economists now essentially know what they are talking about, speak with something resembling one voice, and, despite the politically painful nature of much of their advice, increasingly are being heeded by policymakers. This burgeoning prosperity has not been crucially caused by the rise of democracy, nor will it be in the future—the key to prosperity both for democracies and nondemocracies is to adopt sound economic policies. But the rise of democracy happens to have been accompanied by the capitalist prosperity surge, and democracy may benefit because it will be given undue credit for that surge. And, if the surge continues, such fellow-traveling credit will likely continue to be given.

DEMOCRACY'S CONNECTION TO CAPITALIST GROWTH

Although capitalism can certainly exist without democracy, although it now appears that democracy can exist without capitalism, and although nondemocracies are entirely capable of adopting sound economic policies which can cause them to prosper, democracy may nonetheless, on balance, be beneficial to economic development in several ways.

First, as noted in chapter 6, democracy in practice, if not in Plato's imaginings, does give to property owners a certain confidence that they can protect themselves from arbitrary seizure of their property—or at any rate that they will have recourse if such seizure does take place. Insofar as that confidence is necessary to encourage innovation and capital investment and the beneficial effects these activities have on economic growth and efficiency, democracy will have an economic leg up on authoritarian regimes—or at least on those of the more absolutist sort.[7] Rosenberg and Birdzell point out that "it was not until the nineteenth century that merchants developed enough confidence in governments to invest in large, immobile factories rather than in bills of exchange, ships, and moveable stocks of goods," an important phenomenon that accompanied the rise of democracy and may possibly have been partially caused by it.[8]

Second, although I argued at the end of chapter 4 that quite a bit of capitalist development can take place without much of a legal system as in China today, effective legal systems still do have an economic benefit where they exist—that is, China's economic development would be on even better ground if it had a viable legal system. Insofar as democracy is associated with the rule of law—and, of course, the absence of violence—this association will aid capitalist development. However, if the courts are mainly enforcing business-discouraging laws and regulations as in India for much of its postindependence history, this benefit will be minor.

Third, as noted in chapter 2, businesses which are open and transparent enjoy, on average, a competitive advantage since others are more likely to be willing to deal with them. Therefore an economy with routine and comprehensive openness is likely to develop more prodigiously than one where secrecy prevails. It is certainly possible under democracy to have private business dealings that are secret and opaque, but democracy does foster an atmosphere of openness, whistle-blowing, public prying, and transparency that can be helpful to capitalist development.

Fourth, despite initial appearances, democracy may be better than other forms of government at handing interest-group pressures that harm to the economy. Many economists have bemoaned the economically perverse effects that interest-group politics can have in a democracy. Thus Rosenberg and Birdzell argue that an "adverse political response to organizational innovation is inherent in democratic politics" because an innovation or development that benefits a wide and a diverse group of consumers often threatens existing firms and their employees who are then likely to organize for political action.[9] Although this phenomenon certainly occurs in democracies, it also takes place in nondemocracies. The difference is that in a democracy *all* specially interested people and groups, not just those who happen to be favored by the ruler or the ruling group, are admitted into the fray and may freely seek to manipulate governmental policy to their benefit. Some interests in a democracy do enjoy special privileges, but this is nothing compared to the perks traditionally graced upon preferred groups like the army, the aristocracy, the landed gentry, or the nomenklatura in nondemocracies. In a democracy, interests which are not officially preferred have at least a fighting chance of undercutting favored interests and getting some of the gravy for themselves.

Fifth, democracy, as discussed in chapter 6, is better than other governmental forms at getting rid of failed leaders whereas authoritarian governments, including monarchies, very frequently are incapable of accomplishing this elemental task. For example, it is conceivable that in a democratic China a leader like Mao might have been able to put into place a fanciful economic policy like the Great Leap Forward, but it is inconceivable that he could have remained in office after the policy produced disastrous results including an induced famine in which some fifteen to thirty million perished. In democratic Bulgaria by contrast, the bums were summarily, and peacefully, thrown out in 1996 when their economic policies had merely reduced wages by a factor of ten in a single year and caused the banking system to collapse, wiping out 80 percent of all personal savings in the process.[10] The miserable citizens of mismanaged autocracies like Iraq and Cuba or North Korea do not have the same opportunity. Even where failed leaders are not removed from office in a democracy, their tenure is generally limited by something other than their physical health or their caginess at undercutting coups, so they can often be waited out. Democratic leaders may do dumb things, but their errors—including economic ones—are more likely to be corrected.

Sixth, democracy has come to garner a reputation for stability, and this can enhance the prospects for economic development. Although democracy has not always been known historically as a stable form of government—quite the reverse sometimes— several recent developments may combine to help democracy overcome that image, whether fully deserved or not. Among these are the exhilarating ascendance of democracy of late, the comparative instability recently shown in Communist and military autocracies, the association of democracy with such overwhelmingly, even tediously, stable states as Switzerland and Britain and the United States and Japan, and the clear intention of rich, powerful democracies to assist struggling like-minded countries with their economic development. Since wealth-enhancing investors and entrepreneurs tend to be congenitally fond of stability and predictability, countries held to exhibit those characteristics are accordingly more likely to prosper, something that has greatly benefited impoverished Mali, for example, after it became an effective democracy in 1992 against all transitological odds.[11]

THE CONNECTION OF DEMOCRACY AND CAPITALISM WITH CRIME

Although democracy and capitalism do not, by definition, allow for violence, they may be damaged if they come to be causally (and casually) linked to crime, especially in postcommunist countries. People often look with alarm at the United States where colorful stories of criminal mayhem abound, never at capitalist democracies like Canada, Japan, or Switzerland where crime is low.

Two responses to this concern are unlikely to be very helpful. One is to observe (correctly) that crime in many of the new democracies is, for the most part, actually still quite low, especially compared to that enjoyed in the exemplary United States. The other is to suggest that they must grin and bear it because Western standards of justice require that, essentially, it is better to let a lot of criminals roam free than to imprison a few innocent people. This latter notion merely reinforces the connection of democracy with crime, and the understandable response is to suggest that the choice actually then is between locking up a few innocent people or locking up all of them as, out of fear, they place themselves essentially into house arrest. What good, people may well ask, is "freedom" if one no longer feels free to walk the streets? People are now far freer to speak their minds in the new democracies of course, but not that many people ever say things that anyone, even the most paranoid of dictators, would want to suppress, whereas everybody uses the sidewalks.

Concern about crime has, of course, also been very high at times in the United States, and it can be a hot topic with voters as was shown in the 1994 elections there. An important difference, perhaps, is that concern about crime does not translate in the U.S. into demands to get rid of democracy and capitalism; in some new democracies it conceivably could. Alarmist Hitler analogies should be avoided, but it was the demand for order (in that case from street fighting by political gangs) as much as economic instability that helped him into office.[12]

Obviously, efforts to improve police work could help with this concern. But, as in the United States, the fear of crime is often essentially psychological—concern about crime burgeoned in 1994 even though crime had actually been going down at the time for more than ten years.[13] Moreover, with a free capitalist press, crime, which sells papers everywhere, is more likely to be reported and dwelled upon—often in gruesome detail—and it is likely to be handled in the usual incompetent, anecdotal manner so common in America.[14]

CONCEPTIONAL CONNECTIONS BETWEEN DEMOCRACY
AND CAPITALISM

It has been pointed out at various points in this book that there are a number of conceptual connections between democracy and capitalism. Both rely more on the individual than on the collective; both question authority in one way or another and work best when it is restrained; both allow people the freedom to put an enterprise or a sitting government out of business if they become dissatisfied with its performance; both are notably, if often clumsily, self-correcting; and both leave people substantially free for individual pursuits even though this generally leads to a considerable inequality of result and to a sort of (nonviolent) disorderliness that some find distasteful. Both are also founded on the fundamental—even breathtaking—assumption that it is best, in the end, actually to trust people to understand and to act upon their own interests, and on the related assumption (or hope) that, in the end, you can't fool everybody every time.

Moreover democracy and capitalism are conceptually linked in that each has a kind of "emptiness at the core," as Francis Fukuyama has put it. This quality can be unpleasantly unsatisfying at least to people who aspire to grander goals and who have higher visions: there is, it often seems, no *there* there. What Yergin and Stanislaw say about capitalism can be said about democracy as well: "a system that takes the pursuit of self-interest and profit as its guiding light does not necessarily satisfy the yearning in the human soul for belief and some higher meaning beyond materialism."[15] And it must be granted that democracy and capitalism, at least in the form suggested by the perspective of Ralph's Pretty Good Grocery, really do lack any sort of snappy answer to such great philosophical themes as what is truth? what is good? and what, after all, is the meaning of life? To queries and expostulations about such matters, there is a tendency to shrug, and, like Voltaire's Candide, to suggest exhaustedly, if good-naturedly, "That is well said, but we must cultivate our garden."

Finally, the institutions of democracy and capitalism share a conceptual connection in that both seem routinely to inspire in their constituents a curious incomprehension about the way they work.

Both in mature democracies and in new ones many still cling to a fuzzy, romantic, Rockwellian image that, centuries of experience suggest, is quite fantastic. Democracy, I have argued, is not about active mass participation, enlightened citizen vigilance, heartwarming consensus, or majority tolerance, but the notion that it *ought* somehow to be that way still persists and even prevails.

Similarly, a common view of capitalism, one often held even by capitalists when they trouble to generalize about it, maintains that capitalism is somehow vicious and reprehensible or at least devoid of virtue. This view prevails even though the daily business experience of people in advanced capitalist countries—where they are treated overwhelmingly with honesty, fairness, civility, and even compassion by acquisitive proprietors and deal-makers—constantly belies the negative image. For example, in polls conducted in 1990, the residents of capitalist New York tended to agree with those in still communist Moscow that it is "unfair" for an entrepreneur to raise prices merely because demand increases, and New Yorkers were, if anything, *less* tolerant of economic inequality, *more* distrustful of "speculators," and *less* appreciative of the importance of material incentives. And, although the overwhelming majority of economists insist otherwise, generous portions of the public in capitalist America continue to maintain that downsizing is bad for the economy, that foreign trade agreements cost domestic jobs, and that gasoline prices result mainly from the quest for profits by Big Oil rather than from the normal play of supply and demand.[16]

However, on the brighter side, these faulty popular perspectives—that democracy ought somehow to be much better than experience has shown it to be and that capitalism deep down is somehow really much worse than experience routinely suggests—do not seem to have greatly hampered the fundamental workings of either institution at least in advanced capitalist democracies of late. In operation democracy is far from ideal, but it seems to be the best (or least bad) form of government. And in operation capitalism, for all its real and imagined flaws, seems the best (or least bad) way to run an economy for the greatest benefit of the greatest number.

Hence, although there probably ought to be *some* guiding minds at work for democracy and capitalism to be properly instituted and maintained, it does not appear necessary for people in general fully to appreciate them, or even to believe in them, for them to work. For societies striving to embrace the gains—however limited, modest, and at best pretty good—of democracy and capitalism, that somewhat perverse message could be the most hopeful of all.

* *Appendix* *

AN INVENTORY OF PROPOSITIONS

CAPITALISM

UNDER CAPITALISM, virtue is considerably more than its own reward: contrary to its image, capitalism tends, all other things being equal, systematically, though not uniformly, to reward business behavior that is honest, fair, civil, and compassionate, and it inspires a form of risk-taking behavior that can often be credibly characterized as heroic.

Moreover, since phonies can usually eventually be spotted, people who are genuinely honest, fair, civil, and compassionate are more likely to succeed in business than those who simply feign such qualities.

Since a nice guy will feel bad (punish himself) if he lets somebody down, it is sensible, all other things equal, to prefer to deal with nice guys. As a result, nice guys, on average, have a competitive advantage over non-nice guys and accordingly will tend to prosper—that is, to finish first.

When people generally expect to be treated dishonestly, unfairly, or discourteously in business they will tend to avoid making transactions, and hence there will be less growth because there will be less economic activity.

Virtuous business practices may be financially beneficial in the long term, but in part because of capitalism's traditional image, this reality may not be obvious to the very capitalists who stand to benefit from them. It has apparently often taken an effort for people to grasp the concept of enlightened, long term, economic self-interest.

Since the business virtues are economically advantageous, they can arise and flourish through normal competitive pressures. What seems to be required is the establishment of an important business innovation: since the profitability of virtuous business behavior is apparently often not obvious, a business innovator must discover the economic value of virtue and then act upon this important discovery. Other businesses, noticing the success of the innovator, follow suit.

When dishonest business practices are common, courts or regulatory systems will be swamped. But when honesty is the norm, the courts and regulators will be capable (strongly encouraged by the many honest businesses) of enforcing the comparatively rare infractions, and consequently further encouraging economic growth. It seems likely, then, that effective institutions are more the result of virtuous norms than the cause of them.

As an elaborated, self-conscious principle, the notion that honesty, fair dealing, civility, and compassion bring wealth seems to have been generally discovered, or to have been made clearly explicit, only in the nineteenth century or so. P. T. Barnum's mid-century tract, *The Art of Money-Getting,* may be the earliest publication in which the profitability of virtuous business behavior is specifically and extensively laid out.

The rise of business virtue seems very much to have coincided with the remarkable economic rise of the West in the last two centuries, and probably importantly helped cause it.

The invasion of institutions like McDonald's and K-Mart can have a very beneficial impact on the business climate because such businesses furnish examples of how to prosper through the routine and prominent application of established and tested procedures of honesty, fairness, civility, and compassion to business practices.

Where trust has arduously, and profitably, been built up, efforts to further guarantee honesty by mechanical legalistic devices could actually be counterproductive.

It is desirable to have effective antifraud legislation, but as a practical matter the swindled have very little chance of ever getting their money back even where there is a highly developed and substantially incorruptible court system.

When demand outstrips supply and the seller is unable to raise the price, customers become supplicants, and there is no economic disincentive to incivility, surliness, and arrogance.

The remarkable, historically unprecedented economic expansion of the past two centuries has taken place substantially by accident or default. It was not notably guided by government policy—indeed, it frequently took place *despite* government policy—because it occurred when economists often didn't know what they were talking about or fundamentally disagreed over policy, or, when they could agree, were often ignored by decision makers who were pursuing divergent agendas, were mesmerized by faulty economic folk wisdom or ideology, or were paralyzed by political cowardice.

The random politician or governmental official consulting the random economist only a generation ago might well have gotten the wrong advice. It would have been better, on average, to consult a reader of tea leaves or an astrologer. Now, however, economists appear to have reached a substantial and probably correct (though not necessarily theory-based) consensus about how economies work, and the advice they render is likely—or more likely than not—to be sound.

Moreover, although it is very often politically painful and counterintuitive to act upon such advice, policymakers increasingly are willing do so.

In the process, economists and like-minded idea entrepreneurs seem substantially to have managed to get across four highly consequential and enormously controversial ideas: the growth of economic well-being (as opposed, for example, to the quest for otherworldly eternity and the quest to maintain inborn differences as expressed in class structure) should be a dominant goal; wealth is best achieved through exchange rather than through conquest; international trade should be free; and economies do best when the government leaves them substantially free.

These elemental propositions in combination not only hold the formula for a huge expansion of economic well-being, but they suggest the demise of such central human institutions as empire and war.

War is unlikely if countries take prosperity as their chief goal *and* if they come to believe that trade is the best way to achieve that goal. Thanks in part to the success of economists, both propositions have now gained wide currency.

If people with business motivations had actually been running the world, its history would have been quite a bit different (and generally better).

Free trade furnishes the economic advantages of conquest without the unpleasantness of invasion and the sticky responsibility of imperial control.

Although Kant and many others have posited that increased trade enhances the prospects for peace, history does not suggest that this proposition has much validity: most wars, after all, are civil conflicts, fought between groups which know each other only too well and trade with each other only too much. But a good case could be made for the opposite causal proposition: peace often leads to, or at any rate facilitates, trade.

Advances in economic well-being do not necessarily cause people to think they are happier. Rather, each improvement seems quickly to be taken in stride, and standards are continually raised to compensate. In an important sense, then, things never get better.

However, this curious phenomenon may have a kind of intellectually invigorating quality of its own, and the seemingly unquenchable quest for economic improvement may be useful—crucial, even—for economic advance.

Capitalism is, in an important respect, profoundly irrational. Speculators do worse on average than those who simply and almost randomly buy the market across the board. At the same time, capitalism requires that speculative investment money be generally transferred from bad enterprises to good ones. Therefore, at base, capitalism depends on the self-lacerating thrill of the gamble, and many capitalists effectively act as altruists—that is, they knowingly and systematically take a financial loss in order to better the economic condition of their fellow human beings.

DEMOCRACY

Perfect democracy is an oxymoron.

Democracy, like God, works in mysterious ways its wonders (such as they are) to perform—ways that call into question many theories, hypotheses, expectations, and images generated both by supporters and by opponents about how the institution really ought to work.

Democracy is a form of government in which people are left (equally) free to become politically unequal. It is characterized not by political equality, active participation by the citizenry, and something resembling majority rule and consensus, but by political inequality and substantial apathy—effectively, by minority rule and majority acquiescence.

Democracy is an admirable form of government not because it furnishes a guide to atmospheric and unreachable ideals, but because it is a governmental form, generally compatible with a vigorous and productive society, that functions rather well when people manage, on average, to be no better than they actually are or are ever likely to be: flawed, grasping, self-centered, prejudiced, and easily distracted.

Long experience with democracy suggests that it is scarcely possible to change things a great deal. Inequality, disagreement, apathy, and ignorance seem to be normal, not abnormal, in a democracy, and to a considerable degree the beauty of the form is that it works despite these qualities—or, in some important respects, because of them.

Democracy clearly does not require that people generally be well informed, responsible, or actively attentive. Eternal vigilance has not proven to be the price of democracy—it can come quite a bit cheaper.

Although the advantage is only comparative, democracy seems to do better than other governmental forms at generating effective governments, choosing leaders, addressing minority concerns, creating a livable society, and functioning effectively with real, flawed human beings.

Democracy is a form of government which is necessarily and routinely (though not necessarily equally) responsive. It comes about when the people effectively agree not to use violence to replace the leadership, and the leadership leaves them free to try to dislodge it by any other means: because people are free to develop and use peaceful methods to criticize, pressure, and replace the leadership, the leaders must pay attention to their critics and petitioners.

There are plenty of nonviolent methods for removing officeholders besides elections, and much of what goes on in a democracy comes from petition and pressure, not from elections and legislative voting.

Indeed, it is possible, though not necessarily desirable, to have an effective, responsive democracy even without elections. Like any political device, elections will tend to protect some interests more than others. Moreover, their policy message is almost always ambiguous and often utterly undecipherable.

People excluded from participation in elections, like the feminists of the nineteenth century, have often have nevertheless profoundly affected policy if they have had the right to petition and protest.

Some people, because of their manipulative skills, social position, or sheer luck will do much better under the system than others. Unlike other systems, however, democracy gives to all the opportunity, without regard to social status or ideological conviction, to seek to manipulate the system in their favor.

Because of this characteristic, democracy has been able to survive a potential defect that theoreticians for millennia had concluded was terminal: it allowed democracy to coopt, rather than to alienate, the rich.

While democracy may open up the competition for leadership to all, changes in leadership have not usually been terribly revolutionary: voters have often been inclined to support rich people for office. Democracies, like monarchies, have largely been run by the well connected and the well born.

It is no easy task to persuade free people to agree with one's point of view. What is most difficult of all is to get them to listen in the first place.

Only democracies generally have been able to establish effective review and succession arrangements and thereby solve an elemental problem of governance.

Because of apathy, people, sometimes despite their political predispositions, are often effectively tolerant.

The patent and inevitable contrast between the hopelessly ideal images of democracy and its rough and ready reality often inspires the very cynicism about the democratic process that the idealists continually bemoan and profess to want to reduce.

The quests for equality, for deliberative consensus, for active participation, and for an enlightened citizenry, while not necessarily undesirable, are substantially hopeless.

It is a fundamental property—and perhaps defect—of democracy that citizens may watch laws being made, and when they do so they often compare democracy to its image and then reject the actual process with righteous disdain, even outrage, opaquely dismissing it as bickering and correctly, but uncomprehendingly, labeling it "politics as usual." Effectively, however, politics as usual is the same as democracy in action.

The undisciplined, chaotic, and essentially unequal interplay of "special interests" is a crucial and central part of democracy, not a distortion of it.

The overselling of equality by democratic idealists has encouraged the rise of a destructive and profoundly antidemocratic form when this ideal is transferred to the economic realm. In order really to plunder the propertied it has been necessary to abandon democracy.

Even granting that political cynicism may have risen in recent decades, the quality itself seems more nearly to be a constant than a variable quality in politics. And while this rise of cynicism may be mostly undesirable, it is hardly terminal.

As the futile struggle for campaign finance reform in the United States suggests, people who want or need to influence public policy are very likely to find ways to do so no matter how clever the laws that seek to restrict them.

By just about any standard of what reasonable discourse should be like, there is nothing wrong or indecent about negative campaigning, particularly if it helps to differentiate candidates and issues—as it almost always does.

Democratic theorists and idealists may be intensely interested in government and its processes, but it verges on the arrogant, even the self-righteous, to suggest that other people are somehow inadequate or derelict unless they share the same curious passion.

Democracy does often persecute minorities but, unlike other forms of government, it routinely allows the persecuted to work to change things, a process that has often been remarkably effective even for tiny minorities which are regarded with disgust and contempt by the majority.

Adherence to the democratic image can logically lead some minorities to fear that, if the form is actually about equality, majority rule, and active participation, they stand to be persecuted in a democracy. They can be led to rebel in misguided desperation if they take the democratic ideal too seriously.

Contrary to the ideal image—an image which has often inspired a considerable pessimism about its prospects and one which can furnish authoritarian leaders with a convenient excuse for neglecting reform—democracy is really quite a simple and easily graspable form of government.

Democracy is essentially a governmental gimmick, not a logical or empirical consequence of other factors. A country can quite easily become fully democratic without any special historical preparation and whatever the state of its social or economic development if elites or political activists generally come to believe that democracy is the way things ought to be done and if they aren't physically intimidated or held in check by authoritarian thugs.

Accordingly, the world could just as well have embraced democracy centuries earlier. Or the world could have missed entirely, and we'd still be living, like most of the human race for most of its existence, under the capricious rule of queens and kings and eunuchs.

Democracy's growth has not been the result so much of broader economic, social, or cultural developments. Rather, it has been the consequence of a sort of marketing process that has been characterized by product testing, by luck, by fashion leadership, by the convenient self-destruction of competing institutions, and particularly by the effective propaganda ministrations of idea entrepreneurs—politicians, writers, and organized activist groups.

It was necessary to market-test democracy—to put it into practice somewhere, to show it could actually work. Very much contrary to the anticipations of antidemocrats, it soon became clear that democracy was a rather effective method for choosing and reviewing leaders, and that it does not necessarily mean rule by mobs, incompetents, and demagogues, lead to the persecution of the rich and other minorities, or precipitate a vast social leveling.

Monarchy's amazing longevity over the millennia and in all corners of the globe was probably due chiefly to the fact that it simply had no effective competition as a form of government. Once formidable alternatives were fabricated—chiefly highly flawed democracy—monarchy faded out in rather short order, particularly in the developed world.

Promoters of democracy were lucky that they first test-marketed their product in Britain and America because, in the process, democracy came to be associated with countries which were held to be admirable—that is, which became fashion leaders or role models—for reasons that were often quite irrelevant to the institution itself.

The Islamic countries are kept undemocratic not by the necessary dictates of their culture or by the state of their economic development, but by the will of their leaders.

250

Most of the post-Communist countries of central and eastern Europe as well as many of the new democracies elsewhere have essentially completed their transition to democracy: they are already full-fledged democracies. That is, judging from two hundred years of experience with democracy, what they have now is, pretty much, it.

An overemphasis on the details of democratic transition may cause people in new democracies to continue to think that things may become substantially different—hopefully better—in the future. Thus, not only are transitologists sometimes spreading visions that will never come to pass, but their perspective can inspire or reinforce a short-term point of view that is undesirable from a political standpoint and even more so from an economic one.

Democracies do become more or less democratic, but to seek to establish a point at which a country becomes "consolidated" may not be terribly helpful since, as with Chile in 1973, this condition can be overthrown at any time by sufficiently dedicated and effective antidemocrats—some of whom might even have previously been democrats.

What is most likely to foster democracy in countries that do not now have it, and what is most likely to maintain democracy in ones that do, will not be economic or social development, but rather the desire of ruling elites to emulate the established democracies.

Democracies have often reverted to authoritarian rule historically, but this does not mean that democracy is a peculiarly fragile form: any government can be overthrown by a sufficiently large and dedicated group of thugs with guns. The problem seems to be one of definition. When a democracy gets overthrown we say it has failed, but when one dictator topples another we sometimes see this as persistence of form and a kind of stability.

Although there may well be some softness in the democratic trend of the last decades of the twentieth century, the prospects seem generally rather favorable for further democratic development. In general, economically advanced countries have tended to buy this idea (as well as many other related ones) comparatively earlier, but it is the exertions of idea entrepreneurs that have been more determining of the pace of democratization than the correlated wealth of their customers.

Capitalism and Democracy

Both democracy and capitalism rely more on the individual than on the collective; both question authority in one way or another and work best when it is restrained; both allow people the freedom to put an enterprise or a sitting government out of business if they become dissatisfied with its performance; both are notably, if often clumsily self-correcting; and both leave people substantially free for individual pursuits even though this generally leads to a considerable inequality of result and to a sort of (nonviolent) disorderliness that some find distasteful.

Both are founded on the fundamental—even breathtaking—assumption that it is best, in the end, actually to trust people to understand and to act upon their own interests, and on the related assumption (or hope) that, in the end, you can't fool everybody every time.

Capitalism and democracy are in important respects viscerally unequal and unfair at the systemic level, if not at the personal level, a condition that stems rather naturally and inevitably from the related facts that both institutions leave individuals free to pursue their interests and that some will simply do better at the pursuit than others.

Capitalism will emerge if people are left free to be acquisitive, and democracy can come about if people are left free to complain (and to organize complainants). Neither quality, it seems, is terribly difficult to inspire.

Democracy and capitalism are quite independent. While capitalism can exist without democracy as has often been noted, recent experience in some post-Communist countries suggests that democracy can exist without capitalism as well.

The undeserved association of democracy with capitalist prosperity could lead to destructive disillusion in some places, but it might also help democratic development if the world is really in the process of massive economic improvement.

While democracy may not be necessary for capitalism, democracy probably does benefit capitalist growth by furnishing property owners some potential remedy against governmental confiscation, by establishing the rule of law, by routinely encouraging openness and transparency of information, by allowing *all* interest groups (rather than just a privileged

252

subset) to attempt to influence government policy, by providing a mechanism for removing failed leaders, and, at least lately, by gaining a perhaps undeserved association with stability and predictability.

Democracy and capitalism are conceptually linked in that each has a kind of bland emptiness at the core, a quality that can be unpleasantly unsatisfying to people who aspire to grander goals and who have higher visions.

The faulty popular perspectives that democracy ought somehow to be much better than experience has shown it to be, and that capitalism deep down is somehow really much worse than experience routinely shows it to be, do not seem to have greatly hampered the fundamental workings of either institution, at least in advanced capitalist democracies.

Thus, democracy and capitalism are similar in that they can work pretty well even if people generally do not appreciate them very well, a paradoxical quality that may be one of their most important strengths.

∗ *Notes* ∗

CHAPTER ONE

CAPITALISM AND DEMOCRACY: IMAGES AND IMAGE MISMATCHES

1. Address to a Joint Session of the United States Congress, 21 February 1990.

2. Delli Carpini and Keeter 1996, 22.

3. Kennedy 1964, 539.

CHAPTER TWO

CAPITALISM'S IMAGE

1. Rosenberg and Birdzell 1980, 235. Another definition is: "an economic system with private ownership of land and capital, the individual rights to his (or her) own labor, and the frequency of competitive markets in the determination of prices and quantities for goods and services and for factors of production" (Engerman forthcoming).

2. Macaulay 1963, 63. Stigler 1982, 22. McCloskey 1994, 186. Franklin: *Poor Richard's Almanac,* entry for May 1740. Kavka: quoted in Klein 1997c, 105. See also McCloskey 1994, 183; Wilson 1995, 52–53. On reputational effects, see also Kreps 1990, Axelrod 1984, Klein 1997a, Hardin 1991, Frank 1988, ch. 4.

3. Emden 1939, 17. For a discussion see Nevaskar 1971, especially pp. 219–22. As Nevaskar observes, the same phenomenon characterizes another pacifist group, the Jains of India. See also Klein 1997b, 5. Max Weber once found that Baptists in some areas of the United States had a similar advantage: see Klein and Shearmur 1997, 30.

4. Nevaskar 1971, 130.

5. See Saxon 1989, 334–37.

6. Plowden 1967, 66.

7. Quoted, Weeks 1993, 13. See also Plowden 1967, 67–68.

8. Barnum 1871, 498–99. Of course, such conclusions only hold when governmental policies make it possible to profit honestly.

9. On this issue in postcommunist Europe, where taxi drivers "understand the rules of capitalism in a negative way: as the absence of any rules," see Drakulič 1997, 62–63.

10. See Ramirez 1995.

11. See Klein 1997c, 122–27. On John D. Rockefeller's obsessive concern about protecting the quality of Standard Oil products, see Chernow 1998, 253.

12. Autry 1991, 17. Drucker 1974, 456, 462.

13. Rockefeller: Chernow 1998, 146. Stigler 1975, 179. Barnum 1871, 496. On fairness, see also Brams and Taylor 1999.

14. McCormack 1984, 73, 42, 40; McCormack 1989, 191–92.

15. Kahneman et al. 1986, 738; see also Frank 1988, 176.

16. Thaler 1985, 211–12.

17. The hotels have sometimes found that one acceptable way around this problem is to impose a three-day minimum stay (Thaler 1985, 211).

18. Barnum 1871, 496–97.

19. Barnum 1871, 496.

20. Appel 1930, 55.

21. Peters and Waterman 1982, 29, 157 (emphasis in the original). Cringely 1992, 270. Steinhauer 1998. Templeton: *Wall Street Week with Louis Rukeyser,* PBS, 10 January 1997.

22. Peters and Waterman 1982, 238. See also Schleh 1974, ch. 15; Autry 1991, 122–26; Drucker 1974, 463; Peters 1994, 145; Bittel 1972, 180–214; Vaill 1989, ch. 9; Deep and Sussman 1992, 79–81 and ch. 7. On the honest respect Barnum showed toward his employees, including his many performing freaks, see Saxon 1989, 119.

23. McCormack 1989, 3, 135.

24. H. Smith 1976, 67. Landes 1998, 306n. See also Wilson 1995, 51; Passell 1998.

25. There are remedies against mistreatment by government agencies in a democracy, but they are awkward and indirect: an ill-treated customer can pressure an elected representative who in turn can lean on the agency to treat its customer/supplicants with more civility. (On this issue more generally, see Hirschman 1970.) Among private businesses in the United States, the Toyota experience may most nearly approximate the Soviet one. For quite a while, demand for this car outstripped supply as customers were practically buying them off the boat. Prices rose, but, for various reasons, not to a market-clearing point. Sales approaches developed during that heady time seem to have persisted: in a questionnaire returned by 120,000 car buyers for *Consumer Reports* (April 1995, 270), Toyota placed dead last in expressed satisfaction with the car-buying experience.

26. McCormack 1989, 121. "The pride of man," warns Adam Smith, "makes him love to domineer" (1976, 388 (III.ii)). In his book on man-

agement, James Autry discusses such behavior and supplies a quote from T. S. Eliot: "Half the harm that is done in this world is due to people who want to feel important" (1991, 150). The "harm" in instances like these is to the manager's own bottom line.

27. Barnum 1871, 497. Saxon 1989, 171, 252.

28. Boston CEO (Chad Gifford): *NewsHour With Jim Lehrer,* PBS, 29 April 1997. Cohen and Greenfield 1997, 31.

29. Steckel and Simons 1992, ch. 1. Hood 1996, ch. 2. Advertising's effect: Clancy and Shulman 1994, 140.

30. McCormack 1984, 199–200. Autry 1991, 113.

31. Dunlap 1996, 172–74; emphasis in the original.

32. Quoted, Reder 1994, 7.

33. Failure rate: Clancy and Shulman 1994, 8, 140. It is conventionally estimated that 90 percent of high-tech start-ups fail, though people who have carefully looked at the phenomenon suggest the ratio may be more like 95 percent. Cringely 1992, 232.

34. Nevins 1945, 678. Nevins 1940, 712.

35. Gilder 1984.

36. Wilson 1991, 147. Stigler 1982, 24–25. On this approach in Kant's thought, see Machan 1996, 36.

37. Wilson 1993, 102. Drucker 1974, 462. On this issue, see also Frank 1988, 134–35; Akerlof 1983.

38. McCormack 1984, 4.

39. Autry 1991, 17 (emphasis in the original). For a review of the literature on the malpractice issue, see Levinson 1994.

40. McCormack 1984, 115.

41. Drucker 1974, 456, 462. Saxon 1989, 16.

42. In addition, if the friendship is genuine—that is, if both friends derive some benefit from it—the offended friend can punish the offending friend by withdrawing from the friendship.

43. McCormack 1984, 42 (emphasis in the original). See also McCormack 1989, 2.

44. McCormack 1989, 192.

45. Wilson 1995, 52. Smith 1896, 255.

46. Smith 1976, 898 (V.ii.k). Tilly 1993, 184. A similar moral disconnect can be seen in the behavior of American college students: a student who is known to cheat at exams may well find others doubting the student's general honesty; but one who steals street signs to decorate a dormitory room often will not.

47. Somewhat along the same lines, people who are fundamentally vir-

tuous in their business dealings can also often seek to use government to protect them from competition without necessarily dampening their business reputations, an issue that will be discussed again in chapter 4.

48. Engerman forthcoming. For debate on the business cycle issue, see Kuznets 1961, Lebergott 1964, Romer 1986a, Romer 1986b.

49. Stigler 1984, 149, 155.

50. Tawney 1962, 284. Creating needs: see, for example, Barber 1995, 59.

51. Simon 1995, Rosenberg and Birdzell 1986, Easterlin 1996, Bailey 1995, Stigler 1975, 179.

52. Marshall 1920, 6.

53. Smith 1976, 612 (IV.vii.c). Rockefeller: Chernow 1998, 469.

54. Weeks 1993, ch. 8.

55. Rosenberg and Birdzell 1986, 13.

56. Rickey quoted, Will 1990, 246. Chernow 1998, 101, 133, 197, 284, 557; see also Yergin 1991, 52.

57. One member of the board went along, saying: "I guess I can take the risk if you can," an absurd piece of self-puffery since Rockefeller was clearly taking all the risk himself. Chernow 1998, 285–88.

58. Rockefeller, however, was not always lucky. He made a number of extremely bad, even naive, investments, including the payment of six million dollars for a Colorado company that was not only a money loser, but brought him years of grief and labor turmoil (Chernow 1998, 343, 367–70, 382–85, 556, 571).

59. Cringely 1992, 128–32. Barnum 1871, 476.

60. Nevins 1940, 712.

61. For the bias in full flower, see Brandeis 1934. See also Chernow 1998, 288–89. On the long-term views of large firms, see Chandler 1977, 10.

62. On this issue, see Mueller 1989, 267–69.

63. Barnum 1871, 499. See also McCloskey 1994, 189.

64. Chernow 1998, 467.

65. Rohter 1998.

66. See Bergson 1984; Friedman and Friedman 1980, 146–48; Dye and Zeigler 1988; Kuteinikov 1990; Stigler 1984, 156; Rosenberg and Birdzell 1986, 324; Drucker 1974, 369–72.

67. Ludwig von Mises cites the observations of an eighteenth-century German writer, Justus Möser: "Life in a society in which success would exclusively depend on personal merit would, says Möser, simply be unbearable. As human nature is, everybody is prone to overrate his own worth

and deserts. If a man's station in life is conditioned by factors other than his inherent excellence, those who remain at the bottom of the ladder can acquiesce in this outcome and, knowing their own worth, still preserve their dignity and self-respect. But it is different if merit alone decides. Then the unsuccessful feel themselves insulted and humiliated. Hate and enmity against all those who superseded them must result" (1972, 10–11). Möser therefore advocated promotion by blood lines— though, as the revolutions which began at the end of the eighteenth century were to attest, his method of quality-free promotion actually did inspire quite a bit of resentment.

68. See Malkiel 1996, especially chs. 6, 7, and the bibliography on pp. 492–96. See also Solman 1997, Zweig 1997, and McCloskey 1990, chs. 8–9.

CHAPTER THREE
SOURCES OF CAPITALISM'S NEGATIVE IMAGE

1. Peters 1994, 81.

2. Rosenberg and Birdzell 1986, 181. On this issue see also Hayek 1954, and for a related, balanced discussion of contemporary "sweat shops," Rohter 1996a.

3. A rare exception might be the popular film, *It's a Wonderful Life.* Its economics, however, are bit difficult to dope out. Its good guy businessman hero seems simply to give away money (which, however, saves him in the end since it inspires a charity lovefest in his honor) while the bad guy businessman prospers even though all his customers hate him. Moreover, the plot hinges ultimately on a contrived theft.

4. Many of the businessmen who went bankrupt trying to compete with Rockefeller had it even worse, of course. As the daughter of one of them wrote, "Father went almost insane over this terrible upset to his business. He walked the house day and night. . . . [He] left his church and never entered a church afterward. His whole life was embittered by this experience" (Chernow 1998, 148).

5. Chernow 1998, 121, 122, 260, 319–21, 335, 342, 343, 430, 556.

6. Alger 1876, 312. On this issue, see Scharnhorst 1980, 41–43, 142–44; Scharnhorst 1985, 149–50; Trachtenberg 1990, vi–vii. In his 1980 book Scharnhorst makes a wonderfully wry commentary on the Alger hero in the dedication: "To Sandy, who, though not a banker's daughter, I would save from drowning, if I could swim."

7. Clancy and Shulman 1994, 81–82. On the importance of the pro-

ducer, rather than the various directors, in establishing the Astaire-Rogers phenomenon of the 1930s, see Mueller 1985, 8.

8. Rosenberg and Birdzell 1986, 258. Cringely 1992, 207, 235.

9. Kristol 1978, xi.

10. Stigler 1982, 32. Plato: Machan 1996, 36. McCloskey 1994, 188. Graña 1964, 162. See also Schumpeter 1950, 145–55; Mises 1972, 12–14; Holmes 1993, ch. 13; McCloskey 1998.

11. Havel 1995, 36. See also Gallagher 1990.

12. Jouvenel 1954, 118–21.

13. Havel 1995, 37.

14. Boesche 1988. China: Rosenberg and Birdzell 1986, 88.

15. There seems to be an edge of condescension even in a business magazine, *Fortune,* when it characterizes the operating principles of a successful company ("excellence of quality, reliability of performance, and loyalty in dealer relationships") as a "version of the Boy Scout law" (quoted, Peters and Waterman 1982, 171).

16. Bittel 1972.

17. Kenner 1936, xiii–xiv; emphasis in the original.

18. Graña 1964, 159. Oddly, however, none of this prevents many intellectuals and artists (Lillian Hellman, Charles Dickens, Pablo Picasso, and Bertolt Brecht, for example) from engaging in sharp business practices—even sometimes wallowing in what might be called greed—when their own financial interests are involved.

19. Nozick 1997, 285, 289. He points out that the same mechanism can be used as well to explain the alienation of intellectuals in a communist system (290).

20. Wilson 1991, 139. Smith 1896, 257, 259. Gilder 1984, 16; see also 260. Keynes 1963, 369. Schumpeter 1950, 131; for a critique, see McInnes 1995, 94–97. Fukuyama 1989, 18. On capitalism's supposed alienating and repressive effects on the human personality, see Hirschman 1977, 132.

21. St. Augustine: Hirschman 1977, 9. Stigler 1984, 150.

22. *New York Times,* 3 May 1991, A10.

23. McCloskey 1994, 189. See also Hirschman 1977.

24. Weber 1958, 56. Graña 1964, 172–79.

25. McCormack 1989, 135. Wright 1937, 260–61.

26. Incapable: Smith 1976, 782 (V.i.f). Merchant risk-taking: Smith 1976, 411 (III.iv). Effeminate: Smith 1896, 257–59. Noblest: Smith 1976, 697 (V.i.a).

27. Boesche 1988, 39. Kant 1952, 113.

28. Treitschke readily acknowledged that war had its unpleasant side,

but these defects, he held, were overwhelmed by its many virtues: "War, with all its brutality and sternness, weaves a bond of love between man and man, linking them together to face death, and causing all class distinctions to disappear. He who knows history knows also that to banish war from the world would be to mutilate human nature" (1916, 1:15, 66–67, 2:395–96). Bernhardi 1914, 26. While not a proponent of war, H. G. Wells at times saw considerable virtue in military organization: "When the contemporary man steps from the street of clamorous insincere advertisement, push, adulteration, underselling, and intermittent employment, into the barrack-yard, he steps on to a higher social plane, into an atmosphere of service and co-operation and of infinitely more honorable emulations" (1908, 214–15).

29. Spencer 1909, 664–65. Lea 1909, 45.

30. On this issue more generally, see Mueller 1989, ch. 2.

31. Samuelson: McInnes 1995, 91. Vargas Llosa: Gallagher 1990.

32. Drucker 1974, 373–74; emphasis in the original.

33. On Friedman and philanthropy: Hood 1996. On Hayek: McInnes 1998.

34. Hirschman 1977, 71. Tawney's list is: diligence, moderation, sobriety, thrift (1962, 245).

35. For a balanced account, see Easterbrook 1995. See also Yergin and Stanislaw 1998, 385–86.

36. See also Yergin and Stanislaw 1998, 362, 364. After being ignominiously defeated by Blair's Labour Party, Britain's Conservative Party leader William Hague got around in 1997 to proclaiming at a party conference that "Conservatives ca-a-a-re." Hoggart 1997; White 1997.

37. McCormack 1989, 121.

38. Schulz: Yergin and Stanislaw 1998, 368. Landes 1969, 7.

39. Marshall 1920, 8.

40. Johnson: Burrough and Helyar 1990; the snappy aphorism is prominently displayed on the jacket of the book's hardcover edition. Nevins 1945, 678; see also Hidy and Hidy 1955, 34. Rockefeller accusations: Chernow 1998, 145–48, 168.

CHAPTER FOUR
THE CONSEQUENCES OF CAPITALISM'S IMAGE
FOR ECONOMIC DEVELOPMENT

1. Weber 1958, 57.

2. As Rosenberg and Birdzell put it: "If we take the long view of human

history and judge the economic lives of our ancestors by modern standards, it is a story of almost unrelieved wretchedness. The typical human society has given only a small number of people a humane existence, while the great majority have lived in abysmal squalor. We are led to forget the dominating misery of other times in part by the grace of literature, poetry, romance, and legend, which celebrate those who lived well and forget those who lived in the silence of poverty. The eras of misery have been mythologized and may even be remembered as golden ages of pastoral simplicity. They were not" (1986, 3; see also Marshall 1890, 2–4).

3. Bairoch 1981, 3, 8. Data in figure 4.1: Bairoch 1993, 95

4. Jones 1987. Landes 1969, 19.

5. Rosenberg and Birdzell 1986. McCloskey 1994, 189. See also Landes 1998.

6. North 1990, 123–24.

7. North 1990, 124.

8. They also suggest—wittily, but a bit too ingeniously perhaps—that the "very contempt in which the clergy and the older aristocracy held the rising merchant class could only have encouraged the merchants to develop a code of honor pivoting on scrupulous care in timely payment of debts and on loyalty to superiors—both points of striking weakness in the aristocratic code" (1986, 124–26, 128).

9. Gerschenkron 1962, 48.

10. North 1990, 101. Gerschenkron 1962, 48–49.

11. North 1990, 123.

12. Though, as Richard Tilly has pointed out, this process can also be used to facilitate collusion among businesses and to restrict competition (1993, 200). On the competition-stifling effects of guilds, see also Rosenberg and Birdzell 1986, 51, 174; Landes 1998, 242–45.

13. North 1990, 87.

14. Landes 1998, 493; Rosenberg and Birdzell 1986, 151–53, 159–63, 258.

15. Rosenberg and Birdzell 1986, 11.

16. North 1990, 112–17.

17. Appel 1930, 50–52, 370–73. Barnum's recollection of business in the early part of the century stresses that "sharp trades" and "dishonest tricks and unprincipled deceptions" occurred both in the cities and in the country (Barnum 1855, 39). This observation suggests it may be unwise to assume that transaction costs in the small-scale village are necessarily low because "trade exists within a dense social network" (North 1990, 120).

18. Appel 1930, 54. On the rise of set prices in England, see Alexander 1970, 173–74. There were other advantages to setting prices: a business did not have to rely on an employee's bargaining ability (in contemporary auto sales, the sales manager is usually consulted before a haggled sale is consummated), one could hire less expensive sales clerks, and the process was less time-consuming.

19. Barnum 1871, 496.

20. Haggling also persists in the purchase of houses, but here the amateur usually hires a professional—an attorney and/or a realtor—to check over the deal before it is consummated.

21. McAneny and Moore 1994. On efforts by the National Automobile Dealers Association to "buff the industry's greasy image," see Bennet 1995.

22. *Consumer Reports,* April 1995, 270–71.

23. There are difficulties, however, because new car transactions have traditionally, if illogically, been combined with the purchase by the dealer of a traded-in vehicle for which setting a price is generally impossible (see Wilson 1995, 53n). Also, some auto dealers, unlike Wanamaker, are apparently failing to set their prices low enough, allowing other dealers, in a *New York Times* business reporter's evocative phrase, to "ruthlessly undercut them to capture sales" (Bradsher 1996). To some unsentimental customers, however, it is possible that such "ruthless" behavior might instead look suspiciously like a good deal.

24. McGuire and Olson 1996, 72–73, 76. De Long and Shleifer 1993, 699.

25. McGuire and Olson 1996, 80. De Long and Shleifer 1993, 699.

26. Montesquieu: Hirschman 1986, 107. Smith 1896, 253, 255. Wilson 1991, 148. Klein 1997c, 105. Scottish historian: Hirschman 1977, 61.

27. Smith 1976, 612–13 (IV.vii.c).

28. In his essay, "Advice to a Young Tradesman," Franklin observes, "He that is known to pay punctually and exactly to the time he promises, may at any time, and on any occasion, raise all the money his friends can spare. This is sometimes of great use. After industry and frugality, nothing contributes more to the raising of a young man in the world than punctuality and justice in all his dealings; therefore never keep borrowed money an hour beyond the time you promised, lest a disappointment shut up your friend's purse for ever" (1856, 88). And the entry for May 1740 in Franklin's *Poor Richard's Almanac* declares, "Tricks and treachery are the practice of fools that have not wit enough to be honest."

29. For discussions of such informal institutions in action, see Greif 1993, Benson 1997. See also McCloskey 1994, 183–84.

30. Defoe 1727, 2:34.

31. However, Smith's observation about probity is found not in his published work but rather in notes from earlier lectures taken down by students and published a century after his death. An observation by Defoe, an experienced international trader, essentially suggests that Smith may have been biased because he was living in a comparatively advanced capitalist area: "Our tradesmen are not, as in other countries, the meanest of men" (1727, 1:305).

32. McCormack 1989, 3, 8.

33. Aware that a reputation for bilking the gringos is bad for the economy more generally, the Mexican government has established tourist police to help foreigners maneuver the unfamiliar uncertainties of the marketplace and perhaps to keep them from being taken.

34. Banfield 1958, 64, 79, 93–94. See also Putnam 1993.

35. Rosenberg 1975, 379. Tilly 1993, 188. Poland: Blobaum 1995, 81.

36. Yet Peters and Waterman note that the condition persists in some quarters. They quote a chief of naval operations who says the U.S. Navy assumes "that everyone below the rank of commander is immature," and cite an underground poem circulated among General Motors workers complaining that the company treats them as if they were inmates in an "overgrown nursery" (1982, 235).

37. Tilly 1993, 188–89. Strikes: Greenhouse 1996. Particularly in contrast with General Motors, the Ford Motor Company enjoyed cordial company-union relations in the 1990s, something it considered a competitive advantage (Bradsher 1998). Standard Oil was a generally well-run company, but its antipathy to unionization was so intense as to become economically irrational: see Chernow 1998, 576–81.

38. See Mayo 1933.

39. Peters and Waterman 1982.

40. Defoe concludes by urging that the shopkeeper "should not make a common whore of his tongue" but rather that there exists a "happy medium" in which "the shop-keeper, far from being rude to his customers on the one hand, or sullen and silent on the other, may speak handsomely and modestly of his goods what they deserve, and no other." He goes on to argue that this "way of discoursing to a customer, is generally more effectual, and more to the purpose, and more to the reputation of the shop-keeper, than a storm of words, and a mouthful of common shop-language, which makes a noise, but has little in it to plead, except to here

and there a fool that can no otherwise be prevailed with" (1727, 1:251–56).

41. Frank 1988, 165. There are eerie reflections of Defoe in an article about training schools recently set up by the automobile industry, a retail business that still haggles with customers. When asked, "All buyers are—what?" the salespeople (being trained to become "sales professionals") instantly reply, "liars." The article observes, "Once the negotiating begins, so does the lying . . . every customer suspects the salesman of being slime." To enhance sales, the students are urged to tell the truth, however: it is in their interest to be honest and not to "high gross" their customers: "sacrificing some profit now will yield referrals and repeat business" (Bennet 1995).

42. Tilly 1993, 183–84, 201 n. 13.

43. Marshall 1890, 7.

44. Tilly 1993, 182, 185–86, 199, see also 195. Circus: Plowden 1967, 104; Culhane 1990, 175.

45. Stigler 1982, 23–24. For a history of early efforts, see Kenner 1936. On Underwriters' Laboratories, see Brearly 1997.

46. Gerschenkron 1962, 19.

47. Specter 1995. This process may resemble the adjustments of traditional arrangements that occurred when Japan, China, and Korea were confronted with western capitalism; see Fukuyama 1995, 349–50. On China's efforts to deal with the lingering incivility problem, see Faison 1995; or for East Europe, see Perlez 1993.

48. Tilly 1993, 182, 199–200.

49. Abramovitz 1989, 14–15.

50. Rosenberg 1964, 58–60. See also McCloskey 1998, 311–14.

51. Peters and Waterman 1982, 29.

52. Tilly 1993, 201 n. 10.

53. Marshall also argues that "in every age poets and social reformers have tried to stimulate the people of their own time to a noble life by enchanting stories of the virtues of the heroes of old." Yet, "adulteration and fraud in trade were rampant in the middle ages to an extent that is very astounding when we consider the difficulties of wrong doing without detection at the time." In addition, "No traders are more unscrupulous in taking advantage of the necessities of the unfortunate than the corn-dealers and money-lenders of the East" (1890, 6–7).

54. Quoted, Jones 1987, 235.

55. Klein 1997b, 1. Macaulay 1963, 61, 66. See also Ellickson 1991.

56. Standard Oil: Chernow 1998, 114. Macaulay 1963, 65–67. McCor-

mack, a lawyer himself, contends that "Fights between law firms on behalf of clients are often mere vehicles for firms to charge time and earn money. I feel that if you can put the two parties in most legal disputes in a room by themselves—even two years into the legal dispute—the matter will get resolved, certainly more cheaply, and probably a lot more equitably" (1984, 207).

57. For a similar observation, see Holmstrom and Kreps 1996.

58. Another area in which the courts are likely to be next to useless is the stealing of often unwritten and rarely copyrighted jokes by stand-up comedians. The industry is effectively policed by a newsletter which actively reports on such unsavory business behavior, and performers who get a reputation for lifting the material of others are very likely to lose gigs.

59. Merchant law: Benson 1997. Rosenberg and Birdzell 1986, 116–17; emphasis added. Smith 1976, 412 (III.iv). See also Ellickson 1991.

60. See Wang forthcoming; Yergin and Stanislaw 1998, 206–7.

Chapter Five
Development, Happiness, and the Rise of the Politically Incorrect One-Handed Economist

1. See, for example, Simon 1995; Easterlin 1996, 84, 153; Lebergott 1993; Rosenberg and Birdzell 1986, 333; Jones 1987; Jones 1988; Wattenberg 1997; Landes 1998, ch. 29; Landsburg 1997.

2. Henderson: Gregg 1956, 13. Osler 1932, 123–24. On this issue, see also Kunitz and Engerman 1992.

3. Consumers were quick to respond to the success: by 1929, the amount Americans spent on medicine was nearly seven times higher than in 1900; by 1990 it was seven hundred times higher. Initially in the century, however, life expectancies were raised less by medicine (or "dosing") and surgery than by improved public health—in particular, by better sewage and water supply—and by better housing which reduced the number of germ-carrying people sleeping in the same room (Lebergott 1993, 36–37, 122–23). On the placebo effect, see Blakeslee 1998.

4. For discussions, see Lebergott 1993, Simon 1995, Easterlin 1996. Data in figure 7.1: Sweden and England, Preston 1995 and correspondence with Preston; more developed and less developed countries, Bailey 1995, 403.

5. See, for example, Engerman 1997.

6. For an extended philippic against economic theory, see Cassidy 1996.

7. Summers 1992, 12. Privatization: Yergin and Stanislaw 1998, 114–15.

8. Hellman 1998, Yergin and Stanislaw 1998.

9. Stigler 1975, 57.

10. Brody 1997.

11. Weinstein 1997.

12. Stigler 1975, 57.

13. Kuznets 1966, 12–14. Rosenberg and Birdzell 1986, 309.

14. Wright 1968, 463. Pogge von Strandmann 1988, 97. For an extensive discussion of the varying role of economics as a motivation, or excuse, for war, see Luard 1986.

15. See Jäckel 1981.

16. Russett 1972, 58–60. As Samuel Eliot Morison points out, "The fundamental reason for America's going to war with Japan was our insistence on the integrity of China" (1963, 45). Melvin Small notes that "the defense of China was an unquestioned axiom of American policy taken in along with mother's milk and the Monroe Doctrine. . . . One looks in vain through the official papers of the 1930s for some prominent leader to say, 'Wait a second, just why is China so essential to our security?'" (1980, 238–39). Warner Schilling observes crisply, "At the summit of foreign policy one always finds simplicity and spook," and suggests that "the American opposition to Japan rested on the dubious proposition that the loss of Southeast Asia could prove disastrous for Britain's war effort and for the commitment to maintain the territorial integrity of China—a commitment as mysterious in its logic as anything the Japanese ever conceived" (1965, 389). See also Mueller 1995, 103–8.

17. See Mueller 1993; Mueller 1995, ch. 2; Rush 1993.

18. Mueller 1994a, ch. 8.

19. See also Hirschman 1977; McCloskey 1994, 180–82.

20. Urquhart and Berkowitz 1987.

21. For A. A. Milne's perspective on such thinking, see Milne 1935, 4, 222–23.

22. Buckle 1862, 154, 157. See also Friedman and Friedman 1980, 1–2; Smith 1976, 429–51 (IV.i).

23. On this issue, see also Crawford 1993; Nadelmann 1990; Rosenberg and Birdzell 1986, 17. Beginning in 1908, Angell argued that "It is a logical fallacy to regard a nation as increasing its wealth when it in-

creases its territory." Britain, he pointed out, "owned" Canada and Australia in some sense, yet it certainly did not get the products of those countries for nothing—it had to pay for them just as though they came "from the lesser tribes in Argentina or the USA." The British, in fact, could not get those products any cheaper than the Germans. Thus, he asked, "If Germany conquered Canada, could the Germans get the wheat for nothing? Would the Germans have to pay for it just as they do now? Would conquest make economically any real difference?" He also argued that the popular notion that there were limited supplies in the world and that countries had to fight to get their share was nonsense: "The great danger of the modern world is not absolute shortage, but dislocation of the process of exchange, by which alone the fruits of the earth can be made available for human consumption" (1914, 31; 1933, 108, 175). A half-century later, Malthusian alarmists once again joined in a debate on the issue of scarce resources though they did not advocate conquest as an antidote. For a discussion, see Arndt 1978.

24. Kant 1957, 24; see also Hirschman 1977, 79–80, 134–35. Buckle 1862, 157. Peace activists of the nineteenth century were quick to take up Kant's argument, and often with a similar sense of optimism. Particularly prominent were two Englishmen, Richard Cobden and a Quaker, John Bright, who saw international peace as one of the benefits of free and unfettered trade. And in 1848 John Stuart Mill concurred: "It is commerce which is rapidly rendering war obsolete" (Howard 1978, 37). On booty as an important, though usually not primary, motive for medieval war, see Kaeuper 1988.

25. Mahan 1912, 131. A nation's "wealth, prosperity, and well-being . . . depend in no way upon its military power," Angell argued, noting that the citizens of such war-avoiding countries as Switzerland, Belgium, or Holland were as well off as the Germans, and much better off than the Austrians or Russians (1951, 165; 1933, 89–92, 230; 1914, 36.)

26. Rosecrance 1986, 16, 24. For a discussion of the mechanism by which attitudes toward war have been reshaped, and particularly of the crucial role of World War I in this process, see Mueller 1989 and especially Mueller 1995, ch. 9.

27. Jefferson 1939, 263. The rise of successful capitalism might also affect religion. Modern science and medicine have been destructive of two of religion's once-popular appeals: its ability to explain the physical universe and its ability to heal. (On religion's once-presumed ability to explain the physical universe, see Barr 1987.) And the notion, at one time accepted even by atheists, that religion is vital because it supplies a moral

code, is being undercut when, apparently for the first time in history, many areas in formerly pious Europe have developed societies that are orderly, moral, and generally admirable despite the fact that religion, particularly organized religion, plays little effective part. Now, the newly emerging unselfconscious acceptance of material gain as a dominant goal may tend to devalue another of the church's appeals. As suggested in chapter 3, religion attained prominence in human life in part because it can sometimes supply spiritual uplift as a sort of relief from material woes and fates and because it seeks to give higher meaning to a dreary and difficult life. But if people become primarily materialistic and rich, they may come to feel they need religion less. Of course, in other areas, such as portions of the Islamic world, religiosity may have actually heightened in recent years, and it certainly retains a considerable degree of force in the United States. Thus, whether Europe is a true harbinger remains to be seen. For the argument that it is not, see Berger 1996/97. For the argument that religion is weakest where it is state-dominated, and strongest where there is a vigorous competitive market for religion, see Iannaccone et al. 1997.

28. Actually, to be complete about this, there may be something of a clash between this and the previous proposition. Logically, an ardent free trader should favor conquest—at least ones where damage is minimal and where long-term resentments are not stirred up—since this would expand the free-trade zone to the general benefit. For example, free traders would presumably hold that North Americans would generally benefit if Canada were painlessly and benevolently to conquer the United States, making it, perhaps, its eleventh province.

29. Drew 1994, 338–46.

30. On Nixon and China, see Mueller 1989, 184–85.

31. For a discussion of a somewhat similar development in the 1930s, which depended crucially on the mind-set of a key player, the secretary of state, and on President Franklin Roosevelt's "reliance on economists," see Goldstein 1988, 70–71.

32. Legal restrictions forbidding foreign countries or interests from contributing to political campaigns are, to that degree, unwise policy. See Passell 1998b.

33. Hayek 1988, 45. On the once central, but now abandoned, quest in India for "self-sufficiency" and in Latin America for freedom from "dependency," see Yergin and Stanislaw 1989, chs. 3, 9.

34. Stigler 1975, xi; see also Buchanan 1990. On this process more generally, see also Goldstein 1988.

35. Krugman quoted, *Investor's Business Daily*, 24 August 1998, A6. Friedman and Friedman 1984, 129. However, in the 1930s Keynes advised against the "economic entanglements" of trade (Sachs 1998, 102–3, 110).

36. Waltz 1979, 138.

37. Lip service is often given in the United States to reducing its dependence on oil supplies imported from the politically unstable Middle East, but absent a clear crisis, these warnings have not been very effective. The dependence remains. On the national security imperative Japan once saw in maintaining a domestic oil-refining capacity, see Yergin and Stanislaw 1989, ch. 6.

38. Yardeni forthcoming.

39. Schumpeter 1950, 417; see also Lipset 1993a, Yergin and Stanislaw 1998, 22. Hirsch 1976, 1. Friedman: Hartwell 1995, 165.

40. Heilbroner 1993, 97. Hartwell 1995, 191. On this issue, see Stigler 1959, Yergin and Stanislaw 1998. The Mont Pelerin Society, a group of free-market advocates founded in 1947 to "slow down and stop the march down the road to serfdom," voted "decisively" in 1972 that the world was "still threatened" by such tendencies. However, it happily discovered in the 1990s that its goal was now to "encourage a march down the road to freedom." A role that had been "largely negative and critical" could now be "positive and creative" (Hartwell 1995, 158, 216–17). In 1980, Friedman was willing to suggest that "the tide is turning," while still fearing that the trend "may prove short-lived" (1980, 283).

41. Keynes: Skidelsky 1996, 117. India and Latin America: Yergin and Stanislaw 1998, 215, 234; see also Sachs 1998, 101. Judt 1997.

42. Yergin and Stanislaw 1998, 138. See also Sachs 1998, 99.

43. See Heilbroner 1997; Yergin and Stanislaw 1998.

44. Yergin and Stanislaw 1998, 137.

45. On the once-dominant notion of the "just price" and the "just wage," see Rosenberg and Birdzell 1986, 38. Nixon: Yergin and Stanislaw 1998, 62. In 1973, Milton Friedman warned that "If the U.S. ever succumbs to collectivism, to government control over every facet of our lives, it will not be because the socialists win any argument. It will be through the indirect route of wage and price controls" (Friedman and Friedman 1980, 305).

46. There also seems to be an increasing belief that it may be wise judiciously to regulate the financial system itself because, as one economist has put it, "There's more of a stake in keeping the financial sector honest than there is, for instance, in cosmetics." Yergin and Stanislaw 1998,

373, 349; see also Denny 1997. On the successes of governmental efforts to deal with environmental concerns in the last few decades, see Easterbrook 1995. See also Passell 1998c.

47. Yergin and Stanislaw 1998, 317.

48. See Rosenberg and Birdzell 1986, 119–23; Jones 1987; Weingast 1997; McGuire and Olson 1996; De Long and Shleifer 1993; North and Weingast 1989.

49. For Margaret Thatcher's ready acceptance of this role, see Yergin and Stanislaw 1998, 124.

50. India: Yergin and Stanislaw 1998, 216.

51. Simons 1997, Cohen 1997.

52. It is common to calculate government spending as a percentage of gross domestic product and to conclude that, since this figure has risen in the last decades in most developed countries, governmental "control" over the economy has risen. But most government spending in these countries has not been in consumption but rather in subsidies and transfers, items that do not enter the GDP calculation (Crook 1997, 8). What purports to be a "percentage," therefore, is actually a ratio. Moveover, in assessing "control" of the economy, the rise of transfers may well be far less significant than declines in regulation, in confiscatory taxation, and in once-popular wage and price controls. On this issue, see Nye 1997, 138–41.

53. Aristotle: quoted, Campbell 1981, 56. Slovak film: *Je lepšie byt' bohatý a zdravý, ako chudobný a chorý* by Juraj Jakubisko. Pearl Bailey: quoted, Kunitz and Engerman 1992, 29; Murray (1988, 68) attributes this pithy observation to Sophie Tucker.

54. Easterlin 1974, 90–96, mostly using data and analyses from Cantril 1965. On this issue, see also Murray 1988, ch. 4.

55. Diener 1983, 553. See also Campbell 1981, 241; Easterlin 1974, 99–104; Easterlin 1996, 133–35; Murray 1988, 66–68; Inglehart and Rabier 1986, 22–23. People in wealthy countries may be happier on average than those in poorer ones, but the association is often weak and inconclusive. See Inglehart and Rabier 1986, 40, 44–50; Easterlin 1974, 104–8; Easterlin 1996, 138; but see also Veenhoven 1991, 9–12.

56. Smith 1979; Easterlin 1995, 136, 138; Campbell 1981, 27–30.

57. Veenhoven 1991, 19. Data for Britain and France: Veenhoven 1993, 146–47. See also Murray 1988, ch. 4.

58. Easterlin 1995, 136–40, using data from Veenhoven 1993, 176–77. See also Inglehart and Rabier 1986, 44. Japanese economy: Sullivan 1997.

59. Easterlin 1974, 111–16.

60. Campbell 1981. See also Campbell, Converse, and Rodgers, 1976; Murray 1988, ch. 4.

61. In seeking to explain why professions of happiness did not rise between 1946 and 1977 in the United States, Stanley Lebergott points to a different consideration: the ominous simultaneous expansion in nuclear megatonnage. The considerable increases in measured real incomes during that time, he suggests, could not offset fears of "collective suicide" or of concerns over "poverty, civil rights, nuclear plant explosions, the environment" (1993, 14). The problem with this explanation is that people seem to respond in very personal terms when they are asked about happiness; political considerations like those suggested by Lebergott scarcely enter the happiness calculus unless the question specifically asks about concerns for the nation itself (see Easterlin 1996, 134). Moreover, at the same time the problems Lebergott mentions were rising in the United State, others were dissipating—concerns about food shortages or labor disputes, for example. Even more pointedly, there was actually a considerable decline in fears of atomic war with the relaxation of international tensions that began with the signing of the partial test ban treaty of 1963 (see Mueller 1977, 326–28.).

62. Scitovsky 1992, vi–viii, 4. In like spirit, a letter to the *New York Times* from Latvia worries that youth is being worn down by "grinding affluence" (5 January 1998, p. A24). On the "horrors of prosperity," see Waugh 1986, 49–51.

63. Smith 1976, 782 (V.i.f). Tocqueville 1990, 263. Schumpeter 1950; see also McInnes 1995. See also Keniston 1960.

64. Charles Murray, in line with this proposition, argues that job satisfaction has declined in the U.S. (1988, 134–35). But poll data do not support this conclusion: see, for example, Niemi et al. 1989, 238.

65. Mises 1972, 3. See also Murray 1988, 68–69; Whitman 1998.

66. Lebergott 1993, 15; and, for his authoritative calculation on flies and horse manure, p. 24n. For a rare exception to myopic recollection, see Bettmann 1974.

67. Stanley 1995.

68. For a discussion of ever-rising standards of cleanliness and personal hygiene (at one time people routinely went around encrusted in dirt, rarely washed, and, well, smelled), see Schor 1991, 89–91.

69. Baker 1994–95. See also Whitman 1998, ch. 7.

70. Air quality: Easterbrook 1995, Ellsaesser 1995. People think: *Wash-*

ington Post/Kaiser Family Foundation/Harvard University Survey Project, "Why Don't Americans Trust the Government?" 1996.

71. Rosenberg and Birdzell 1986, 6, also 265. However, improvement was evident to economist Alfred Marshall when he published the first edition of his classic textbook in 1890 (pp. 3–4).

72. Woolsey 1993.

73. Kraus 1962, 394.

74. Data: Mueller 1995, 23.

75. For additional doomsaying on international issues, see Kennedy 1987, 1993; Brzezinski 1993. For an extended critique, see Mueller 1994b.

76. Overchoice: Williams 1990. Buridan's ass comparison suggested by Stanley Engerman.

77. Rosenberg and Birdzell 1986, 5. Hume 1955, 14. For Pope John Paul II's very contrasting take on all this, see Elshtain 1995, 13–14.

78. Easterlin 1996, 153. Hume 1955, 21; see also Murray 1988, ch. 7.

Chapter Six
Images and Definitions

1. Lindberg 1996, 42.

2. See also Schmitter and Karl 1991, 84–85.

3. Huntington 1991, 7. In other places (1991, 16), however, Huntington uses as a democratic criterion the requirement that 50 percent of adult males be eligible to vote. James Bryce similarly gets entangled in the suffrage issue when he attempts to define democracy (1921, ch. 3).

4. Dahl 1971, 1. Riker 1965, 31. Wiebe 1995, 263–64. Mencken 1920, 203. See also Schmitter and Karl 1991, 76.

5. A similar approach is adopted by Linz 1978, 5–6. For a critique of the rather murky "civil society" or "civic culture" concept, concluding that the "norms of a civic culture are better thought of as a *product* and not as a producer of democracy," see Schmitter and Karl (1991, 83, emphasis in the original). See also Laitin 1995.

6. Riker 1965, 25.

7. Pomper 1974, 37.

8. Bailey 1950, 237.

9. Vote communication: Verba, Schlozman, and Brady 1995, 13. Contract: CBS News/*New York Times* Poll release, 14 December 1994; Toner 1995.

10. Almond and Verba 1963, 37, 473. Mexican observer (Rodrigo Gar-

cía Treviño) quoted, Scott 1959, 298. Needler 1990, 3, 130–31. Scott 1959, 15. See also Yergin and Stanislaw 1998, 252–53.

11. See Scott 1989, Mosher 1991.

12. On this issue, see Fenno 1973; Schlozman and Tierney 1986; Rosenstone and Hansen 1993.

13. Plato 1957, 316.

14. On this issue, see also Riker 1982, 7–8. "Not the privilege": Riker 1965, 20. Locke 1970, 322.

15. There is also the issue of equality before the law (see Riker 1982, 14–15). Thus an aristocrat who killed someone in a drunken brawl would be held as accountable as a commoner who did so. But it seems entirely feasible to have that sort of legal equality under an authoritarian system—it might have been achieved as much in Nazi Germany or Communist Russia as in democratic England or America.

16. Jefferson 1939, 126–27. Pericles: Thucydides 1934, 104.

17. For a discussion, see Dahl 1956, 112–18; Fishkin 1995, 35–36.

18. See also Schmitter and Karl 1991, 83–84; Dahl 1956, ch. 4.

19. Another way to look at all this would be as follows. Opposition and petitioning cost time and money. Democracy takes effect when the government does not increase this cost by harassing or jailing the petitioners and the opposition, or by imposing additional economic or other sanctions on them. The costs of opposition and petition are not equal because some people have more time, money, or relevant skills than others. Elections do have something of an equalizing effect because the cost of this form of political expression is much the same for everybody. However, the political impact of a single vote is so small that unless one gets a psychological charge out of the act, it makes little sense to go through the exercise.

20. Plato 1957, 316, 325–27; see also Elshtain 1995, 96–104. James Madison's solution to the Platonic puzzle was typically gimmicky and institutional and, moreover, highly unlikely to convince Plato. Should a majority yearn for an "improper or wicked project" such as paper money or an equal division of property, such yearnings could be adequately finessed, he proposed in *Federalist Paper* number 10, if the country were large and if governing were done by representatives rather than directly by the passionate masses.

21. On this issue, see also Popkin 1991, 21; McGuire and Olson 1996, 94.

22. Plato 1957, 328. Mencken 1920, 221. Mark Antony's demagogic fu-

see Fishkin 1995; for a critique of the results, see Merkle 1996. On the use of random methods to choose leaders in Greek democracy, see Dahl 1989, 19.

21. In Russell Baker's modest estimation, Capra's "Mr. Smith Goes to Washington" is a "childish slur on the American political system" and "the worst movie ever made about a politician." "The portrait of the Senate is absurd and vicious. Mr. Smith himself is a boob so dense that he should never have been allowed to go to Podunk, much less to Washington" (1998).

22. Dionne 1991, 354.

23. This process is central to Riker's analysis of democracy (1982).

24. See Patterson and Magleby 1992, 544; Mueller 1994a, 180; Hibbing and Theiss-Morse 1995, 14.

25. See Toner 1994.

26. Broder and Johnson 1996, 628.

27. Berke 1994.

28. Nelson observes that "in 1992, the same voters who in 14 states imposed term limits on members of Congress reelected all but six of the 116 incumbents who were running for reelection in their states, including 70 who had been in office longer than the term limit those voters were imposing" (1995, 76).

29. Dionne 1991, 15.

30. Riker 1996, ch. 5; see also Popkin 1991, 234-36.

31. Ansolabehere and Iyengar 1995, 8-9, 12, 14, 16, 145, 150-56.

32. *Economist*, 16 May 1991, 48.

33. Hibbing and Theiss-Morse 1995, 18, 19, 157.

34. In general, local television news is more highly evaluated and trusted than national television in surveys in the United States, a difference that may arise from the fact that local news tends to avoid controversy while national news frequently wallows in it.

35. For data: *Gallup Poll Monthly*, February 1998, 16. On this phenomenon more generally, see Hibbing and Theiss-Morse 1995, 36.

36. Hibbing and Theiss-Morse 1995, 81, 105.

37. Hibbing and Theiss-Morse 1995, 157. Mortimer quoted, Harrison 1997.

38. Lienesch 1992, 1011. Delli Carpini and Keeter 1996, 224. Junn 1991, 193. Ansolabehere and Iyengar 1995, 145. Fishkin 1995, 176.

39. Lijphart 1997, 5. Conway 1991, ch. 1. Switzerland: Teixeira 1992, 8; Lijphart 1997, 5; Burnham 1987, 107.

40. Lijphart 1997, 5.

279

41. Teixeira 1992, 101. Lijphart 1997, 2–5.

42. Teixeira 1992, 101–3.

43. Ansolabehere and Iyengar 1995, 145.

44. Burnham 1987, 99.

45. Policy agenda: Teixeira 1992, 102. Rosenstone and Hansen 1993, 228–29; see also Rothenberg 1992.

46. Some analysts, like Putnam, argue for participation more broadly and contend that the key to making democracy work is not so much political participation as the presence of "dense networks of social exchange." (Actually, however, he seems to be arguing that such networks may be more helpful for effective government than for democracy itself when he concludes that "*good government*" is a "by-product of singing groups and soccer clubs" [1993, 172, 196, emphasis added; see also Laitin 1995, 173].) Putnam has extrapolated these conclusions, developed from an analysis of Italy, to the United States, but fails to demonstrate that the lamented decline in such things as PTA membership and the rise of television viewing has had detrimental policy consequences (1995a, 1995b; for critiques, see Lemann 1996; Norris 1996; Ladd 1996; *Economist,* 18 February 1995, 21–22; Schudson 1998, 294–314).

47. Quoted, Delli Carpini and Keeter 1996, 1.

48. Bryce 1921, 1:48. Mann quoted, Sandel 1996, 165.

49. Lienesch 1992, 1011; Lakoff 1996, 326; Bellah et al. 1991, 273. One observer urges rather improbably that America will get back on the road to the democratic ideal "only when we have figured out how to use television to teach the essence of citizenship, the virtues of individual sacrifice in the common good and the nobility necessary to make democracy work" (Squires 1990).

50. Delli Carpini and Keeter 1996. See also Berelson 1952, 318.

51. CBS News/*New York Times* Poll release, December 14, 1994. Toner 1995.

52. *Washington Post*/Kaiser Family Foundation/Harvard University Survey Project, "Why Don't Americans Trust the Government?" 1996. See also Morin 1996.

53. Delli Carpini and Keeter 1996, 22. As so often happens, this statement ignores the country's notably unstable Civil War.

54. Holmes 1996, 33–34.

55. Tocqueville 1990, 1:201.

56. McGuire and Olson 1996, 94. Reviewing several studies of new democracies, Nancy Bermeo observes, to her dismay, that "in every en-

during case, dramatic redistributions of property were postponed, circumscribed, or rolled back" (1990, 365). See also Przeworski 1986, 63.

57. Lenin 1932, 73, 82. See also Meyer 1957, 66–70.

58. See Meyer 1957, 19–56, 92–103; Cook 1991, 248–56.

59. For a discussion, see Cohen 1995, 131, 246; Bennett 1995, 137–42; Woodward 1995, 228, 241, 279.

60. See Gordon and Troxel 1995; Ganev 1997; Châtelot 1997; Stokes 1993, 701.

61. See also Stokes 1993, 701–4; Marody 1997.

62. None too surprisingly, cynicism about democracy has flourished in the new democracies of eastern and central Europe. See Gati 1996. Of course, politicians there have to deal daily there with messy issues that are hugely difficult and painful: in the early 1990s, as American politicians agonized over whether flag burning should be banned or whether the gasoline tax should be raised a few cents, politicians in Poland alone privatized more businesses than had previously been privatized in the entire history of the human race and created a banking system in less time than it takes in the West to train a bank examiner (Fischer and Gelb 1991, 99, 100). For all that, however, cynicism may not be much greater than in the "mature" democracies of the West. One analyst is shocked at a poll showing that 79 percent of the Romanian population feels politicians were "ready to promise anything to get votes" while 65 percent say politicians are more interested in strengthening their own parties than in solving the country's problems (Shafir 1993, 18)—disapproval rates likely to be found in the West as well. Another asserts that Russian voters have "lost their faith in all politicians" (Rutland 1994/95, 6). However, while only 6 percent of polled in Russia in 1994 said they trust political parties (Rose 1994, 53), a poll in the United States in the same year discovered only 10 percent willing to rate the "honesty and ethical standards" of congressmen as "very high" or "high," tidily placing them twenty-fifth on a list of twenty-six, just ahead of car salesmen (McAneny and Moore 1994, 2–4), and a 1995 poll in Britain found that 73 percent of Britons considered the ruling Conservative Party to be "very sleazy and disreputable" (*Harper's,* February 1995, 11). Richard Rose argues that "the communist regime has left a legacy of distrust" (1994, 53), but, as noted earlier, there is plenty of evidence to suggest the United States has managed to pick up the legacy without that experience. He also concludes that "An election produces a representative government if those elected are trusted representatives of those who voted for them. The current Russian govern-

ment is democratically elected but distrusted" (Rose 1994, 53), but much the same could be said for the United States at almost any point in its history. On a scale of political distrust developed from polls conducted in the 1990s, Japan scored highest; Poland, Russia, and Estonia registered on the same plane as Britain; East Germany, Bulgaria, and the Czech Republic were all a bit lower than West Germany; and Slovenia was level with the United States (Mason 1995, 69).

63. On this issue, see also Holmes 1996. Actually, the theory-derived notion that low participation implies low legitimacy can be dangerously self-fulfilling. For example, a romanticism about political participation has helped lead to the rather bizarre and even potentially disruptive legal requirement in some postcommunist countries that at least 25 or 50 percent of the electorate must participate for an election to be valid. If this were the law in the United States, of course, huge numbers of elected offices would be vacant.

64. There can also be definitional turmoil. By the definition used by Higley and Gunther in one able effort to deal with this tricky concept (1992), it seems likely that Canada could not be considered to be a "consolidated" democracy since devoted secessionists are numbered among its political elite.

65. Actually, if broad political participation is an important standard, many postcommunist countries are *more* democratic than the United States. For example, in the 1994 parliamentary elections in Ukraine some 5,833 candidates competed in the country's 450 electoral districts, and of these, 62 percent were put forward by "simple groups of voters." Moreover, turnout "reached a surprisingly high average of about 75 percent" (*RFE/RL Daily Report,* 1 March 1994; 29 March 1994). And, by contrast with the American public's impressive ignorance about who Newt Gingrich might be, a poll conducted in Slovakia in October 1993, when the country was only ten months old, asked its respondents about a long list of thirty-one politicians, many of them quite obscure, and found only eight cases in which the Slovak public's ignorance level reached that of the Americans' about Gingrich (FOCUS 1993, 10–11).

66. Michnik 1997, 18.

CHAPTER EIGHT
THE RISE OF DEMOCRACY

1. Fukuyama 1989, 6; Dahl 1971, 181–82.
2. Gellner 1988, 3–4.

3. Engerman 1986, 339. See also Drescher 1987, Eltis 1987.

4. Dahl 1989, 251. See also Burkhart and Lewis-Beck 1994, Inglehart 1997, ch. 6.

5. Dahl 1989, 253; Dahl 1971, 186.

6. Moore 1966, 418. See also Huntington 1984, 204.

7. As Huntington observes, in 1981 almost all countries with per capita gross national products over $4220 were *either* democratic *or* Communist (1984, 202).

8. Huntington 1984, 200.

9. Huntington 1991, 108, 316; see also Lipset 1993a, 1993b. Di Palma 1990, 6–7.

10. For some analysts, however, this will take a long time: looking at Spain a full twenty-one years after it became a democracy, Harry Eckstein acknowledges that the country "seems well on the way to becoming a stable democracy," but still insists that "the returns are not yet all in" (1996, 24).

11. Whitehead 1986, 38.

12. Rustow 1970, 361; for a more recent expression of this perspective, see Eckstein 1996. Dahl 1971, 45, 47. Dahl 1989, 264. By contrast, see Plattner 1988.

13. Wiarda 1976, 51–52.

14. Huntington 1984, 218; emphasis added.

15. Kaufman 1986, 85.

16. Barro 1993, 1994. On the pessimism issue, see also Fukuyama 1992, ch. 1; Muravchik 1992, ch. 6.

17. Di Palma 1990, 4. African leaders: French 1996. Democratic dispositions: Elshtain 1995, 2. Thatcher: speech presented on C-SPAN, 29 December 1996.

18. Dahl 1989, 260, 262. See also Dahl 1971, 126. On elite transformations, see Higley and Gunther 1992.

19. Dahl 1971, 188.

20. On this process, see also Mueller 1995, ch. 10.

21. Voltaire: Chodorow and Knox 1989, 609. Berlin 1969, 129–30. Huntington 1991, 28.

22. A related development took place with respect to the democracy-enhancing fiction that the government owes its authority to the consent of the governed. In some self-serving battles with the king in the seventeenth century, the English Parliament sought to undermine the monarchy's putative direct connection to God by repackaging and selling the ancient notion that government actually owed its existence and legiti-

macy to the consent of the people (who, in turn, somehow embodied the voice of God). But Parliament's objective in all this was, as Edmund Morgan observes, "to magnify the power not of the people themselves, but of the people's representatives." Then the monarchists helped to bring out the democratic implications of the fiction: zeroing in on an apparent weakness in the Parliament's self-serving conceit, they argued that if the people could revoke the King's powers, they could also revoke those of the Parliament. The monarchists took this tack in part because they believed, probably correctly, that in any straight electoral contest with the Parliament, the king would win. But in the process, observes Morgan, "they expanded the dimensions of the fiction and contributed to its future success as the basis of modern government." Thus, by 1650 the notion of the consent of the governed had been substantially accepted, a fiction that could later be used to imply democracy (Morgan 1988, 17, 56, 58, 62, 63).

23. Huntington 1991, 78, 84.

24. Palmer 1959, 239–40.

25. On this process, see also Geoghegan 1983, 156.

26. Jefferson 1939, 279.

27. Seward 1991, 85. Catherine: O'Connor 1994.

28. Tocqueville 1990, xx–xxi.

29. Riker 1965, 12. It is possible, however, that democracy's crisis in America was not all that deep. If the South had won the war or if it had been allowed peacefully to secede, it seems likely that the major portion of the country would have continued to be a democracy.

30. On the unpopularity of war in Germany, see Mueller 1989, 64–68; Mueller 1991; Steinert 1977, 40–41, 315, 341; Kershaw 1987, 122–47, 229, 241. On the unpopularity of war in Italy, see Mueller 1989, 62–63; Knox 1982. On Japan, see Mueller 1989, 71–77.

31. Huntington 1991, 36, 45–46.

32. Huntington 1997, 5, 10.

33. Moynihan 1975, 6. Brandt: Crozier et al., 1975, 2. On these issues, see also Plattner 1988.

34. Huntington 1984, 206; emphasis in the original.

35. Huntington 1991, 88; see also Gershman 1989, 127–28.

36. See Yergin and Stanislaw 1998, ch. 9.

37. Whitehead 1986, 6.

38. O'Donnell and Schmitter 1986, 31, emphasis in the original. Hardest questions: Schemo 1997. Ridiculous antics: Kamm 1990.

39. Rohter 1996b. See also Brooke 1990.

40. *Economist,* 18 May 1991, 48. Brooke 1993.

41. Huntington 1984, 212.

42. Thailand: Kahn 1998. Pakistan: Dugger 1998.

43. The role of the Soviet Union in this enterprise, declared Josef Stalin, was to serve as a "base for the overthrow of imperialism in all countries" or as a "lever for the further disintegration of imperialism." He concluded that "The struggle between these two centers for the possession of the world economy will decide the fate of capitalism and Communism in the whole world," and he would often quote Lenin on such matters: "the existence of the Soviet Republic side by side with the imperialist states for a long time is unthinkable. In the end either one or the other will conquer." As Lenin had also vividly put it, "as soon as we are strong enough to fight the whole of capitalism, we shall at once take it by the neck." Meanwhile, the official Party history proclaimed its "confidence in the final victory of the great cause of the party of Lenin and Stalin, the victory of Communism in the whole world" (Historicus 1949, 198, 200, 203–4; Leffler 1994, 17).

44. For a discussion and an assessment, see Mueller 1989, chs. 5–9.

45. President's Commission on National Goals 1960, 1–2. CIA: Reeves 1993, 54. On the Soviet Union's apparent economic strength at the time, see also Yergin and Stanislaw 1998, 22, 272.

46. For contemporary Western analyses, see H. Smith 1976, Pipes 1984, and Bialer 1986. See also Kennedy 1987, 488–514.

47. See Bunce 1985.

48. As late as the 1970s quite a few people—not only Communists—were still working up enthusiasm for violent, undemocratic revolution. For example, in her multiple-award-winning book about Vietnam, *Fire in the Lake,* American journalist Frances Fitzgerald fairly glowed with anticipation at what successful revolutionaries could bring to Southeast Asia: "when 'individualism' and its attendant corruption gives way to the revolutionary community," she breathlessly anticipated, "the narrow flame of revolution" will "cleanse the lake of Vietnamese society from the corruption and disorder of the American war" (1972, 589–90). Neither corruption nor disorder were eradicated when revolution's narrow flame sliced through Vietnam, and evils far worse were perpetrated.

49. See Mueller 1986; Mueller 1989, 262.

50. On this point, see also Dahl 1989, 263; Huntington 1984, 214. The 1989 experiences also suggest that, from his standpoint, Brezhnev was correct in 1968 when he sent tanks forcefully to stifle Czechoslovak liberalization on the grounds that, although its leaders protested much to

the contrary, the country was on the slippery slope out of the Soviet bloc and into Western democracy.

51. Huntington 1984, 217.

52. Diamond 1996, Gati 1996. See also Zakaria 1997.

53. Collins 1997, 19. The trend toward democracy is also understated when one calculates democracies as a percentage of all countries (as in Diamond 1996, for example). The Soviet Union garnered a rank zero, of course, but the territories it once constituted now make up not one, but fifteen countries which are free to various degrees. To make things comparable it might be sensible to recalculate, counting the old Soviet Union not as one unfree country, but as fifteen unfree ones.

54. Rowen 1996. See also Manion 1996; Pei 1998; Yergin and Stanislaw 1998, 231; Collins 1997; Harding 1998, 12–13. At the end of 1997, it was announced that democracy would be advanced to the township level. In many areas, people can complain all they want, as long as they do not organize: Faison 1998.

55. Huntington 1984, 216.

56. On Qatar, see Jehl 1997. On Iran, see Bakhash 1998.

57. See French 1996.

58. Perlez 1990a; see also Legum 1990; Perlez 1990b, 1990c.

59. Zakaria 1997, 42.

60. Machiavelli 1950, 265.

CHAPTER NINE
DEMOCRACY AND CAPITALISM: CONNECTIONS AND DISCONNECTIONS

1. Lindblom 1977, 116, see also 161–69. Berger 1986, 81. Friedman 1962, 10. Dahl 1990, 80. See also Kristol 1978, xi; Huntington 1984, 204–5, 214. For a useful overview of aspects of this issue, see Almond 1991.

2. Yergin and Stanislaw 1998, 25, 366.

3. See Ganev 1997, Hockstader 1997.

4. Riker 1982, 7.

5. Friedman 1962, 16–18.

6. See, for example, Barro 1993. See also Schmitter and Karl 1991, 85.

7. Mueller 1992a, 990; Olson 1993; *Economist* 1994, 17.

8. Rosenberg and Birdzell 1986, 121–22.

9. Rosenberg and Birdzell 1986, 309. See also Barro 1993, Olson 1982, Buchanan 1990.

10. China: Ashton et al., 1984; Riskin 1995, 414. Bulgaria: Ganev 1997, 131, 136.

11. French 1996. On the foreign policy of the wealthy democracies, see Mueller 1996b. See also Friedman 1997.

12. Bullock 1993, 309–10.

13. See Warr 1995. Although Mayor David Dinkins could correctly point to statistics that showed crime had gone down in New York City during his tenure, this did him little good in his reelection campaign: for example, *New York Times* columnist A. M. Rosenthal actually referred to the "trivializing statistics" that "are supposed to convince us that crime is going down" (1993). For data showing that crime peaked in New York in 1990 and declined steadily thereafter, see *New York Times,* 19 February 1998, A16.

14. For example, buried in a sensational story in *USA Today* about "driveway robberies" in Dallas was the observation that, actually, violent crime had dropped 32 percent in that city in the previous two years (Potok 1994).

15. Fukuyama 1989, 14. Yergin and Stanislaw 1998, 389.

16. Moscow and New York: Shiller et al., 1991, 1992. Economists and the public: Brossard and Pearlstein 1996. When gasoline prices soared during the Gulf War crisis, the public overwhelmingly blamed manipulation by the oil companies, not normal market forces (Mueller 1994a, 151–52, 346 n 10). Much of the outrage against Standard Oil in the nineteenth century stemmed from a similar economic perspective: see Chernow 1998, ch. 12.

* *References* *

Abramovitz, Moses. 1989. *Thinking About Growth and Other Essays on Economic Growth and Welfare.* New York: Cambridge University Press.

Akerlof, George A. 1983. Loyalty Filters. *American Economic Review* 73, no. 1 (March): 54–63.

Alexander, David. 1970. *Retailing in England during the Industrial Revolution.* London: Athlone.

Alger, Horatio, Jr. [1876]. *Shifting for Himself or Gilbert Greyson's Fortunes.* New York: A. L. Burt.

Almond, Gabriel A. 1950. *The American People and Foreign Policy.* New York: Harcourt Brace.

———. 1991. Capitalism and Democracy. *PS: Political Science & Politics* 24, no. 3 (September): 467–74.

Almond, Gabriel A., and Sidney Verba. 1963. *The Civic Culture: Political Attitudes and Democracy in Five Nations.* Princeton, N.J.: Princeton University Press.

Altschuler, Glenn C., and Stuart M. Blumin. 1997. Limits of Political Engagement in Antebellum America: A New Look at the Golden Age of Participatory Democracy. *Journal of American History* 84, no. 3 (December): 855–85.

Angell, Norman. 1914. *The Great Illusion: A Study of the Relation of Military Power to National Advantage.* London: Heinemann.

———. 1933. *The Great Illusion 1933.* New York: Putnam's.

———. 1951. *After All: An Autobiography.* New York: Farrar, Straus and Young.

Ansolabehere, Stephen, and Shanto Iyengar. 1995. *Going Negative: How Attack Ads Shrink and Polarize the Electorate.* New York: Free Press.

Appel, Joseph H. 1930. *The Business Biography of John Wanamaker, Founder and Builder: America's Merchant Pioneer from 1861 to 1922.* New York: Macmillan.

Arndt, H. W. 1978. *The Rise and Fall of Economic Growth: A Study in Contemporary Thought.* Melbourne: Longman Cheshire.

Ashton, Basil, Kenneth Hill, Alan Piazza, and Robin Zeitz. 1984. Famine in China. *Population and Development Review* 10, no. 4 (December): 613–45.

Autry, James A. 1991. *Love and Profit: The Art of Caring Leadership.* New York: William Morrow.

Axelrod, Robert. 1984. *The Evolution of Cooperation.* New York: Basic Books.

Bailey, Ronald, ed. 1995. *The True State of the Planet.* New York: Free Press.

Bailey, Stephen Kemp. 1950. *Congress Makes a Law: The Story Behind the Employment Act of 1946.* New York: Columbia University Press.

Bairoch, Paul. 1981. The Main Trends in National Economic Disparities since the Industrial Revolution. In *Disparities in Economic Development since the Industrial Revolution,* ed. Paul Bairoch and M. Levy-Leboyer, 3–17. London: Macmillan.

———. 1993. *Economics and World History: Myths and Paradoxes.* Chicago: University of Chicago Press.

Baker, Nicholson. 1994–95. From the Index of First Lines. *New Yorker,* December 26–January 2, 83.

Baker, Russell. 1998. What! No Buster Keaton? *New York Times,* 19 June, A29.

Bakhash, Shaul. 1998. Iran's Remarkable Election. *Journal of Democracy* 9, no. 1 (January): 80–94.

Banfield, Edward C. 1958. *The Moral Basis of a Backward Society.* Glencoe, Il: Free Press.

Barany, Zoltan. 1998. Ethnic Mobilization and the State: The Roma in Eastern Europe. *Ethnic and Racial Studies* 21, no. 2 (March): 308–27.

Barber, Benjamin R. 1995. *Jihad* vs. *McWorld.* New York: Times Books.

Barnum, P. T. 1855. *Life of P. T. Barnum Written by Himself.* New York: Redfield.

———. 1871. *Struggles and Triumphs: Or, Forty Years' Recollections of P. T. Barnum, Written by Himself.* New York: American News Company.

Barr, James. 1987. Biblical Chronology: Legend or Science? Ethel M. Wood Lecture. Senate House, University of London, 4 March.

Barro, Robert J. 1993. Pushing Democracy Is No Key to Prosperity. *Wall Street Journal,* 14 December, A16.

———. 1994. Democracy: A Recipe for Growth? *Wall Street Journal,* 1 December, A18.

Bellah, Robert N., Richard Madsen, William M. Sullivan, Ann Swidler, and Steven M. Tipton. 1991. *The Good Society.* New York: Knopf.

Bennet, James. 1995. A Charm School For Selling Cars: In Class, Making Peace With Buyers; Then There's the Real World. *New York Times,* 29 March, D1.

Bennett, Christopher. 1995. *Yugoslavia's Bloody Collapse: Causes, Course and Consequences.* New York: New York University Press.

Benson, Bruce L. 1997. The Spontaneous Evolution of Commercial Law.

In *Reputation: Studies in the Voluntary Elicitation of Good Conduct,* ed. Daniel B. Klein, 165–89. Ann Arbor: University of Michigan Press.

Berelson, Bernard R. 1952. Democratic Theory and Public Opinion. *Public Opinion Quarterly* 16, no. 3 (Fall): 313–30.

Berelson, Bernard R., Paul F. Lazarsfeld, and William N. McPhee. 1954. *Voting: A Study of Opinion Formation in a Presidential Campaign.* Chicago: University of Chicago Press.

Berger, Peter L. 1986. *The Capitalist Revolution: Fifty Propositions About Prosperity, Equality, and Liberty.* New York: Basic Books.

———. 1996/97. Secularism in Retreat. *National Interest,* Winter, 3–12.

Bergson, Abram. 1984. Income Inequality Under Soviet Socialism. *Journal of Economic Literature* 22, no. 3 (September): 1052–99.

Berke, Richard L. 1994. Victories Were Captured By G.O.P. Candidates, Not the Party's Platform. *New York Times,* 10 November, B1.

Berlin, Isaiah. 1969. *Four Essays in Liberty.* London: Oxford University Press.

Bermeo, Nancy. 1990. Rethinking Regime Change. *Comparative Politics* 22, no. 3 (April): 359–77.

Bernhardi, Friedrich von. 1914. *Germany and the Next War.* New York: Longmans, Green.

Bettmann, Otto L. 1974. *The Good Old Days—They Were Terrible!.* New York: Random House.

Bialer, Seweryn. 1986. *The Soviet Paradox: External Expansion, Internal Decline.* New York: Knopf.

Bittel, Lester R. 1972. *The Nine Master Keys of Management.* New York: McGraw-Hill.

Blakeslee, Sandra. 1998. Placebos Prove So Powerful Even Experts Are Surprised. *New York Times,* 13 October, D1.

Blobaum, Robert E. 1995. *Rewolucja: Russian Poland, 1904–1907.* Ithaca, N.Y.: Cornell University Press.

Boesche, Roger. 1988. Why did Tocqueville Fear Abundance? or The Tension Between Commerce and Citizenship. *History of European Ideas* 9, no. 1: 25–45.

Bradsher, Keith. 1996. Sticker Shock: Car Buyers Miss Haggling Ritual. *New York Times,* 13 June, D1.

———. 1998. At G.M., Can They Get Along? *New York Times,* 29 July, C1.

Brams, Steven J., and Alan D. Taylor. 1999. *The Win-Win Solution: Guaranteeing Fair Shares to Everybody.* New York: Norton.

Brandeis, Louis D. 1934. *The Curse of Bigness: Miscellaneous Papers of Louis D. Brandeis.* Ed. Osmond K. Fraenkel. New York: Viking.

Brearly, Harry Chase. 1997. A Symbol of Safety: The Origins of Under-writers' Laboratories. In *Reputation: Studies in the Voluntary Elicitation of Good Conduct,* ed. Daniel B. Klein, 75–84. Ann Arbor: University of Michigan Press.

Broder, David S., and Haynes Johnson. 1996. *The System: The American Way of Politics at the Breaking Point.* Boston: Little, Brown.

Brody, Jane E. 1997. Personal Health: The Nutrient That Reddens Toma-toes Appears to Have Health Benefits. *New York Times,* 12 March.

Brooke, James. 1990. Colombian Guerrillas Forsake the Gun for Politics. *New York Times,* 2 September, 14.

———. 1993. Governing Party's Candidate Wins Paraguay's Presidential Election. *New York Times,* 11 May, A10.

Brossard, Mario A., and Steven Pearlstein. 1996. Great Divide: Econo-mists vs. Public. *Washington Post,* 15 October, A1.

Bryce, James . 1921. *Modern Democracies.* New York: Macmillan.

Brzezinski, Zbigniew. 1993. *Out of Control: Global Turmoil on the Eve of the 21st Century.* New York: Scribner's.

Buchanan, James. 1990. Socialism Is Dead; Leviathan Lives. *Wall Street Journal,* 18 July, A8.

Buckle, Henry Thomas. 1862. *History of Civilization in England.* New York: Appleton.

Bullock, Alan. 1993. *Hitler and Stalin: Parallel Lives.* New York: Vintage.

Bunce, Valerie. 1985. The Empire Strikes Back: The Evolution of the East-ern Bloc from a Soviet Asset to a Soviet Liability. *International Organi-zation* 39, no. 1 (Winter): 1–46.

Burkhart, Ross E., and Michael S. Lewis-Beck. 1994. Comparative De-mocracy: The Economic Development Thesis. *American Political Science Review* 88, no. 4 (December): 903–10.

Burnham, Walter Dean. 1987. The Turnout Problem. In *Elections Ameri-can Style,* ed. A. James Reichley, 97–133. Washington, D.C.: Brookings Institution.

Burrough, Bryan, and John Helyar. 1990. *Barbarians at the Gate: The Fall of RJR Nabisco.* New York: Harper & Row.

Campbell, Angus. 1981. *The Sense of Well-Being in America: Recent Patterns and Trends.* New York: McGraw-Hill.

Campbell, Angus, Philip E. Converse, and Willard L. Rodgers. 1976. *The Quality of American Life.* New York: Russell Sage Foundation.

Cantril, Hadley. 1965. *The Pattern of Human Concerns.* New Brunswick, N.J.: Rutgers University Press.

Cassidy, John. 1996. The Decline of Economics. *New Yorker,* 2 December, 50–60.

Chandler, Alfred D., Jr. 1977. *The Visible Hand: The Managerial Revolution in American Business.* Cambridge, Mass.: Harvard University Press.

Châtelot, Christophe. 1997. Bulgaria Learns to Live with Its Turks. *Guardian Weekly,* 11 May, 17.

Chernow, Ron. 1998. *Titan: The Life of John D. Rockefeller, Sr.* New York: Random House.

Chodorow, Stanley, and MacGregor Knox. 1989. *The Mainstream of Civilization.* 5th ed. New York: Harcourt Brace Jovanovich.

Churchill, Winston S. 1950. *Europe Unite: Speeches 1947 and 1948.* Ed. Randolph S. Churchill. Boston: Houghton Mifflin.

Clancy, Kevin J., and Robert S. Shulman. 1994. *Marketing Myths That Are Killing Business: The Cure for Death Wish Marketing.* New York: McGraw-Hill.

Cohen, Ben, and Jerry Greenfield. 1997. *Ben & Jerry's Double Dip: Lead with Your Values and Make Money, Too.* New York: Simon & Schuster.

Cohen, Lenard J. 1995. *Broken Bonds: Yugoslavia's Disintegration and Balkan Politics in Transition.* 2d ed. Boulder, Colo.: Westview.

Cohen, Roger. 1997. The Cries of Welfare States Under the Knife. *New York Times,* 19 September, A1.

Collins, Walton R. 1997. Gale Force. *University of Chicago Magazine* 90, no. 2 (December): 16–21.

Conway, M. Margaret. 1991. *Political Participation in the United States.* 2d ed. Washington, D.C.: CQ Press.

Cook, Terrence. 1991. *The Great Alternatives of Social Thought.* Savage, Md.: Rowman & Littlefield.

Crawford, Neta C. 1993. Decolonization as an International Norm: The Evolution of Practices, Arguments, and Beliefs. In *Emerging Norms of Justified Intervention,* ed. Laura W. Reed and Carl Kaysen, 37–61. Cambridge, Mass.: American Academy of Arts and Sciences.

Cringely, Robert X. 1992. *Accidental Empires: How the Boys of Silicon Valley Make Their Millions, Battle Foreign Competition, and Still Can't Get A Date.* Reading, Mass.: Addison-Wesley.

Crook, Clive. 1997. The Future of the State. *Economist,* 20 September, 5–48.

Crozier, Michel, Samuel P. Huntington, and Joji Watanuki, eds. 1975. *The Crisis of Democracy.* New York: New York University Press.

Culhane, John. 1990. *The American Circus.* New York: Holt.

Dahl, Robert A. 1956. *A Preface to Democratic Theory*. Chicago: University of Chicago Press.

———. 1971. *Polyarchy*. New Haven, Conn.: Yale University Press.

———. 1989. *Democracy and Its Critics*. New Haven, Conn.: Yale University Press.

———. 1990. *After the Revolution? Authority in a Good Society*. Rev. ed. New Haven, Conn.: Yale University Press.

De Long, Bradford, and Andrei Shleifer. 1993. Princes and Merchants: European City Growth Before the Industrial Revolution. *Journal of Law and Economics* 36 (October): 671–702.

Deep, Sam, and Lyle Sussman. 1992. *What to Say to Get What You Want*. Reading, Mass.: Addison-Wesley.

Defoe, Daniel. 1727. *The Complete Tradesman in Familiar Letters, Directing him in all the several Parts and Progressions of Trade*. 2d ed. London: Charles Rivington. Repr. New York, 1969: Augustus M. Kelley.

Delli Carpini, Michael X., and Scott Keeter. 1996. *What Americans Know about Politics and Why It Matters*. New Haven, Conn.: Yale University Press.

Denny, Charlotte. 1997. World Bank in Surprise Policy U-Turn. *Guardian Weekly*, 6 July.

Di Palma, Giuseppe. 1990. *To Craft Democracies: An Essay on Democratic Transitions*. Berkeley: University of California Press.

Diamond, Larry. 1996. Is the Third Wave Over? *Journal of Democracy* 7, no. 3 (July): 20–37.

Diener, Ed. 1983. Subjective Well-Being. *Psychological Bulletin* 95, no. 3 (May): 542–75.

Dionne, E. J., Jr. 1991. *Why Americans Hate Politics*. New York: Simon & Schuster.

Dostoyevsky, Fyodor. 1945. *The Brothers Karamazov*. Trans. Constance Garnett. New York: Random House.

Drakulić, Slavenka. 1997. Café Europa: Life after Communism. New York: Norton.

Drescher, Seymour. 1987. *Capitalism and Antislavery: British Mobilization in Comparative Perspective*. New York: Oxford University Press.

Drew, Elizabeth. 1994. *On the Edge: The Clinton Presidency*. New York: Simon & Schuster.

Drucker, Peter F. 1974. *Management: Tasks, Responsibilities, Practices*. New York: Harper & Row.

Dugger, Celia W. Pakistan Premier Prevails in Clash with General. *New York Times*, 20 October, A4.

Dunlap, Albert J. 1996. *Mean Business: How I Save Bad Companies and Make Good Companies Great.* New York: Times Books.

Dye, Thomas R., and Harmon Zeigler. 1988. Socialism and Equality in Cross-National Perspective. *PS: Political Science & Politics* 21, no. 1 (Winter): 45–56.

Easterbrook, Gregg. 1995. *A Moment on the Earth: The Coming Age of Environmental Optimism.* New York: Viking.

Easterlin, Richard A. 1974. Does Economic Growth Improve the Human Lot? Some Empirical Evidence. In *Nations and Households in Economic Growth: Essays in Honor of Moses Abramovitz,* ed. Paul A. David and Melvin W. Reder, 89–125. New York: Academic Press.

———. 1996. *Growth Triumphant: The Twenty-first Century in Historical Perspective.* Ann Arbor, Mich.: University of Michigan Press.

Eckstein, Harry. 1996. Lessons for the "Third Wave" from the First: An Essay on Democratization. Irvine: Center for the Study of Democracy, School of Social Sciences, University of California.

Economist. 1994. Democracy and Growth: Why Voting is Good for You. *Economist,* 27 August, 15–17.

Ellickson, Robert C. 1991. *Order Without Law: How Neighbors Settle Disputes.* Cambridge, Mass.: Harvard University Press.

Ellsaesser, Hugh W. 1995. Trends in Air Pollution in the United States. In *The State of Humanity,* ed. Julian Simon, 491–502. Cambridge, Mass.: Blackwell.

Elshtain, Jean Bethke. 1995. *Democracy on Trial.* New York: Basic Books.

Eltis, David. 1987. *Economic Growth and the Ending of the Transatlantic Slave Trade.* New York: Oxford University Press.

Emden, Paul H. 1939. *Quakers in Commerce: A Record of Business Achievement.* London: Sampson Low, Marston.

Engerman, Stanley L. 1986. Slavery and Emancipation in Comparative Perspective: A Look at Some Recent Debates. *Journal of Economic History* 46, no. 2 (June): 317–39.

———. 1997. The Standard of Living Debate in International Perspective: Measures and Indicators. In *Health and Welfare During Industrialization,* ed. Richard Steckel and Roderick Flood. Chicago: University of Chicago Press.

———. Forthcoming. Capitalism. In *Oxford Companion to United States History,* ed. Paul Boyer. New York: Oxford University Press.

Faison, Seth. 1995. Service With Some Bile. *New York Times,* 22 October, 4-4.

————. 1998. Cry Goes Up: Let a Hundred Garbage Cans Bloom!. *New York Times,* 23 April, A4.

Fenno, Richard F., Jr. 1973. *Congressmen in Committees.* Boston: Little, Brown.

Fischer, Stanley, and Alan Gelb. 1991. The Process of Socialist Economic Transformation. *Journal of Economic Perspectives* 5, no. 4 (Fall): 91–105.

Fishkin, James S. 1995. *The Voice of the People: Public Opinion and Democracy.* New Haven, Conn.: Yale University Press.

Fitzgerald, Frances. 1972. *Fire in the Lake: The Vietnamese and Americans in Vietnam.* New York: Vintage.

FOCUS. 1993. *Current Problems of Slovakia After the Split of the CSFR (October 1993).* Bratislava, Slovak Republic: Center for Social and Market Analysis.

Forster, E. M. 1951. *Two Cheers for Democracy.* New York: Harcourt, Brace & World.

Frank, Robert H. 1988. *Passions Within Reason: The Strategic Role of the Emotions.* New York: Norton.

Franklin, Benjamin. 1856. *The Works of Benjamin Franklin.* Ed. Jared Sparks. Boston: Whittlemore, Niles, and Hall.

French, Howard W. 1996. In One Poor African Nation, Democracy Thrives. *New York Times,* 16 October, A3.

Friedman, Milton. 1962. *Capitalism and Freedom.* Chicago: University of Chicago Press.

Friedman, Milton, and Rose Friedman. 1980. *Free to Choose: A Personal Statement.* New York: Harcourt Brace Jovanovich.

————. 1984. *Tyranny of the Status Quo.* San Diego, Calif.: Harcourt Brace Jovanovich.

Friedman, Thomas L. 1997. Berlin Wall, Part 2: Asia's New Route to Democracy. *New York Times,* 22 December, A21.

Fukuyama, Francis. 1989. The End of History? *National Interest,* Summer, 3–18.

————. 1992. *The End of History and the Last Man.* New York: Free Press.

————. 1995. *Trust: The Social Virtues and the Creation of Prosperity.* New York: Free Press.

Gallagher, David. 1990. Vargas Llosa Pans His Political and Intellectual Peers. *Wall Street Journal,* 6 April, A19.

Ganev, Venelin I. 1997. Bulgaria's Symphony of Hope. *Journal of Democracy* 8, no. 4 (October): 125–39.

Gati, Charles. 1996. If Not Democracy, What? Leaders, Laggards, and Losers in the Postcommunist World. In *Postcommunism: Four Perspectives,* ed. Michael Mandelbaum, 168–98. New York: Council on Foreign Relations.

Gellner, Ernest. 1988. Introduction. In *Europe and the Rise of Capitalism*, ed. Jean Baechler, John A. Hall and Michael Mann, 1–5. London: Basil Blackwell.

Geoghegan, Vincent. 1983. Marcuse and Autonomy. In *Democratic Theory and Practice*, ed. Graeme Duncan, 156–72. Cambridge: Cambridge University Press.

Gerschenkron, Alexander. 1962. *Economic Backwardness in Historical Perspective*. Cambridge, Mass.: Harvard University Press.

Gershman, Carl. 1989. The United States and the World Democratic Revolution. *Washington Quarterly* 12, no. 1 (Winter): 127–39.

Gilder, George. 1984. *The Spirit of Enterprise*. New York: Simon and Schuster.

Goldstein, Judith. 1988. Ideas, Institutions, and American Trade Policy. *International Organization* 42, no. 1 (Winter): 179–217.

————. 1989. The Impact of Ideas on Trade Policy: The Origins of U.S. Agricultural and Manufacturing Policies. *International Organization* 43, no. 1 (Winter): 31–71.

Gordon, Ellen J., and Luan Troxel. 1995. Minority Mobilization without War. Paper Delivered at the Conference on Post-Communism and Ethnic Mobilization. Cornell University, 21–22 April.

Graña, César. 1964. *Bohemian Versus Bourgeois: French Society and the French Man of Letters in the Nineteenth Century*. New York: Basic Books.

Greenhouse, Steven. 1996. Strikes Decrease To a 50-Year Low. *New York Times*, 29 January, A1.

Gregg, Alan. 1956. *Challenges to Contemporary Medicine*. New York: Columbia University Press.

Greif, Avner. 1993. Contract Enforceability and Economic Institutions in Early Trade: The Maghribi Traders' Coalition. *American Economic Review* 83, no. 3 (June): 525–48.

Hardin, Russell. 1991. Trusting Persons, Trusting Institutions. In *Strategy and Choice*, ed. Richard J. Zeckhauser, 185–209. Cambridge, Mass.: MIT Press.

Harding, Harry. 1998. Will China Democratize? The Halting Advance of Pluralism. *Journal of Democracy* 9, no. 1 (January): 11–17.

Harris, Richard. 1966. *A Sacred Trust*. New York: New American Library.

Harrison, David. 1997. Unquenchable Thirst for Freedom. *Guardian Weekly*, 29 December, 20.

Hartwell, R. M. 1995. *A History of the Mont Pelerin Society*. Indianapolis, Ind.: Liberty Fund.

Havel, Václav. 1995. The Responsibility of Intellectuals. *New York Review of Books,* 22 June 1995, 36–37.

Havelock, Eric A. 1957. *The Liberal Temper in Greek Politics.* New Haven, Conn.: Yale University Press.

Hayek, F. A., ed. 1954. *Capitalism and the Historians.* Chicago: University of Chicago Press.

———. 1988. *The Fatal Conceit: The Errors of Socialism.* Ed. W. W. Bartley, III. Chicago: University of Chicago Press.

Heard, Alexander. 1960. *The Costs of Democracy.* Chapel Hill: University of North Carolina Press.

Heilbroner, Robert. 1993. *21st Century Capitalism.* New York: Norton.

———. 1997. Economics by the Book. *Nation,* 20 October, 16–19.

Hellman, Joel S. 1998. Winners Take All: The Politics of Partial Reform in Postcommunist Transition. *World Politics* 50, no. 2 (January): 203–34.

Hess, Stephen. 1987. "Why Great Men Are Not Chosen Presidents": Lord Bryce Revisited. In *Elections American Style,* ed. A. James Reichley, 75–94. Washington, D.C.: Brookings Institution.

Hibbing, John R., and Elizabeth Theiss-Morse. 1995. *Congress As Public Enemy: Public Attitudes toward American Political Institutions.* New York: Cambridge University Press.

Hidy, Ralph W., and Muriel E. Hidy. 1955. *History of Standard Oil Company (New Jersey): Pioneering in Big Business, 1882–1911.* New York: Harper.

Higley, John, and Richard Gunther, eds. 1992. *Elites and Democratic Consolidation in Latin America and Southern Europe.* Cambridge: Cambridge University Press.

Hirsch, Fred. 1976. *The Social Limits to Growth.* Cambridge, Mass.: Harvard University Press.

Hirschman, Albert O. 1970. *Exit, Voice, and Loyalty: Responses to Decline in Firms, Organizations, and States.* Cambridge, Mass.: Harvard University Press.

———. 1977. *The Passions and the Interests: Political Arguments for Capitalism before Its Triumph.* Princeton, N.J.: Princeton University Press.

———. 1986. *Rival Views of Market Society and Other Recent Essays.* New York: Viking.

Historicus [George Allen Morgan]. 1949. Stalin on Revolution. *Foreign Affairs* 27, no. 2 (January): 175–214.

Hockstader, Lee. 1997. Bulgaria Slides Into Economic Collapse. *Guardian Weekly,* 16 February, 19.

Hoggart, Simon. 1997. A Thunderously Adequate Performance. *Guardian Weekly,* 19 October, 8.

Holmes, Stephen. 1993. *The Anatomy of Antiliberalism*. Cambridge, Mass.: Harvard University Press.

———. 1996. Cultural Legacies or State Collapse? Probing the Postcommunist Dilemma. In *Postcommunism: Four Perspectives,* ed. Michael Mandelbaum, 22–76. New York: Council on Foreign Relations.

Holmstrom, Bengt, and David M. Kreps. 1996. Examples for and Questions about: An Economic (?) Theory of Promises. Lionel McKenzie Lecture, University of Rochester, 28 March.

Hood, John M. 1996. *The Heroic Enterprise: Business and the Common Good.* New York: Free Press.

Howard, Michael. 1978. *War and the Liberal Conscience*. New Brunswick, N.J.: Rutgers University Press.

Hume, David. 1955. *David Hume: Writings on Economics.* Ed. Eugene Rotwein. Madison: University of Wisconsin Press.

Huntington, Samuel P. 1984. Will More Countries Become Democratic? *Political Science Quarterly* 99, no. 2 (Summer): 193–218.

———. 1991. *The Third Wave: Democratization in the Late Twentieth Century.* Norman: University of Oklahoma Press.

———. 1997. After Twenty Years: The Future of the Third Wave. *Journal of Democracy* 8, no. 4 (October): 3–12.

Iannaccone, Lawrence K., Roger Finke, and Rodney Stark. 1997. Deregulating Religion: The Economics of Church and State. *Economic Inquiry* 35, no. 2 (April): 350–64.

Inge, William Ralph. 1919. *Outspoken Essays.* London: Longmans, Green.

Inglehart, Ronald. 1997. *Modernization and Postmodernization: Cultural, Economic, and Political Change in 43 Countries.* Princeton, N.J.: Princeton University Press.

Inglehart, Ronald, and Jacques-Rene Rabier. 1986. Aspirations Adopt to Situations—But Why Are the Belgians So Much Happier Than the French? In *Research on the Quality of Life,* ed. Frank M. Andrews, 1–56. Ann Arbor: Institute for Social Research, University of Michigan.

Jäckel, Eberhard. 1981. *Hitler's World View: A Blueprint for Power.* Trans. Herbert Arnold. Cambridge, Mass.: Harvard University Press.

Jefferson, Thomas. 1939. *Democracy.* Ed. Saul K. Padover. New York: Appleton-Century.

———. 1944. *The Life and Selected Writings of Thomas Jefferson.* Ed. Adrienne Koch and William Peden. New York: Modern Library.

Jehl, Douglas. 1997. Persian Gulf's Young Turk: Sheik Hamad, Emir of Qatar. *New York Times,* 10 July, A1.

Jones, E. L. 1987. *The European Miracle: Environments, economies, and geopol-*

itics in the history of Europe and Asia. 2d ed. Cambridge: Cambridge University Press.

———. 1988. *Growth Recurring: Economic Change in World History.* Oxford: Oxford University Press.

Jouvenel, Bernard de. 1954. The Treatment of Capitalism by Continental Intellectuals. In *Capitalism and the Historians,* ed. F. A. Hayek, 93–123. Chicago: University of Chicago Press.

Judt, Tony. 1997. The Longest Road to Hell. *New York Times,* 22 December, A21.

Junn, Jane. 1991. Participation and Political Knowledge. In *Political Participation and American Democracy,* ed. William Crotty, 193–212. New York: Greenwood Press.

Kaeuper, Richard W. 1988. *War, Justice, and Public Order: England and France in the Later Middle Ages.* New York: Oxford University Press.

Kahn, Joseph. 1998. The Latest Asian Miracle: Chaos Without Coups. *New York Times,* 26 July, 4–5.

Kahneman, Daniel, Jack L. Knetsch, and Richard Thaler. 1986. Fairness as a Constraint on Profit Seeking: Entitlements in the Market. *American Economic Review* 76, no. 4 (September): 728–41.

Kamm, Thomas. 1990. Democracy in Argentina Buoyed as Armed Revolt Is Ended Fast. *Wall Street Journal,* 5 December, A13.

Kant, Immanuel. 1952. *The Critique of Judgement.* London: Oxford University Press.

———. 1957. *Perpetual Peace.* Trans. Louis White Beck. Indianapolis, Ind.: Bobbs-Merrill.

Kaufman, Robert R. 1986. Liberalization and Democratization in South America: Perspectives from the 1970s. In *Transitions from Authoritarian Rule: Comparative Perspectives,* ed. Guillermo O'Donnell, Philippe C. Schmitter, and Laurence Whitehead, 85–107. Baltimore: Johns Hopkins University Press.

Keniston, Kenneth. 1960. Alienation and the Decline of Utopia. *American Scholar* 29, no. 2 (Spring): 161–200.

Kennedy, John F. 1964. *Public Papers of the Presidents of the United States: John F. Kennedy, 1963.* Washington, DC: United States Government Printing Office.

Kennedy, Paul. 1987. *The Rise and Fall of the Great Powers.* New York: Random House.

———. 1993. *Preparing for the Twenty-first Century.* New York: Random House.

Kenner, H. J. 1936. *The Fight for the Truth in Advertising: A Story of What Business Has Done and Is Doing to Establish and Maintain Accuracy and Fair*

Play in Advertising and Selling for the Public's Protection. New York: Round Table Press.

Kershaw, Ian. 1987. *The "Hitler Myth": Image and Reality in the Third Reich.* New York: Oxford University Press.

Keynes, John Maynard. 1963. *Essays in Persuasion.* New York: Norton.

Klein, Daniel B., ed. 1997a. *Reputation: Studies in the Voluntary Elicitation of Good Conduct.* Ann Arbor: University of Michigan Press.

————. 1997b. Knowledge, Reputation, and Trust, by Voluntary Means. In *Reputation: Studies in the Voluntary Elicitation of Good Conduct,* ed. Daniel B. Klein, 1–14. Ann Arbor: University of Michigan Press.

————. 1997c. Trust for Hire: Voluntary Remedies for Quality and Safety. In *Reputation: Studies in the Voluntary Elicitation of Good Conduct,* ed. Daniel B. Klein, 97–133. Ann Arbor: University of Michigan Press.

Klein, Daniel B., and Jeremy Shearmur. 1997. Good Conduct in the Great Society: Adam Smith and the Role of Reputation. In *Reputation: Studies in the Voluntary Elicitation of Good Conduct,* ed. Daniel B. Klein, 29–45. Ann Arbor: University of Michigan Press.

Knox, MacGregor. 1982. *Mussolini Unleashed 1939–1941: Politics and Strategy in Fascist Italy's Last War.* New York: Cambridge University Press.

Kraus, Sidney, ed. 1962. *The Great Debates: Kennedy vs. Nixon, 1960.* Bloomington: University of Indiana Press.

Kreps, David M. 1990. Corporate Culture and Economic Theory. In *Perspectives on Positive Political Economy,* ed. James E. Alt and Kenneth A. Shepsle, 90–143. New York: Cambridge University Press.

Kristol, Irving. 1978. *Two Cheers for Capitalism.* New York: Basic Books.

Kunitz, Stephen, and Stanley L. Engerman. 1992. The Ranks of Death: Secular Trends in Income and Mortality. *Health Transition Review* 2 (supplementary issue): 29–46.

Kuteinikov, Andrei. 1990. Soviet Society—Much More Unequal Than U.S. *Wall Street Journal,* 26 January, A14.

Kuznets, Simon. 1961. *Capital in the American Economy: Its Formation and Financing.* Princeton, N.J.: Princeton University Press.

————. 1966. *Modern Economic Growth: Rate, Structure, and Spread.* New Haven, Conn.: Yale University Press.

Ladd, Everett C. 1996. The Data Just Don't Show Erosion of America's "Social Capital." *Public Perspective,* June/July, 1, 5–6.

Laitin, David D. 1995. The Civic Culture at 30. *American Political Science Review* 89, no. 1 (March): 168–73.

Lakoff, Sanford. 1996. *Democracy: History, Theory, Practice.* Boulder, Colo.: Westview.

Landes, David S. 1969. *The Unbound Prometheus: Technological Change and*

Industrial Development in Western Europe from 1750 to the Present. Cambridge: Cambridge University Press.

————. 1998. *The Wealth and Poverty of Nations: Why Some Are So Rich and Some So Poor.* New York: Norton.

Landsburg, Steven E. 1997. *Fair Play: What Your Child Can Teach You About Economics, Value, and the Meaning of Life.* New York: Free Press.

Lea, Homer. 1909. *The Valor of Ignorance.* New York: Harper.

Lebergott, Stanley. 1964. *Manpower in Economic Growth: The American Record since 1860.* New York: McGraw-Hill.

————. 1993. *Pursuing Happiness: American Consumers in the Twentieth Century.* Princeton, N.J.: Princeton University Press.

Leffler, Melvyn P. 1994. *The Specter of Communism: The United States and the Origins of the Cold War, 1917–1953.* New York: Hill and Wang.

Legum, Colin. 1990. The Coming of Africa's Second Independence. *Washington Quarterly* 11, no. 1 (Winter): 129–40.

Lemann, Nicholas. 1996. Kicking in Groups. *Harper's,* April, 22–26.

Lenin, Vladimir I. 1932. *State and Revolution.* New York: International Publishers.

Levin, Murray B. 1960. *The Alienated Voter: Politics in Boston.* New York: Holt.

Levinson, Wendy. 1994. Physician-Patient Communication: A Key to Malpractice Prevention. *JAMA* 272, no. 20 (23/30 November): 1619–20.

Lienesch, Michael. 1992. Wo(e)begon(e) Democracy. *American Journal of Political Science* 36, no. 4 (November): 1004–14.

Lijphart, Arend. 1997. Unequal Participation: Democracy's Unresolved Dilemma. *American Political Science Review* 91, no. 4 (March): 1–14.

Lindberg, Tod. 1996. Ready for Round Two? *Policy Review,* September–October, 38–42.

Lindblom, Charles E. 1977. *Politics and Markets: The World's Political-Economic Systems.* New York: Basic Books.

Linz, Juan J. 1978. *The Breakdown of Democratic Regimes: Crisis, Breakdown, and Reequilibration.* Baltimore: Johns Hopkins University Press.

Lipset, Seymour Martin. 1993a. Reflections on Capitalism, Socialism and Democracy. *Journal of Democracy* 4, no. 2 (April): 43–55.

————. 1993b. A Comparative Analysis of the Social Requisites of Democracy. *International Social Science Journal,* May, 155–75.

Luard, Evan. 1986. *War in International Society.* New Haven, Conn.: Yale University Press.

McAneny, Leslie, and David W. Moore. 1994. Annual Honesty & Ethics Poll. *Gallup Poll Monthly,* October, 2–4.

McCloskey, Deirdre W. 1998. Bourgeois Virtue and the History of *P* and *S*. *Journal of Economic History* 58, no. 2 (June): 297–317.

Macaulay, Stewart. 1963. Non-Contractual Relations in Business: A Preliminary Study. *American Sociological Review* 28, no. 1 (Fall): 55–69.

McCloskey, Donald N. 1990. *If You're So Smart: The Narrative of Economic Experience*. Chicago: University of Chicago Press.

———. 1994. Bourgeois Virtue. *American Scholar* 63, no. 2 (Spring): 177–91.

McCormack, Mark H. 1984. *What They Don't Teach You at Harvard Business School*. New York: Bantam.

———. 1989. *What They* Still *Don't Teach You at Harvard Business School*. New York: Bantam.

McGuire, Martin, and Mancur Olson. 1996. The Economics of Autocracy and Majority Rule: The Invisible Hand and the Use of Force. *Journal of Economic Literature* 34 (March): 72–96.

Machan, Tibor R. 1996. Business Bashing: Why Is Commerce Maligned? *Jobs & Capital*, Winter, 35–40.

Machiavelli, Niccolò. 1950. *The Prince and the Discourses*. Trans. Luigi Ricci. New York: Modern Library.

McInnes, Neil. 1995. Wrong for Superior Reasons. *National Interest*, Spring, 85–97.

———. 1998. Hayek's Slippery Slope. *National Interest*, Spring, 56–66.

Madison, James. 1788. *Federalist Papers, No. 10*. Various editions.

Mahan, Alfred Thayer. 1912. *Armaments and Arbitration: The Place of Force in the International Relations of States*. New York: Harper.

Malkiel, Burton G. 1996. *A Random Walk Down Wall Street*. New York: Norton.

Manion, Melanie. 1996. The Electoral Connection in the Chinese Countryside. *American Political Science Review* 90, no. 4 (December): 736–48.

Mansbridge, Jane. 1997. Normative Theory and *Voice and Equality*. *American Political Science Review* 91, no. 2 (June): 423–25.

Marody, Mira. 1997. Post-Transitology: Is There Any Life After Transition? *Polish Sociological Review*, 13–21.

Marshall, Alfred. 1890. *Principles of Economics*. London: Macmillan.

———. 1920. *Principles of Economics*. 8th ed. London: Macmillan.

Mason, David S. 1995. Justice, Socialism, and Participation in the Post-communist States. In *Social Justice and Political Change: Public Opinion in Capitalist and Post-Communist States*, ed. James R. Kluegel, David S. Mason and Bernd Wegener, 49–80. New York: Aldine De Gruyter.

Mayo, Elton. 1933. *The Human Problems of an Industrial Civilization.* New York: Macmillan.

Mencken, H. L. 1920. *Prejudices: Second Series.* New York: Knopf.

Merkle, Daniel M. 1996. The National Issues Convention Deliberative Poll. *Public Opinion Quarterly* 60, no. 4 (Winter): 588–619.

Meyer, Alfred G. 1957. *Leninism.* Cambridge, Mass.: Harvard University Press.

Michnik, Adam. 1997. Gray Is Beautiful: Thoughts on Democracy in Central Europe. *Dissent,* Spring, 14–19.

Milne, Alan Alexander. 1935. *Peace with Honour.* New York: Dutton.

Mises, Ludwig von. 1972 [1956]. *The Anticapitalistic Mentality.* Grove City, Pa.: Libertarian Press.

Moore, Barrington. 1966. *Social Origins of Dictatorship and Democracy.* New York: Basic Books.

Morgan, Edmund S. 1988. *Inventing the People: The Rise of Popular Sovereignty in England and America.* New York: Norton.

Morin, Richard. 1996. Who's in Control? Many Don't Know or Care. *Washington Post,* 29 January, A1.

Morin, Richard, and Dan Balz. 1996. Americans Losing Trust in Each Other and Institutions. *Washington Post,* 28 January, A1.

Morison, Samuel Eliot. 1963. *The Two-Ocean War: A Short History of the United States Navy in the Second World War.* Boston: Little, Brown.

Mosher, Stacy. 1991. Hong Kong: The Governor's Men. *Far Eastern Economic Review,* 3 October, 11–13.

Moynihan, Daniel Patrick. 1975. The American Experiment. *Public Interest,* no. 41 (Fall): 4–8.

Mueller, John. 1973. *War, Presidents and Public Opinion.* New York: Wiley.

———. 1977. Changes in American Public Attitudes toward International Involvement. In *The Limits of Military Intervention,* ed. Ellen Stern, 323–44. Beverly Hills, Calif.: Sage.

———. 1979. Public Expectations of War during the Cold War. *American Journal of Political Science* 23, no. 2 (May): 301–29.

———. 1984. Reflections on the Vietnam Protest Movement and on the Curious Calm at the War's End. In *Vietnam as History,* ed. Peter Braestrup, 151–57. Lanham, Md.: University Press of America.

———. 1985. *Astaire Dancing: The Musical Films.* New York: Knopf.

———. 1986. Containment and the Decline of the Soviet Empire: Some Tentative Reflections on the End of the World as We Know It. Paper given at the Annual Convention of the International Studies Association. Anaheim, Calif., 25–29 March. (http://www.rochester.edu/College/psc/Mueller)

———. 1988. Trends in Political Tolerance. *Public Opinion Quarterly* 52, no. 1 (Spring): 1–25.

———. 1989. *Retreat from Doomsday: The Obsolescence of Major War.* New York: Basic Books.

———. 1991. Is War Still Becoming Obsolete? Paper given at the Annual Meeting of the American Political Science Association. Washington, D.C., 29 August–1 September. (http://www.rochester.edu/College/psc/Mueller)

———. 1992a. Democracy and Ralph's Pretty Good Grocery: Elections, Inequality, and the Minimal Human Being. *American Journal of Political Science* 36, no. 4 (November): 983–1003.

———. 1992b. Theory and Democracy: A Reply to Michael Lienesch. *American Journal of Political Science* 36, no. 4 (November): 1015–22.

———. 1993. The Impact of Ideas on Grand Strategy. In *The Domestic Bases of Grand Strategy*, ed. Richard Rosecrance and Arthur A. Stein, 48–62. Ithaca, N.Y.: Cornell University Press.

———. 1994a. *Policy and Opinion in the Gulf War.* Chicago: University of Chicago Press.

———. 1994b. The Catastrophe Quota: Trouble After the Cold War. *Journal of Conflict Resolution* 38, no. 3 (September): 355–75.

———. 1995. *Quiet Cataclysm: Reflections on the Recent Transformation of World Politics.* New York: HarperCollins.

———. 1996a. Democracy, Capitalism and the End of Transition. In *Post-Communism: Four Views*, ed. Michael Mandelbaum, 102–67. New York: Council on Foreign Relations.

———. 1996b. Policy Principles for Unthreatened Wealth-Seekers. *Foreign Policy*, Spring, 22–33.

Muravchik, Joshua. 1992. *Exporting Democracy: Fulfilling America's Destiny.* Washington, D.C.: AEI Press.

Murray, Charles. 1988. *In Pursuit: Of Happiness and Good Government.* New York: Simon & Schuster.

Nadelmann, Ethan A. 1990. Global Prohibition Regimes: The Evolution of Norms in International Society. *International Organization* 44, no. 4 (Autumn): 479–526.

Nardulli, Peter F., Jon K. Dalager, and Donald E. Greco. 1996. Voter Turnout in U.S. Presidential Elections: An Historical View and Some Speculation. *PS: Political Science & Politics* 29, no. 3 (September): 480–90.

Needler, Martin. 1990. *Mexican Politics: The Containment of Conflict.* 2d ed. New York: Praeger.

Nelson, Michael. 1995. Why Americans Hate Politics and Politicians. *PS: Political Science & Politics,* 28, no. 1 (March): 72–77.

Neuman, W. Russell. 1986. *The Paradox of Mass Politics: Knowledge and Opinion in the American Electorate.* Cambridge, Mass.: Harvard University Press.

Nevaskar, Balwant. 1971. *Capitalists without Capitalism: The Jains of India and the Quakers of the West.* Westport, Conn.: Greenwood.

Nevins, Allan. 1940. *John D. Rockefeller: The Heroic Age of American Enterprise.* New York: Scribner's.

———. 1945. Letter to the Editor. *American Historical Review* 50, no. 3 (April): 676–89.

Niemi, Richard G., John Mueller, and Tom W. Smith. 1989. *Trends in Public Opinion: A Compendium of Survey Data.* Westport, Conn.: Greenwood.

Norris, Pippa. 1996. Does Television Erode Social Capital? A Reply to Putnam. *PS: Political Science & Politics* 29, no. 3 (September): 474–80.

North, Douglass C. 1990. *Institutions, Institutional Change and Economic Performance.* Cambridge: Cambridge University Press.

North, Douglass C., and Barry R. Weingast. 1989. Constitutions and Commitment: The Evolution of Institutions Governing Public Choice in Seventeenth-Century England. *Journal of Economic History* 49, no. 4 (December): 803–32.

Nozick, Robert. 1997. *Socratic Puzzles.* Cambridge, Mass.: Harvard University Press.

Nye, John V. C. 1997. Thinking About the State: Property Rights, Trade, and Changing Contractual Arrangements in a World with Coercion. In *The Frontiers of the New Institutional Economics,* ed. John N. Drobak and John V. C. Nye, 121–42. San Diego, Calif.: Academic Press.

O'Connor, John J. 1994. A Museum That's Its Own Best Exhibit. *New York Times,* 9 September.

O'Donnell, Guillermo, and Philippe C. Schmitter. 1986. *Transitions from Authoritarian Rule: Tentative Conclusions about Uncertain Democracies.* Baltimore: Johns Hopkins University Press.

Olson, Mancur. 1982. *The Rise and Decline of Nations: Economic Growth, Stagflation, and Social Rigidities.* New Haven, Conn.: Yale University Press.

———. 1993. Dictatorship, Democracy, and Development. *American Political Science Review* 87, no. 3 (September): 567–76.

Osler, William. 1932. *Aequanimitas: With Other Addresses to Medical Students, Nurses and Practitioners of Medicine.* 3d ed. Philadelphia: Blakiston.

Page, Benjamin I., and Robert Y. Shapiro. 1992. *The Rational Public: Fifty Years of Trends in American Policy Preferences.* Chicago: University of Chicago Press.

Palmer, R. R. 1959. *The Age of the Democratic Revolution: A Political History of Europe and America, 1760–1800: The Challenge.* Princeton, N.J.: Princeton University Press.

Passell, Peter. 1995. Economic Scene: Battered but Not Broken, the Honey Lobby Is Back and Winning. *New York Times,* 13 April, D2.

———. 1998a. Economic Scene: Socialism and Its Long Lines Are Alive and Well as Disneyland. *New York Times,* 2 April, C2.

———. 1998b. Economic Scene: Salmon Eaters Salute a Victory against the Protectionists. *New York Times,* 22 January, C2.

———. 1998c. Economic Scene: A New Project Will Measure the Cost and Effect of Regulation. *New York Times,* 30 July, C2.

Pateman, Carole. 1970. *Participation and Democratic Theory.* London: Cambridge University Press.

Patterson, Kelly D., and David B. Magleby. 1992. Trends: Public Support for Congress. *Public Opinion Quarterly* 56, no. 4 (Winter): 539–51.

Pei, Minxin. 1998. Is China Democratizing? *Foreign Affairs* 77, no. 1 (January/February): 68–82.

Perlez, Jane. 1990a. East-Bloc's Admirers in Africa Draw Line at Multiparty Politics. *New York Times,* 22 April, 12.

———. 1990b. Is Botswana a Model for Democracies in Africa? *New York Times,* 16 May, A6.

———. 1990c. For Democracy, Just a Nod at an African Meeting. *New York Times,* 10 July, A3.

———. 1993. In East Europe, Kmart Faces an Attitude Problem. *New York Times,* 7 July, D1.

Pessen, Edward. 1984. *The Log Cabin Myth: The Social Backgrounds of the Presidents.* New Haven, Conn.: Yale University Press.

Peters, Thomas J. 1994. *The Tom Peters Seminar: Crazy Times Call for Crazy Organizations.* New York: Vintage.

Peters, Thomas J., and Robert H. Waterman, Jr. 1982. *In Search of Excellence: Lessons from America's Best-Run Companies.* New York: Warner Books.

Pipes, Richard. 1984. *Survival Is Not Enough.* New York: Simon & Schuster.

Plato. 1957. *The Republic.* Trans. A. D. Lindsay. New York: Dutton.

Plattner, Marc F. 1988. Democracy Outwits the Pessimists. *Wall Street Journal,* 12 October, A18.

Plowden, Gene. 1967. *Those Amazing Ringlings and Their Circus.* Caldwell, Idaho: Caxton Printers.

Pogge von Strandmann, Hartmut. 1988. Germany and the Coming of War. In *The Coming of the First World War,* ed. R. J. W. Evans and Hartmut Pogge von Strandmann, 87–123. Oxford: Clarendon.

Pomper, Gerald M. 1974. *Elections in America: Control and Influence in Democratic Politics.* New York: Dodd, Mead.

Popkin, Samuel L. 1991. *The Reasoning Voter: Communication and Persuasion in Presidential Campaigns.* Chicago: University of Chicago Press.

Potok, Mark. 1994. Fear Grips Dallas after Driveway Attacks. *USA Today,* 22 March, 8A.

President's Commission on National Goals. 1960. *Goals for Americans.* New York: Prentice-Hall.

Preston, Samuel H. 1995. Human Mortality throughout History and Prehistory. In *The State of Humanity,* ed. Julian Simon, 30–36. Cambridge, Mass.: Blackwell.

Przeworski, Adam. 1986. Problems in the Study of Transition to Democracy. In *Transitions from Authoritarian Rule: Comparative Perspectives,* ed. Guillermo O'Donnell, Philippe C. Schmitter and Laurence Whitehead, 47–63. Baltimore: Johns Hopkins University Press.

Putnam, Robert D. 1993. *Making Democracy Work: Civic Traditions in Modern Italy.* Princeton, N.J.: Princeton University Press.

———. 1995a. Bowling Alone: America's Declining Social Capital. *Journal of Democracy* 6, no. 1 (January): 65–78.

———. 1995b. Tuning In, Tuning Out: The Strange Disappearance of Social Capital in America. *PS: Political Science & Politics* 28, no. 4 (December): 664–83.

Ramirez, Anthony. 1995. A Crackdown on Phone Marketing. *New York Times,* 10 February, D1.

Reder, Alan. 1994. *In Pursuit of Principle and Profit: Business Success Through Social Responsibility.* New York: Putnam's.

Reeves, Richard. 1993. *President Kennedy: Profile of Power.* New York: Simon & Schuster.

Riker, William H. 1965. *Democracy in the United States.* 2d ed. New York: Macmillan.

———. 1982. *Liberalism Against Populism.* San Francisco: Freeman.

———. 1996. *The Strategy of Rhetoric: Campaigning for the American Constitution.* New Haven, Conn.: Yale University Press.

Riskin, Carl. 1995. Feeding China: The Experience since 1949. In *The Po-*

litical Economy of Hunger, ed. Jean Drèze, Amartya Sen, and Athar Hussain. Oxford: Oxford University Press.

Rohter, Larry. 1996a. To U.S. Critics, a Sweatshop; To Hondurans, a Better Life. *New York Times,* 18 July, A1.

———. 1996b. A Chastened Latin Left Puts Its Hope in Ballots. *New York Times,* 29 July, A6.

———. 1998. Pope Asks Cubans to Seek New Path Toward Freedom. *New York Times,* 26 January, A1.

Romer, Christina. 1986a. Spurious Volatility in Historical Unemployment Data. *Journal of Political Economy* 94, no. 1 (February): 1–37.

———. 1986b. New Estimates of Prewar Gross National Product and Employment. *Journal of Economic History* 46, no. 2 (June): 341–52.

Rose, Richard. 1994. Getting By Without Government: Everyday Life in Russia. *Daedalus* 123, no. 3 (Summer): 41–62.

Rosecrance, Richard. 1986. *The Rise of the Trading State: Conquest and Commerce in the Modern World.* New York: Basic Books.

Rosenbaum, David E. 1997. Against the Current, Republican Senator Is Trying to Block Fund-Raising Restrictions. *New York Times,* 29 September, A12.

Rosenberg, Nathan. 1964. Neglected Dimensions in the Analysis of Economic Change. *Oxford Bulletin of Economics and Statistics* 26, no. 1 (February): 59–77.

———. 1975. Adam Smith on Profits—Paradox Lost and Regained. In *Essays on Adam Smith,* ed. Andrew S. Skinner and Thomas Wilson, 377–89. Oxford: Clarendon Press.

Rosenberg, Nathan, and L. E. Birdzell. 1986. *How the West Grew Rich: The Economic Transformation of the Industrial World.* New York: Basic Books.

Rosenberg, Tina. 1993. Meet the New Boss, Same as the Old Boss. *Harper's,* May, 47–53.

Rosenstone, Steven J., and John Mark Hansen. 1993. *Mobilization, Participation, and Democracy in America.* New York: Macmillan.

Rosenthal, A. M. 1993. New York to Clinton. *New York Times,* 1 October, A31.

Rothenberg, Lawrence S. 1992. *Linking Citizens to Government: Interest Group Politics at Common Cause.* New York: Cambridge University Press.

Rowen, Henry S. 1996. The Short March: China's Road to Democracy. *National Interest,* Fall, 61–70.

Rush, Myron. 1993. Fortune and Fate. *National Interest,* Spring, 19–25.

Russett, Bruce. 1972. *No Clear and Present Danger: A Skeptical View of the United States' Entry into World War II.* New York: Harper and Row.

Rustow, Dankwart A. 1970. Transitions to Democracy: Toward a Dynamic Model. *Comparative Politics* 2, no. 3 (April): 337–63.

Rutland, Peter. 1994/95. Has Democracy Failed Russia? *National Interest,* Winter, 3–12.

Sachs, Jeffrey. 1998. International Economics: Unlocking the Mysteries of Globalization. *Foreign Policy,* Spring, 97–109.

Samuelson, Robert J. 1995. The Price of Politics: Campaign Contributions Haven't Corrupted Congress. *Newsweek,* 28 August, 65.

Sandel, Michael J. 1996. *Democracy's Discontent: America in Search of a Public Philosophy.* Cambridge, Mass.: Harvard University Press.

Saxon, A. H. 1989. *P. T. Barnum: The Legend and the Man.* New York: Columbia University Press.

Scharnhorst, Gary. 1980. *Horatio Alger, Jr.* Boston: Twayne.

Scharnhorst, Gary, and with Jack Bales. 1985. *The Lost Life of Horatio Alger, Jr.* Bloomington: Indiana University Press.

Schemo, Diana Jean. 1997. Ecuador's Military Code: Democracy Is Better. *New York Times,* 11 February, A3.

Schilling, Warner R. 1965. Surprise Attack, Death, and War. *Journal of Conflict Resolution* 9, no. 3 (September): 285–90.

Schleh, Edward C. 1974. *The Management Tactician: Executive Tactics for Getting Results.* New York: McGraw-Hill.

Schlozman, Kay Lehman, and John T. Tierney. 1986. *Organized Interests and American Democracy.* New York: Harper & Row.

Schmitter, Philippe, and Terry Lynn Karl. 1991. What Democracy Is . . . And Is Not. *Journal of Democracy* 2, no. 3 (Summer): 75–88.

Schor, Juliet B. 1991. *The Overworked American: The Unexpected Decline of Leisure.* New York: Basic Books.

Schudson, Michael. 1998. *The Good Citizen: A History of American Civic Life.* New York: Free Press.

Schumpeter, Joseph A. 1950. *Capitalism, Socialism and Democracy.* 3d ed. New York: Harper & Row.

Scitovsky, Tibor. 1992. *The Joyless Economy: The Psychology of Human Satisfaction.* Rev. ed. New York: Oxford University Press.

Scott, Ian. 1989. *Political Change and the Crisis of Legitimacy in Hong Kong.* Honolulu: University of Hawaii Press.

Scott, Robert E. 1959. *Mexican Government in Transition.* Urbana: University of Illinois Press.

Seward, Desmond. 1991. *Metternich: The First European.* New York: Viking.

Shafir, Michael. 1993. Growing Political Extremism in Romania. *RFE/RL Research Report,* April, 18–22.

Sherrill, Kenneth. 1996. The Political Power of Lesbians, Gays, and Bisexuals. *PS: Political Science & Politics* 29, no. 3 (September): 469–73.

Shiller, Robert J., Maxim Boychko, and Vladimir Korobov. 1991. Popular Attitudes toward Free Markets: The Soviet Union and the United States Compared. *American Economic Review* 81, no. 3 (June): 385–400.

———. 1992. Hunting for *Homo Sovieticus:* Situational versus Attitudinal Factors in Economic Behavior. *Brookings Papers on Economic Activity* 1: 127–181, 193–194.

Simon, Julian L., ed. 1995. *The State of Humanity.* Cambridge, Mass.: Blackwell.

Simons, Marlise. 1997. Dutch Take "Third Way" to Prosperity. *New York Times,* 16 June, A6.

Skidelsky, Robert. 1996. *Keynes.* New York: Oxford University Press.

Small, Melvin. 1980. *Was War Necessary? National Security and U.S. Entry into War.* Beverly Hills, Calif.: Sage.

Smith, Adam. 1896. *Lectures on Justice, Police, Revenue and Arms.* Oxford: Clarendon.

———. 1976 [1776]. *An Inquiry into the Nature and Causes of the Wealth of Nations.* Oxford University Press. Oxford.

Smith, Hedrick. 1976. *The Russians.* New York: Quadrangle.

Smith, Sydney. 1956. *Selected Writings of Sydney Smith.* Ed. W. H. Auden. New York: Farrar, Straus and Cudahy.

Smith, Tom W. 1979. Happiness: Time Trends, Seasonal Variations, Intersurvey Differences, and Other Mysteries. *Social Psychological Quarterly* 42, no. 1 (March): 18–30.

Solman, Paul. 1997. Mutual Bet. PBS, *The NewsHour with Jim Lehrer,* 1 October.

Sorauf, Frank J. 1988. *Money in American Elections.* Glenview, Ill.: Scott, Foresman.

Specter, Michael. 1995. Borscht and Blini to Go: From Russian Capitalists, an Answer to McDonald's. *New York Times,* 9 August, D1.

Spencer, Herbert. 1909. *The Principles of Sociology.* New York: Appleton.

Squires, Jim. 1990. Television's Civil War. *Wall Street Journal,* 8 October, A12.

Stanley, Alessandra. 1995. A Toast! To the Good Things About Bad Times. *New York Times,* 1 January, 4-1.

Steckel, Richard, and Robin Simons. 1992. *Doing Best by Doing Good: How to Use Public-Purpose Partnerships to Boost Corporate Profits and Benefit Your Community.* New York: Dutton.

Steinert, Marlis G. 1977. *Hitler's War and the Germans: Public Mood and Attitude during the Second World War.* Athens: Ohio University Press.

Steinhauer, Jennifer. 1998. The Undercover Shoppers: Posing as Customers, Paid Agents Grade the Stores. *New York Times,* 4 February, C1.

Stigler, George J. 1959. The Politics of Political Economists. *Quarterly Journal of Economics* 73, no. 4 (November): 522–32.

———. 1975. *The Citizen and the State: Essays on Regulation.* Chicago: University of Chicago Press.

———. 1982. *The Economist as Preacher and Other Essays.* Chicago: University of Chicago Press.

———. 1984. *The Intellectual and the Marketplace.* Cambridge, Mass.: Harvard University Press.

Stokes, Gale. 1993. Is It Possible to Be Optimistic about Eastern Europe? *Social Research* 60, no. 4 (Winter): 685–704.

Sullivan, Kevin. 1997. Cost of Economic Equality Questioned. *Guardian Weekly,* 8 June, 17.

Summers, Lawrence H. 1992. The Next Chapter. *International Economic Insights,* May/June, 12–16.

Tawney, R. H. 1962 [1926]. *Religion and the Rise of Capitalism.* Gloucester, Mass.: Peter Smith.

Teixeira, Ruy A. 1992. *The Disappearing American Voter.* Washington, D.C.: Brookings Institution.

Thaler, Richard. 1985. Mental Accounting and Consumer Choice. *Marketing Science* 4, no. 3 (Summer): 199–214.

Thucydides. 1934. *The Pelopennesian War.* New York: Modern Library.

Tilly, Richard. 1993. Moral Standards and Business Behaviour in Nineteenth-Century Germany and Britain. In *Bourgeois Society in Nineteenth-Century Europe,* ed. Jürgen Kocka and Allen Mitchell, 179–206. Oxford: Berg.

Tocqueville, Alexis de. 1990. *Democracy in America.* Trans. Henry Reeve. New York: Vintage.

Toner, Robin. 1994. Pollsters See a Silent Storm That Swept Away Democrats. *New York Times,* 16 November, A14.

———. 1995. G.O.P. Gets Mixed Reviews From Public Wary on Taxes. *New York Times,* 6 April, A1.

Trachtenberg, Alan. 1990. Introduction. In *Ragged Dick, Or, Street Life in New York with the Boot Blacks.* by Horatio Alger, Jr. New York: Signet.

Treitschke, Heinrich von. 1916. *Politics.* New York: Macmillan.

Troy, Gil. 1997. Money and Politics: The Oldest Connection. *Wilson Quarterly* 21, no. 3 (Summer): 14–32.

Urquhart, John, and Peggy Berkowitz. 1987. Northern Angst. *Wall Street Journal,* 22 September, 1.

Uslaner, Eric M. 1993. *The Decline of Comity in Congress.* Ann Arbor: University of Michigan Press.

Vaill, Peter B. 1989. *Managing as a Performing Art: New Ideas for a World of Chaotic Change.* San Francisco: Jossey-Bass.

Veenhoven, Ruut. 1991. Is Happiness Relative? *Social Indicators Research* 24 (February): 1–34.

———. 1993. *Happiness in Nations: Subjective Appreciation of Life in 56 Nations 1946–1992.* Rotterdam: Erasmus University of Rotterdam Department of Social Sciences.

Verba, Sidney, and Norman H. Nie. 1972. *Participation in America: Political Democracy and Social Equality.* New York: Harper & Row.

Verba, Sidney, Kay Lehman Schlozman, and Henry E. Brady. 1995. *Voice and Equality: Civic Voluntarianism in American Politics.* Cambridge, Mass.: Harvard University Press.

Verba, Sidney, Kay Lehman Schlozman, Henry E. Brady, and Norman E. Nie. 1993. Citizen Activity: Who Participates? What Do They Say? *American Political Science Review* 87, no. 2 (June): 303–18.

Waltz, Kenneth N. 1979. *Theory of International Politics.* Reading, Mass.: Addison-Wesley.

Wang, Hongying. Forthcoming. *Law, Diplomacy and Transnational Networks: The Dynamics of Foreign Direct Investment in China.* New York: Oxford University Press.

Warr, Mark. 1995. Trends: Public Opinion on Crime and Punishment. *Public Opinion Quarterly* 59, no. 2 (Summer): 296–310.

Wasilewski, Jacek. 1998. The Fates of Nomenklatura Elites in Postcommunist Eastern Europe. In *Elites, Crises, and the Origins of Regimes,* ed. Mattei Dogan and John Higley. Boulder, Colo.: Rowman & Littlefield.

Wattenberg, Ben. 1997. Going Ga-Ga over the Golden Age. *Washington Times,* 20 March, A17.

Waugh, Auberon. 1986. *Brideshead Benighted.* Boston: Little, Brown.

Weber, Max. 1958 [1904–5]. *The Protestant Ethic and the Spirit of Capitalism.* Trans. Talcott Parsons. New York: Scribner's.

Weeks, David C. 1993. *Ringling: The Florida Years, 1911–1936.* Gainesville: University Press of Florida.

Weingast, Barry R. 1997. The Political Foundations of Limited Government: Parliament and Sovereign Debt in 17th- and 18th-Century England. In *The Frontiers of the New Institutional Economics,* ed. John N. Drobak and John V. C. Nye, 213–46. San Diego, Calif.: Academic Press.

Weinstein, Michael M. 1997. Dr. Doom Becomes Dr. Pangloss. *New York Times,* 18 August, A18.

Weissberg, Robert. 1998. *Political Tolerance: Balancing Community and Diversity.* Thousand Oaks, Calif.: Sage.

Wells, H. G. 1908. *First and Last Things: A Confession of Faith and a Rule of Life.* New York: Putnam's Sons.

West, Rebecca. 1941. *Black Lamb and Grey Falcon: A Journey through Yugoslavia.* New York: Viking.

White, Michael. 1997. We Care Too, Says Hague. *Guardian Weekly,* 19 October, 8.

Whitehead, Laurence. 1986. International Aspects of Democratization. In *Transitions from Authoritarian Rule: Comparative Perspectives,* ed. Guillermo O'Donnell, Philippe C. Schmitter, and Laurence Whitehead, 3–46. Baltimore: Johns Hopkins University Press.

Whitman, David. 1998. *The Optimism Gap: The I'm OK–They're Not Syndrome and the Myth of American Decline.* New York: Walker.

Wiarda, Howard J. 1976. *Transcending Corporatism? The Portuguese Corporative System and the Revolution of 1974.* Columbia: Institute of International Studies, University of South Carolina.

Wiebe, Robert H. 1995. *Self-Rule: A Cultural History of American Democracy.* Chicago: University of Chicago Press.

Will, George F. 1990. *Men At Work: The Craft of Baseball.* New York: Macmillan.

Williams, Lena. 1990. Free Choice: When Too Much Is Too Much. *New York Times,* 14 February, C1.

Wilson, James Q. 1961. The Strategy of Protest: Problems of Negro Civic Action. *Journal of Conflict Resolution* 5, no. 3 (September): 291–303.

———. 1991. *On Character.* Washington, D.C.: The AEI Press.

———. 1993. *The Moral Sense.* New York: Free Press.

———. 1995. Capitalism and Morality. *Public Interest,* Fall, 42–60.

Woldman, Albert A. 1950. Lincoln Never Said That. *Harper's,* May, 70–74.

Woodward, Susan L. 1995. *Balkan Tragedy: Chaos and Dissolution After the Cold War.* Washington, D.C.: Brookings Institution.

Woolsey, R. James, Jr. 1993. Testimony before the Senate Intelligence Committee. 2 February.

Wright, Richard. 1937. *Black Boy.* Cleveland, Ohio: World.

Wright, Quincy. 1968. War: The Study of War. In *International Encyclopedia of the Social Sciences,* 16: 453–68.

Yang, Alan S. 1997. Trends: Attitudes toward Homosexuality. *Public Opinion Quarterly* 61, no. 3 (Fall): 477–507.

Yardeni, Edward. Forthcoming. The Economic Consequences of the Peace. In *Peace, Prosperity, and Politics,* ed. John Mueller. New York: Westview.

Yergin, Daniel. 1991. *The Prize: The Epic Quest for Oil, Money, and Power.* New York: Simon & Schuster.

Yergin, Daniel, and Joseph Stanislaw. 1998. *The Commanding Heights: The Battle between Government and the Marketplace That Is Remaking the Modern World.* New York: Simon & Schuster.

Zakaria, Fareed. 1997. The Rise of Illiberal Democracy. *Foreign Affairs* 76, no. 6 (November/December): 22–43.

Zweig, Jason. 1997. How to Beat 77% of Fund Investors Year after Year: That's What Indexers Have Done for More than Two Decades. *Money,* August, 136–39.

* Index *

Barnum, P. T. (*cont.*)
  virtues, 80–81; on fair dealing, 28;
  on fortune favoring the brave, 50–
  51; on money getters as benefac-
  tors, 53; on profitable philanthropy,
  34; respect toward his employees,
  256n.22; "there's a sucker born
  every minute," 24, 275n.23; "you
  can't fool all of the people all of the
  time," 275n.23
Barnum and Bailey circus, 25, 91
Barr, James, 268n.27
Barro, Robert, 201–2, 286nn. 6, 9
Bellah, Robert N., 280n.49
Ben and Jerry's ice cream, 34, 40
Bennet, James, 263n.21, 265n.41
Bennett, Christopher, 281n.59
Bennett, Robert, 172
Benson, Bruce L., 264n.29, 266n.59
Berelson, Bernard R., 275n.28,
  280n.50
Berger, Peter L., 232, 269n.27
Bergson, Abram, 258n.66
Berke, Richard L., 279n.27
Berkowitz, Peggy, 267n.20
Berlin, Isaiah, 206–7
Bermeo, Nancy, 280n.56
Bernhardi, Friedrich, 67
Better Business Bureau, 23, 27, 63, 91
Bettmann, Otto L., 272n.66
Beverly Hillbillies, 185
Bialer, Seweryn, 285n.46
bigness, resentment focused on, 51
Birdzell, L. E., 132; on acquisitiveness,
  79; on business morality's rise, 76,
  262n.8; capitalism as defined by, 22;
  cited, 258nn. 51, 55, 66, 260n.14,
  262n.12, 266n.1, 267n.23, 270n.45,
  271n.48; on commercial legal sys-
  tem, 97; on economic misery in
  human history, 261n.2; on the factory system, 58, 78–79; on innovation, 60, 107, 236, 237; on the
  West's economic growth, 73–74,
  130
Bismarck, Otto von, 9, 174, 175, 179
Bittel, Lester R., 62, 256n.22

black Americans, 159, 189, 277n.42
Blair, Tony, 69
Blakeslee, Sandra, 266n.3
Blobaum, Robert E., 264n.35
Blumin, Stuart M., 278n.5
Boesche, Roger, 260nn. 14, 27
boom-and-bust cycles, 122
boredom, 126–27
Bosnia-Hercegovina, 188
Botswana, 198, 199, 225
Bradsher, Keith, 263n.23, 264n.37
Brady, Henry E., 273n.9, 278nn. 13,
  16
Brams, Steven J., 256n.13
Brandeis, Louis D., 258n.61
Brandt, Willy, 214
Brazil, 201
Brearly, Harry Chase, 265n.45
Brecht, Bertolt, 260n.18
Brezhnev, Leonid, 156, 221, 285n.50
Bright, John, 268n.24
Britain: Blair, 69; Channel Tunnel,
  117; commerce and the legal system in, 97; consent of the governed
  in, 283n.22; Conservative Party as
  viewed in, 281n.62; contested suc-
  cessions in, 276n.38; decolonization, 215; as a democracy, 138, 144;
  democracy's rise in, 199, 203, 209,
  250; empire of, 268n.23; happiness
  and wealth associated in, 124;
  Labour Party clause on common
  ownership, 232; life expectancy
  at birth, 102; Smith on London
  merchants, 84; stability of, 238;
  Thatcher, 69, 103, 202, 271n.49;
  transition from monarchy to
  democracy, 108; Victoria, 209; virtuous business behavior in, 44, 90
Broder, David S., 173, 176, 278nn. 15,
  16
Brody, Jane E., 267n.10
Brontë, Charlotte, 12
Brooke, James, 284n.39, 285n.40
Brossard, Mario A., 287n.16
Brothers Karamazov, The (Dostoyevsky),
  153–54

The Court and the Country

The Court
and the Country

The Beginning of
the English Revolution

PEREZ ZAGORIN

Atheneum   NEW YORK

1970

To H.S. and A.D.Z.

'Grau, teurer Freund, ist alle Theorie
Und grün des Lebens goldner Baum.'

Contents

Preface

The revolution of 1640–1660 is the highest mountain in the English seventeenth-century landscape, towering over events before and after. I have sought in the following work to add to the general understanding of the English revolution from its origins to the inception of the civil war in 1642. My aim throughout has been to penetrate the specific factors, political, social, and religious, that engendered the revolt against Charles I and determined its character and progress. Comparative considerations relative to the sixteenth–seventeenth-century revolutions in general have not been absent from my mind and are taken up especially in the first two chapters. They have been strictly subordinated, however, to the task of investigating the process of revolution in England. As far as any single theme predominates, it is the organization, tactics, principles, and ideas of the movement of opposition to the Stuart régime. I have attempted to trace these from the formation of the Country opposition in the 1620s to the emergence of the Parliamentarian party in 1641–42. The method I have chosen is as far as possible interpretative and analytic. Accordingly, when I give any connected narrative of events or transactions, as is particularly the case in chapters seven through nine, I do so in order to clarify and set in relief the themes and problems which have claimed my interest.

This book doubtless contains many weaknesses, but it would contain still more, had I not been able to draw freely on the writings of other scholars who have done significant work on the period with which I deal. The amount of research in sixteenth–seventeenth-century British history has become enormous during the past twenty years—more, indeed, than a single student can possibly control. As regards learning, originality, and suggestiveness, some of it stands on the highest level of the historical scholarship of our time. I have tried to avail myself of this to the best of my ability, and hope that my notes give an adequate indication of my indebtedness. Of the older writers, I have had frequent recourse to the great work of S. R. Gardiner.

Preface

At this date his history of England from the time of James I to the Cromwellian protectorate is perhaps more to be consulted than read. It remains indispensable, nevertheless, in the masterly scope, accuracy, and detail of its narrative, while in part, at least, its interpretation of the English conflict still continues to hold sway.

Among the manuscripts I have used, the most important is Sir Simonds D'Ewes's Journal of the Long Parliament in the Harleian manuscripts at the British Museum. D'Ewes, who represented Sudbury in the House of Commons, left an incomparable record of the Commons' transactions down to 1645. In 1923, when Professor Wallace Notestein of Yale University published an edition of D'Ewes's Journal for the period 3 November 1640–20 March 1641, he declared in the Preface: 'No private journal of Parliament during the seventeenth century, or for that matter in any century, can compare in importance with that of Sir Simonds D'Ewes.' Nearly twenty years later, Professor Willson Coates of the University of Rochester published a further edition of D'Ewes covering the period 12 October 1641–10 January 1642. I am indebted to both these editions. At present, however, though nearly a half-century has elapsed since Notestein's words, far the greater part of D'Ewes's Journal is still unpublished. This can only be described as a scandal to Anglo-American scholarship and a glaring void in the considerable body of work devoted to parliamentary history in recent years.

I have incurred numerous obligations in writing this book, which I acknowledge with gratitude. Fellowships from the Canada Council and the Social Science Research Council enabled me to do a considerable part of my research in England. At a subsequent stage, a fellowship from the Folger Library in Washington, awarded while I was visiting professor of history at the Johns Hopkins University, provided me with invaluable facilities as well as the unexcelled amenities of a great research institution. My thanks are due to the librarians and staffs of the following: the British Museum Reading Room, North Library, and Department of Manuscripts; the Public Record Office; the City of London Guildhall Record Office; Dr. Williams's Library; the Bodleian Library; the Sheffield Central Library; the Folger Library; and the libraries of McGill University, the University of Rochester, and Yale University.

To the following I express appreciation for materials they have allowed me to use: Viscount De L'Isle, for permission to read his manuscripts in the Public Record Office; the Marquess of Salisbury, for permission to read the Cecil manuscripts in microfilm deposited in the British Museum; Earl Fitzwilliam and the Trustees of Earl Fitzwilliam's Wentworth Estates Company, for permission to read the Strafford manuscripts in the Sheffield Central Library.

Preface

I also thank: Professor H. N. Fieldhouse, Academic Vice-Principal Emeritus of McGill University; Mr. Roger Ellis, Secretary of the Historical Manuscripts Commission; Dr. L. B. Wright, Director of the Folger Library, who procured at my request a microfilm of D'Ewes's Journal; Professor Willson Coates of the University of Rochester, who permitted me to use his transcript of the portion of D'Ewes's Journal from 11 January to 21 March 1642; Mr. John Bebbington, Sheffield City Librarian, who provided me with the microfilm of a document in the Strafford manuscripts; the Warden and Fellows of Wadham College, who gave me hospitality as a member of their Senior Common Room when I resided in Oxford.

I have had the assistance of my graduate students, Mrs. Susan Guralnik and Mrs. Jean Woy, in preparing this book for publication. Mrs. Claire Sundeen, who typed my manuscript, has rendered invaluable service.

I have given dates according to the 'Old Style' or Julian calendar, which still prevailed in England in the seventeenth century; by contrast, however, I have reckoned the year as beginning on 1 January, rather than, as the contemporary English usage was, on 25 March. Most of the seventeenth-century works cited were published in London. In transcribing documents, I have consistently followed the originals in all points of grammar, spelling, and syntax, except when changes became necessary for the sake of intelligibility.

P. ZAGORIN

Abbreviations

Add.	Additional manuscripts.
B.M.	British Museum.
C.J.	*Journal of the House of Commons.*
C.S.P.D.	*Calendar of State Papers Domestic.*
C.S.P.V.	*Calendar of State Papers . . . in the archives and collections of Venice. . . .*
Clarendon, *Life*	*The life of Edward earl of Clarendon written by himself,* Oxford, 1843 [bound in and paginated continuously with *The history of the rebellion*].
Clarendon, *Rebellion*	Edward earl of Clarendon, *The history of the rebellion and civil wars begun in the year 1641,* ed. W. D. Macray, 6 v., Oxford, 1888 [references are to book and paragraph].
Coates, *D'Ewes*	*The journal of Sir Simonds D'Ewes from the first recess of the Long Parliament to the withdrawal of King Charles from London,* ed. W. Coates, New Haven, 1942.
D.N.B.	*Dictionary of National Biography.*
E.H.R.	*English Historical Review.*
An exact collection	*An exact collection of all remonstrances, declarations, votes, orders, ordinances, proclamations, petitions, messages, answers, and other remarkable passages betweene the Kings most excellent Majesty and his high court of Parliament . . . December 1641 . . . untill March the 21, 1643,* 1643.

Abbreviations

S. R. Gardiner, *History*	S. R. Gardiner, *History of England from the accession of James I to the outbreak of the civil war, 1603–42*, 10 v., L., 1883–84.
Harl.	*Harleian manuscripts.*
H.M.C.	*Reports and calendars issued by the Royal Commission on Historical Manuscripts.*
Journal	Journal of the common council of the city of London, Guildhall record office.
L.	London, used in footnotes as place of publication.
L.J.	*Journal of the House of Lords.*
Notestein, *D'Ewes*	*The journal of Sir Simonds D'Ewes from the beginning of the Long Parliament to the trial of the earl of Strafford*, ed. W. Notestein, New Haven, 1923.
P.R.O.	Public Record Office.
Repertories	Repertories of the aldermanic bench of the city of London, Guildhall record office.
J. Rushworth	J. Rushworth, *Historical collections of private passages of state*, 8 v., L., 1682–1721.
S.P.	State Papers.

1

Introduction

In the middle years of the seventeenth century, a tempest of rebellions and civil wars broke over the greatest of the European monarchies and for a space engulfed them. The nations were already treading a grisly dance of death in the long war which, beginning in 1618 with the Bohemian insurrection, had gradually grown into a general conflict of the powers. Smitten by a flail of iron, the provinces of Germany and other seats of war bled under the marchings and devastations of the soldiery. Then to this sanguinary international rivalry of dynasties was added the further affliction of domestic insurrections and internal wars. Widespread revolts spanned the years of the 1640s and '50s. Scotland, England, and Ireland, the kingdoms of the Stuart, Charles I; Catalonia, Portugal, Sicily, and Naples, the realms of the Spanish Habsburg, Philip IV; France of the young Bourbon, Louis XIV: in all these lands the flocks threw off their subjection and about the princely shepherds of the people the storm winds blew, menacing their authority, threatening the loss of great domains long in possession, even endangering their thrones.

Civil disturbances, though for the most part of lesser dimension, also overtook other of the states of Europe. The Dutch republic passed through a sharp tussle with its princely family of Orange which resulted in the extinction of the latter's power and a new form of republican regime for many years. Sweden under Queen Christina was wracked simultaneously by a deep constitutional and social crisis. In the Swiss cantons a peasant Jacquerie broke out. The Ukraine, then ruled by the King of Poland, was the ground of one of the greatest serf and Cossack insurrections ever to occur in eastern Europe.

Was there an identical conjuncture of malign planets presiding at that period over the destinies of the unlucky governors of states whose influence can account for these many rebellions and disturbances? Did the latter possess a common character and result from the same set of causes? Did they belong, as it were, to a single constellation and

1

thus constitute what has been called a 'general crisis' of the seventeenth century?[1]

Contemporaries impressed by the extent of the revolts occasionally noted resemblances but were unable to go beyond this. An English writer compared the rebellion of Ireland to that of Catalonia and Portugal, while several Italians composed meagre chronicles of the, civil wars of their time.[2] The councillors of Queen Christina interested themselves in news from England and France and spoke forebodingly of the 'spiritus vertiginis' abroad.[3] The Brandenburg Elector, Frederick William, accused the Estates in his recently acquired Rhenish principalities of seeking to emulate the English Parliamentarians.[4]

Such commonplaces aside, a close view of the struggles in question would show at best a series of partial parallelisms with little inner connection, rather than a general crisis.[5] Not only the rebellions against the different sovereigns, but even those within the realms of the same prince, originated and developed in almost complete independence of each other. The closest link was that between Scotland and England, where the heads of the resistance to Charles I actually established mutual relations. But no such thing happened in the Spanish empire, and the risings of Catalonia and Portugal in 1640, of Sicily and Naples in 1647, proceeded entirely separately.[6]

[1] An attempt to deal with the seventeenth-century revolutions collectively was made by R. B. Merriman, *Six contemporaneous revolutions*, Oxford, 1938. More recently there has been much discussion of the 'crisis of the seventeenth century'; cf. E. Hobsbawm, 'The crisis of the seventeenth century', *Past and present*, 5, 6 (1954), a brilliant but unconvincing account premised on the (to-say-the-least) questionable Marxian view that the crucial problem of early modern history is the transition from feudalism to capitalism. A better analysis, though also unconvincing, is H. R. Trevor-Roper's 'The general crisis of the seventeenth century', *ibid.*, 16 (1959). A symposium on the seventeenth-century revolutions is in *ibid.*, 13 (1958), and a discussion of Trevor-Roper's article by E. H. Kossmann, E. J. Hobsbawm, J. H. Hexter, R. Mousnier, J. H. Elliott, and L. Stone appears in *ibid.*, 18 (1960). The contribution by M. Roberts, 'Queen Christina and the general crisis of the seventeenth century', *ibid.*, 22 (1962), should also be read. Some of these papers previously printed in *Past and present* are now collected in *Crisis in Europe 1560–1660*, ed. T. Aston, L., 1965.
[2] H.G., *England's present distractions paralleled with those of Spaine, and other foraigne countries*, 1642; Masolino Bisaccioni, *Historia delle guerre civili di questi ultimi tempi*, Venice, 1653; G. B. Birago-Avogadro, *Delle historie memorabili che contiene le sollevationi di stato di nostri tempi*, Venice, 1653.   [3] M. Roberts, *op. cit.*
[4] F. L. Carsten, *Princes and parliaments in Germany*, Oxford, 1959, 302.
[5] Justifiable scepticism as to the 'general crisis' has been expressed by E. H. Kossmann, *Past and present*, 18 (1960), 8–11 and Q. Skinner, *E.H.R.*, LXXXI, 321 (1966), 791–5.
[6] It has been pointed out, however, that in Palermo, where the Sicilian

Moreover, the many elements that determined the nature of these revolts also differed largely. There were significant contrasts in the groups and classes who rose, in the aims pursued by their leaders, in their programmes and ideas, as well as in the depth and intensity of the rebellions, the stages through which they passed, and their ultimate results.

The grievances, too, that produced the secret swellings and hollow gusts before the tempest varied considerably from state to state. As to these in general, we may take a hint from Francis Bacon. A thinker in an age when public order was always precarious, a councillor who had seen how the Netherlands rebellion and the French wars of religion caused mighty monarchies to totter, Bacon had reflected deeply on the causes of revolution in his time. The grounds of troubles in states, he said, are

innovation in religion; taxes; alteration of laws and customs; breaking of privileges; general oppression; advancement of unworthy persons; strangers; dearths; disbanded soldiers; factions grown desperate; and whatsoever in offending people joineth and knitteth them in a common cause.[1]

Add to this list religious persecution and provincial oppression (if Bacon's account does not already imply them) and we should have the complete repertoire of motives to sedition in the sixteenth- and seventeenth-century rebellions.

Although some of these were common to more than one state, their incidence and the circumstances in which they manifested themselves formed in every case a pattern of particular causes incommensurable with that prevailing elsewhere. Ireland, for instance, like Catalonia, found a cue to revolt in the alien rule from which it suffered. But here resemblance ended. For Ireland's subjection to England was far greater than Catalonia's to its Spanish master. If Ireland before its rebellion had been governed too hard, Catalonia had been governed too little. Sudden withdrawal of a strong arm in the one, attempts to introduce fresh pressures in the other, alike ended in revolt. In addition, while the Catholic Catalans were ruled

---

[1] F. Bacon, *Essays*, 'Of seditions and troubles.'

---

revolt broke out in May 1647, the news of the revolt of Naples two months later may have influenced the guilds and their consuls to think of overthrowing the Spanish regime. At the beginning the slogan of the Sicilian rising had been, 'Long live the King and down with the taxes and the bad Government'; cf. H. L. Koenigsberger, 'The revolt of Palermo in 1647' *Cambridge historical journal*, VIII, 2 (1945), 133, 135.

by a dynasty of the same faith as their own, the Irish felt their hardships doubled in having to endure the persecution of a heretical religion.[1]

Probably the most common condition making for rebellion in these star-crossed decades was the strain resulting from the Thirty Years War. The prolonged military operations and the maintenance of armies on a scale never before attained, necessitated crushing costs and burdens. These the beset combatants endeavoured to meet by fiscal demands and exactions which eventually provoked resistance not only from the peasants and urban poor but also from the aristocratic and privileged orders. The hatred which the cardinals Richelieu and Mazarin aroused in France, and the count-duke of Olivares in Spain, was partly a consequence of the financial expedients to which these prepotent ministers were constrained to resort. Neither for the first nor last time war, and for Spain grave defeats as well, proved to be the midwife of revolt.

Yet even the frictions generated internally by the Thirty Years War were restricted in their range. Charles I's kingdoms had no share in them. Only France and the possessions of imperial Spain were affected, and of the latter, the kingdom of Portugal and the principality of Catalonia, whose burdens were least, revolted, while Castile, the most severely exploited of all Philip IV's realms, remained quiescent.[2]

Amidst these differences and the prevalence of particular causes, one broad feature nevertheless characterized in some degree the context of nearly all the mid-century rebellions. Most of them were directed against a monarchical power which, however vulnerable at the moment of revolt because of war or other difficulties, had grown during the preceding decades more centralized, more capable of imposing its will, more uniform in controlling and disciplining all ranks of its subjects. The outstanding exception was the Dutch republic, where the process had been checked through the prosperous outcome of the rebellion against Spain. There, too, however, it was opposition to the ambition of the stadholder Prince of Orange that

---

[1] Comparing the situation of the Irish with that of the Dutch, Lord Burghley once remarked that 'the Flemings had no such cause to protest against Spanish oppression as the Irish against the tyranny of England'; cf. C. Read, *Lord Burghley and Queen Elizabeth*, L., 1960, 9. Catalonia's relation to the monarchy of Spain is described in J. H. Elliott's notable work, *The revolt of the Catalans*, Cambridge, 1963.

[2] The importance of the effects of the Thirty Years War in provoking revolution has been stressed by Mousnier and Elliott, *Past and present*, 18 (1960), 23–4, 29–30, and by H. L. Koenigsberger, 'The revolt of Palermo in 1647,' *loc. cit.*, 130; cf. also J. H. Elliott, *The revolt of the Catalans*, chs. XVII–XVIII and E. H. Kossmann, *La Fronde*, Leiden, 1954, ch. II.

led to the commotions of 1650.[1] Elsewhere in the foremost states of Europe the progress of royal authority had been in full career for more than a hundred and fifty years. Despite intervals of retrogression, that authority was increasing in all the attributes which could make its rule over its subjects an untrammelled reality. Everywhere there were groups, orders, and whole regions upon whom regal sovereignty fell as a vexation and a burden. The inherited and prescriptive privileges of assemblies of estates, the liberties of provinces and of degrees of men, were pared down, became thin and emaciated, or were rendered lifeless at the feet of the all-conquering Leviathan. And at the same time the administrative apparatus of the crowns expanded, the costs of their government rose, and expenditure for the maintenance of courts and the support of wars became more prodigal. To finance government, war, and courts, the princes challenged or obtained a taxing power that invaded their subjects' security of property. It was inevitable that so far-reaching an application of royal power among peoples not yet fully habituated to bear the yoke should give rise to popular and aristocratic reaction.

2

Such in its general complexion was the background against which the seventeenth-century revolutions took place. The investigation of their detailed similarities and differences could, of course, be extended with illuminating results. What is especially pertinent to our present purpose, however, is to observe that of all these occurrences only one, the English revolution, possesses a significance transcending the restricted national history of which it is part. By common consent the rebellion against Charles I belongs to the handful of the 'great revolutions' of Europe and the West—cataclysms which appear to mark the turning of times and to signify some fundamental change in the condition of humanity. Ranke spoke of the 'universal historical importance of these contests in Great Britain,' declaring his conviction that 'it is an event which concerns all, this shaking of the foundations of the old British state.'[2] Lord Acton called England's revolution 'the point where the history of nations turned into its modern bed' and 'the second stage on the road of revolution, which started from the Netherlands, and went on to America and France, and is the centre of the history of the modern world.'[3] More recently,

---

[1] P. Geyl, *The Netherlands in the seventeenth century, Part two, 1648–1715*, L., 1964, 13–19.
[2] L. von Ranke, *A history of England principally in the seventeenth century* (trans. of *Englische Geschichte*, 1859–69), 6v., Oxford, 1875, II, 331.
[3] Lord Acton, *Lectures on modern history*, L., ed. 1952, 205.

Trotsky, maker and theorist of revolution in one, found it natural, when writing his *History of the Russian revolution*, to refer to the English struggle as constituting part of a mighty succession of ideas and forms that passed through France to attain a new and higher stage of the Bolshevik conquest of power in 1917.[1]

These judgments as to the importance of the English revolution are well founded. The great revolutions are those in which the pace of change is suddenly accelerated and in which, as Macaulay wrote, 'the experience of years is crowded into hours' and 'old habits of thought and action are violently broken.'[2] Political and social conflict brought to white heat creates a forcing-house that permits every existent tendency to realize itself with startling rapidity. Programmes and shibboleths, ideas and myths, come to birth which will engross the deepest efforts not only of the present contestants but of others in time to come. Perspectives are announced which may require fifty years, a century, or longer for their fulfilment; utopias are envisioned whose being can never be seen on land or sea. In a few weeks or months, venerable monuments are overthrown before which men's forefathers had made reverential obeisance. Amidst the convulsive heavings of an enraged generation, great reforms are effected and powerful energies released which elevate the character and raise the power of the revolutionary state among the nations.

If the English alone of the seventeenth-century rebellions belongs to the category of 'great revolutions' and is thus fittingly linked with the American and French revolutions of the next century, this is because it, too, like these latter, was a decisive event in the emergence of a liberal political order in the world. In the range of its constitutional and religious experimentation, the fertility of its public discussion, and the extremity to which it was carried by the abolition of kingship and the establishment of a republic, it far exceeded the other rebellions of its time. Moreover, in longer perspective, both its practical attainments and ideal aims may be seen as expressive of the aspirations of the epoch at whose threshold it stood. Popular sovereignty; representative rule through parliamentary bodies; the accountability of kings and magistrates; the bounding of government by law; the liberty of the religious conscience; the disestablishment of all ecclesiastical dominion; individual consent to subjection as a natural and human right; written constitutions; republicanism: in short, many of

---

[1] L. Trotsky, *The history of the Russian revolution*, tr. M. Eastman, 3v., N.Y., 1936, I, 14–15, 208–9. Trotsky's references to the English revolution in this work are not always on the mark. Mr. Isaac Deutscher in his great biography of Trotsky also invokes the English revolution for comparison from time to time, with results no more consistently correct.

[2] T. B. Macaulay, *History of England*, 5v., Philadelphia, n.d., II, 451.

the principles and demands that were to subvert the European *ancien régime* made their appearance in England at some time or other between 1640 and 1660.

The wider significance here ascribed to the English revolution has been commonly acknowledged. But almost as a direct result, serious misconceptions have often arisen concerning its nature and origins. For the recognition of the revolution's place as precursor in the course of subsequent development has not infrequently been the cause of an inability to perceive how much its history was peculiar to itself and to its own immediate age.

This failure is due mainly to the influence of the Marxian theory of revolution. According to Marx and Engels, the bourgeois revolution formed a necessary general stage of the historical process leading to capitalism, so that each of its instances bore substantially the same character and resembled the others in essential respects. It thus became possible within the Marxian ambit of ideas to describe the English conflict as 'a bourgeois revolution . . . of classical type, to be closely compared with the French revolution of 1789.'[1] Inevitably, the revolution in France, owing to its thoroughness and universal scope, was taken by Marx and his followers as the model to which the interpretation of other revolutions considered 'bourgeois' could be assimilated. This was not, however, the conclusion of research, but the presupposition through which the entire subject was approached.[2] Thus, in its social origins, in the nature of the contending forces, in the stages through which it passed, the French revolution provided the pattern which, *mutatis mutandis*, was believed a sufficient explanation of the revolution in England.[3]

In consequence of this view the grossest errors and distortions have been committed. It enabled Marx to call the civil war

the victory of bourgeois over feudal property, of nationality over provincialism, of free trade over the guilds, of sub-division of property

[1] Cf. C. Hill, 'The English civil war interpreted by Marx and Engels', *Science and society*, XII, 1 (1948), which conveniently summarizes the Marxian analysis of the English revolution with appropriate citations.

[2] Cf. the apt remark of J. Plamenatz concerning the 'great error of the Marxists, which is to search hard for the causes of things before they have looked carefully at the things themselves. They know, so they think, what revolutions are, and they also know what kind of events their causes must be. This knowledge they acquire not from history but from philosophy; and their task as historians is to discover not what happened but what must have happened.' *The revolutionary movement in France 1815–1871*, L., 1952, x.

[3] The Marxian class analysis which in one form or another has dominated the historiography of the French revolution for many years is the subject of critical treatment in the recent work by A. Cobban, *The social interpretation of the French revolution*, Cambridge, 1964.

over primogeniture, of landownership over the subordination of the
owner by means of the land ... of the family over family title, of
industry over heroic idleness. ....[1]

In a similar way, it has allowed recent historians, despite the weight
of evidence to the contrary, to speak of England in 1640 as a predominantly feudal society and to pronounce the revolution the
conflict of a progressive mode of production and way of life against
the trammels of a surviving feudalism.[2]

Such aberrations are a natural result of the presupposition which
Marx maintained and are bound to persist while it is taken seriously.
It is therefore essential to realize that there is no model of revolutions,
bourgeois or other, no 'classical type,' which can yield the secret of
the specific phenomenon we are studying. Comparisons otherwise
instructive will lead only to error so long as they are based on the
fallacious belief that a single morphological structure exists to which
the explanation of events of a certain kind must necessarily conform.

In particular, as regards the English revolution, we must cast aside
the categories elaborated by historians and sociologists for the
revolution in France and examine it in its own right. At once vital
differences appear. One of the most striking was remarked on over a
century ago by the historian, Guizot, to whom the civil war was a
subject of absorbing study. In an implied contrast to France he
declared:

*It was the peculiar felicity of England in the seventeenth century that the
spirit of religious faith and the spirit of political liberty reigned
together. . . .*
*All the great passions of the human soul were thus excited and brought
into action, while some of the most powerful restraints by which they
are controlled remained unbroken. . . .*
*The two parties fought with the most determined acrimony; but, in the
midst of mortal struggle, they did not renounce all sentiments of order
and peace. There were no sanguinary riots, no judicial massacres. There
was civil war, fierce, obstinate, full of violence . . . but without cynical*

---

[1] Cited in C. Hill, 'The English civil war interpreted by Marx and Engels"
loc. cit., 143.

[2] C. Hill, *The English revolution*, 3rd rev. ed., L., 1955 and 'The agrarian
legislation of the Revolution,' *Puritanism and revolution*, L., 1958, 154, 156.
A similar conception informs M. Dobb's discussion of the revolution in
Studies in the development of capitalism, L., 1947, ch. IV. Cf. also 'Tercen-
tenary number on the English revolution,' *Modern quarterly*, IV, 2 (1949)
and A. Meusel, *Aus der Vorgeschichte der bürgerlichen Revolution in England*,
*Sitzungsberichte der Deutschen Akademie der Wiss. zu Berlin, Klasse für
Gesellschaftswissen*, 1954.

or atrocious excesses, and restrained by the general manners of the
people within certain bounds of justice and humanity.[1]

The essential truth of Guizot's perhaps slightly hyperbolic statement is, of course, undeniable. The English revolution did not devour
its own children. Neither side resorted to systematic and ideologically
buttressed destruction of political enemies, and there was no 'Red'
terror while the revolutionary governments were in power and no
'White' terror at the Restoration.

We could easily add further contrasts as well. Thus, we do not find
among any of the opponents of Charles I a party remotely similar to
the Jacobins in organization, vigilance, and ideological passion. We
do not see in England the prevalence of the extravagant hopes and
boundless combinations which exercised the minds of the revolutionary leaders in France. Most important of all, perhaps, we do not
discover a class conflict to underlie the origins of the English revolution or to be its cause; and we observe that through political change
and upheaval the social order remained unshaken at its foundations,
emerging intact in the aftermath of the cataclysm on the same
continuum along which it had been evolving before.

3

To cite these differences is, of course, to specify a problem. What *was*
the nature of the English revolution? Why did it occur? What made
it what it was? It will be our aim in the present work to answer these
questions, if possible, with some precision, and to delineate the
physiognomy of the revolution in its own right—not, indeed, over the
full extent of its twenty years, but from its origins to the onset of the
civil war, the period which witnessed the dissolution of the inherited
governmental order and the inauguration of a long series of political
expedients and experiments.

In order to proceed to our task, however, we must first inquire
whether and how far the seventeenth century itself possessed a conception of revolution. This is a topic which historians of the rebellions
and civil wars of the time have seldom considered, though it is of high
interest and importance. For while we, the retrospective analysts at
three centuries' distance, rightly describe English occurrences after

[1] F. Guizot, *On the causes of the success of the English revolution of 1640–
1688*, L., 1850, 3, 18. Sainte-Beuve's essay on this work (*Causeries du Lundi*,
4 Feb. 1850) points out how much its judgment on the English revolution
was formed in reaction against the French. It should be recalled that Guizot
wrote it after the collapse of the July monarchy in 1848 and his own exile to
England.

1640 as a revolution, the contemporaries and actors of these events did not—or certainly not, at any rate, in our sense. Is it not therefore apparent that a revolution initiated by men who had no thought of what *we* have come to understand by 'revolution' and, moreover, no awareness of being revolutionaries, must present, in significant respects, another character than the type of revolutionary change predominant in aftertimes? It is to this preliminary question that we here wish to address ourselves.

If we reflect on our present-day conception of 'revolution,' we shall observe that besides its having proliferated into many diverse contexts such as the economic, scientific, military, and even aesthetic, it has also acquired on its political side an enormous amplitude of meaning. It stands here for the conscious, unremitting will to transform fundamentally the condition of humanity. Far more comprehensive than rebellion, it signifies the attempt not only to overthrow a regime, but to change society. The merely 'political' does not exist for it, premissed as it is upon the complete interpenetration of the political and social realms and the controlling relevance of politics for every field of action. Its characteristic note is orientation and commitment towards the future as a history to be made in full awareness. Hence, when this conception issues forth as a deed, the latter aims at nothing less than total emancipation from the old society and creation of the new, to which end the conquest of state power is instrumental.

That this idea has not only entered deeply into the texture of modern politics, but has actually conditioned and guided the greatest revolutions of our time, is incontestable. Its materialization in world events would suffice of itself to confirm the frequently expressed conviction as to the overwhelming part which revolution has played in the history of the twentieth century.[1]

Whence, however, did such a conception derive?[2]

[1] Cf. H. Arendt, *On revolution*, N.Y., ed. 1965, Intro., and the contributions to the theory and history of revolution collected in *Revolution, Nomos*, VIII, ed. C. J. Friedrich, N.Y., 1966. Cf. also the useful survey by L. Stone, 'Theories of revolution,' *World politics*, XVIII, 2 (1966). Within the typology of revolution, what S. Neumann and C. Johnson have called the Jacobin Communist Revolution—'a sweeping fundamental change in political organization, social structure, economic property control and the predominant myth of a social order . . .' (cited in L. Stone, *op. cit.*, 163)—is, in fact, the preeminent type of revolution of this century. The description, 'Jacobin Communist,' however, is somewhat misleading, as the Nazi movement belongs to it as well. This appears with great clarity in H. Rauschning, *The revolution of nihilism*, tr. E. W. Dickes, N.Y., 1939, a work which remains fundamental for the understanding of German national-socialism.

[2] The history of the idea and terminology of revolutions has been treated by E. Rosenstock-Huessy, 'Revolution als politischer Begriff in der Neuzeit,'

Introduction

Undoubtedly, its immediate origin lay in the thought of Marx, just as it also attained its fullest development in Marxist theory, which holds as a basic proposition that 'revolutions are the locomotives of history.'[1] In becoming a practical will, as it did with Lenin and the Bolsheviks, the Marxian revolutionary idea revealed its elemental potency. The nature of its operation appears to perfection in the brilliant pages of Trotsky's *History of the Russian revolution*, permeated as the latter is by the consciousness of moulding history and the belief that 'never in all the past have the conceptions of a revolution in the minds of revolutionists approached so closely to the actual essence of the events as in 1917.'[2]

But prior to the theoretical enthronement of revolution in Marxism occurred the *fact* of the French revolution. Originating like nearly all the European revolts of the previous age in a resistance of the aristocratic order—a *révolte nobiliare*, it then rapidly grew into a vast popular movement which drove on with unexampled dynamism to extremes of violence and struggle. Here for the first time, beyond the aims of securing a constitution and specific reforms, the will to regenerate mankind became during the Jacobin ascendancy a ruling passion.[3] Amidst the colossal events through which France passed, the idea and terminology of revolution expanded and acquired an extraordinary resonance. Their new significance was symbolized in the well-known saying of the Duc de Rochefoucauld-Liancourt on the morrow of the fall of the Bastille. To Louis XVI's question,

[1] K. Marx, *The class struggles in France 1848–50, Selected works*, ed. V. Adoratsky, 2v., N.Y., n.d., II, 283; cf. K. Griewank, *op. cit.*, 270–9 and R. C. Tucker, 'The Marxian revolutionary idea,' in *Revolution, Nomos*, VIII.

[2] L. Trotsky, *op. cit.*, III, App. III, 380. Cf. also the remark, 'You may say of the Bolsheviks ... they were adequate to their epoch and its tasks; curses in plenty resounded in their direction, but irony would not stick to them—it had nothing to catch hold of.' *Ibid.*, II, vii.

[3] Cf. the numerous texts cited in J. L. Talmon, *The origins of totalitarian democracy*, N.Y., ed. 1961, pt. II.

Festgabe ... für Paul Heilborn, Breslau, 1931 and in the same writer's *Out of revolution*, N.Y., 1938, *passim*. The fullest account of the subject is K. Griewank's posthumously published *Der neuzeitliche Revolutionsbegriff*, Weimar, 1955, which, in agreement with Rosenstock-Huessy, establishes convincingly that revolution as word and concept 'ist in seiner politischen Anwendung ein Erzeugnis der Neuzeit' and 'ist ... erst möglich geworden auf Grund eines spezifisch modernen Weltverständnisses', *ibid.*, 1, 8. Cf. also A. Hatto, 'Revolution: an enquiry into the usefulness of an historical term,' *Mind*, LVIII, 232 (1949) and V. Snow, 'The concept of revolution in seventeenth-century England,' *Historical journal*, V, 2 (1962). The relation of the idea of reform to revolution and other renewal concepts is discussed by G. Ladner, *The idea of reform*, Cambridge, 1959, ch. 1.

'C'est une révolte?', the Duc replied, 'Non, Sire, c'est une révolution.'[1] Already for some of its contemporaries and participants the revolution was a *mystique*—the expression of humanity's advance into the realm of freedom. The word itself annexed this novel meaning. Adding the definite article and capitals, it was invoked as *La Révolution*. And further, as has been strikingly observed,

it now becomes one of the most individual of words, one of the most powerful. He who could say now, 'La révolution, c'est moi,' *would wield a greater, a more violent power, than had he who said,* 'L'état, c'est moi.' La Révolution, *in the minds of many, now replaces* l'état, le gouvernement, l'église, le roi. . . . *It has swept all these from their seats of authority.*[2]

From hence, too, after 1789 came the mintage of related terms such as 'revolutionary,' 'revolutionize,' and 'counter-revolutionary,' which seem not to have been in use before. Thus, the Convention's wartime decree of 10 October 1793 proclaimed the government of France to be '*révolutionnaire*' until the peace.[3] A Jacobin notable, insisting in 1793 that only severe measures could save the republic, wrote,

. . . la Révolution n'est point faite, et il faut bien dire . . . à la Convention nationale: 'Vous êtes une assemblée révolutionnaire.'[4]

To the Girondist, Condorcet, who composed a tract, *Sur le sens Du mot révolutionnaire* (1793), the word, 'revolutionary,' applied only to revolutions which have liberty as their object.[5] Presently it appeared in English dress and was used pejoratively by Edmund Burke in a diatribe against the French revolution: 'Everything is new, and according to the fashionable phrase, revolutionary.'[6]

These verbal elaborations answered to the need to describe a fresh reality. They were recognitions in the realm of language, the infallible register of men's consciousness, of a phenomenon new in human affairs—the emergence of what Tocqueville, the profoundest his-

---

[1] This is mentioned by E. Rosenstock-Huessy, *Out of revolution*, 130.
[2] H. J. Swann, *French terminologies in the making*, cited in E. Rosenstock-Huessy, *Out of revolution*, 129–30. Cf. also the account of the idea and language of revolution in France after 1789 in K. Griewank, *op. cit.*, ch. IX.
[3] Cited in J. L. Talmon, *op. cit.*, 111. The decree originated with Saint-Just.
[4] Jeanbon de Saint-André, cited in J. L. Talmon, *op. cit.*, 291–2.
[5] Condorcet remarks: 'De *révolution*, nous avons fait révolutionnaire,' and gives various acceptations of the word. He defines '*contre-révolution*' as a revolution against liberty, *Oeuvres*, 12v., Paris, 1847–9, XII, 615, 619.
[6] *Fourth letter on the proposals for peace with the regicide directory of France, 1795, Select works*, ed. E. J. Payne, new ed., 3v., Oxford, 1892, III, 261.

torian of the French revolution, called the 'revolutionary spirit' and a 'race of revolutionaries' dedicated to changing the world.[1]

4

It is the total absence of this highly charged idea of revolution born in France and elevated to a theoretical principle by Marx that we have to notice as we look back across the abyss of time to the 1640s. 'Revolution' had then another, mainly non-political meaning. If the contemporaries of Charles I's deposition used the word in a political context at all, they did so without any of the dynamic connotations it later acquired. Neither did the historiography of the seventeenth century attain to the conception of England's civil conflict as a revolution. To Clarendon, it belonged to the familiar and long-established category of rebellion, the name he gave it in his great work, *The history of the rebellion and civil wars in England*. Not until after the assimilation of post-1789 French experience, it seems, was historical thought able to grasp the revolt against Charles I's government as an authentic *revolution*. The earliest historian to do so systematically was Guizot, whose writings on the subject, begun in 1826, treated the decades 1640–60 and their antecedents for the first time as 'the English revolution.'[2]

The predominant meaning which 'revolution' possessed for the thought and language of the seventeenth and preceding centuries was astronomical. Both in Latin and the vernacular it denoted the rotation of bodies, as in the title of Copernicus's celebrated treatise, *De revolutionibus orbium coelestium* (1543). Belonging thus to a cosmo-logical context, its chief attribute was *circularity*—motion returning to its point of origin.[3]

When occasionally historians or political writers took over the term, it retained this sense. In their usage, it signified political change proceeding cyclically and describing in its course an alternation of rise and fall of powers. Thereby it might include the notion of upheaval and turbulence, but not that of the creation of a new order of things. Machiavelli, though he hardly ever used the word, under-stood it in this way speaking in *The prince*, for instance, of '*tante*

---

[1] Cf. the valuable essay by M. Richter, 'Tocqueville's contributions to the theory of revolution,' *Revolution, Nomos*, VIII, 86–8.

[2] *Histoire de la révolution d'Angleterre depuis l'avènement de Charles Ier jusqu'a sa mort*, 2v., Paris, 1826. In his preface Guizot placed the English and French revolutions on a level, calling the former 'avant la révolution française . . . le plus grand évènement que l'Europe eût à raconter.' Cf. also R. C. Latham, 'English revolutionary thought, 1640–1660,' *History*, n.s., XXX, iii (1945), 39.

[3] Cf. V. Snow, *op. cit.*, 167–8.

revoluzioni d'Italia.' On the other hand, his customary expression for changes in states was the neutral *mutazione* or some variant thereof like *alterazione* or *variazione*.[1] So far was Machiavelli from the later idea of revolution that he declared the only salutary *alterazioni* in republics to be those that bring them back (*riducano*) to their founding principles.[2] Jean Bodin in his *De republica* (1576) likewise characterized the transformation of states merely as *conversio, alteratio*, or *changement* in the French version, terms which his English translator of 1606 rendered simply as 'change.'[3]

In the seventeenth century the astronomical sense of revolution still prevailed over any other. Hence, even as applied to politics, instead of betokening the event which engenders a new political order, revolution, by a curious irony, described the opposite: the return of the cycle of change to its beginning, or else the reversals and overturnings attendant on the cycle. And this conception was often tinged with a pessimistic implication of fatality, as though the rotations of human affairs were subject to the same irresistibility as the orbits of the planets.

In just such a way did a seventeenth-century lover of antiquity refer to 'The revolution of families now wholly extinguished' and confess that

The supreme powers have framed all sublunary things transitory and subject to revolution.[4]

Some writers, with the cyclical image in mind, called the Stuart restoration of 1660 a 'revolution.' Alluding to Charles II's re-establishment on the throne, Thomas Hobbes declared:

I have seen in this Revolution a circular Motion of the Sovereign Power, through two Usurpers, from the late King to this his Son ... where long may it remain![5]

---

[1] *Il principe*, c.26; *Discorsi*, III, vii ('*mutazioni dalla libertà alla servitù*'), viii ('*alterare una republica*'); cf. K. Griewank, *op. cit.*, ch. IV.
[2] *Discorsi*, III, 1.
[3] *De republica*, IV, c. 1, 2, translated into English by Richard Knolles, *The six books of a commonweale*, 1606.
[4] Robert Reyce, *The breviary of Suffolk*, 1618, ed. F. Hervey, L., 1902, 2. Cf. also Chief Justice Crewe's well-known lament over the passing of families in the Oxford peerage case of 1625: '... time hath his revolution; there must be a period and an end to all temporal things ... an end of names and dignities. ... For where is Bohun? Where's Mowbray? Where's Mortimer? ... nay, which is more, and most of all, where is Plantagenet? They are intombed in the urns and sepulchres of mortality.' C. H. Firth, *The House of Lords during the civil war*, L., 1910, 7.
[5] *Behemoth*, in F. Maseres, *Select tracts*, L., 1815, pt. 2, 652.

Introduction

The diplomat, Sir William Temple, spoke similarly of 'the revolution of England in the year sixty. . . .' The associated aspect of overturning is suggested by another of Temple's remarks concerning the Dutch republic invaded by Louis XIV in 1672:

. . . such a greatness, and such a fall of this State, seem revolutions unparalleled in any story. . . .[1]

The analogous thought appears in the few instances where mid-century writers termed the civil conflicts of their time 'revolutions'. They intended no more by the expression than reversals or a *peripeteia* of state. An Italian account of the Neapolitan rising bore the title, *Le rivolutioni di Napoli*.[2] After Charles I's deposition, the English political theorist, Anthony Ascham, published a work called *Of the confusions and revolutions of governments* (1649).[3] Another tract of the 1650s, *Of the origin and progress of the revolution in England*, presupposed the cyclical character of political change both in its title and in its author's reference to 'the strange revolutions we have seen.'[4]

Unrelated to 'revolution' and possessing an entirely different import was 'rebellion.' The former, with its rooted associations in the image of cosmic motion, was an occurrence, not an act. 'Rebellion,' on the other hand, referred indisputably to human conduct; and since it denoted treasonable resistance to authority, it bore the taint of illegality and sin. Hence, none of the rebels of the age admitted to being such. All pleaded grounds of law or religion to repel the accusation from themselves. This was equally true of Charles I's opponents, of the French Fronde, and of the revolt of the Catalans.[5] John Locke, in justifying the right of rebellion, went so far as to turn the charge of rebel against bad rulers. It is they, he said, who incur the responsibility of rebellion by illegal actions contrary to the ends for which government is ordained.[6]

[1] Sir William Temple, *Works*, 4v., L., 1757, I, 57, 59.
[2] Alessandro Giraffi, *Le rivolutioni di Napoli*, Venice, 1647; cf. also in the same sense an account of the Catalan rebellion by Luca Assarino, *Le rivolutioni di Catalogna*, Bologna, 1648.
[3] On Ascham, cf. P. Zagorin, *A history of political thought in the English revolution*, L., 1954, 64–7. Cyclical conceptions with a strong note of pessimism are a prominent feature of Ascham's political ideas.
[4] Matthew Wren, *Of the origin and progress of the revolution in England*, in J. Gutch, *Collectanea curiosa*, Oxford, 1781, 170.
[5] Recent historians of the Fronde and the Catalonian rebellion have stressed the conservatism and appeal to law of both these revolts; cf. P. Doolin, *The Fronde*, Cambridge, 1935, xii–xiii; E. Kossmann, *La Fronde*, ch. I; J. H. Elliott, *The revolt of the Catalans*, 549.
[6] *Two treatises of government*, ed. P. Laslett, Mentor ed., N.Y., 1965, ch. XIX, par. 227.

The event in the seventeenth century that contributed most to infuse the idea of revolution with an enduring political content was James II's deposition and the enthronement of William and Mary.[1] To contemporaries, 1688 was a 'revolution' and such it remained to posterity as well.[2] Yet here also, despite the establishment of a new royal line, the concept still preserved its attribute of circularity. Locke, in the preface to his *Two treatises of government*, published in 1690, called King William 'our Great Restorer,' thereby sufficiently indicating how he viewed the revolution. In the *Two treatises* themselves, now known to have been written mainly before 1688, the term only occurs twice, and exclusively in its cyclical sense, as in the allusion to 'the many Revolutions . . . seen in this Kingdom, in this and former Ages. . . .'[3]

On the same premiss the revolution was represented by its makers as a restoration. The Convention Parliament of 1689, which laid the foundation of the revolution settlement, took care to avoid any suggestion of innovation. Although in fact a revolutionary body, in form its work was conservative. It professed only to restore and preserve the laws and liberties violated by a law-breaking King.[4] This enabled Burke a century later to boast of the finality of the revolution of 1688 and of its close continuity with the historic past.[5]

5

The foregoing account has shown that revolution had not yet become a fundamental and actuating concept of politics in the seventeenth century. Not till 1688 did it even possess itself of a definite political meaning. Only thereafter did it also begin to acquire for the contemporary mind a close and invincible connection with liberty. Even at this stage, however, the idea of revolution remained devoid of dynamism and attached to its restorationist premiss. There was paradox, too, in the fact that 1688, a substitution of rulers accomplished peacefully with the least possible breach of continuity, should

[1] Cf. K. Griewank, *op. cit.*, 179–80.
[2] Cf. Evelyn's remark on 2 Dec. 1688, when declarations for the Prince of Orange were pouring in: 'it lookes like a Revolution,' John Evelyn, *Diary*, ed. E. S. de Beer, Oxford, 1959, 895; an earlier mention of a 'sad revolution' threatening 'this sinfull Nation,' *ibid.*, 891.
[3] *Two treatises of government*, Preface, and *Second treatise*, ch. XIX, par. 223, 225. For the dating of Locke's work, see P. Laslett's introduction, pt. III.
[4] This view appears clearly in the Declaration of Rights, 1 Will. and Mary, Sess. 2, c.2, *Statutes of the realm*, VI, 142–5; cf. also the remarks of G. N. Clark, *The later Stuarts*, 2nd ed., Oxford, 1961, 146–7.
[5] *Reflections on the revolution in France*, 1790, *Select works*, I, 18–22.

have become known as a revolution; while 1640–60, a period of violence and unprecedented innovation, did not receive the name.

But this, in turn, reflected a view of things which inevitably influenced the nature of the actual revolutions of the age. The political outlook that held so limited an idea of revolution belonged to societies still strongly bound to their traditions. It pertained to social structures dominated by aristocratic and privileged élites in whose opposition most of the significant rebellions and civil wars of the sixteenth and seventeenth centuries arose. The men of that time tended to look backward rather than forward. Conservatives at heart, they were not magnetized by an ideal of the future, and preferred to find their justifications in the precedents of the past and the wisdom of ancestors. They groped blindly towards the new, instead of boldly embracing it. The revolutions of which they were the authors occurred, as it were, behind their own backs.

We shall see these characteristics at the inception of the English revolution. The inspirers of resistance to Charles I never dreamed of being revolutionaries. They opened a course of unimaginable change contrary to their own intentions. Having promoted a civil war, they prepared the way for the momentary appearance of a radicalism which did, indeed, proclaim in political terms the goal of a new order of freedom and justice. It was a Leveller pamphleteer in 1646 who denounced Magna Charta as 'a beggarly thing, containing many markes of intollerable bondage. ...' It was the same writer who imperiously declared that

whatever our Fore-fathers were; or whatever they did or suffered, or were enforced to yield unto, we are the men of the present age, and ought to be absolutely free from all kindes of exorbitancies, molestations or Arbitrary Power. ...[1]

Here we perceive the germ of a political doctrine new to Europe which, by its appeal to reason and natural right, would at a later day help to remould the institutions of the Western peoples. But not even the Levellers could emancipate themselves completely from the myth of the past; and their thought faced backward as well in its invocation of a primitive Anglo-Saxon freedom to be restored after centuries of Norman tyranny.[2]

Outside these audacious democrats and a few fellow radicals, the only other belief in a new age to appear during the revolution took the familiar form of religious millenarianism. Expectation of a

---

[1] [Richard Overton], *A remonstrance of many thousand citizens*, 1646, 16, 5,
[2] Cf. C. Hill, 'The Norman yoke,' in *Puritanism and revolution*; P. Zagorin, *op. cit.*, 27–8.

supernatural reign of righteousness excited some of the Puritans in the early 1640s, and gave rise in the '50s to the Fifth Monarchy movement, which looked impatiently for the Second Coming and the rule of the saints.[1] At no time, however, did a will to secular transformation determine the revolution's course. Millenarianism, a phenomenon recurrent in Christian history, was politically sterile; while Leveller democracy was too far in advance of its age to achieve power or play a directive role.

Undoubtedly, the revolution administered a great shock to the inherited order. Yet notwithstanding, most Englishmen and their governors remained under the spell of continuity with the past. They did not wish to cut loose from the generations or to venture on a terrain bare of landmarks. This abiding trait in the political mentality of the old societies conditioned the revolution in its origins, just as it resulted at its end in the restoration of kingship.

---

[1] P. Zagorin, *op. cit.*, ch. VIII.

Social Structure and the Court and the Country

It has become a virtual axiom for the scientific study of revolutions that the latter as a general phenomenon are held to reflect a severe structural crisis in society. Insofar as this view forces inquirers to look closely at the connection between revolution and the social system, it is incontrovertible. Often, however, it is associated with the theoretical conviction (of Marxian provenance but by no means exclusively Marxist) that every revolution is necessarily a class struggle—that economic classes are the dominant collectivities whose conflict lies at the root of revolution. This, as a general proposition, is certainly false. Besides its inapplicability to other prominent cases in the sixteenth and seventeenth centuries, it cannot account for the English revolution. Hence, if the cleavage that underlay the revolt against Charles I is to be properly understood, it is essential to dispose of this opinion in regard to England together with the picture of the pre-revolutionary society on which it is based.

The question of English social structure thus presented has been widely discussed of recent years. In particular, it has figured as an issue in the brilliant display of intellectual fireworks known as the gentry controversy, perhaps the most notable historical debate of this generation. The subject of that debate, broadly stated, is the direction of social-economic change in the century preceding 1640 and the connection of the latter with the English revolution. On one side, the thesis advanced by Professor Tawney held that a large-scale shift of landed property away from the crown, the church, and aristocracy resulted in the rise to economic supremacy of a new class of gentry; and further, that it was this class, a species of 'agricultural capitalists,' whose bid for state power overthrew the monarchical regime.[1] On the other side, Professor Trevor-Roper's counter-thesis asserted that economic conditions were unfavourable to gentry

---

[1] R. H. Tawney, 'The rise of the gentry, 1558–1640,' *Economic history review*, XI, 1 (1941); 'Harrington's interpretation of his age,' *Proceedings of the British Academy*, XXVII, 1941.

prosperity from the profits of landholding alone; that far from rising, the gentry declined as a class, save for a fortunate minority who also possessed non-agrarian sources of income such as crown offices or the law; and that the revolution was the rebellion of the 'declining mere gentry' against a hated court and the system of royal benefit and patronage from which they were excluded.[1]

It is not our purpose to review the details of the gentry controversy or the large body of research and criticism it has generated. This has been done in several writings which contain effective assessments of the discussion.[2] What rather calls for notice here are the conceptual and terminological confusions respecting the social structure that still persist. Was the gentry a class? Ought it to be distinguished from, or contrasted with, the aristocracy? Did economic factors determine the form of stratification at that period? Did they determine political organization? These questions remain undecided.[3] Tawney's anatomy of the English social order was framed entirely on quasi-Marxian lines of class, and against this Trevor-Roper directed a powerful critique. His own conception, however, if closer to the realities of seventeenth-century society, runs counter to obvious facts (for it is incorrect that the revolution was the act of a declining gentry) and is therefore only slightly less unsatisfactory. Most recently, Professor Stone, after first concurring with Tawney and then modifying his views in response to criticism, has thrown a penetrating light on the social order in his magisterial study of the peerage.[4] Yet this work manages at the same time to perpetuate some of the muddle concerning social condition. It speaks of the aristocracy when it means the peerage, thus conveying the misleading suggestion that the

[1] H. R. Trevor-Roper, 'The Elizabethan aristocracy: an anatomy anatomized,' *Economic history review*, 2nd ser., III, 3 (1951); *The gentry, 1540–1640*, Cambridge, 1953.

[2] J. H. Hexter, 'Storm over the gentry,' in *Reappraisals in history*, L., 1961; C. Hill, 'Recent interpretations of the civil war,' in *Puritanism and revolution*; P. Zagorin, 'The social interpretation of the English revolution,' *Journal of economic history*, XIX, 3 (1959). A good selection of writings and documents relating to the gentry controversy is contained in Lawrence Stone (ed.), *Social change and revolution in England 1540–1640*, L., 1965, which also has a useful bibliography.

[3] It is worth noticing that similar differences over social classification and terminology exist concerning France in the seventeenth century and at the revolution; cf. R. Mousnier, 'Problèmes de méthode dans l'étude des structures sociales des seizième, dix-septième, dix-huitième siècles,' *Spiegel der Geschichte. Festgabe für Max Braubach*, ed. K. Repgen and S. Skalweit, Münster, 1964, and A. Cobban, 'The vocabulary of social history,' *Political science quarterly*, LXXI, 1 (1956) and *The social interpretation of the French revolution*, chs. II–III.

[4] *The crisis of the aristocracy 1558–1641*, Oxford, 1965; cf. also Stone's introduction to *Social change and revolution in England 1540–1640*.

two were identical although in fact the first, a broader category than the second, included the gentry as well.[1]

If we wish to grasp the relation between politics and the social system, we must take care not to use categories that are classificatory constructions and nothing more. The nature of such categories is purely artificial. However usefully they may serve certain purposes of inquiry, they do not define real collectivities whose actuality and common consciousness is attested in documents.

The failure to recognize this has been a cause of error in the gentry controversy. Much of the argument has turned on disagreements concerning the economic developments of the century. The period was evidently one that witnessed exceptional fluctuations in the composition of landed society. In the present state of knowledge it appears nearly certain that the price revolution and rising population established conditions conducive to the prosperity of landlords. There is a good deal of evidence to indicate that landed incomes, especially from the late sixteenth century on, rose steeply.[2] It is very probable that the gentry grew in numbers and wealth on the profits from land; and it is also likely that relative to the gentry, the land-holdings and wealth of the peerage somewhat declined.[3]

But if this description be correct, there is still no reason to suppose that the trends in question produced a different type of social structure than before. Nor is it the case that a classification founded on changes in the distribution of the ownership of land or wealth necessarily coincides with one that delineates real social groups. Tawney's rising gentry, Trevor-Roper's declining gentry (in this respect like the fictitious progressive landlords who, according to the

---

[1] Stone writes of the Tudor period, for instance, 'If the gentry were the ruling, the aristocracy were the governing class.' (*The crisis of the aristocracy*, 55.) The meaning of this statement is unclear and the distinction it asserts untenable. England was governed under the crown by an aristocratic order that consisted of both the titular nobility or peerage and the gentry.

[2] Cf. E. Kerridge, 'The movement of rent, 1540–1640,' *Economic history review*, 2nd ser., VI, 1 (1953); M. Finch, *The wealth of five Northamptonshire families 1540–1640, Northamptonshire record society*, XIX, 1956; A. Simpson, *The wealth of the gentry 1540–1640*, Chicago, 1961; L. Stone, *The crisis of the aristocracy*, App. XVIB.

[3] The movement of yeoman families into the lesser gentry on an unprecedented scale has been frequently remarked; cf. M. Campbell, *The English yeoman under Elizabeth and the early Stuarts*, New Haven, 1942, 34–42, and W. G. Hoskins, *Provincial England*, L., 1963, 151. The expansion of the gentry is also attested by the statistics representing the increase in the number of armigerous families and grants of knighthood; cf. L. Stone, *The crisis of the aristocracy*, 66–82 and App. III. For the financial decline of the peerage relative to the gentry, cf. *ibid.*, 129–64. W. K. Jordan, *Philanthropy in England 1480–1660*, L., 1959, 333n., has also commented on the striking numerical expansion of the gentry.

orthodox Marxian interpretation, were in conflict with a semi-feudal monarchy[1]) are at best economic abstractions. They are categories that do not reach the operative distinctions in the society nor the actual basis of its political behaviour and division.

The social system in which the revolution occurred was not based on economic classes. It was based, rather, on status, and the terms in which we must perforce delineate it—peers, gentry, yeomen, citizens, etc.—are fundamentally not economic classifications at all.[2] Indeed, none of these categories possesses a distinct economic correlate. If, for example, we refer either to economic function or source of income, then the peerage and the gentry compose a single undifferentiated body. Rising or declining, richer or poorer, ancient family or recent, all were landlords living from the rights they possessed over land, which might be materialized as rents and fines, as profits from the direct sale of agricultural commodities like wool, or as the royalty or other return on mineral resources belonging to their estates. If, on the other hand, we refer to the economic developments that occupied Tawney, then peerage and gentry would have to be alike divided, since within both some prospered by the more efficient exploitation of their estates on capitalist lines, while others did not. These categories do, it is true, imply a financial criterion in that the social sense of the sixteenth century deemed it fitting that a peer's income should exceed a knight's or an esquire's. As contemporaries

[1] Cf. C. Hill, *The English revolution 1640*.

[2] The concept of class is one of the most complex and disputed problems in both history and sociology. Its difficulty is increased because, as has been well-remarked, it is used 'with equal frequency and intensity, as a descriptive category, and as a symbol of demand and identification. . . .' (H. Lasswell and A. Kaplan, *Power and society*, L., 1952, 62). Marx himself, while employing it constantly, yet never defined it or provided a formal analysis of its character as a category of social description. As will be seen from the remarks that follow in the text, I have preferred to distinguish status from class as alternative types of social organization. Historically, the first precedes the second as the form of social structure in Western Europe. Classes are primarily economically-determined collectivities; they lack religious or legal sanction, and membership in them confers no special rights; moreover, the boundaries between them are undefined. Status groups differ from classes in all of these respects (cf. T. B. Bottomore, *Classes in modern society*, L., 1955, 14). The emergence of economic classes as the basis of social structure and social consciousness proceeded *pari passu* with the disintegration of the status system and the coming of industrialism. The revolutions of the sixteenth and seventeenth centuries took place in status, not class, societies. On the distinction of status and class, cf. P. Sorokin, 'What is a social class?', F. Tönnies, 'Estates and classes,' Max Weber, 'Class, status, party,' all in R. Bendix and S. Lipset (eds.), *Class, status, and power*, Glencoe, 1953; T. H. Marshall, 'The nature of class conflict,' in *Class conflict and social stratification*, ed. T. H. Marshall, L., 1938; W. G Runciman, *Social science and political theory*, Cambridge, 1963, ch. VII.

22

well realized, however, this conventional assumption was not infrequently falsified; and Thomas Wilson, writing in 1600, had to observe that some knights, 'cheefe men in their Countryes both for livinge and reputacions ... equall the best Barons and come not much behind many Erles. ...'[1]   •

In reality, what the nomenclature of peers, gentry, etc., envisaged was a system of status defined mainly by non-economic criteria such as titles of honour, ancestry, legal and customary privilege, deference, and service to the prince.[2] Of this system the ruling principle was honour and the dignity attaching to way of life. The most elementary distinction it enforced was between those who were gentlemen and those not.[3] Around this, however, further and more complex differentiations were elaborated. It was status that conditioned men's social awareness; equally, it was status that provided the frame of political action. In view of the determinative influence of this type of social organization, its basic features may be more fully depicted.

2

To the observation of the sixteenth and seventeenth centuries, society appeared as a hierarchy of orders or degrees of men, graduated from the prince at the top, through the peerage, gentry, and other estates, down to the artificers, husbandmen, and labourers at the bottom. Such was the conception everywhere implicit in the religious, didactic, and imaginative literature of the age, and incorporated as well in formal accounts of their society by contemporary thinkers.[4]

Writing in Henry VIII's time, Sir Thomas Elyot defined the *republica* as a 'body ... compact or made of sundry estates and degrees of men ... disposed by the order of equity and governed by the rule and moderation of reason.' Of this body the king was head, with magistrates under him as governors 'chosen out of that estate of

[1] Thomas Wilson, *The state of England (1600)*, ed. F. J. Fisher, *Camden miscellany*, XVI, 1936, 23.
[2] Cf. R. Mousnier's forceful critique of the attempts to analyse the society of the *ancien régime* on lines of economic class and his account of the actual basis of its stratification, 'Problèmes de méthode dans l'étude des structures sociales des seizième, dix-septième, dix-huitième siècles,' *loc. cit.*
[3] The importance of the difference between the gentleman and others has been stressed by P. Laslett, who speaks of it as 'the exact point at which the traditional social system divided up the population into two extremely unequal sections.' He has confused the matter, however, by picturing the society as composed of many status groups and only one class, that of the gentlemen; cf. *The world we have lost*, L., 1965, ch. II.
[4] Cf. R. Mohl, *The three estates in medieval and renaissance literature*, N.Y., 1933 and R. Kelso, *The doctrine of the English gentleman in the sixteenth century*, Urbana, 1929.

men which be called worshipful.'[1] Thirty-five years later under Queen Elizabeth, Sir Thomas Smith divided Englishmen into the four degrees of gentlemen, citizens or burgesses, yeomen, and labourers. The gentlemen consisted of the prince, a *nobilitas maior* composed of the peerage, and a *nobilitas minor* of knights, esquires, and gentlemen *simpliciter*.[2] At the beginning of the seventeenth century Thomas Wilson employed a nearly identical classification in which the uppermost order was a two-fold *nobilitas* formed of the peerage proper and of a lesser nobility of knights, esquires, and gentlemen.[3] In James I's reign, Robert Burton, author of *The anatomy of melancholy*, characterized the society as an 'inequality of States, orders, and degrees,' appointed by God.[4] Henry Peacham, a prolific commentator on social custom, described the preeminence of noblemen and gentlemen, who were to be preferred in 'honours, offices, and other dignities of command and government.'[5] Another writer listed seven 'degrees of callings' whose three highest, respectively, were the peerage, the 'degree of Gentry called Knighthood,' and 'Gentlemen of Auncestry. . . .'[6]

Forty years passed, the revolutionary upheaval was subsiding, but the schematism of status persisted. The political theorist, Harrington, by conviction a republican, still took it for granted that the task of government was a thing 'peculiar unto the Genius of a Gentleman.'[7] A pamphleteer at the Restoration spoke of the gentry as a dominant order that 'live plentifully and at ease upon their rents' and hold 'the command of this nation. . . .'[8] Even at the end of the century, the founders of the science of Political Arithmetic, the earliest quantitative investigation of national wealth and population, continued to analyse the social structure in terms of status. In 1685, Sir William Petty divided the kingdom for tax purposes into a number of 'orders' of which the titular nobility was first, followed by knights, esquires,

---

[1] Sir Thomas Elyot, *The book named the governor*, 1531, Everyman ed., L., 1962, 1, 12, 13.

[2] Sir Thomas Smith, *De republica Anglorum*, written 1565, published 1583, ed. L. Alston, Cambridge, 1906, 31–40.

[3] Thomas Wilson, *The state of England (1600)*, *loc. cit.*, 17. Wilson notes five divisions to Smith's four: noblemen, citizens, yeomen, artificers, and labourers.

[4] Robert Burton, *The anatomy of melancholy*, 1621, ed. A. R. Shilleto from the 6th ed., 3v., L., 1904, II, 196.

[5] Henry Peacham, *The complete gentleman*, 1622, ed. V. Heltzel, Ithaca, 1962.

[6] R. Reyce, *A breviary of Suffolk*, 56–72. Reyce's other degrees are the poor, husbandmen, yeomen, and townsmen.

[7] James Harrington, *Oceana*, 1656, ed. S. B. Liljegren, Lund and Heidelberg, 1924, 35.

[8] Cited in C. Hill and E. Dell, *The good old cause*, L., 1950 471.

and gentlemen.[1] The most elaborate classification made up to that time, however, was Gregory King's table of incomes and expenditure of all English families for the year 1688. He distinguished twenty-six 'Ranks Degrees Titles and Qualifications.' At the summit were some 16,500 families of temporal and spiritual lords, baronets, knights, esquires and gentlemen; at the foot, 849,000 families of labourers, cottagers, paupers, common seamen, common soldiers, and vagrants.[2]

We could add almost indefinitely to these illustrations, but they should suffice to show how strongly status dominated the contemporary perception of the social order. Nor should we imagine that the notion of status was merely a myth, an illusory form of consciousness, falsifying for those who thought in its categories the reality in which they lived. However it might distort by idealizing a system of inequality, it nevertheless corresponded to an objectively-given structure of distinctions. For the society itself, in its resistance to the pretensions of money and riches as such, and in the gradations of privilege and disability, authority and subordination, deference and disesteem which it incorporated, made manifest in innumerable ways that status was its effective mode of differentiation.

Both by law and common practice, every man was known not only by his name, but by his rank.[3] Esquires and gentlemen might have their names prefixed by 'Master,' while yeomen were to be called 'John' or 'Thomas,' 'Goodman Smith' or 'Goodman Coot.'[4]

Parliamentary statutes, royal proclamations, town ordinances, and gild regulations all concurred in their deference to status by confining certain apparel and recreations to particular ranks. Elizabethan proclamations, for instance, minutely prescribed the degrees of persons permitted to use satin, silk, cloth of gold, and other rich materials in their outer garments.[5] An act of 1566 regulating hat

[1] *The Petty papers*, ed. Lord Lansdowne, 2v., L., 1927, I, 182–4.
[2] Gregory King, *Natural and political observations*, 1696, in *Two tracts*, ed. G. E. Barnett, Baltimore, 1936, 31. Commenting on King's classification, Professor G. N. Clark has criticized it for attaching too much importance to rank as compared with wealth (*Three aspects of Stuart England*, L., 1960, 39). King, however, as his writings show, took a wide and informed interest in all matters of money, finance, and political economy; and if he differentiated the higher orders according to status (he used occupational and economic criteria for some of the middle and inferior grades), this was because the society itself did so.
[3] Cf., e.g., the act of 1413 which required that original writs in legal proceedings should contain the defendant's 'Estate or Degree, or Mystery ...', *Statutes of the realm*, II, 171.
[4] William Harrison, *Elizabethan England* [*Description of England*, first printed in Holinshed's *Chronicle*, 1577], ed., L. Withington, L., n.d., 8, 13, 16.
[5] R. Steele, *Tudor and Stuart proclamations*, 2v., Oxford, 1910, 517, 717, 890. These proclamations were issued to enforce statutes of Henry VIII and Philip and Mary against excess in apparel.

manufacture was characteristic in ordering that no one 'under the degree of a knight, or of a lord's son' should wear a hat or cap of velvet.[1] Servants and labourers in husbandry were indicted for playing such games as bowls or football legally prohibited to their rank.[2]

Gentlemen whose status had been traduced could seek redress in the Court of Chivalry, a tribunal restored by James I after a long eclipse.[3] The court possessed jurisdiction over wrongs done to gentlemen, and during the 1630s it heard many cases in which aggrieved parties alleged that their gentility had been denied or defamed by 'scandalous words.' The procedure in such suits was for the plaintiff to bring evidence of his rank. He might do this by producing a pedigree or coat of arms, but more commonly he offered proof that he had always lived in the manner of a gentleman and was so reputed; or he might show that his father was a gentleman and known as 'Mr. Rigby,' never 'Goodman Rigby.'

The prevailing mentality accepted these distinctions as belonging to the nature of things. The general attitude was reflected in the recollections of a seventeenth-century clergyman, a yeoman's son, looking back to his childhood in the reign of Charles I. 'Freeholders' daughters,' he said,

were then confined to their felts, pettiecoates and waistcoates, crosse handkerchiefs about their neckes, and white cross-clothes upon their heads. . . . Tis true the finest sort of them wore gold or silver lace upon their wastcoates, good silk laces (and store of them) about their pettiecoates, and bone laces . . . about their linnens. But the proudest of them (below the gentry) durst not have offered to weare an hood, or a scarfe . . . noe, nor soe much as a gowne, till her wedding day. And if

---

[1] F. E. Baldwin, *Sumptuary legislation and personal regulation in England*, Baltimore, 1926, 210. The statutes of apparel were repealed in 1604, *ibid.*, 249.

[2] Cf. indictments in 1621 and 1637, *Nottinghamshire county records*, ed. H. H. Copnall, Nottingham, 1915, 52. The inferior orders were confined to archery and sports believed necessary to condition them for martial action.

[3] G. D. Squibb, *The high court of chivalry*, Oxford, 1959, chs. III, XII. The Long Parliament abolished the Court of Chivalry (the Earl Marshal's court) in 1641 as having no foundation in law. Five years later, however, it appointed a successor commission composed of the earl of Northumberland and other lords and members of the Commons to prevent 'Abuses in Heraldry' and the wrongful assumption of arms (C. H. Firth and R. Rait, *Acts and ordinances of the interregnum*, 3v., L., 1911, I, 838–9). 'The Parliamentarians,' writes the court's historian, 'numbered many armigerous men in their ranks and the prospect of heraldic chaos can have held no attraction for them.' G. D. Squibb, *op. cit.*, 68.

any of them had transgressed these bounds, she would have been accounted an ambitious foole.[1]

From the same angle a gentleman of Kent in 1642 defended his intention to marry beneath his status:

There is one objection, which I doubt not but in the course of my life I shall heare often, and that is my Mistress was a Yeoman's daughter; True itt is her father was a Yeoman, but such a Yeoman as lived in his house, in his company, and in his sportes and pleasures like a gentleman . . . and . . . hee bred his daughter . . . mayntaining her 4 yeares at schoole, amongst other gentlemen's daughters, at the same costs and charges. . . .

He added—a striking remark, in view of the impending civil war— '. . . my former highlie esteeming of politicall nobilitie I now reckon amongst the follies of my youth.'[2]

The highest places in the status system belonged to the peerage and gentry, which were separate ranks. Each of these was further differentiated internally in accordance with such factors as age of title and family eminence, crown office, territorial or neighbourhood importance, size of landed income, and opulence in the aristocratic way of life. Except for titles and the order of precedence they conferred, these were informal criteria: but they effectually stratified landed society, giving rise within the latter to an uppermost layer of lords and greater gentry of particular distinction and prestige.

At the same time, however, peerage and gentry together constituted an aristocratic order. Of this aristocracy, the peerage formed a hereditary nobility recognized by law, while the gentry did not. The peerage thus enjoyed legally sanctioned privileges peculiar to itself, among which was the right to be summoned by individual writ to sit in the House of Lords. But in a social, if not a legal sense, the gentry was also a nobility. It was the English equivalent of the lesser nobilities of the continental states, as appears plainly from contemporary descriptions of it as a '*nobilitas minor.*'[3]

Beneath the aristocratic order came the middle and low degrees. Their inferiority was founded on the practice of occupations or

---

[1] *The life of Adam Martindale . . . by himself*, ed. R. Parkinson, *Chetham society*, IV, 1845, 6–7. This was written in 1685.
[2] *The Oxinden letters, 1607–1642*, ed. D. Gardiner, L., 1933, 278, 279.
[3] Cf. *supra*, 24 and A. R. Wagner, *English genealogy*, Oxford, 1960, 89. Bacon declared in his Star Chamber speech of 1618 that 'here in England are noblemen and gentlemen incorporated' and alluded to knights and gentlemen as '*minores nobiles,*' *Works*, ed. J. Spedding, D. Heath, and R. Ellis, 14v., L., 1859–74, XIII, 303.

functions lacking in honour. In rural society were many yeomen freeholders and copyholders of substance—men who might employ a little agricultural labour and who gained a profitable living from the land. Although deemed a worthy status, they were not gentlemen because they engaged in manual pursuits and attained their prosperity by thrifty ways incompatible with the leisure and display of gentry existence.[1]

In urban society, trade disqualified its practitioners from the status of gentleman. A small minority of merchants might acquire grants of arms, put 'gent.' after their names, or receive knighthoods. The prevailing attitude, however, refused to acknowledge such persons as authentic gentlemen and as a rule classified the mercantile part of the community among the 'citizens and burgesses.'[2]

As for the remaining and still lower levels of the status structure, which of course meant the great majority of the kingdom, their position was summarily defined as having

no voice nor authoritie in our common wealth, and no account is made of them but onelie to be ruled, and not to rule other. . . .[3]

Sir Thomas Smith's words, written in 1565, were equally applicable seventy-five years later when the Long Parliament met. In this category—'lowe and base persons,' according to Smith—he placed day labourers, poor husbandmen, copyholders, many merchants and retailers, and all artificers.[4] At the end of the next century, Edmund Burke, goaded to fury by French revolutionary levelling, expressed the same sentiments:

The occupation of a hair-dresser, or of a working tallow-chandler, cannot be a matter of honour to any person—to say nothing of a number of other more servile employments. Such descriptions of men ought not to suffer oppression from the state; but the state suffers oppression if such as they, either individually or collectively, are permitted to rule.[5]

A type of social organization so congruent with the past in which

---

[1] Cf. Sir Thomas Smith's account of yeomen, *op. cit.*, ch. 23, and the authoritative discussion of yeoman status in M. Campbell, *op. cit.*, ch. II. In current usage the yeoman was in the next degree above husbandman and was a prosperous small farmer, whether he held by freehold tenure of 40s. p.a., as the law defined him, or by copyhold tenure.

[2] Cf. *infra*, ch. V for a fuller discussion of this subject.

[3] Sir Thomas Smith, *op. cit.*, 46.

[4] *Ibid.*, 46.

[5] *Reflections on the revolution in France, Select works*, II, 58.

for centuries lordship of the soil had been the title to authority—so buttressed, too, by law and custom, so rooted in current values, so sanctified by religion as the terrestrial analogy of God's cosmos: this was a resistant and perdurable thing. Under the impact of the economic changes of the pre-1640 century, it responded to new pressures, but was far from being displaced. In England its barriers had never been impassable, and the higher reaches of the status hierarchy were not quasi-castes, as the French *noblesse* tended to be. Loosened by inflation and lubricated by wealth, the structure became less rigid, circulation within it more frequent and rapid.

Contemporaries attributed the accelerated mobility to riches. Robert Burton's jaundiced comment was characteristic:

Thy great great great grandfather was a rich citizen, and then in all likelihood a usurer, a lawyer, and then . . . a Country Gentleman, and then he scraped it out of sheep.[1]

That the heralds of the College of Arms took bribes from aspirants to gentility in return for granting them coat armour contrived under the pretence of antiquity was well known.[2] The relentless social ambition of a climbing age effected a broadened definition of the gentleman. The trend was indicated by Smith's observation that 'gentlemen . . . be made good cheape in England'; and he did not consider the English way amiss that a man who 'can live idly . . . without manuall labour, and will beare the port, charge and countenaunce of a gentleman,' should be accounted one. Thus the university graduate, the student at the Inns of Court, the practitioner of a liberal profession, could style themselves gentlemen.[3] In England, wrote Thomas Fuller in 1642 in his essay on the yeoman, 'the temple of honour is bolted against none. . . .'[4]

What should be obvious, nevertheless, is that the new wine of riches flowed into the old bottles of status. For while the minimal condition for gentility became more easily attainable and the financial buoyancy of the age enabled families to rise in larger numbers, this did not alter the social framework. The status system remained intact and, as before, to belong to the higher orders meant to be or to become of a certain quality and to live in a certain way. The gentleman was still preeminently one 'extracted from ancient and worshipful parentage.' His ambit continued to be landed society. He displayed the hospitality, apparel, recreations of a gentleman and

[1] Robert Burton, *op. cit.*, II, 159.
[2] A. R. Wagner, *op. cit.*, 112.
[3] Sir Thomas Smith, *op. cit.*, 39–40.
[4] Thomas Fuller, *The holy state*, L., ed. 1840, 91.

married according to his rank.[1] It was incumbent on him to show a 'bountifuller liberalitie than others, and keepe about him idle servauntes, who shall doe nothing but waite upon him.'[2] In short, he exhibited the 'ancient characters of true Gentry,' and as the exemplar of an aristocratic ethos, was expected to be 'more affable, courteous, gently disposed . . . of a more magnanimous, heroical, and generous spirit' than the '*vulgus hominum*.'[3]

3

Where status constitutes the prevailing mode of stratification, there also exists a socially sanctioned inequality of living standards between the degrees of men as well as a great inequality of political rights and privileges. But these differentiations are able to survive because such a society tends to develop in its members the type of mentality appropriate to their place in the general scheme. The assumption is assiduously maintained that each order contributes to the welfare of the body politic and that the superior legitimately utilize the inferior for the benefit of all. No provision is made for any bargaining respecting status itself or the marked distinctions it entails. The lower orders, the ruled, must accept their subordination. For them there is virtually no middle course between complete acquiescence and outright rebellion.

Social criticism, of course, issues in abundance from preachers and publicists and is occasionally capable of penetrating insights. Almost invariably, however, its assumptions are fixed within the inherited scheme of inequality, which it seldom questions. Criticism reserves its severest condemnation for the defections of the respective estates from their duties and obligations to the commonweal and one another; it stigmatizes alike the insubordination of the low and the acquisitiveness of the high; if it recommends measures of reform besides the moralist's change of heart, their purpose is to enable the various estates to maintain their way of life within the customary system.[4]

In this profoundly unequal society—it is the society in which the sixteenth and seventeenth revolutions occurred—the power of political and constitutional initiative, of manoeuvre, of obstruction, is

---

[1] *Ibid.*, ch. XL, 'The true gentleman.'

[2] Sir Thomas Smith, *op. cit.*, 40.

[3] Robert Burton, *op. cit.*, II, 165.

[4] On social criticism and the defections of estates, cf. R. Mohl, *op. cit.*, chs. VII–IX and H. C. White, *Social criticism in popular religious literature of the sixteenth century*, N.Y., 1944. A sign of changing times in the sixteenth century was that the remedies proposed against prevailing evils often took the form of legislation.

30

largely restricted at the outset of any struggle to the superior orders. They are the community's governors under the prince; and if we speak henceforth of a governing or dominant class, we shall mean by this the persons who occupy the aristocratic and the privileged sectors of the status hierarchy. These possess in special measure an ascendancy over the rural countryside and its inhabitants; they hold the higher and more honorific offices bestowed by the prince; they are present with influential voice in the assemblies of estates which the prince convokes when he wishes to consult or tax his subjects;[1] their social and political importance entitles them to deference from even the wealthiest *bourgeoisie* and the magistrates of the town corpora- tions.

Thus, when a conflict destined to rend the body politic occurs, its inception is inevitably dominated by the action, the manoeuvres, and the fissions of members of the governing class. Uprisings of the inferior and contemned, such as peasant insurrections, for instance, break out as a rule with sudden violence and are quickly suppressed by the united power of an affrighted society. In some of the greatest rebellions of the age, however, the throne-shaking movements that become protracted civil wars, nobilities and aristocracies take a leading part. These alone possess the authority to draw other orders of men into resistance against divinely appointed sovereigns.

In the French and Netherlands revolts of the sixteenth century, it was seigneurial Protestantism and the adherence of members of the high nobility, such as the princes of the house of Bourbon, the Montmorency family, and William of Orange, that made the Calvinist parties so formidable. The French Huguenot leaders, wrote the Venetian envoy, were 'tutti gentiluomini onorati, e di sangue nobile.' If the reformed churches provided the organizational discipline and sustaining faith in these struggles, the nobility provided the military cadres and political direction. It was no accident, either, that the Calvinists' justification of rebellion was commonly couched in aristocratic terms, placing in aristocracies of 'inferior magistrates' the right and duty to resist tyrannous kings.[2]

The phenomenon of governing class opposition was equally conspicuous in some of the mid-seventeenth-century rebellions. The

---

[1] The relations of assemblies of estates to the society of legalized privilege and inequality is discussed by O. Hintze, 'Typologie der ständischen Verfassungen des Abendlandes,' *Gesammelte Abhandlungen*, 3v., Leipzig, 1941, I.
[2] Cf. H. G. Koenigsberger, 'The organization of revolutionary parties in France and the Netherlands,' *Journal of modern history*, XXVII, 1 (1955) and R. M. Kingdon, 'The political resistance of the Calvinists in France and the Low Countries,' *Church history*, XXVII, 3 (1958). The dissemination of Calvinism within the French social structure is described in L. Romier, *Le royaume de Catherine de Médicis*, 2v., Paris, 1922.

revolt of Catalonia would have been impossible without the concurrence of the native aristocracy and its disaffection from the government in Madrid.[1] Members of the nobility appeared in the forefront of the Scottish Covenanters' resistance to Charles I.[2] In France, the initiators and chiefs of the Fronde were officials of the King's sovereign courts, princes of the blood, and persons belonging to the highest aristocracy.[3] It has been shown as well that French peasant outbreaks of the earlier seventeenth century were frequently inspired by local officials and noblemen; the latter were able to instigate a resistance of diverse strata to the fiscality of the royal regime.[4]

So, too, *mutatis mutandis*, the case was in England. The fundamental cleavage of the decades before the civil war was that which opened *within* the dominant class between the crown and its adherents on the one side, and its opponents on the other. Around this widening split, all the various conflicts in the kingdom gradually became polarized. The antagonism was thus not a lateral one between the orders of society; it was vertical, by degrees dividing the peerage, the gentry and the merchant oligarchies of the towns. At last it drew in also the unprivileged and normally inarticulate mass of men.

As the cleavage grew, the opposing sides acquired names. They began to be called the Court and the Country. The appearance of these terms was of great symptomatic importance. It was a sign of recognition by politically conscious Englishmen of the bitter struggle developing in their midst. It was a sign as well of the progressive deterioration of the unity of the governing class around the crown.

In the strife of the Court and the Country—if diffuse, yet real, not fictitious, collectivities—the English revolution had its origins. And the names themselves are of moment. For when understood they reveal to us how the contemporary mind saw the schism that completely transformed public life between Queen Elizabeth's death and the meeting of the Long Parliament. We shall therefore consider the evolution and meaning of this political terminology, in order that we may then pass in the next chapters to an account of the substance of what it represented.

---

[1] J. H. Elliott, *The revolt of the Catalans*, 485–6.

[2] S. R. Gardiner, *History*, VII, 304–5, 313.

[3] E. Kossmann, *La Fronde*, chs. II, V.

[4] Cf. R. Mousnier, 'Recherches sur les soulèvements populaires en France avant la Fronde,' *Revue d'histoire moderne et contemporaine*, V (1958). This is a critique of B. Porchnev, *Les soulèvements populaires en France de 1623 à 1648* (Moscow, 1948) Paris, 1963. See on the controversy concerning these risings the review by M. Prestwich, *E.H.R.*, LXXXI, 320 (1966), 565–72.

4

To begin with the Country: this was the label most commonly applied to the opposition to the crown before the civil war.[1] Occasionally other terms, such as 'patriots' and 'parliamentarians,' were employed,[2] but 'Country' was becoming current in the 1620s and appears to have been in fairly wide use by the commencement of Charles I's reign.[3] Its emergence reflected the hardening of political differences in these final years of King James and the first of his son. A coalescence of several meanings with subtle overtones and connotations, the name throws a flood of light on the opposition movement's self-conception and the impression it made on the political scene.

The oldest use of the word, dating apparently from the fourteenth century, signified 'county,' and it continued to retain this sense for centuries. Somewhat later, it acquired the further meaning of rural and distant from cities and courts, instances of which occur from the sixteenth century on.[4]

By Queen Elizabeth's time, its meaning as 'county' was becoming fused—doubtless because of the rapid development of parliament at this period—with the general idea of representation and the public interest. Members of the Commons now talked of their duty to their 'Countries' or 'Country.' Thus, when the Privy Council sequestered Strickland in 1571 for his conduct in the House, it was protested 'in regard of the Country, which was not to be wronged,' the debarred member being not a private person but the representative of a multitude. In the monopolies debate of 1601, a member referred to the heavy grievances suffered by the 'Town and Country for which I serve. . . .' When a subsidy was under consideration in 1593, the poverty of 'the Country' was adduced, and a member declared, '. . . our Countries are poor, and we must respect them that sent us hither.'[5] In 1621, Edward Alford, one of the most vocal of the

---

[1] Cf. also P. Zagorin, 'The Court and the Country: a note on political terminology in the earlier seventeenth century', *E.H.R.*, LXXVII, 303 (1962).
[2] For 'patriots,' cf., e.g., the description of Sir Henry Neville's conduct in the parliament of 1610, when he was said to have 'ranged himself with those Patriots that were accounted of a contrary faction to the Courtiers . . .', *H.M.C. Buccleuch*, I, 102. 'Parliamentarians'—'*li parlamentarii*'—occurs frequently in the Venetian despatches, e.g., *C.S.P.V. 1623–25*, 568, 574, *ibid., 1625–26*, 298, 425.
[3] The currency of 'Country' was first pointed out by W. Notestein, 'The winning of the initiative by the House of Commons,' *Proceedings of the British Academy*, XI, 1924–25, 152n. Cf. also D. H. Willson, *The privy councillors in the House of Commons*, Minneapolis, 1940, 122–3.
[4] *Oxford English dictionary, s.v.*, 'Country.'
[5] S. D'Ewes, *A compleat journal of the . . . House of Commons throughout the*

Country opposition, complained that parliament 'had given away our two subsidies and donne no good for our Countrie. . . .'[1] Four years later, a tax proposal in Charles's first parliament was criticized, said a news writer, 'by three or four of the principall speakers who usually stand stiffest for the country. . . .'[2]

Besides the meanings already illustrated, there was also another conception, very familiar in the seventeenth century, of the Country as a mode of existence to be favourably contrasted with the Court. It was implied, for instance, in a remark of the third earl of Southampton, a peer who had gained sad experience of courts as the friend and fellow conspirator of the earl of Essex and who belonged to the opposition in the parliament of 1621. He wrote from his mansion at Titchfield in December 1623:

I have been wholy a country man and seldom seen either the Court or London. . . . In this life I have found so much quiet and content, that I thinke I should hardly ever brooke any other; sure I am I envy none.[3]

Calidore in *The Faerie Queene* expressed the same feeling when he resolved to

> *set his rest amongst the rusticke sort*
> *Rather than hunt still after shadowes vaine*
> *Of courtly favour fed with light report*
> *Of every blast. . . .*[4]

An amusing tract by Nicholas Breton, *The Court and Country* (1618) treated this theme by comparing the two modes of life.[5] Breton, of course, had no intimate knowledge of courts, and his standpoint was solidly burgher rather than aristocratic. He elaborated, however, a conception of the country as the symbol of simplicity and wholesome pleasures based on religion and respect for tradition. Against this he set the court with its sophistication and search for novelty, its moral and financial dangers. There was no suggestion in

[1] *Commons debates 1621*, ed. W. Notestein, F. Relf, H. Simpson, 7v., New Haven, 1935, III, 435n.
[2] *Commons debates in 1625*, ed. S. R. Gardiner, *Camden society*, n.s., 1873, 155–6.
[3] C. C. Stopes, *The life of Henry, third earl of Southampton*, Cambridge, 1922, 449.
[4] Book VI, canto x, 2.
[5] Printed in *Inedited tracts, Roxburghe library*, 1868.

whole reign of Queen Elizabeth, 2nd ed., L., 1693, 175, 645, 646, 490, 491; cf. L. F. Brown, 'Ideas of representation from Elizabeth to Charles II,' *Journal of modern history*, XI, I (1939).

Breton's writing that the two might also stand for opposed political positions, but such a view was already emerging in parliamentary affairs.

There the types of Court and Country first represented the distinction between men officially connected with the Court and royal government and private members not resident in the capital. In 1587, a Puritan member zealous for reformation chided the privy councillors in the Commons for their lack of initiative on this important subject and told them:

. . . if any of the inferior sort here amongst us do happen in some zeal to overstrain himself, surely ye that are honorable . . . ought in equity to bear with them, because the fault is in yourselves. . . . It is wondered at . . . that simple men of the country should be so forward; and it doth amaze us in the country that wise men of the Court should be so backward. . . . Is it fault in a private man to be too busy and can it be excused in a Councillor to be too sleepy?[1]

By the middle years of James I's reign, the unconnected member had passed through a metamorphosis. He now appeared as the honest, disinterested country gentleman, an ideal aura about him. When the privy councillors preparing for the parliament of 1621 were considering how to forestall a general outcry against monopolies, they decided that

the most convenient way will be, if some grave and discreet gentlemen of the country, such as have least relation to the court, make at fit times some modest motions touching the same. . . .[2]

A speaker in the parliament of 1625 described himself as 'neither Courtier nor Lawyer but a plaine Countrey Gentleman;' apparently this description was held to be a sure warrant of a man's candour and lack of prejudice.[3] In 1626, a paper of advice drawn up by Sir Dudley Digges on the King's relations with parliament told Charles to put his trust in these members:

. . . if Your Majesties Grave Counsellours, such as are reverenced for their worth, shall make known your engagements and your wants, the honest Countrie knights . . . will soone shew their Affections. . . .[4]

[1] Cited in J. E. Neale, *Elizabeth I and her parliaments 1584–1601*, L., 1957, 150.
[2] F. Bacon, *Works*, XIV, 146.
[3] *Commons debates in 1625*, 158. The speaker was the oppositionist, Sir Robert Phelips.
[4] P.R.O. S.P. 16/19, no. 107.

All these intimations and aspects of 'Country' were closely inter-woven in its use as the name of the opposition. It referred at one and the same time both to those who on grounds of public interest actively resisted the Court and those who, lacking any connection with the Court, would stand for their 'Country.' Sir John Eliot, a leader of the Country, employed it indiscriminately in both senses. Writing of a debate in the Commons he declared that '. . . it was begun by a gentleman of the Countrie . . . unexpected to the Cour-tiers. . . .'; and alluding to the small attendance in the House on a certain occasion, he remarked, 'ther were hardlie threescore in the house, & of these, countrimen not the most.' His description of the parliament of 1625 contrasted the 'Courtiers' with the 'Countrie,' the antagonists, as he conceived it, in the political struggle.[1]

Evidently Eliot's view was widespread, for in the parliament of 1626 Sir George Goring

tooke exception how the name of Courtyer was a woyrd of faccion, and how he thought that Courtyers were as honest men as any . . . in the house and did interest themselves as much in the good of the State.'[2]

In 1629, the Chancellor of the Duchy, Sir Humphrey May, was provoked into telling the House, 'I wish we heare noe more of the distinction between Courtiers and country gentlemen . . .'[3]

In similar fashion, peers opposed to the King were sometimes known as 'country lords.' Thus did Lord Robartes call them, who was of their number.[4] Lord Savile, an oppositionist who went over to the Court, was regretfully spoken of as 'one of the stoutest Lords in all England for the countrey . . . at first. . . .'[5] The oppositionist, Sir Anthony Weldon, complained of the courtiers' insolence 'to any Country Nobleman, that was not in the Court favour.'[6] A sym-pathetic portrait of the first Lord Spencer, an opposition peer whose wealth came from sheep, depicted him as one that

made the Countrey a vertuous Court, where his Fields and Flockes broughte him more calme and happie contentment, than the various and mutable dispensations of a Court. . . . and when he was called to the

---

[1] Sir J. Eliot, *Negotium posterorum*, ed. A. Grosart, 2v., p.p., 1881, I, 75, 118, II, 49.
[2] Cited in D. H. Willson, *op. cit.*, 213n.
[3] *Commons debates, 1629*, ed. W. Notestein and F. Relf, Minneapolis, 1921, 236.
[4] J. L. Sanford, *Studies and illustrations of the Great Rebellion*, L., 1858, 496.
[5] R. Baillie, *Letters and journals*, ed. D. Laing, 3v., *Bannatyne Club*, 1841, I, 348.
[6] Cited in G. E. Aylmer, *The King's servants*, L., 1961, 463.

Social Structure and the Court and the Country

Senate, was more vigilant to keep the Peoples Liberties from being a
prey to the incroaching power of Monarchy, than his harmless and
tender Lambs from Foxes and ravenous Creatures.[1]

The term, 'Country,' thus suggested that the men it designated were
persons of public spirit, unmoved by private interest, untainted by
court influence and corruption—representatives, in short, of the
highest good of their local communities and the nation in whose
interest they, and they only, acted. It described those members of
parliament who believed that

being chosen for the Country, they are to be all for the Country, for the
Liberty of the Subject, for the freedome of Speech, & to gain as much
and as many Priviledges for the Subject from the King, as is possible.
And if they stand stiffely out in the deniall of Subsidies, to save their
owne & their Countries purses, then they are excellent Patriots, good
Commonwealthsmen, they have well & faithfully discharg'd the trust
reposed in them by their City or Country.[2]

Between men of this political tendency and the court only hostility
could prevail. Hence, according to Thomas Fuller, 'The country
hath constantly a blessing for those for whom the court hath a
curse.'[3] Equally, it was the conviction of the political writer, Henry
Parker, that '. . . we have ever found enmity and antipathy betwixt
the Court and the country. . . .'[4] Clarendon often expressed his
awareness of the differences between the two, and when narrating his
peaceful life before the Long Parliament, he wrote of himself: 'As he
had . . . many friends in court, so he was not less acceptable to
many great persons in the country, who least regarded the court, and
were least esteemed by it. . . .'[5]
But despite the political significance of the name, it cannot be
likened with any accuracy to a modern party title, any more than
those associated in or related to the Country can be supposed to have
constituted a party in the modern sense. A man could be 'of the
Country,' or 'for the Country,' but nowhere at this period is the

[1] Arthur Wilson, *The history of Great Britain*, 1653, 162–3.
[2] [Anon.], *A true presentation of forepast parliaments*, 1629, B. M. Lansdowne, 213, f. 162.
[3] *The church history of Britain*, 1655, ed. J. Nichols, 3v., L., 1842, III, 350.
This remark appears under the year 1627, in Fuller's account of Archbishop
Abbott, whose 'averseness to . . . court-designs' incurred the King's displeasure.
[4] Henry Parker, *Observations upon some of his majesties late answers and*
expresses, 2nd ed., 1642, 11.
[5] *Life*, 931.

37

expression, 'country party,' met with, such as came into use later in the century during the reign of Charles II.[1] The word was both vaguer and less determinate than a modern party name and far more comprehensive in its possible reference. Indeed, its pronounced implication of general interest, and the absence of any explicit association with the idea of party, show how reluctant the men of the time still were to acknowledge the legitimacy of self-constituted organizations coming into being to pursue political ends of their own.[2] Had Eliot, Pym, Phelips, or other opposition leaders in parliament been willing to concede that the Country was anything like a party at all, it could only have been in the exalted sense laid down many years later by Lord Bolingbroke when he stated that

A country party must be authorized by the voice of the country. It must be formed on principles of common interest. It cannot be united and maintained on the particular prejudices . . . or . . . particular interests of any set of men whatsoever. It is the nation, speaking and acting in the discourse and conduct of particular men. . . .[3]

'Court,' the term for the crown's adherents, may be dealt with quite summarily. It was the customary collective designation of the monarch, his residence, council, officials, and courtiers.[4] But coupled as a label with Country, it meant that the King, his councillors, officials, and supporters had become the recognized partisans in a political struggle. Thus, Sir Henry Spelman, the great antiquarian, disclaimed any intention of studying the calamitous history of the parliaments of his own time lest the results should 'displease both Court and Country. . . .'[5] In 1640, a Kentish candidate for election to the Short Parliament was warned that a rival '. . . hath endeavoured . . . to poyson the good opinion the Country hath of you, by professinge . . . howe diligent & eager a servant you were for the Court. . . .'[6] Lord Digby declared after the outbreak of the civil war that he had hoped

---

[1] Cf. G. Burnet, *History of my own time*, pt. I, *The reign of Charles II*, ed. O. Airy, 2v., Oxford, 1897, I, 489, II, 82n.; H. C. Foxcroft, *A supplement to Burnet's history*, Oxford, 1902, 99n., 151, 258; D. Ogg, *England in the reign of Charles II*, 2v., 2nd ed., Oxford, 1955, II, 477, 526–7. On the persistence of Court and Country as political divisions, cf. K. Feiling, *History of the Tory party 1660–1714*, Oxford, 1924, 145, 277.
[2] Cf. C. Robbins, 'Discordant parties: a study of the acceptance of parties by Englishmen,' *Political science quarterly*, LXXIII, 4 (1958).
[3] Lord Bolingbroke, *A dissertation on parties*, Works, 5v., L., 1754, II, 68.
[4] *Oxford English dictionary*, s.v., 'Court.'
[5] Cited in J. G. Pocock, *The ancient constitution and the feudal law*, Cambridge, 1957, 120–1.
[6] Sir John Sedley to Sir Edward Dering, B. M. Stowe 743, f. 140.

for a reconciliation which would make 'The Court and the Country ... to be all of a piece. ...'[1] Related to 'Court' was 'courtier,' mentioned by Pym and Eliot in connection with parliamentary affairs with the implication that the defenders of royal policy were dependents of the crown.[2] Another less frequent term for the crown's supporters was 'royalist,' used as early as 1612 by Francis Bacon,[3] and from time to time also in the Venetian dispatches.[4]

The appearance of *Court* and *Country* as political descriptions signalized the enlarging conflict within the upper ranks of English society. It meant that the organic body politic of the sixteenth century was in process of dissolution and that the bonds which had so intimately united the prince and his subjects in the governing class were falling away. No longer could the King and Court stand as the highest unchallenged expression of an integral authority. Royal power was forced into a certain isolation when it took shape as the Court, one side of the deepening division in political and public life. At the same time, the vagueness and imprecision of 'Court' and 'Country' reflected the transitional character of political affairs from the 1620s onwards, as well as the loose and somewhat unstable composition of the antagonistic groupings. But a new relationship of power in the state was in prospect. What Lord Bolingbroke said of a country party was soon to come to pass:

> ... *whenever such a party finds it difficult to prevail, our constitution is in danger; and when they find it impossible, our constitution must in fact be altered.*[5]

[1] *The Lord George Digbie's apologie*, 1643, 11.
[2] Sir John Eliot, *op. cit.*, I, 75, II, 49; *Commons debates 1621*, IV, 281.
[3] Bacon to King James, May 1612: '. . . I was a perfect and peremptory royalist, yet ... never one hour out of credit with the lower house. ...', *Works*, XI, 280. The word also occurs in the same connection in the first Lord Brooke's *Life of ... Sir Philip Sidney*, *Works*, 4v., ed. A. Grosart, p.p., 1870, IV, 187, which was written in James's reign.
[4] *C.S.P.V. 1628–29*, 580; *ibid.*, *1632–36*, 256 ('*Realisti*').
[5] *Op. cit.*, II, 66.

3

The Court

In an age of personal monarchy, when the prince ruled as well as reigned and his favour conferred riches or power, all roads of advancement led to the Court. The Court was a lottery of fortune. There, ambition might achieve its furthest ends and disaster, political and financial, overwhelm the unlucky.

Kingship was not conceived merely abstractly. It was incarnated in the ruler's person, the sun whose warming rays fructified the body politic. 'The fountain of honour is the king,' wrote Bacon, 'and the access to his person continueth honour in life, and to be banished from his presence is one of the greatest eclipses of honour that can be.'[1] The sovereign possessed a sacral character. 'Ye are Gods,'—so said the Scripture of kings, an image James I liked to invoke and on which the seventeenth century, pondering its meaning, reared an imposing structure of exegesis and commentary.[2] The *mystique* of kingship was expounded in the thought of the theologian and the lawyer. It was blazoned forth with a deep and solemn pomp in the coronation rite. It was vivified in the services of the church in the prayers and homilies. Rebellion was the compound of all sins, civil war the worst of evils.[3] The King's touch could cure, so that common men hastened to his presence to beseech the mysterious gift. On Good Friday 1639, despite the gathering wave of resistance to Charles I's rule, two hundred persons attended on him at York Cathedral to receive his touch.[4] Regality was the sustaining principle of order in the state, the prince's fitness to govern the condition of its peace and well-being. What the prince did, who were the recipients of his

[1] Cited in F. H. Anderson, *Francis Bacon*, Los Angeles, 1962, 46.
[2] Psalm 82.6; cf. *The political works of James I*, ed. C. H. McIlwain, Cambridge, 1918, 307.
[3] Cf. Homily XXI, 'Against disobedience and wilful rebellion,' ed. 1623, reprinted in *Certain sermons or homilies*, Oxford, 1840. Article XXXV of the Thirty-nine Articles authorized the homilies to be read in the churches. Canon XLVI of the Canons of 1604 required them to be read on any Sunday when there was no sermon.
[4] F. Drake, *Eboracum*, 2v., ed. 1788, I, 156.

bounty or ill will, 'who loses and who wins; who's in, who's out;'[1]—these topics provided the talk and cynosure of the body politic.

A throng of ministers, courtiers, officials, and servants belonged to the Court, for the latter in the broadest sense embraced all the organs of central and regional government, all who had to do with the ceremonial position of the monarch as the fountain of honour and head of his people, and all who served him as the greatest landowner and chief feudal lord of the realm. Thus, the Privy Council, the secretaries of state with their staff, the diplomatic personnel, and great departments such as the Exchequer and Court of Wards were part of the Court; so were the courts of common law and equity and the prerogative tribunals—the Star Chamber and the High Commission; so too were the King's household and the households of the Queen and the Prince of Wales. Beyond the seat of government at London, the Court swept out to include officials in every area of the kingdom: receivers of royal revenue and feodaries of the Court of Wards in the counties; persons connected with the Admiralty, the customs, the Duchy of Lancaster, the Councils of the North and in Wales; keepers and surveyors, constables, stewards, and under-officers of royal castles, manors, and forests. All these, in the capital and in the countryside, were the ministers, officials, and servants of the prince, receiving by his authority the fees and perquisites of their places.[2]

What was *not* part of the Court was the structure of county government. The sheriffs, the justices appointed to the commission of the peace, the lords lieutenants and their deputies, were unpaid officers of the crown. The men serving these places were the more important members of the governing class for whom the county was a natural sphere of public activity. They undertook their functions as a duty to prince and community and because of the prestige associated with such offices in landed society. Some of the incumbents might also, of course, be of the Court: the lords lieutenants, for instance, were usually peers or privy councillors, like Viscount Wentworth, who in the 1630s was at the same time President of the Council of the North, Lord Deputy of Ireland, and lord lieutenant of Yorkshire.[3] On the county notables and municipal magistracies depended local administration, civil and military, and the execution of the crown's mandates.[4]

[1] *King Lear*, V, 3, l. 15.
[2] Cf. the account of the personnel of governmental institutions at the time of Charles I by G. E. Aylmer, *The King's servants*, ch. 2.
[3] Cf. Wentworth's letter to his deputy lieutenants of Yorkshire, W. Knowler, *The letters and dispatches of the earl of Strafforde*, 2v., L., 1739, II, 284–5.
[4] Cf. the accounts of the process and personnel of county government by W. B. Willcox, *Gloucestershire . . . 1590–1640*, New Haven, 1940 and T. G. Barnes, *Somerset 1625–1640*, Cambridge, 1961.

The Court and the Country

The seat of a royal power so essentially personal in its nature and so frequently capricious in its operation, the Court was a scene of ceaseless competition for the prizes obtainable by the favour of the King and those who possessed his confidence.[1] Hobbes's analysis of human nature might have been taken thence, where life was a race and envy, joy, and sorrow the passions of the participants as they advanced or fell behind in the contest. The privy councillors advised the ruler in an individual capacity, not as a body endowed with a common voice. At the pinnacle of the Court, they were themselves rivals for the high offices and grants that would increase their wealth and multiply the suitors who crowded their doors. They formed factions that might be associated with differences of policy, but whose principal aim was to extend their influence over the King and form an exclusive channel for the receipt and distribution of the ensuing rewards.

Almost everything at the Court was done by means of patronage and intermediaries. This was the normal accompaniment both of the concentration of personal power in the monarch and of the differentiation and subordination of ranks in society at large. Patronage existed not only in the Court but in the relations between the more and the less powerful everywhere. Government was not conducted by an administrative bureaucracy trained in loyalty to an abstract state, discharging its functions in conformity with objective norms, and recruited according to fixed and impersonal criteria of competence. The King exercised his authority through such instruments as he pleased. To obtain a favourable decision in any business, much depended on the propitiation and support of those with influence. It was essential to gain the countenance of ministers, courtiers, favourite, or of persons near to them.

Moreover, the prevalence of status as the mode of stratification entailed the result that an acknowledged personal dependence should exist between those in authority and their inferiors. At a remoter time, such dependence had commonly rested on a tenurial basis; later, in the decaying feudalism of the fifteenth century, it took the form of good lordship and retainership.[2] By the end of the sixteenth century, though the forms of dependence were much vaguer, the latter still remained a potent factor. It now manifested itself as patronage and influence. Persons desiring success in a suit or advancement attached themselves to men of rank in order to obtain their recommendation. 'The gentleman that shall present these lines'—so went a letter in 1637 from the earl of Dorset to the Lord Deputy of

---

[1] Cf. J. E. Neale, 'The Elizabethan political scene,' *Proceedings of the British Academy*, XXXIV, 1948.

[2] Cf. W. H. Dunham, *Lord Hastings' indentured retainers*, New Haven, 1955.

Ireland, Viscount Wentworth, craving the latter's favour for a friend —'. . . is the descendant of a family that hath for three descents depended on mine. His father, grandfather and now himselfe have ever been owned by us . . . more out of there own inclination then any benefitt . . . myself be able to deserve.'[1] In this way, clients and followings would form around the great and the powerful. A peer or great official who controlled some parliamentary seats might obtain a small following as a result. A landlord of broad possessions with places of profit to grant in the administration of his estates might have numerous dependents in his neighbourhood, while his influence could extend over scores or even hundreds of freeholders. A minister would always be sought out by petitioners wanting his backing. In using their influence on behalf of dependents, men in great place enhanced their own standing and proclaimed the advantage their good will conferred.[2]

Inevitably, the nature of Court life evoked ambivalent attitudes in all who had to do with it. A veteran courtier dismissed from the service of the Prince of Wales, the future Charles II, declared, 'Were I to live a thousand years I would never sett my foott within a court againe, for there is nothing in itt butt flattery and falshood.'[3] Dependence frequently led to humiliation and patient merit was often spurned. At the age of forty-six, Francis Bacon, still unsuccessful in his pursuit of office, petitioned his cousin, the earl of Salisbury, James I's chief minister, for the Solicitor's place—though he knew, he said, 'how mean a thing I stand for. . . . For . . . it is not the thing it hath been.' He reminded Salisbury of his hopes, 'your Lordship being pleased to tell me, during the course of my last service, that you would raise me; and that when you had resolved to raise a man, you were more careful of him than himself. . . .' Bacon obtained his desire, but after Salisbury's death, he affirmed that his relation to the minister had been that of 'a hawk tied to another's fist, that mought sometimes bait and proffer but could never fly.'[4]

The 'aulical faculty' requisite to success in the Court came far short of the standard of conduct demanded by a moralist. Sir Robert Naunton, a cold-eyed observer of court ways, Master of the Wards under James and Charles, told of the saying of one of Elizabeth's

---

[1] Strafford MSS., v. 22, no. 136.
[2] On the role of patronage under Elizabeth and in the early Stuart period, cf. J. E. Neale, 'The Elizabethan political scene,' *loc. cit.*; W. T. MacCaffrey, 'Place and patronage in Elizabeth politics,' *Elizabethan government and society*, ed. S. T. Bindoff, J. Hurstfield, and C. Williams, L., 1961; D. Mathew, *The social structure in Caroline England*, Oxford, 1948, 4–6.
[3] *The autobiography of Anne, Lady Halkett*, ed. J. G. Nichols, *Camden society*, n.s., XIII, 1875, 30. The remark was made by Will Murray.
[4] *Works*, X, 296–7, XI, 279.

peers '(and it did him no good), That he was none of the *Reptilia*, intimating that he could not creep on the ground, and that the Court was not his element.' Another courtier, an unfortunate Deputy of Ireland, was 'a person who loved to stand too much alone, and on his own legges . . . a fault . . . incompatible with the wayes of Court and favour.'[1] Elizabeth's favourite, the earl of Leicester, was noted by Sir Henry Wotton, another Jacobean commentator on court practices, to be 'a great Artizan of Court,' one who did 'nothing by chance nor much by affection.'[2] Bacon's essays contained sombre reflections on the nature of courtly advancement. 'All rising to great place,' he wrote, 'is by a winding stair. . . .' The rising

is laborious . . . and it is sometimes base; and by indignities men come to dignities. The standing is slippery, and the regress is either a downfall, or at least an eclipse, which is a melancholy thing.[3]

Although tradition idealized the courtier-type as the incarnation of high virtues, the reality was commonly otherwise.[4] Sir John Harington, having spent years in a frustrated quest for the prizes of courtiership under Elizabeth and James, held that 'He that thryveth in a Courte must put halfe his honestie under his bonnet. . . .'[5] The poet, Wither, an opposition sympathizer, wrote in 1628:

The Court is fraught with bribery, with hate,
With envie, lust, ambition, and debate;
With fawnings, with fantasticke imitation,
With shamefull sloth, and base dissimulation.
True Virtue's almost quite exiled thence. . . .[6]

A treatise on courts composed in the reign of Charles I pictured the courtier as driven by ambition and avarice to

contrive strange plotts, basely serve others turnes and use all . . . artifices to compasse his projects; and this is the reason hee putte himselfe to the sea of the court, hoping by that voyage to gett the golden

[1] Sir R. Naunton, *Fragmenta regalia*, 1641, *Harleian miscellany*, 12v., L., ed. 1811, V, 137, 140.
[2] Sir H. Wotton, *A parallel betweene Robert, late earle of Essex, and George, late duke of Buckingham, Reliquiae Wottonianae*, 3rd ed., L., 1672, 162.
[3] 'Of great place.' Cf. also the essays, 'Of followers and friends' and 'Of suitors.'
[4] Cf. the account of the literature of English courtiership in J. E. Mason, *Gentlefolk in the making*, Philadelphia, 1935, ch. VII.
[5] *Nugae antiquae*, ed. H. Harington, 3v., L., 1779, II, 153.
[6] G. Wither, *Britain's remembrancer*, 1628, 195–6.

The Court

Peru, and to finde out a Magelan advancement. . . . There is noe
Machiavilian politie which he diveth not into . . . nor sordid actions
which he doth not accomplish. . . . [Courtiers] nourishe Oppositions and
factions to make the pathe more facill for their endes. . . . Theire Motto
is; Qui nescit dissimulare nescit vivere. . . .[1]

The Court was not known for loyalty or disinterested friendship.
'. . . a cashiered Courtier,' said Bishop Williams after Charles I
dismissed him as Lord Keeper, 'is an Almanack of the last Year,
remembered by nothing but the great Eclipse.'[2] The declension of a
courtier or minister was the signal of an imminent redistribution of
places of profit. On the disgrace of the earl of Somerset, King James's
favourite, Viscount Lisle, commander of the English garrison at
Flushing, was informed by a dependent, 'Undoubtedly their will be
by this man's fall manye good things in his Matys. guifte againe. I
beseache your Lordship take this Occation . . . to move for sumthing
for me unto his Maty.' Naturally, the author of this request hoped
too that 'this great man's fall will rayse your Lordship and some of
your nobell friendes to your just and worthye demerits. . . .'[3]

Despite the dangers of the Court, every man of rank understood
the importance of having good connections there. Lord Burghley
advised his son, Robert:

Be sure to keep some great man thy friend, but trouble him not for
trifles. Compliment him often with many, yet small gifts, & of little
charge. And if thou hast cause to bestow any great gratuity, let it be
something which may be daily in sight. Otherwise, in this ambitious age,
thou shalt remain like a hop without a pole, live in obscurity, & be made
a foot-ball for every insulting companion to spurn at.[4]

Widely circulated, Burghley's precept was frequently cited by
aristocratic fathers in the seventeenth century. Sir John Holles, later
earl of Clare, addressed the same counsel to his heir, as did the earl
of Derby, who added, however, that 'Court friendship is a cable that
in storms is ever cut.' The chief thing, he asserted, was that his heir
should look well to his estate: for 'though a friend at court be . . .
better than a penny in the purse, yett keepe your owne estate & a

---

[1] Edward Payton, *A discours of Court and courtiers*, 1633–4, B. M. Harl.
3364, ff. 29–30. Dedicated to the young duke of Lennox, this writing preserves, despite its strictures, the idealistic tradition of courtier literature.
[2] J. Hacket, *Scrinia reserata*, L., 1693, pt. II, 26.
[3] *H.M.C. De L'Isle and Dudley*, V, 340, 344 (Sir John Throckmorton to Lord
Lisle, Nov. 1615).
[4] Printed in F. Peck, *Desiderata curiosa*, L., ed. 1779, Bk. I, 49.

penny to spare, & you will create friends in court or countrey at any time.'[1] The earl of Huntingdon recommended his son to go to the Court for brief visits no more than once or twice yearly: 'I should be sorry that you should like a court life too well, for it is but a *splendida miseria.* . . .'[2]

If some got wealth in the Court, others squandered it. Viscount Wentworth impressed his youthful nephew and ward, Sir William Savile, with the financial risks to be run there:

. . . think not of putting yourself into Court before you be thirty years of Age at least, till your Judgment be so awakened, as that you may be able to discover and put aside such Trains, as will always infallibly be laid there for Men of great Fortunes, by a Company of Flesh Flies, that ever buzze up and downe the Palaces of Princes; and this let me tell you, I have seen many men of great Estates come young thither and spend all, but did I never see a good Estate prosper amongst them that put itself forward before the Master had an Experience and Knowledge how to husband and keep it. . . .[3]

A Court life, often extremely costly, could make deep inroads on a man's fortune. The Kentish baronet, Sir William Twysden, left his son a heavily encumbered inheritance because of his extravagant expenditure at Court.[4] The earl of Carlisle, another of James I's favourites, had tasted the royal bounty to the extent of many thousand pounds; yet so great was his outlay that in 1622 he complained that he could not subsist without further help from the King. At his death in 1636 his debts were said to exceed £120,000.[5] The pursuit of office put the earl of Newcastle into debt for £40,000. In 1633 he told Wentworth that debt and disappointment made him resolve to press his suit no longer: 'It is better to give over in tyme wth some losse than lose all. . . .'[6] The position and success of Court luminaries, like that of the glittering figures in the cinema capitals of the twentieth century, depended so much on spectacular spending and dazzling consumption that men of large inherited estates might

---

[1] *The letterbook of Sir John Holles, H.M.C. Portland,* IX, 6; *Stanley papers,* pt. iii, *Chetham society,* LXX, 1867, 45; F. Peck, *op. cit.,* Bk. XI, 443.

[2] *H.M.C. Hastings,* IV, 333, II, 70–1.

[3] *The earl of Strafforde's letters,* I, 169–70.

[4] F. W. Jessup, *Sir Roger Twysden,* L., 1965, 11–12, 19–21.

[5] Carlisle, then still Viscount Doncaster, to Buckingham, B.M. Harl. 1581, ff. 335–8; *C.S.P.V. 1632–36,* 558.

[6] *The earl of Strafforde's letters,* I, 101–2; G. E. Cokayne, *Complete peerage,* rev. ed., 13v., L., 1910–49, *s.v.,* 'Newcastle, 1st earl.' In 1638 the earl's ambition was finally gratified when the King appointed him governor of the Prince of Wales.

well think it prudent not to venture themselves in the Court's dangerous waters.[1]

Beyond all these considerations, great rising and an eminent career in the Court were attended by envy, hatred, and faction. 'Happy the favourite,' wrote Fuller, 'that is raised without the ruin of another.'[2] The actors on the Stuart political scene long retained the memory of the rivalry between the Essex and Cecil factions and of Essex's fall and execution at the setting of Queen Elizabeth's reign. The reigns of James and Charles likewise witnessed the disgrace of such Court personages as the earls of Somerset and Suffolk, Bacon, and Bishop Williams, whose calamity pointed up the perils incident to high office. The weightiest words on the subject were those Sir Edward Stanhope addressed in intimate friendship to Viscount Wentworth, vainly imploring the nobleman not to accept the Irish deputyship then dangling before him. 'How manye men,' Stanhope warned,

. . . have endeavored to sease on the hyghest and most honorable places in the state, and having reached their desiered prey, before they could feed enough to satisfye their exorbitant appetites, have miserably fallen . . . into disgrace and infamye. . . . How many have purchased their owne ruin att a deare rate . . . by contracting for the greate and burthensom offices of the Kingdom? . . . How many greate officers in our times made, in our times unmayde agayne. . . . Som thrust out by heade and shoulders, some led out . . . som for pleasing others, som for being corrupt, som for integritye . . . soe have greate offices bin purged, and the officers, som with detestation and infamye eiected, som like excrements that every man avoyds both sight and sence of. . . . And yet how many competitors have striven whoe shall succeede, and then the next that fills itt is the next (before warme in itt) that leaves itt for another.[3]

This foreboding letter was penned in 1631. Ten years later, with the spectacle of Wentworth's disastrous end before his eyes, Stanhope could only have exclaimed, 'O my prophetic soul!'

2

The Court's resources for gratifying the hope of preferment were of diverse kinds. They ranged from the bestowal of titles and places of

[1] This point has been stressed by M. Finch, *Five Northamptonshire families*, 63.
[2] T. Fuller, *op. cit.*, LXVI, 'The favourite.'
[3] P. Zagorin, 'Sir Edward Stanhope's advice to Thomas Wentworth, Viscount Wentworth, concerning the deputyship of Ireland: an unpublished letter of 1631,' *Historical journal*, VII, 2 (1964), 316–17.

honour, through rewards of land or money, grants of valuable fiscal privileges under the royal prerogative, such as monopolies and customs farms, miscellaneous rights in the crown's gift that could be a source of profit to their recipients, and appointment to office. The commonest aim, however, of the seeker after advancement was office, which might also afford access to other benefits obtainable in the Court. We shall therefore confine our attention to the nature and significance of office.[1] In particular, we shall wish to consider how far officials constituted a *bloc* committed to the support of the King's power and whether they were a body socially distinct from men without Court affiliation.

The fundamental feature determining the nature of office in the seventeenth century was that the latter was usually a species of property which belonged to its occupant in the same way as did his land. This characteristic derived from feudal times, when public functions of all sorts were granted out to private men as property to be held on certain terms. Despite the lapse of centuries, offices preserved this peculiarity. Both they and the emoluments pertaining to them were regarded as a form of freehold from which their possessors could not be legally disseized.[2] The King, according to Bacon, 'can no more take away the profits of a man's office, than . . . the profits of his land.'[3]

To be sure, the tenure specified in grants of office varied. A sampling, for instance, from the reign of Charles I contains offices conferred for life, for two lives, for thirty-one years, during pleasure, during good behaviour, and hereditarily in a few cases where the grant was made to a man and his heirs.[4] The principle of life tenure, however, had steadily gained ground in the royal service since the fifteenth century, so that by the seventeenth the majority of offices, including occasionally even such high political appointments as the secretaryship of state, appear to have been granted for life.[5] Many

---

[1] Office in England in the earlier seventeenth century is the subject of comprehensive treatment in G. E. Aylmer's *The King's servants*; cf. also his paper, 'Office holding as a factor in English history, 1625–42,' *History*, XLIV, 152 (1959).

[2] Cf. the account of the legal position of office as property in Sir W. Holdsworth, *A history of English law*, 13v., L., ed. 1922–52, I, 246–8.

[3] F. Bacon, *Works*, XIII, 295; instances of contemporary legal opinion to the same effect respecting office and its profits are given in Sir W. Holdsworth, *op. cit.*, I, 260 and J. Wilson, 'Sir Henry Spelman and the Royal Commission on Fees 1622–1640,' *Studies presented to Sir Hilary Jenkinson*, Oxford, 1957, 467.

[4] These specimens are taken at random from grants of office under the privy seal printed in T. Rymer, *Foedera*, 20v., L., 1704–32, XIX, *passim*.

[5] On the tenure of offices, cf. G. E. Aylmer, *The King's servants*, 106–25; A. F. Havighurst, 'The judiciary and politics in the reign of Charles II,' pt. I,

office holders thus enjoyed great security in their places. An objectionable official with life tenure might be interdicted from exercising his functions, but to remove him was extremely difficult.[1] The easiest way was to procure a candidate as his successor who would offer a pecuniary inducement sufficient to make him relinquish his place voluntarily.

The usual means of obtaining office were purchase and patronage. These were not mutually exclusive, as patronage was often exercised in behalf of someone who wished to buy an office in which other competitors were interested. It was also possible to succeed to an office by acquiring the reversion; and if an official owned the reversion to his place, he could bequeath it to an heir. Through the device of reversions, a hereditary element was introduced into the crown service, resulting in an association between certain families and offices or departments that might last for generations, like that of the Fanshawes, Osbornes, and Crokes with the Exchequer.[2]

Although legally the buying and selling of offices was forbidden—at any rate in the law courts and revenue departments—the prohibition was ineffectual and trafficking in office a common occurrence.[3] Wither adverted bitterly to the practice in 1628:

> *Nor will this Iland better dayes behold,*
> *So long as offices are bought and sold.*
> *Nor shall I ever think that any one,*
> *Much cares, what right or injury be done,*
> *That buyes or sels an Office. . . .*[4]

[1] Officials appointed for life could be removed only if convicted of high treason or of contravening the act of 1552 against the sale of offices. The latter, however, seems to have been nearly a dead letter.

[2] Cf. G. E. Aylmer, 'The officers of the Exchequer, 1625–1642,' *Essays in the economic and social history of Tudor and Stuart England,* ed. F. J. Fisher, Cambridge, 1961, 172–4.

[3] Sir W. Holdsworth, *op. cit.*, I, 246–8, 250–1, has summarized the legislation concerning venality of office. There is a brief account of the practice in England in K. Swart, *Sale of offices in the seventeenth century,* The Hague, 1949, ch. III. Cf. also the discussion and instances in D. Mathew, *The Jacobean age,* L., 1938, 209–15 and G. E. Aylmer, *The King's servants,* 225–39.

[4] G. Wither, *Britain's remembrancer,* 189.

Law quarterly review, LXVI (1950), 64–5; and J. C. Sainty, 'The tenure of offices in the Exchequer,' *E.H.R.,* LXXX, 316 (1965). Sainty has commented on the increase of life tenure in office and has attributed the phenomenon to the growing replacement of clerical by lay officials. As regards the secretaryship of state, F. M. G. Evans declares that the office was granted during pleasure and the salary for life (*The principal secretary of state,* Manchester, 1923, 211). Sir George Calvert, however, was appointed for life in 1619 (*C.S.P.D. 1619–23,* 14).

The character of such a transaction in the upper reaches of the crown's service may be illustrated from the attempt by Sir Dudley Carleton, ambassador in Holland, to purchase one of the two secretaryships of state in 1624. The office was held by Sir George Calvert, appointed for life in February 1619. Carleton, who had been seeking further preferment for some time, was informed that Calvert wished to retire because of ill-health and would sell his place for £6,000. The price seemed reasonable, as the secretary's office was said to be worth £2,000 *per annum* and £7,000 and £8,000 had been offered for it prior to Calvert's appointment. Naturally, the King would have to sanction an arrangement by which one of his secretaries left to make way for another. But Carleton was unlucky. He was passed over on Calvert's resignation and the office obtained by Sir Albertus Morton, Clerk of the Privy Council. On the latter's death a few months later, the secretaryship went to Sir John Coke, a client of the King's favourite, the duke of Buckingham. Carleton was told that he had been denied promotion because he had fixed his dependence on persons averse to Buckingham and all his undertakings.[1]

In contemporary France, venality of offices, however strongly deplored, was an established policy of the crown and a regular source of the King's revenue.[2] This was not the case in England. While both James I and Charles I sometimes sold offices, they did not institutionalize the practice; nor was it mainly the crown that profited from the sale of places in its service. The beneficiaries were the courtiers and ministers who used their influence for money. In addition, officials themselves also profited from venality. Some of them possessed in right of their office the gift of appointment to subordinate posts in their departments: this was a feature of certain offices, for instance, in the law courts and the Exchequer. Naturally, the officials enjoying this privilege commonly exercised it only in favour of one prepared to offer a good bargain. The gains thus made were a recognized item in the profits of office.

Salaries, generally fixed long before the seventeenth century, were small and usually represented the least part of office-holders' income. Far more important were the various perquisites, the scheduled fees exacted from those using their services, and confidential gratuities and bribes. The latter kinds of payment were the inevitable consequence

---

[1] The details of this transaction may be followed in *C.S.P.D. 1619–23*, 14, *ibid. 1623–25*, 231, 450, 457, 472, *ibid. 1625–26*, 100. Carleton had actually tried to win Buckingham's support by sending him from the continent a costly gift of marble for his building. Carleton later achieved his ambition, becoming, as Viscount Dorchester, Secretary of State in 1629.

[2] Cf. R. Doucet, *Les institutions de la France au XVIe siècle*, 2v., Paris, 1948, I, ch. XVIII and R. Mousnier, *La vénalité des offices sous Henri IV et Louis XIII*, Rouen, 1945.

of low official remuneration. The earl of Dorset, Chamberlain to the Queen, asserted during a Star Chamber suit in 1635 in which an officer stood accused of fraud that 'he did not think it a crime for a Courtier that comes up to Court for His Majestie's service, and lives at great expence in his attendance, to receive a reward to get a business done by a great man in Power. . . .'[1] Dorset's remark merely reflected the current attitude, which maintained a tenuous distinction between the permissible present or *douceur* and the impermissible bribe, thus tolerating practices which a later age would unhesitatingly pronounce corrupt.

Besides irregular gifts and rakeoffs, there was a steady tendency for the fees demanded by officials to increase in size and number.[2] The proprietary conception of office doubtless encouraged incumbents to make what gains they could. Wither blamed their extortions on the system of venality:

> *It is a sum of money that prefers*
> *To ev'ry place; and that makes knaves, and sharks,*
> *Of Sergeants, Waiters, and of Under-clarks.*
> *This maketh Registers, in ev'ry Court,*
> *And other Ministers, so much extort:*
> *This makes them seek out knots, demurs, delayes,*
> *And practise many unapproved wayes,*
> *To make up that which foolishly they paid:*
> *. . . .*[3]

In the parliament of 1621 there was a strong protest against exactions by officials: Bacon's impeachment as Lord Chancellor on the charge of bribery was connected with this outcry. In 1610 criticism of the rapacity of office-holders had resulted in the first of a series of royal commissions to investigate excessive fees in offices. Although these commissions functioned intermittently until 1640 and gathered a large quantity of information on the malpractices of officials, they appear to have done little to reform the abuses complained of by parliamentary orators.[4]

It has been pointed out that the payments which officials took

---

[1] J. Rushworth, II, 313.

[2] Cf. the fees taken in the Court of Wards and Liveries, H. E. Bell, *An introduction to the history and records of the Court of Wards & Liveries,* Cambridge, 1953, 36.

[3] *Britain's remembrancer,* 190–1.

[4] Cf. J. Wilson, 'Sir Henry Spelman and the royal commission on fees 1622–1640,' *loc. cit.* and the less favourable verdict on these commissions by G. E. Aylmer, 'Charles I's commissions on fees, 1627–1640,' *Bulletin of the Institute of Historical Research,* XXXI, 83 (1958) and *The King's servants,* 182–203.

beyond their remuneration from the crown were in effect an indirect tax levied on the public to finance the costs of administration. The royal government was thus spared the necessity of having to draw on its own hard-pressed income to raise its servants' pay, grown totally inadequate in the seventeenth century after decades of inflation.[1] Of the economic significance of this *de facto* transfer of costs by the monarchy there can be little question. An estimate for the early 1630s suggests its magnitude. At that time, when Charles I's ordinary annual revenue averaged about £618,000, the fees and gratuities of officials have been reckoned at between £250,000 and £400,000. A sum that may possibly have exceeded 40 per cent of ordinary revenue was thus paid, in lieu of crown remuneration, as an indirect tax to officials by the persons who, for whatever reasons, used their services.[2]

It must not be supposed, however, that office was in itself a high road to fortune, for the places in which spectacular gains were possible were relatively few. Families such as Cecil, Montagu, Villiers, Feilding, Goring, Wentworth, and Weston, who established peerages on the riches acquired through office or favour in the Court were not typical of the official class as a whole. The enormous sums, licit and illicit, which Robert Cecil, first earl of Salisbury, realized by his ministerial posts under King James as Treasurer, Master of the Wards, and Secretary of State were most exceptional—an Eldorado to which only a tiny minority could hope to gain admittance.[3]

Moreover, office was desired for diverse reasons and incumbents treated it in various ways. It might be wanted to provide a regular income—a consideration which, in the absence of an organized system of pensions and annuities, often entered into the purchase of offices and reversions.[4] When Sir Henry Wotton, thrice ambassador to Venice, returned from his last embassy in 1623, he sought an office on which to live. By Buckingham's intercession he obtained the provostship of Eton. This gave him security in his old age (he was then fifty-six), though besides his residence and perquisites, his stipend came to only £140 per annum.[5] On the other hand, office

[1] Cf. J. Hurstfield, *The Queen's wards*, L., 1958, 348.
[2] These figures come from G. E. Aylmer, *The King's servants*, 246–8. Aylmer's estimate of ordinary revenue appears to have been taken from Gardiner, *History*, X, App. I.
[3] Cf. L. Stone, 'The fruits of office: the case of Robert Cecil, first earl of Salisbury, 1596–1612,' *Essays in the economic & social history of Tudor and Stuart England*.
[4] D. Mathew, *The Jacobean age*, 209–10, has stressed this aspect of office.
[5] L. P. Smith, *The life and letters of Sir Henry Wotton*, 2v., Oxford, 1907, II, 284, I, 200–1, 204–5. Wotton also received a pension of £200 *p.a.* from the King in 1611 which was increased in 1632 to £500. He owned two reversions which he surrendered to Buckingham in exchange for the office of Provost of Eton.

might be desired as a form of investment to yield a high return on capital. Such a purpose probably actuated Paul D'Ewes, the father of the parliamentary diarist, Sir Simonds D'Ewes, to buy a Six Clerks office in the Court of Chancery for nearly £5,000 in 1607: the elder D'Ewes kept the place for twenty-three years, realizing about £32,500 from it.[1]

In contrast to officials who wanted a regular income or a return on capital, others used their position like entrepreneurs. Richard Boyle exploited his offices in Ireland with such success that he made a great fortune and secured Irish peerages for himself and two of his sons.[2] Sir Arthur Ingram was another who became extremely rich by exploiting office and other devices of profit obtainable in the Court.[3]

Some aspirants looked for office only as a means to further promotion. A feodary's place in the Court of Wards was described as one '. . . not of profit, but rather an introduction to better fortunes.'[4] At the other extreme, office was sought for its political importance and honorific status as much as for its pecuniary value. Great places like that of Lord Treasurer, Lord Admiral, Lord Chamberlain, and Lord Steward were of this kind. The occupants of these in the seventeenth century were privy councillors *ex officio*: personages, it was said, 'by place and office soe interested in the businesses of state as they are of the Councell.'[5]

Since office was frequently property and commonly viewed in that light, its rationale was not exclusively one of service to prince or public. This circumstance was profoundly important for the political consequences of office holding. Undoubtedly, so far as concerned high officials in the executive, the legal departments, and the household, the aspect of service to their royal master would be prominent: though most of them, too, were keenly interested in their private enrichment. But in general, the idea of office as a trust entailing the disinterested performance of public duties was little developed. Rather, the usual concern in office was primarily with its pecuniary side, and only secondarily with its public features. Hence office-holders did not necessarily favour the royal government's policy or

---

[1] *The autobiography and correspondence of Sir Simonds D'Ewes*, ed. J. O. Halliwell, 2v., L., 1845, I, 179.
[2] Cf. T. O. Ranger, 'Richard Boyle and the making of an Irish fortune, 1588–1614,' *Irish historical studies*, IX (1957) and *Lismore papers*, ed. A. B. Grosart, 10v., pp., 1886–8, II, 239.
[3] Cf. A. F. Upton, *Sir Arthur Ingram*, Oxford, 1961.
[4] *C.S.P.D. 1629–31*, 373. Bishop Goodman took a more favourable view of a feodary's office; cf. G. Goodman, *The court of James I*, ed. J. S. Brewer, 2v., L., 1839, I, 271.
[5] Cf. E. R. Turner, *The Privy Council of England in the seventeenth and eighteenth centuries*, 2v., Baltimore, 1927, I, 77.

invariably feel themselves obliged to support it. Considerations of this sort had little to do with the motives of most seekers and occupants of Court places. In parliament's conflict with the King after 1640, some officials remained neutral, while others, if they did not adhere to parliament, nevertheless complied with it. A prudent care for their stake in office might lead them to such a course. The official of the posts in Durham who declared during the protectorate of Oliver Cromwell that he had bought his place in 1637 for £120 and intended 'to be true to any government established' expressed a view easily comprehensible in revolutionary times.[1] The Long Parliament itself was sensible of the claims of office-holders and disposed to give them compensation if their places were extinguished by its reform measures.[2]

Notwithstanding the great patronage resources at the crown's disposal and the many motives inducing men to the Court, the latter was a much less solid body politically than might be expected. In the intermediate ranks of the royal service were men who belonged to the Country opposition or were in some way related to it.[3] Even courtiers and ministers in the highest positions, however, were not always steady in their adherence to the King's policies. Factional differences and personal rivalries often caused them to hinder crown measures underhand and give covert support to oppositionists. Bacon warned James I of the evil consequences of Court disaffection. As long as turbulent spirits, peevish Puritans, and popular men, he said, should be able when opposing the King's causes to 'have a retreat . . . in the favour of some great person, let his Majesty look for nothing but tempest.'[4] In the parliament of 1614, the earl of Northampton, a privy councillor, incited a member to denounce the favour shown by the King to the Scotsmen at Court.[5] Great peers and councillors such as the third earl of Pembroke, who was Chamberlain and afterwards Lord Steward, and his brother and heir, the fourth earl, who also became Chamberlain, did not hesitate to abet oppositionists. Intent on extending their personal power against competitors, they gave their countenance at different times both to the Country leaders and to those who were discontented in the Court. The fourth earl was reputed a protector of the Puritans, and had the habit of 'speaking frankly of the oversights of the Court that he might not be thought a slave to it.'[6]

[1] J. Thurloe, *State papers*, 7v., L., 1742, IV, 283.
[2] Cf. the pensions which the Houses assigned to be paid to the officers of the Court of Wards, abolished in 1646, H. E. Bell, *op. cit.*, 160–1.
[3] Cf. *infra*, ch. IV.   [4] *Works*, XII, 188–9.
[5] Cf. T. L. Moir, *The addled parliament of 1614*, Oxford, 1958, 138, 140.
[6] Clarendon, *Rebellion*, I, 122, VI, 399; *C.S.P.V. 1636–39*, 571. Pembroke's steward at Baynard's Castle, Nathan Walworth, was certainly a Puritan; cf.

In parliament men with Court connections did not form a disciplined group always ready to follow the lead of councillors and ministers. The parliamentary transactions of the time were studded with episodes in which members of the lower House who enjoyed office or favour either acted independently or refused to rally behind the government's spokesmen. Bacon asserted that one of the great problems of political management was the 'drawing of that body of the house which consisteth of courtiers and the K[ing's] servants to be . . . sure and zealous for the K[ing] and not fearful or popular.'[1] In the parliaments of 1621 and 1625, the opposition received support from many who held offices.[2] After the Long Parliament met, a number of officials in great or profitable places abandoned the Court and went over to its enemies. In short, not all attached to the Court were deeply or unalterably committed to it; not all officials who enjoyed advancement there would remain loyal in the struggle for power that impended.

When we turn to the social basis of the Court, nothing stands out to distinguish the members in its intermediate and highest regions from the dominant class as a whole. Socially speaking, they were more or less homogeneous with the general body of gentlemen who governed England. As a rule, their family origins lay in the gentry.[3] Economic interests in the land, kinship, and neighbourhood associations linked them with their fellows of the aristocratic order who lacked Court connection. Like the latter, they usually owned landed properties out of which they derived a portion of their income. Together with the latter, they might be appointed to the commission of the peace. If they left office, it was to the land they went and in landed society that they took, or aspired to take, their place.

In these respects there was no perceptible difference between the peers, knights, and gentlemen in Court offices and their counterparts in the Country opposition. Of course, the fortunate insiders who profited from monopolies and other crown rewards thereby acquired pecuniary interests not shared beyond the favoured circle. But the dislike these parasitic devices of enrichment provoked was not a

---

[1] *Works*, XI, 366.

[2] Cf. W. F. Mitchell, *The rise of the revolutionary party in the House of Commons*, N.Y., 1957, 90 and J. N. Ball, 'Sir John Eliot at the Oxford parliament, 1625,' *Bulletin of the Institute of Historical Research*, XXVIII, 78 (1955), 115. D. H. Willson, *The privy councillors in the House of Commons 1604–1629*, also gives numerous instances of the disunity and disaffection of courtiers and officials in the Commons.

[3] Cf. the social description of Charles I's officials in G. E. Aylmer, *The King's servants*, ch. 5.

The correspondence of Nathan Walworth and Peter Seddon, ed. J. S. Fletcher, *Chetham society*, CIX, 1880.

manifestation of social antagonism. It was simply the reaction of men who saw the King's power and resources used for purposes they condemned, or who perhaps in an occasional instance envied the opportunities beyond their reach. The conflict between the Court and the Country was therefore not rooted in social or economic contradictions. Fundamentally, it expressed a *political* opposition among the governing and wealthy members of the society, divided by their attachment or hostility to the operation of the authority and prerogative power of the crown.

Because the Court and the Country were formations within the governing class, no rigid barrier separated the two. It was possible, therefore, for men connected with the Country to pass over to the Court. All that was necessary was a political change of front. A number of instances of this kind took place in the 1620s and '30s, just as the reverse movement occurred afterwards when the Court collapsed in 1640–1.

Sir Dudley Digges, for example, was a prominent opponent of the crown in the House of Commons and in 1626 served as one of the House's managers in its impeachment of the duke of Buckingham. But having shown his disapproval of the opposition's conduct at the parliamentary dissolution of 1629, he obtained the reversion to the important office of Master of the Rolls, actually succeeding to the place in 1636.[1] William Noy, a great lawyer in his day, took a similar course. Conspicuous as an oppositionist in the parliaments of the 1620s, he made a political turnabout, became the King's Attorney-General in 1731, and lived to devise the execrated ship money tax.[2] Another instance was Sir Henry Yelverton, who was first an oppositionist and then, on obtaining the King's good will, became successively Solicitor-General and Attorney-General. Next, a quarrel with Buckingham caused his disgrace and in 1621 he attacked the favourite when called before the House of Lords to give evidence on monopolies. Four years later he pleaded to be restored to favour, and having made his political peace, was appointed a judge of the Court of Common Pleas.[3]

But the most momentous of political reversals was that accomplished by Sir Thomas Wentworth, later famous as Viscount Wentworth and earl of Strafford. Member of an important Yorkshire family, heir to a baronetcy and a great estate, Wentworth did not require Court infusions to supplement his fortune. The earlier part of

---

[1] Gardiner, *History*, VI, 99; *C.S.P.D. 1627–28*, 2, *ibid. 1629–31*, 392; *D.N.B., s.v.*

[2] *D.N.B., s.v.*

[3] Gardiner. *History*, IV, 22–3, 111–15; *C.S.P.D. 1623–25*, 461; *D.N.B., s.v.*

his public career was a record of opposition and of slights from the King. By his second marriage in 1624 to Arabella Holles, daughter of the earl of Clare, he was related as well to a prominent opposition family. Wentworth's actions in the parliament of 1625 incurred the disfavour of both Charles I and Buckingham. In consequence, he and other Country spokesmen were pricked as sheriffs to render them ineligible for election to the House of Commons in the following year.[1] This disqualification, Lord Clare wrote him, 'me thinkes ... putts a marke of estimation uppon you & your fellowes, for perseqution is oftner a sumtome of virtu, then reward.'[2] In 1626 he suffered the further humiliation of being summarily dismissed from his dignity as *custos rotulorum* of the Yorkshire commission of the peace.[3] A year later, when the King exacted a forced loan from his subjects, Wentworth appeared amongst the principal resisters, being summoned by the Council and committed for his defiance.[4] The climax of his political association with the Country came in the parliament of 1628, where he virtually led the House of Commons in its efforts to secure the liberties of the subject.[5]

Yet throughout his years of opposition, Wentworth repeatedly sought admission to the Court. He aspired to a peerage, sued for office, and tried unavailingly to make a bargain of support with the favourite, Buckingham. Then in July 1628, shortly after the close of the parliamentary session in which he had distinguished himself, he attained his aim. He received a peerage and several months later was appointed President of the Council of the North. To this high place was added in 1632 the great office of Lord Deputy of Ireland.[6]

Did Wentworth, then, adhere to the Country from conviction, or because he wished to become so considerable in opposition that the King would think him a personage worth gaining for the Court? The answer must remain uncertain. What is undeniable, however, is that if he held any principles, his conduct was no less marked by mercenary self-interest and lack of scruple. These traits appeared fully in his political *volte-face*, whose nature is revealed in the letter sent him in 1631 by his intimate and kinsman, Sir Edward Stanhope. In this extraordinary communication, from which we have already cited,

[1] Cf. Sir Arthur Ingram's letter, *The earl of Strafforde's letters*, I, 28.
[2] Strafford MSS., v. 22, no. 53.
[3] *The earl of Strafforde's letters*, I, 36.
[4] *Ibid.*, I, 37–8.
[5] C. V. Wedgwood, *Thomas Wentworth first earl of Strafford*, L., 1961, ch. V.
[6] Wentworth's approaches to the Court are summarized in P. Zagorin, 'Sir Edward Stanhope's advice to Thomas Wentworth, Viscount Wentworth, concerning the deputyship of Ireland,' *loc. cit.*, 301–2.

Stanhope conveyed the truth of Wentworth's entry to the Court.[1] He there drew an imaginary picture of the voice of malice speaking of Wentworth to Charles I as follows:

Sir you have bin of late pleased to cast a speciall eye of Royall favor on Sir Thomas Wentworth. Why, I know not, unless itt hath bin to with draw him (beinge but a private Gentleman, which maks the wonder greater) from his vyolent and refractory courses against you and your iust designs, which rather should have provoked you to have showred downe tempests of your displeasure on his disobedient head and heart. But you whoe have ever desiered more to shew mercye and win favor then to inforce by vyolence ... have honored him by creatinge him a Baron ... and a Peere of the Realme. ... being perswaded by the Duke of Buckingham (whoe receaved his informatione from the Lord Treasurer [Sir Richard Weston] that undertooke to reduce him to a mylder temper and make him his creature). ...[2]

Wentworth thus abandoned the Country for the King's service on his agreeing to become the duke of Buckingham's dependent—a transaction in which the Treasurer Weston, another of Buckingham's clients, was the intermediary. In this way did he enter the path to preferment and power. And so, too, did destiny set him on the course which led him thirteen years later to Tower Hill and the executioner's axe, the most hated minister in three kingdoms.

3

It was in 1616 that George Villiers, the future Buckingham, began his career as favourite. Supported by the affection of two kings, he rose to the meridian of power, there to shine in blazing splendour until the knife of an assassin extinguished his light. With his beauty of

---

[1] Both H. F. Kearney (*Strafford in Ireland*, Manchester, 1959, 27–8) and C. V. Wedgwood (*op. cit.*, 68) connect Wentworth's entry into the Court with the reorientation of English policy towards Spain. According to them, Wentworth disliked the war against Spain, begun in 1624, and as soon as the government started to veer towards peace and friendship with Spain in 1628, he had no further reason to continue his political opposition. This explanation of his conduct appears to me implausible and I know of no convincing evidence to support it.

[2] P. Zagorin, 'Sir Edward Stanhope's advice to Thomas Wentworth, Viscount Wentworth, concerning the deputyship of Ireland,' *loc. cit.*, 314. C. V. Wedgwood alludes briefly to this letter (*op. cit.*, 122), thirty-five folio pages in length, which the present writer first published in 1964 from the Strafford MSS. Inexplicably, she fails to quote from it or to observe its significance for the comprehension of Wentworth's personality and political career.

person and his adeptness in the complimenting ways of courts, the youthful Villiers became the recipient of the most lavish gifts both James I and Charles I could bestow. A golden shower of wealth and offices descended on him. Swift promotion through the peerage brought him in 1623 to the culminating honour of the dukedom of Buckingham. By King James's aid he secured an earl's daughter for his wife. The rays of princely benefaction fell equally on his kindred and dependents, fructifying them with titles of nobility and grants of money, land and office. Never did a subject wield greater influence or grow to such prodigious height under the sun of royal favour.[1]

Buckingham's domination formed an epoch of critical importance in the pre-history of the revolution. It deformed the workings of the King's government and the patronage system. It sowed disaffection in the Court and was a prime cause of enmity on the political scene. It brought the royal regime into hatred and contempt. To the favourite's ascendancy must be ascribed in no small measure the decline of the crown's moral authority—an authority indispensable to government which, once lost, can hardly ever be recovered.

With all his sway over affairs, Buckingham had no real policy or extended aims. Unlike his contemporary ministers, Richelieu and Olivares, his predominant purpose in the use of power was to aggrandize himself and his dependents. Both the maxims of statecraft and the examples of prudent rulers warned princes to beware of permitting any subject a monopoly of rewards and influence.[2] Thus had Elizabeth governed, and in her greatest indulgences to favourites she took care to balance her generosity to one by the countenance she gave to another.[3] But James and Charles were neither as strong nor shrewd as the great Queen. The result was that they allowed Buckingham to secure virtually complete control of the higher administration and the machinery of patronage, thereby inflicting incalculable harm upon the monarchy.

Of all the organs of authority, the Council was the most important. The nerve and brain of regal power, on its right functioning the effectiveness of the King's government depended, and every episode of feeble or uncertain rule in the previous century had been connected with its impairment or debility. The establishment of Buckingham's

---

[1] *D.N.B.*, *s.v.*, 'George Villiers, first duke of Buckingham' and cf. also the sketch of Buckingham's rise and relation to the King by G. P. V. Akrigg, *Jacobean pageant*, Cambridge, 1962, ch. XVII and M. A. Gibb, *Buckingham*, L., 1935.

[2] Cf. Charles V's so-called political testament of 1543 to his son, Philip II, in K. Brandi, *The Emperor Charles V*, tr. C. V. Wedgwood, L., 1939, 490–2.

[3] Cf. the observations of Sir R. Naunton, *Fragmenta regalia*, *loc. cit.*, V, 123–5, and of Fulke Greville, Lord Brooke, *The life of . . . Sir Philip Sidney*, *Works*, IV, 176, 181.

dominion was quickly followed by the Council's decline. Privy Councillors became his mouthpieces or feared to express their views. The Council toiled at routine business, while great matters were reserved for private consultation between the King and favourite.[1] This condition, prevalent in James I's later years, continued after Charles I's accession. In the first Council meeting of the new reign, the earl of Arundel, a Privy Councillor since 1616, protested against the Council's exclusion from affairs, but to no avail.[2] With perfect justification did the Venetian envoy write in a *relazione* of England that 'There was no longer any Council' since Buckingham alone 'with three or four creatures constituted it.'[3]

While rendering the Council impotent, Buckingham also fastened his grip on key positions in the King's government. The machinery of promotions and favour in the Court could operate with full political advantage to the crown only if its fruits were not at the disposal of a single faction. Some rough parity, at least, between rivals was essential. But under the favourite's rule, the system of patronage which sustained the Court suffered the severest distortion. The principal levers were in his hands. It was him, not the King, whom suitors had to propitiate for benefits sought, and him whom they must thank for what was received. He alone could open the door to offices of importance in the royal service. The resentment his control aroused only made his hold the tighter, lest his enemies dislodge him from his eminence. Thus, what ought to have been a powerful asset in the strength of the crown became a source of weakness; and while the Country opposition denounced him, in the bitter words which Tacitus used of Sejanus, as a man 'audax, sui obtegens . . . superbus . . . clientes suos provinciis adornare,'[4] the Court itself was divided and some of its great personages disaffected.

For himself, Buckingham obtained a collection of honourable offices providing rich opportunities for influence and the gratification of dependents. During his primacy he became Master of the Horse; Lord Admiral; Lord Warden of the Cinque Ports; Warden, Chief Justice, and Justice in Eyre of the forests this side of Trent; Constable of Windsor Castle; and Chancellor of the University of Cambridge. He held, besides, a place in the royal household as Gentleman of the Bed Chamber. To diminish criticism, he resigned his wardenship of the Cinque Ports shortly before his death to the earl of Suffolk, 'a mean spirited man, his creature and humble servant. . . .'[5] When the

---

[1] *C.S.P.V. 1621–23*, 229, ibid., *1625–26*, 603, ibid., *1626–28*, 22, 128.
[2] *Ibid., 1625–26*, 12, 21.   [3] *Ibid., 1625–26*, 603.
[4] This expression was quoted by Sir John Eliot in a speech during the impeachment proceedings against the duke in 1626; cf. J. Rushworth, I, 355.
[5] *C.S.P.V. 1628–29*, 213.

Lord Steward's place fell vacant in 1625 through the death of the duke of Richmond, he was urged by his dependent, the Lord Keeper, Bishop Williams, to take it for himself. 'It keeps you,' Williams pointed out,

in all Changes and Alterations of years, near the King; and gives unto you all the Opportunities of Accesses, without the Envy of a Favourite. . . . It gives you Opportunities to Gratifie all the Court, great and small, Virtute Officii . . . which is a thing better accepted of, and interpreted, than a Courtesie from a Favourite; because in this you are a Dispenser of your own, but in the other (Say many envious men) of the King's Goodness. . . .[1]

Buckingham, however, had sufficient restraint to let this dignity go to the earl of Pembroke, the Lord Chamberlain, in an ineffectual attempt to purchase the latter's support.[2]

In addition to these places, the duke enjoyed lucrative royal grants and gifts of land. In 1623, his income exceeded £15,000 per annum. A sinecure in the Court of King's Bench alone yielded £4,500, while a grant on the customs of Ireland gave him £3,100 and an Exchequer pension £1,000. His lands in five counties produced nearly £6,000 more.[3]

The royal service, furthermore, was staffed with his clients, and his correspondence a tale of sycophantic requests for his favourable notice.[4] The Secretaries of State, Sir John Coke and Viscount Conway, made their careers by his patronage and were wholly at his bidding.[5] The Lord Keeper, Bishop Williams, rose in the same way, and lost his post after he fell into disfavour.[6] He was succeeded by Sir Thomas Coventry, still another dependent.[7] Sir Lionel Cranfield

---

[1] *Cabala*, 3rd ed., L., 1691, 280–1.
[2] Cf. *C.S.P.V. 1625–26*, 500, 515.
[3] These figures are taken from a report made in July 1623 by commissioners whom Buckingham appointed to ascertain his estate; cf. P.R.O. S.P. 14/149, no. 91. His expenses, made high by the requirements of Court display, almost equalled his income. They amounted to £14,700, £3,000 of which was spent on housekeeping, £2,500 on charges at Court, £2,000 on servants' wages and pensions, £1,200 on the stable, £1,500 on wearing apparel, and £2,000 on private expenses for rewards. Letters to Buckingham on the care of his estate are contained in B.M. Harl. 1581, *passim*.
[4] Cf. the letters in B.M. Harl. 1580, 1581, and *Fortescue papers*, ed. S. R. Gardiner, *Camden society*, n.s., I, 1871.
[5] For Coke, cf. *C.S.P.V. 1625–26*, 168, and D. Coke, *The last Elizabethan*, L., 1937. Conway's letters and references to the duke are those of client to patron; cf. *C.S.P.D. 1627–28*, 224, 225, 434.
[6] J. Hacket, *op. cit.*, pt. II, 24.
[7] *C.S.P.V. 1625–26*, 238.

became Master of the Court of Wards and was promoted to Treasurer and the earldom of Middlesex with Buckingham's support.[1] Sir Richard Weston's advancement in the royal service also occurred under his auspices.[2] The Admiralty was filled with his creatures, Sir James Bagg, Vice-Admiral in Cornwall, subscribing himself in letters as the duke's 'humble servant and slave.'[3] Prominent courtiers like George Goring furthered their aims as his dependents. '... I so sucked in debt from my cradle,' Goring told Buckingham, 'as I never knew what freedom was. ... with hope and my eyes well fixed upwards I have as your Lo:p sees yet lived.'[4] To ambitious gentlemen who aspired to noble titles, the duke became a broker, procuring peerages for them at a price. Clerical careerists besought his aid. By the duke's 'sole procurement,' said Bishop Laud, 'I am made a Governour [in the Church].'[5] '... one blast of your Breath,' Bishop Field of Llandaff prayed, 'is able to bring me to the Heaven where I would be. ...'; the bishop meant the see of Ely or of Bath and Wells.[6] What Lord Keeper Williams told the favourite was not far from the truth: 'Lett all our Greatness depend ... upon youres, the true Originall. Lett the kinge be Pharao, youre self Joseph, and lett us com after as your halfe Brethren.'[7]

Buckingham's unprecedented sway aroused intense antagonism, but as James continued, despite all criticism, to support the duke, the latter became a heavy liability to the crown and a prime cause of political enmity. In the Court the strongest resentment was felt towards the man who engrossed the favour of two princes, the setting and the rising sun, King James and Prince Charles. The duke of Richmond, Lord Steward and a cousin of the monarch, strove to unseat Buckingham from the royal affections.[8] During the second session of the parliament of 1625, the earls of Arundel and Pembroke consulted frequently with members of the Commons against him.[9] In the 1626 parliament, Pembroke employed his territorial influence and his office of Warden of the Stannaries to elect opponents of Buckingham and the Court. The first to call for the duke's impeachment in

[1] B.M. Harl. 1581, ff. 89–90; *Cabala*, 263; cf. also R. H. Tawney, *Business and politics under James I*, Cambridge, 1958, 125–6.
[2] B.M. Harl. 1581, ff. 202, 204.
[3] *C.S.P.D. 1627–28*, 444, 447.
[4] B.M. Harl. 1580, f. 405.
[5] *Cabala*, 108.
[6] *Ibid.*, 111.
[7] *Ibid.*, 263.
[8] *Letters of John Chamberlain*, ed. N. E. McClure, 2v., Philadelphia, 1940, II, 542. Richmond's dislike is seen in a letter sent in 1623 to Lord Herbert, ambassador in France, P.R.O. Powis MSS. 30/53/10, f. 165.
[9] Sir Arthur Ingram to Wentworth, November 1625, *The earl of Strafforde's letters*, I, 28.

this parliament was a member returned to the Commons with Pembroke's aid.[1] There is no doubt that Charles I's difficulties with parliament were acutely aggravated because of the support discontented courtiers gave the Country leaders in their attacks on the duke and his measures.

Once, and once only, did Buckingham try to win over the Country opposition by identifying himself with a popular policy. Successful at first, the attempt ended in failure, an episode that pointed up the complexity of the political scene before public differences hardened beyond any likelihood of reconciliation.

As early as 1621, the favourite had been persuaded to make a tentative move to mollify his antagonists. On the advice of a kinsman who suggested that he 'oblige the Puritans, and lay a groundwork for his own security, if tempests should arise,'[2] he secured the appointment of John Preston, a clergyman who was spiritual guide to some of the principal Puritan gentry, as Prince Charles's chaplain.[3] Compounding this good office, he then assisted Preston the next year to become Master of Emmanuel College, Cambridge. Preston's promotion was the first step towards a tactical alliance between the Court and the Country. It was not till 1624, however, in consequence of a sharp reversal in the King's foreign policy, that a *rapprochement* became possible.

King James had long pursued a Spanish marriage for his son, and with it also the chimerical hope of Spain's assistance for the restoration of the Palatinate, his son-in-law's principality occupied by the Catholic-Imperialist forces at the beginning of the Thirty Years War. In 1623, Buckingham and Charles journeyed to Madrid to press the long-discussed marriage treaty in person—an imprudent venture, exposing the prince to unnecessary danger, which aroused strong criticism at home. English opinion, in any case, heartily disliked the proposed alliance, as it saw in Spain the national enemy and the supreme menace to continental Protestantism. At Madrid negotiations proved unsuccessful. Buckingham, therefore, to remove the odium they brought on him, resolved to sponsor a fresh policy. He returned from Spain determined to end the Spanish connection with parliament's backing and to make a French marriage alliance instead. This was an objective the Country opposition could support. The result of the agreement was seen in the parliament of 1624, where the

---

[1] *C.S.P.D. Addenda 1625–49*, 112–13; *H.M.C. Mar and Kellie, Supplementary*, 237; V. Rowe, 'The influence of the earls of Pembroke in parliamentary elections 1625–41,' *E.H.R.*, L, 198 (1935), 247–8.

[2] T. Ball, *Life of John Preston* in S. Clarke, *A general martyrologie*, L., 1677, pt. 2, 49–50.

[3] Cf. Christopher Hill's essay on Preston in *Puritanism and revolution*, ch. 8.

duke and Charles, who concurred in the new line, found themselves for the first and only time exponents of a policy that parliament endorsed.[1]

On behalf of the Country leaders in the House of Commons, Buckingham pressed the unwilling King for concessions. James, he insisted, should allow him to 'assure some of them underhand' that their advice for a war with Spain and a grant of money for this purpose would be accepted. He further told the monarch of the fear 'that when your turns are served, you will not call them together again to reform abuses. . . . and the making of laws for the good government of the country. . . .' James must therefore show himself in love with parliaments, and to prove his sincerity must permit a parliamentary committee to supervise the expenditure of moneys raised for the war.[2] Throughout this time, the duke was in cordial association with principal men of the opposition, and together with the Prince an advocate of all popular courses.[3] 'I did never see,' wrote an old Scottish courtier, '. . . onye Parliament lyke to it, whitche dois evrye daye grate upone the King's prerogative soe mutche. . . . It is verrye strange to see the Prince goe on soe in applawding all or the most pairt of their doeings, whitche . . . monye thinks he shall never recover againe. . . .'[4]

Buckingham and the opposition got their war. Negotiations were started for a match with France which led the next year to Charles's marriage to Henrietta Maria, sister of Louis XIII. Parliament was permitted freely to debate foreign policy matters and to impeach the unpopular Treasurer, the earl of Middlesex, who fell out of the duke's good graces because he disliked the break with Spain on grounds of economy. Parliament's Subsidy Act trenched deeply on the King's prerogative, giving the lower House supervision of the collection and expenditure of the money voted for the war.[5] But notwithstanding these concessions, the agreement with the Country did not last. The oppositionist leaders and the Commons, wanting a sea war accom-

---

[1] An account of the short-lived alliance between Buckingham and the Country is given in I. Morgan's biography of John Preston, *Prince Charles's Puritan chaplain*, L., 1958; cf. also J. F. Maclear, 'Puritan relations with Buckingham,' *Huntington Library quarterly*, XXI, 1 (1957).

[2] *Hardwicke state papers*, 2v., L., 1778, II, 466, 467–8. A similar letter of advice to James from the earl of Carlisle (*Cabala*, 197–8) seems also to be connected with Buckingham's strategy.

[3] Cf. his letters to Sir Robert Phelips, *Cabala*, 314–15, and Richard Knightley, *Fortescue papers*, 196–7.

[4] The earl of Kellie to the earl of Mar, May 1624, *H.M.C. Mar and Kellie, Supplementary*, 200.

[5] Cf. the act in J. R. Tanner, *Constitutional documents of the reign of James I*, Cambridge, 1930, 374–9 and the remarks of C. Roberts, *The growth of responsible government in Stuart England*, Cambridge, 1966, 39–40.

panied by penetration of Spain's American empire, showed themselves unprepared to support the cost of land hostilities on the continent. In addition, their suspicion of Buckingham remained invincible. The love of the Puritans 'is yet but green towards [you],' Bacon had informed the duke. '. . . there are a great many that will magnify you and make use of you for the . . . putting the realm into a war, which will after return to their old bias.'[1] Bacon's forecast proved correct, and the period immediately following Charles I's accession saw the liaison of the Court and the Country draw to an end. In the first parliament of the reign, the strain became great during the second session as the Country leaders opposed further money grants and conditioned for religious and other reforms.[2] By the time the parliament of 1626 met, the alliance lay in ruins and Buckingham confronted the prospect of impeachment.

The destruction of the political *rapprochement* was at the same time also of considerable consequence for the Church of England. Previous to this, Buckingham's policy of conciliating the Puritans made it uncertain that the Arminian and high-church party[3] would be allowed to prevail in the Anglican establishment.[4] The duke gave his support to silenced Puritan ministers,[5] and Preston even went so far as to broach a project for solving the crown's financial difficulties by the confiscation of episcopal lands. There were reports, too, that Charles I would appoint Preston Lord Keeper in succession to Bishop Williams.[6] In February 1626, while parliament was sitting, Buckingham sponsored a conference at his London house where a number of theologians publicly debated the merits of the Arminian position. Preston was one of the disputants, but the Calvinistic divines failed to convince the duke; indeed, their opponents had the best of the argument.[7] After this, Puritan influence swiftly waned, while the oppositionists' attack in parliament on Buckingham and

---

[1] *Works*, XIV, 442.

[2] Cf. the speeches of Sir N. Rich and Sir R. Phelips in H. Hulme, *The life of Sir John Eliot*, L., 1957, 89, and J. N. Ball, 'Sir John Eliot at the Oxford Parliament, 1625,' *loc. cit.*

[3] The nature of the Arminian movement in the church is discussed below in ch. VI.

[4] The persistent anxieties of high-church clergymen at this period appear in Richard Montague's letters to John Cosin; cf. *Correspondence of John Cosin*, ed. G. Ornsby, *Surtees society*, LII, 1869, 98, 100, 103.

[5] The eminent ministers, John Dod and Arthur Hildersam, were permitted to resume preaching, I. Morgan, *op. cit.*, 42 and Dr. Williams's Library, Morrice MSS., G., f. 841.

[6] J. Hacket, *op. cit.*, pt. I, 204; G. Burnet, *op. cit.*, I, 27–8.

[7] This conclusion can be drawn from a reading of the debate in J. Cosin, *The sum and substance of conferences lately had at York House, Works*, ed. J. Sansom, 5v., Oxford, 1843–5, II.

the King's policy removed all further incentive to conciliate the Puritans. Preston himself, according to his contemporary biographer, '. . . finding that his standing at Court was undermined . . . resolved upon Buttresses to underprop him in the Countrey.'[1] It was now that Bishop Laud, who enjoyed Buckingham's patronage, was able to consolidate his own and the intolerant Arminian ascendancy over ecclesiastical affairs. Thus, the resumption of the conflict between the Court and the Country gave the administration of the church to men as responsible as any for provoking revolution.

The next three years witnessed the aggravation of political and religious division, while the King's governmental methods aroused growing resistance. The levying of loans and taxes widely regarded as illegal, imprisonment of the crown's opponents, general hatred of the favourite—these provoked what by 1629 was very nearly a revolutionary situation.[2] Military failure added to the regime's discredit. Operations against Spain were signally unsuccessful and war with France, begun in 1627 in support of the Huguenots, equally so. In August 1628 Buckingham was assassinated. The following March Charles dissolved his third parliament in an atmosphere of bitterest animosity. Henceforth he determined to rule without summoning again a body he had found to be unmanageable. He adhered to this resolution until the Scottish rebellion, breaking out in 1638, led on to its eventual denouement in the convening of the Long Parliament and the rout of the Court.

4

In the decade before the revolution, the King did nothing to remove the causes of his subjects' discontents. At home he showed himself altogether unforeseeing of the dangerous weather that lay close ahead. Abroad, his policy aimed at avoiding any undertakings which he could not sustain without parliamentary assistance. To this end he made peace with France in 1629, with Spain in 1630. The ministers managing affairs had all enjoyed Buckingham's patronage. None succeeded to the duke's position, however, and Charles never again gave his unreserved friendship to anyone. Sir Richard Weston, appointed Lord Treasurer in 1628 and subsequently created earl of Portland, was the leading minister, the one, it was stated, 'who moves all the wheels of this government as he pleases. . . .' Joined with him was his colleague, Lord Cottington, Chancellor of the Exchequer and Master of the Court of Wards.[3] These men were clever politicians, in

[1] T. Ball, *Life of John Preston, loc. cit.*, pt. 2, 108. Preston died in 1628.
[2] Cf. *infra*, 110–11.
[3] *C.S.P.V. 1629–32*, 588, *ibid., 1632–36*, 55–6.

no wise statesmen, agile enough on the slippery paths of the Court, but unfit to steer a state should waves run high. On Portland's death in 1635, Archbishop Laud became the most considerable person in the Privy Council. The archbishop's importance was the most conspicuous sign of the increase of clerical influence in the Court that contributed so much to envenom politics and estrange even the crown's supporters.

Translated from London to the archbishopric of Canterbury in 1633, Laud already possessed control of the church because of the King's confidence in him and the displeasure into which his predecessor, Archbishop Abbott, had fallen. Once primate, he was able to place the full resources of his metropolitan authority behind his ecclesiastical programme. This was inspired by the grand conception of a national church, uniform in worship and doctrine, acknowledging its affinities with the historic Catholicism of Rome but purged of Rome's errors, and submissive to God's vicegerent, the King, and to God's spiritual representatives, the bishops. Such a uniformity, however, resting on clericalism and ceremonialism, could not be attained: both Puritan opposition and the prevailing moderate Anglicanism of the laity forbade it. But the archbishop had no indulgence for those who differed. Personally insecure, troubled by fears that he would fall out of favour, he detested every challenge to his position.[1] Thus when he met resistance, he pursued his goal by means of the whip, the pillory, and the prison. To English Protestantism he became what the Counter-Reformation was to the Protestantism of the continent. His pressures for a church order towards which most of his countrymen were antipathetic brought both himself and the royal regime into odium.

And the weight of Laud's power was felt in other matters besides religion. '. . . this is the great man,' said a courtier of him in 1635, 'made now of the Commissioners of the Treasury and the First of the Junto of Foreign Affairs, and in the greatest esteem with his Majesty of any in my observance.'[2] He took a conspicuous part in the Court of Star Chamber. He was active on the commission to investigate enclosures. In 1636 his influence secured the appointment of his episcopal colleague, Juxon, Bishop of London, as Treasurer. He was, indeed, a ubiquitous presence in the King's government. Charles trusted Laud for his reverence of monarchy, his loyalty, and his lack of opportunism. So great a political role permitted an ecclesiastic was

---

[1] The deeper recesses of Laud's personality are glimpsed in his diary, printed in *Works*, ed. W. Scott and J. Bliss, 7v., Oxford, 1847–60, III. Cf. also the sketch of his life by S. R. Gardiner in *D.N.B., s.v.* and H. R. Trevor-Roper, *Archbishop Laud*, L., 1940.

[2] Sir T. Roe to the Queen of Bohemia, *C.S.P.D. 1635*, viii.

unprecedented since the Reformation. It touched the nerve of English anti-clericalism and prepared the storm of condemnation that was about to break upon the church.

Ablest of the King's ministers during the 1630s was Wentworth. With all his defects of character and vision, he alone of those in the Court had perhaps some quality of greatness in him. His imperious nature, his heroic energy, and his proconsular confidence in the invulnerability of the King's power made him a formidable royal servant.[1] In office he distinguished himself at once by his capacity and rigour. Lacking the politic pliability of weaker men, he suffered no hindrance to the crown's authority or to himself as its instrument. '... this is an arrogance grown frequent now-a-days,' he declared, that

every ordinary man must put himself in balance with the King. . . . Silly wretches! Let us not deceive ourselves. . . . The ground whereupon Government stands will not so easily be washed away, so as the sooner we unfool ourselves of this error, the sooner we shall learn to know ourselves, and shake off that self-pride, which hath to our own esteem represented us much bigger, more considerable, than indeed there is cause for.[2]

As a minister Wentworth did not fail to exploit his position to enrich himself greatly; in 1637 his annual income, by his own account, was £27,000.[3] But at the same time he strove unsparingly to render the crown independent and powerful. He was resolved that the King must conquer what he called 'The universal Distemper of this Age, where the Subjection nestles itself too near the Sovereignty, where we are more apt wantonly to dispute the Powers which are over us than in former times.'[4] That he himself had but recently exemplified this same distemper, irony, of course, can hardly overlook. Nevertheless, only Archbishop Laud among the other councillors was actuated with equal inflexibility by the same purpose, and the two men were united in a policy of Thorough, as they named it. The

---

[1] Wentworth's best biography is C. V. Wedgwood's, *op. cit.*, which gives an absorbing account of his life and career; cf. J. P. Cooper's review in *E.H.R.*, LXXIX, 311 (1964). Suggestive observations will also be found in H. D. Traill, *Strafford*, L., 1889 and D. Mathew, *The age of Charles I*, L., 1951, ch. VI.

[2] *C.S.P.D. 1631–33*, xxv.

[3] So Wentworth told his friend, Lady Carlisle, *H.M.C. De L'Isle and Dudley*, VI, 90. On Wentworth's financial dealings, cf. J. P. Cooper, 'The fortune of Thomas Wentworth, earl of Strafford,' *Economic history review*, 2nd ser., XI, 2 (1958).

[4] *The earl of Strafforde's letters*, II, 161.

injustices each committed in his official career were to bring the day of reckoning upon them both. In the Council Wentworth was disliked and resented for his arrogance, energy, and success. He was incapable of forming a faction of his own, so that despite Laud's friendship and support, he remained isolated in the Court.[1] 'I procure daily so many Ill-Wishers,' he told the archbishop,

keep the Friends I have with so much difficulty in this rigid Way I go for my Master's Service, as almost makes Business unwelcome unto me, yet so long as I do serve, I will Thorough *by the Grace of God. . . .*[2]

When Wentworth was offered the Irish deputyship in 1631, Sir Edward Stanhope warned him that the appointment was a plot of his Court rivals, Weston and Cottington, who sought his removal from England. Eager to dissuade his friend, Stanhope described the Irish office as a burden too heavy for the shoulders of Atlas and Ireland as 'the last refuge of desperate hope . . . whither never man of eminency went, but was driven as the surest meanes of his over-throw. . . .'[3]

Nevertheless, Wentworth's record in Ireland seemed for long to defy these gloomy prognostications. He dominated the subject kingdom as none of its former governors could. Mastering every element of Irish society, he made all interests yield to the King's and not least those of the ruling English colonial minority.[4] But in the end, his severe and unscrupulous rule drove Ireland to revolt, while it convinced the Country oppositionists in England that there was no safety for them if he lived.[5]

The King himself, although conscious of Wentworth's exceptional services, remained cold and aloof towards him for a long time. Evidently something in Wentworth's forceful personality grated painfully on Charles. Twice the minister petitioned to be made an earl as a fresh sign of royal esteem, requests the King denied in chill and lapidary words.[6] As the emergency of the Scottish insurrection grew, however, Charles at length turned to Wentworth as the strongest pillar of his state. In the fall of 1639 he summoned the

---

[1] Cf. his remarks to the earl of Newcastle in 1638, *The earl of Strafforde's letters*, II, 174.

[2] *Ibid.*, II, 250.

[3] P. Zagorin, 'Sir Edward Stanhope's advice to . . . Viscount Wentworth, concerning the deputyship of Ireland,' *loc. cit.*, 303–6, 308.

[4] Wentworth's Irish administration is definitively treated by H. F. Kearney, *op. cit.*; cf. also T. Ranger, 'Strafford in Ireland: a revaluation.' *Past and present*, 19 (1961).

[5] The Irish rebellion is discussed *infra*, 254–9.

[6] *The earl of Stafforde's letters*, I, 331–2, II, 32.

Deputy home and shortly gave him coveted promotion as Lord Lieutenant of Ireland and earl of Strafford. Now, in the King's extremity, Strafford became the most great and trusted of councillors. It was what he had wanted all his life. Unflinchingly he took the fate of the monarchy upon his shoulders, and both he and it were to be overwhelmed in the same catastrophe.

As the 1630s drew towards a close, the King's difficulties multiplied, while the Court presented a scene of disunity and hidden discontent. Scotland was in revolt, incited by Laud's attempt to impose his ceremonialism on the Scottish church. Charles's rule in his northern kingdom was tottering, its nobility unreliable, its populace shaken by a deep tremor of hatred for the episcopal church and the royal supremacy in religion. At home money was scarce to pay the forces being raised against the Scots. None of the fiscal expedients devised since parliament last met was sufficient. Without a parliament no relief from financial stringency, no support against Scotland, would be forthcoming. But parliament was a dangerous medicine that might kill rather than cure. Everywhere in England a spirit of sullen resentment and opposition prevailed. '. . . what with Scottish brags,' wrote Laud despondently at the end of 1638, 'and desire of a Parliament, and a Puritan fashion, and a discontented subject, and a wasted estate. . . . The case at best is bad enough, not to add court divisions and jealousies.'[1]

In the cold world of the Court, distrust and rivalry between the councillors weakened the government's ability to deal with the crisis. The archbishop suspected Cottington of wanting a parliament so as to drive him from power and become Treasurer in place of Bishop Juxon.[2] The Treasurer of the Household, Sir Henry Vane, who became Secretary of State early in 1640, hated Strafford and hoped for his ruin.[3] The earl of Holland, a great courtier friend of the Queen, was thought to be cultivating his Puritan connections. He, too, was Strafford's enemy.[4] The Lord Admiral, the earl of Northumberland, one of the foremost noblemen in the kingdom, was disaffected. 'Such Incendiaries are here amongst us,' he complained of his fellow councillors, 'that . . . I do not see how we shall possibilie avoid falling into great Misfortunes. . . . To think well of the [Reformed Religion] is cause enough to make [Laud] . . . Ene-

---

[1] *Works*, VII, 513.

[2] *Ibid.*, VII, 568, Laud to Wentworth, May 1639.

[3] *C.S.P.D. 1639–40*, 436; Sir Edward Walker, *Historical discourses*, L., 1705, 305.

[4] Viscount Conway to Laud, June 1640, *C.S.P.D. 1640*, 278. Laud referred frequently in his letters to the enmity of Holland and Strafford, *Works*, VII, *passim*. The former was the brother of the great oppositionist peer, the earl of Warwick.

mie. . . .'[1] Although appointed in January 1640 to command against the Scots, Northumberland had no sympathy with his task. To Lord Mandeville, a Puritan oppositionist peer, he wrote excusing himself for his new employment 'against our brethren in Scotland . . . this Generallship will I feare utterly ruine my reputation, and make me be thought allmost as greate a reprobate as any Bishop. . . .'[2]

The regime faced the crisis disunited internally, surrounded from without by enmity and suspicion. The King was estranged from his subjects, though he lacked the political insight or imagination to gauge the depth of animosity against his rule. His own strong sense of kingship, the dominant idea of his life, deprived him of any comprehension of the convictions that sustained the angry energies of his opponents.

The Court's atmosphere emphasized its isolation. Its higher circles breathed an artificial air. Its theatricals with their precious, sentimental love themes were the amusement of a coterie. They induced a feeling of exclusiveness and aristocratic intimacy amongst the courtiers.[3] The poets who reflected the Court's taste flattered the King and Queen in exquisite verses conveying slight awareness of the differences in public life. The literature responsive to the Court's sensibility expressed a spirit of make-believe in such representative lines as the following by Abraham Cowley:

> *Happy who did remain*
> *Unborn till Charles's reign!*
> *Where, dreaming chymics! is your pain and cost?*
> *How is your oil! How is your labour lost!*
> *Our Charles, blessed alchemist! (Though strange,*
> *Believe it, future time!) did change*
> *The iron-age of old*
> *Into an age of gold!*[4]

Not only Cowley, but other writers like Carew, Shirley, Waller, and Davenant all fostered the illusion of a contented state in love with its royal master that was very far from the reality of the 1630s.[5]

---

[1] Northumberland to the earl of Leicester, Dec. 1639, A. Collins, *Letters and memorials of state*, 2v., L., 1746, II, 623, bracketed words in cipher.
[2] P.R.O. Manchester MSS., 30/15, no. 471.
[3] Cf. A. Harbage, *Cavalier drama*, Oxford, 1936, chs. I, II, IV and M. B. Pickel, *Charles I as patron of poetry and drama*, L., 1936, chs. III, VI, VII.
[4] *Ode in commendation of the time we live under, the reign of our gracious King Charles.*
[5] Cf. C. V. Wedgwood, *Poetry and politics under the Stuarts*, Cambridge, 1960, ch. II.

The Court and the Country

A Catholic element in the Court also promoted its remoteness from the prevailing temper. Queen Henrietta Maria was the centre of a fashionable Catholicism which the King, secure in his unswerving Anglicanism, treated with courtesy and toleration. There were aristocratic converts in Court society. Ministers such as Portland had Romanist sympathies. Catholics freely frequented the Queen's chapel at Somerset House. The King received the pope's diplomatic agents.[1] Naturally, such things aroused the dislike and mistrust of the robust Protestantism in country houses and tradesmen's shops.

Connected with this Catholic note was the impression the King conveyed as a collector and connoisseur. Charles had a keen love of art, and at a time when English taste was still provincial and little guided by knowledge, his own cultivated preferences led him to the art associated with the world of the courtly baroque and the Counter-Reformation. He admired such masters as Raphael, Titian, Caravaggio, and Rubens, the last of whom painted for him a rich glorification of Stuart kingship in the banqueting house at Whitehall.[2] This was the taste, then shared by few Englishmen, which the King exemplified in the formation of his great collections.[3] Outside the Court it could only have seemed a further manifestation of the ornate ceremonialism and subtle sensibility to be stigmatized as Romanist or crypto-Catholic.

In the portraits of Van Dyck, who worked in England under royal patronage from 1632 to his death nine years later, the image of Charles's court was enshrined forever on the eve of its passing. King, Queen, ministers, courtiers, noblemen, were represented in romantic grandeur. Elevated by the sumptuous, aristocratic imagination of the artist, the figures appear somewhat remote in their self-conscious elegance. The King gazes with a distant majesty in his equestrian portraits. The earl of Strafford and the opposition peer, Lord Warwick, both share the same withdrawn quality. The charm of the Queen and the royal children is enclosed within a cool hauteur. Van Dyck's vision was the definitive formulation of the Court's mood of delusive security about to be swept away.[4] In 1630, a courtier poet had celebrated the King's pacific reign:

White Peace (the beautifull'st of things)
Seems here her everlasting rest

---

[1] Cf. G. Albion, *Charles I and the court of Rome*, L., 1935, ch. VIII and M. J. Havran, *The Catholics in Caroline England*, Stanford, 1962, ch. VIII.
[2] Rubens's ceiling at Whitehall is analysed in P. Palme, *Triumph of peace*, Stockholm, 1962, 230–62.
[3] M. Whinney and O. Millar, *English art 1625–1714*, Oxford, 1957, ch. I.
[4] Cf. *ibid.*, ch. IV.

The Court

To fix, and spreads her downy Wings
Over the nest.[1]

Ten years later England's boasted calm was ready to expire in the heat of public strife. Under a darkening sky the Court advanced towards its defeat and dissolution.

[1] Sir Richard Fanshawe, *An ode, upon occasion of his Majesties proclamation in the year 1630. Commanding the gentry to reside upon their estates in the countrey.*

The Country

The Country was the first opposition movement in English history whose character transcended that of a feudal following or a faction. One hundred and fifty years before the seventeenth century, when the kingship itself was at stake in the broken world of the declining Middle Age, the protagonists were a handful of dynasts, their retainers, soldiers, and servants. The mass of Englishmen looked on while the lords of a moribund feudality fought each other to death. During the sixteenth century, after Henry VII established domestic peace, political differences lay centred chiefly about the court. The organic Tudor commonwealth allowed no place for an independent political life. The ruler's will was to be supreme in the determination of policy, the state a unity under its sole head, the prince. No legitimacy or tolerance could be accorded to public argument in which men joined openly to promote a policy contrary to the prince's. When tendencies of this kind appeared, as they did most notably in the Puritan and parliamentary opposition of Queen Elizabeth's reign, they were quashed. Thus, the normal form of political contention was the factional grouping ranged around rival ministers. The latter, competitors for power and favour, held their adherents together by patronage and the prospect of reward. Issues of high policy, inextricably bound up with the differences of factions, were decided in contests waged in court and council to gain the approval of the prince. This was a phenomenon consequent on the nature of personal monarchy, an ineluctable trait of its political system. The rivalry between Essex and the Cecils, the supreme faction struggle of the sixteenth century, was only the last of a number of such quarrels which exercised a deep influence on the internal measures and the course of religion, foreign relations, and war in the Tudor age.

The Country was essentially different from the factional groupings that dominated the Elizabethan scene. Its name, as has been seen, first became current as a political label in the 1620s, and its appearance in this sense signified the formation of a new type of opposition. The Country was not constituted as a system of dependency under

the personal authority of great men who aspired to a preponderant share in the prince's favour and the shaping of his policy. Fundamentally, it consisted, rather, of a loose collaboration or alliance of men in the governing class, peers and gentlemen of assured position and often of substantial fortune, alienated for a variety of reasons from the Court. Principles counted for it more than persons. It found its main focus of action in parliament, and to a lesser extent in local government, in both of which it eventually secured an ascendancy beyond the monarch's ability to control.

If faction and party be considered as alternative types of political structure, then the Country approximated more nearly to party, notwithstanding that it was yet far from having evolved into one. It lacked the consciousness of party and possessed none of the formalized mechanisms of leadership, organization, discipline, and propaganda which create such a body and keep it in being. On the other hand, like a party it had some organization, even if informal; it stood for certain policies and opinions which it sought to carry into public life; and it gathered adherents among those persons who concurred with its outlook. It was thus the potential rallying point for a mass disaffection from the King's rule, and this is what it became at the close of the 1630s.

Two conditions made it possible for the Country to take shape as a new kind of opposition movement in the seventeenth century. One was the further growth of parliament under the Tudors, the other the changed circumstances prevailing after the accession of James I.

Parliament's evolution was, together with the progress of monarchical authority and institutions, the most important political fact of the sixteenth century. Fundamentally, both were aspects of the same process. Usually the monarch's cooperative and obedient instrumentality, parliament was employed to effect the greatest acts of state. The reformation under Henry and Edward was its work, as was the Elizabethan settlement of religion. The royal power was buttressed and extended by its enactments. Statute sanctioned the crown's ecclesiastical supremacy, gave it the wealth of the monasteries, authorized some of its new administrative bodies, and erected for its security a formidable barrier of treason legislation. Thus, while representative assemblies elsewhere in Europe were falling into desuetude and decay, or consuming themselves in strife between their constituent orders, parliament went from strength to strength. Statute acquired an immensely broader scope. Procedure and privilege underwent a notable expansion. The size of the House of Commons rose from 298 members in Henry VIII's first parliament to 467 in the first parliament of James I, an increase resulting mainly from the

striking extension of borough representation.[1] The calibre of members improved as competition for seats grew and as university and legal education became more common in the governing class.[2] By the end of Queen Elizabeth's reign, parliament occupied a place far greater than ever before. So far as the political nation had a voice, it spoke in the House of Commons.[3]

Opposition to the royal will did not fail, of course, to appear in Tudor parliaments, but its advocates never attained a position of dominance in parliamentary transactions. In Henry VIII's reign, there was outspoken criticism of financial measures and resistance to the passage of the Statutes of Uses and of Proclamations. Under Mary, the government's opponents were sufficiently well-organized in 1555 to defeat a bill in the Commons aimed against the English refugees abroad.[4]

Such intermittent occurrences, rather obscure from paucity of evidence, gave place to repeated and persistent manifestations of opposition in Elizabethan parliaments. Throughout most of her reign, as Professor Neale's masterly researches have shown, the Queen encountered concerted defiance from members in the lower House.[5] These men were the forerunners of the later Country which began to emerge as a proto-party in the 1620s. Like most of the Country leaders of Charles I's time, the Elizabethan oppositionists were Puritan sympathizers, critical of the church establishment and bent on further reformation. They hated Spain, the pope, and Mary Queen of Scots. They judged Elizabeth too *politique* in her policy and blamed her refusal to provide for the succession. Their sort introduced a new figure to the political scene: the man of rigid principles, the idealist with a religious conscience. Of such stuff was the foremost of them, Peter Wentworth, made. The bluntest of the Queen's critics, the most audacious champion of parliamentary privilege, he would have been comfortably at home in the Long Parliament.[6]

Oppositionist activity in the Elizabethan House of Commons was part of an organized campaign of the Puritan clergy and their lay

[1] These figures come from J. R. Tanner, *Tudor constitutional documents*, 2nd ed., Cambridge, 1940, 514–15.
[2] Cf. J. E. Neale, *The Elizabethan House of Commons*, New Haven, 1950, ch. XV.
[3] Cf. *ibid.*, and for a concise survey of parliamentary development in the sixteenth century, G. R. Elton, *The Tudor constitution*, Cambridge, 1962, ch. 8.
[4] Cf. *ibid.*, 22, 305–7; J. E. Neale, *Elizabeth I and her parliaments 1559–81*, L., 1953, 23–6; D. M. Loades, *Two Tudor conspiracies*, Cambridge, 1965, 242–3.
[5] J. E. Neale, *Elizabeth I and her parliaments 1559–81*; *Elizabeth I and her parliaments 1584–1601*, L., 1957.
[6] Cf. J. E. Neale, 'Peter Wentworth,' *E.H.R.*, XXXIX, 2 pts., 153, 154 (1924).

patrons to win parliament's support for church reform. The attention the Puritans gave to petitions and bills was one of their most prominent traits.[1] Theirs was the earliest attempt to create a broad movement agitating openly for its demands in defiance of authority and censorship. The collisions of Puritan members with the government's spokesmen in the Commons, their strainings against the Queen's direction of the House, provided the main impulse in the sixteenth-century parliament's struggle to win a wider liberty. They were the ones who

taught the House of Commons methods of concerted action and propaganda. Indeed, the art of opposition, which might be considered the outstanding contribution of the Elizabethan period to Parliamentary history, was largely learnt from them or inspired by them.[2]

In spite of their challenge, however, the Queen retained control of parliament throughout her long reign. Firmness tempered by occasional concession, and the blandishments, amounting almost to a magical spell, with which she woo'd her subjects' affections, enabled her to keep the House of Commons in tutelage. The oppositionists were only a small number, in any case, and while they sometimes enjoyed the House's sympathy, they could not count on its support. They themselves, moreover, were intensely loyal to Elizabeth. They might chafe at her domination of parliament and press reform upon her, but they well knew that she was the Deborah of their English Israel, the protectress of the Dutch, the enemy of the pope and Spain, the stay of Protestantism in Europe. With her great personal popularity and the successes of her government in diplomacy and the war with Spain, the Queen remained unshakeable. The process which engendered the division between the Court and the Country had not yet begun.

The accession of James I opened a new period in many ways. The Spanish danger had passed and peace was made in the first year of the new reign. With the war's conclusion, a factor promoting the unity of ruler and subject was no longer operative. The King lacked Elizabeth's personal authority and her arts of management. A foreigner, his experience in Scotland did not prepare him for relations with an English parliament. Inflation, heavy debts inherited from the war, and his own extravagance placed his government under continuous financial strain.

[1] Cf. P. Collinson, 'John Field and Elizabethan Puritanism,' *Elizabethan government and society.*
[2] J. E. Neale, *Elizabeth I and her parliaments 1584–1601*, 436; cf. the remarks of A. F. Scott Pearson, *Church & state*, Cambridge, 1928, 95–7.

James therefore found it impossible to exercise the same mastery over parliament as his predecessor. As his reign proceeded, issues of division multiplied. Constitutional disagreements about the limits of the King's prerogative; dislike of the action of the royal supremacy in religion and of the jurisdiction of the ecclesiastical courts; financial grievances; the domination of Buckingham—these were some of the points on which serious differences and political opposition to the crown were gathering.

The place occupied by parliament made it inevitably the focus and *point d'appui* of the movement which then gradually began to take shape as the Country. By the start of James's reign, the corporate consciousness of the House of Commons and traditions favourable to its independence were already well developed. In the King's first parliament, the House ventured boldly on an unprecedented declaration to the monarch in defence of its privileges. These, the members asserted, were no donative from the crown, but belonged to them as a right not to be denied or impaired 'but with apparent wrong to the whole state of the realm.'[1] During the following years the Commons became ever more difficult to manage, so that control slipped from the King's grasp. The crown's financial necessity offered a lever susceptible to pressure. Bacon stated that once parliament

was . . . in taste with matter of bargain and contribution and retribution and . . . quid pro quo, the generous disposition of free giving unto the King, and the politic argument of persuading it upon reason of estate, became dry things, and the endeavour grew . . . to draw from the King. . . .[2]

By the 1620s opposition existed also in the House of Lords, while in the lower House the influence of the privy councillors waned disastrously and leadership of the Commons passed to 'popular men.'[3] The growth of procedure assisted this result. Through the device of the committee of the whole, first used in 1607, the House could turn

---

[1] *The form of apology and satisfaction of the House of Commons*, 1604, in J. R. Tanner, *Constitutional documents of the reign of James I*, Cambridge, 1930, 221. G. R. Elton has wrongly contended that the *Apology* was never adopted by the House and 'virtually forgotten' afterwards ('A high road to civil war?', *From the Renaissance to the Counter-Reformation. Essays in honor of Garrett Mattingly*, ed. C. H. Carter, N.Y., 1965). In the 1621 parliament, however, when members were discussing the defence of their privileges, the *Apology* of 1604 was frequently cited as a precedent by Coke, Crew, Hakewill, Phelips, and others, and referred to as an act of the House of Commons; cf. *Commons debates 1621*, II, 505, 525, 526, 533, 538, 541, V, 433.

[2] *Works*, XII, 179; cf. an earlier letter on the same theme, *ibid.*, XI, 313.

[3] C. H. Firth, *The House of Lords during the civil war*, ch. II; D. H. Willson, *op. cit.*

itself into a great committee, elect a chairman, and thus evade the rule of the Speaker, who was in effect the crown's nominee. At these occasions members had also the right to speak more than once to a motion. Committees of the whole functioned concurrently for various purposes, employing sub-committees in their work. In 1610, a committee of the whole was first appointed for grievances, thereby giving that irritant subject a sharper emphasis.[1] The consequence of these changes, leading to 'the winning of the initiative by the House of Commons,' was stated tartly by Charles I upon the dissolution of his intractable third parliament in 1629:

We are not ignorant, how much the House hath of late years endeavoured to extend their Privileges, by setting up general Committees for Religion, for Courts of Justice, for Trade, and the like; a course never heard of until of late: So as, where in former times the Knights and Burgesses were wont to communicate to the House, such business, as they brought from Their Countries; now there are so many chairs erected, to make enquiry upon all sorts of men, where complaints of all sorts are entertained, to the unsupportable disturbance and Scandal of Justice and Government, which having been tolerated a while by Our Father, and Our Self, hath daily grown to more height. . . .[2]

Together with procedural developments and the intensification of political conflict, early Stuart parliaments saw an increasing number of opposition sympathizers in the Commons. This was in contrast to the three parliaments of Elizabeth's last decade, in which, according to Professor Neale, opposition diminished considerably due to the passing of earlier militants and the government's suppression of the Puritans' organization.[3] In the parliaments of James I and Charles I, however, a largely new generation of activists became prominent. Although some died before the Long Parliament and others abandoned the Country, their presence ensured an unbroken and strengthening continuity of oppositionist personnel.

Sir Edwin Sandys, Nicholas Fuller, William Hakewill, Edward Alford, and Sir Dudley Digges, for instance, attended all or most of the parliaments convened between 1604 and 1628. Sir Robert Phelips,

---

[1] Cf. W. Notestein, 'The winning of the initiative by the House of Commons,' *loc. cit.* The device of a committee of the whole seems also to have come into use at about the same time in the House of Lords; cf. E. R. Foster, 'Procedure in the House of Lords during the early Stuart period,' *Journal of British studies*, V, 2 (1966), 67–9.

[2] J. Rushworth, I, App., 7.

[3] *Elizabeth I and her parliaments 1584–1601*, 241–2, 325–6, 370–1, 436–7. Neale holds that even in the monopolies dispute in 1601 the royal prerogative was less contested than in the parliaments previous to the 1590s.

Sir John Eliot, Sir Thomas Wentworth, William Mallory, and Sir Walter Erle first entered the House in 1614. Sir Edward Coke, the oracle of the law, returned to the Commons after a long absence in 1621. John Pym, John Hampden, and Sir Francis Seymour were elected the first time in this same year. Denzil Holles and William Strode first sat in 1624, Oliver Cromwell in 1628.

Besides these and other oppositionists of note, repeated contingents of the Country's supporters entered the early Stuart House of Commons. This can be seen clearly from the fact that the Long Parliament contained one hundred and twenty-eight Parliamentarian members who had also sat in parliament prior to 1640. Of this body of royal opponents, ninety-one were members of the Commons in 1628–9.[1] The latter parliament was remarkable for another circumstance as well: with the exception of St. John, Nathaniel Fiennes, and the younger Vane, all the subsequent leaders and managers of the Long Parliament were present in it.

Nothing was more significant in early Stuart parliaments than the Country leaders' efforts to concert their tactics through private consultations. The House of Commons was a body vulnerable to the influence of an organized minority. Since parliaments met irregularly and members came from all parts of the realm, most were strangers to one another. Many, too, having no parliamentary experience, lacked knowledge of procedure and precedents. In the growing state of public differences, therefore, an able group of men who worked together could have an effect in the House out of all proportion to their number.

Signs of oppositionist organization appeared first in the parliament of 1604–10. The presence in the Commons of such vocal critics as Sir Edwin Sandys and Sir Roger Owen was one reason this parliament produced frequent clashes with the King.[2] But there was more to the story than this: for Lord Ellesmere, the Chancellor, touched one of the secrets of the parliament in some 'Special Observations' he wrote about it after its conclusion. In later sessions a group of opposition members 'kept ... privy conventicles and conferences' to plot 'the carrying of business in the House according to their own humor ... and ... in the weightiest and most important causes. ...' They defeated a subsidy bill by devising that six of them who 'did bear great sway in the House' should speak against it. They talked con-

---

[1] Cf. W. M. Mitchell, *The rise of the revolutionary party in the House of Commons*, N.Y., 1957, 51–4, 122–3; T. L. Moir, *The addled parliament*, Oxford, 1958, 159–60; D. Brunton and D. H. Pennington, *Members of the Long Parliament*, L., 1954, 14–15.

[2] Cf. T. K. Rabb, 'Sir Edwin Sandys and the parliament of 1604,' *American historical review*, LXIX, 3 (1964) and D. H. Willson, *op. cit.*, 120–1.

stantly of grievances and delivered contemptuous speeches against the King's prerogative and regal power. Ellesmere saw a portent in these 'rare and strange proceedings.' Since the beginning of James's reign, he noted,

the popular state . . . hath grown big and audacious, and in every session of parliament swelled more and more. And if way be still given unto it . . . it is to be doubted what the end will be. . . . Great and dangerous inundations happen for the most part by reason that small breaches are neglected and not . . . stopped in the beginning.[1]

In the parliament of 1621, the Country opposition again made use of similar methods. The examination of members whom the King committed for their refractory conduct revealed that they had held private meetings on parliamentary business. Sandys was charged with conspiring to organize a petition against a threatened dissolution. He was further accused of corresponding with Puritan exiles in Amsterdam and was commanded to explain a suspicious writing he had composed on the power of kings. The earl of Southampton, an opposition peer in spite of his being a privy councillor, had taken part in these conferences. He was accused of consulting with members of the lower House at his residence and in the Lord's committee room concerning the passage or defeat of bills. All inflammatory speeches were said to have been delivered by his bosom friends.[2]

These tactics go some way to explain the aggressions which the 1621 parliament committed. Articulating the general sense of grievance, it set out in full cry against the patents of monopoly conferred by the King under his prerogative. The Houses revived impeachment, a procedure in disuse for over one hundred and fifty years, in order to attack dishonest royal officials and patentees.[3] The Commons tried to extend its privilege of free speech to deal with the hitherto forbidden subject of foreign affairs, persisting in its attempt despite the King's prohibitions.[4] The parliament's carriage aroused strong misgivings in James and provoked him to declare: '. . . he that will have all doon by Parliament is an enemie to Monarchie and a traitor to the King of England.'[5]

---

[1] Printed in *Proceedings in parliament 1610*, ed. E. R. Foster, 2v., New Haven, 1966, I, 276–83.
[2] *Proceedings and debates of the House of Commons in 1620 and 1621*, ed. T. Tyrwhitt, 2v., Oxford, 1766, II, Appendix; Sir Lionel Cranfield to James I, July 1621, *Commons debates 1621*, VII, 615ff.
[3] Cf. C. Roberts, *The growth of responsible government in Stuart England*, Cambridge, 1966, ch. 1.   [4] Cf. *infra*, 88.
[5] *Notes of the debates in the House of Lords. A.D. 1621 . . . 1628*, ed. F. Relf, *Camden society*, 3rd ser., XLII, 1929, 14.

There were also indications of oppositionist parliamentary organization in 1624 and 1628–9. The *rapprochement* of 1624 between the Court and the Country could only have been effected by Buckingham's consultations with leading opposition members.[1] In 1628, a group of Country oppositionists met at Sir Robert Cotton's house prior to the opening of parliament. Those present included Pym, Eliot, Wentworth, Phelips, Coke, and Holles. They decided not to renew Buckingham's impeachment from the last parliament, but to concentrate on grievances.[2] When Eliot delivered a bitter attack on the government's misdeeds later in the session, a crown supporter[3] charged that his speech had been planned at 'private counsels and conference. . . .' To this Wentworth replied with a justification of such proceedings:

God forbid but we may speak one with another out of that House concerning those things which concern this House, and yet no confederacy. And this tends much to the disservice of this House not to confer with one another. A man may light his candle at another man's fire.[4]

During the second session in 1629, Eliot, Holles, and several other Country M.P.s conferred at the Three Cranes tavern to decide their course in view of the anticipated adjournment. The result was the unprecedented scene of disorder in the House of Commons on 2 March, when Eliot read out the opposition's resolutions against Arminianism and illegal tonnage and poundage, while his friends forcibly restrained the Speaker from executing the King's command to adjourn.[5] Later that year Eliot was brought to trial for his actions, and his counsel stated in his defence that 'members of the House may advise of matters out of the House, for the House itself is not so much for consultation as for proposition. . . .'[6]

---

[1] Cf. *supra*, 63–5.

[2] J. Forster, *Sir John Eliot*, 2v., L., 1865, II, 114; but cf. the critical remarks on Forster's account by H. Hulme, *The life of Sir John Eliot*, L., 1957, 184.

[3] Sir William Beecher.

[4] H. Hulme, *op. cit.*, 246. As Lord Deputy of Ireland, Wentworth afterwards took a different view of private consultations by M.P.s. He denounced them in a speech to the Irish parliament in 1634, warning that they were punishable, and said, 'I never knew them in all my experience to doe any good, to the publique. . . .', Strafford MSS., v. 21, 119.

[5] Cf. I. H. C. Fraser, 'The agitation in the Commons, 2 March 1629, and the interrogation of the anti-court group,' *Bulletin of the Institute of Historical Research*, XXX, 81 (1957).

[6] *State trials*, ed. T. B. Howell, 21v., L., 1816, III, 298. Eliot was charged with seditious speeches, contempts to the King in resisting the adjournment, and conspiracy with other M.P.s to restrain the Speaker.

Perhaps there were other oppositionist attempts at parliamentary organization in the 1620s; from the exiguous surviving evidence it is impossible to tell. These experiments afterwards bore fruit, however, in the Long Parliament. If Pym and his friends manifested some of the characteristics of a party in the House of Commons in 1640–1, and if by this means they were able to manage the House, it was due in part to opposition members' experience in the organization of their forces in previous parliaments.

2

Although the Country conducted a lengthy resistance to various powers claimed by the crown, its leaders produced no original political doctrine of their own. Moreover, the ends they sought, their conception of their struggle, must be mainly inferred from scattered utterances such as speeches in parliament or the law courts, since they refrained from composing elaborate theoretic justifications. The reason was not that they were intellectually unequipped for such a task. The contrary was rather the case. The opposition movement contained lawyers, learned scholars, gentlemen widely read in the political literature of Europe. That they created little in the way of theory was, in fact, a result of their political mentality and, as such, highly revealing.

The Country was a conservative opposition. Its adherents had no prejudice in favour of change. Certainly, in contesting with James I and Charles I, they did not set out to alter the government. They felt no necessity to rationalize a new version of the state or the English constitution because they conceived themselves defenders of an immemorial legal order of rights and liberties against which the King was the transgressor. He, not his antagonists, was the innovator—so it seemed to the Country.[1]

In 1610, in the great Commons debate over the King's right to impose customs duties of his sole will, Hakewill asserted that such a power in the crown entailed the 'utter dissolution' of the 'politic frame and constitution of this commonwealth. . . .' Pym declared, similarly, in 1629 that the law requiring the subject's consent in parliament to a tax 'was not introduced by any Statute, or by any Charter or Sanction of Princes, but was the antient and fundamental

---

[1] Cf. the full account of the political ideas of the opposition and the King's supporters by M. Judson, *The crisis of the constitution*, New Brunswick, 1949, and the discussion in J. W. Allen, *English political thought*, L., 1938, 3–47; C. H. McIlwain, *Constitutionalism ancient and modern*, rev. ed., Ithaca, 1947, chs. V–VI; G. Mosse, *The struggle for sovereignty in England*, Lansing, 1950, chs. IV–VII; J. W. Gough, *Fundamental law in English history*, Oxford, 1955, chs. IV–V.

law issuing from the first frame and constitution of the Kingdom.'[1] This conviction passed with the Country's supporters for an axiom. Thus, they took their stand on the law and the ancient constitution— a position they abandoned only after 1640, when circumstances gradually compelled the leaders of the Long Parliament to embark on a course of revolutionary change.[2]

The Country's supporters fully accepted, of course, the monarchical government inherited from their ancestors and advanced no claim to a sovereignty on parliament's behalf which excluded the King. Indeed, they seem not to have recognized sovereignty anywhere in the state, for they could not believe in a power that gave law to all while legally unlimited itself.[3] They held that the King's authority rested on law and must be exercised legally. The law also, in their view, secured the right of the subject, combining both elements in a well-poised balance. What they conceived themselves as contesting, therefore, were those invasions of power that deranged the equilibrium and violated law. For the King to levy impositions on merchandise; to exact forced loans and benevolences; to commit men to prison without showing lawful cause; to lay a direct charge on his people without their common consent in parliament—these things, done by James I or Charles I, they condemned as altogether illegal.

Against this assertion there was no general claim on the King's part to be exempt from law. The constitutional issue between him and his opponents centred on the nature of his prerogative and his powers under it. The question came before the courts in several great cases of the earlier seventeenth century.[4] In each, the judges, deciding for the King, enunciated a doctrine of the prerogative to justify those exercises of authority which the crown's opponents challenged.

Their opinions freely acknowledged that in many matters respecting

---

[1] J. R. Tanner, *Constitutional documents . . . James I*, 253; J. Rushworth, I, 596.

[2] Cf. the discussion of the intellectual traits of the 'common-law mind' by J. G. Pocock, *op. cit.*, ch. II.

[3] Whitelocke's argument in the Commons debate on impositions in 1610 was perhaps an exception. He denied the King's right to impose customs duties because the sovereign power in England lay not with the King alone, but with the King-in-parliament. The King therefore required parliament's assent for his action (J. R. Tanner, *Constitutional documents . . . James I*, 260–1). An echo of this idea appeared in the House's petition of grievances, 7 July 1610, in the reference to impositions (G. R. Prothero, *Select statutes and other . . . documents . . . Elizabeth and James I*, 4th ed., Oxford, 1913, 302). The conception of sovereignty remained uncommon, however, and scarcely figured in the armoury of oppositionist argument. Probably not even Whitelocke, moreover, would have allowed that the sovereign power of King-in-parliament was unlimited.

[4] In Bate's case, 1606, the Five Knights' case, 1627, and the Ship-money case, 1637; cf. *State trials*, II, III, for the texts.

private rights the King had to contain himself within the ordinary rules of law. But they declared that his prerogative included a power to act for the general good and safety in which he was not thus limited. This power, the special province of policy and 'matter of state,' they called his 'absolute' prerogative. Further, the King alone was judge of the circumstances in which he might use his 'absolute' prerogative. When he did so, he was to be presumed acting for the welfare of his subjects. Such a power the judges pronounced inherent in his monarchical office.[1]

This doctrine of the prerogative was by no means new. It had respectable mediaeval and Tudor antecedents.[2] Only in the reigns of James and Charles, because of unprecedented parliamentary recalcitrance to the King's will and attacks on his authority, it was magnified to new proportions by elaborate judicial exposition on the royal behalf. Naturally, the Country would have nothing to do with the idea. The crown's opponents admitted that many great powers belonged exclusively to the King under his prerogative, but none to act outside the law. They denied that the ancestral polity allowed him this power. They foresaw the danger that absolute prerogative would eat out liberty and property. Sandys told the House of Commons in 1614 that 'the mayne liberty of the people' was involved in the question of impositions; if the King had power to impose by his sole authority, 'no man Coulde knowe his right and propertye in his owne goodes. . . .'[3] That the judges sanctioned the absolute prerogative did not alter the oppositionists' mind.[4] On the contrary, it caused them increasingly to doubt the integrity and independence of the judiciary. The ship-money decision of 1637, in particular, was popularly regarded as a flagrant example of judicial subservience.

It would be strange, nevertheless, if the Country opposition, for all its professed conservatism, did not somewhere betray the radical implications of its conduct and intimate its gropings towards a new balance of political forces. For there can be no doubt that its adherents, greatly as they respected the *mos maiorum*, were unconsciously shaping a different conception of the polity—one that gave the power

[1] Cf. F. Wormuth, *The royal prerogative*, Ithaca, 1939, ch. II; M. Judson, *op. cit.*, ch. IV; P. Zagorin, *A history of political thought in the English revolution*, 192–4.

[2] Cf. C. H. McIlwain, *op. cit.*, 111, 127–9.

[3] *Commons debates 1621*, VII, 653, 654 (from a diary of proceedings in the House of Commons in 1614).

[4] Sandys, for instance, said in 1614: '. . . wheras the kinge dothe alledge that he had a Judgement . . . that he might Laye impositions by his sole Authoritie . . . the Judges had nothing to doe to decide that question, for they are not to meddle with two thinges, viz. the title of the Crowne and Libertie of the kingdome. . . .', *ibid.*, VII, 54.

of decision over policy to parliament, rather than the King. This was especially evident in two particulars: first, in the Country's intense awareness of parliament as the people's representative and trustee; second, in its championship of parliamentary privilege on that account.

That parliament represented the kingdom was no more than a constitutional truism in the sixteenth century: as the first statute of James's reign expressed it, in parliament 'all the whole body of the realm, and every particular member thereof, either in person or by representation ... are by the laws of this realm deemed to be personally present.'[1] The Country, however, gave the notion of representation a new meaning. Its supporters manifested a sort of 'constituency-consciousness' and set themselves against the royal will on the ground of their public trust.[2]

Opposition speakers in parliament repeatedly employed the theme of representation in their arsenal of argument. Coke told the House in 1621: '... when the kinge sayes he cannot allowe our liberties of right, this strikes at the roote. Wee serve here for thousands and tenn thousands.' William Mallory declared: 'We are entrusted for our country. If we lose our privileges, we betray it.' And Edward Alford: '... lett us remember that England sent us. That must be satisfied.'[3] In 1626 the Commons informed the King that unless members searched into grievances, 'we could neither be faithful to your Majesty, nor to the Countrey that doth trust and employ us. ...'[4] Protesting the imprisonment of men by martial law, Sir Robert Phelips said in 1628: 'The County I serve for were pleased to command me to seek the removal from them of the greatest burthen that ever people suffered. ... it concerns us to preserve the Countrey in freedom. ...' Of the Commons' privileges he asserted, 'If we suffer the liberties of this House ... to be abused, we shall give a wound to the happiness of this Kingdom. ...'[5] Coke laid it down that 'the freedom of this House is the freedom of the whole land. ...'[6] Sir John Eliot solemnly stated,

[1] The Succession Act, 1 Jac. I, c. I, in J. R. Tanner, *Constitutional documents ... James I*, 11; the identical thought in Sir T. Smith, *op. cit.*, 49; R. Hooker, *Laws of ecclesiastical polity*, VIII, c. vi, 11; W. Lambarde, *Archeion*, 1635, written c. 1591, ed. C. H. McIlwain and P. Ward, Cambridge, 1957, 126. Those deemed personally present are the King and the temporal and spiritual peers.
[2] Cf. C. H. McIlwain, *op. cit.*, 115, and A. F. Pollard, *The evolution of parliament*, 2nd ed., L., 1926, for remarks on the changing conception of representation.
[3] *Commons debates 1621*, V, 240, 219, II, 484.
[4] J. Rushworth, I, 401.
[5] J. Rushworth, I, 503; *Commons debates for 1629*, 7. Phelips was knight for Somerset in the 1628–9 parliament.   [6] *Commons debates 1621*, II, 57.

That which is more than lives . . . than all our goods, all our interests and faculties, [is] the life, the liberty of the Parliament, the privileges and immunities of this House which are the bases and support of all the rest.[1]

In like vein, Pym declared, 'The peace of this kingdom consists in the peace of this House.'[2]

This profound devotion to parliament was gradually replacing the profound devotion the preceding age had accorded the prince. It was a momentous shift of sentiment—from the exaltation of the godly head to the exaltation of the representative body. With such a view, opposition supporters could not but feel anxiety when they considered that the King might succeed in dispensing with parliament altogether. Fears on this score aggravated political differences. '. . . if this power of imposing were quietly settled in our Kings,' Whitelocke said in 1610, 'considering . . . the greatest use they make of assembling of Parliaments, which is the supply of money, I do not see any likelihood to hope for often meetings in that kind.'[3] The Country's leaders did not fail to mark the fate of continental assemblies at the hands of absolute kings. 'Wee are the last monarchy in Christendome,' exclaimed Phelips, 'that retayne our originall rights and constitutions.'[4] Whitelocke noted the decline of the Estates General of France, and Pym the debility of the Estates of Normandy, their privileges devoured by the taxing power conceded the French king.[5] If the House of Commons permitted its privileges to be impaired, Alford warned, it would be 'farewell Parliaments and farewell England.'[6] Charles I stated the danger bluntly when he informed the Houses in 1626 that the existence of parliaments depended entirely on his will: 'therefore as I find the fruits of them good or evil, they are to continue, or not to be. . . .'[7]

The Country's supreme regard for parliament led, logically, to the conclusion that the latter should possess the deciding voice over the King in all matters of public concernment. This outcome, if still not anticipated, was definitely foreshadowed in the efforts of the House

[1] Cited in H. Hulme, *op. cit.*, 190.
[2] *Commons debates 1621*, II, 95.
[3] J. R. Tanner, *Constitutional documents . . . James I*, 262.
[4] *Commons debates in 1625*, 110.
[5] J. R. Tanner, *Constitutional documents . . . James I*, 262; J. Rushworth, I, 601.
[6] *Commons debates 1621*, VI, 155.
[7] J. Rushworth, I, 225. The King's threat was subsequently amplified in a speech by Sir Dudley Carleton, a privy councillor, who, after describing the decline of representative assemblies throughout Christendom, begged the Commons not to trench on the royal prerogative lest parliaments in England be overthrown; *ibid.*, I, 359.

of Commons under oppositionist leadership to intrude into areas of policy hitherto reserved by precedent for the crown alone. When warned off these forbidden topics, the House invoked its privilege of liberty of speech in justification.

As the privilege had grown up in the preceding century, it did not signify the members' right to treat what subjects they pleased. The official position, successfully enforced by Queen Elizabeth, was that they might express their minds freely (though without license) on matters properly within their purview or referred to them by the crown.[1] Numerous questions of high policy were denied them leave to consider. Stuart parliaments, however, abandoned former limits, and the House asserted its privilege of free speech in far more comprehensive terms—to embrace war, peace, foreign relations, and other prerogative matters pertaining to the King's personal decision.

Already in 1610, commanded by James not to discuss the legality of impositions, the members replied with the general claim that everything of concern to the King's subjects lay within the House's 'ancient and undoubted right . . . to debate freely. . . .'[2] Again in 1621, when defending its right to treat of foreign policy, the House made the blanket avowal, '. . . we cannot conceive that the honour and safety of your Majesty . . . the welfare of religion, and state of your kingdom, are matters at any time unfit for our deepest consideration in . . . Parliament.'[3] This contention, submitted in a petition, brought from the exasperated monarch the answer:

. . . this Plenipotency of yours, invests you in all power upon Earth, lacking nothing but the Popes to have the Keys also both of Heaven and Purgatory. . . . For what have you left unattempted in the highest points of Sovereignty, in that Petition of yours, except the striking of Coin? For it contains the violations of Leagues, the particular way how to govern a War, and the marriage of our dearest Son. . . . These are unfit

[1] The Lord Keeper's speech in 1593 was the best expression of the official Elizabethan view of the House's privilege of free speech; cf. G. R. Elton, *The Tudor constitution*, 266–7, for the text. Oppositionists like Peter Wentworth championed a far broader interpretation of the privilege. Though not successful under Elizabeth, their position was adopted by the House of Commons in the next reign.

[2] J. R. Tanner, *Constitutional documents . . . James I*, 246. In the debate preceding the adoption of this statement, Bacon defended James's command and pointed out to no avail that Queen Elizabeth had frequently inhibited the House from treating of matters within her prerogative; *Parliamentary debates in 1610*, ed. S. R. Gardiner, *Camden society*, LXXXI, 1862, 38–9. One of the extraordinary features of Stuart parliamentary history was the rapidity with which the House of Commons possessed itself of an 'ancient right.'

[3] J. R. Tanner, *Constitutional documents . . . James I*, 281.

things to be handled in Parliament, except your King should require it of you. . . .[1]

The Commons nevertheless refused to yield, and adopted a protestation which declared forthrightly that all the arduous affairs of King and state, the defence of the realm, the church, and the redress of mischiefs and grievances were proper subjects for counsel and debate in parliament.[2] Here the elastic privilege of freedom of speech, stretched to its widest extent thus far, became a claim not much short of the demand that the King should answer to parliament in every province of government. No symptom was more revealing of the challenge parliament and the Country were gradually generating against the King's supremacy.

The latent possibilities in the House's position, however, were destined to remain unacted till after 1640. During the 1620s parliament's predominant concern was to contain the King's power within bounds of law. This in the main determined the opposition movement's perspective. Needless to say, there was as yet no question, even when relations with Charles I were at their worst, of forcible resistance or a right of rebellion. Such an idea was far from the Country's mind, imbued as it was with the long tradition of loyalty to the monarchy built up in the union of Protestantism and patriotism from Queen Elizabeth's days.

The Petition of Right in 1628 represented parliament's extreme effort prior to the revolution to fortify the subject's liberty by means of law. It was called forth by certain arbitrary acts of Charles I— forced loans, imprisonment of refusers, execution of men by martial law, billeting of troops on unwilling householders. The Petition declared these to be grievances contrary to law, and asked the King to confirm Magna Charta and other good laws which secured his subjects in their rights and property.[3] That parliamentary and oppositionist pressure compelled Charles to assent was no inconsiderable achievement. Nevertheless, the Petition had no practical effect at the time. The conflict between the King and parliament, Court and Country, was more than legal; it involved serious political and religious disagreements as well, and to these the Petition was irrelevant. Moreover, the Petition provided no means for deciding what future exercises of power might be illegal, and contained no machinery of enforcement in case the King should break the law. Control without accountability remained in the crown, and Charles did not

[1] *Ibid.*, 285, 286.
[2] *Ibid.*, 289.
[3] Cf. the text in S. R. Gardiner, *The constitutional documents of the Puritan revolution*, 3rd ed., Oxford, 1936, 66–70.

deem himself to have parted with any of his prerogative powers by his assent to the Petition.[1]

At such a juncture more was required than a restatement of old law on the subject's behalf. The true situation was that parliament was pulling one way, the crown another. Both were essential elements in the polity, but in the past the King's will, not parliament's, had prevailed. Now the royal will was persistently contested and obstructed. There could be no arbitrator or legal remedy for this division. The character of Charles I's government from 1629 to 1640, when no parliament met, sufficed to show how little the methods of the Petition of Right availed. The King's opponents were to see that political reforms to curb the crown must be effected and guarantees devised. This aim was to be the first preoccupation of the Country politicians when they led the Long Parliament in a wholesale assault on a large part of the monarchy's traditional authority.

3

The outstanding characteristic of the Country from a social-structural standpoint was its uniformity with the governing class. To imagine the Country as 'progressive' in the sense of incarnating, even unwittingly, a new ordering of society, is completely erroneous. Equally so is the supposition that its relation to the Court was the antipathy of 'Outs' to 'Ins'—the social resentment of men denied admission to influence and favour. What made the Country so formidable was that its adherents were pillars of society. They belonged to the elite of Englishmen who owned the soil and administered the law to its inhabitants. They were noblemen, lords of manors, justices, lawyers, members of parliament. Beneficiaries of the society established, they entertained no thought of changing it, much less of overthrowing it. Singular destiny that such men should become revolutionaries! But they were surely the most conservative revolutionists who ever lived. It was not possible that they should foresee the overturnings consequent on the constitutional revolution they accomplished . . .

The Country's social substance and its close integration with the dominant class can best be seen from a review of some of the types drawn into its orbit. First to be noticed must be the peerage: for there was no more sinister omen to the crown than the formation of an alliance of noble oppositionists. They were not a great number, but as the personal embodiment of the regime of privilege which sanctioned their hereditary honours, they brought to the struggle against the King an invaluable prestige. Without their backing, the Country could not have sustained its character as the reaction of the

[1] Cf. F. H. Relf, *The Petition of Right*, Minneapolis, 1917, 56–8.

nation to the dangerously misguided policies of a purblind Court. In the well-founded judgment of Sir Edward Walker, a contemporary chronicler of their order, 'if the Nobility had been unanimous to have defended the just Rights of the King ... it had never been in the power of the Commons to have begun their Rebellion.'[1]

The alienation of part of the peerage began with Buckingham's domination and was soon reflected in parliament and elsewhere. The House of Lords' resumption in 1621 of its power of judicature in cases of impeachment was an effect of it. So also was the Lords' support of the Petition of Right in 1628. Both these notable episodes of cooperation with the House of Commons occurred because of widespread discontent in the upper House and an active oppositionist presence there.[2]

Some seventeenth-century commentators thought political disaffection in the nobility to be the result of the lavish distribution of titles by James I and Charles I. It was a fact that under the early Stuarts the peerage went through one of the most rapid transformations in its history. Queen Elizabeth, as parsimonious with honours as with money, authorized the creation or recognition of only 18 titles. When she died the English nobility stood at 55. James created 65 peers during his reign and Charles did about the same, half of them before the civil war. Between 1615 and 1628, the period of most frequent creations, the peerage grew from 81 to 126, earldoms alone rising from 27 to 65.[3] In addition to English titles, numerous Scotch and Irish peerages were bestowed. Some of these creations were merely the crown's acknowledgment of the claim of distinguished commoner families to be raised to noble rank. Others, however, lacked this justification, being given more in recognition of wealth or to gratify a favourite than as a sign of family distinction and eminent services to the crown. After 1615, moreover, noble titles were frequently sold, a practice never permitted in Elizabeth's time. These mercenary transactions, from which Buckingham and other courtiers profited as intermediaries, ceased only with the favourite's death, and aroused widespread resentment and disapproval.[4]

---

[1] Sir Edward Walker, *op. cit.*, 304.

[2] Cf. C. H. Firth, *The House of Lords during the civil war*, ch. II; *Notes of the debates in the House of Lords A.D. 1621 ... 1628*, Introduction; J. L. Sanford, *op. cit.*, 109n.

[3] It is not suggested that this increase in earldoms represented new creations. Most were due to promotions of peers to higher rank. A rise of earls by over 100 per cent in such a short time was extraordinary, nevertheless; how much so appears from L. Stone's table of the numbers and composition of the peerage 1487–1641, *The crisis of the aristocracy*, App. VI.

[4] *Ibid.*, ch. III and App. III–VI, a definitive treatment of the inflation of honours and the sale of titles; cf. also C. H. Firth, *The House of Lords during*

Sir Edward Walker, who as a herald had a professional interest in the nobility, expatiated at length on the unhappy consequences of its enlargement. He believed that the older aristocracy became antagonized because it felt itself undervalued when it saw men ennobled by the patronage of the favourite or the 'Riches . . . gotten in a Shop. . . .' Most harmful, in his opinion, was the King's inability to reward the entire peerage with offices or gifts, with the result that the noblemen overlooked became envious and factious: 'whereas had the number been smaller, they might every one had opportunity to have tasted of the royal favours.' The same view was expressed by the duke of Newcastle in looking back on the revolution.[1]

Walker's explanation, however, exaggerated the importance of personal motives in the formation of a peerage opposition, and it erred as well in suggesting a connection between these noble oppositionists and antiquity of title that never, in fact, existed. It was, indeed, exactly the sort of opinion to be expected in the Court, where the tendency was to visualize all issues in terms of the manoeuvres for favour so characteristic of the royal milieu. Desire for office and influence was doubtless a strand—but only a strand—in the opposition of the peers. But in that aspect which was politically significant, it was joined with the further aim of effecting a change in policy, to which a change of ministers and the oft-demanded removal of 'evil counsellors' would necessarily be instrumental. This was what made the involvement of certain noblemen with the Country a matter of consequence. So long as the state remained effectively monarchical, so long also did the service of the King present itself as the only means of playing a political role that would be positive and not merely obstructive. In the 1620s and '30s, no other perspective on the exercise of power could be thought of. The partial fulfilment of this point of view, in which a change of men was to confirm a change of measures, occurred in early 1641, when a few of the Country leaders in both Houses received offices of state. By then, however, such reconciling methods had ceased to be effective.[2]

A mixed bag of peers were active in the opposition. One of the most prominent was Robert Rich, earl of Warwick. The Riches were

[1] Sir Edward Walker, *Observations upon the inconveniences that have attended the frequent promotion to titles of honour*, [1653], *op. cit.*, 304–5; S. A. Strong, *A catalogue of documents . . . at Welbeck*, L., 1903, App. I, 215; C. H. Firth, *The House of Lords during the civil war*, 33. Cf. John Selden's remark, 'The making of new lords lessens all the rest.' *Table talk*, L., ed. 1894, 102.

[2] Cf. *infra*, 214–16.

---

the civil war, ch. II and C. R. Mayes, 'The sale of peerages in early Stuart England,' *Journal of modern history*, XXIX, 1 (1957) and 'The early Stuarts and the Irish peerage,' *E.H.R.*, LXXIII, 287 (1958).

the principal landed family in Essex, and in 1635 the earl owned sixty-five manors in the county. He was a great patron of the Puritans, his house, Lees Priory, being known as 'The common Randezvous of all Schysmaticall Preachers.' The friend of Sir John Eliot and other Country notables, he inspired the resistance in Essex to the King's forced loan and the ship-money tax.[1] Even more conspicuous as an oppositionist was William Fiennes, Viscount Saye and Sele, a Puritan of the Puritans. He was a man of rigid character who unfailingly contradicted every act of state he deemed illegal—forced loans, compulsory billeting of soldiers, ship money. In 1625 Saye was promoted from the degree of baron (he was the fourth of the title) to a viscountcy, an honour which Buckingham secured for him during the Court's brief *rapprochement* with the Country. A story in Saye's family described the favourite's flattering addresses—'that it may be writ upon my Tombe, Here Lies the man who did . . . Lord Say a kindnesse. . . .' But no blandishments could win him over: 'his ambition,' said Clarendon, 'would not be satisfied with offices . . . without some . . . alterations in ecclesiastical matters.' In truth, he wanted nothing less than the removal of bishops. There was not in the 1630s a firmer antagonist of the royal regime than this nobleman.[2]

Robert Greville, Lord Brooke, shared Saye's enmity towards the bishops. His cousin, the poet, Fulke Greville, whom he succeeded in the title, was a courtier and had been Chancellor of the Exchequer under King James. In spite of this, Brooke allied himself with the opposition. He was a youthful idealist of rare intellectual gifts, a Puritan who detested the clerical presumption of the Laudian churchmen and sympathized even with separatists.[3]

William Seymour, earl of Hertford, also adhered to the Country. He was a magnate in Somerset and the west and was esteemed by his contemporaries as a figure of honour. In 1610 he aroused the high displeasure of the King by marrying a royal cousin, Arabella Stuart. Following her death he took as his second wife the sister of the earl of Essex, another noble dissident. His closest associations, wrote Clarendon, were with men who loved the Court least and 'engaged most factiously and furiously against the King.' Nevertheless, he

---

[1] F. Hull, *Agriculture and rural society in Essex 1560–1640*, University of London Ph.D. thesis, 1951; Clarendon, *Rebellion*, III, 27; *A letter from Mercurius Rusticus to Mercurius Civicus*, 1643, 8; *C.S.P.D. 1627–28*, 43, 150; *D.N.B., s.v.*

[2] *C.S.P.D. 1627–28*, 589; *H.M.C. Rutland*, I, 507–8; Clarendon, *Rebellion*, III, 26; Dr. Williams's Library, Morrice MSS., v. G., f. 841; *D.N.B., s.v.*

[3] R. E. Strider, *Robert Greville, Lord Brooke*, Cambridge, 1958; *D.N.B., s.v.* The quality of Brooke's mind and the range of his sympathies are revealed in his published writings, *The nature of truth*, 1640, and *A discourse . . . of . . . episcopacie . . . in England*, 1642.

abandoned his friends after 1640 and supported Charles I, one of the few Country peers to do so. Very likely a strong sentiment of personal loyalty to Charles prompted his reversal.[1]

Edward Montagu, Viscount Mandeville, belonged to the Country as well, although there were a host of Court connections in his background. His uncle was Bishop of Winchester. His father made his career as a lawyer in the royal service, attained the earldom of Manchester, and was Lord Privy Seal from 1628 to his death in 1642. Mandeville began as a courtier and friend of Buckingham, whose patronage obtained him the unusual honour of elevation to a peerage in his father's lifetime. His first wife—he had five—was Buckingham's kinswoman, but after her death in 1625 he married a daughter of the earl of Warwick. Having thus contracted an affinity with a great opposition peer, he detached himself completely from his former associations. He became a Puritan, a resolute opponent of the crown, who believed according to Clarendon, that 'the Court was inclined to hurt and even to destroy the country....'[2]

Another of the Country's noble adherents was Robert Devereux, earl of Essex, son of the unhappy second earl executed for treason in 1601. James I restored Essex in blood and title, only to humiliate him a few years later by aiding his wife to obtain a divorce so that she might marry the earl of Somerset, the King's protégé. Perhaps this and family tradition first led him into the oppositionist camp. He engaged in numerous actions against royal power. For combating Charles I's forced loan he was deprived of his lord lieutenancy of Staffordshire. His friendships were with other opponents of the regime, and he appointed the earl of Warwick, Hampden, and St. John among the executors of his will. A member of his household wrote that he 'ever affected (out of the nobleness of his mind) a naturall & just freedom for the subject.' He enjoyed a reputation for integrity and a personal popularity inherited from his father which made his political support a great resource in the conflict with the crown.[3]

Still another lord in the fraternity of oppositionists was Francis

---

[1] *D.N.B., s.v.*; Clarendon, *Rebellion*, IV, 296, VI, 385.

[2] *D.N.B., s.v.*; Clarendon, *Rebellion*, VI, 407, III, 27.

[3] *D.N.B., s.v.*; Clarendon, *Rebellion*, V, 32; W. B. Devereux, *Lives ... of the Devereux*, 2v., L., 1853, II, 471n. The quotation is from Arthur Wilson (author of the *History of Great Britain*, 1653), who was first in Essex's service and then became steward to the earl of Warwick; F. Peck, *op. cit.*, pt. II, 470. Cf. also V. Snow, 'Essex and the aristocratic opposition to the early Stuarts,' *Journal of modern history*, XXXII, 3 (1960). B.M. Add. 46188, pt. 7 contains Essex's correspondence relating to his lieutenancy; B.M. Add. 46189, pts. 2, 4, includes correspondence with Warwick, Hertford, and John Selden.

Russell, earl of Bedford. A Puritan magnate, the owner of a great estate, he was an entrepreneur in the development of his London property and the draining of the fens. Among his close associates were Pym and St. John. The former sat in six parliaments for Tavistock, a Devon borough under Russell patronage. The latter was the earl's relation and lawyer and by his interest was elected to parliament in 1640 for Totnes.[1]

These were some of the opposition peers, though by no means all. The earl of Southampton has already been mentioned.[2] His heir, the fourth earl succeeding in 1624, continued to hold to the same position as 'a high assertor of the rights of his country. . . .'[3] Lord Spencer and the earl of Clare, who died before the Long Parliament, were both connected with the Country.[4] Clare's younger son, Denzil Holles, became a noted oppositionist in the House of Commons. The Puritan earl of Lincoln stood out against the forced loan and belonged to the inner circle of the crown's opponents.[5] Other titled dissidents in the 1630s were the earls of Danby, Mulgrave, and Bolingbroke, and lords Paget, Robartes, Savile, Wharton, and Willoughby of Parham.[6] Most of the Country peers—the main exceptions were Hertford, Southampton, and Paget—became Parliamentarians in the civil war, along with a group of noblemen who switched their allegiance from the Court after the assembling of the Long Parliament.

Save for their political and religious position, this gallery of peers differed in no respect from the rest of their order. Some held older, others more recent titles. In fortune they varied from the very rich, such as Warwick, Bedford, and Clare, to those whose estates were moderate or even straitened, such as Saye and Mandeville. What they had in common was precisely their antagonism to the crown's policy and methods, which they expressed sufficiently openly to

---

[1] *D.N.B., s.v.*; G. S. Thomson, *Life in a noble household 1641–1700*, L., 1937, ch. I; L. Stone, *The crisis of the aristocracy*, 355–7, 360–1; Clarendon, *Rebellion*, III, 32; M. Keeler, *op. cit.*, 318, 330.

[2] Cf. *supra*, 81.

[3] *D.N.B., s.v.*, 'Thomas Wriothesley;' H. C. Foxcroft, *op. cit.*, 56.

[4] *D.N.B., s.v.*, 'Robert Spencer;' G. Holles, *Memorials of the Holles family*, ed. A. C. Wood, *Camden society*, 3rd ser., LV, 1937, 106–9; A. Thomson, 'John Holles,' *Journal of modern history*, VIII, 2 (1936). In a letter to Wentworth in January 1628 Clare expressed his fears concerning the operation of regal power, Strafford MSS., v.22 (10).

[5] G. E. Cokayne, *op. cit.*, VII, 696–7; *C.S.P.V. 1626–28*, 126, 160; *C.S.P.D. 1628–29*, 498–9.

[6] Danby: *C.S.P.V. 1636–39*, 110–11; Mulgrave: *D.N.B., s.v.*, 'Edmund Sheffield;' Bolingbroke: *D.N.B., s.v.*, 'Oliver St. John;' Paget: Clarendon, *Rebellion*, III, 339; Robartes: *D.N.B., s.v.*, 'John Robartes;' Savile: *D.N.B., s.v.*, 'Thomas Savile;' Wharton: *D.N.B., s.v.*, 'Philip Wharton;' Willoughby of Parham: *D.N.B., s.v.*, 'Francis Willoughby.'

leave some record of their sentiments. Most also had Puritan sympathies, and there can be no doubt that the Puritanism of the peerage was heavily concentrated among these noblemen.

Another type represented in the Country was the royal official. There were not many such in the 1630s, but enough to illustrate the complete social resemblance of the groupings from whose conflict the revolution arose. Sir Robert Harley, Master of the Mint, may be taken as an instance. He was a prosperous Herefordshire gentleman, prominent in county affairs, and a member of parliament five times before November 1640. In 1623 at the age of forty-five, already twice a widower, he married the daughter of Sir Edward Conway, Secretary of State and Buckingham's dependent. With such a father-in-law he soon tasted favour. In 1626 the office of Master of the Mint was conferred on him for life at a salary of £500.[1] Harley had thus become affiliated with the Court, but he was out of sympathy with it all the same. A story in his family told how Buckingham, inviting him to a private meeting, tried vainly to gain his support.[2] The truth was, he was the friend of oppositionists and a Puritan.[3] Both he and his wife looked sourly on bishops, and in the parliament of 1628-9, in spite of his being elected with his father-in-law's help, he was a vocal assailant of the Arminian clergy who enjoyed the King's protection.[4]

It was his Puritanism that got Sir Robert into difficulty. In 1634, by his own account, 'falling under the disfavour of those ... then powerfull at Court, especially the ... Bishop of Canterbury,' a writ of *scire facias* was brought against his patent of office by Attorney General Noy. His offence was his support and patronage of nonconforming ministers. Since he was appointed for life, it appears that he was not legally deprived of his place. He was not allowed to exercise his function, however, or to receive any income from it. The Long Parliament restored Harley, but he had incurred a loss which he estimated at £3,875 for setting religious principles higher than office.[5]

[1] *D.N.B., s.v.; C.S.P.D. 1625–26,* 573, 577; *H.M.C. Portland,* III, 21.
[2] *The character of Sir Robert Harley,* B.M. Loan 29/124, no. 57. This story was recorded in the early eighteenth century.
[3] Cf. the letter to Sir Robert in February 1637 from Nathaniel Fiennes, Lord Saye's son, which speaks of their frequent meetings, B.M. Loan 29/119, pt. 4.
[4] *Commons debates for 1629,* 116. Harley represented Evesham, to which Conway wrote on his behalf, *C.S.P.D. 1627–28,* 562.
[5] Harley's narrative of his trouble over his office is in B.M. Loan 29/124, no. 65. For his support of nonconformist clergy, cf. *C.S.P.D. 1637–38,* 249, and his correspondence with the Rev. Stanley Gower, the Puritan rector of

Harley's example suggests that oppositionists in office saw nothing questionable about their situation. In any case, not being in the greatest positions, they bore no responsibility for the crown's measures. They were at most administrators, not devisers of policy. So we find Sir Gilbert Gerrard, Bt., an activist in the Country, serving at the close of the '30s as clerk to the Council of the Duchy of Lancaster—a place occupied by his father before him.[1] So, too, John Hutchinson, a Nottinghamshire Puritan hostile to the regime, tried about 1639 to buy an office in the Court of Star Chamber; before his negotiation could bear fruit, wrote his wife ingenuously, 'it pleased God ... that arbitrary court was, by the parliament then sitting, taken away.'[2] The Suffolk gentleman, John Winthrop, another Puritan, held an attorneyship in the Star Chamber. Assiduously as he had sought the office, he resigned it in the dark year 1629, when the Country's hopes were at a low ebb, in order to emigrate to New England as governor of the Massachusetts Bay Company.[3] The Surveyor of the Court of Wards, Sir Benjamin Rudyard, was associated in the '30s with leading oppositionists.[4] Even John Pym, while not to be classified as an official, was Receiver General of royal revenues for three counties from about 1607 to 1636.[5]

Just as Sir Thomas Wentworth left the Country for office and the Court, so in a corresponding reversal Sir John Eliot left the Court and office for the Country. The latter's was the outstanding case of this kind in the opposition movement. And if Wentworth's change of front gave him power, Eliot's brought him fame as one of the greatest parliamentary champions of his time. Born of a Cornish gentry family, he became attached to the Court in consequence of an early friendship with Buckingham. He was knighted in 1618 through the favourite's influence and four years later Buckingham as Lord Admiral gave him the profitable office of Vice-Admiral of Devon.[6] Here he was shortly in trouble. In 1624, Sir John Coke, the duke's assistant in naval matters, accused him of financial malfeasance in his

[1] M. Keeler, *op. cit.*, 186.
[2] Lucy Hutchinson, *Memoirs of Colonel Hutchinson*, ed. C. H. Firth, 2v., L., 1885, I, 95, 96–7.
[3] R. C. Winthrop, *Life and letters of John Winthrop*, 2v., Boston, 1864, I, 214; C. M. Andrews, *The colonial period of American history*, 4v., New Haven, 1934–8, I, 384–7.
[4] *D.N.B.*, *s.v.*
[5] M. Keeler, *op. cit.*, 318.
[6] H. Hulme, *op. cit.*, 17–19, 26, 30, 32.

his own parish, B.M. Loan 29, *passim*. The account of Harley in the preceding two paragraphs of the text derives from material collected prior to the publication of G. E. Aylmer's *The King's servants*, which also uses him as an illustration. Our discussions differ in a few details.

vice-admiralty. He also quarrelled bitterly with the Vice-Admiral of South Cornwall, Sir James Bagg, who denounced him to Buckingham as obstructive in naval affairs in Devon.[1]

Despite these frictions, Eliot was still loyal to the Court.[2] The duke's help secured his election to parliament in 1624 and 1625; and though in the latter he showed himself somewhat critical of the government, he refrained from joining the attack on the all-powerful minister.[3] The next year, however, with political division hardening and in the background the failure of the English expedition against Cadiz, he broke completely with his patron. Returned to the parliament of 1626 for St. Germans, the borough neighbouring his own estate, he delivered 'the sharpest denunciation of the government ... ever ... heard in the House of Commons.' It was a powerful appeal to patriotic feeling in condemnation of the dishonour and loss brought by evil counsellors upon the King and kingdom. A few weeks later he assailed Buckingham as the cause of all the nation's ills. The House chose him, together with Pym, Digges, Erle, Selden, and three others, to manage the duke's impeachment.[4]

Eliot thus renounced the Court to ally himself with the politicians of the Country. His oratorical talents and fearless espousal of the popular cause put him immediately in the front rank of oppositionists in parliament. His conduct did not go unscathed, however. Although never formally removed from his vice-admiralty, in 1626 proceedings were instituted against him for abuses in office and an order of the Privy Council suspended him from his functions.[5] There is scarcely any reason to doubt that his change of front was dictated by political dislike of crown policy and the sincere conviction that Buckingham's domination meant ruin. He was, according to his most painstaking biographer, 'an idealist in government ... so loyal to his convictions that he was eager to fight and willing to die for them.'[6]

We have mentioned peers and royal officials among the types represented in the Country. There were also citizen and merchant supporters who will be noticed in the following chapter. The predominant element in the opposition movement, however, was the gentry, in particular the upper gentry. The men in the House of

[1] *C.S.P.D. Addenda 1625–49*, 203; *H.M.C. Cowper*, I, 177, 190.
[2] Cf. his letter to Buckingham, April 1625, *C.S.P.D. 1625–26*, 5.
[3] H. Hulme, *op. cit.*, 43, 75, 89, 91–3. Eliot represented Newport in these parliaments. He was first elected to the House in 1614; he was not returned in 1621.
[4] *Ibid.*, 104–7, 117–19, 131.
[5] *Ibid.*, 152–4, 165.
[6] *Ibid.*, 13–14.

Commons who led the struggle for parliamentary privilege, liberty of the subject, and security of property; their friends and associates outside parliament; the persons who showed themselves most refractory to forced loans, ship money, and other devices of the regime: they were almost all gentry. Such, to cite a representative sample of families whose members defied the royal power at one time or another in the 1620s and '30s, were Phelips, Seymour, Strangeways, Erle, Ayscough, Armyne, Irby, Wray, Hampden, Luke, Goodwin, Haselrig, Barnardiston, Cheeke, Barrington, Rous, Masham, Buller, Grenville, Stephens, Pelham, Dryden, Knightley, Heyman, Mallory, Belasyse.

Here was a portent. A growing section of the aristocratic order—the privileged elite of landlords and local governors on whose loyalty and obedience the monarchy's stability depended—was hostile to the crown. When a growing body of men in the governing class could be provoked into opposition, a revolutionary situation was in the making. It only remained for Charles I, driving forward on his purblind course in the 1630s, to bring the revolutionary situation to birth.

4

Considered as a whole, the opposition engendered by the rule of Charles I was not an organized affair. If we were to collect from the surviving evidence the name of every one in England and Wales who showed himself in any way recalcitrant towards the royal authority in these years, the result would be a list of hundreds of individuals, most of them personally unknown to each other. There was no coordination, no connection, no design in this large and amorphous mass. Acts of disobedience were frequently spontaneous or due to the force of example, a product of common grievances and sympathies, rather than of planning and calculation.

But at the centre of the Country was something more. Here a definite organization existed: a group united by conviction, linked through family and friendship, meeting to concert the tactics of opposition. In structure an informal alliance of like-minded men, this group was the nucleus of the Country. It was that part of the opposition movement in which the reaction to Stuart rule had produced an organized political force, the embryo of a party. To it belonged the gentlemen with whom the regime had most to reckon, the most resourceful and determined antagonists of the royal power.

A vague but illuminating description of this organization of opposition leaders was set down late in the seventeenth century by the Tory antiquarian, Anthony Wood. According to his account, the

Puritan Lord Saye, godfather of the 'discontented party,' was endeavouring to incite a rebellion and held meetings of his friends at his Oxfordshire house, Broughton Castle,

where was a room and passages thereunto, to which his Servants were prohibited to come near: and when they were of a compleat number, there could be great noises and talkings heard among them, to the admiration of those that lived in the House, yet could they never discern their Lord's Companions. At other times he would be present at their meetings in the House of [Richard] Knightley at Fawsley in Northamptonshire; where, as at other places in the Kingdom, they had their Council Chambers and chief Speakers: And what Embryo's were conceived in The Country, were shaped in Greys-Inn-Lane near London, where the Undertakers for the Isle of Providence did meet....[1]

A pamphlet written forty years earlier, from which Wood drew some of his material, added the detail that John Hampden went annually to Scotland, thereby implying a connection between the Country nucleus and the Scottish rebels. It also reported that John Pym 'rode a Circuite into divers Counties, to promote Elections of men of the Faction' to the Long Parliament.[2]

That a group of the kind pointed at in these statements really existed is beyond question. It is impossible, however, to determine precisely how it came into being or to throw much light on its inner transactions. Opposition was dangerous, meetings were illicit conspiracies, and these Country politicians must surely have been careful to destroy compromising communications and to cover their deliberations with secrecy. Yet despite these difficulties an idea of its nature and activities can be formed.

Probably the group took shape through the cooperation of certain of the principal Country members and their friends in parliament. We have already mentioned some of their private consultations to influence the House of Commons. Then, after the dissolution of 1629 and the cessation of parliaments, they had to establish other means through which to maintain their collaboration. The Country leaders apparently found a solution in several of the companies for colonization. These enterprises, in which the English Puritans took a

[1] Anthony Wood, *Athenae Oxonienses*, 2nd ed., 2v., L., 1721, II, 273–4. The room at Broughton Castle where, according to tradition, these meetings took place, is still shown to visitors.

[2] *Persecutio undecima*, 1648, 55–6. Wood took some of his material from this tract, and both he and it also depended heavily on *A letter from Mercurius Civicus to Mercurius Rusticus*, 1643, which appears to have been their common source. For the latter pamphlet, cf. *infra*, 287.

54367

strong interest, were created to finance and support settlement in the lands across the Atlantic. They were legal incorporations, managing their own affairs under a charter from the crown. In the shelter of their meetings, it was possible to discuss much else besides company business when the occasion warranted. Thus, within some of these bodies, like the Providence Island enterprise founded in 1630, which Wood mentioned, and the Saybrooke patentees of 1632, a virtual interlocking directorate of oppositionists was formed. Its members were the militant Puritan centre of the struggle against Charles I before and after 1640—Pym, Hampden, St. John, Knightley, Sir Thomas Barrington, Sir Gilbert Gerrard, Sir Thomas Cheeke, and a number of others, as well as such noblemen as Warwick, Saye, Brooke, Robartes, and Mandeville.[1] Most likely Eliot would have been associated with them, had he not been put in prison for sedition in 1629, dying there three years later the victim of royal displeasure.

An astonishing number of threads joined these men and led out from them to other enemies of the King's rule. So thick were their ties of family that altogether they resembled a large kith or clan. Thus, both Mandeville and Robartes married daughters of the earl of Warwick. Warwick's sister was married to the Essex oppositionist, Sir Thomas Cheeke. Mandeville's third wife was Cheeke's daughter. Lord Brooke was the son-in-law of the earl of Bedford and his sister married Sir Arthur Haselrig, a Leicestershire adherent of the Country. Of Lord Saye's children, one daughter married the oppositionist earl of Lincoln, another the son of the Dorset oppositionist, Sir Walter Erle. Saye's younger son, Nathaniel Fiennes, was Sir John Eliot's son-in-law. His older son, James Fiennes, and Lord Willoughby of Parham, a Country peer, both married sisters. Richard Knightley and John Hampden were connected by marriage, while the relatives of Sir Thomas Barrington, an Essex member of this inner circle, included Hampden, St. John, Sir Gilbert Gerrard, as well as Oliver Cromwell and such opposition families as Masham in Essex, Luke in Bedfordshire, and Wallop in Hampshire. Warwick and Mandeville were also related to still other supporters of the Country—to the Wrays, the Irbys, and the Ayscoughs in Lincolnshire, who were in turn linked through marriage to each other.[2]

---

[1] The discovery of the role of the colonizing companies in the organization of opposition to Charles I was due to A. P. Newton, *The colonizing activities of the English Puritans*, New Haven, 1914, a work to which I am indebted.
[2] On these kinship connections, cf. A. P. Newton, *op. cit.*, *passim*; J. H. Hexter, *The reign of King Pym*, Cambridge, 1941, ch. IV; and biographical accounts under the names mentioned in M. Keeler, *op. cit.*, G. E. Cokayne, *op. cit.*, and *D.N.B.* A genealogical chart in J. W. F. Hill, *Tudor and Stuart Lincoln*, Cambridge, 1956, 127, shows the relationships of some of the oppositionist families of Lincolnshire.

Close bonds of friendship, too, held these men together. The correspondence of Sir Thomas Barrington included familiar letters from or allusions to Hampden, St. John, the earl of Warwick, and other political confidants.[1] In 1630 Barrington informed his mother of the possibility that Pym would occupy Barrington Hall 'till winter.'[2] Pym addressed Sir Thomas as 'brother,' the term Puritans often used towards one another in recognition of their spiritual bond.[3] A further impression of these friendships cemented by common convictions comes from the prison correspondence of Sir John Eliot. Warm and sympathetic letters passed between him and Hampden, the earls of Warwick and Lincoln, Denzil Holles, and Sir Oliver Luke. To his great friend, Richard Knightley, a pillar of Northamptonshire Puritanism, he signed himself 'brother'—an expression which, like his account of his spiritual experience as a prisoner, shows that he became a Puritan in the last years of his life.[4]

In spite of the obscurity surrounding the Country nucleus during the 1630s, several important manifestations of its political activity can be traced. One was its role in the resistance to ship money. The King introduced this tax in 1634, giving as ground the necessity to raise a fleet for the security of shipping and the defence of the realm.[5] First imposed only on the port towns, the next year it was made into a general levy. As a device which was in fact, if not in form, a direct impost ordained without assent of parliament, ship money provoked strong protest everywhere. It was seen as a move in Charles I's possible plan to dispense forever with the representative body of the kingdom.

In December 1636 the earl of Danby took the bold step of writing the King to denounce ship money as illegal and ask for the summoning of parliament. The Venetian ambassador, Correr, reported that Danby's letter was the 'long premeditated' result of 'consultation' among leading men. A month later Correr mentioned 'secret meetings' by 'leading men . . . determined to make a final effort to bring the forms of government back to their former state.' He thought they would issue a public call for a parliament and offer the King some

---

[1] B.M. Egerton MSS. 2645, *passim.*

[2] *Ibid.,* f. 184.

[3] B.M. Egerton MSS. 2643, ff. 6, 14. Cf. Wentworth's remark in 1637 about the Puritan Hampden: he 'is a great Brother, and the very Genius of that Nation of People leads them always to oppose . . . Authority. . . .', *The earl of Strafforde's letters,* II, 138.

[4] *The letter-book of Sir John Eliot,* ed. A. Grosart, 2v., p.p., 1882, 52, 55, 63; J. Forster, *op. cit.,* II, 642–5; H. Hulme, *op. cit.,* ch. XV. Eliot seems to have passed through a conversion in prison.

[5] Cf. the text of the writ ordering the levy of ship money in S. R. Gardiner *Constitutional documents of the Puritan revolution,* 105–8.

concessions as an inducement.[1] If such was the oppositionists' purpose, nothing further was heard of it, but meanwhile they were preparing to challenge ship money in the courts. With the aim of laying the basis of a case, both Saye and Hampden had formally refused payment.[2] At the end of February 1637 the directors of the Providence Island Company held several meetings in Northamptonshire at Preston Capes, a house belonging to Richard Knightley not far from his mansion at Fawsley.[3] Pym, Saye, Brooke, Mandeville, Knightley, and doubtless Hampden, too, attended. Probably they discussed the ship-money question, since a declaration by the judges in favour of the King's power to levy the tax had just been made public.[4] At any rate, within two weeks, on 9 March 1637, Hampden's name was certified as a refuser and the legal proceedings thus instituted in which he as defendant and St. John as counsel were soon to win fame for their opposition to taxation without the consent of the subject in parliament.[5]

There is further evidence of the political activity of the inner circle of Country politicians in connection with the Scottish rebellion. They did not fail, of course, to realize the significance of the rising which broke out in the northern kingdom in 1638. The adverse decision of the judges in the ship-money case had made them so despairing of the trend of events that some of them even contemplated emigration across the Atlantic.[6] But then, as if by providence, a storm blew up in Scotland that threatened the carefully erected edifice of arbitrary rule. Sharing the Scots' hatred of Laud, the English oppositionists saw the revolt as the occasion that might reinstate liberty and religion in England: for in the face of danger and possible invasion from the north, the King would have to seek his subjects' aid in parliament. There is no doubt that they sent the rebels secret encouragement. Late in 1639 Lord Saye addressed a message to the earl of Loudoun, one of the Scot leaders. It was carried by Henry Lawrence, a Huntingdon neighbour of Mandeville and Oliver Cromwell, and declared that the English people would oppose a war against the Scots if the latter 'did unanimouslie resolve . . . to come in for the publique

---

[1] *C.S.P.V. 1636–39*, 110–11, 125, 136.
[2] S. R. Gardiner, *History*, VIII, 271.
[3] *Victoria county history, Northamptonshire, Genealogical vols.*, II, 171, 185.
[4] The probable connection between the February meetings of the Providence Island Company and the ship-money struggle is discussed by A. P. Newton, *op. cit.*, 242–3. The judges' declaration justifying ship money was read in the Star Chamber on 14 Feb. 1637, *State trials*, III, 839–44. It was not a judicial decision, but an opinion solicited by the King.
[5] The chronology of the case can be gathered from *State trials*, III, 846. The suit did not come to trial until November.
[6] A. P. Newton, *op. cit.*, 245.

liberties of both kingdomes. ....' Saye's son, Nathaniel Fiennes, subsequently joined Lawrence at Edinburgh in order to represent the state of English affairs to the Scots.[1]

The King, meanwhile, having lost hope of any agreement with his rebellious subjects in Scotland, decided in December 1639 to summon a parliament to assist him against them. The Short Parliament met on 13 April 1640 and lasted only three weeks. It refused to vote a penny to put down the Scots unless English grievances were first redressed. When Charles learned that Pym and a group of fellow M.P.s were about to offer a petition in the House of Commons against a war, he hastily dissolved the parliament.[2] Two months later, as the Scottish army prepared to march south, the rebel leaders communicated with the opposition peers in England to ask assurances of support. The noblemen who replied—Bedford, Essex, Warwick, Brooke, Saye,[3] Mandeville, and Savile—refused to extend an invitation to the Scottish army to enter England, since that would be treason. On the same ground they would make no specific offers of aid. But they pointed out that if the Scots entered England 'in their own just Right ... we are resolv'd to do more, and more effectually, for obtaining their and our honest Ends' than the assistance requested would provide. Between Scotland and England, they said, 'the Enemies are all one, the common Interest one, the End is all one; a free Parliament to try all Offenders, and to settle Religion and Liberty.'[4]

Nothing could have been more clearsighted than this appraisal of the bearing of the Scottish rebellion upon English affairs and the political objectives of the Country. The King's game was now about played out. At the end of August an army of 25,000 Scotsmen crossed the border, occupied Newcastle, and brought most of the north under its power. Disorganized, poorly led, disaffected, the King's forces offered no resistance. The time had come for the opposition leaders to make a last attempt, as they had promised the Scots, to obtain a parliament that would do the work of both. At London

[1] The evidence for this episode is an anonymous paper in *The Hamilton papers*, ed. S. R. Gardiner, *Camden society*, n.s., XXVII, 1880, 264–6. It was probably written in 1640, and though mentioning no dates, seems to refer to the later months of 1639. The 'Lawrence' of whom it speaks can be identified by the allusion to his stay in Holland, where he had been a religious exile; cf. *D.N.B.*, *s.v.*, 'Henry Lawrence.'

[2] An account of Pym's consultations with the purpose of laying the case of the Scots before the Commons was given to the Privy Council; cf. *C.S.P.D. 1640*, 144–5.

[3] Not Lord Scrope, given by Gardiner, *History*, IX, 179.

[4] J. Oldmixon, *The history of England during the reigns of the royal house of Stuart*, L., 1730, 142–3. The original of this letter is not extant and is known only from the copy printed by Oldmixon. Its genuineness has been challenged, but is convincingly defended by Gardiner, *History*, IX, 179n.

discussions took place between Essex, Warwick, Saye, Brooke, Bedford, the latter's son, Lord Russell, Pym, Hampden, St. John, and perhaps other participants. The Privy Council, learning of these meetings, feared 'some dangerous practice or intelligence with the Rebels of Scotland.'[1] The outcome of the oppositionists' deliberations was a petition to the King drafted by Pym and St. John in the name of twelve peers. The petitioners recited the evils and dangers threatening church and state by reason of the Scottish war, religious innovations, ship money, and other burdens. They dwelt, too, on the grief caused Charles's subjects by the long intermission and the dissolution of parliaments. To compose the Scottish troubles without bloodshed, to remove the people's grievances and punish those responsible, they asked that a parliament be promptly summoned.[2]

The demand thus voiced was universal—the expression of national feeling too imperious to be withstood. On 24 September at York, where he had summoned a council of the whole nobility, Charles yielded. Devoid of money for war, beset by a Scottish army and the clamour of his discontented people, he announced the convening of a parliament for 3 November.

Although Pym and his friends must have bent all their energies to secure the return to the House of Commons of members favourable to the Country, scarcely any evidence of their election preparations has survived.[3] It is not difficult, however, to imagine the hopes and fears with which they faced the immediate future. Through years past they had done what lay in their power to sustain the political struggle against the crown. The parliament about to meet would present them with the gravest challenge and the greatest opportunity. The prospect existed of enacting measures to put an end to methods of arbitrary rule so productive of animosity and division in the '20s and '30s. For this more than a talent for opposition would be required. Amidst the deepest political crisis in more than a century members from all parts of the kingdom were assembling to take their seats at Westminster. It remained to be seen whether the Country leaders could maintain their unity and apply the lessons of their collaboration to guide parliament in achieving a great work of constructive reform.

[1] Secretary Windebanke to the King, 31 Aug. 1640, *Clarendon state papers*, ed. R. Scrope and T. Monkhouse, 3v., Oxford, 1767–86, II, 94–5.
[2] Printed in S. R. Gardiner, *The constitutional documents of the Puritan revolution*, 134–6. Pym's and St. John's authorship of the petition was attested by Lord Savile, who had joined in the previous message to the Scots and was in a position to know; cf. Savile to Lady Temple, November 1642, *Camden miscellany*, VIII, 1883, 2.
[3] A few scanty indications of the Country group's electioneering activity preliminary to the Long Parliament are mentioned by M. Keeler, *op. cit.*, 9 68, 166.

The period that witnessed the generation of the Country's conflict with the Court also saw a great awakening of political awareness in society at large. There was a heightened interest everywhere in public questions, along with growing hostility to the Court and royal government. Beneath the surface of events, profound tremors of popular discontent made themselves felt. Sectional grievances resulting from one or another aspect of the crown's policy were merging behind the spokesmen of the Country in a broad front of opposition. Sullen and resentful, the offended hosts of sufferers from the prerogative and prerogative courts, financial exactions, monopolies, and religious repression were drawing together in one swelling mass of enmity, their hope of redress and a day of reckoning centred on the opposition movement. A formidable insurgent temper was taking possession of the English people which in the end endowed the Country leaders with power to impose their will on Charles I.

The awakened political consciousness of the 1620s had its origin in the attention with which the public mind followed the fortunes of continental Protestantism and the progress of controversies in parliament. A decade of defeat for the Protestant forces in central Europe, Germany, and France made it appear that the princes and peoples adhering to the Reformation might be overwhelmed by a rising tide of Catholic conquest. The failures of Stuart foreign policy and the reverses which Charles I encountered against Spain and France became matters for general comment and criticism. Together with angry disputes in parliament and dislike of Buckingham and royal financial pressures, they raised the political temperature to fever height.

Under these circumstances, a rapid evolution of public opinion occurred. The Venetian ambassador told his government at the end of 1620: '. . . this kingdom has never had its eyes so wide open . . . and it has never been so teeming and pregnant with ideas and grievances as now.'[1] Preoccupation with governmental affairs was widespread. '. . . now-a-days,' said Bacon, 'there is no vulgar, but all statesmen.'[2] On the eve of the parliament of 1621, King James found it necessary to issue a proclamation against 'excesse of lavish Speech of Matters of State.' It declared that 'there is at this tyme a more licentious Passage of lavish Discourse and bould Censure in matters of State than hath been heretofore or is fitt to be suffered.' James commanded his presumptuous people not to meddle with 'Causes of

[1] *C.S.P.V. 1619–21*, 490.
[2] *Works*, XIV, 129.

State and Secretes of Empire either at Home or abroade, but containe themselves within that modest and Reverend Regard of Matter above the Reach and Calling that to good and dutiful Subjects appertaineth.'[1] This royal attempt to silence public discussion was fatuous, however, in the face of powerful domestic and international forces whose effect everyone could feel or see.

Just at this time, appropriately enough, in December 1620, the first English newspaper or coranto saw the light. Printed at Amsterdam and translated from Dutch, it was imported into England to supply the demand for information about the European war. Some of the corantoes published the next year were printed in London, but bore a fictitious Dutch imprint to defeat government attempts at suppression.[2] A second proclamation issued in July 1621 against the 'inordinate libertie of unreverent Speech touching Matters of high Nature unfit for vulgar Discourse,' was probably aimed partly at them.[3] From the middle of 1622, however, weekly news sheets began to be printed in England by rival writers with the consent of authority.[4] These confined themselves to dry accounts of foreign occurrences, leaving domestic topics alone. The government allowed them because the appetite for such news was too keen to be stifled by prohibition.

In general, anything of immediate political relevance was seized on avidly by a growing public. *Vox Populi*, a tract published in 1620 against a Spanish marriage alliance, won instant notoriety and its Puritan author, the Rev. Thomas Scott, had to flee the kingdom.[5] Three years later, Thomas Middleton's play, *A Game At Chesse*, a sharp-witted satire that took off the Spanish ambassador, Gondomar, to the life, became a nine-day-wonder—the longest run of any play to that time. It 'hath ben followed'—so wrote the best of all Jacobean news correspondents—'with extraordinarie concourse, and frequented by all sorts of people old and younge, rich and poor, masters and servants, papists and puritans ... churchmen and statesmen. ...'[6]

But the chief focus of political attention in the 1620s was parliament. Concentration on its proceedings produced an extraordinary

[1] T. Rymer, *Foedera*, ed. 1742, VII, pt. 3, 187. The proclamation was dated 24 Dec. 1620.
[2] Cf. L. Hanson, 'English newsbooks, 1620–1641,' *The library*, 4th ser., XVIII, 4 (1938) and J. Frank, *The beginnings of the English newspaper*, Cambridge, 1961, ch. I.
[3] T. Rymer, *op. cit.*, VII, pt. 3, 207.   [4] L. Hanson, *op. cit.*
[5] *Letters of John Chamberlain*, II, 339; *D.N.B.*, *s.v.*, 'Thomas Scott.' *Vox populi* went through four editions in 1620. Scott's writings as an anti-Spanish publicist are discussed by L. B. Wright, 'Propaganda against James I's "Appeasement" of Spain,' *Huntington Library quarterly*, VI, 2 (1943).
[6] *Letters of John Chamberlain*, II, 578.

increase in the dissemination of parliamentary news and speeches, so that the import of the conflict at Westminster between the Court and the Country was communicated to every quarter. Debate, of course, was supposed to be secret and members' revelation of parliamentary business a breach of privilege. The tendency, however, of the oppositionists to carry their fight in an appeal beyond the walls of parliament caused the restraints against disclosure to be seriously undermined. Manuscript copies of speeches, petitions, and declarations circulated far and wide. Such 'separates' of parliamentary utterances began first to appear in small numbers in the middle of Elizabeth's reign. Gradually increasing in volume, their quantity reached new proportions amidst the bitter arguments of the 1620s. From this time, parliamentary affairs were conducted in an unprecedented glare of publicity, while the words of Pym, Eliot, Coke and other oppositionist orators were studied and preserved in scores of country houses. Members themselves passed around manuscripts of their own and other men's speeches to the end, said an unfriendly critic, 'That all the people might take notice of the zeal they had to the common liberty of the nation.'[1] Private intelligencers, procuring copies, sold them to subscribers; writers of news letters summarized them in accounts of parliamentary transactions. These expanding facilities for learning of what passed in parliament developed in almost direct relation to the progress of political opposition. They were at one and the same time both a consequence of enlarged public awareness and a further means of stimulating its growth.[2]

Revolution is never a sudden birth. It must ripen through a considerable period of gestation. Before the decisive battle is joined, there are preliminary skirmishes and engagements. Usually the men in power repel the first challenges. The attacking forces fall back momentarily, fatigued and defeated, while the disturbed political atmosphere settles down for a little. But soon a new crisis erupts creating fresh difficulties for the regime. Opposition revives with resurgent energy, the struggle against the government attains greater dimensions than before, and this time its enemies are victorious. Such was the phasing of the course of events between the inception of Charles I's rule and the meeting of the Long Parliament. From 1625 to 1629 the deterioration of relations between the King and his subjects brought England close to rebellion. The period ended with the temporary defeat of the Country, and an interval of quiescence ensued. Then after 1635 occurred the growing reaction against ship

[1] P. Heylyn, *Examen historicum*, 1656, pt. 2, 74, cited in *Commons debates for 1629*, xxviii.
[2] Cf. *ibid.*, Intro., chs. III–IV, for an account of the circulation of parliamentary news and separates.

money, the renewal of open conflict in the wake of the disturbances in Scotland, and the generalization of disaffection throughout the kingdom. When revolution came, it was because an invincible body of support had gathered about the opposition leaders which the King was powerless to resist.

The first outbreak of large-scale disobedience to the royal government occurred in 1626–7 in consequence of the forced loan. Repulsed in his attempt to obtain a money grant from the parliament of 1626 for the Spanish war, Charles resorted to a device the Tudor rulers occasionally employed and commanded the levying of a loan. It was to be demanded from everyone liable to the payment of parliamentary subsidies. In palliation of the measure, the King published a proclamation promising that it would not be made a precedent nor used to evade the future summoning of parliament.[1] These professions had no effect, and during the next months a spirit of insubordination burst forth throughout the kingdom. Frequently, men appointed as commissioners for the loan would neither perform their duty nor lend themselves. In some counties the principal gentry refused to lend and also influenced the freeholders to follow their example. The Privy Council was kept busy summoning recalcitrants before it to warn them of the penalties of their defiance. In Northamptonshire the Council learned that twenty-two gentlemen had drawn half the county into opposition and threatened to infect the neighbouring shires by their conduct. Two hundred and five freeholders there were reported as refusers.[2] Sizeable opposition manifested itself in Somerset and Gloucestershire; in the latter, twelve of the twenty-five loan commissioners would give no money for reasons of conscience.[3]

Many refusers also appeared in Yorkshire: one landlord was haled to the Council board for saying that no one who lent should hold land of him.[4] In Cornwall three justices were ordered removed from the commission of the peace for their opposition while in Norfolk some of the loan commissioners went on a sort of strike, declining to attend meetings of their body.[5] A numerous group of refusers gave

[1] S. R. Gardiner, *History*, VI, 143; R. Steele, *op. cit.*, I, 1494.

[2] *C.S.P.D. 1627–28*, 15; *The court and times of Charles I*, I, 184. Several striking instances of defiance by Northamptonshire gentlemen summoned before the Privy Council appear in *Acts of the Privy Council, Jan.-Aug. 1627*, 42, 62.

[3] *C.S.P.D. 1627–28*, 58–9, 76; W. B. Willcox, *op. cit.*, 117–20; T. G. Barnes, *op. cit.*, 165–7.

[4] *C.S.P.D. 1627–28*, 32, 194; *Fairfax correspondence*, ed. G. W. Johnson, 2v., L., 1848, I, 73–4; *Acts of the Privy Council Jan.–Aug. 1627*, 54, 67.

[5] *C.S.P.D. 1627–28*, 231; *State papers relating to musters, beacons, ship money in Norfolk*, ed. W. B. Rye, Norwich, 1907, 83–4.

the Council trouble in Lincolnshire, Essex, and Warwickshire.[1] In several London parishes the loan provoked riots. The refusers were many and the constables would not distrain upon their goods as ordered.[2] Six hundred persons in Hertfordshire subscribed a letter to their lord lieutenant, the earl of Salisbury, protesting the loan.[3] Some of the nobility were adamant in their refusal of money. A servant of the earl of Lincoln was apprehended for dispersing letters against the loan among freeholders inscribed, 'To all true-hearted Englishmen.' '. . . this scattering of letters,' reported a news writer, 'is grown rife in divers parts, and they are but ill symptoms.'[4] At the beginning of 1628, according to the Privy Council's records, seventy-eight men were still in prison or under some form of restraint for their disobedience. The list included twenty-six knights, fifteen esquires, three gentlemen, and twenty-three described as Londoners.[5]

Although only a small minority stood forth openly against the loan, they expressed the sentiment of multitudes. The angry kingdom stirred with unrest. A hard will against giving to the King in any but a parliamentary way had been revealed. Furthermore, with all the pressures the crown could apply, fourteen months after the loan was undertaken it was still over £55,000 short of its estimated total of £300,000. The balance was never obtained.[6]

During 1628 and 1629, the political mood worsened. While the resentments of the forced loan lingered, abuses from the billeting of soldiers and the operation of martial law added to the general sense of grievance.[7] At the ports, the customs officials extracted tonnage and poundage duties from unwilling merchants without a grant from parliament for the purpose. Buckingham was universally execrated. In June 1628 a London mob lynched Dr. Lambe, a quack astrologer reputed to have some shady connection with the duke. The city officials did nothing to suppress this outbreak of violence.[8] Two months later Buckingham himself was murdered by an assassin who said he acted solely for patriotic and public reasons.[9] The elections to

[1] *C.S.P.D. 1627–28*, 81; *The court and times of Charles I*, I, 207; P.R.O. S.P. 16/56, no. 70.
[2] *The court and times of Charles I*, I, 154, 157.
[3] *Ibid.*, I, 176.
[4] *Ibid.*, I, 172, 177, 202, 207; *C.S.P.D. 1627–28*, 43.
[5] *Acts of the Privy Council Sept. 1627–June 1628*, 217–18.
[6] W. R. Scott, *The constitution and finance of English . . . joint-stock companies*, 3v., Cambridge, 1910–12, I, 190. I have preferred these figures to those given by S. R. Gardiner, *History*, VI, 219–20.
[7] Cf. the Privy Council's letter of June 1628 about the opposition to billeting, *Acts of the Privy Council Sept. 1627–June 1628*, 490, and L. Boynton, 'Martial law and the Petition of Right,' *E.H.R.*, LXXIX, 311 (1964).
[8] *Acts of the Privy Council Sept. 1627–June 1628*, 492.
[9] *The court and times of Charles I*, I, 387.

the parliament of 1628, which were held in February and early March, provoked more excitement than any since the Stuart accession. 'All the counties,' the Venetian ambassador reported, 'have uniformly rejected candidates who had even a shadow of dependence upon the Court, electing members who refused the late subsidies ... now everywhere called good patriots.'[1] Loan refusers and oppositionists were returned as knights of the shire in Kent, Essex, Dorset, Northampton, Yorkshire, Norfolk, Cornwall, Gloucester, Lincoln, and elsewhere.[2] The first session saw the passage of the Petition of Right after a hard fight; but in the second, rancorous quarrels ensued because of the King's collection of tonnage and poundage and his patronage of well-known Arminian divines. The resolutions condemning these royal acts which Eliot and his friends forced through the Commons on the eve of dissolution raised passions to white heat. Not all the Country's sympathizers approved of their conduct. Some, like the Puritan Sir Simonds D'Ewes, blamed it as imprudent and extremist—the work of 'fiery spirits.'[3] Their unprecedented defiance of the Speaker, however, backed by the House, was a sign that confidence in the King had sunk nearly to the vanishing point.

It was in these months that the likelihood of rebellion was spoken of here and there for the first time. The Venetian ambassador had been expecting an outbreak all along. In September 1626 he considered one to be imminent because of the intense popular dissatisfaction.[4] At the end of 1627 a Suffolk clergyman confided a similar belief to his diary, the result of political discussions with his acquaintances. In June 1628 he mentioned rumours of a secret intent to depose Charles in favour of his sister, Queen Elizabeth of Bohemia. 'Our King's proceedings,' he wrote, 'have caused mens mindes to be incensed, to rove, and projecte. ...'[5] From 1626 onward, Salvetti, the agent of the Grand Duke of Tuscany, also repeatedly reported to his government on the prospects of a rising. In May 1628 he held it certain that serious disorders would occur. At the end of the year, he reiterated his prediction, in view of the 'growing and daring opposition of the people.'[6]

Perhaps if the Country leaders had believed in the right of forcible

---

[1] *C.S.P.V. 1628–29*, 21.

[2] Cf. on the elections to the parliament of 1628 H. Hulme, *op. cit.*, 173–6 and W. M. Mitchell, *op. cit.*, 114–16. The list of M.P.s is printed in *Members of Parliament. Return of the names of every member ... to the present*, 1878, pt. 1, 474–9.

[3] *The autobiography and correspondence of Sir Simonds D'Ewes*, I, 402.

[4] *C.S.P.V. 1625–26*, 548, 511–12.

[5] *Diary of John Rous ... 1625 to 1642*, ed. M. A. E. Green, *Camden society* LXVI, 1856, 11–12, 19.

[6] *H.M.C. Skrine*, 44, 48, 150, 172.

resistance, there really would have been a rebellion. But their legalist, constitutionalist convictions precluded such a course. Non-violent, civil disobedience was still as far as they were prepared to go. Their influence in this direction, however, made itself strongly felt even after parliament's dissolution in March 1629 and the arrest of Eliot and eight other M.P.s. The Commons' resolutions had denounced anyone who voluntarily paid tonnage and poundage as an enemy to the liberties of the kingdom. In consequence, a stoppage of foreign trade occurred for some weeks, the merchants preferring to suspend business rather than pay the duties. The Merchant Adventurers Company ceased to ship cloth and the foreign commerce of London came nearly to a halt. In April it was reported that the King, 'who usually obtained 500 l. sterling a day from the duties, has not obtained 30 l. in the last three weeks.'[1] At the port of Colchester the merchants refused to pay duties, but offered to enter bond for such customs as the next parliament should establish.[2] When April ended there was still only a trickle of duties coming into the custom house in London. The Council was told that many are 'terrified at Sir John Eliot's *brutum fulmen*. . . . The ill spirit of obstinacy lies . . . in the merchants' breasts. . . .'[3] In May, Richard Chambers, a London merchant, was fined £2,000 in the Star Chamber for seditious words spoken in condemnation of the duties, and sentenced to prison till he acknowledged his offence.[4] This example and economic necessity broke the mercantile boycott. Later in the month the Merchant Adventurers agreed to resume trading and others followed suit.[5] For the time being the government had won.

Besides political and religious differences, hard times aggravated the mood of resentment. Between 1620 and 1624 a severe trade depression occurred from which the recovery was only partial. The end of the '20s and most of the '30s were again a period of slump and stagnation due to foreign competition, the contraction of established markets, and currency manipulations abroad. The textile industry, the most important non-agricultural occupation in the national economy, was particularly affected. The hard-hit clothing districts in East Anglia, Yorkshire, and the counties of the west and southwest experienced widespread unemployment and wage-cuts. Misery and unrest were rife. In 1630–1 the position was worsened by poor harvests, which raised the price of grain to famine levels.[6]

[1] *C.S.P.V. 1629–32*, 7–8, 19, 29.
[2] *Acts of the Privy Council July 1628–April 1629*, 378–9.
[3] *C.S.P.D. 1628–29*, 524.
[4] Cf. his trial, *State trials*, III, 373ff.   [5] *C.S.P.D. 1628–29*, 550.
[6] W. R. Scott, *op. cit.*, I; B. Supple, *Commercial crisis and change in England 1600–1642*, Cambridge, 1959, chs. III, V–VII; C. Wilson, *England's apprenticeship 1603–1763*, L., 1965, 52–7; instances of distress and unrest in the

While the Privy Council exerted itself vigorously to enforce the poor laws and control the price of grain, other aspects of royal intervention in the economic field during the '30s increased hardship and discontent so much that, on balance, the antagonism the crown created far outweighed any gratitude it may have derived from its efforts to mitigate the effects of depression. The most conspicuous grievances were the monopolies granted by Charles I for mainly fiscal reasons, which not only injured existing trading and industrial interests but also raised prices—and this in a time of slump. Rights to the manufacture or sale of salt, glass, coal, and wine, for instance, were all vested or reinforced in monopolist companies in return for a revenue promised the crown. Since in addition to domestic use soap was required in the textile industry, salt in fishing, and coal for diverse industrial purposes, the injurious effects were broadly felt. A further factor was the bad feeling and resistance, occasionally breaking out in violence, of the sellers and producers whom the royal patentees either excluded or subjugated.[1]

The government's agrarian policy also provoked serious repercussions during these depressed years. Its disafforesting and enclosure of royal forests in Wiltshire, Dorset, and Gloucester, undertaken between 1628 and 1631 for revenue purposes, led to some of the largest disturbances before the civil war. In the forests of Braydon, Gillingham, and Dean, hundreds of armed commoners rioted in defence of their customary rights threatened by enclosures.[2] Such men of little means were extremely vulnerable to the effect of short-term economic fluctuations, and a royal measure so plainly detrimental to their interests inevitably produced a violent reaction. Compared with such enclosures effected on royal initiative, the results obtained by the government's Depopulation Commission, created in 1633 to protect small tenants against enclosing landlords, were

[1] W. R. Scott, *op. cit.*, I, 216–17: W. H. Price, *The English patents of monopoly*, Cambridge, 1906, chs. III, VI, X, XI; E. Lipson, *The economic history of England*, 3v. (v. II–III, 7th ed.), L., 1943, III, 362–72; *Extracts from the records of the Company of Hostmen of Newcastle* . . . , ed. F. W. Dendy, *Surtees society*, CV, 1901, xxxiii, 78n.; J. U. Nef, *Industry and government in France and England 1540–1640*, Philadelphia, 1940, 113–17. For examples of the independent producers' defiance of the soap monopoly, cf. *C.S.P.D. 1634–35*, 218, 358, 393 and R. Steele, *op. cit.*, I, 1680.

[2] Cf. instances of these outbreaks in *C.S.P.D. 1631–33*, 67, 74, 87, 88, 90, 178, 182, 190–1 and *Acts of the Privy Council June 1630–June 1631*, 284, 352–3, 390–1; an account of the whole episode is given by D. G. C. Allan, 'The rising in the west 1628–1631,' *Economic history review*, 2nd ser., V, 1 (1952).

clothing districts appear in *C.S.P.D. 1628–29*, 521, 554, *ibid. 1629–31*, 8, 20 391, 419, *ibid. 1631–33*, 14, 37.

negligible.[1] In Wiltshire, for instance, the thousands of acres enclosed at the King's command overshadowed all the enclosures of the preceding century. Because of them, many of the inhabitants of the affected areas must have come to regard Charles I as an implacable foe.[2]

Although the symptoms foreshadowing the breakdown of the King's authority were gradually maturing, the government weathered its difficulties for the present. Once parliament ended, it was free to deal with its enemies in church and state without hindrance. In the next few years, while Laud ascended to Canterbury and Wentworth was at Dublin, the King ruled without concession. Opposition fell to its lowest ebb. A reflection of the gloomy mood among the Country's close adherents was contained in a paper distributed in Puritan circles in the summer of 1629 to justify the intended migration to New England. With one eye on the evil auguries to religion from the condition of English politics, and the other on the recent disasters of continental Protestantism, the paper declared:

All other churches of Europe are brought to desolation ... & whoe knowes, but that God hath provided this place to be a refuge for many whome he meanes to save out of the general calamity ... seeing the Church hath no place lefte to flie into but the wildernesse. ...[3]

No doubt, to many of the regime's Puritan opponents it must have seemed in the early '30s that prayer or flight were the sole recourses left them.

Not until after ship money was made a general tax in 1635, with the manifest likelihood that it would become a permanent impost, did the national movement against the crown revive. Then, aided by the pressure of the Scottish rebellion, the flood of opposition rose until it overwhelmed the King's authority. Most pronounced was the resistance in the governing class: the 'knowing gentry,' commented a contemporary, 'expressed great discontent at this new ... burden as an imposition against law and the rights of the subject.'[4] The scope of ship money, reaching to both real and personal property and falling with annual regularity upon thousands of small owners and

[1] The commission was issued to inquire into depopulation and the conversion of arable to pasture since the tenth year of Queen Elizabeth; J. Rushworth, II, 333. Cf. the summary of government measures in the '30s regarding enclosures in E. Lipson, *op. cit.*, II, 404–6.
[2] E. Kerridge, 'The revolts in Wiltshire against Charles I,' *Wiltshire archaeological and natural history magazine*, CCVI, 1958.
[3] *Reasons to be considered for iustifeinge the undertakers of the intended plantation in New England, Life and letters of John Winthrop*, I, 309.
[4] B. Whitelocke, *Memorials*, 4v., Oxford, 1853, I, 69–70.

householders, also contributed to the popular reaction against it. The entire responsibility for the collection lay with the sheriffs in the counties, who were to be assisted by the justices, the deputy lieutenants, and the constables of the hundreds. Some showed their antagonism by openly condemning the tax, others by the sluggishness with which they performed their duty. Many of the previous opponents of the forced loan renewed their disobedience. Considerable remissness appeared among the high and petty constables ordered to distrain on the goods of non-payers. Complaints about inequities in assessing the tax on the different parts of the counties repeatedly became a pretext for default and obstruction. To try to cope with the insubordination of the magisterial order, the Privy Council commanded in November 1636 that lords lieutenants, deputy lieutenants, and justices who refused or forbore to pay ship money should be discharged from their offices.[1]

Through 1638 and 1639 opposition mounted. From all parts of the realm accounts came in of refractoriness. Men chosen as sheriffs and deputy lieutenants did everything in their power to evade office.[2] The sheriff of Norfolk declared that he had become odious by carrying out his duties.[3] From Gloucestershire it was reported that if all the refusers were committed there would not be jails enough to receive them.[4] A general backwardness showed itself in Huntingdon, Surrey, Bedfordshire, Buckinghamshire, Oxfordshire, and Northamptonshire.[5] The Somerset grand jury in the summer of 1638 blamed the high price of grain on 'the great and heavy taxations by new invented ways. . . .'[6] In Derbyshire hundreds of defaulters let their goods be distrained rather than pay.[7] During the summer and fall of 1639 the Privy Council wrote the sheriffs admonishing them for lack of affection and diligence in the work of collection.[8]

One more prophecies of revolt appeared, together with strong expressions of support for the Scots. The Venetian ambassador again looked for an outbreak.[9] Most Englishmen were so discontented, said the earl of Northumberland, that they 'will be readier to join with the Scots than to draw their swords in the King's service.'[10]

---

[1] *C.S.P.D. 1636–37*, 181; cf. the excellent account of the operation of ship money in Somerset and the progressive resistance to it in T. G. Barnes, *op. cit.*, ch. VIII. Documents illustrating the sheriff's difficulties in Buckingham are printed in *Ship money papers and Richard Grenville's note-book*, ed. C. G. Bonsey and J. G. Jenkins, *Buckinghamshire record society*, XIII, 1965. The Gloucestershire opposition is described by W. B. Willcox, *op. cit.*, 124–33.
[2] A. H. Dodd, *Studies in Stuart Wales*, Cardiff, 1952, 63.
[3] *C.S.P.D. 1638–39*, 48–9, 61.
[4] *Ibid. 1637–38*, 337.
[5] *Ibid.*, 420, 432, 337.
[6] *Ibid.*, 551.
[7] *Ibid. 1638–39*, 29.
[8] *Ibid. 1639, passim.*
[9] *C.S.P.V. 1636–39*, 273, 297, 429–30.
[10] *The earl of Strafforde's letters*, II, 186.

Laud began to read the writing on the wall. 'The minds of men are mightily alienated,' he told Wentworth at the end of 1638: '. . . I fear you will see the King brought upon his knees to a parliament. And then farewell church and ship monye.'[1] In gentry houses in the south-west an anonymous paper circulated which said that if the King put down the Scots, England would be reduced to slavery.[2]

By the middle of 1640 Charles's power was visibly disintegrating. The nation was on a tax strike and the latest levy of ship money far in arrears. In May the Privy Council issued an order against 'the great and supine negligence of the high sheriffs of divers counties in executing the last writs for ship money.' It required the attendance of the sheriffs of London and Middlesex, Yorkshire, Berkshire, Surrey, Leicester, Essex, and Northamptonshire, and threatened them with trial in the Star Chamber for their contempt and neglect.[3] All was to no avail. Local government was ceasing to respond to royal command. Strong in their sense of grievance, the worshipful gentlemen who controlled its machinery had fallen under the Country's political influence. The complete defeat of ship money was attested by the collection figures for 1640. The King demanded for this year a total of £214,400; of that amount, only £43,417 was paid.[4] The remainder was never obtained.

On the eve of the Long Parliament, the structure of royal sovereignty had virtually crumbled. Although not a single hand had risen against it in England, in the face of universal insubordination and disaffection Charles and his Council were powerless to rule. What occurred was possible only because the King had no independent force at his disposal with which to scourge and chastise his refractory subjects. Totally dependent on the support of the aristocratic order to carry out his mandates, he was helpless the moment it ceased to obey. By its folly and blindness, the royal government had enabled the Country to attain political ascendancy over a great part of the dominant class and the kingdom as a whole. It was to the men prominent in opposition that the King's subjects now looked to direct them on the road to redress. While the governing class stood largely united around the Country, royal authority would remain in eclipse.

The elections to the Long Parliament, held in October, completed the rout of the Court. The issue lay between the Court and the Country—between those who, in the common belief, bore respon-

---

[1] *Works*, VII, 502.

[2] *The Buller papers*, ed. R. N. Worth, p.p., 1895, 27.

[3] *C.S.P.D. 1640*, 126.

[4] M. D. Gordon, 'The collection of ship money in the reign of Charles I,' *Transactions of the Royal Historical Society*, 3rd ser., IV, 1910, 144.

sibility for the discredited policies of the King's government, and those determined on redress and reform. As yet Royalist and Parliamentarian, the parties that formed in 1642 as civil war loomed up, had no being in either name or fact. Electoral contests took place in about seventy of the existing two hundred and fifty-nine constituencies. They were fought most hotly in the shire elections, at which the freeholders voted in thousands.[1] Sometimes keen personal rivalry between candidates from leading county families figured as much or more than politics in these contests.[2] As in the past, too, the majority of members were elected unopposed and frequently as a result of personal or official influence on their behalf.

The fundamental point about the elections, nevertheless, was that they occurred on a flood-tide of animosity against the regime which had no parallel in living memory. In whatever circumstances members reached the House of Commons, most were imbued with the prevailing sentiment when the Long Parliament began. Thus the political composition was strongly adverse to the King. Charles's most resolute and active opponents were returned to the House. Of the original 547 members elected,[3] nearly 60 had resisted his demand for loans; 18 of these had been imprisoned for their refusal to lend; an additional 20, not part of the former, had been imprisoned for other expressions of opposition; 50 members had stood out in some way against ship money; 14 others had been sheriffs who incurred the Privy Council's displeasure for their failures in the administration of ship money. Altogether, the known number of members who had demonstrated their antagonism to the crown, or whose close relatives had done so, was 143, more than one out of four.[4]

The decay of the crown's electoral influence was noticeable.[5] 'The court laboured to bring in their friends,' wrote Bulstrode Whitelocke, a Country M.P., 'but those who were most favoured at court had least respect in the country . . . so that very few of that party had the favour to be chosen members of this parliament.'[6] The Duchy of

[1] M. Keeler, *op. cit.*, 7.

[2] This was apparently the case in the Somerset election, *ibid.*, 61. T. G. Barnes, *op. cit.*, has stressed the importance of the rivalry of eminent families in Somerset affairs. By contrast, in Suffolk political issues were uppermost. Over two thousand freeholders voted for the two victorious Puritan gentlemen as knights of the shire. The loser by about seven hundred votes was a Court sympathizer; cf. M. Keeler, *op. cit.*, 64.

[3] Cf. M. Keeler, *op. cit.*, 6. By her tabulation the 547 members consisted of 493 elected before 3 November 1640 when the Long Parliament met; 14 elected for boroughs which were given representation soon after 1640; 40 who replaced others or were replaced themselves before January 1642.

[4] Cf. the discussion in M. Keeler, *ibid.*, 13–15.

[5] This has been remarked on by D. Brunton and D. H. Pennington, *op. cit.*, 8–9.

[6] *Op. cit.*, I, 107.

Cornwall failed to elect a single one of eight nominees whom it recommended to the Cornish boroughs under its jurisdiction.[1] In the Cinque Ports, where royal patronage operating through the Lord Warden, was usually decisive, nine of the fourteen members elected were supporters of the Country. Of twelve men, ten of them law officers of the crown, for whom the Secretary of State was instructed to find seats, only three were returned.[2] What was said about the county election in Kent was quite generally the case: '. . . the common people had been so bytten with shippe money they were very averse from a courtyer.'[3]

Even though it was true that by no means all the Country's sympathizers were passionately committed to struggle against the King, that many were moderates and others lukewarm or opportunists, the victory of Charles's opponents was a great one. In an election in which issues of policy predominated as never before, the political nation had spoken unequivocally. It had voiced its confidence in the cause of the Country's leaders, who now held the initiative in their hands.

[1] D. Brunton and D. H. Pennington, *op. cit.*, 134; M. Keeler, *op. cit.*, 37; M. Coate, 'The Duchy of Cornwall: its history and administration 1640–1660,' *Transactions of the Royal Historical Society*, 4th ser., X, 1927, 156.

[2] R. N. Kershaw, 'The elections for the Long Parliament, 1640,' *E.H.R.*, XXXVIII, 152 (1923), 497, 499. Cf. M. Keeler's account of the election of the Puritan Edward Partridge as M.P. for Sandwich as an instance of what happened in the Cinque Ports.

[3] *Proceedings . . . in . . . Kent*, ed. L. B. Larking, *Camden society*, LXXXI, 1862, 6. The remark was Sir Roger Twysden's.

The Citizen Element

Below the aristocratic and elite groups in the social order that formed the substance of the Court and the Country lay the broadly extended intermediate strata in which the nation's citizen and commercial elements were comprised. By seventeenth-century observers searching the causes of the revolution, the spread of the insurrectionary contagion to these strata was remarked as one of the most unfortunate fatalities in the overthrow of the King's power. There was a note both of snobbery and of the immemorial suspicion of the country-bred man for the town dweller in the acid comments in which the friends of royal authority summed up the apostasy of their fellow-subjects in the towns. '. . . 'tis notorious,' said a writer after the Restoration, 'that there is not any sort of people so inclineable to seditious practices as the trading part of a nation. . . . And, if we reflect upon our late miserable distractions, 'tis easy to observe how the quarrel was chiefly hatched in the shops of tradesmen. . . .'[1] It was considered almost a truism that in 'Market-Towns . . . the People . . . were more apt to Faction and Innovation than in other places. . . .'[2] James Howell, the epistolarian, fancied he saw an anti-monarchical tendency in the members of parliament who sat for towns: they 'are the for the most part all tradesmen, and being bred in corporations . . . are more inclining to popular government and democracy.'[3] Hobbes, with his eye fixed on London, asserted that 'those great capital Cities, when Rebellion is entered—into upon Pretence of Grievances, must needs be of the Rebel Party: because the Grievances are but Taxes, to which Citizens, that is Merchants (whose Profession is their private Gain), are naturally mortal Enemies.'[4] Clarendon, speaking of Manchester, referred to the 'factious humour which possessed most corporations, and the pride of their wealth'; while

---

[1] S. Parker, *Discourse of ecclesiastical politie*, 1671, cited in C. Hill and E. Dell, *op. cit.*, 238.
[2] P. Heylyn, *Cyprianus Anglicanus*, 1671, 198.
[3] James Howell, *Some sober inspections*, 1655, 36–7, cited in C. Hill and E. Dell, *op. cit.*, 239.
[4] T. Hobbes, *Behemoth, loc. cit.*, II, 576.

London he described, *tout court*, as 'the sink of all the ill humour of the kingdom. . . .'[1]

These statements provide an interesting revelation of Royalist opinion, but they certainly cannot qualify as an adequate description of the role of the citizen element in the genesis of the revolution. The political stand of the urban segment of the society was, in fact, by no means uniform. To say that most of its members had become, like other Englishmen, estranged from the crown by 1640 would probably be true, but insufficient as a rendering of the complex reality. A diversity of circumstances governed the outlook of the citizen and trading part of the kingdom, and it is only in the light of them that its political posture amidst the deepening conflict of the Court and the Country can be understood.

If the revolution begun in 1640 may be regarded as 'bourgeois' in the very general meaning which this expression has come to possess in historical discourse, it was not one in the strict and etymologically precise sense of 'bourgeois'—*burgenses*, the descendants in status of the inhabitants of the *burgi* of the Middle Ages in whom the awakening commercial life of Europe was first incarnated. When we consider the English burghers of the sixteenth and seventeenth century, we have to observe that they had no living traditions of political struggle for liberty like those that once animated the citizens of the great towns of Italy and Flanders. Their predecessors had lived for the most part in faithful obedience to kings; they had not risen in rebellion against emperor or count to win a jealousy-guarded self-government or independence for their communities. They had not taken a leading part in the trade and diplomacy of Europe, as had the Venetians and Florentines, or parleyed on terms of relative equality with popes and secular princes. Nor had these predecessors, not even those of London, belonged to world-cities whose merchant statesmen watched with an imperial eye for every shift of the political weather and its effect on the destinies of their commerce. Up through the sixteenth century, the story of the English towns is mainly a tale of provincial occurrences, hardly a record of events of wider European significance such as occur in the Florentine histories of Compagni, Villani, and Machiavelli.

English towns in the earlier seventeenth century, except for London, were small and could not compare in population or economic importance with many continental cities. London's population about 1640 has been estimated at 350,000,[2] but the capital towered as far

---

[1] *Rebellion*, VI, 271, III, 57.

[2] W. K. Jordan, *The charities of London*, L., 1960, 16. At the beginning of the century the capital's population has been estimated at 250,000 and 300,000; cf. C. Wilson, *op. cit.*, 45 and G. N. Clark, *The wealth of England*

over other urban centres as Everest over its foothills. Not a single provincial town important to the national economy—not Bristol or Norwich, for example, which came next after London—had more than 15,000 inhabitants.[1] So far, therefore, as urban wealth and economic power might be a force to reckon with politically, only London possessed sufficient leverage to make its resources and sentiments count for something truly formidable in the constitutional conflict. But apart from this, there were other factors which made it impossible that citizen wealth and opinion should play an initiating or dominant part on the political scene. These had to do with the inferior position in the social structure of the *bourgeoisie* as a whole, with the internal differentiation of the strata belonging to it, and with the sectional and protectionist spirit that still widely prevailed in urban life and economy.

We have previously emphasized the persisting significance of status in the society of the earlier seventeenth century. Within the hierarchy of orders in which every rank was assigned its place, the *bourgeoisie* was lumped together as a single entity occupying a middle position respectable but nevertheless distinctly subordinate. Sir Thomas Smith classified townsmen as 'citizens' or 'burgesses,' Dr. Wilson similarly as '*cives*'; and both expressed contemporary opinion in setting them firmly below the gentlemen, the *nobiles* greater and lesser, to whom the highest honour and authority were due.[2] It is possible that in wealth the greatest merchants in the citizen body exceeded every other order in England, except the very richest of the nobility.[3] But if this was so, it did not suffice to remove the stigma of inferiority from men whose fortunes were acquired by trade and finance and in daily resort to a warehouse or a shop. The burgher style of life left no place for the prestigeful pursuits of aristocratic existence. '. . . when we do not hunt we hawk. . . .'—so wrote a carefree peer before the civil war—'the rest of the time is spent in tennis, chess, and dice, and in a word we eat and drink and rise up to play; and this is to live like

---

[1] Bristol's population at the beginning of the seventeenth century has been estimated at 12,000 and Norwich's at 15,000; J. Latimer, *The annals of Bristol in the seventeenth century*, Bristol, 1900, 34, and *The records of the city of Norwich*, ed. W. Hudson and J. C. Tingey, 2v., Norwich, 1906–10, II, cxxviii. Cf. also on the population of London and provincial towns the figures given by J. N. L. Baker in *An historical geography of England before A.D. 1800*, ed. H. C. Darby, Cambridge, 1936, 441–2.

[2] Cf. *supra*, 27.

[3] The size of mercantile wealth, especially London's, in the earlier seventeenth century, has been emphasized by W. K. Jordan in his monumental study of wills, *Philanthropy in England*, 335–6.

---

from 1496 to 1760, Oxford, 1946, 93. In 1636, according to James Howell, the lord mayor made an informal census and estimated London's population at 700,000 (*Londinopolis*, 1657, 403). This figure is incredible.

121

a gentleman, for what is a gentleman but his pleasure.'[1] It was not by such recreations nor in such leisure that burgher fortunes were gained and preserved.

In the urban community itself, the highest status belonged to the merchant, a designation which, in the parlance of the time, referred not to any mere retailer, but, more particularly, to the minority of men engaged in wholesale trade or foreign commerce.[2] Yet however secure and authoritative the merchant's position was among his fellow townsmen—and it was such as he who almost invariably formed the magistracy of the urban corporations—his status in the general body politic was much lower and even somewhat contemptible to those above him. A scattering of merchants might achieve knighthood as the reward of valuable financial services rendered the crown or in recognition of their business eminence; a tiny few, such as Cranfield, Robartes, Hicks, or Bayning, might move from the highest regions of commerce and money lending into the peerage, as all of them did in the 1620s, and then hope in a generation or so to leave the aroma of the counting-house behind. But the majority of merchants had no such opportunity; and these, according to the aristocratic standard of the time, were disqualified by their vocation from any claim to real gentility.

Ample testimony bears witness to the defensive and self-justifying attitude which the merchant and his advocates adopted in the face of this upper-class prejudice.[3] '... I cannot wonder,' wrote the antiquarian, Gervase Holles, a kinsman of the earl of Clare, whose family was established on the land by the wealth of a London lord mayor of Henry VIII's reign, 'at the vanity and folly of many of our English gentry who, in the sickness of their understanding, apprehend this worthy calling of a merchant to be but ignoble and derogatory to the honour of a gentleman. All ... are not of this opinion, but the generality are.'[4] Bishop Goodman, of mercantile stock himself, defended the honour of the merchant against the complaints of the base origin of Sir Lionel Cranfield, who began his career in the City.[5] Another exponent of the merchant's worth denied that sons of gentlemen apprenticed in trade lost their status. '... such Gentlemen

---

[1] Viscount Conway's words, cited in W. Woodfill, *Musicians in English society from Elizabeth to Charles I*, Princeton, 1953, 221. It should be noted that these sentiments would not have been endorsed by noblemen and gentlemen of Puritan or other serious religious persuasion.
[2] Cf. J. Stow, *A survey of London*, ed. C. Kingsford, 2v., Oxford, 1908, II, 207. This was first published in 1598.
[3] A good survey of contemporary writings on the citizen's status is given in L. B. Wright, *Middle class culture in Elizabethan England*, Ithaca, 1958, ch. II.
[4] G. Holles, *Memorials of the Holles family*, 18. This was written in the 1650s. [5] G. Goodman, *op. cit.*, I, 297–8.

are much deceived,' he asserted, 'which no sooner heare one named to be of this, or that Societie, or Colledge of trade in London, as of Grocers, Haberdashers, Fishmongers . . . but they forthwith entertaine a low conceit of the parties quality, as too much beneath their owne ranck, and order. . . .'[1]

The playwrights of the age were wont to underscore the prejudice against trade by depicting its practitioners more often than not as cheats, usurers, and social climbers.[2] Ben Jonson's goldsmith, Guilt-Head, declares:

> *We live, by finding fooles out, to be trusted.*
> *Our shop-bookes are our pastures, our corngroundes,*
> *. . . .*
> *Wee Citizens never trust, but wee doe coozen. . . .*[3]

Quomodo, the woollen draper in Middleton's *Michaelmas Term*, orders his accomplice:

> *Go, make my coarse commodities look sleek;*
> *With subtle art beguile the honest eye.*

When by deceit he has the land of Easy, an Essex gentleman, within his grasp, he exults:

The land's mine . . . now shall I be divulged a landed man throughout the livery. . . . Now come my golden days in. Whither is worshipful Master Quomodo . . . rid forth? To his land in Essex. Whence come those goodly loads of logs? From his land in Essex. Where grows this pleasant fruit, says one citizen's wife in the row? At Master Quomodo's orchard in Essex. O, O, does it so? I thank you for that good news, i' faith.[4]

The rule by which the Court of Wards guided itself, a good index to social custom, also assumed the inferiority of the merchant. The court was required not to give a ward in marriage to his disparagement, and even in the seventeenth century, it seems, this was held to mean that one of gentle rank should not be wed to a burgher. Sir Edward Coke, as well, listed marriage with a *burgensis* as a disparagement to a ward.[5] A parallel instance of the grudging conception taken

---

[1] [E. Bolton], *The cities advocate, in this . . . question . . . whether apprenticeship extinguisheth gentry*, 1628, 45, 46–7.
[2] Cf. L. C. Knights, *Drama & society in the age of Jonson*, L., 1936, chs. VII, IX.
[3] *The divell is an asse*, III, 1, ll. 16–17, 22.
[4] Cited in C. W. Camp, *The artisan in Elizabethan literature*, N.Y., 1924, 95–7.   [5] Cf. J. Hurstfield, *op. cit.*, 139–40.

of the merchant was the case of Humphrey Chetham, a great Lanca-shire business man and money lender. Appointed sheriff of his county in 1634, he undertook to display armorial bearings as part of the pomp appropriate to his office. This was regarded by his social superiors as an act of rash presumption, and he was informed that 'some malicious knaves have endeavoured to disgrace you about your Coate of Armes' and that 'Gentlemen in the Countie are aggrieved and will have the truth tryed. . . .' Through the influence of friends, however, and a payment to Sir Henry St. George, Norroy herald, Chetham succeeded in having his arms confirmed.[1]

Of course, in point of fact the interrelations between trade and aristocracy were much closer than the status ideology and its atten-dant snobbery made out. That had always been the case to a certain extent, and was doubtless far more so in the economic conditions of the sixteenth and seventeenth centuries. A thin top layer of merchants was continuously abandoning trade for the land and entrance to the lower levels of county society;[2] marriage between the ranks was an old story, more than one nobleman matching with the heiress to a commercial fortune;[3] and sons of gentlemen were regularly appren-ticed in mercantile pursuits.[4] But so long as distinction of degree

[1] F. R. Raines and C. W. Sutton, *Life of Humphrey Chetham, Chetham society*, n.s., 2v., XLIX, L, 1903, I, 102, 104.

[2] The recruitment of landed society from merchant families at this period has not been systematically studied. The impression derived from recent research is that it was not a sizeable phenomenon. Of Exeter, for instance, it has been said that while 'most . . . merchants put some money into land . . . very few had purchased enough to secure independence from mercantile pursuits.' (W. T. MacCaffrey, *Exeter 1540–1640*, Cambridge, 1958, 260–1, 266). Similar observations have been made about London and Bristol merchants; cf. T. W. Willan, *The Muscovy merchants of 1555*, Manchester, 1953, 73, and P. McGrath, *Merchants and merchandise in seventeenth century Bristol, Bristol record society*, XIX, 1955, xxiv. The gentry of Kent, near as the county lay to London, were largely indigenous and descended from the pre-Tudor gentry; few came of transplanted London stock; cf. C. W. Chalklin, *Seventeenth-century Kent*, L., 1965, 192–4. A historian of Norwich merchants, however, has seen a steady movement of its ruling families on to the land; cf. Bruce Allen, *The social and administrative structure of the Norwich merchant class*, Harvard Ph.D. thesis, 1951, 355–6, 368–9.

[3] Instances in L. Stone, *The crisis of the aristocracy*, 628–32. The proportion of intermarriage between peers and merchants was small, however. Stone's figures on the status of the wives of 465 noblemen married between 1540–1659 shows only 17 or 4 per cent to have been of merchant stock. Only 5 marriages of 129 noblemen between 1600–29 were to wives of merchant rank. Most noblemen married within their own order or the gentry.

[4] Some indication of the social origin of merchants can be obtained from apprenticeship records. Between January 1600 and May 1660, the New-castle Merchant Adventurers Company admitted 749 apprentices. The status of their fathers was as follows: gentleman, including 24 clergy, 324;

retained its hold on contemporary attitudes and behaviour, the political influence of the *bourgeoisie* on the national scene was bound to be limited and its role one of follower, not leader.

As a consequence, it was extremely rare for a merchant to rise to high ministerial office, and this continued to be equally the case under the revolutionary governments of the 1640s and '50s. The career of Sir Lionel Cranfield, Buckingham's client, who became Master of the Wards, Treasurer, and earl of Middlesex, was most exceptional. Cranfield, indeed, was elevated by James I because of his financial expertise and in the hope that his administration would effect much-needed economies in crown expenditure. He strove vigorously, but when Buckingham abandoned him and he was impeached by the Commons, there is no doubt that the prejudice of members against the insolence of a *parvenu* aggravated his faults and contributed to his downfall.[1] On the whole, it is unlikely that even the greatest merchants entertained high political ambitions or aims. Their interest was mainly in business, and the rewards they sought were usually of the tangible pecuniary sort.[2]

Although the citizen element formed a middle order in the body politic, it was itself differentiated internally by profound inequalities of status and wealth which had considerable bearing on the outlook of its component strata. Stow, the memorialist and historian of London, anatomized the city's population on lines broadly applicable to the urban structure as a whole at this period. Its four main divisions, according to him, were the merchants, the retailers, the handicraftsmen, and the hired labourers. The merchants, though least in number, were first in wealth, together with some principal retailers. The next place pertained to the other retailers, who with the craftsmen also made up the larger part of the inhabitants. Economically, the craftsmen came after the retailers and 'have not much to

---

[1] Cf. R. H. Tawney, *Business and politics under James I*, Cambridge, 1958.

[2] Miss Thrupp's remarks on this point in connection with the mediaeval merchant are applicable also to his sixteenth- and early seventeenth-century successor; S. Thrupp, *The merchant class of medieval London*, Chicago, 1948, 55. Cf. also A. H. Dodd, 'Mr. Myddelton the merchant of Tower Street,' in *Elizabethan government and society*, 266. Dodd remarks what was probably true of the great majority of merchants: 'Business, religion, family: these were Myddelton's three dominant interests . . .' (*ibid.*, 277).

---

yeoman, 188; merchant or craftsman, 169; other or status undetermined, 68; figures from *Records of the Merchant Adventurers of Newcastle*, 2v., ed. J. R. Boyle and F. W. Dendy, *Surtees society*, 93, 101, 1895–9, II, *ad finem*. At Bristol, merchants admitted 377 apprentices between 1600–30. Their fathers' status or occupation was: gentleman, 88; merchant, 70; yeoman, 37; husbandman, 24; mariner, 11; vintner, 11; mercer, 10; clerk, 2; bishop, 1; miscellaneous trades and crafts, 123; P. McGrath, *op. cit.*, App. B.

spare,' while the labourers, who were in the lowest position, 'have neede that it were given unto them.'[1] A considerable proletariat existed in London and the same class was present as well in smaller numbers in the main provincial towns. Composed of porters, car men, floating labourers, wage earners in the textile industry, the tailoring trades, brewing, dyeing, wire and pin manufacture, this portion of the population lived in grinding poverty and hardship.[2] Several evidences from Professor Jordan's study of the charitable donors of the sixteenth and seventeenth centuries show how pronounced was the disparity of wealth in the urban sector of society. In London, for instance, 7,391 charitable benefactors have been traced over the period 1480–1660. Four hundred and thirty-eight merchants of this number—less than 6 per cent of the entire body of givers—contributed nearly 50 per cent of all the city's gifts, a total amounting to the huge sum of more than £907,000. The scale of mercantile riches in the years preceding the revolution is suggested by the fact that 40 per cent of this total was provided by merchants between 1611 and 1630.[3] At Bristol as well, the same overwhelming pre-eminence of mercantile wealth can be inferred from the philanthropy of its inhabitants.[4]

As we might expect in a privilege-ridden age, the minority of citizens distinguished for their money and success in commerce dominated all aspects of municipal life. Every important town without exception was ruled by a small and virtually self-perpetuating body of such men, for the urban constitutions were invariably oligarchical, vesting the substance of power in organs little subject to popular check or dismissal. The gilds and companies, in which the urban division of labour was broadly organized, were equally controlled by the few who were masters, wardens, assistants, and members of the livery. The journeymen and yeomanry of these associations, though comprising the majority, had scarcely any voice in their affairs.[5] It was characteristic of this oligarchic pattern that when King James gave new charters to nine of London's twelve great livery companies, he confined their narrow structure of rule still further. Their govern-

---

[1] J. Stow, *op. cit.*, II, 207–9.

[2] J. L. Archer, *The industrial history of London 1603–1640*, London M.A. thesis, 1934, 140–3; W. K. Jordan, *Philanthropy in England*, 329. W. G. Hoskins has stressed the number and poverty of town wage-earners in Tudor times; cf. 'English provincial towns in the early sixteenth century,' *Provincial England*, L., 1963.

[3] W. K. Jordan, *The charities of London*, 50–1, 64–5, 71, 321n.

[4] W. K. Jordan, *The forming of the charitable institutions in the west of England*, Philadelphia, 1960.

[5] G. Unwin, *Industrial organization in the sixteenth and seventeenth centuries*, Oxford, 1904, and the same writer's *The gilds and companies of London*, L., 1909, ch. XIV.

ing bodies were given life-tenure, made self-elective, and authorized as well to enact ordinances for the whole membership.[1]

Nowhere was the prevalence of status and privilege in the distribution of power within the municipalities more strikingly evident than in the capital. Here, both the restrictions on the popular element and the narrow composition of even the latter relative to the inhabitants as a whole were equally pronounced.[2]

London's government rested on three main institutions: the lord mayor and court of aldermen, the court of common council, and the court of common hall. Far the most powerful of these was the first, since the mayor and the twenty-six aldermen possessed the entire executive authority. The aldermen, who were required to have a £10,000 property qualification for their office, held their places for life. Such was their wealth that Sir Ralph Freeman, mayor in 1633, boasted that he and his aldermanic brethren could buy out a hundred burgomasters of Amsterdam.[3] They co-opted their members from the nominees presented to them by the wards, and the lord mayor was customarily chosen each year from the senior among them.

The court of common council was the city's legislative body with a membership of about two hundred and fifty.[4] Contemporary writers likened it and the court of aldermen to parliament, the former resembling the lower House, the latter the upper one.[5] In theory the choice of councilmen belonged to the freemen—citizens—i.e., to all persons free of any of the city companies and hence possessed of the right to trade—who constituted the wardmote for this purpose. Practice, however, had come to limit the election of councilmen to a minority of well-to-do residents who had usurped the wardmote's power. In much the same way, the nomination of aldermen was made not by the freemen, but only by those citizens who were either councilmen or members of the livery of their companies.[6] John

---

[1] W. Herbert, *History of the twelve great livery companies of London*, 2v., L., 1836–7, I, 186–7.

[2] G. A. Williams, *Medieval London. From commune to capital*, L., 1963, describes the earlier history of London's governmental structure. For the sixteenth and early seventeenth century, a definitive account is given by V. Pearl, *London and the outbreak of the Puritan revolution*, Oxford, 1961, ch. II. I have drawn for the following paragraphs on the latter and also on J. Strype's ed. of J. Stow, *Survey of London*, 2v., L., 1720, II, ch. V. Useful also is *The corporation of London. Its origin, constitution, powers and duties*, Oxford, 1950.

[3] J. Howell, *op. cit.*, 389.

[4] This was the figure given by John Bellamie, *A plea for the commonalty of London*, 1645, 15. J. Strype (ed.), *op. cit.*, II, 375, gives the number of councilmen as two hundred and thirty-four.

[5] *Ibid.*, II, 375; J. Howell, *op. cit.*, 38.

[6] J. Strype (ed.), *op. cit.*, II, 157.

Strype, the learned eighteenth-century editor of Stow's *Survey of London*, declared that the common council was 'in Representation many Thousands.'[1] While that may have been so, it nevertheless exercised its functions in strict subordination to the mayor and court of aldermen. Convened only a few times a year, its summons and dissolution, its agenda and proceedings, were controlled by the mayor and his colleagues, who met with it and had a veto on its deliberations.

Lastly, the court of common hall was the assembly that elected the four city M.P.s and submitted nominations for mayor and certain other officers to the court of aldermen from which the latter made choice. Only the liverymen of the companies had the right to vote in it, and these were said to number about four thousand in the middle of the century. The common hall was the most broadly constituted of London's organs of government, yet the small proportion of liverymen to unenfranchised freemen-citizens merely emphasized how tightly power was concentrated in the great and populous capital. In 1646 it was stated that the ratio of liverymen to freemen was one to three hundred.[2] While this estimate was certainly too high, company records confirm that the difference was substantial. In the Drapers Company, for instance, one of the twelve great companies of the city, the masters, wardens, assistants, and liverymen never exceeded 136 during the reign of James I, while the highest number of freemen was 2,106.[3] In the Goldsmiths, another of the twelve great companies, there were 90 wardens, ex-wardens, and liverymen in 1641, and 373 freemen.[4] Many of these freemen without voice in the common hall were also of low economic condition, as appears from the poll tax levied by the Long Parliament in 1641. Of the 1,427 freemen of the Drapers Company assessed £2 or less, only 835 could pay, and a considerable number were too poor even to pay their quarterly fees to the gild.[5] In the Goldsmiths Company, most of the freemen were able to pay only one shilling.[6]

The government of the principal provincial towns resembled London's in being similarly constituted by a small minority of rich citizens who dominated affairs.[7] At Norwich, it was the mayor and

---

[1] *Ibid.*, II, 375.

[2] J. Lilburne, *Londons liberty in chains discovered*, 1646, 52.

[3] A. H. Johnson, *The history of the worshipful Company of Drapers of London*, 4v., Oxford, 1914–22, III, 87–8.

[4] *Memorials of the Goldsmiths Company*, ed. W. S. Prideaux, 2v., L., n.d., I, App.

[5] A. H. Johnson, *op. cit.*, III, 194.

[6] *Memorials of the Goldsmiths Company*, I, App.

[7] Historical accounts of the government of the English towns containing material applicable to the earlier seventeenth century are to be found in

twenty-four aldermen who possessed the preponderant authority with broad civil and judicial powers.[1] At Bristol, the twelve aldermen recruited their own body and also had the dominant share in choosing the common council. The affairs of the city, probably the second in commercial importance after London, 'were in the hands of about forty-five individuals who elected themselves and were . . . answerable only to themselves.'[2] At Exeter, the government was closely concentrated in a self-perpetuating chamber of twenty-four.[3] At Newcastle, power over the municipality was confined to a couple of dozen men who elected and co-opted each other.[4]

The men of this kind in the more important towns formed an urban sector of the governing class. Mayors and aldermen, sheriffs and justices of the peace within their municipalities, they ruled their fellow citizens in the same way that the gentry ruled the countryside and county communities. Although socially below the aristocratic order and certainly less weighty in the kingdom's political affairs, they bore an equal responsibility in their own jurisdiction for the execution of the crown's mandates. As a dominant minority, they were very conscious of their position and strongly apprehensive of every sign of disturbance or unrest among the citizenry or the poor. Perhaps one-half the urban population lived near or below the subsistence level, vulnerable in the extreme to any adverse movement of prices and the trade cycle.[5] The spectre of riot and anarchy breaking out in this poverty-stricken mass haunted the town rulers, causing them to show a compulsive concern with the poor rate and the maintenance of civic order and discipline. Police forces were non-existent, and other resources available for the preservation of the peace slender and inadequate. The urban magistrates practised a ceaseless vigilance and refused to tolerate the slightest gesture of disrespect for their persons or dignity. Not infrequently they had to invoke the support of the

[1] Cf. *Minutes of the Norwich court of mayoralty 1630–31*, ed. W. L. Sachse, *Norfolk record society*, XV, 1942, Introduction.
[2] *Bristol charters 1509–1899*, ed. R. C. Latham, *Bristol record society*, XII, 1946, 17.
[3] W. T. MacCaffrey, *Exeter 1540–1640*, 29–30; cf. also W. G. Hoskins, 'The Elizabethan merchants of Exeter,' *Elizabethan government and society*, 165.
[4] Cf. the Newcastle charter of 1600 in J. Brand, *The history and antiquities . . . of Newcastle*, 2v., L., 1789, II.
[5] Cf. the remarks of W. G. Hoskins, 'An Elizabethan provincial town: Leicester,' *Studies in social history*, ed. J. H. Plumb, L., 1955, 45, W. T. MacCaffrey, *Exeter 1540–1640*, 249, and W. K. Jordan, *Philanthropy in England*, 66–72.

First report on municipal corporations, Parliamentary papers, vols. XXIII–XXVI, 1835, and S. and B. Webb, *English local government . . . the manor and the borough*, 2v., L., 1908.

Privy Council to render their action more effective or to assist them in coping with local difficulties of scarcity, high food prices, and unemployment. They were also continually appealing to the royal government for measures to strengthen the town's economy against competitors.

These circumstances naturally influenced the political conduct of the municipal elite. The masters of the towns looked to the King to support their privileges and were imbued by their responsibilities of rule with a conservative bent. They shared Charles I's solicitude, communicated on one occasion to the magistrates of Norwich, 'that the orderly gouvernment of cittie and corporacions should be maynteined, and that popular and factious humours that trouble the same should be supprest and punisht.'[1] Hence, in spite of antagonism among them to the Court, they were not of one political mind nor disposed to make forthright commitments. Surveying their position, a variety of responses appeared as the conflict grew between the King and his opponents. Many inclined to hedge, restrained by their care for civic stability and the perpetuation of their own authority. Others sided with the King. A greater militancy, on the other hand, was likely to exist in the outer edge of the urban governing class, in men of substance who were not, however, at the pinnacle of civic wealth and power. Situated on the fringe of the ruling oligarchy, these obtained an opportunity in the conflict to enlarge their importance in their communities' affairs. As for the citizens of lesser status, such of them as were sensible of their slight or non-existent voice in the civic order also frequently showed themselves favourable to the Country's cause. Finally, the effects of Puritanism at all levels of the urban social structure must be taken into account.[2] All susceptible to its influence—and the citizen element was markedly so—were likely to develop a distrust and hostility towards the Court which figured significantly in turning many townsmen against Charles I's regime during the '30s.

A last factor affecting the political position of the citizen element was the predominance of sectional and protectionist concerns in the urban economies. The English *bourgeoisie* was not yet a national *bourgeoisie*. Merchants and retailers tended to be particularist in their aims, while the towns were divided by keen commercial rivalry and by the exclusiveness which they all showed to outsiders. To prevent strangers from acquiring any share in the town's trade; to uphold the regulatory power of its companies and gilds and confine commerce and crafts solely to their members; to secure, if possible, a privileged or monopoly position for its merchants in their trading

[1] *Acts of the Privy Council Sept. 1627–June 1628*, 141.
[2] Cf. *infra*, ch. VI.

130

area;—such were the ends at which municipal policy commonly aimed. The outports resented the supremacy of London, through which the largest part of the kingdom's foreign trade passed, and endeavoured to preserve their own markets and commerce against the competitive pressure of the Londoners. The pursuit of similar objectives appeared in the relations between the municipalities and the royal government. The businessmen who directed urban affairs were not champions of economic freedom or opposed on principle to the controls which the crown laid on commercial and industrial enterprise. Every town and every association liked controls beneficial to itself and protested against others not to its advantage. In consequence of the persistence of the protectionist spirit, the economic interest of the trading part of the nation was fixed first and foremost in its own communities. When merchants and retailers appraised national developments, appreciation of the impact of events and policies on their town was always an important and sometimes a decisive consideration. Their civic allegiance conditioned their political consciousness more decidedly than any general interests they may have shared as an order. With such parochialism of outlook, the citizen element was incapable of leadership in the kingdom's affairs. The wealth of the towns might be an invaluable asset to the side that could gain their support, but they were too intent on their single advancement, too unaccustomed to cooperation, to assume an independent or initiating part in matters of general political import.

2

As the supreme patron in a patronage-ridden society, the crown naturally distributed some of its favours in the urban section of the population—not, of course, gratuitously, but in return for the advantages thereby to be obtained for royal finance. The men who were thus drawn into the Court were not the common-garden variety of merchants. They were the magnates of the financial world, a handful of outstandingly successful London businessmen, customs farmers, and revenue officials of the crown; in fact, the germ of what subsequently came to be designated in its financial connotation as the City. The nature of this important minority has been admirably described by Professor Tawney. Entrepreneurs on a great scale, their activity transcended the conventional boundaries between the different lines of business activity that prevailed lower in the economic hierarchy of the municipalities. Having accumulated large capitals in commerce, they moved from one venture to another, ready to exploit an opportunity as it arose even while they continued to carry on their

regular trade. Heavy lenders to the crown both for themselves and on behalf of others with whose money they were entrusted, established in the royal financial administration, they were indispensable instruments of government finance. Promoters as well as merchants, their forte was the 'deal,' that typical progeny of the union of political connections and business acumen. 'With a footing in more than one world and fingers, if they please, in every pie . . . so closely interlocked that the ledger of an important figure can contain a substantial assortment of them; propitiating, when expedient, ministers and courtiers with tips as to possibilities in the wind, and sometimes . . . with more material rewards,' these men, the tycoons of commerce, were of all the citizen element the closest to the crown.[1]

The favoured position enjoyed by these capitalists was due to the effectiveness with which they mobilized the resources of private enterprise to provide for the revenue needs of the King's government. The activity of the customs farmers was the prime example of this function.[2] From the middle years of Elizabeth's reign, the crown adopted the practice of leasing the collection of its customs to businessmen who, in return, paid a lump sum for the contract and an annual rent. After 1604, the scale of this operation became larger as most species of duties were consolidated in a single great farm which was then let competitively to the syndicate that offered the best bargain. The magnitude of the transaction appears from the annual rent which the farmers of the great customs undertook to pay: £112,400 in 1604–5, rising steadily to reach £160,000 from 1621 to 1625; then, after a drop to £150,000 during the depressed years of the later 1620s and earlier '30s, rising once more to £172,500 in 1638–9.[3] The reasons that the crown preferred to lease the customs to private concessionaires instead of directly administering them with its own servants had to do with the urgency of its fiscal requirements. It was prepared to forego the gain which direct administration might have yielded for the sake of rendering its customs revenue certain year by year and, perhaps even more important, because the financial ability of the customs farmers made them a major source of government loans. The arrangement was founded on a *quid pro quo*: in return for its profits, the syndicate used its immense resources to enable the King to anticipate his revenue by allowing advances on its rent for

[1] R. H. Tawney, *Business and politics under James I*, 79–81.

[2] The following remarks on the customs farmers are based on W. P. Harper, 'The significance of the farmers of the customs in public finance in the middle of the seventeenth century,' *Economica*, X, 25 (1929) and especially on the penetrating account by R. Ashton, *The crown and the money market 1603–1640*, Oxford, 1960, ch. IV and 'Revenue farming under the early Stuarts,' *Economic history review*, 2nd ser., VIII, 3 (1956).

[3] Cf. the tables in R. Ashton, *The crown and the money market*, ch. IV.

current and future years and by outright loans—both, naturally, bearing interest.[1]

The farmers' efficiency in supplying the royal demand for funds was based on their own large fortunes and on their credit and reputation in the business world. Those of Charles I's reign included some of the foremost figures in London commerce. Sir Paul Pindar, Sir John Wolstenholme senior, Sir Nicholas Crispe, Sir John Harrison, Sir Job Harby, Sir Abraham Dawes, and Sir John Jacob were prominent merchants, speculators, and financial experts who, beside their share in the customs farm, were active in the East India, the Levant, and other companies and were repeatedly called on by the royal government for advice in questions of economic and trade policy.[2] The function of these men was to serve as intermediaries through whom the profits of trade found an investment outlet in government borrowing; and through their instrumentality, in turn, the revenue needs of the crown promoted the growth of financial capitalism. A major source of their loanable funds was the mercantile community as a whole, since numerous persons lent them as if they were bankers the money which they in turn advanced to the King.[3] Thus, while the customs farmers themselves were few and exceptional in their privileges, a good many others had a stake in their favoured position and stood to lose if they failed to meet their obligations.

The farmers of the customs were not the only business men who enjoyed a profitable relation to the Court. Others willing to assist the regime in providing for its financial requirements obtained similar advantages. Sir William Russell, a great merchant and one of the directors of the East India Company, acquired the treasurership of the navy under Charles I, in which place he became a substantial

---

[1] The farmers' profits arose from the surplus over their rent in the proceeds of the customs; from the interest they received on their loans and advances; and from the large cash balances which they had on hand for considerable periods and could invest on their own account. Their reputation also made it possible for them to borrow money from others at a lesser rate of interest than the crown paid them. According to Ashton, the profits of the farmers cannot be accurately estimated; 'Revenue farming under the early Stuarts,' *loc. cit.*, 319n. A report made on 22 May 1641 by a House of Commons committee on the customs farmers contains information concerning their various gains; cf. D'Ewes, Journal, B.M. Harl. 163, ff. 219–22.

[2] Most of these men are listed in the *D.N.B.* Their participation in the customs is described by R. Ashton, *The crown and the money market, passim.* Their names occur frequently in the state papers of James's and Charles's reigns in connection with service on government commissions and with topics of economic significance on which they were consulted.

[3] The dependence of the farmers on loans from others has been stressed by W. P. Harper, *op. cit.*, 69, who describes them as resembling bankers or financial agents, and by R. Ashton, 'Revenue farming under the early Stuarts,' *loc. cit.*, 320.

lender to the crown, recouping himself by means of the opportunities his office put in his way.[1] The viscountcies given in 1628 to the merchants, Sir Baptist Hicks and Sir Paul Bayning, were also probably a reward for the large sums these money lenders had advanced the King.[2]

Apart from the matter of loans, the government's impact on the contemporary economy was so extensive, the details of its regulation so complex, that, inevitably, some business groups benefited considerably from its policies.[3] The Statute of Monopolies of 1624, the culmination of thirty years of complaint in parliament, had excepted incorporated companies from its provisions. In consequence, the monopolies of Charles I's reign differed from their predecessors in being granted, not to a limited number of private persons, but to corporations in order to evade the statute.[4] The practice of conferring monopoly rights over a particular trade upon companies in return for a revenue to the crown reached a height in the '30s. Due to the corporate character of these enterprises, they created a net of business interests closely dependent on the crown. These, at any rate, had little to complain of from royal economic intervention, however outraged were the protests against monopolies in other quarters.

Involved so deeply in the royal revenue system, the magnates of the customs farm probably had a greater stake in the survival of Charles I's rule than any other business group. Their economic well-being was based on the King's ability to meet his obligations and to enforce the powers he claimed under his prerogative. There was nothing surprising, therefore, in the fact that the farmers supported the crown in its conflict with the Country opposition. During the first fifteen years of the reign, they continued to collect the tonnage and poundage duties declared unlawful by parliament and which the Commons' resolutions of 1629 had condemned. Nor did they fail to come to the King's assistance when the outbreak of the Scottish rebellion put a new strain on royal finances. While the Privy Council was meeting the severest difficulty in raising money elsewhere because of the political isolation of the Court and the decline in the King's credit, the farmers utilized their own great resources on the crown's behalf.

[1] Cf. *D.N.B.*, *s.v.* and R. Ashton, 'The disbursing official under the early Stuarts: the cases of Sir William Russell and Philip Burlamachi,' *Bulletin of the Institute of Historical Research*, XXX, 82 (1957).
[2] Cf. L. Stone, *The crisis of the aristocracy*, 534–5. Hicks became viscount Campden, Bayning viscount Bayning. Their loans to the King are mentioned by R. Ashton, *The crown and the money market*, *passim.*
[3] Cf. R. Ashton, 'Charles I and the City,' *Essays in the economic & social history of Tudor & Stuart England.*
[4] W. H. Price, *op. cit.*, ch. III; C. T. Carr (ed.), *Select charters of trading companies A.D. 1530–1707*, *Selden society*, XXVIII, 1913, lxxii.

Sir Paul Pindar personally advanced £85,000 in 1638–9, while the syndicate formed in 1640 through a merger of two previous groups of farmers provided well over £100,000 and perhaps as much as a quarter of a million.[1]

Faithful to Charles I in the period of parliament's eclipse, they thereby incurred the ruin which the wrath of the Long Parliament brought on them. In 1641 they were declared delinquents and guilty of heinous crimes for their unlawful collection of customs duties. Besides the loss of the huge sums they lent the King, the farmers were fined £150,000 and left to confront the claims of the creditors on whom they had now defaulted.[2] The greatest capitalists in the kingdom, their estates were wrecked in the collapse of the King's power.

3

The one municipality whose magnitude made its political sympathies a factor of crucial importance was London. The residence of the King and royal family, the seat of the central government and the law courts, the resort of the wealthier gentry who came to further their litigious concerns, to take part in the season that was just then starting to be a feature of the city's social life, and to patronize the shops where European luxuries might be obtained, the capital was already a great metropolis. Two-thirds or more of England's foreign trade was exported there. It was equally preeminent industrially and as a centre of consumption whose economic impact was felt throughout the kingdom and whose expanding demand provided the chief stimulus to its own industrial development.[3]

The extraordinary growth of London was a phenomenon that staggered and dismayed contemporaries. The thousands of workmen who lived in the city and its suburbs made industrial regulation exceedingly difficult and created serious problems of government and public order.[4] Administratively, the municipality was encumbered by anomalies inherited from the past. Within and about it were liberties and franchises, once the property of religious houses, that had passed to new lay and clerical owners after the dissolution of the monasteries and were exempt in whole or part from the jurisdiction of the lord

[1] R. Ashton, *The crown and the money market*, 175, 110–11.
[2] *Ibid.*, 111–12; Notestein, *D'Ewes*, 197–200; *C.J.*, II, 157, 163–4.
[3] Cf. F. J. Fisher, 'London's export trade in the early seventeenth century,' *Economic history review*, 2nd ser., III, 2 (1950) and 'The development of London as a center of conspicuous consumption in the sixteenth and seventeenth centuries,' *Transactions of the Royal Historical Society*, 4th ser., XXX, 1948; J. L. Archer, *op. cit.*, 47–54.
[4] Cf. V. Pearl, *op. cit.*, ch. I.

mayor and aldermen. Here dense populations resided, including many aliens, who, as Stow said, enjoyed the *quondam* clerical immunities now 'wrested to artificers, buyers and sellars. . . .'[1] The suburbs also, though integral to the city's economy and peace, were only partially subject to its authority. To accommodate London's increasing numbers, cheap dwellings were erected and large houses, formerly monastic or noble establishments, subdivided by landlords into 'small tenements, letten out to strangers, and other meane people.'[2] In such slums a large miscellaneous population swarmed, complicating the task of the municipal magistrates. As an instance of the resultant crowding, in 1607 the recorder of London described four large buildings which housed eight thousand inhabitants, of whom eight hundred had died in the last plague visitation: '. . . if it be not reformed,' he stated, 'the people cannot have food nor can they be governed.'[3]

Alarmed by the capital's growth, Elizabeth, James, and Charles all tried to control it by publishing proclamations against new buildings and sub-division. The Privy Council in 1613 referred to the 'inconveniences which cannot be avoyded by the swelling multitudes of people . . . drawne hether from all partes of the Kingdome, and that as well in regard of the price of victuall . . . as also in respect of government and order.'[4] Prohibition was ineffectual, however, and new construction continued to go up in hundreds during the earlier years of the century. 'The desire of Profitte greatly increaseth Buyldinges,' wrote a Jacobean pamphleteer,

and so much the more for that this great Concourse of all sortes of people drawing nere unto this Cittie, everie man seeketh out places, highewayes, lanes and coverte corners to buylde upon, yf it be but sheddes, cottages, and small tenements for people to lodge inn which have not any meanes either to live or to imploye themselves. . . . This sorte of covetous Buylders exacte greater renttes, and daiely doe increase them, in so much that a poore handiecraftsman is not able by his paynefull laboure to paye the rentte of a small tenement.[5]

When Stow published his *Survey of London* in 1598, he took note of the apprehension which the city's disproportionate size and wealth had already created. At the end of his work he appended a discourse on the advantages of cities, 'Written by way of an Apologie (or

[1] J. Stow, *op. cit.*, I, 309.
[2] *Ibid.*, I, 163.
[3] Cited in N. G. Brett-James, *The growth of Stuart London*, L., 1935, 83–4.
[4] Cited in *ibid.*, 87–8.
[5] Cited in *ibid.*, 98–9.

defence) against the opinion ... that the greatnes of [London] standeth not with the profit and securitie of this Realme.' As well as stressing the close connection between cities and a civilized, religious life, he took pains to emphasize that great towns, if rightly ordered, are a bulwark of aristocracy and just kingship. Rebellions, he pointed out, are the offspring of ambition or covetousness. Hence they are likely to be incited either by high and noble personages or by unthrifts and needy men who may be numerous in the city but have no part of its rule. Although the capital had supported some rebellions, it had opposed others and was never the author of any; nor could it be so long as it continued to be well governed. But he had to confess that 'London is a mighty arme and instrument to bring any great desire to effect, if it may be woon to a man's devotion; whereof ... there want not examples in the English Historie.'[1]

This was a lesson Charles I failed to learn. The citizens' deep-rooted feeling for property and their hard religious sensibilities were, indeed, dangerous to offend. The mass of apprentices, workmen, and shopkeepers who inhabited the city's parishes and suburbs could not be controlled when they assembled in angry multitudes to shout their will. If the Londoners withdrew their allegiance, the King would suffer a calamitous reverse. Yet with the shortsightedness that marked so much of his rule, his treatment of the capital produced exactly this result.

In the relations between Charles I and London, the financial aspect was inevitably uppermost. The King's treatment of his capital was aptly described by Clarendon: 'The City of London,' he wrote, 'was looked upon too much of late time as a common stock not easy to be exhausted, and as a body not to be grieved by ordinary acts of injustice.'[2] It is impossible to pinpoint any one particular act of state which focused all the resentment provoked by the crown's projects to exploit the wealth of London. But in the twenty years or so before the revolution, there was not a single financial transaction between the crown and the city of London as a corporate body in which the royal government behaved toward its municipal creditor with the probity essential in maintaining its respect and credit within the business community. In 1617, the Corporation of London stood guarantor for a loan to the King of nearly £100,000 which was raised among the wealthier citizens with repayment promised in a year at ten per cent interest. The royal pledge was not kept, and for over a decade there were repeated prolongations of the debt, while most of the interest due remained unpaid. In the meantime, the crown obtained what was in effect a conversion of the terms of its loan, when an act of 1624 fixed eight per cent as the statutory maximum

[1] J. Stow, *op. cit.*, II, 196ff.   [2] *Rebellion*, IV, 179.

that could be charged for interest. While repayment of the loan of 1617 hung fire, Charles I soon after his accession borrowed another £60,000 also underwritten by the Corporation of London. He undertook to repay both this and the earlier debt within a year. Once more, however, the crown defaulted on its obligation. In 1628, an expedient was agreed upon to satisfy the citizen creditors to whom the Corporation of London stood bound. The latter advanced another £120,000 to the King, much of it raised by assessments which the city authorities levied on the livery companies; in return, crown lands were conveyed to the Corporation which it was to sell, the proceeds being applied to the repayment of the several loans. The scheme went into operation, but four years later, the government accused the city of misconduct in its role as contractor of royal lands. There was in fact some profiteering by land purchasers; yet it was scarcely the part of the crown to reproach the Corporation of London for its management of an arrangement it had been persuaded to accept as the only means of recovering debts legally due it and long outstanding. Although the city finally decided to compound for its alleged offence, the dispute retarded the further disposal of royal lands, and during the 1630s the loans of 1617, 1625, and 1628 were still being repaid. Even in the '40s not all the creditors had yet received their principal and accumulated interest.[1]

Another notable instance in which London discovered the baneful effects of royal bad faith was the Star Chamber prosecution against the city in connection with the Londonderry plantation. Like the royal loans, the plantation in Ireland was a project undertaken by the Corporation of London at the crown's behest and in which some of the money raised was lent with considerable unwillingness. The task of assisting to colonize and anglicize Ulster was first laid upon London by King James in 1610, the necessary capital being advanced at the Corporation's call by the livery companies, who assessed their members for the purpose. The enterprise in the end yielded no profit: in fact, the contributing companies incurred a net loss of more than £50,000. However, in 1631 the Attorney General entered a bill against the Corporation in the Star Chamber, charging it with fraud and excessive profit in its administration of the Londonderry plantation. The political significance of the case was perhaps as great as the financial. The prosecution was instituted after Charles had resolved to summon parliament no more and his subjects had shown strong signs

---

[1] Cf. for the details of these transactions the account by R. Ashton, 'Deficit finance in the reign of James I,' *Economic history review*, 2nd ser., X, 1 (1957) and *The crown and the money market*, chs. V–VI. The mode of raising these loans in the city is described in R. Sharpe, *London and the kingdom*, 3v., L., 1894–5, II, 70, 104–5.

of disaffection. According to Secretary of State Coke, if the King won the suit, 'Hee may breake the confidence of the times that have encroached uppon him and increase his royalties and revenue in an ample and faire manner.'[1] The trial took place in 1635 and lasted over the unprecedented time of thirteen days. Its conclusion was probably predictable. The Corporation was sentenced to a fine of £70,000 and the forfeiture of its Irish lands. Although the fine was subsequently mitigated to £12,000, the city's loss was nonetheless substantial. Their treatment must have left a sour taste in many citizens' mouths and could only have contributed to bring both the Court of Star Chamber and the royal government into discredit. Even Wentworth was of the opinion that the Londoners, 'out great Sums upon the Plantation,' had been dealt with too severely.[2]

In spite of the royal exactions to which the city was subjected, its government was too closely connected with the crown to become a sounding board for the swelling animosity of the citizens. The lord mayor and aldermen did try to defend the corporate interests of the municipality, as in 1626, when they demurred to the King's demand for twenty ships from the city, and in 1634, when they with the common council petitioned that London by reason of its privileges should be exempt from ship money.[3] But they invariably yielded in these instances under the slightest pressure from the crown; and equally important, they carefully avoided taking up the larger political issue implicit in the King's attempt by his fiscal measures to gain a revenue independent of parliamentary assent. Neither to the forced loan of 1627 nor to ship money, the supreme national grievance of the 1630s, did the city of London express any official opposition. The municipal authorities were even fortified in their adherence to the King when he permitted the city to compound in 1638 for various offences of which it stood accused and granted it a new charter amplifying some of its privileges.[4]

The crown's laxity in paying its debts had so seriously impaired its credit in the capital that from 1628 to the outbreak of the Scottish rebellion it made no further attempt to raise any loans through the Corporation of London. Its borrowing needs in these years were mainly met by the customs farmers supplemented by a number of individual lenders and companies to whom it had granted monopoly

---

[1] Sir John Coke to Viscount Dorchester, August 1630, cited in T. W. Moody, *The Londonderry plantation 1609–41*, Belfast, 1939, 259. The account in the above paragraph is based on this excellent work.

[2] *The earl of Strafforde's letters*, II, 25.

[3] R. Sharpe, *op. cit.*, II, 98–9, 113–14; M. Wren, 'London and the twenty ships, 1626–27,' *American historical review*, LV, 2 (1950).

[4] Cf. V. Pearl, *op. cit.*, 82–7, for an account of the negotiations that led to the 1638 charter.

privileges.[1] The Scottish crisis, however, forced the King to turn to the city once more, and in June 1639 the Corporation was asked for a loan of £100,000. The consequences of the crown's former bad faith to its creditors now declared themselves. The lord mayor and aldermen denied the request, though as a sop they offered a free gift of £10,000. Their refusal was based primarily on financial grounds, but must have been reinforced by their awareness that the unpopularity of the Scottish war in the capital would have created serious difficulties in persuading citizens to lend.[2]

In the spring of 1640, they were once more approached for a large loan. The crown's credit was worse than ever and they again refused. By now the King's insistent pressure on them for money provoked a small reaction even in the aldermanic bench. When the aldermen were commanded to submit lists of the richest citizens in their wards from whom contributions could be demanded, four declined to do so, and were jailed by the Council for a few days.[3] This was the limit of opposition to the King in the governing body of London. Sir Henry Garway, mayor in 1639–40, had close financial ties with the crown, and he and most of the aldermen were well disposed towards Charles, as they were to show at a heavy cost to themselves in the months to come.[4] They were all accustomed to serve the royal power both as magistrates and as business men frequently summoned to advise on trade matters. But their unwillingness at such a time to open the city's purse without good security was disastrous for the King. It made his financial plight so desperate that no recourse was left him but to throw himself upon parliament. And, in fact, not until October, after the summons of parliament had been announced and ten peers had given their personal security in anticipation of a parliamentary grant, did the capital's authorities become cooperative and agree to assess the livery companies for an advance of £50,000.[5] No doubt, London lenders and moneyed men believed that parliament's recall after its long intermission promised the end of extraordinary fiscal exactions and the regularization of the entire financial position of the crown.

In contrast to the attitude of the official municipality, there was an

---

[1] Cf. R. Ashton, *The crown and the money market*, ch. VII.

[2] R. Sharpe, *op. cit.*, II, 120–1.

[3] *Ibid.*, II, 122–4, 125. The four aldermen were Rainton, Gayer, Soame, and Atkins.

[4] The Garways were one of the wealthiest merchant families in London and participated as principals or under-sharers in some of the syndicates that farmed the customs under James and Charles; cf. the references to them in R. Ashton, *The crown and the money market*, *passim*, and the account of Sir Henry in V. Pearl, *op. cit.*, and *D.N.B.*, *s.v.*, 'Sir Henry Garraway.'

[5] R. Sharpe, *op. cit.*, II, 128–30; R. Ashton, *The crown and the money market*, 181–2.

organized opposition to the royal government within the citizen body. Its core was a group of merchants who were allies of the Country leaders and united through their Puritan convictions and support for the claims of parliament. Their political activity is shrouded in obscurity, but they probably were behind some of the attempts in London to challenge the King's power. Their chief bond of association was the Massachusetts Bay Company, which paralleled the Providence Island Company as a centre for the London elements of the anti-Court party that was taking shape before 1640. In May 1628, when certain adventurers received a grant from the Council for New England, an earlier colonizing enterprise, for settlement in Massachusetts, twenty-two of the original forty-three participants were London merchants. These included Mathew Cradock and John Venn, both of whom represented London in the Long Parliament as adherents of the Country leaders. A few months later, Samuel Vassall, another future London M.P. of identical sympathies, became an adventurer.[1] We can well believe that the hearts of these men must have been deeply committed to this enterprise, under whose auspices the great Puritan migration to Massachusetts began. When, as the sequel to this undertaking, the Massachusetts Bay Company was formed in the following year, its charter appointed Cradock as governor and mentioned Venn and Vassall as founder members. Vassall had already suffered imprisonment for refusing to pay tonnage and poundage, and a few years afterwards the Privy Council noted him as friendly to the Scottish rebels. Some of the other men among the company's first investors—Thomas Andrewes, William Perkins, Owen Rowe, Nathaniel Wright, and William Spurstowe—became well known in London after 1640 as enemies of the Court. Spurstowe, who resisted the forced loan in 1627, possessed family and trading connections with Shrewsbury and was elected one of its M.P.s in the Long Parliament, where he showed himself keen for political and religious reform. The others in 1641–2 were active in the struggle to align the government of the capital behind Pym, Hampden, and their party in parliament.

With the probable exception of Cradock and Spurstowe, none of these London supporters of the Country was in the first rank of citizen wealth; but almost all were men of substance—rich or prosperous merchants, exporters with interests in several trading companies, members of the urban governing class well qualified to take a prominent share in the political life of the city.[2]

[1] Cf. F. Rose-Troup, *John White, the patriarch of Dorchester*, N.Y., 1930, 111–12, 122, and the same writer's *The Massachusetts Bay Company and its predecessors*, N.Y., 1930, 19–21.

[2] Cf. *Records of the governor and company of . . . Massachusetts Bay*, ed.

A direct connection existed between the London oppositionists and the men involved in another enterprise dear to the heart of Puritan England. This was the Feoffees for Impropriations, a body of trustees formed in 1625 to finance the purchase of places in the church for Puritan clergy.[1] John White, the Massachusetts Bay Company's counsel, was one of these feoffees. He represented Southwark in the Long Parliament and was a supporter of the Country. Another lawyer in the Bay company, also a feoffee, was Samuel Browne, first cousin to Oliver St. John and future M.P. for Dartmouth. Three other feoffees in the Bay company—George Harwood, Francis Bridges and Richard Davis—were all London merchants. John Davenport, the Puritan vicar of St. Stephen's Coleman Street in London until his emigration to New England in 1633, was likewise both a feoffee and a charter member of the Massachusetts Bay Company.[2]

Besides the feoffees, there were looser associations through the Bay company between the Londoners and some of the Country peers and gentry. Two of the subscribers to the company's capital were brothers-in-law of the opposition nobleman, the earl of Lincoln.[3] Another subscriber was a son of Lord Saye.[4] Sir William Brereton, an oppositionist who subsequently represented Cheshire in the Long Parliament, and Henry Darley, whom the Country leaders later sent as their intermediary to the Scots, also a future M.P., were both stockholders in the Bay company.[5] As president of the Council for New England, the earl of Warwick gave substantial support to the promoters of the Massachusetts enterprise.[6] Thus, the merchant group, while not of the inner circle of the opposition movement, was related in various ways to its leaders. Once again, in these multi-

[1] On the Feoffees for Impropriations, cf. *infra,* 179–82.

[2] The feoffees' names are listed in I. Calder, *Activities of the Puritan faction of the Church of England,* L., 1957, x–xi. Those mentioned in the text are included in the list of adventurers in the Bay company in F. Rose-Troup, *The Massachusetts Bay Company and its predecessors,* ch. XVI.

[3] These were John Humphrey and Isaac Johnson; cf. C. M. Andrews, *op. cit.,* I, 355, 360.

[4] Charles Fiennes.

[5] M. Keeler, *op. cit., s.v.*

[6] F. Rose-Troup, *The Massachusetts Bay Company and its predecessors,* 45; C. M. Andrews, *op. cit.,* I, 366–7.

N. B. Shurtleff, 5v., Boston, 1853, I, 11, and the list of adventurers in F. Rose-Troup, *The Massachusetts Bay Company and its predecessors,* ch. XVI. Biographical references to, or accounts of, the names mentioned in the text may be found in M. Keeler, *op. cit., D.N.B.,* and V. Pearl, *op. cit., passim.* Cf. also the cordial letter sent by Cradock and Owen Rowe to John Winthrop on the transfer of the company's government to New England, *Winthrop papers,* III, 226, 377.

farious connections, we have a sight of the uncanny ability of the Puritan oppositionists to devise methods of organization and common action, even at the time the King's power seemed at its highest. In London as elsewhere, the forces were forming whom Pym and his collaborators could mobilize when the hour came.

While the city's governing body consistently refrained from taking a stand in the political conflict, the temper of its citizens was increasingly hostile toward the crown. Considerable resistance appeared to the forced loan, and in 1629 the King's collection of tonnage and poundage provoked a trade stoppage for several weeks by the protesting merchants.[1] Political sentiment in London found an opportunity to manifest itself unmistakably in the election to the parliament of 1628. The choice of London's members lay with the liverymen assembled in the court of common hall. What occurred may well have been planned in advance by opposition elements in the city. The recorder, customarily always returned as one of London's members, was ignominiously rejected. Instead, the electors named as two of their four representatives Alderman Bunce and Henry Waller, both known to be opponents of the Court. Bunce had stood out against the forced loan; Waller was a good friend of Sir John Eliot and subsequently a subscriber to the Massachusetts Bay Company.[2] During the later '30s, the levying of ship money was also met by the Londoners with a recalcitrance and dislike that no threats from the Privy Council could subdue.[3] A pointed symptom of London's discontent was the unwillingness of qualified citizens to accept municipal office, particularly the place of sheriff, on which the burden of the ship-money collection lay. At the end of 1639, an act of the common council was constrained to take notice of this state of affairs. Remarking on 'the greate number of Commoners men of good worth and ability ... elected to the place of Sherivalty ... refusing the same,' it removed the disabilities which an act of common council a century before had imposed on such refusers.[4]

During 1640, as the unpopularity of the royal government reached an extreme, signs of a revolutionary situation began to appear in the great city. The spring election to the Short Parliament went strongly against the Court. Besides Cradock and Vassall, who belonged to the group of city oppositionists, two junior aldermen, Thomas Soame and Isaac Penington, were returned. Neither had taken part in previous

---

[1] Cf. *supra*, 110, 112.

[2] Cf. the account of the London election in a news letter to Lord Fairfax, February 1628, *Fairfax correspondence*, I, 89; J. Forster, *op. cit.*, II, 100, 592, 596; F. Rose-Troup, *The Massachusetts Bay Company and its predecessors*, 91, 157; P.R.O. S.P. 16/89 no. 2.

[3] Cf. V. Pearl, *op. cit.*, 89–91.

[4] Journal, 39, f. 36.

manifestations of resistance to the King, but Penington, who became an alderman early in 1639, was a prominent Puritan and proved himself an uncompromising enemy of the royal power.[1] In May, dislike of the Scottish war broke out in rioting in Lambeth and Southwark against Archbishop Laud. An angry mob of hundreds attacked the archiepiscopal residence, forcing Laud to flee across the river to Whitehall for safety. Insulting placards were posted denouncing the Queen and popery. A royal proclamation ordering the repression of these 'late Rebellious and Traiterous assemblies' gave some indication of the social status of the rioters. It commanded the arrest for treason of John Archer, glover, George Seares, poulterer, and William Seltrum, shoemaker. Archer and several others were executed for their share in the outbreak.[2] Clearly, a spirit of rebellion was springing to dangerous life among the heaving mass of apprentices, artificers, and tradesmen in the capital. The fears of wealthy citizens were aggravated by the spectre of violence from below, while they worriedly watched the King's desperate efforts to find money for the war against the Scots. Having failed to obtain a loan from the city government, in July Charles seized the bullion deposited by merchants and goldsmiths at the royal mint and threatened to debase the coinage unless financial help from London were forthcoming. This last scheme, commented a privy councillor, 'is conceived the most mischievous thing that could be thought on, and would be the destruction of all trade if it should go on. All the merchants and monied men in the citty are much troubled at this project. . . .'[3]

At the beginning of September, with the Scottish Covenanters already in occupation in the north, London heard the first justification of forcible resistance against the King to issue from an English pulpit. The Puritan preacher was Dr. Calybute Downing, his auditors the members of the Artillery Company of London. Other than the trained bands, the Artillery Company was the only organization in the capital exercised to the use of arms. Vassall, Venn, Rowe, and other militant oppositionists belonged to it; Henry Waller, the London M.P. in 1628, had once been its commander. Evidently it had become notorious as a centre for anti-Court citizens.[4] It could hardly have been by chance that Downing addressed his insurrectionary

---

[1] Cf. on Penington the account in M. Keeler, *op. cit., s.v.,* and V. Pearl, *op. cit.,* 176–84.
[2] R. Steele, *op. cit.,* I, 1817; S. R. Gardiner, *History,* IX, 132–3, 141.
[3] The earl of Northumberland's statement; *H.M.C. Third report,* 82. Cf. the petitions of the merchants, goldsmiths, and Merchant Adventurers Company against the seizure of their bullion, *C.S.P.D. 1640,* 543–4.
[4] Cf. *A letter from Mercurius Civicus to Mercurius Rusticus,* 8–9, and V. Pearl, *op. cit.,* 170–2. Waller died in 1631.

sermon to this body. Taking his text from Deuteronomy, the preacher declared that the injurious treatment of the people of Israel by their ungodly enemies gave an example of 'all the justifiable causes of a legall warre. . . .' '. . . for the safety of the Body of the State,' he said, 'there are . . . Latitudes allowed. . . .' The application to the Scots in arms could not have been more clear. But the preacher left the 'chief Legionaries of this royall City' in no doubt about their own duty. There is in England, he told his congregation, a 'Jesuited faction' which must be destroyed as the Israelites of old righteously destroyed their persecutors, the Amalekites. 'Be wise, be resolute,' was his conclusion, 'you have Amalekites amongst you.'[1] After this discourse, Downing, no longer able to remain safely in London, went for refuge to the earl of Warwick's house in Essex.[2]

As pressure on the King intensified to force the summoning of another parliament, many Londoners threw their weight into the effort. In September, just after the petition of the twelve peers for a parliament,[3] a petition to the same effect was circulated among the citizens. This was an organized campaign to back up the demand of the opposition noblemen with London's numbers. The government received information that nearly three hundred persons had consulted about the petition and that a secret press existed in the city to print seditious literature. Despite the Privy Council's attempt to stop the proceedings and the petition's disavowal by the aldermanic bench, it was delivered to the King at York with ten thousand signatures.[4] A hard indictment of royal misrule, it complained of unlawful taxation, monopolies, religious innovations, and the spread of popery. The petitioners asserted that they could obtain no redress through ordinary justice and demanded that a parliament be called.[5]

Tension in London ran high and the annual election of lord mayor to succeed Sir Henry Garway took place at the end of the month in a disturbed and tempestuous atmosphere. A disorderly crowd assembled in a common hall, with many 'young mechanics' present who had no right to vote. Altogether, about fifteen hundred votes were cast. In a violation of long established usage, the electors passed over the senior alderman, Sir William Acton, whose loyalty to the Court was well known, and nominated two other aldermen for mayor instead, Edmund Wright and Thomas Soame. Wright's choice had

---

[1] C. Downing, *A sermon preached to the renowned Company of the Artillery*, 1641, 10, 11, 37, 39. The sermon, delivered on 1 September 1640, was published by Downing the following year in response to widespread demand.
[2] *A letter from Mercurius Civicus to Mercurius Rusticus*, 8–9.
[3] Cf. *supra*, 105.
[4] *C.S.P.D. 1640–41*, 67, 72, 84; Repertories, 54, f. 307b.
[5] Cf. the text of the citizens' petition in *C.S.P.D. 1640–41*, viii.

no political import, but Soame had recently become popular for disregarding the Privy Council's order to the aldermen to give in lists of the rich men in their wards. The Council was gravely concerned about the result of common hall's departure from tradition. If it were not reversed, wrote Secretary of State Windebank to the King, 'the government of the City is utterly lost.' In the end, after consultation with the Council, the court of aldermen selected Wright, the next in seniority to Acton, as mayor, and he proved to be a dependable friend of royal authority.[1]

Although the Court thus retained its hold on London's government, the citizenry had turned against the crown. At the October election to the Long Parliament, the recorder, Thomas Gardiner, on whose return the Privy Council counted, was rejected. The members of the previous spring—Cradock, Vassall, Soame, and Penington— were again chosen to represent the capital.[2] All four took their stand in the House of Commons with the Country leaders. A contemporary tract stated the reasons for their election:

... Alderman Soame for his imprisonment in denying ship-money, Vassall for his obstinacy against Customes, Craddock for the Cause of New-England, Alderman Pennington for his knowne zeale by his keeping a fasting Sabboth throughout his Shirifalty. ...[3]

There remained, nevertheless, a formidable obstacle to the supremacy of the oppositionists in London. So long as the mayor and majority of aldermen favoured the King, they would stand in the way of every effort to throw London's voice and resources behind the leaders of opposition in parliament. London's M.P.s might represent the political feeling of the citizens, but they could not speak for the aldermanic bench which dominated the official municipality. The anomalous situation that existed was clearly revealed when the mayor and aldermen on 1 December 1640 named a committee of twenty-three persons to consult on matters to be propounded to parliament on the city's behalf. Not one of London's representatives in the House of Commons was appointed.[4] Evidently the London magistracy had no confidence in its own M.P.s. Thus, if the Country's London sympathizers were to be free to work their will in the capital, they would either have to circumvent the mayor and aldermen

---

[1] *C.S.P.D. 1640–41*, 115; *Clarendon state papers*, II, 124–5, 128. A detailed account of the mayoralty election is contained in V. Pearl, *op. cit.*, 110–12. Biographical notices of Acton, Wright, and Soame are in *ibid.*, App. I and M. Keeler, *op. cit.*, 345–6 (Soame).

[2] M. Keeler, *op. cit.*, 55; Gardiner, *History*, IX, 220.

[3] *Persecutio undecima*, 57. Penington was sheriff in 1638.

[4] Cf. V. Pearl, *op. cit.*, 195–6.

or annul their power under the civic constitution. This was the task the fraternity of London oppositionists confronted in the months ahead. The struggle against Charles I had acquired a momentum that was to subvert the traditional structure of rule in the capital.

4

The reaction of the towns of provincial England to the crisis of 1640 is much less documented than London's. The impact of national events and the state of local opinion are often impossible to ascertain. All municipal authorities preferred to maintain the fiction of a harmonious community. Their practice, therefore, was to exclude from official records as much as possible any traces of dissension in the urban corporation or the citizenry. In the case of London, the limitations of the official evidence can be somewhat overcome by means of the considerable information to be derived from state papers, letters, and pamphlets. Such supplementary sources of knowledge are far fewer for other towns, and the history of their relation to the developing revolution is accordingly more obscure. Despite the paucity of evidence, however, there is no reason to doubt that factors similar to those in the capital were operative in the political stand of the provincial *bourgeoisie*. Again there was a deep and widespread dissatisfaction with the crown among the citizens. Again the urban governing bodies usually hesitated or evinced a conservative tendency, notwithstanding the grievances royal policy and financial exactions had inflicted on their communities. Bristol, Newcastle, and Norwich, three leading provincial towns, may serve as illustrations. Here lived business men inferior only to the Londoners in wealth. The cross-currents and play of forces in these lesser centres throw a further light on the posture of the citizen element as revolution approached and the Court's power disintegrated.

Bristol, the metropolis of its region and the second trading city in the kingdom, had suffered numerous difficulties from the royal government. Its merchants, carrying on a large commerce with France and the Iberian peninsula, complained frequently of the duties levied on their wine imports by the customs farmers. There were city petitions to parliament against these duties in the 1620s; and after the first session of the 1628 parliament, the Bristol members, we are told, 'laid before the common council six books concerning the liberty of the subject.'[1] These probably related to the Petition of Right. In 1631 the prohibition of tobacco importation through any port but London adversely affected an important Bristol trade, while

---

[1] J. Latimer, *op. cit.*, 84, 89, 101.

the monopolies which the crown granted to the London companies of soap makers and vintners also did injury to the city's economy.[1] Leading merchants suffered harassment from royal agents and were even prosecuted in the Star Chamber for illegal trade in prohibited goods.[2]

As against these grievances, on the other hand, there were royal measures calculated to gain the city's favour. The municipal corporation realized a long-standing desire when the King gave it sole jurisdiction over Bristol castle and precincts, till then part of Gloucestershire. The limitation of tobacco imports to London was lifted in 1639, and the Merchant Venturers Society, the dominant factor in the city's political and economic life, received an ample confirmation of its privileges from the crown.[3] Moreover, the peace made with France and Spain at the end of the '20s led to a period of expanding trade and prosperity in Bristol. Its substantial commerce with Ireland also benefited by royal action to suppress piracy in the Irish channel.[4]

In 1640 Bristol appointed a deputation to represent its mistreatment to the Short Parliament.[5] Yet however much their grievances aroused the rancour of the citizens, they did not suffice to turn the leading men of the municipality against the crown. This was made clear in the election to the Long Parliament. The parliamentary franchise was confined to the officers of the urban corporation and the resident freeholders. Mere citizen-freemen had no vote and vainly protested their exclusion in a petition to the city government. Even if their request had prevailed, however, the enlargement of the electorate would have been negligible, since it appears that from 1619 to 1699 only five hundred and fifty persons were admitted to the freedom of the city.[6] The members elected were two aldermen, Humphrey Hooke and Richard Long, each in the top rank of Bristol's mercantile elite. Although both had tried to defend the city's interests in their dealings with the royal government, neither was in the least disaffected to the crown or the church. In May 1642 the House of Commons expelled them as monopolists, in spite of their contention that they had cooperated in the wine monopoly of the London

---

[1] *Ibid.*, 116, 121–2; *Proceedings . . . of the Company of Soapmakers 1562–1642*, ed. H. E. Matthews, *Bristol record society*, X, 1940, 3; *Records relating to the Society of Merchant Venturers of . . . Bristol*, ed. P. McGrath, *Bristol record society*, XVII, 1951, 223–5.

[2] *C.S.P.D. 1634–35*, 177; *ibid. 1637–38*, 168–9; *ibid. 1639–40*, 39–40.

[3] J. Latimer, *op. cit.*, 90–1, 144; J. Latimer, *The history of the Society o Merchant Venturers of Bristol*, Bristol, 1903, 87–8.

[4] P. McGrath, *op. cit.*, xix.

[5] J. Latimer, *The annals of Bristol in the seventeenth century*, 147.

[6] *Ibid.*, 147–8; P. McGrath, *op. cit.*, ix, n.

Vintners only to avoid exclusion from the trade entirely. Both became Royalists in the civil war.[1]

Other Bristol notables, indistinguishable from Hooke and Long in social or economic terms, supported the Country, judging by some of the aldermen who later appeared as active partisans on the Parliamentarian side in the civil war.[2] In 1640, however, the aldermanic body as a whole was either too cautious to commit itself against the King or averse from doing do. Apparently, the political alignment in Bristol at the convening of the Long Parliament was not very different from what it was to be two years later, when a native stated, '. . . here are many malignants of the great ones amongst us . . . yet I conceive that the Major part of this City . . . stand firm for the Parliament.'[3]

Newcastle, the centre of the English coal industry, supplied London with all its mineral fuel. A great provincial town, it was described by a traveller in the 1630s as 'inferior for wealth and building to no city save London and Bristow. . . .'[4] Here the 'lords of coal' resided. These colliery owners and merchants maintained a monopoly through the Hostmen's Company of Newcastle, whose members, in return for a shilling duty to the crown on every chaldron shipped, possessed the sole right to buy and sell coal on the Tyne. It was a token of the dominance of this association of coal traders in Newcastle that the same royal charter of 1600 which completed the town's oligarchical constitution also established the privileges of the Hostmen.[5] So close was the relation between the Hostmen and Newcastle's government that every mayor in the earlier seventeenth century was a leading figure in the company.[6]

Charles I's undeviating support of the political and commercial privileges of Newcastle's ruling minority caused most of its members to favour the Court. A few signs of opposition to the oligarchy's dominance, nevertheless, appeared in the town. In 1633, the freemen petitioned the Privy Council against the misgovernment of the mayor

---

[1] Biographical notices of Hooke and Long are contained in M. Keeler, *op. cit.*, *s.v.* The former also represented Bristol in the Short Parliament. The Bristol merchants' defence of their collaboration in the wine monopoly is printed in *Records relating to the Society of Merchant Venturers of* . . . *Bristol*, 223–5. When the House expelled Hooke and Long, it declared that they were beneficiaries of the wine monopoly, but not its projectors, *C.J.*, II, 567.

[2] Cf. *infra*, 339–70.

[3] *A declaration from the city of Bristol . . . sent from M. John Bell*, 1642, 1–3.

[4] Sir W. Brereton, *Travels*, ed. E. Hawkins, *Chetham society*, I, 1844, 85.

[5] For the history and privileges of the Newcastle Hostmen, cf. *Extracts from the records of the Company of Hostmen*.

[6] Cf. J. U. Nef, *The rise of the British coal industry*, 2v., L., 1932, II, 126.

and aldermen. They complained of corruption in the disposal of town revenues and leases and asked for an addition to Newcastle's charter to curb the excessive power of the mayor and his brethren. Their petition was referred to the Council of the North at York which, as might have been expected, upheld the magistrates in their powers. The Council's report on the case expressed a keen awareness of the need for subordination in a centre so important to the King's service. Newcastle, it stated,

is now growne to be very populous . . . the farr greater parte of the Com'ons consisting . . . of Mariners . . . Watermen, Colliers, Keelmen and other people of mean condition, who are apt to turne every pretence and color of grievance into uproare and seditious mutinye. . . .

Again in 1638 the freemen made a similar protest against the civic government, but with no greater effect than before.[1]

The chief threat of political disaffection in Newcastle came not from the commonalty, but from a few influential citizens—a threat the more serious because of the town's strategic importance in the defence of the north against the Scottish Covenanters. There was a small Puritan group in Newcastle; and at the autumn mayoralty election in 1639, Robert Bewick, who belonged to it and was believed sympathetic to the Scots, was chosen mayor. The Privy Council, although warned of the danger of his election, was unable to prevent it.[2] A prominent Hostman, son of a former mayor and already once mayor himself as well as sheriff of Northumberland, Bewick's status fully qualified him for his position. No accusation was made of any irregularity in his election. But in spite of his being one of the oligarchy, his reputation as a Puritan made him deeply suspect to his fellows in the town elite.[3] During his mayoralty, Newcastle manifested dislike of ship money, and the Privy Council was told that some of the magistrates refused to be assessed, 'pretending the tax . . . an unjust pressure on them.'[4] Moreover, on the eve of the Short Parliament, several merchants organized a petition instructing

[1] R. Welford, *History of Newcastle and Gateshead*, 3v., L., 1884–7, III, 315–16, 359–62. The report of the Council of the North and other documents relating to the free burgesses' protest are printed in C. S. Terry, 'The visits of Charles I to Newcastle,' *Archaeologia Aeliana*, n.s., XXI, 1891, 91–5.
[2] *C.S.P.D. 1639*, 450–1, 480.
[3] Cf. *The mayors and sheriffs of Newcastle*, ed. C. H. Hunter Blair, *Archaeologia Aeliana*, 4th ser., XVIII, 1940, 53. Bewick participated in the cartel agreement of the Hostmen to limit the sale of coal in order to maintain the price; cf. *Extracts from the records of the Company of Hostmen*, 66, 69, 73. His Puritan sympathies are mentioned in *C.S.P.D. 1639–40*, 346, 402.
[4] *C.S.P.D. 1639–40*, 460.

the municipal M.P.s to oppose Laud's religious innovations and preserve the liberty of the subject. The ringleader in this move was Anthony Errington, the warden of the Newcastle Merchant Adventurers Company. The organizers were denounced to the Privy Council by a number of aldermen, who called the petition 'as ill as the covenant of Scotland.'[1]

The dissatisfaction in the town towards Charles I's regime was registered at the election to the Long Parliament. What the parliamentary franchise was is uncertain, but probably it was broader than the franchise in civic elections. Perhaps the presence of the Scots, who were already at Newcastle, also had some effect on the outcome. At any rate, both the members chosen were supporters of the Country. Sir Henry Anderson, scion of a family prominent in public affairs and the coal trade, was one of the representatives.[2] The other was John Blakiston, not one of the inner circle of Newcastle wealth or power, but a prosperous merchant who had recently been in trouble with the Court of High Commission for religious nonconformity.[3] His return, in particular, must have reflected the oppositionist sentiments of the electors.

There can be no doubt that the election result was decidedly unwelcome to almost all Newcastle's notables. These—Marlays, Davisons, Carrs, Coles, Liddells, Riddells, and their like—adhered from first to last to the King, the buttress of their privileges. One of them, Sir Nicholas Cole, succeeded Bewick as mayor, an indication of their determination to keep the town in line with their own position. They afterwards swelled the roll of Royalists in the civil war, while even Sir Henry Anderson in a couple of years went over to the King's party.[4] In 1640–1, with some of the freemen aroused against the Court and a few of the elite estranged, the town government's power may have been momentarily impaired. This is particularly suggested by an order of December 1641 giving the common council a voice in the disposition of the corporation's revenues and leases.[5] Eight years previously the freemen had petitioned in vain for such an arrangement. But if the oligarchy's position was indeed shaken, the situation

---

[1] *Ibid.*, 600–4; *Memoirs of Ambrose Barnes*, ed. W. H. D. Longstaffe, *Surtees society*, L, 1867, App., 329–30.

[2] Cf. M. Keeler, *op. cit.*, *s.v.*

[3] *Ibid.*, *s.v.* and *Acts of the High Commission Court . . . of Durham*, ed. W. H. D. Longstaffe, *Surtees society*, XXXIV, 1858, 157–8. Blakiston was named in a disputed return with Sir John Melton, Secretary of the Council of the North. Melton's death a few weeks after parliament's opening enabled Blakiston to take his seat without further difficulty; cf. M. Keeler, *op. cit.*, 59.

[4] Cf. *infra*, 339, and M. Keeler, *op. cit.*, 59, 87.

[5] *Extracts from the Newcastle . . . council minute book 1639–1650*, ed. M. H. Dodds, *Newcastle upon Tyne records committee*, I, 1920, 7–10.

did not last. For it was not many months until the coal masters of Newcastle turned their town into a royal stronghold completely subservient to their will.

Norwich, the third city in the kingdom, owed its importance to its position in the East Anglian textile industry. Long a centre of the worsted manufacture, in the reign of Queen Elizabeth several thousand Protestant refugees from the Low Countries were permitted to settle there, and they introduced to Norwich the making of the 'new draperies,' the lighter woollens on which its prosperity in the earlier seventeenth century was principally based.[1] As elsewhere, so at Norwich the governing court of mayoralty was composed of merchants and well-to-do retailers in the textile and a few other trades vital to the urban economy.[2]

The civic rulers were indebted to the crown in more than one respect for its favour to themselves and the cloth manufacture. Under its fifteenth-century charters, power in the municipality was centred in the mayor and twenty-four aldermen, the latter of whom possessed life tenure. Some scope still remained for the popular element, nevertheless, since the general body of citizens had the right to nominate the mayor and his brethren, while the choice of common councillors lay with the resident householders in the four wards. In 1619, after a disputed mayoralty election, a royal order curtailed the citizens' privileges. To quash 'factious opposition,' it was decreed that henceforth the office of mayor should be annually filled by the senior alderman who had not yet served. Another alteration in 1621 confined aldermanic office to men who had previously been sheriffs, and also transferred the nomination of aldermen from the citizens to the mayor and his sitting colleagues. In this way, the participation of the citizen-freemen was all but eliminated and the control of the oligarchy fixed more firmly than ever. The crown showed its determination to preserve this state of affairs when it upheld the mayor and aldermen in a disputed shrievalty election in 1627 that had caused disturbance in the city.[3]

---

[1] Cf. E. Lipson, *The history of the woollen and worsted industries*, L., 1921, 21–4. A document of 1575 attests the benefits the Dutch and Walloon refugees brought Norwich; cf. R. H. Tawney and E. Power (eds.), *Tudor economic documents*, 3v., L., 1924, I, 315–16.

[2] Cf. *Minutes of the Norwich court of mayoralty 1630–1631*, 21–3. Of the mayors and aldermen in the earlier seventeenth century, merchants, grocers, mercers, and drapers exceeded all other occupations.

[3] A full account of the evolution of Norwich's government is contained in *The records of the city of Norwich*, I, Introduction; a shorter sketch is given in *Minutes of the court of mayoralty 1630–1631*, Introduction. For crown

To Norwich's textile industry the crown also extended its support. In 1610, for instance, the Privy Council helped the mayor to suppress a strike of journeymen and apprentices directed against the employment of weavers who had not passed their apprenticeship in the trade. The strikers' complaint was justifiable under the Statute of Artificers of 1563, yet such was the magistrates' fear of insubordination that the ringleaders were brought to trial for conspiracy and sedition by the Council's intervention.[1] Again, in 1638 when a royal proclamation ordered that all cloth shipped to London for sale should be inspected in the capital, Norwich woollens were exempted on the mayor's petition. Thus the magistrates retained the authority to supervise the quality of the stuffs manufactured in their city.[2] In general, it was only because the King sustained their privileges that the civic rulers were able to exercise a comprehensive regulation of the cloth industry.

Despite these benefits, there was much enmity to the Court both among the citizens and the governing elite. The chief reason for this was Charles I's religious policy. Puritanism had struck deep roots in Norwich, and Archbishop Laud's rule of the church helped to alienate people in every stratum of the community.[3] The threat of action by the ecclesiastical authorities made the inhabitants circumspect, yet signs of religious disaffection were apparent. In 1627 and 1636 a number of citizens petitioned for liberty of preaching and for lectures.[4] Four aldermen belonged to a group of trustees who, like the London Feoffees for Impropriations, were engaged in securing places for Puritan ministers in Norwich and Norfolk.[5] One of them was Alderman Thomas Atkins, a cloth merchant who left Norwich in 1637 owing to Bishop Wren's prosecution of citizens for nonconformity. Settling in London where he had business connections, he became an alderman there and won renown in 1640 for resisting the King's financial demands upon the capital.[6]

Bishop Wren's pressures in the diocese of Norwich from 1635 to 1638 aroused particular antagonism. As the collaborator of Laud, he did everything in his power to carry the archbishop's programme into effect. He imposed the Anglo-Catholic ritualistic innovations on the

[1] J. U. Nef, *Industry and government in France and England 1540–1640*, 40–1.
[2] *Records of the city of Norwich*, II, 259–66.
[3] The extent of Puritanism in Norwich is stressed by Bruce Allen, *op. cit.*
[4] F. Blomefield, *An essay towards a . . . history of . . . Norfolk*, 2nd ed., 11v., L., 1805–10, III, 374, 379.
[5] P.R.O. S.P. 16/531 no. 134.
[6] *C.S.P.D. 1637*, 219 and *supra*, 170.

action in behalf of the civic oligarchy, cf. *Acts of the Privy Council Jan. 1618–June 1619*, 484, *ibid. Sept. 1627–June 1628*, 75, 114. 140–1: *C.S.P.D. 1627–28*, 348.

churches and purged the city's pulpits of their Puritan incumbents and lecturers. Eight ministers in Norwich were thus deprived for non-conformity in 1636.[1] Besides the rigour of his visitations, he touched Norwich's inhabitants in a sore place when he forced them to increase their tithes to the parish clergy. To consolidate this achievement, he procured a royal order commanding all disputes on tithes to be heard in Chancery or his own episcopal court, to the exclusion of common law jurisdiction.[2]

These proceedings turned Norwich against the crown. The sequel was seen in 1640. To the Short Parliament the city elected its ex-alderman, Thomas Atkins, and Alderman John Tooley, another Puritan and one of the Norfolk feoffees.[3] The franchise must have been open to all freemen, since more than a thousand citizens voted in the fall election of the Long Parliament.[4] Again two M.P.s opposed to the Court were returned. They were Alderman Richard Harman, mayor in the previous year, and Richard Catelyn, who did not reside in the city but possessed long-standing family connections with it. In due course, Catelyn became a Royalist; his membership in the Norfolk feoffees, however, indicates that he supported the Country when elected.[5] A minority of the ruling oligarchy took a different stand, to judge from the Norwich merchants who later became notorious Royalists in the civil war.[6] But in 1640 most of the court of mayoralty undoubtedly favoured the opponents of Charles I. Strong oppositionist sentiment also probably accounted for the citizens' resumption in 1641 of their privilege of nominating the mayor, which they had lost twenty-two years before. They used their newly regained power to nominate a mayor whose political sympathies accorded with their own.[7]

---

[1] *H.M.C. Gawdy*, 158. One of the deprived was William Bridge, later a well-known Independent, on whose behalf a committee of aldermen petitioned in 1634. He had been rector of St. Peter's Hungate and curate of St. George's in Norwich; *Minutes of the Norwich court of mayoralty 1630–1631*, 49–50 and J. Browne, *History of Congregationalism in Norfolk and Suffolk*, L., 1887, 105, 107.

[2] *State trials*, IV, 35; cf. Norwich's petition to parliament in December 1640 against Bishop Wren and his tithe exactions, *C.J.*, II, 56.

[3] *Members of parliament*, 491; P.R.O. S.P. 16/531, no. 134 lists Tooley's name among the Norfolk feoffees.

[4] M. Keeler, *op. cit.*, 57n.

[5] On the Norwich members, cf. M. Keeler, *op. cit.*, *s.v.* Catelyn is mentioned as a feoffee in P.R.O. S.P. 16/531 no. 134.

[6] Cf. *infra*, 339.

[7] F. Blomefield, *op. cit.*, III, 381. The citizens first nominated Alderman Thomas Carver, and after he died they named Adrian Parmenter, sheriff in 1632, who was to become a strong Parliamentarian (*ibid.*, III, 383–4, 388, 398).

The outstanding conclusion to emerge from this survey of the citizen element before and during the crisis of 1640 is the absence of any simple uniformity in its political stand. Like the aristocratic order it was divided. But this division, of course, was far from equal. Even as in 1640 the greater part of the nobility and gentry stood with the leaders of the Country and endorsed their insistence on redress of grievances and reform, so did the greater part of the *bourgeoisie*. That was the meaning of the Court's deep isolation at the moment when the Long Parliament assembled.

Yet, as has been seen, important sections of the mercantile elite either continued to support the King or at any rate failed to take a public position against his government. In the case of the customs farmers the reason was obvious: so involved were their pecuniary interests with crown finance that they necessarily stood and fell with the regime. In other instances, however, *bourgeois* dependence on the crown was less close. Had the coal capitalists of Newcastle not shown themselves hostile to the partisans of the opposition movement in their town, they might have retained their privileges with the Long Parliament's sanction, instead of incurring its enmity as they soon did. The mayor and aldermen of London supported the crown partly because they were accustomed to do so, partly because they knew that the struggle against Charles I would provoke unrest in the capital and place their own authority in question. Even so, their refusal to lend to the King in his time of need spelled ruin for the Court. As for other town corporations, many, we may be sure, harboured a hostility to the crown which they refrained from expressing. If they failed to pronounce an official condemnation of ship money or to make a public demand for a parliament, it was because they were too cautious to do so. It was not in their power to give a political lead, and they did not care to jeopardize their civic interests by risking royal displeasure. They chose the unheroic course and awaited the initiative of the peers and gentlemen who were the natural and inevitable spokesmen of the kingdom's grievances.

6

Puritanism

Puritanism first became a force on the political scene in the reign of Queen Elizabeth. Its early adherents by their pressure helped shape the religious settlement of 1559; and soon after, they turned towards parliament to obtain its support in imposing their design of reformation upon an unwilling Church of England. Between the coming forth in 1572 of the famous Puritan manifesto, *An Admonition To The Parliament*, and the prospect of reform that opened at last with the Long Parliament's assembly, more than three generations elapsed: long years during which the Puritans wandered in the wilderness, far from the Canaan for which their souls thirsted. Suppressed by the Queen and Archbishop Whitgift, the organized Puritan movement broke up and its inspirers, Cartwright, Field, Travers, together with their great lay patrons of the Elizabethan age, passed from the scene.[1] The successors of these militants preserved the hope of reformation, but with a more temperate zeal. Kept down, like their predecessors, by the crown and the ecclesiastical authorities, they found an outlet for their energies in preaching and writing. From pulpit and press they unceasingly propagated the Puritan scheme of life and way of salvation. And thus in the first two Stuart reigns there grew up an active clergy and a numerous laity whose moral ideals and spiritual temper were deeply stamped by Puritan teaching.[2] Here began the incorporation of Puritanism as a formative element in English civilization and character, which was to be its enduring legacy after the revolutionary gales of the seventeenth century had blown themselves out. But before the long post-revolutionary epilogue set in, the tale of Puritanism militant and Puritanism suffering was to culminate in a third act of Puritanism triumphant: a triumph prepared by the reaction of hatred to the rule of Archbishop Laud, and achieved in the alliance of Puritanism with the Country opposition.

The singular fact about Puritanism was that it survived and

[1] Cartwright died in 1603, his last years having been spent relatively remote from former controversies; Field died in 1588; Travers lived until 1635, but remained in obscurity during the Stuart reigns.

[2] Cf. the account of Puritan preaching and writing by W. Haller, *The rise of Puritanism*, N.Y. 1938.

tenaciously preserved its identity in the Church of England through seven decades of repression and postponed hopes. Never extirpated and never assimilated, it never ceased to manifest its powerful energies in the cultivation of its own religious ethos and the defiance of ecclesiastical authority. So prolific was it that the era of its predominance after 1640 became the climax of the English reformation. We can think of no other instance in the history of revolutions of a movement that maintained itself in the abundance of its creative strength for so long a period.

We have already referred frequently to Puritanism in preceding chapters. We must now take a closer view of it: our purpose will be to ascertain its relation to the revolution that was in the making prior to 1640. Much confusion will be avoided if we state at the outset what is to be understood by 'Puritan.' First used in the mid-1560s, the name, like that of all broad movements which attract many and diverse supporters to their cause, quickly acquired an overlay of various meanings.[1] The commonest was an abusive one designating the censorious rigorist who professed to take his moral and religious duties with greater earnestness than other men. 'Who are so much branded with vile terms of Puritans and Precisians,' asked the famous Puritan divine, William Perkins, 'as those, that most endeavour to get and keepe the puritie of heart in good conscience?'[2] 'To bewail the distresses of God's children,' said a Puritan member of parliament in 1587,

it is puritanism. To reprove a man for swearing, it is puritanism. To banish an adulterer out of the house, it is puritanism. . . . I fear me we shall shortly come to this, that to do God and her Majesty good service shall be counted puritanism. . . .[3]

Praising the Puritan clergy, another lay favourer in 1576 referred to them as 'those faithfull ministers whom none can justly reprove . . . in doctrine or life, and yet of the wicked worldlings and vaine courtiers falsly termed Puritanes. . . .'[4]

[1] Thomas Fuller placed the origin of 'Puritan' in 1564, *The church history of Britain*, 1651, 3rd ed., ed. J. Nichols, 3v., L., 1842, II, 474; A. F. Scott Pearson assigns the term to 1564 or 1566, *Thomas Cartwright and Elizabethan Puritanism*, Cambridge, 1925, 18 and n.; M. Knappen, in his account of the history of the name, traces it to 1567–8, *Tudor Puritanism*, Chicago, 1939, 488–91. Many illustrations of the word are given by C. Hill, *Society and Puritanism in pre-revolutionary England*, L., 1964, ch. I.

[2] William Perkins, *An exposition upon Christs sermon on the mount, Works*, 3v., 1626–31, III, 15.

[3] Job Throckmorton, cited by J. E. Neale, *Elizabeth I and her parliaments 1584–1601*, 151.

[4] *Letters of Thomas Wood, Puritan, 1566–1577*, ed. P. Collinson, *Bulletin of the Institute of Historical Research supplement*, 5 (1960), 16.

Undoubtedly this description, though the Puritans repudiated it, closely approximated the traits of character and behaviour they tended to display. However, it provides no criterion by which to identify Puritanism as a factor in the ecclesiastical and political conflicts of the age. For this purpose another usage of contemporaries affords a guide. From the time it first became current, 'Puritan' retained one indisputable sense with considerable consistency whatever other meanings of a more ambiguous kind were added to it. It regularly signified those members of the Church of England who opposed its hierarchy and many of its ceremonies, while rejecting on principle any separation from it. People who adopted this position in the established church were known as *non-conformists*; and thus, following the practice of the church historian, Fuller, and many other writers and controversialists of the time, Puritanism may be regarded as synonomous with non-conformity and with sympathy for non-conformity, in any of the latter's numerous manifestations.[1]

It is undeniable, of course, that those who separated from the Church of England were offshoots of Puritanism, with which they shared some important characteristics. But in the context of ecclesiastical and political controversy, Puritanism and the varieties of separatism were distinct phenomena and were so conceived by their respective adherents. A Puritan confession of faith of 1572, in stigmatizing withdrawal from the public assemblies of the church, declared, 'we thincke it not meete for private persons of their own auctoritie . . . to establish churches. . . .'[2] The Puritan author of the Marprelate tracts pointed out that he 'doth account no Brownist [separatist] to be a Puritan. . . .'[3] Thomas Cartwright, the foremost Elizabethan champion of Puritan reform, maintained throughout his career a consistent stand against separatism.[4] A Puritan clergyman, the Rev. John White of Dorchester, remarked, 'we doe and ought to put a great difference between Separation and Non-conformity.'[5] Such statements, which could be added to indefinitely, expressed the general Puritan attitude towards separation right down to the era of the revolution. On the other hand, the animosity of the separatists against the Puritan 'reformists' was scarcely less bitter than their

[1] *The church history of Britain*, II, 474–5. Fuller declared that when referring to the Puritans, 'The reader knoweth that only nonconformists are thereby intended.'
[2] Drawn up by John Field and Thomas Wilcox, *The seconde parte of a register*, ed. A. Peel, 2v., Cambridge, 1915, I, 86.
[3] *Hay any worke for a cooper*, 1589, cited in F. J. Powicke, *Henry Barrow separatist*, L., 1900, 83.
[4] Cf. A. F. Scott Pearson, *op. cit.*, for numerous illustrations of Cartwright's opinion.
[5] Cited in P. Miller, *Orthodoxy in Massachusetts*, Cambridge, 1933, 141.

feeling towards the bishops and 'pontifical clergy.' Henry Barrow assailed the Puritans as 'enemies of Christ's kingdome, the pharisees of these times . . . great learned preachers . . . that sigh and grone for reformation, but their hands with the sluggard denie to worke. . . .'[1] Henry Ainsworth voiced the common separatist attitude when he said of the Puritans, 'all that know the truth of God . . . aright have just cause to blame them for their long halting and dissembling.'[2]

Our concern in the following pages is with Puritanism alone, since its role in the genesis of the revolution was incomparably greater than that of any other species of religious dissent. This was so precisely because of its refusal to abandon the Church of England. Had it done so, Puritanism would have been reduced to impotence. Separation would have cut it off from almost all its patrons in the governing class who, as pillars of society, were hardly likely to jeopardize their social dominion, renounce their public privileges, and expose themselves to the penalties of the law—all of which would have certainly been the consequence of secession from the national church. Correspondent to this, it was revelatory of the political potentialities of the Puritan movement that it never merely sought toleration for itself in a community estranged from its beliefs. Its outlook was imperial: determinedly clinging to its lodgment in the church, it aimed at mastery, the power to impose its system on the whole of religious life. There was here an affinity with the mentality of its aristocratic lay sympathizers. Such men, landlords, magistrates, law-makers, statesmen, were accustomed to rule. They could far more easily understand and support the Puritan attempt to transform and dominate the national church than they could those who by their withdrawal appeared to generate an anarchy of sects. And in point of fact, while Puritanism attracted adherents of high rank and influence, the disciples of separatism before the revolution belonged almost exclusively to the inferior and labouring orders of the society.

In the largest sense, Puritanism was a reaction not merely against the survival of Catholic practices in the established church, but even more, against the plight of religion rendered subservient to the political expediencies of the crown and placed at the mercy of a rapacious and unscrupulous laity. Already in a decadent condition at the end of the Middle Ages, the church was further weakened by the Henrician reformation and the vicissitudes of the reigns of Edward and Mary. The spoliations committed on its wealth by Henry VIII

[1] Henry Barrow, *A brief discoverie of the false church*, 1590, *The writings of Henry Barrow, 1587–1590*, ed. L. Carlson, L., 1962, 556–7.
[2] Henry Ainsworth, *Counterpoyson*, 1608, cited in B. Hanbury, *Historical memorials relating to the Independents or Congregationalists*, 3v., L., 1839, I, 171.

and his successors, and by the officials and nobility whom they allowed to share in the plunder, did it grave damage. With the loss of corporate autonomy went the church's ability to enforce its will on those who defied it. It became completely dependent on the secular power. The clergy were notoriously poor. Their educational qualifications were grossly inadequate and few could preach. Pastoral efficacy fell to a low ebb. In the later sixteenth century, therefore, the restoration of the church's institutional life, its spiritual strength, and its material resources became for many conscientious men a matter of urgent necessity. Puritanism was one form of response addressing itself to this extraordinarily difficult task. The means which it chose, however, placed it in antagonism to both royal and episcopal authority and thus set it on a course of opposition for decades to come.[1]

The palpable presence of a dissident Puritan party first became evident in the 1560s, when a number of clergy demonstrated their dissatisfaction with certain externals of church worship and the vestments prescribed for ministers. Denouncing both as Romish and unfit for a reformed church, they conducted an agitation that gave serious trouble to Archbishop Parker of Canterbury. Here already, in their disobedience to their ecclesiastical superiors, the Puritans showed how stiff they could be in non-conformity. Although they were unsuccessful in this campaign and had to submit, they did not resign themselves to its outcome. It was, in fact, only the first engagement in a prolonged struggle.[2]

As the Puritan movement evolved in the next years, it advanced well beyond the ground on which its early encounters were fought. This Puritanism was more radical than its predecessor of the '60s. Its leaders were new and younger men, exponents of a programme which became the standard of a rebellious generation.[3] The intellec-

---

[1] On the condition and difficulties of the established church in the later sixteenth century, cf. W. H. Frere, *The English church in the reigns of Elizabeth and James I*, L., 1904, R. G. Usher, *The reconstruction of the English church*, 2v., N.Y., 1910, and C. Hill, *Economic problems of the church from Whitgift to the Long Parliament*, Oxford, 1956.

[2] Cf. M. Knappen, *op. cit.*, for a general account of this and the subsequent stages in the history of sixteenth-century Puritanism. P. Collinson's *The Elizabethan Puritan movement*, L., 1967, which is now the best and fullest treatment of the subject, appeared too late for use by the present writer.

[3] The age of the Puritan leaders in 1572, when the *Admonition* appeared, is suggestive. Cartwright, the oldest, was 37; Walter Travers (whose birthdate has been settled by S. J. Knox, *Walter Travers: paragon of Elizabethan Puritanism*, L., 1962, 14) was 24; John Field and Thomas Wilcox, the *Admonition*'s authors, were respectively 27 and 23. In 1583, Archbishop Whitgift told some Puritan ministers: 'You are . . . but boyes in comparison of us, who have studied divinity before you for the most part were borne'

tual inspirer of this fresh phase was Thomas Cartwright, chief theorist of the Puritan party, who held a divinity professorship at Cambridge until ousted by the authorities in 1570. As their central tenet, the Puritans now demanded the abolition of the ecclesiastical hierarchy and its replacement by a presbyterian polity in the national church. The *Admonition to the parliament* of 1572 declared their position with unsurpassed trenchancy; while two years later, Walter Travers's *Ecclesiasticae Disciplinae ... Explicatio* (for which Cartwright provided the preface) expounded it more fully and systematically.[1]

'... we in England are so fare of, from having a church rightly reformed,' said the *Admonition*, '... that as yet we are not come to the outward face of the same.'[2] It went on to present a formidable indictment of the state of the church, noting unsparingly the incapacity of the clergy, the transgressions of the bishops, and the prevalence of popish abuses contrary to God's word in the service and prayer book. Here for the first time the Puritans adopted the doctrine that 'ecclesiastical discipline' is one of the essential marks of a true Christian church.[3] This the *Admonition* concisely explained as church government by ministers, elders, and deacons, the 'order left by God ... wherby men learne to frame their wylles and doyngs accordyng to the law of God. ...' It offered parliament a scheme of reform which touched every aspect of the ecclesiastical system. The proposals included election of ministers by their congregations and elimination of impropriations, patronage, and advowsons. The spiritual rulers of the church, the ministers and elders, were to exercise the power of excommunication against the carnal and unrepentant in independence of the secular authority. The unscriptural superiority of bishops was to give place to the equality of the clergy. Parliament, the *Admonition* concluded, must 'go foreward to a thorow and a speedy reformation.' The task was no longer to 'patch and peece,' but to 'remove ... Antichrist, both head body and branch, and perfectly plant that puritie of the word, that simplicitie of the

---

[1] Cf. S. J. Knox, *op. cit.*, ch. II and F. Paget, *An introduction to the fifth book of Hooker's ... Laws of ecclesiastical polity*, Oxford, 1899, 52–63, for an analysis of Travers's work.

[2] I cite the text of the *Admonition* from *Puritan manifestoes*, ed. W. H. Frere and C. E. Douglas, L., repr. 1954.

[3] The two other marks of a true church were the 'preaching of the worde purely' and the 'ministring of the sacraments sincerely.'

(Cited in A. F. Scott Pearson, *op. cit.*, 242). Both Gordon Donaldson, *The Scottish reformation*, Cambridge, 1960, 187–90 and P. Collinson, *op. cit.*, 136–7, have rightly stressed that it was a Puritan party under new leaders that opened the attack on episcopacy.

sacraments, and severitie of discipline, which Christ hath commanded. . . .'

Voice and temper in this manifesto were nearly as significant as its substance. The reproving sharpness, the peremptory dismissal of all that hindered reformation, the religious superiority assumed by the sponsors—these notes of a self-accrediting intransigent righteousness were to characterize the Puritan movement during its heroic age. As for the revolutionary essence of the *Admonition*, that lay in ecclesiastical discipline—the presbyterian system of church government and censure derived from the influence and practice of Beza and Calvin in Geneva. Since the Discipline, as it became known, would have not only abolished bishops, but would also have established the church's independence from the civil magistrate, it was no way compatible with the ecclesiastical supremacy of the crown.[1] No wonder that the Queen felt compelled to proceed severely against a movement so corrosive of royal power in a vital department of state.

Much of the subsequent activity of Elizabethan Puritanism aimed at putting the presbyterian church order into effect in despite of the crown. In localities where their influence predominated, the Puritan clergy introduced instalments of the Discipline on their own initiative and altered the liturgy and service to accord with their views.[2] Essex, Northamptonshire, Warwickshire, and London were the main scenes of this attempt, which was well organized and hard to check. After 1583, however, when John Whitgift became Archbishop of Canterbury, the government took vigorous measures to deal with nonconformity. The archbishop insisted on strict obedience to the ordinances of the church and, with the backing of the Queen, brought the repressive machinery of the High Commission and the Star Chamber to bear against the Puritan ministers. By the end of the reign the firmness of the ecclesiastical authorities had attained success. The movement for the Discipline was shattered and its promoters driven into silence or submission. Cartwright, its leading ideologue, withdrew himself from the struggle under the government's pressure. Retreat and tribulation were the lot of Puritanism in the setting years of Elizabeth's reign.

While Puritanism continued to be a significant factor in the national church, its presbyterian phase was over for the time. It was to reappear forty years afterward, fanned into life by the revolution, when the Long Parliament began to canvass models for a reformed

---

[1] On the political bearings of the Discipline, cf. A. F. Scott Pearson, *Church & state.*

[2] Cf. the texts and introduction in *The presbyterian movement in the reign of Queen Elizabeth*, ed. R. G. Usher, *Camden society*, 3rd ser., VIII, 1905.

church.[1] The demand to abolish bishops now receded into the background. At James I's accession, it was not mentioned in the proposals for reformation which the Puritan clergy gave the new ruler in their Millenary Petition of 1603.[2] Neither did their spokesmen talk of eliminating episcopal church government at the Hampton Court conference, which the King held the next year to discuss the Puritans' desires. The subject was too inflammatory to be touched. Henceforth Puritan non-conformity expressed its persistent defiance of ecclesiastical authority in other ways. There was even perhaps a possibility that, having laid aside the Discipline, the Puritans could have been brought gradually to live at peace in the church by moderate concessions from the crown. But if such a chance did exist in the earlier seventeenth century, it was never taken. James yielded little to Puritan wishes,[3] while its harsh treatment by Charles and Laud made it intractable.

2

The impact of Puritanism, as we have already suggested, depended on the retention of its hold in the established church; and that, in turn, required the presence of a clergy able to sustain it through all its trials by their teaching and example. From the outset of the movement Puritan ministers confronted some painful dilemmas of conscience: how to justify remaining in the church in view of the blemishes which disfigured it; and how far to persist in non-conformity if threatened with suspension or deprivation (expulsion) from their spiritual functions. These questions, canvassed in the heyday of the movement's Disciplinarian phase, continued to be equally pressing in the earlier seventeenth century. The problem of conscience was aggravated after 1583, as a result of the oath of three articles imposed on the clergy by Archbishop Whitgift, which was later incorporated in the canons of 1604 and thus made the law of the church. Under its provisions every ecclesiastical person had to subscribe on oath *ex animo* acknowledging the royal supremacy in religion and declaring that the prayer book, the ordination service, and the thirty-nine articles of religion contained nothing contrary to

[1] Cf. W. Shaw, *A history of the English church . . . 1640–1660*, 2v., L., 1900, I, 5–6 and C. Hill, *Society and Puritanism in pre-revolutionary England*, 502.
[2] Cf. the text of the petition in J. R. Tanner, *Constitutional documents . . . James I*, 56–60. The Oxford vice-chancellor and heads of houses, indeed, denounced the petition, contending that the framers really aimed at the Discipline, though not daring to avow it. The Puritans replied repudiating the accusation; cf. S. B. Babbage, *Puritanism and Richard Bancroft*, L., 1962, 54.
[3] On the King's concessions, cf. M. Curtis, 'The Hampton Court conference and its aftermath,' *History*, XLVI, 156 (1961).

the word of God.[1] This subscription, of course, was devised to coerce the Puritans. The latter, however, were neither hypocrites nor cowards. They remained fast in their hope of a national church that would yet be rightly reformed; and while a few were deprived of their clerical office, most demonstrated remarkable ingenuity in avoiding this fate. In consequence, the Puritans succeeded in preserving a considerable place for themselves in the ministry right down to the meeting of the Long Parliament.

The premiss of their conduct was relatively simple. They believed that it was right and lawful to remain in communion with the Church of England, which possessed the *esse* of a church, if not yet the *bene esse*;[2] and they attached such value to the work of the ministry that they held it justifiable to bear with the church's shortcomings if loss of their vocation should ensue from refusal. There may be added the more mundane consideration that the average clergyman, entirely dependent on his small professional income to support himself and his family, had a strong inducement against quitting his place. Since the Puritans, however, displayed a more than ordinary readiness for self-sacrifice, the influence of conscientious motives upon their actions must be fully acknowledged.

The view we have described was strongly stated by Thomas Cartwright in the Puritan argument with separatism. On this ground, in a 'Resolution of Doubts touching a mans entrie into ye Ministrye,' he defended the church against its separatist critics and vindicated the assumption of the ministerial function within it.[3] When consulted, he advised Puritan clergymen to bear with popish cermonies if necessary rather than renounce their calling.[4] Most non-conformists held this opinion. In 1578, for instance, seven suspended ministers of Norwich made their submission in order to be restored to preaching. The ceremonies and government of the church, they declared, 'are so farre tolerable that for the same no man ought to withdrawe himselfe . . . neither ought any minister for these to refuse to preche the Worde of God and to administer the Sacraments.'[5] The position was most clearly formulated nearly forty years later in an admirable work

---

[1] Whitgift's oath became, with slight changes, canon XXXVI in the canons of 1604. The texts of both, together with earlier precedents for subscription, are printed in R. G. Usher, *op. cit.*, II, 293–310.

[2] So Cartwright argued; cf. A. F. Scott Pearson, *Church and state*, 57–8, who ascribes Cartwright's opinion to the influence of the Aristotelian doctrine of the gradations of reality.

[3] Printed in *Cartwrightiana*, ed. A. Peel and L. Carlson, L., 1951. Cf. also his defence of remaining in the national church in *An answere unto a letter of Master Harrisons*, in *ibid*.

[4] *The seconde parte of a register*, I, 137–43.

[5] *Ibid.*, I, 146.

written by the Rev. John Sprint, a Gloucestershire Puritan. He contended that deprivation for non-conformity did more harm to religion than conforming, and that the good received from the preaching of ministers outweighed the inconvenience of objectionable ceremonies. A reply to his tract pointed out that though many clergy were ready to conform, they could not subscribe the oaths ordained by the canon of 1604. To this Sprint returned the revealing answer, 'it is well known, that for these later 5. or 6. yeares, subscription hath not been urged to Incumbents or settled Ministers, but meere conformity. ...' Thus, as he saw it, the choice was conformity vs. deprivation, not subscription vs. deprivation, and he was convinced that conformity ought to be preferred.[1]

Undoubtedly subscription was the chief stumbling block to the Puritan non-conformists. Of the oaths required of them, their reservations were not directed against the acknowledgment of the crown's religious supremacy. Well before the canons of 1604 and Whitgift's three articles, the Supremacy Act of 1559 had exacted a similar oath from the clergy. Even the presbyterian proponents of the Discipline could and did subscribe to the supremacy, despite its apparent contradiction to their conception of an autonomous church order of which Christ alone, not the Queen, was head. They were able to do so because the explanation of the nature of the royal supremacy contained in the thirty-nine articles was such as to allay their scruples.[2] The real difficulty lay in subscribing that the prayer book and articles of religion were throughout agreeable to the word of God. At the Hampton Court conference, a Puritan spokesman told King James what a heavy burden this was and entreated that it should not be imposed.[3] In 1607 some Puritan clergy issued a declaration that they desired the continuance of their ministry 'above all earthly things,' but could not subscribe to the whole of the prayer book.[4] On the other hand, as Sprint pointed out, if a man conformed, subscription was sometimes waived.

This stemmed from the policy of Archbishop Bancroft, Whitgift's successor, in administering the 1604 canons. Though a notorious opponent of the Puritans, he instructed his episcopal colleagues to distinguish between two sorts of 'Revolters' among the clergy: the

[1] *Cassander Anglicus, showing the necessitie of conformitie to the prescribed ceremonies of our church, in case of deprivation*, 1618, 211–12, 237. Sprint was vicar of Thornbury in Gloucestershire; he is noticed in *D.N.B., s.v.*
[2] Article XXXVII, 'Of the civil magistrate.' Cf. the valuable account of the grounds on which the Puritans acknowledged the crown's ecclesiastical supremacy in A. F. Scott Pearson, *Church and state*, 54–7.
[3] T. Fuller, *The church history of Britain*, III, 206.
[4] *The ministers reasons for refusal of subscription to the Book of Common Prayer*, 1607, cited in B. Hanbury, *op. cit.*, I, 128–9.

one 'promiseth conformitie, but is as yet unwillinge to subscribe;' the other 'in his obstinacie will be induced to yield to neither.' Bancroft directed that subscription should be respited the former sort in the hope that they would eventually change their minds.[1] Accordingly, the canons did not lead to a grand purge of Puritan churchmen. Altogether, the number actually deprived in their aftermath was between eighty and ninety. These were the most inflexible who refused both conformity and subscription.[2] Most Puritan ministers— they must have amounted to some hundreds—survived.[3]

At a pinch even subscription could be swallowed. The authors of the Millenary Petition told King James,

... divers of us that sue for reformation have formerly, in respect of the times, subscribed to the Book [of Common Prayer], some upon protes-tation, some upon exposition given them, some with conditions, rather than the Church should have been deprived of their labour and ministry. ...[4]

After the enactment of the canons, some ministers found it possible to subscribe with explicit provisos that satisfied conscience. 'I doe ... willingly subscribe,' wrote one, 'soe as I may be allowed to interpret the things in the fayrest sense which the words of subscription ... may beare. ...'[5]

In fact, then, several alternatives were open to the Puritan clergy. They might subscribe, perhaps with conditions or qualifications; or they might submit to a merely partial and occasional conformity just sufficient to retain their place. If they cooperated thus far, they gained the inestimable consolation of being able to continue their spiritual calling. This, as Laud sardonically pointed out, was on the whole the policy of the Puritan clergy of his time. Ever since the Hampton Court conference, he said,

they have put in practice, and have yeilded a kind of Conformity; not that they thought any whit better of the things, but for that they held

[1] Cf. the text of Bancroft's letter to the bishops, December 1604, in S. Babbage, *op. cit.*, 110–12.

[2] Historians have variously estimated the number of ministers deprived by the enforcement of the canons. The subject has been carefully investigated afresh by S. Babbage, *op. cit.*, ch. 6, whose conclusions I have adopted.

[3] All figures as to the number of Puritans in 1605 are mere guesswork. R. G. Usher's total of 281 is incredibly low; by another computation which he cites, it would be 746 (*op. cit.*, I, 249–51). According to a report of the bishops, there were in 1603 about 10,000 clergy in England altogether (*ibid.*, I, 207).

[4] J. R. Tanner, *Constitutional documents ... James I*, 58.

[5] S. Babbage, *op. cit.*, 227–9.

them (though in themselves unlawfull) not to be such as for which a man ought to hazard (not his lyving, that might savour of covetousnes, but) his Mynisterie, and the good which gods people might by that meanes receave.[1]

An incident from Laud's visitation of his London diocese in 1631 was characteristic of the situation. At Braintree, the Rev. Stephen Marshall, one of the foremost Puritans of Essex, came before him together with other ministers accused of non-conformity. They denied the charge and Marshall told the bishop he was misinformed. 'Ay,' declared Laud,

but do you conforme always? He answered he did some times but not always. . . . The Bishop answered, your preaching I like wel and your Catechising wondrous wel but I mislike your answers . . . you wear the Surpless sometimes, and then you lay it aside from you for a long time. . . .

The narrator of this scene commented:

these good men cannot abide these ceremonies, and if they might they would never use them: But to avoid the Persecution of these Bishops that would fetch them up to the High Commission . . . these good men are fain to stoop to them sometimes.[2]

Undoubtedly, this story was many times paralleled. A Puritan thus described the years of his ministry in London up to 1640:

I never had a canonical coat . . . took not the canonical oath, declined subscription for many years . . . (though I practised the old conformity,)[3] *would not give ne obolum quidem against the Scots, but dissuaded other ministers; much less did I yield to bow to the altar, and at the name of Jesus, or administer the Lord's supper at a table turned altarwise, or bring the people up to the rails, or read the Book of Sports. . . .*[4]

[1] Cited in S. Babbage, *op. cit.*, 225.
[2] *Winthrop papers*, III, 59.
[3] The 'old conformity': acceptance of the form of church services before the Laudian innovations.
[4] Thomas Edwards, *Gangraena*, pt. I, 1646, cited in D. Williams, 'London Puritanism: the parish of St. Botolph without Aldgate,' *Guildhall miscellany*, II, 1 (1960). In 1629, Edwards, then lecturer at St. Botolph without Aldgate, was in trouble for non-conformity and had to promise to conform and to preach a sermon on obedience to superiors, *C.S.P.D. 1628–29*, 543, 593, *ibid. 1629–31*, 1.

The Rev. John Carter, a Suffolk minister for over fifty years, 'was always a Non-conformist, one of the good old Puritans of England. He never swallowed any of the Prelatical Ceremonies against his Conscience.'[1] The Rev. Richard Mather, minister of Toxteth in Lancashire, confessed that he did not wear the canonical surplice once in fifteen years.[2] The Rev. Thomas Toller, vicar of Sheffield for nearly forty years until finally suspended for non-conformity in 1635, used almost none of the services prescribed in the prayer book, and neither he nor his assistant ever wore a surplice or a hood.[3]

There were other ways by which the Puritans could indulge their scruples. John Cotton, later famous in the New England ministry, was a non-conformist when vicar of St. Botolph's in Boston, Lincolnshire; by arrangement a fellow clergyman performed those ceremonies Cotton refused to practise.[4] The non-conformist could seek shelter in a lectureship, where his main business was preaching and he was only required by canon law to read divine service twice a year. Arthur Hildersam, a patriarch of Stuart Puritanism, having been deprived in 1605 as vicar of Ashby-de-la-Zouch, became lecturer there four years later, and engaged a curate to perform the services.[5] This harbour was only temporary, however, for he was suspended in 1613 and was afterwards often in trouble.[6]

If the Puritan had the luck to live under a lenient or moderate bishop, he might remain unmolested in his non-conformity. A speaker in the parliament of 1625 pointed out that 'moderate Bishopps' did not demand subscription, a statement that was certainly correct.[7] This, of course, was before the severe rule of Archbishop Laud and his brethren turned the Puritans into unforgiving enemies. While Archbishop Mathew, for instance, governed the diocese of York between 1606 and 1628, numerous clergy refusing conformity on conscientious grounds were allowed to go their way.[8] The administration of the Laudian Archbishop Neile (1632–40), one of Mathew's successors, was quite a different story. Bishop Bayley of Bangor ordained the Rev. John Angier in 1629 without subscription

---

[1] Carter died in 1634; cf. his life in S. Clarke, *A collection of the lives of ten eminent divines*, 1662.

[2] S. Clarke, *The lives of sundry eminent persons*, 1683, pt. 1, 130. Mather went to New England after suspension in 1634; cf. *D.N.B.*, *s.v.*

[3] R. H. Marchant, *Puritanism and the church courts in the diocese of York*, Cambridge, 1960, 68–73.

[4] L. Ziff, *The career of John Cotton*, Princeton, 1962, 50–6.

[5] S. Babbage, *op. cit.*, 229.

[6] *D.N.B.*, *s.v.* Hildersam died in 1632.

[7] *Commons debates in 1625*, 26. The speaker was Sir Benjamin Rudyard.

[8] R. H. Marchant, *op. cit.*, 166.

and was believed partial to non-conformists.[1] Bishop Williams of Lincoln, while trying to persuade John Cotton to use the ceremonies, took no measures against him for non-conformity.[2] Bishop Hall of Norwich instituted the Rev. Samuel Fairclough to a Suffolk living without subscription.[3] There were frequent examples of this kind in the annals of Puritan biography.

In the last resort, the Puritan minister might simply conform, resolved to possess his soul in patience until the day of reformation. When Richard Baxter was ordained in 1638, he carefully studied the case for non-conformity, and then decided to conform despite his dislike of certain ceremonies.[4] The Rev. John Davenport, vicar of St. Stephen's Coleman Street in London, left his living in 1633 because of the

alteracion of my iudgment in matters of conformity to the ceremonies whereby I cannot practise them as formerly I have done. Wherein I doe not censure those that doe conforme (nay I account many of them faithfull, and worthy instruments of Gods glory, and I know that I did conforme with as much inward peace, as now I doe forbeare, in both my uprightness was the same, but my light different).[5]

Such a 'faithfull and worthy instrument' was Robert More, the Puritan rector of Guiseley in Yorkshire, who left in his will an illuminating explanation of his conformity. '. . . though many learned and good men,' he said,

have always holden and doe still hold, and that with great reason that needles Ceremonyes . . . remaneing still in our Church are very inconvenient and daingerous. . . . for my selfe, I doe confesse that as I could never take upon me to bee a resolute Patron of such humane ordinances, soe could I never find iust cause of sufficient waight to warrant my selfe or any other to oppose or renounce them being commanded by lawfull Authority; but rather regardinge the peace of our Church, the liberty of the Gospell and obedience to Authoritie; I have held it to bee fitt . . . to submitt my selfe to a wise and discreete Tolleratinge and using of them till the tyme of reformacion. . . .[6]

[1] O. Heywood, *The life of John Angier*, ed. E. Axon, *Chetham society*, n.s., XCVII, 1937, 56–7.　　　　[2] L. Ziff, *op. cit.*, 55–7.
[3] S. Clarke, *The lives of sundry eminent persons*, pt. 1, 163.
[4] F. J. Powicke, *A life of the Reverend Richard Baxter*, 2v., L., 1924–7, I, 22–3.
[5] John Davenport to Lady Vere, *Letters of John Davenport*, ed. I. Calder, New Haven, 1937, 39.
[6] Quoted in R. H. Marchant, *op. cit.*, 213–14. More, rector of Guiseley since 1587, died in 1642.

These various practices go far to explain the impossibility of rooting Puritanism out of the church. Through difficult times the Puritan clergy held their ground, while by their ministrations they fortified the consciences of a laity who with hard assurance would tread the government of Charles I under foot.

3

If the clergy were the teachers and ideologues of Puritanism, the laity were its patrons who provided it with an indispensable assistance. Without lay backing, the Puritan movement would have remained an exclusively clerical tendency and could never have acquired the power to shake church and state. The Puritan ministers realized fully, of course, the necessity of support from persons of substance. 'The countenance,' wrote one of them, '. . . which a man of great Estate and Power doth give to a Minister is of great import and influence unto his Ministry.'[1] Enemies saw the ties between the non-conformist clergy and their patrons in the governing class as the fruit of deliberate policy. According to Richard Bancroft, the Puritans 'will have the chiefest and the richest, to be their Elders.' They

doe practize daylie how they may not onlye creep into noble & gentlemens bosomes in the Contrye . . . but also thrust themselves forward by all the power of their frendes, to be . . . Readers, but I feare Seducers in the Innes of Courte. . . . Verye manye gentlemen . . . and some others of greater calling (as it is thought) have ioyned themselves in this faction, and are become great favourers and maynteyners thereof, who beinge manye of them Iustices of peace &c, doe not only countenance theire leaders, but discourage with all theire might the rest of [the] ministerie.[2]

Nor did Bancroft feel any doubt concerning the motives of these lay protectors of the Puritan movement:

Certaine hypocriticall Brethren of the Laytie have clapped [the clergy] uppon the shoulders, followed their sermons, set them at the upper ende of their tables, and sought by all their strength to procure them credit & favour with the people: not that they cared either for them, or for Religion . . . but hopinge that by the violent course, which they saw these men run into, the Bishops, & the rest of the Cleargie, would growe . . . to be so odious: as it would be a very small matter, to disposses

[1] S. Clarke, *The lives of sundry eminent persons*, pt. 1, 169.
[2] *A survay of the pretended holy discipline*, 1593, 154; *Tracts ascribed to Richard Bancroft*, ed. A. Peel, Cambridge, 1953, 57, 71.

them of all their livings, whereof some portion might come to their shares.[1]

Perhaps Bancroft's explanation of the laity's attitude applied in a few instances; but, in general, it was a prejudiced description from one of the Puritans' bitterest enemies. Writing under Elizabeth, he must have been referring to someone like the earl of Leicester, the Queen's favourite, whose unscrupulous ambition and help to non-conformists were both equally well known. Leicester, however, was hardly representative of the Puritan laity. While sharing the Puritan hatred of the pope and Spain, he knew little or nothing of the spiritual side of religion. His interventions on behalf of Cartwright and other ministers were probably less the result of zeal than strata-gems in the factional manoeuvres which formed the substance of Elizabethan politics and at which he was a master.[2] In any event, he contained his support of the movement within prudent limits. Once when reproved for lukewarmness by a friend of the Discipline, his answer was, 'I am so resolved to the defence of that ... already established, as I mean not to be a mayntaynor or allower of any that wold troble or disturbe the quiett proceeding thereof.'[3] Even finan-cially, his interests were better served by the continuance of the existing church establishment than by the Puritan programme. His great position at court allowed him to enrich himself at the church's expense without the disendowment of the bishops; whereas if the Puritans had been able to effect their reformation, they would have stopped the depredation of ecclesiastical property and would have used episcopal revenues to improve the lot of the parish clergy.[4]

Thus it was not of such as Leicester that the Puritan laity were formed. First and foremost, they were men of firm religious convic-tions, diligent attenders at sermons, sharp reprovers of swearing, drunkenness, and sexual transgressions. Often they had undergone a spiritual conversion. Psychologically speaking, conversion was the core of Puritan experience and from it arose the unwavering faith and sense of righteousness (and frequently of self-righteousness) so prominent in the Puritan temper.[5] Filled with the awareness of a new birth, having won through to the knowledge that God, in spite of their transgressions, had predestined them among the elect, they could never imagine they were wrong. Men like these were dedicated to

[1] *A survey of the pretended holy discipline*, 246.
[2] The famous libel against the earl, *Leycesters commonwealth*, 1584, con-nected his patronage of the Puritans with his factional purpose of building up a structure of clientage.
[3] Leicester to Thomas Wood, August 1576, *Letters of Thomas Wood*, 13–15.
[4] Cf. the editor's remarks, *ibid.*, xix, xxiii.
[5] Cf. A. Simpson, *Puritanism in old and New England*, Chicago, 1955, 2.

warfare against sin. They sustained and protected the non-conformist clergy and collaborated in the opposition to Charles I's methods of government. Once their loyalty turned to disaffection, nothing could gain on their intransigence. The King's worst blunder was that he alienated them irrevocably.

Puritan biographies and letters offer lively revelations of these laymen and the sources of their moral and spiritual strength. 'I remember,' wrote one, a Yorkshire gentleman connected with the Barringtons of Essex and other notable Puritan families in the Country opposition,

in the beginninge of my conversion my soule was so abundantlie ravished with the beautie of the lambe, that trulie I was scarce wel when my toungue was not speakinge of the infinitenes of that mercie to me so unworthye a wretche. . . .[1]

Oliver Cromwell described his spiritual experience to his cousin, the wife of Oliver St. John, so as

to honour my God by declaring what He hath done for my soul, in this I am confident, and I will be so. . . . Oh, I lived in and loved darkness, and hated the light. I was . . . the chief of sinners. . . . yet God had mercy on me. O the riches of his mercy! Praise Him for me, pray for me, that He who hath begun a good work would perfect it to the day of Christ.[2]

John Winthrop, the leader of the Puritan migration to New England, gave a similar account of his religious travail. At the age of eighteen,

I married into a family under Mr. Culverwell his ministry in Essex; and living there sometimes I first found the ministry of the word to come to my heart with power.

He wrestled stubbornly with his carnality and so arrived 'to some peace and comfort in God.'

I honoured a faithful minister in my heart and could have kissed his feet. . . . I had an unsatiable thirst after the word of God and could not misse a good sermon, though many miles off, especially of such as did search deep into the conscience.

[1] Thomas Bourchier to Lady Joan Barrington, undated, but probably written at the end of the 1620s, B. M. Egerton MSS. 2650, f. 205.
[2] Written October 1638, W. C. Abbott, *Writings and speeches of Oliver Cromwell*, 4v., Cambridge, 1937–47, I, 96–7.

Finally, after many sore afflictions, Christ was revealed to him when he was thirty years old, and he saw clearly 'into the covenant of free grace.'[1]

Sir Nathaniel Barnardiston, Bt., of whom a pious biographer left an edifying narrative, belonged to this type of Puritan layman in the aristocratic order. Born in 1588 of a distinguished family, he was the 'Top-Branch of the Suffolk Cedars,' the twenty-third knight in lineal descent. In his youth he passed through a religious conversion: this was the 'second Birth' which confirmed his faith in his salvation. He prayed daily, read the Scripture much, and was always careful to sanctify the Sabbath, while 'his preparation for the Sacrament of the Lord's Supper was transcendent.' Few could outdo him in his 'constant attendance upon the Ministration of the Word, publickly dispensed. ...' A warm friend of the Puritan clergy, he was of the mind that 'he had rather fall with the Ministry of England, than stand in greatest power with their enemies.' He sat in all the parliaments of Charles I. As a public man, 'none could put on a braver obstinacy, or more peremptory refusal ... to the most lofty Commands, or most zealous Importunities, even of the greatest Man, if what was urged was unjust, or against his happy Rule of Life, the Word of God.' Thus he exposed himself 'to a Gulph of Hazards' in defence of the liberties of his country because he resisted the forced loan and ship money. It was a note of Sir Nathaniel's patriotism that he annually celebrated Queen Elizabeth's accession day. When he went as Suffolk's senior knight to the Short Parliament, he declared that God's 'covenant and call is the only supporter of my faith. ...' Barnardiston was one of many like-minded religious gentlemen whose wrath the King and Archbishop Laud had to face in 1640.[2]

Ignatius Jurdain, merchant, alderman, and mayor of Exeter, was another of this sort of layman whose stiff rectitude presented a front of iron to the pressures of Charles I. Converted at fifteen, according to his biographer, he continued in the life and power of religion until his death at the age of seventy-nine in 1640. He was a great reader of the Bible, of books of practical divinity, and had gone through Foxe's *Martyrs* seven times. Sermons were a strong interest. He took notes regularly in church, 'not for his own benefit alone, but for the good of his Family to whom he did constantly repeat the Sermons.' As a magistrate, 'the Stocks and Whipping-post could testifie what

---

[1] *Winthrop papers*, I, 155–6, 158–9. Winthrop wrote this history of his progress in religion when he was forty-nine. Cf. also E. S. Morgan, *The Puritan dilemma. The story of John Winthrop*, Boston, 1958, ch. I.
[2] S. Clarke, *The lives of sundry eminent persons*, pt. 2; *Winthrop papers*, IV, 218. The local importance of Sir Nathaniel and his family is noticed in *Suffolk and the great rebellion*, ed. A. Everitt, *Suffolk records society*, 3, 1960.

swearers, drunkards, unclean persons ... were punished by his indifferent execution of justice.' At one time he accepted usury for loans; but some ministers having convinced him this was wrong, he made restitution of his gains and thereafter took no more for a loan than the borrower would freely give. Twice he represented his city in parliament where he 'was a great stickler to have the Bill passed for the punishment of Adultery with death. ...' This became known as 'Mr. Jurdains Bill.' It failed because 'those times would not bear it.' He interceded for non-conformist clergy and did not fear to write Charles I protesting the profanation of the Sabbath by the King's encouragement of Sunday sports. It was of Alderman Jurdain that the satiric Bishop Corbett spoke in his poem on the parliament of 1628, joining him with Pym and William Prynne:

> *A sad presage of dainger to this land*
> *When lower strive to gett the upper hand:*
> *When Prince and Peeres to Peysants must obey,*
> *When Lay-men must their Teachers teach the way:*
> *When Pym and Prinn and Jourdain must define*
> *What Lords are het'rodox and what divine*
>
> *. . .*
>
> *It is a Paritie must sett all right:*
> *Then shall the Gospell shine like Phoebus bright.*[1]

There were many men of this pious kind in the civic oligarchies and landed society. On them the interest of religion as they conceived it exercised a profound influence. Knowing their importance, the Puritan clergy laboured painfully to shape their faith from earliest youth. The Rev. John Preston, referred to previously in another connection,[2] while a teacher at Cambridge was the 'greatest pupil-monger in England ... having sixteen fellow commoners (most heirs to fair estates) admitted in one year.' Among his pupils he counted such offspring of opposition families as the earl of Lincoln and sons of Lord Saye and the earl of Warwick.[3]

The same devout laity figured among the benefactors of non-conformity whom Puritan hagiography delighted to honour. There was, for instance, Mr. Taylor, the recorder of Richmond in York-shire, 'a very Gaius or Onesiphorus to the silenced ministers of

[1] S. Clarke, *A collection of the lives of ten eminent divines ... and of some other eminent Christians*, 1662; 'Against the opposing the duke in parliament, 1628,' *The poems of Richard Corbett*, ed. J. A. W. Bennett and H. R. Trevor-Roper, Oxford, 1955.
[2] Cf. *supra*, 63, 65–6.
[3] T. Fuller, *The worthies of England*, ed. P. A. Nuttall, 3v., L., 1840, II, 1517; I. Morgan, *op. cit.*, 28–31.

England;' the 'honourable and Elect Lady, the Lady Bowes,' who gave £1,000 a year to maintain preachers in the north and Derbyshire, all of them formerly 'silenced men by reason of Non-conformity;' Lady Margaret Bromley in Shropshire, 'a constant and unparallel'd favourer of all good Ministers . . . who suffered under Prelaticall pressures. . . .'[1] Of a slightly earlier generation was the zealous Sir Francis Hastings, brother of the third earl of Huntingdon, whose incessant efforts in behalf of non-conformist clergy provoked James I to remove him from the commission of the peace and the deputy lieutenancy.[2] Equally representative of the type were the Hereford-shire gentleman, Sir Robert Harley, and his wife, both strict Sab-batarians, observers of fast days, and stout friends of the Puritan ministry. To her son of fourteen at Oxford, Lady Brilliana Harley wrote urging him on in his reading of Calvin. The Scottish rebellion naturally claimed all her sympathy, so that she thought 1639 'the yeere in which . . . Antichrist must beginne to falle.' Soon after the Long Parliament's assembling, where her husband represented his county, Lady Brilliana was saying that the church hierarchy 'must downe, and I hope now.'[3]

Moral narrowness and intolerant incomprehension of other forms of religion than their own were a common characteristic of these Puritan laymen. Perhaps without such qualities they might not have been so inflexibly resolute in withstanding the frowns and distaste of royal authority. Yet to this type there were striking exceptions. In a Cromwell or a Milton, for instance, austerity mingled with an idealist passion and heroic spirituality that raised them far above the average Puritan. Such men were destined to a pilgrimage of conquests and chastenings that opened their field of vision to truths altogether beyond the ken of the Barnardistons and Jurdains. Theirs were natures no orthodoxy could confine.

Moreover, as the mention of Milton should suggest, there was no hostility towards culture in these Puritan adherents. While the revolution was in embryo, the youthful Milton dedicatedly pursued his studies, fitting himself for his high vocation as a poet who would teach virtue to nations, fusing in his artist's imagination the didactic aims of the Puritan with the idealism of Plato.[4] The Country noble-man, Lord Brooke, was another inspired by Platonist influence. Revealed in his work, *The Nature of Truth* (1640), was a mind seeking a harmony between Puritan moralism and the humanist exaltation of

[1] S. Clarke, *A generall martyrologie*, 2nd ed., 1660, pt. 2, 88, 157, 195.
[2] C. Cross, *The Puritan earl*, N.Y., 1966, 49–51. Sir Francis died in 1610. The third earl, who died in 1595, was also a great Puritan patron.
[3] *Letters of the Lady Brilliana Harley*, ed. T. Lewis, *Camden society*, LVIII, 1854, 20, 41, 111.   [4] Cf. W. Haller, *op. cit.*, ch. VIII.

reason as the divine faculty in man. Sir Robert Harley, though disliking the bishops, was the friend of John Donne, of George Herbert, and of the latter's philosophic brother, Lord Herbert of Cherbury. With Lord Herbert he exchanged letters on deism; and such was his affection for George Herbert's piety that he was solicited to assist in the posthumous publication of *The Country Parson*.[1] Further indicative of the cultural range of an ordinary Puritan gentleman is the list of books bought between 1635-9 by the Essex oppositionist, Sir Thomas Barrington. The one hundred and six titles included not only legal texts, biblical commentaries, Catholic and Protestant controversy, and popular Puritan treatises, but also the poems of George Herbert, writings by Erasmus and Raleigh, and the works of Shakespeare.[2]

It was the constant support of such well-disposed persons in the governing class that more than anything else insured the survival of Puritanism. The Puritan ministers recognized the debt and expressed their gratitude in the writings they dedicated to their aristocratic patrons. Leading oppositionists were among the recipients of these tributes. Cornelius Burges dedicated *Baptismall Regeneration* (1629) to the earl of Bedford in thanks to 'that Ancient, Noble, and much honoured Family, to which I was, and ever will be a faithfull & humble servant.' Jeremiah Burroughs's *The Excellency of A Gracious Spirit* (1638) and Richard Sibbes's *Bowels Opened ... The Love Betwixt Christ And The Church* (1639) were dedicated to Lord Mandeville. One of the most popular Puritan devotional works, John Preston's *The New Covenant* (1629), was published with dedications to Lord Saye and the earl of Lincoln. Several other writings of Preston, *The Breast-Plate of Faith And Love* (1630) and *The Golden Sceptre* (1638), were dedicated respectively to the earl of Warwick and Richard Knightley. Warwick also received the dedication of Thomas Stoughton's *The Christians Sacrifice* (1622). '. . . God himselfe,' wrote the author,

hath now honored your Noble house, and made it renowned in the

[1] *H.M.C. Portland*, III, *passim*, contains Harley's correspondence with Donne, Herbert, and Herbert of Cherbury. A letter to him from Robert Cooke in 1641, asking his aid on behalf of Herbert's *The Country Parson*, begins, 'Mr. George Herbert (whose memory I love as well as you did his person) . . .', B.M. Loan 29, 119, pt. 3. The work was not published until 1652 in *Herbert's remains*. A point of affinity between Herbert and Harley is suggested by the former's well-known line referring to the Puritan migration, in which religion stands 'on tip-toe in our land, Readie to passe to the American Strand.'

[2] M. E. Bohannon, 'A London bookseller's bill: 1635-1639,' *The library*, 4th ser., XVIII, 4 (1938). Barrington owned Shakespeare's second folio of 1632, bought for 18s. 6d.

Church, both by the profession of the Gospell, and also by the protection of the possessors thereof, even now to the third generation of your name. . . .

To Richard Knightley, the venerable John Dod dedicated *A plaine . . . . exposition on the lords prayer* (1635), a 'testimony . . . of mine unfeined and hearty thankfulnesse, for all your favours and goodnesse to mee and mine.'[1]

In view of the close connections between the Puritan clergy and their protectors in the governing class, descriptions of the former as 'alienated intellectuals' and as an 'intelligentsia' cut off from tradition and seeking a new order have an altogether anachronistic ring.[2] It is doubtful that the ministers were intellectuals at all in the modern sense. At any rate, they contributed virtually nothing to the work of universal desacralization and de-mystification of society and nature which has probably been the foremost function of the intellectual in recent times. Certainly, they were not alienated from traditional society. Whatever their religious discontents, they accepted unquestioningly the inherited status order in which their own calling held an acknowledged place. Their preaching was all of social subordination to superiors; for they knew, as one of the most admired of them wrote, that

God hath appointed . . . in every society one person should bee above or under another; not making all equall, as though the bodie should bee all head and nothing else: but even in degree and order, hee hath set a distinction, that one should be above another.[3]

It was with a grateful unction that the Puritan ministers invoked God's blessing on the citizen worthies and well-descended gentlemen who were their supporters and defenders.

No contribution of these same laymen to the cause was more important than their use of ecclesiastical patronage. By installing Puritan ministers in church livings, lectureships, and chaplaincies, they secured them both a haven and a fruitful field of activity as

[1] I have found these dedications by means of F. B. Williams (ed.), *Index of dedications and commendatory verses in English books before 1641*, L., 1962. Several of the works cited were published posthumously with dedications by their editors, Puritan clergymen of note.
[2] Cf. M. Curtis, 'The alienated intellectuals of early Stuart England,' *Past and present*, 23 (1962) and M. Walzer, *The revolution of the saints*, Cambridge, 1965, 121, 124–7.
[3] William Perkins, 'A treatise of callings,' *Works*, I, 755. The conservative nature of Puritan social attitudes is well brought out by C. and K. George *The Protestant mind of the English reformation*, Princeton, 1961.

pastors and preachers. In Lincolnshire before 1640, for instance, a group of Puritan adherents of the Country—Sir William Wray, Sir George St. Paul, Sir William Armyne, Sir Thomas Grantham, and the earl of Lincoln—held twenty-seven advowsons between them which were available to clergy of their own persuasion.[1] In 1628, with the help of the earl of Warwick, the Puritan Samuel Clarke obtained a lectureship in the town of Warwick. When he was forced out five years later for non-conformity, Lord Brooke gave him a rectory in Warwickshire. There he also received the protection of Richard Knightley.[2] The Essex oppositionist, Sir William Masham, known to Laud as 'a very factious Puritan,' had the ministers, John Norton and the famous Roger Williams, as chaplains before their emigration to New England.[3] Sir Nathaniel Barnardiston, we are told, always took care to present the church livings in his possession to 'eminent and worthy Divines. . . .' Most of the other leading families of Suffolk, like the Heveninghams, Parkers, Bacons, Gurdons, and Playters, were also Puritan and bestowed their patronage in the same way.[4]

Where Puritan influence could exert itself in corporate bodies, these, too, assisted non-conformists with their patronage. In the 1630s, the Haberdashers and Mercers companies of London appointed Puritans to curacies and lectureships in their gift in Cheshire, Gloucestershire, and Durham.[5] The English churches in the Dutch republic belonging to the Merchant Adventurers Company were notorious havens not only for non-conformists but even for dissenters of a more extreme kind. An official account drawn up in 1632 described them as 'Seminaries of disorderly preachers' who hold 'continuall Correspondence with the Refractories in England.'[6] The vestrymen of the London parish of St. Stephen's Coleman Street, one

[1] J. W. F. Hill, *op. cit.*, 112–15.
[2] S. Clarke, *The lives of sundry eminent persons*, Preface.
[3] H. Smith, *The ecclesiastical history of Essex under the Long Parliament and Commonwealth*, Chelmsford, 1933, 26–7, 51.
[4] S. Clarke, *The lives of sundry eminent persons*, pt. 2, 112; *Suffolk and the Great Rebellion*, 18.
[5] *C.S.P.D. 1631–33*, 36; *ibid. 1633–34*, 444; *ibid. 1636–37*, 549–50; *ibid. 1639–40*, 104–5.
[6] *C.S.P.D. 1631–33*, 432; P.R.O. S.P. 16/224 no. 57. Cf. R. P. Stearns, *Congregationalism in the Dutch Netherlands*, Chicago, 1940; A. C. Carter, 'The ministry to the English churches in the Netherlands in the seventeenth century,' *Bulletin of the Institute of Historical Research*, XXXIII, 88 (1960); and documents printed in C. Burrage, *The early English dissenters*, 2v., Cambridge, 1912, II, App. XVII. The Merchant Adventurers churches in the Low Countries had conformed to the Dutch church with its presbyterian discipline since 1579 by agreement between the English government and the Dutch authorities.

of the few parishes in the capital that owned the presentation to its church, showed their Puritan sympathies under Charles I by appointing John Davenport and John Goodwin as vicars.[1] In York, the mayor, John Vaux, obtained the appointment in 1637 of a non-conformist, John Shaw, as lecturer of the church of All Saints. Shaw was summoned before Archbishop Neile, who declared, '. . . you are brought in by the lord mayor . . . to head the Puritan party against me, but . . . I will break Vaux and the Puritan party.'[2] The York church of St. Martin's Micklegate, whose advowson was in the hands of citizen trustees, had Puritan vicars during most of the earlier seventeenth century.[3] Several York aldermen during the '30s were Puritans, including Thomas Hoyle and Sir William Allanson, the city's future representatives in the Long Parliament. In consequence, the corporation encouraged non-conformity under Laud and petitioned against episcopacy in 1641.[4]

But all these efforts to entrench the Puritan clergy in the church through patronage were overshadowed by the ambitious scheme undertaken by the Feoffees for Impropriations. Their project gave further proof of the immense resourcefulness the Puritan movement displayed in promoting its aims despite royal and ecclesiastical disfavour. Founded in 1625 as a group of twelve unincorporated trustees, the Feoffees' object was to raise money for the purchase of impropriated tithes and other church revenue and appointments, which were to be used in the maintenance of a preaching ministry. The members, all well-known London Puritans, consisted of four clergymen, four lawyers, and four, later five, merchants. Such a venture could only have taken shape as a result of extensive consultation and planning by important laymen and ministers. There was thus good reason for the hostile contemporary judgment which traced the scheme to 'a secret combination of the brotherhood, to advance their projects;' not one man amongst them, the same writer added, 'wished well to the present government.'[5]

One of the Feoffees' rules specified that they should assist none but conformable men. This may have been a blind, however, for some whom they helped were non-conformists. Perhaps they even adopted

---

[1] E. Freshfield, 'Some remarks upon the . . . parish of St. Stephen Coleman Street . . . ,' *Archaeologia*, L (1887) and D. A. Williams, 'London Puritanism: the parish of St. Stephen Coleman Street,' *Church quarterly review*, CLX, 337 (1959).

[2] *The life of Master John Shaw*, ed. C. Jackson, *Yorkshire diaries, Surtees society*, LXV, 1877, 129.

[3] R. H. Marchant, *op. cit.*, 75–6.

[4] *Victoria county history. City of York*, 201–2.

[5] P. Heylyn, *Examen historicum*, 1659, 208–9, cited in C. Hill, *Economic problems of the church*, 255.

it for the record in the event of future legal trouble.[1] As their transactions required the avoidance of publicity, they refrained from incorporating themselves. This was cited against them by Attorney General Noy in 1633, when they were dissolved as unlawful, in proof of their policy of secrecy.[2] Their method was to retain ownership of the tithes, revenues, and appointments they acquired, and to grant them only conditionally to such clerical beneficiaries as they approved. They thus had complete discretion in selecting the recipients of their help, who in turn were wholly dependent on the Feoffees' bounty. They extended their patronage chiefly to curates and lecturers, since these, unlike beneficed men, could be appointed and removed without episcopal permission. By this expedient they were able to function with almost complete freedom from interference by the church officials.[3]

In their eight years of existence, the Feoffees' achievement was an impressive one. According to their accounts, they received more than £6,300, almost all of it in contributions from sympathizers. The smallest individual gift was six shillings, the largest £500, some hundreds of men and women having provided donations and legacies to further their work. With this money, the Feoffees bought impropriations, advowsons, and nominations of curacies, lectureships, and school masters in numerous counties. Their greatest acquisition was the nomination of the six lecturers of St. Antholin's London, an old and famous lectureship, which they obtained from the vestry of the parish in 1628. The fact that the rector of the church, Charles Offspring, was a Feoffee, no doubt facilitated this notable transaction. Another piece of patronage was the impropriation of the vicarage of Presteigne in Herefordshire, which they bought from Sir Robert Harley for £1,400 at ten years purchase. Sir Robert added the advowson gratis.[4]

That a group of Puritans should dispose of patronage on such a scale was manifestly dangerous to the crown and the ecclesiastical order alike. Accordingly, in 1632 the government, spurred on by Laud, proceeded against the Feoffees in the Court of Exchequer,

[1] *Activities of the Puritan faction of the Church of England 1625–33*, ed. I. Calder, L., 1957, 55–6, 82. This book prints the documents in the Exchequer case against the Feoffees, from which almost all that is known of them has to be derived. Cf. also the accounts by E. Kirby, 'The lay feoffees: a study in militant Puritanism,' *Journal of modern history*, XIV, 1 (1942), I. Calder, 'A seventeenth century attempt to purify the Anglican church,' *American historical review*, LIII, 4 (1948), and C. Hill, *Economic problems of the church*, ch. XI.

[2] *Activities of the Puritan faction of the Church of England*, 54, 78.

[3] *Ibid.*, 50, 52.

[4] *Ibid.*, 28–36, 37–42, 85.

charging them with acting illegally as a corporation and usurping on the King's regality. Policy rather than law was the real issue and Attorney General Noy drew forcible attention to the implications of the Feoffees' aims. '. . . to what end tendeth this?', he asked.

If they goe this way to buy up all impropriations, They may get almost halfe the Churches in England. . . . They might come to be supreme Patrons. . . . And to make great a number of Clergy men dependant on them to follow their wills. . . . They place men in eminent places, meane places they doe not ayme at, But London, Hertford, Cirencester, Shrewsburye, Dunwich, and good Borough townes.

Moreover, as he showed with examples, 'their eyes are upon factious men . . . such they deall with, and labor to uphold.'[1]

The Exchequer judges reinforced Noy's argument in rendering judgment against the Feoffees. '. . . for a Corporation,' declared Baron Trevor,

or theis men that are like a Corporation, to ioyne together to get into their hands a multitude of Church livings to dispose as they please, this is to beare a great stroak in the Comonwealth, and it tendeth to make a new Church, A Church in a Church. It is so great a matter as it toucheth the Kings aucthority.[2]

A vigilant government thus frustrated the scheme the Feoffees had at heart. To their Puritan contributors and well-wishers the Feoffees' dissolution with the loss of all the patronage they had acquired must have come as a heavy blow. It taught the lesson that methods of private enterprise and unofficial initiative must fail against the hostility of the regime. Viewing the destruction of their pious work, politically conscious men could only have concluded that the power of the state itself must be in friendly hands if the cause of religion were to be made secure and flourishing.

4

It is much harder to form a conception of the Puritan laity outside the privileged elite of wealth and status. We can sometimes see as individual beings the gentlemen and prosperous citizens who left some record of their spiritual journey; whereas the poor and inferior we have perforce to look at mostly in the mass, though now and again the darkness that encircles them is lighted up by a surviving bit of evidence. These largely unknown men and women were 'the Religious

---

[1] *Ibid.*, 51, 53, 61, 82.   [2] *Ibid.*, 113.

serious People' whom Richard Baxter knew from his own experience of ministering to them, who had

a suspicion of all that is Ceremonious in Gods Service, and of all which they find not warrant for in Scripture, and a greater inclination to a rational convincing earnest way of Preaching and Prayers, than to the written Forms of Words, which are to be read in Churches. And they are greatly taken with a Preacher that speaketh to them in a familiar natural Language and exhorteth them as if it were for their Lives. . . .[1]

In short, they were Puritans, with a spiritual outlook probably no way different from the Puritan laity superior to them in worldly station or riches. We discover such men in the two hundred yeomen of Essex parishes who petitioned King James in behalf of the nonconformist clergy.[2] We meet them in a minister's description of the Puritan people that 'do heare sermons, talke of the scriptures, singe Psalmes together in private houses. . . .'[3] We see them in Baxter's industrious flock of weavers at Kidderminster who 'as they stand in their Loom . . . can set a Book before them, or edifie one another.'[4] We notice their zeal in religious exercises in an account composed by the Rev. Samuel Clarke of his ministry in the late 1620s in a part of Cheshire where he was almost the only preacher. Lacking a regular benefice, he was maintained by voluntary offerings, and Sunday by Sunday the people came to hear him in all weathers. Every three weeks he held a day of conference for Scripture discussion and prayer, 'unto which repaired all the Professors, both Men and Women, out of all the Country.' 'I was never acquainted,' Clarke recorded, 'with more understanding Christians in all my Life, though the best of them went but in Russet Coats, and followed Husbandry.'[5]

The sermon had far the strongest effect in forming the religious personality of the Puritan people. On Sundays Englishmen were at church, and many attended at least once more in the week as well if there were a lecture to supplement the work of the Sabbath. In that plain, practical preaching which was a calculated point of style with Puritan clergymen, their congregations had set before them the great epic of the spirit—the radical depravity of man, free grace and the election of the saints, God's covenant with the chosen ones, their perseverance, sanctification, and glory. Sermons of this kind, diversi-

---

[1] R. Baxter, *Reliquiae Baxterianae*, 1696, pt. I, 32.
[2] H. Smith, *op. cit.*, 19–20.
[3] Josias Nichols, *The plea of the innocent*, 1602, 12.
[4] R. Baxter, *op. cit.*, pt. I, 89.
[5] S. Clarke, *The lives of sundry eminent persons*, Preface, which contains a narrative of the author's life.

fied by forceful disquisitions on moral duties, displaying frequently a strong common sense and a keen perception into the psychological condition of the soul fearful and uncertain of its salvation—these were the staple of the Puritan pulpit. Never was there a more verte-brate faith, a tougher moral and social discipline, than that which the Puritan preachers inculcated in their auditories.[1] It could act on the souls of common men with consoling assurance, fortifying their self-respect according to a divine standard above the judgments of the world.

An indication of its educative power may be gathered from a memoir by William Kiffin, who experienced it fully as a young apprentice. In 1629 at the age of thirteen, Kiffin, later to become a wealthy merchant, was bound in London to a 'mean calling.' Two years after he began to consider his spiritual state and fell into a deep melancholy. It was the Puritan preachers who sustained and helped him in his depression. At St. Antholin's, where there was a lecture six mornings a week, he heard Thomas Foxley and John Norton. At St. Stephen's Coleman Street he drew comfort from the sermons of John Davenport and John Goodwin. All these lights of the Puritan ministry were to feel the persecution of Archbishop Laud. Several apprentice friends shared Kiffin's religious concerns, and 'our constant practice,' he said, was

to attend the morning lecture, which began at six o'clock. We also appointed to meet together an hour before service, to spend it in praying, and in communicating to each other what experience we had received from the Lord; or else to repeat some sermon which we had heard before.[2]

So did the clergy effect the youth's conversion to the narrow way of faith. Kiffin's history belonged to the authentic milieu of the Puritanism of the inferior order: the life of hard work, the bareness and discipline, and the relief which the consolations of spiritual achievement gave to straitened circumstances.

It would be easier to judge the impact of Puritanism within the humbler strata of society if it were possible to estimate the extent of literacy at this period. For second only to the pulpit as a factor in the spread of Puritan sympathies were the scores of books of practical

[1] Cf. the account of the Puritan preachers and their work in W. Haller, *op. cit.* Useful observations are also contained in W. F. Mitchell, *English pulpit oratory from Andrewes to Tillotson*, L., 1932.

[2] *Remarkable passages in the life of William Kiffin*, ed. W. Orme, L., 1823, 4–12. An account of the St. Antholin's sermons which Kiffin attended is given by I. Calder, 'The St. Antholin lectures,' *Church quarterly review*, CLX, 334 (1959).

divinity and of religious and moral exhortation written by the clergy, as well as the Bible itself viewed through the glass of Puritan interpretation. The works of divines like William Perkins, Richard Sibbes, and John Preston, were widely read and offered both instruction and comfort to people of every condition. They did not, of course, touch the controversies that were dividing the body politic, but their temper and teachings were infinitely remote from the theology and ritualism of the Laudian church and from the religious sensibility prevalent around Charles I and Henrietta Maria. The men and women nursed at the breasts of the Puritan writers could have felt only hostility at the course of religion and politics under the first two Stuart kings.

Possibly the literacy of the humbler laity, and hence its access to such books, was more widespread than might be supposed in a society where inequality was so pronounced.[1] In quantitative terms, benefactions for education rose enormously during the earlier seventeenth century, a goodly proportion of the donors being merchants of Puritan persuasion. One consequence was the endowment of many new grammar schools.[2] These, of course, taught Latin and Greek, not English; but their growth may also have reflected an increased opportunity of other kind for poor and middle people to acquire a degree of literacy. Nehemiah Wallington, an anti-prelatical London craftsman, studied Richard Sibbes's The *bruised reed*, Thomas Beard's *Theatre of God's judgements*, and the Geneva translation of the Bible.[3] Kiffin, the young apprentice, drew strength from reading Thomas Goodwin's *Childe of light* and Thomas Hooker's *The souls preparation for Christ*; and it must be assumed that boys like him put into trade could read and write, however they learned to do so. Moreover, the torrential output of pamphlets during the revolution would be inexplicable without the existence of a substantial readership among the great London populace.

Literacy, however, was not essential to holding strong views on religion. In 1641, when many parishes were petitioning a sympathetic parliament against Laud's ceremonial innovations, some of the protesters could not write their names. From Kent came denunciation of clergymen who required the people to 'cringe and bowe' at the name of Jesus, who introduced 'superstitious ceremonyes,' and who abused their opposers as 'itching Puritans.' The authors of these

[1] This has been suggested for the fifteenth and sixteenth centuries by J. W. Adamson, 'The extent of literacy in England in the fifteenth and sixteenth centuries: notes and conjectures,' *The library*, 4th ser., X, 2 (1929).
[2] Cf. W. K. Jordan, *Philanthropy in England*, 281–91.
[3] N. Wallington, *Historical notices*, ed. R. Webb, 2v., L., 1869, I, xxv. Wallington, a turner, kept a shop in Eastcheap.

complaints, obscure church wardens, parish constables, and over-
seers, being illiterate, had to make their mark.[1]

Had Puritanism a determinate basis in the social structure? Was
it bound up with a particular kind of economic existence? Were
sympathy for the non-conforming clergy, dislike of ceremonies and
bishops, responsiveness to Puritan moral preachment determined by
social situation? It must be answered at once that any connections of
this sort except of the most general and tenuous kind would be
extremely difficult to prove; while to demonstrate a causal relation
between Puritanism and status or class would be even harder.

What seems least disputable concerning the social incidence of
Puritanism is that it was greatest in the towns and trading part of the
nation. On this the judgment of both contemporaries and most
modern historians concur. The Arminian Richard Montague, for
instance, called Coventry 'a second Geneva,' and an associate of
Laud characteristically remarked, '. . . where are all these pestilent
nests of Puritans hatched, but in corporations, where they swarm and
breed like hornets in a [dead] horse's head.'[2] Similarly, A. F. Scott
Pearson expressed the common opinion of modern scholars in stating
that the majority of Puritan adherents were to be found in the towns.[3]
It has further been noted that Puritanism flourished especially in the
textile districts—in places such as Essex, Suffolk, Norfolk, Warwick,
the West Riding of Yorkshire, and parts of Somerset, Wiltshire, and
Lancashire: so much so that one writer has even asked, 'why was
industrial England Puritan England.'[4] To this may be added that
some of these Puritan areas also had a long history of receptiveness
to heresy. The parts of Essex about Colchester and Dedham where
Puritanism took root were formerly centres of Lollardy and early
Lutheranism. Moreover, most of the county's victims in the Marian
persecutions derived from there.[5] This was true as well of the textile
communities in the West Riding, which having previously shown

---

[1] *Proceedings in Kent*, ed. L. B. Larking, *Camden society*, LXXX, 1861,
102ff., *passim*.

[2] *The correspondence of John Cosin*, 66; *C.S.P.D. 1639–40*, 515–20.

[3] A. F. Scott Pearson, *Church & state*, 104–5; cf. C. Hill, *Society and
Puritanism in pre-revolutionary England*, 235–6, for the same view that the
Puritan appeal was especially to the urban middle class and 'industrious'
people.

[4] G. C. Homans, 'The Puritans and the clothing industry in England,' *New
England quarterly*, XVI, 3 (1940). The Puritanism of the Lancashire textile
towns has been stressed by F. Walker, *Historical geography of Southwest
Lancashire*, *Chetham society*, n.s., CIII, 1939, 76–7. On Yorkshire, cf. R. H.
Marchant, *op. cit.*, 51 and M. E. François, 'The social and economic
development of Halifax 1558–1640,' *Proceedings of the Leeds philosophical
and literary society. Literary and historical section*, XI, pt. VIII (1966), 271–7.

[5] H. Smith, *op. cit.*, 6.

themselves hospitable to Lollard and Protestant beliefs, then became strongly Puritan under Elizabeth and the early Stuarts.[1]

That Puritanism exercised a strong appeal to the citizen element is explicable both on social and psychological grounds. Its members, even the wealthy who enjoyed the privileges of town rule, held an inferior position by the aristocratic standards of the society. To them the doctrines of election and the covenant, a religion of personal experience sealed by conversion, must have given a powerful access of esteem and consciousness of worth. The moral code taught by the Puritan ministers would have had the same effect. That code was not one, as has sometimes been thought, which sanctioned capitalist acquisitiveness. It stressed, rather, the religious and ethical value of work in one's calling, and exalted habits of sobriety, decorum, and self-discipline in all stations of life.[2] It rigorously subjected worldly activity to religious ends, thereby investing such activity, when conducted under proper restraints, with genuine spiritual significance.[3] Possibly it also provided the middle people with a subjectively secure ground from which to direct their moral opprobrium and indignation at the Court way of life so alien to their own.[4]

However, the tendency of Puritanism to take root in the town was no more than that. Certainly, not all citizens were Puritans, and there is no way of knowing whether even most were. Moreover, the Puritan laity included, as has been seen, numerous persons belonging to the aristocratic order as well as others of inferior status who lived by husbandry. As to the dissemination of Puritanism in the textile districts, this was probably due to causes not directly related to the social structure. The East Anglian and Yorkshire areas which became successively centres of Lollard, Protestant, and Puritan sympathies were particularly susceptible by geographic situation and commercial intercourse to continental influence. They were thus easily accessible

---

[1] A. G. Dickens, *Lollards and Protestants in the diocese of York*, L., 1959 247–8.

[2] Cf. the account of Calvinist Puritanism as a work ethic, rather than a capitalist ethic, by C. H. George, 'English Calvinist opinion on usury, 1600–1640,' *Journal of the history of ideas*, XVIII, 4 (1959) and the discussion of the calling in C. H. and K. George, *The Protestant mind of the English reformation*, 169–72.

[3] The affinity between Puritanism and burgher values appears clearly in William Scott's *An essay of drapery, or the compleate citizen*, 1635, ed. S. Thrupp, Cambridge, 1953. Described as 'the first substantial . . . writing known in English that exalts business as a career' (*ibid.*, 1), Scott's tract gives emphatic expression to the conception of trade as a calling and discipline in the world, while also advocating cultural pursuits as both profitable and pleasant to the merchant.

[4] Cf. S. Ranulf, *Moral indignation and middle class psychology*, Copenhagen, 1938.

to the heresies appearing on the continent, especially those coming out of the Low Countries and Germany. Lollardy was largely indigenous; but Lutheranism and Calvinism found their earliest hospitality in England among the eastern communities and ports in closest contact with the Netherlands and the lower Rhine. Religious influences from the continent became even stronger in the later sixteenth century, as refugee industrial groups in flight from the Catholic repression in France and the Netherlands arrived in England. The Fleming and Walloon craftsmen who brought the manufacture of the New Draperies to Essex, Suffolk, and Norfolk also carried with them their Calvinist church polity and worship which they continued to practise with the permission of Queen Elizabeth and James I. Residing for decades in those counties, they must certainly have promoted the spread of extreme Protestant beliefs. It was no wonder that Archbishop Laud, seeing a cause of infection in the foreign congregations, determined to break them up and make their members attend the parish churches under episcopal jurisdiction.

In truth, whatever its particular appeals, the sway of Puritanism extended over a broad social spectrum of the laity. Though it doubtless flourished more in the urban, citizen environment, it was by no means limited to the latter. This constituted a fundamental feature of its political significance. Religion here became the bond uniting a large, composite mass of the laity in common sympathies and antagonisms. It cut across diversities of status and neighbourhood to form a movement of high and low that was potentially revolutionary if once roused to wrathful resistance. Puritanism thus resembled the part played previously by Calvinism in engendering the revolutionary parties of France and the Netherlands in the sixteenth century.[1] But while in the Netherlands rebellion and the French wars of religion Protestantism had been fighting a life-and-death struggle for survival, there was no such issue at stake in England, where a Protestant state church had existed since Elizabeth's time. It should have been one of the foremost tasks of Stuart rule to deal cautiously and moderately with the Puritans in the established church. Instead, by his support of Laud's severity against them, Charles I drove the Puritans to revolt. In this way the opposition to his policies became for many people a holy war involving not only the liberty of the subject and the future of parliament, but even the fate of religion itself.

---

[1] Cf. H. Koenigsberger, 'The organization of revolutionary parties in France and the Netherlands during the sixteenth century,' *loc. cit.* and R. M. Kingdon, 'The political resistance of the Calvinists in France and the Low Countries,' *loc. cit.*

If not for Archbishop Laud's administration, Puritanism might have continued to live in its restless and uneasy peace within the Church of England. Troublesome as the ecclesiastical authorities found non-conformity to be, it was nevertheless a long-established trend in religious life which they might have contained and controlled as they had done in the past. Certainly, Puritanism was too rooted and widespread for any policy to succeed that aimed at extirpating or silencing it. Just this, however, is what Laud, with the crown's endorsement, set out to do.

The nature of the Laudian rule must be correctly stated, for it was not its intolerance as such that made it hateful. The Puritans were themselves intolerant; had they possessed the power, most would not have hesitated to silence their opponents. But Laud's programme signified in certain respects an abandonment of the Protestant foundations of the national church as fixed in the Elizabethan settlement now three generations old. Hence it awoke the fears not only of the Puritans, but of all those Anglicans—and they were the majority—who could not share the archbishop's prepossessions, driving the two into a common front. Indeed, it permitted the Puritans to stand forth as the champions-in-chief of English Protestantism threatened by what appeared an attempt to subvert it from within.

The Laudians constituted an Anglo-Catholic or High Church party in the Anglican establishment.[1] Because they repudiated the doctrine of predestination, they were known to their enemies as Arminians, after the theologian, Jacobus Arminius and his disciples, the intellectual critics of Calvinist orthodoxy in the Dutch Republic during the early seventeenth century. The Laudians, however, were not influenced by Arminius, nor was the religious latitudinarianism and rationalism which animated Dutch Arminianism characteristic of their outlook. 'Anglo-Catholic' and 'High Church,' accordingly, describe their position much more appropriately.[2]

---

[1] 'Anglo-Catholic' is used by A. W. Harrison, *Arminianism*, L., 1937, 132 and W. K. Jordan, *The development of religious toleration in England*, II, 115–16, 'High Church' by W. R. Fryer, 'The High Churchmen of the earlier seventeenth century,' *Renaissance and modern studies*, V (1961). In calling the Laudians Anglo-Catholics, I am mindful of their differences from the Anglo-Catholic tractarians of the nineteenth century, which are well brought out in *ibid.*, 115–16.

[2] Both W. K. Jordan, *The development of religious toleration in England*, II, 115 and W. R. Fryer, *op. cit.*, App. A, recognize the inapplicability of the term 'Arminian' to the Laudians. It is worth noting as an instance that Richard Montague, one of the best known Arminian churchmen, said in

Puritanism

The Anglo-Catholicism of the Laudians represented a high clericalist reaction in the church and a reaching out towards a conception of catholicity in which Rome and Canterbury could both share. The jettisoning of Calvinist theology was a necessary phase of the movement. For of all the creeds to emerge from the Reformation, Calvinism alone appeared as a comprehensive and systematized structure standing in uncompromising antithesis at every point to the teachings of Rome. Owing to this immense achievement, Calvinism became the greatest intellectual influence in European Protestantism, its sway extending beyond as well as within the Reformed churches. On the theological side, and apart from issues of ecclesiastical polity, the Church of England itself was largely Calvinistic. Most Elizabethan divines regarded predestination and election as points of orthodoxy, interpreting the Thirty-Nine Articles in that sense; and though these doctrines never became canonical, they received a quasi-authoritative expression in the Lambeth Articles of 1595.[1] The prevalence of Calvinistic theology persisted into the seventeenth century. The religious controversies of the Dutch republic were observed from England with close interest, and the churchmen whom King James sent to the Synod of Dort in 1618 took part with the majority in condemning the Arminians.[2] Predestination was commonly thought fundamental to Protestant belief. By denying free-will in man to obtain merit before God, it humbled the sinful pride of human nature and exalted God's incomprehensible power and mercy. It left no slightest room for the apparatus of priestly intercession and sacramentalism which the Roman church provided to help believers to salvation. Thus when Anglo-Catholics rejected predestination, they rejected a tenet long received in the Anglican church and supposed to be essential in differentiating Protestant from Catholic principles. It was from this standpoint that in 1629 a sub-committee on religion of the House of Commons condemned Arminianism as contrary to the doctrine publicly professed in the Church of England and all reformed churches.[3]

Their enemies grossly libelled and gravely misinterpreted the Anglo-Catholics when they called them papists. Yet Laud, Richard

[1] Cf. the excellent account of the Elizabethan controversy over predestination and assurance of election by H. C. Porter, *Reformation and reaction in Tudor Cambridge*, Cambridge, 1958, chs. 13–16.

[2] The disputes within Dutch Calvinism are described by D. Nobbs, *Theocracy and toleration*, Cambridge, 1938.

[3] Printed in S. R. Gardiner, *Constitutional documents of the Puritan revolution*, 80–1.

1626 that he had only just read Arminius for the first time. He added: 'The man had more in him than all the Netherlands.' (*Correspondence of John Cosin*, I, 90.)

Montague, John Cosin, and other doctors of the school felt a nostalgia for the ancient catholicity of an undivided church which the militant, embattled Protestantism of their time did not share and could not fail to misunderstand. They held that Rome for all its errors was a true church in which salvation was possible; and they showed a warmer interest in the practices of Roman Catholic worship than for the other Protestant communions of Europe. Devoted to ritual, they imitated Rome by introducing ceremonies emblematic of the believers' adoration of the holy mysteries of religion. They liked crossings and bowings, candles and incense; they cared much more for liturgy and sacrament than for edification through preaching; and they turned the communion table into an altar surrounded by a rail, at which they required communicants to kneel. These ceremonial innovations ran counter to Anglican tradition and gave great offence. The Anglo-Catholics called them decency and order; their enemies, idolatry, superstition, and popery.

Finally, the Anglo-Catholics took a different view of episcopacy from that prevailing earlier in the Anglican church. They did not merely justify the episcopate as an institution sanctioned by historic tradition and expedient to the monarchical regime. They exalted it as a divinely commissioned order appointed by God to be the stay of religion and the church. His external legal jurisdiction, said Laud, he and all bishops derive from the King; 'but my order, my calling, my jurisdiction *in foro conscientiae*, that is from God and from Christ, and by divine and apostolical right.'[1] It was for the bishops and their clergy to proclaim religious truth and what was to be publicly professed; it was for the laity to hearken and obey. Nothing was better calculated to release the spring of anti-clericalism in Puritan and non-Puritan alike. In fact, by these pretensions the Anglo-Catholics brought obloquy and ruin upon the episcopacy they wished most dearly to uphold.

The Anglo-Catholics, though a minority, were able to enforce their dictates because they possessed Charles I's support. Laud's highest goal was an outward uniformity and order, and he imagined that severity could establish the peace of the church. He set out to suppress the Puritans as disturbers of religion and enemies to monarchy. It was only natural that the Anglo-Catholic divines should exalt the crown's powers to the fullest. '. . . defend thou me with the sword,' Richard Montague addressed the King in *Apello Caesarem* (1625), 'and I will defend thee with the pen.' Other clergy of the party preached compliance with forced loans and royal exactions as a religious duty.[2] If their doctrines were true,

[1] Cited in W. R. Fryer, *op. cit.*, 135–6.
[2] Cf. Robert Sibthorpe, *Apostolike obedience*, 1627; Roger Manwaring,

said the oppositionist, John Selden, 'there is no *meum* or *tuum* in England.'[1]

Inevitably, Puritan and moderate Anglican opposition to the Anglo-Catholics merged with the Country's political opposition to Charles I. Their coalescence occurred as the direct consequence of the alliance between the crown and Anglo-Catholics. In the first three parliaments of the reign Country supporters led the House of Commons in a repeated hue-and-cry against the High Churchmen.[2] Not the least of the causes inflaming hostility was the favour Charles showed them. He protected them from parliament's anger and gave them preferment. In 1628, Montague received the bishopric of Chichester; the Anglo-Catholic Neile was translated from Durham to Winchester and thence to York in 1632; Laud, already the governing influence in the church, went to London in 1629 and four years later to Canterbury; Roger Manwaring, a notorious object of parliament's displeasure, became bishop of St. David's in 1635; Matthew Wren was appointed to Hereford in 1635 and next year to Norwich.

In full control during the '30s, the Laudians crowned their dominance by the canons which the clerical convocation passed in the spring of 1640. These enacted their programme into ecclesiastical law binding clergy and laity alike. They prescribed the ceremonial practices the archbishop favoured, and they imposed an oath on ministers and various classes of laymen promising never 'to alter the government of this Church by archbishops, bishops, deans, and archdeacons, &c. as it stands now ... and as by right it ought to stand. ...'[3] The canons were the Laudians' last act before the rage of the Long Parliament drove them from power.

Because of Charles's patronage of the Anglo-Catholics, 'Puritan' turned into a catchword covering every form of opposition to the regime. This only confused its meaning further, but was nevertheless a clear indication that the religious and political struggles had become completely identified with one another. Oppositionists charged in parliament that the Arminians 'under the name of Puritanes ... collecteth the greatest parte of the King's true subjects. ...'; and that 'to be an honest man is now to be a Puritan. ...'[4]

---

[1] *D.N.B.*, *s.v.* 'Robert Sibthorp.'
[2] Cf. the account of parliamentary attacks on the Anglo-Catholic clergy in W. K. Jordan, *The development of religious toleration in England*, II, 117–29.
[3] H. Gee and W. J. Hardy, *Documents illustrative of English church history* L., ed. 1921, 535–6.
[4] *Commons debates in 1625*, App., 180–4; *Commons debates, 1629*, 178.

Religion and allegiance, 1627; cf. the discussion of the political opinions of the Anglo-Catholic clergy in J. W. Allen, *op. cit.*, pt. II, ch. IX and M. Judson, *op. cit.*, ch. V.

On the other hand, the Laudian view held that 'Puritanism is the root of all rebellious and disobedient intractableness in Parliament . . . and all schism and sauciness in the country. . . .'[1]

In 1641, with revolution under way, the consequences of labelling all opposition as Puritanism were astutely described by Henry Parker, one of the keenest writers of the time. 'Puritans,' he pointed out, '. . . were at first Ecclesiasticall only . . . but now it is come about, that by a new enlargement of the name, the world is full of nothing else but Puritans. . . .' Thus,

whole Kingdoms are familiarly upbrayded with this sinne of Puritanisme: As for example, All in Scotland, who wish well to the Covenant, though some Papists, some Courtiers, and almost all the whole body without exception have now declared themselves for it, yet all these are manifest Puritans. So also in England, all the Commons in Parliament, and almost all the ancient impartiall temporall Nobility, and all such as favour . . . the late proceedings of both the houses, which is the mayne body of the Realme . . . all these are Puritans. They which deprave this great Councell of the Kingdome, suggest to the King that the major part is gull'd . . . by the Puritan party. . . .

In fact, Parker suggested, the Scottish rebellion, the eleven-year cessation of parliaments in England, and the King's estrangement from his subjects were 'all caused by the abusive mistake and injurious misapplication of this word *Puritan*.'[2] His analysis attested that hostility to the government, become well-nigh universal, extended far beyond the Puritans. It attested, too, that Charles's policies had forced every sort of antagonism into a united front of disaffection.

6

Religious controversy in the pre-revolutionary years took on an almost unprecedented bitterness. Puritan rancour towards the church hierarchy found vent in incendiary writings by men willing and eager to undergo martyrdom for their beliefs. The anti-prelatical pamphlets of William Prynne, Alexander Leighton, John Bastwick, and Henry Burton expressed an implacable hatred, testifying that a spirit of unrelenting fanaticism was loose in the land.[3] Councillors might

---

[1] *C.S.P.D. 1629–31*, 411.

[2] [Henry Parker], *A discourse concerning Puritans*, [January] 1641, 10–11, 41–2.

[3] Cf. the account of these writings by W. Haller, *op. cit.*, ch. VII. The nature of Prynne's attitude toward the Laudian clergy is discussed by W. M. Lamont, *Marginal Prynne*, L., 1963, ch. I.

well have reminded themselves of Bacon's warning that religious innovation was a main cause of disturbance in states. Despite their execrations on 'Popish Arminians,' these works steadfastly, and doubtless sincerely, avowed their authors' loyalty to the King. Yet they could only have had the effect upon sympathetic readers of discrediting the crown for its support of the Anglo-Catholic party in the church.

The government found it impossible to stop such writings. The Court of High Commission, charged with enforcement of the crown's ecclesiastical supremacy, dealt with religious dissent; while the Court of Star Chamber had jurisdiction over the press and could punish the publication of unlicensed works.[1] The boldness of authors and printers, however, defeated censorship and attempts at suppression. Produced secretly at home, or else smuggled into England from Dutch presses abroad, anti-Laudian propaganda circulated along a transmission belt of Puritan sympathizers in London and other towns. In 1637, for instance, a wax chandler of St. Clement Danes parish in the capital was brought before the High Commission for selling prohibited books by Bastwick and others, and a Gloucester clothier was accused of receiving a hundred copies of Prynne's *News From Ipswich* to dispose in the neighbourhood at eightpence apiece.[2] A Norwich citizen was examined on suspicion of distributing *News From Ipswich* and *The Divine Tragedie*, another of Prynne's tracts. It appeared that he got fifty copies of both in London from one, Stephen Moor, 'a packer of stuffs in Philpot Lane.'[3] John Lilburne, then a London apprentice and soon to emerge as the greatest agitator of the revolution, first tasted persecution in 1637 when the Star Chamber sentenced him to prison, whipping, and the pillory for importing seditious books from Holland.[4]

Since the government could not suppress anti-prelatical pamphlets, it retaliated by punishing the authors. Bastwick, Burton, and Prynne became the most notorious victims of the repression of Puritanism by the King's prerogative tribunals, the High Commission and the Star Chamber. Of the three, only Burton was a clergyman; Bastwick was a physician, Prynne a lawyer. All, however, had attacked the Arminian clergy and bishops with envenomed pens. After several less grave encounters with the law, they were brought into the Star Chamber in 1637 charged with seditious libel. They were convicted,

[1] Cf. F. S. Siebert, *Freedom of the press in England 1476–1776*, Urbana, 1952, chs. 5–7.
[2] *C.S.P.D. 1636–37*, 546; *The court and times of Charles I*, II, 273–4.
[3] *C.S.P.D. 1636–37*, 427.
[4] Lilburne arranged to print Bastwick's *The letany of John Bastwick* in Holland and then brought it into England.

sentenced to have their ears cut off and ordered committed to distant prisons. Such were their provocations that they must have expected severe punishment and even desired it in order to bear witness to their faith. When it came upon them, they embraced it with the zeal of martyrs. Their bearing turned the scene into a demonstration of their own righteousness before the unchristian cruelty of their judges. A wave of sympathy went out to them from the spectators, and later from the crowds who gathered to see them on their way to prison. When Prynne passed Chester, his well-wishers were so many that the ecclesiastical authorities threatened some with punishment. At Coventry, the citizens' warm reception of Burton caused a *quo warranto* proceeding to be instituted against the town's charter.[1] It was said that the brand of S.L. for *Seditious Libeller* burned on Prynne's cheek really stood for *Sion's Lawyer*. 'You may say what you wil,' wrote one of his sympathizers in Essex, 'the King hath a wife, and he loves her wel, and she is a papist and we must al be of her Religion, and thats the thing the Bishops aime at. . . .'[2]

The harsh treatment of dissent by the Star Chamber and High Commission brought both tribunals into discredit. Such cases were merely a small fraction of their judicial business, but they left a strong impression on the public mind. The Star Chamber, in particular, long considered by English legal opinion as a court of the highest dignity in Christendom, declined in reputation. Its identification with the policy of Laud, who sat as a judge with the other privy councillors and did not hesitate to shed blood, helped make it unpopular.[3] The High Commission, on the other hand, had always possessed a questionable reputation. Under Elizabeth and James, Puritan clergymen and common lawyers denied its legality and attacked its procedures and jurisdiction. These assaults were repelled, so that the court was never busier than in Charles's reign. Moral delinquencies and Catholic recusancy occupied far more of its time than non-conformity. Yet its role in the religious repression and its power to fine and imprison even laymen without appeal reinforced its image as the epitome of clerical injustice and arrogance.[4] No institution was more detested in the '30s. Probably many would have echoed the sentiments of a

---

[1] Edward Burghall, *Providence improved*, ed. J. Hall, *Lancashire and Cheshire record society*, XIX, 1889, 13; *C.S.P.D. 1638–39*, 142; *H.M.C. House of Lords, XI, Addenda 1514–1714*, 380.

[2] *Winthrop papers*, III, 486.

[3] Cf. H. E. I. Phillips, 'The last years of the Court of Star Chamber 1630–41,' *Transactions of the Royal Historical Society*, 4th ser., XXI, 1939.

[4] R. G. Usher, *The rise and fall of the High Commission*, Oxford, 1913. Usher greatly underestimates the extent of opposition to the court over the years preceding its abolition.

prominent Northumberland gentleman haled before it in 1633 who hoped that

if ever a parliament came . . . it would pull downe and abate the pride of the usurping bishops. . . . for these courtes . . . are but bawdy courtes, and merely to oppresse people and get monie for themselves.[1]

Ever since Queen Elizabeth's time, the Puritans' enemies had warned that their attacks on the church would lead to revolution. Whitgift, Bancroft, and Laud all considered them potential rebels who, as Laud said about Prynne and his fellows, 'do but begin with the Church, that they might after have freer access to the State. . . .'[2] This was a plausible opinion in the sixteenth century because of the affinity between Elizabethan Puritanism and the beleaguered Calvinist parties in Scotland, France, and the Netherlands. The theorists of these parties expounded a right of resistance to princes; and since Calvinism was an international movement, Bancroft attributed the same doctrine to the English Puritans. He taxed them with taking over the 'most strange and rebellious propositions' of Buchanan's *De jure regni apud Scotos*, Beza's *De jure magistratuum in subditos*, and the *Vindiciae contra tyrannos*. '. . . your drift,' he charged Cartwright on trial before the High Commission in 1591, '. . . is to bring in the further reformacion against the Princes will by force and armes.'[3]

It was indeed true that two of Calvin's English disciples, Christopher Goodman and John Ponet, had written boldly in justification of rebellion against ungodly rulers. That, however, was in relation to the Catholic reign of Elizabeth's sister, Mary, and her husband, Philip II of Spain.[4] After Elizabeth's accession no such doctrine was ever maintained by any Puritan advocate, and for more than seventy-five years the non-conformists remained at one with English Protestantism in upholding the duty of obedience and non-resistance to princes. Even under the tribulations of the Laudian rule they continued to adhere to this position.

---

[1] This was the case of Robert Brandling, previously sheriff of the county, who was cited before the High Commission at Durham for adultery and other misdemeanours; *The acts of the High Commission Court within the diocese of Durham*, 64.

[2] *The earl of Strafforde's letters*, II, 101.

[3] A. F. Scott Pearson, *Thomas Cartwright and Elizabethan Puritanism*, 462; *Church & state*, 89–90.

[4] Christopher Goodman, *How superior powers ought to be obeyed*, 1558 (published in Geneva); John Ponet, *A short treatise of politike power*, 1556; cf. the discussion of these writings by J. W. Allen, *Political thought in the sixteenth century*, 116–20.

The Court and the Country

The views of the London minister, Henry Burton, one of Laud's victims, were typical of the Puritan attitude. Intemperately as he condemned the prelates, his political professions were of quite another character. The little liberalism they possessed appeared only incidentally. In a writing addressed to the parliament of 1628, for instance, he warned 'The Lay Elders of Israel' against the 'Arminian Papists' who 'daily creep into high favour in Court,' telling the King he is omnipotent and not bound by laws.[1] Or again, in 1636 he referred to 'the mutual stipulation in covenant which the King and his subjects make at his coronation,' and called the Petition of Right a 'solemn covenant.'[2] Such assertions that the King was under law were political commonplaces and not in the least novel. Moreover, Burton joined them to emphatic declarations of the duty of subjection and non-resistance. Even commands contrary to God's law, though they ought to be disobeyed, were no justification for rebellion. 'It is one thing,' he said,

not to obey; and another to be rebellious: Superiors ought not to be obeyed, if they command against God. Yet this is no rebellion—where men are ready to yield passive obedience to their unjust cruelty, by not resisting it; though they detest, and deny active obedience, to their unjust commands. . . . Thus all God's true-bred children have, and will do.[3]

John Lilburne held the same position. Writing in 1639 as a martyr to the prelates' rage, he declared that the King's authority is from God, so that to disobey it is to disobey God. If the King commands something against God's work, he would refuse obedience and submit his body for punishment: 'for I doe hold it unlawfull for any of Gods people, in their greatest Oppression by the Majestrate, to rebell or take up any Temporall armes. . . .'[4]

Burton and Lilburne were only restating the traditional doctrine of English Protestantism respecting the limits of obedience. It could provide a religious rationale for defiance of the Laudian hierarchy. Politically, however, it was at most a basis for obstruction, never for revolution.

Yet just as in the sixteenth century the restraints which European Calvinism maintained against resistance gave way under the sword of Catholic persecution, so was the same pattern soon to repeat itself

---

[1] Henry Burton, *Israel's fast*, 1628, Prefatory epistle, cited in B. Hanbury, *op. cit.*, I, 481–3.

[2] Henry Burton, *For God and the King*, 1636, cited in *ibid.*, I, 549–51.

[3] Henry Burton, *The law and the gospel reconciled*, 1631, cited in *ibid.*, I, 507.

[4] John Lilburne, *Come out of her my people*, 1639, 14.

with English Puritanism. Calvin had forcibly enjoined the duty of non-resistance to superiors, leaving, however, one loophole: in kingdoms where inferior magistrates, such as the estates of the realm [*in singulis regnis tres ordines*] were ordained *ad moderandam regum libidinem*, they had the right to oppose tyrants with force.[1] Out of this and a motley assortment of other conceptions, John Knox, Beza, Hotman, and the whole company of European Monarchomachs forged a justification for rebellion in Scotland, France, and the Netherlands. Incited by Laud's ecclesiastical government, moved, too, by an almost hysterical fear of popery, Puritanism was at length to react in an analogous way.

The Scots gave the signal earliest, when they began their revolt in 1638 against the new liturgy the King and archbishop commanded to be used in the Scottish church. In England, nevertheless, despite widespread sympathy with the Scots, two years elapsed before any public justification of resistance appeared. It came in September 1640 in the Rev. Calybute Downing's sermon to the London Artillery Company.[2] Delivered even before the Long Parliament met, the sermon was a straw in the wind. The Puritan clergyman was no daring speculator. On the contrary, his ideas were familiar and unoriginal. Precisely this gave his sermon its significance. He was as far as known the first preacher to express openly the momentous reversal that was occurring in Puritan opinion. Drawing on the Old Testament and 'Rationall Grotius' to justify the Scottish rebellion, he merely stated what many Englishmen had become ripe to consider: that resistance to the King might be a religious duty as well as a political necessity. Evidently the belief in subjection and non-resistance, entrenched and reiterated for decades, was starting to crumble. With the meeting of the Long Parliament before it, Puritanism was about to set forth on a revolutionary path whose consequences it was far from perceiving.

[1] J. Calvin, *Institutio religionis Christiani*, IV, xx, 31.
[2] Cf. *supra*, 144–5.

The Country and the
Constitutional Revolution

It is a universal characteristic of revolutions that their course can neither be predicted nor controlled. Their occurrence brings with it such a multiplication and acceleration of political forces that every stage of their progress forms an equation of unknown quantity. The agitation during the period of preparation has already undermined the habitual obedience and unreflecting loyalty which ensure the equilibrium of states. When the revolutionary gale then breaks upon the body politic, it shatters them completely. The men who lead the movement in the beginning must necessarily sharpen and inflame the popular temper in order to use it for their ends. Thereby they call up a spirit from the vasty deep that once having learned its strength will not be so easily commanded. Criticism and propaganda expose the *arcana imperii* to the light of common day. Subjects ask if they should obey, and whom, and why. Authority is constrained to plead its case with reasons or impose itself by violence. In either instance it has lost its virtue: for while authority remains itself, it neither argues nor coerces, but merely speaks and is accepted. Upon the complex scene already charged with tense uncertainties, unexpected fresh initiatives supervene. Negotiations and threats are followed by civil war. And while the original parties are locked in their angry struggle, they find themselves joined by other combatants. Limited aims in time give way to more extended ones. With an unlooked-for dynamism the movement advances, generating utopian passions and idealistic rage. Partisan love and hate fashion objects for themselves equal to their own ample dimensions. Thus public and private life become thoroughly deranged. Driven by incalculable combinations of force and intrigue, of heroism and vileness, of principled action and unscrupulous manoeuvre, the revolution proceeds through its successive stages to its conclusion and liquidation.

The men who assembled at Westminster on 3 November 1640 could not know that this was the earthquake history about to be enacted in their land. The meeting of the Long Parliament, however,

marked the beginning of the revolution in England as definitely as the convening of the Estates General in the next century dated the commencement of the revolution in France. The parliament set out to obtain redress and reform. But before its unprecedented thirteen-year life was done, it stayed to wage a war against the King and to raise the whirlwind that destroyed the monarchy. It outlived its first great leaders, and many of its members fell away in enmity or dis-illusion. At last a military dictatorship by the general of its own creation put an end to it.[1] Such was the unimagined journey, carrying the kingdom far from its old moorings, on which a revolutionary parliament launched England in 1640.

From the day it opened the parliament met continuously to 9 September 1641, when the Houses, exercising a newly acquired power, voted to adjourn for six weeks to 20 October.[2] The first sitting, therefore, occupied ten months: a period forming a definite epoch in the revolution's progress. The alliance that had taken shape in support of the Country then accomplished its main work. While the ranks behind them were still more or less united, the Country leaders effected a constitutional or legal revolution, shearing away by statute a century and a half's accretion of royal power. In this interval of relative consensus, the last that revolutionary England was to know for many a year, the heritage of the Tudor monarchy was taken to pieces. But this achievement, instead of producing a settlement, left a void. Fixed in a posture of extreme distrust, the King and his opponents could not collaborate to work the new arrangements. The need for security and guarantees gave rise to fresh demands; the fresh demands only widened the gulf. Reform, accordingly, did not beget a new political equilibrium. It brought on, rather, a violent struggle for sovereignty.

When parliament met, the auspices strongly favoured the Country leaders. The King's government was completely discredited and the ministers feared the wrath of the Houses. In the north, the intimidating presence of the Scottish rebel army enforced the pressure at Westminster for reform. A cessation of arms made with the Scots in October left them in occupation of Durham and Northumberland until the conclusion of a peace treaty, which was to be negotiated at London with their commissioners. In the meantime the King was obliged to maintain them at a cost of £850 a day. Facing the Scots

[1] Even Cromwell's expulsion of the Long Parliament in 1653 was not its final demise. It went through two resurrections, another expulsion, and a last dissolution by its own vote during the political unsettlement of 1659–60.

[2] *C.J.*, II, 289; *L.J.*, IV, 396. The act against dissolving the present parliament without its consent (16 Car. I, c. 7, *Statutes of the realm*, V, 103–4) provided also that neither of the Houses should be adjourned except by its own order.

199

lay the King's army, which was also to remain in being pending a treaty. Parliament alone could provide the great sums needed to support the two armies: Charles would have to pay the price in concessions.

What was to be hinged largely on the oppositionist leaders' strategy and their ability to sway the parliament. Here their informal organization of recent years stood them in good stead. Accustomed to consultation and common action, they were able by these means to govern the proceedings of the House of Commons. No body of men brought together as were its members could possibly achieve any constructive result without direction from one quarter or another. Even with direction the task was sufficiently formidable. The odium of the privy councillors was such that they could not exert the least influence upon the House. The Country with its numerous supporters supplied the control and cohesion that could come from nowhere else. In the prevailing temper the renown of its leaders as defenders of the kingdom's rights gave them an immediate authority. Pym, Hampden, St. John, Holles, Nathaniel Fiennes, and others of their political circle therefore took the management of the Commons into their hands from the very outset.

For them to retain their ascendancy, however, was no easy matter. Theirs was only an embryo or proto-party, and they wielded neither the powers of discipline nor the blandishments of patronage by which modern politicians secure their rule. Lacking these resources, the heads of the Country had to exercise control in other ways. The basis of their strength was superiority of organization and adeptness in the methods always indispensable to the government of great assemblies. As most of them were veterans of earlier parliaments, they possessed a solid acquaintance with the details of procedure. They were knowledgeable about precedents and privilege, never failing to appear as the most conspicuous champions of the House's liberties. They understood the necessity of making their presence felt in important committees. They gave themselves up to a multitude of parliamentary labours with incessant energy. By their denunciations of grievances and continued warnings of plots and dangers, they roused the members' passions and never allowed them to flag. Such a mastery of tactics reaped its reward. Aided by the general animosity against the Court, it gained the party managers a dominion from which they could not be deposed.

Of the Country leaders, none acquired so commanding an authority as did Pym. To him both the opposition movement and the House of Commons owed an incalculable debt. He was a man who lived wholly for the public cause and whose being became merged in it. His private personality was thus so much obscured by the events

The Country and the Constitutional Revolution

in which he took part that he remains least known among the prominent figures who most influenced the revolution's course. But while the depths of his character and the circumstances of his intimate life are closed to us, it is possible to discern the nature of his leadership. Pym possessed in a supreme degree the art of parliamentary management. Of tireless industry and great practical sense, he was a committee-man of genius. He knew how to make men work together and how to promote his party's enterprises among them without noise or vanity. Although he had firmness and strong principles, he was neither a doctrinaire nor a radical. He always tried to moderate differences on his own side, and whenever it was compatible with the safety of his cause he was ready for conciliation. To these qualities as a politician he united the gifts of an orator who could address his fellow members in memorable words. Nowhere did the faith and fears of the parliamentary leaders attain more eloquent expression than in his speeches. But the final secret of his power was that while his abilities were superior to most in the Commons, his ideas were not. With all his militancy against the Court, he was conservative and old-fashioned. He believed himself a preserver of old ways, not a shaper of new ones. He harboured the same convictions and prejudices, the same hopes and anxieties as the majority of members. That was why they trusted him and permitted him to achieve a position among them rarely equalled in parliamentary annals.

By comparison with the House of Commons, the House of Lords was much less susceptible to control. When parliament began it consisted of one hundred and twenty-four lay and twenty-six spiritual peers.[1] It prided itself on its greatness and did not intend to be a subordinate partner of the lower House. The basis of its corporate consciousness was the conviction that its role ought to be one of mediator between the King and the Commons. This was the position the peers strove to occupy in the constitutional disputes preceding the Petition of Right and towards which most of them probably aspired in 1640. It was notable that in the abortive Short Parliament the Lords had dissented from the Commons, a majority voting that supply should come before grievances.[2] Haughtiness of rank, ancestry, and wealth made many noblemen moderates by every inclination. When that posture eventually became untenable, honour or interest drove them towards royalism or withdrawal from public life. Nonetheless, within the upper House the Commons managers also possessed some firm allies. Bedford, Warwick, Essex, Saye, and Mandeville belonged to the Country's innermost counsels, while a number of others shared

[1] C. H. Firth, *The House of Lords during the civil war*, 74 and n.
[2] *Ibid.*, 66–7.

201

their political sympathies. Noble defectors in Court offices, like the earls of Northumberland, Pembroke, and Holland, Warwick's brother, could also be counted as friends of the opposition. There was in consequence an active sentiment among the peers favourable to close cooperation with the lower House.

The Country had a considerable organization in the House of Commons, though its detailed workings cannot be traced precisely. The leaders of course consulted frequently. Pym was known to hold meetings with political associates and friends at his lodgings in a house behind Westminster Hall.[1] The parliamentary diarist, Sir Simonds D'Ewes, M.P. for Sudbury and our incomparable informant about the transactions of the Commons, gives us a rare and tantalizing glimpse of a private conference on the night of 10 June 1641, where Pym, Hampden, Sir Robert Harley, the Rev. Stephen Marshall, and some others decided that the bill against episcopacy should be moved next day in the House: 'for Mr Hampden out of his serpentine subtletie did still putt others to move those businesses that he contrived.'[2] This was undoubtedly how the party chiefs directed affairs from behind the scenes. In one such earlier meeting, to be noticed presently, the leaders in both Houses worked out their strategy at the opening of the parliament.[3]

The machinery of the Commons was subjected to the Country through the prevalence of its supporters on committees.[4] In grand committees of the whole House, which any member could attend, men became prominent by diligent participation and by exploiting the general animosity against the Court. When we find, for instance, John White, M.P. for Southwark, reporting to the House for the grand committee on religion in the early days of the parliament, and George Peard, M.P. for Barnstaple, reporting for the grand committee on courts of justice, it is likely that oppositionist influence in these committees was pretty considerable.[5] White, a Puritan lawyer, was one of the old Feoffees for Impropriations and connected also with the Massachusetts Bay Company. Peard had spoken strongly against ship money in the Short Parliament of the preceding spring.[6]

Oppositionist ascendancy was equally pronounced in select com-

---

[1] Clarendon, *Life*, 936.
[2] D'Ewes, Journal, B.M. Harl. 163, f. 306b. Gardiner's statement (*History*, X, 77n.) that D'Ewes's reference to Hampden was inserted long after the date in which it is placed in the Journal is not borne out by the manuscript.
[3] Cf. *infra*, 207.
[4] Cf. M. Keeler, ' "There are no remedies for many things but by a parliament." Some opposition committees, 1640,' *Conflict in Stuart England*, ed. W. A. Aiken and B. Henning, L., 1960.
[5] Cf., e.g., *C.J.*, II, 35, 70, 72.
[6] M. Keeler, *The Long Parliament*, 299, 390.

mittees. This was especially true of the small committee which bore responsibility for the most crucial of all the Commons' early enterprises, the preparation of the case against Strafford. The eight members appointed on 11 and 12 November included the opposition chiefs and trusted associates: Pym, Hampden, St. John, Holles, William Strode, Sir John Clotworthy, and Sir Walter Erle. Only Lord George Digby, the earl of Bristol's son, had no connection with the party: he was probably chosen because of his and his father's known zeal against the Court.[1] The large committee on privileges, established on 6 November to report on disputed elections, was another instrument of the Country's purpose. Its supporters, who were heavily represented, used the committee to strengthen the party's hold by deciding contested returns against opponents. Sir Edward Osborne, for instance, Strafford's friend and Vice-President of the Council of the North, was returned in a disputed election at Berwick. The committee recommended that his return should be void. Osborne was thus kept out of parliament, where he might have been able to help Strafford.[2] John Hampden was also named in a disputed return for Buckinghamshire. The esteem the House felt for him was shown by its vote when appointing the committee on privileges that his election for the county should not be questioned.[3]

A major factor contributing to the Country's ascendancy was the intensification of political consciousness in the kingdom at large. The crisis at the close of the '30s infused a fresh vigour into public discussion, which developed after November 1640 with extraordinary rapidity. The result was a veritable transformation of the political scene. For the first time, decisions affecting the common lot had to be taken amidst incessant popular argument and scrutiny. Greater numbers than ever before—people on the margins of the political nation, even elements within the traditionally mute and inarticulate mass—concerned themselves with questions of the day. Aroused by hatred of Laud and Strafford, this powerful upsurge of popular awareness ranged itself almost entirely behind the opposition party, a force to be reckoned with and appeased.

The press, no longer controllable by the palsied hand of the regime, poured forth a torrent of publication to sustain the general interest in

---

[1] *C.J.*, II, 26, 27; *D.N.B.*, *s.v.*, 'George Digby, second earl of Bristol,' 'John Digby, first earl of Bristol.' On the 12th Holles asked to be excused, doubtless because Strafford was his brother-in-law. He was replaced by Harbottle Grimston, recorder and M.P. for Colchester, one of the most Puritan towns in the most Puritan county in England. On 23 January 1641, the lawyers, Selden, Whitelocke, Palmer, and Maynard were added to the committee, *C.J.*, II, 72.

[2] *C.J.*, II, 20–1, 47; Clarendon, *Rebellion*, III, 12; M. Keeler, *The Long Parliament*, 10 and n.   [3] Notestein, *D'Ewes*, 3n.

public affairs. The most impressive evidence of its output during the revolutionary years is the British Museum's great Thomason collection—the collection of books, pamphlets, and newspapers formed by the London bookseller, George Thomason, between 1640–61. Amounting to nearly 30,000 titles, the writings Thomason gathered by unsparing effort and expense equal or perhaps exceed the sum of works printed in all languages in the British Isles and in the English language abroad during the whole period 1475 to 1640.[1] The entire mind of the revolution survives in this collection; and though it contains titles of the utmost diversity, from *belles lettres* to joke books, its greater part relates directly to political, religious, and economic controversies. According to a tabulation of its contents, 721 publications appeared in 1641, 2,134 in 1642, the latter the highest total in any year up to the Restoration: a fact that sufficiently demonstrates the accelerated preoccupation with political-ecclesiastical issues in the first stages of the revolution's progress.[2]

But Thomason's collection should not be regarded only as an endlessly rich hunting ground for subsequent generations of historians. For his undertaking was in itself a sign of the growth of contemporary consciousness under the influence of the opposition movement's struggle. Thomason, strongly sympathetic to the Country in the early '40s, realized from the beginning that the Long Parliament's meeting was a great historic event. He therefore resolved, he said, to make 'an Exact Collection' of everything published from November 1640 onwards, in the conviction that it would be both useful for his own age and 'of greate Advantage to Posterity.' He found the amassing of his collection a 'chargeable and heavy . . . Burthen. . . .'; but the prescience that led him to attempt it has attached his name permanently to the greatest of all sources of knowledge of the revolutionary epoch.[3]

Nothing attracted more public attention than occurrences in parlia-

---

[1] *A short-title catalogue . . . 1475–1640*, ed. A. W. Pollard and G. R. Redgrave, L., ed. 1946, lists 26,143 publications from 1475–1640. More will be added in a second ed. now in progress. This number, however, includes hundreds of royal proclamations, statutes, and different editions of the same work. In comparison, Thomason estimated his collection at nearly 30,000 items, while modern writers using other modes of computation have counted the total as 26,000 and 22,255; cf. L. Spencer, 'The professional and literary connexions of George Thomason,' *The library*, 5th ser., XIII, 2 (1958). G. K. Fortescue, editor of the Thomason catalogue, believed the collection was nearly complete for the years it covered; cf. *Catalogue of the pamphlets . . . George Thomason*, 2v., L., 1908, I, xxii.
[2] *Ibid.*, I, xxi.
[3] Cf. Thomason's statement of his purpose and methods in L. Spencer, *loc. cit.*, 114–15. The fullest account of Thomason is in *ibid.* and the same author's 'The politics of George Thomason,' *The library*, 5th ser., XIV, 1

ment. The stationers catered to this interest by printing speeches in large numbers. The spread of political division had already undermined the restraints on the disclosure of proceedings in the earlier parliaments of Charles I, and after 1640 all barriers were down. Although the House of Commons made occasional gestures to suppress the 'License of Printing,' they were quite ineffectual.[1] Frequently members themselves gave the stationers the text of their remarks or connived in some other way at publication. More commonly stationers obtained a copy from a scrivener working from second-hand reports and hence likely to make errors or even to resort to wholesale fabrication where knowledge failed him.[2]

The circulation of speeches probably helped considerably to advance members' reputations as well as to form opinion. Every major speech by Pym and St. John, for instance, got into print, thus reinforcing their authority as leaders. Numerous speeches on grievances, on Strafford's misrule, and on church government, replete with citations of legal precedent, political writers, and scriptural texts, opened every issue of controversy to ordinary readers. The great majority of printed speeches embodied the oppositionist standpoint and were highly critical of royal policies and ministers. When members published unpopular views, they ran the risk of retaliation by the Commons. Lord Digby learned this to his cost after he put into circulation the speech he delivered in April 1641 denouncing the legality of Strafford's attainder. He gave the text to one, Moore, 'a common writer,' to make twenty copies. Through the latter it came to Parslow, a stationer, who printed an edition of five hundred which was then distributed with the help of Digby's relative, Sir Lewis Dyve. The lower House was so provoked that it authorized a committee to investigate the circumstances of publication. On receiving the committee's report, the members voted that the speech was false and its appearance in print defamatory to the House. Moore, Parslow, and Dyve were declared delinquents and the speech was ordered burned by the common hangman. As for Digby, who had recently been summoned by the King to the House of Lords, they resolved on a petition requesting Charles to refrain from conferring any honour or employment upon him.[3]

[1] Cf. *C.J.*, II, 168, 5 June 1641, an order of the House to the Master and Wardens of the Company of Stationers to take measures against the licence of printing speeches and other pamphlets.

[2] For an account of the publication and circulation of parliamentary speeches, cf. *Commons debates for 1629*, Introduction, and Coates, *D'Ewes*, xx–xxiii.   [3] D'Ewes, Journal, B.M. Harl. 163, f. 396b; *C.J.*, II, 208–9.

(1959), and cf. also the introduction to the *Catalogue of the pamphlets . . . George Thomason*, I.

Together with speeches a great spate of pamphlets poured from the press to gratify an increasing demand. The minds of Englishmen were in a ferment. Political and religious argument became the daily diet of people who read, and the appetite for information and controversy grew by what it fed on. It was in this setting that the first weekly newspapers reporting parliamentary and national affairs appeared in London. There had been nothing of their kind before in England, since their predecessors, the corantoes of the '20s, limited themselves strictly to continental news.[1] The earliest, *The heads of several proceedings in this present parliament*, came out in the week of 22–29 November 1641. The work of an enterprising publisher, it was soon followed by competitors, two in December, still others in 1642. These newspapers of 1641 were cheaply printed in eight pages, badly written, and devoid of personality. They sold in the capital for a penny. Their publication day was Monday, in time for the mail which left London for the north on Tuesday mornings. Primitive though they were, they were the forerunners of a journalistic phenomenon that was to propagate itself during the following years with astonishing fecundity. The issues of newspapers acquired by Thomason from 1641 to 1660 fill sixty-eight pages in the catalogue of his collection. '. . . when these diurnalls were first printed,' said a parliamentary speaker in March 1642,

ther came out but one each weeke, & then ther was some moderate truth in them. But now ther are sometimes printed twelve or fourteene in a week, & they commonlie labour in that worke all the Lords day, to gett them readie by monday morning.[2]

This was already the power of the press on an unexampled scale. And it was to continue to grow, so that in the civil war and after, newspapers became regular party organs and propaganda instruments written by men of real literary ability.[3] The appearance of the newspaper in 1641 was an indication of how far political life had broken through its former limits. Opposition to the regime had engendered a broad public which wished both to participate and to be informed. To mobilize popular support and stiffen conviction, the press was indispensable. The systematized provision of news, the presence of the journalist and publicist, were the necessary adjuncts of an energized politics.

[1] Cf. *supra*, 107.
[2] From a speech by D'Ewes, Journal, B.M. Harl. 163, f. 52b.
[3] Cf. J. Frank, *op. cit.*

Immediately after the opening of parliament, the chief oppositionists met to work out their strategy. Viscount Mandeville, one of those present, later described their deliberations in his memoirs. '. . . some of the members of both houses,' he recorded, 'had private meetings and consultacons how to direct their parliamentary resolutions in order to a present redresse and future security. . . .' They concluded that 'the most certaine way, and most consistent with the duty and allegiance of Subjects' was 'to fix their complaints and accusations upon evill Councellors, as the imediate actors in the tragicall miseries of the Kingdome, rather then upon the personall faileings and male administrations in the King.' In particular, they decided to aim their attack at the judges, the bishops, and the privy councillors, and especially against Laud, Strafford, Cottington, and the marquis of Hamilton, the King's representative to the rebellious Scots.[1] Hamilton's inclusion with the other malefactors was significant: the English and Scottish oppositions were clearly working together and intended to coordinate their blows against the ministers.

The assault began on 7 November—perhaps therefore even before the party leaders' meeting—in a powerful speech delivered by Pym.[2] In it he called for a reformation and for the discovery and punishment of the authors of the kingdom's ills. Surveying in detail the recent misrule in church and state, he linked it with the malignity of the Arminian clergy and the secret influence of papists on the King's affairs. In all that had occurred he saw evidence of a sinister design. And he gave the first intimation of what was to form the foundation of the House of Commons' charge against Strafford: that an attempt of the highest treason was under way to change the form of government to a despotism, for which purpose it had been planned to bring an Irish army into England.[3]

Pym's address, together with the decisions he and his friends had made, marked out the line on which they tried to lead parliament during the following months. Their strategy was eminently sound. In refraining from a direct attack on the King, these conservative

[1] B.M. Add. 15,567, f. 30. This anonymous manuscript is easily identifiable from internal evidence as a fragment of Mandeville's memoirs. Passages from it have been printed in J. Nalson, *An impartial collection*, 2v., 1682–3, II, 689, and J. L. Sanford, *op. cit.*, 307ff. I am indebted to Dr. De Lloyd Guth and Mrs. Susan Guralnik for making a transcript of this manuscript for me.

[2] Mandeville mentions no dates, but says the oppositionists' consultations occurred after the kingdom's grievances had been declared in the House; Pym's speech was such a declaration.

[3] Notestein, *D'Ewes*, 7–11.

revolutionists acted in keeping with the strongest instincts of constitutional propriety. They left inviolate the profession of loyalty to the monarch's crown and person which was a primary article in the creed of the governing class. The rank-and-file member could support them in good conscience, his sentiments of respect for the King unimpaired. Pym's accusation of an Arminian-popish conspiracy was false, but it reflected a rooted popular prejudice that could be used against the Court with deadly effect. Finally, the determination to fix responsibility on ministers carried far-reaching implications. If the parliamentary leaders succeeded, Charles would be forced to take new councillors.[1] He would have to receive men into his service who could reconcile King and parliament, Court and Country, because their presence would be the sign and guarantee of a change of policy. Only those who possessed parliament's confidence could undertake the task. The perspective of the oppositionists therefore envisaged the assumption of ministerial offices by some of themselves as an indispensable step towards the goal of reform. Had they attained their aim of entering the King's service as effective agents of a parliamentary and popular will, there would have been no civil war. Their failure inevitably advanced the revolution to a further stage that required more drastic solutions.

Parliament pressed its offensive with unremitting vigour over the next months. Needing no prodding, the members loosed a storm of anger on the ministers and servants of royal misgovernment. The first and greatest victim was Strafford, whom the party leaders needed to immobilize to succeed in their attack against the Court. They intended to impeach him and had made careful preparations to this end. A key role was assigned to Sir John Clotworthy, an Irish landowner elected to the Commons for the town of Maldon through the influence of the earl of Warwick. Clotworthy was a Puritan, a friend of John Winthrop and Pym, who possessed family and business connections with Strafford's greatest enemies in Ireland. His return to the House had been contrived so that he could expose the record of the Lord Lieutenant's Irish administration and its dangerous implications for the liberty of England.[2] Pym had also secretly obtained vital evidence against Strafford through his friendship with

---

[1] In this connection, a comment made in December 1640 by Robert Baillie, one of the Scottish commissioners in London, is significant. Among the aims he ascribed to the parliamentary leaders was 'the displanting the Court' and 'the planting the Court'; *The letters and journals of Robert Baillie*, I, 285.

[2] M. Keeler, *The Long Parliament*, *s.v.*; H. F. Kearney, *op. cit.*, 199–200; *Winthrop papers*, III, 190. Clotworthy was also returned to parliament for Bosinney, probably by the patronage of the earl of Pembroke, Lord Warden of the Stannaries. This suggests that Pembroke's assistance was available to the party leaders; cf. V. Rowe, *loc. cit.*, 253.

Sir Henry Vane junior, son of the King's co-Secretary of State. Notwithstanding his father's position, the younger Vane's religious and political sympathies lay altogether with the Country. In October he had shown Pym without his father's knowledge a copy of notes of a Council meeting held the previous 5 May after the Short Parliament's refusal to grant the King money against the Scots. According to these notes, Strafford advised Charles that he was now absolved from law and spoke words that could be construed as urging the introduction of an Irish army to compel England to obedience. The army referred to was one Strafford had raised in 1640 to assist the King to crush the Scottish rebellion, but which had not got into action and remained on foot in Ireland. Secretary Vane destroyed his original notes at the King's order before the Long Parliament opened. Pym, however, had made a copy of his own. The damning statements confirmed his worst fears and were to form the substance of the gravest charge in the Lord Lieutenant's impeachment.[1]

Strafford was too bold and resourceful merely to await his enemies' onslaught. He arrived in London from Yorkshire on 9 November planning to accuse the opposition leaders in both Houses of high treason for complicity with the Scots. Learning of his purpose from connections at the Court, Pym acted hastily to forestall its execution.[2] Clotworthy had already denounced Strafford's oppressions in Ireland in a long speech on the 7th.[3] Four days later the blow against him fell. On the 11th the House was tense with wild rumours of Strafford's intentions and reports of a far-reaching Catholic plot. Clotworthy related a story from Ireland that Strafford had promised the King he should be able to do as he pleased in England with the help of the Irish army. Thoroughly worked up, the members appointed a committee to frame a charge against the earl.[4] That same day Pym took the charge to the House of Lords and there in the Commons' name impeached Strafford of high treason. The Lord Lieutenant was not permitted to make a reply. In response to Pym's request, the peers sequestered him from his seat in their House and committed him to custody.

The party leaders thus removed the most dangerous of the King's ministers from the political scene. Although they still had to make good their case in Strafford's trial, they were meanwhile free to press

---

[1] On 10 April 1641, during the proceedings against Strafford, the younger Vane told the lower House how he had obtained his father's notes and shown a copy to Pym, D'Ewes, Journal, B.M. Harl. 164, ff. 162a–b, 163a.
[2] Mandeville relates in his memoirs the story of Strafford's reported intention and the oppositionists hastening their impeachment, B.M. Add. 15,567, f. 31.
[3] Notestein, D'Ewes, 13–14.
[4] Ibid., 24–9; C.J., II, 26–7.

the House's assault on the Court with increased momentum. On 18 December Laud was impeached and sent to the Tower. Sir Francis Windebank, the other Secretary of State, had already taken flight to France rather than face the members' accusations of favouring Catholic recusants. He was joined there by the Lord Keeper, Lord Finch, charged with treason on 21 December for his earlier conduct as a judge in the ship-money case. The other six judges who had upheld the legality of ship money were also accused in the House, and on 12 February Sir Robert Berkeley, justice of the King's Bench, was impeached.[1]

The first rule of revolutionaries is to preserve the initiative and to advance more boldly with each success. Within a couple of months, the parliamentary attack on ministers had done the Country's work. Too weak to resist, the Court disintegrated as a political force. The King was powerless. His councillors could neither help him nor find safety in his protection. Their only hope was to seek their preservation from the favour of parliament. Cottington, Master of the Wards and Chancellor of the Exchequer, saved himself by pledging to give up his offices so that they would be available to the parliamentary leaders. The marquis of Hamilton averted the storm by a promise to promote the aims of the oppositionists and their Scottish allies.[2]

Along with ministers, lesser officials and beneficiaries of royal favour who sat in parliament joined the general defection. Fear or opportunism, sympathy with the Country, hatred of Strafford and Laud, were amongst the several motives determining their conduct. Sir Miles Fleetwood and Sir Benjamin Rudyard, occupants of important places in the Court of Wards; Sir Robert Pye, Auditor of the Exchequer; Sir Henry Mildmay, Master of the Jewel House; Sir Arthur Ingram, Sir John Hippesley, Cornelius Holland, and Lawrence Whitaker, all monopolists and profiteers through Court patronage; every one of them attached himself to the opposition party.[3] Although the lower House voted to expel monopolists, Mildmay, Whitaker, and their like retained their seats as a result of their zealous cooperation with the party managers.[4]

With the Court routed, it became likely that a redistribution of offices would occur. At this stage, however, the question of office appeared under a double aspect. To the parliamentary leaders, office was not the goal of a merely personal policy inspired by the desire for

[1] *C.J.*, II, 44, 54, 55, 56, 83; Notestein, *D'Ewes*, 103, 175–6.

[2] Mandeville mentions these bargains in his memoirs, B.M. Add. 15,567, ff. 30–1.

[3] Cf. the biographies of these officials in M. Keeler, *The Long Parliament*, and the account of Sir Arthur Ingram's political stand by A. F. Upton, *op. cit.*, ch. X.

[4] *C.J.*, II, 24; Clarendon, *Rebellion*, III, 13.

emoluments and honour. It was, on the contrary, a serious political objective. Assuming the continuance of the monarchical regime—and of course they did not consider any other possibility—ministerial office was essential to the realization of their aims. But they had not risked royal disfavour for so many years only to abandon their principles at this juncture. If they entered Charles's service, it would be for a public purpose: to resolve the crisis and reconcile the King to parliament by carrying out a new policy in his name.

On the other hand, the Court's disruption and the expectation of changes naturally introduced an element of opportunism into the situation as well. Its centre was the Queen, whose influence on her husband was a factor that could affect the choice of ministers. Henrietta Maria did not understand the depth of political and religious differences from which the quarrel in the state arose. To her the dispute was predominantly a contest for places and honours, and from this frivolous premiss all her interventions proceeded. It was her intent to become the channel through which promotion flowed and thus to fix the dependence of all men on herself. She imagined that in this way, by bargaining with offices, she would gain the leading politicians for the King.[1] The opposition leaders, of course, were hardly likely to tolerate the Queen in such a mischievous role. For a moment, however, while she tried to play it, aspirants eager for promotion on any terms had a keen incentive to enlist her support on their behalf.

This opportunist aspect of the pursuit of office was most markedly exemplified by the earl of Leicester, the King's ambassador in France. Through his marriage to Lady Dorothy Percy, the nobleman belonged to an aristocratic Court circle. His brothers-in-law were the earl of Northumberland, Lord Admiral, and Henry Percy, a favourite courtier in the Queen's household. His sister-in-law was the dowager countess of Carlisle, an intimate of the Queen and of Strafford, one of those *grandes dames* who aspire to affect the course of affairs behind the scenes by their friendship with the great. Although Leicester possessed no special fitness to be a minister, he was nevertheless strongly ambitious for higher office, and at the end of the '30s had hoped to become Secretary of State or to replace Wentworth in Ireland.[2] The King's dislike of him, however, and Laud's enmity disappointed these designs.[3] At the same time, while cultivating his

---

[1] Cf. Clarendon's description, *Rebellion*, II, 130.

[2] Leicester became ambassador to France in 1636. For his earlier attempts at promotion, cf. *H.M.C. De L'Isle and Dudley*, VI, 77, 182, 192, 203–4, 211; A. Collins, *op. cit.*, II, 604, 618, 631, 634.

[3] Laud suspected Leicester's opinions and spoke of him as 'a most dangerous practicing Puritan. . . .' (*Works*, VII, 568). He was certainly wrong in this belief, since the earl's chaplain and occupant of the living at Penshurst was

Court connections for all they were worth, he did not fail to keep up friendly relations with the oppositionist, Lord Mandeville, to whom he professed his warm sympathies for the Puritans.[1]

Neither Leicester nor Northumberland agreed with the policies that brought disaster on the King in 1640. But in their frigid, self-centred world, political judgments were invariably dominated by hard material calculations as to the effect of events on their own personal position. Feeling little loyalty to their royal master, they viewed his plight without commiseration and prepared to exploit his weakness to the best advantage. Thus less than three weeks after parliament began, Northumberland found himself able to write Leicester in France of the splendid prospects now opening:

Both howses understand one an other so well, and are so fully resolved upon a reformation of all things that I do verily beleeve we shall see many persons questioned that within these 6 months thought themselves in great securitie, and such are the Kings necessities that he will not be any way able either to defend those men or to helpe himselfe, be their proceedings never so distastefull to him. . . . I should be glad to know which . . . offices . . . [Leicester] doth most affect. . . . if [Treasurer] can not be had [Northumberland] may use his best endevors to gett some of the others for him.[2]

In truth, what Leicester wanted was nothing less than the lord lieutenancy of Ireland as Strafford's successor. Accordingly, while Northumberland undertook to see that his nomination should be acceptable to the party managers in parliament,[3] Leicester himself began an intrigue to secure the Queen's support of his appointment. In this his intermediary was his old family friend, Sir John Temple, whose letters to the earl, chafing with impatience in Paris, described the labyrinthine progress of the negotiation.[4] On the Queen's side, the agent with whom Temple conducted most of his dealings was

---

[1] P.R.O. Manchester MSS. 30/15/466.

[2] *H.M.C. De L'Isle and Dudley*, VI, 343, some words in cipher. In a previous letter, Northumberland had suggested the posts of Treasurer, Irish Deputy, or Secretary of State; A. Collins, *op. cit.*, II, 663.

[3] Northumberland's good relations with the opposition leaders had lost him the King's favour, but he thought he could get parliament to recommend Leicester for the Irish office; A. Collins, *op. cit.*, II, 665, 666.

[4] On Temple, cf. *D.N.B.*, *s.v.* He was born and educated in Ireland and had Irish interests. Early in 1641, contemporaneously with his efforts on Leicester's behalf, he was made Master of the Rolls in Ireland in succession to Strafford's kinsman, Sir Christopher Wandesford.

Henry Hammond, a clergyman firmly attached to the Anglican establishment; cf. on the latter *D.N.B.*, *s.v.*

her Vice-Chamberlain, Henry Jermyn, who enjoyed her full confidence.[1]

Having begun his approach early in January 1641, Temple soon reported that while the King was averse to Leicester, the Queen was well-disposed; Jermyn, however, would do nothing without money.[2] He therefore took the liberty of offering Jermyn £4,000 on his principal's behalf. He justified this on the ground that the Queen's power 'will not long continew in this heigth' and that once the opposition leaders were settled in office, as he expected, they would 'find a way to cutt short Jermyn so as he will not have power to doe ... that service he now desires.'[3] Leicester was prepared for a bribe, but not so large a one, and on learning the amount, he angrily disavowed it as excessive.[4] Jermyn nevertheless professed himself still willing to continue his efforts and wait for his recompense; but Temple attributed some of the subsequent delay in the business to the earl's reluctance to provide Jermyn with an incentive to make him prompt and stirring.[5]

As the transaction dragged on, Temple's letters alternated between gloom and optimism. At the end of January he wrote that the Queen still could not overcome the King's dislike of Leicester's appointment.[6] In February, Jermyn secured from Strafford in the Tower a letter expressing readiness to resign his office in Leicester's favour. This letter was made known to Charles by the Queen, who now promised to press hard to obtain the settlement of Ireland on the earl.[7] Still no result ensued, and in March Temple thought the Irish appointment would be held up until the outcome of Strafford's trial should become clear. He also reported that he had sounded Sir John Clotworthy, who declared that Leicester was not '[Puritan] enough.'[8] The earl had already tried to correct this impression by writing early in February to Lord Mandeville to express his good will and desire 'to live in the good opinion of the brethren. . . .'[9] But Temple now took the further precaution of sending Leicester's son, Lord Lisle, down to the family residence at Penshurst to remove some incriminating pictures from the chapel, lest the earl's lapse towards ceremonialism become known and arouse the animosity of parliament.[10]

In spite of these actions, Leicester's suit still continued without

---

[1] On Jermyn, cf. *D.N.B.*, *s.v.* Temple did some of his business with Jermyn through Robert Long, Surveyor of the Queen's lands, *H.M.C. De L'Isle and Dudley*, VI, 360, 362–3.   [2] *Ibid.*, VI, 362–3.   [3] *Ibid.*, VI, 366–7.
[4] *Ibid.*, VI, 369, 375–6. Leicester's replies to Temple are not extant and have to be inferred from Temple's letters.
[5] *Ibid.*, VI, 379, 391.   [6] *Ibid.*, VI, 369.   [7] *Ibid.*, VI. 379, 382.
[8] *Ibid.*, VI, 288, bracketed word in cipher.
[9] P.R.O. Manchester MSS. 30/15/488.
[10] *H.M.C. De L'Isle and Dudley*, VI, 388–9.

issue, and in April Temple indicated that the managers in the House of Commons felt some suspicion of him as having formerly been a friend of Strafford. He urged the nobleman in the strongest terms to come at once to England, as nothing but his own presence could rectify him.[1] After some hesitation, Leicester accepted this advice and left unannounced for home near the end of the month.

With his departure from Paris, Temple's letters to him ceased so that it becomes impossible to follow the intrigue to its conclusion. His return, however, accomplished its purpose, and on 14 June 1641, a month after Strafford's execution, he was finally created Lord Lieutenant of Ireland. By this time the Queen was thoroughly discredited and under fierce attack for complicity in a plot to use elements of the King's northern army against parliament, while Jermyn, who was also involved, had fled to France. All this was a matter of complete indifference to Leicester, now that he had attained his goal. By his wife the news of his promotion was received with appropriately pious gratitude. 'God has been mercifull to us in a great preportion,' she wrote, 'and I doe beseche him to give us such a thankefulnes as may be acceptable to him.'[2] Unfortunately, Lady Leicester's acknowledgment of divine favours was premature: for the Irish rebellion, breaking out in the following autumn, ruined her husband's prospects, and he never arrived in Ireland to exercise his office.

Leicester's sordid intrigue represented the quest for office in its most unscrupulous form. Meanwhile, however, the momentous question of office for the opposition leaders was also under consideration. The earliest intimation of its possibility came at the end of December 1640 in reports that the 'ruling partie in . . . parliament' expected the earl of Bedford to be made Treasurer. A month later rumour added that Pym would become Chancellor of the Exchequer and Lord Saye Master of the Wards. Sir John Temple thought that the 'new men' would take office 'to make up an entire union betweene the Kinge and his people. . . .'[3] The first honours bestowed on the party chiefs were nevertheless of a more modest character than the current gossip predicted. At the end of January St. John was named Solicitor, a legal post devoid of political significance, and three weeks later the King created Bedford, Essex, Saye, Mandeville, and Hertford privy councillors. The latter appointments were procured by the marquis of Hamilton as one of his services to his new-found Country

---

[1] *Ibid.*, VI, 399.
[2] P.R.O. De L'Isle and Dudley MSS., XIII, 214. This passage is omitted from the published calendar.
[3] A. Collins, *op. cit.*, II, 666; *C.S.P.D. 1640–41*, 439; *H.M.C. Cowper*, II, 272; *H.M.C. De L'Isle and Dudley*, VI, 367–8.

allies.[1] Although the King's promotion of these noblemen looked like a concession, it was in reality only a gesture, since the new councillors held a merely honorary position and their advice counted no more after their elevation than before.

In fact, behind the scenes the Queen was endeavouring with the bait of office to win concessions from the parliamentary managers. Prior to Strafford's trial, which began on 22 March, and while it was in progress, she talked secretly with Pym, Bedford, and Saye to offer them advancement in return for Strafford's life.[2] In April the King gave audience to Pym with the same object.[3] But no inducement could move Pym and his collaborators from their determination to pursue Strafford to the death.[4]

It was indeed the King's unhappiness that while he could be driven so far in his adversity as to confer a few offices on the opposition leaders, he never made these grants the foundation of a fresh orientation of his government. Because he gave the shadow and withheld the substance, his appointments effected nothing. In the middle of May Saye was created Master of the Wards in Cottington's stead.[5] Bedford would probably have been named Treasurer if not for his unexpected death about the same time.[6] Bishop Juxon in any case ceased to be Treasurer in May and the office was at once put in commission of which Saye was made a member.[7] In May also the earl of Essex was appointed lord lieutenant of Yorkshire and two

[1] S. R. Gardiner, *History*, IX, 264, 292. On 27 April the earl of Warwick was also made a privy councillor, *H.M.C. Cowper*, II, 280. Hamilton's role in the oppositionists' promotions was noted by the Scotsman, Baillie (*op. cit.*, I, 305) and by Sir John Temple (*H.M.C. De L'Isle and Dudley*, VI, 367).
[2] *H.M.C. Cowper*, II, 272; B. Whitelocke, *op. cit.*, I, 120. In the account she gave Mme. De Motteville, Henrietta Maria said she held interviews with the 'most wicked.' She obviously thought the parliamentary managers were animated solely by personal and factious motives (*Mémoires de Mme. De Motteville*, ed. Petitot, Paris, 1824, 98–9).
[3] *C.S.P.D. 1640–41*, 560.
[4] According to the story told by Clarendon, Bedford complained of parliament's passion against Strafford and tried to persuade his friends to concur with the King in sparing the earl's life on condition of his exclusion from all employment and banishment or prison (*Rebellion*, III, 161–2). It is impossible to believe, however, that Bedford could have been divided from Pym and St. John on so crucial a point. Firth expressed the opinion that Clarendon's story contained 'manifest impossibilities.' (*D.N.B.*, *s.v.*, 'Edward Hyde').
[5] S. R. Gardiner, *History*, IX, 374.
[6] That Bedford's appointment was probably intended appears from the detailed memorandum on the King's revenue which was prepared for him in April, *C.S.P.D. 1640–41*, 565–7.
[7] *D.N.B.*, *s.v.*, 'William Juxon'; *H.M.C. Cowper*, II, 284. The treasury commission was established on 18 May with Lord Keeper Littleton as its head, *D.N.B.*, *s.v.*, 'Edward Littleton.'

months later he succeeded the earl of Pembroke as Lord Chamberlain.[1] During the summer of 1641 there were rumours of further appointments, as that Hampden or Holles would become Secretary of State, Saye Treasurer, and Lord Brooke a privy councillor; but nothing came of these.[2]

The sum of places conferred by Charles on the opposition leaders therefore did not amount to very much in political terms. It was further noticeable that Pym and Hampden, in spite of their great authority in the House of Commons, were overlooked. Most important, perhaps, the recipients well understood that they derived their advancement only from their reputation in parliament, not from the King's esteem or desire to receive their advice. Lacking any testimonial of his confidence and intention to rely on them, they resolved, as Clarendon pointed out, 'to keep up principally the greatness of that place to which they thought they owed their greatness.'[3]

The King's refusal to make effective use of a policy of 'bridge appointments'[4] was a great error that brought many subsequent evils upon him. Had he been willing to take the Country leaders unreservedly into his service and cooperate fully with their counsels, the political crisis might have been overcome before it became intractable. No doubt this step would have entailed some painful consequences: disavowal of the measures of the previous years, abandonment of old servants, acceptance of permanent restrictions on his prerogative powers. Yet in the long run he would have served his crown better if he had given his countenance to the parliamentary managers. Once in office as ministers on whose advice the King was seen to depend, Pym and his associates could have closed up the schism in the body politic. Their parliamentary ascendancy would have secured the penurious crown a revenue. Charles, devoid of reliable advice because of the attack on the Court, would have gained the aid of a council composed of some of the ablest and most popular men in the kingdom.

Because the opportunity was let slip to build on office a bridge to draw King and people, Court and Country, together, parliament's attitude inevitably hardened. If the King would not of his own will confide the management of affairs to men parliament trusted, he must be forced to do so: the revolutionary consequence could not be avoided. Thus it soon came about that the parliamentary choice and

---

[1] J. Nalson, *op. cit.*, II, 247; *C.S.P.D. 1641–43*, 59. In July, prior to the King's departure for Scotland, Essex was also made lieutenant-general south of Trent (Clarendon, *Rebellion*, III, 248).

[2] *C.S.P.D. 1641–43*, 53, 63.

[3] *Rebellion*, III, 54.

[4] This excellent phrase is B. H. G. Wormald's, *Clarendon*, Cambridge, 1951.

control of councillors—a new fetter forged to bind the royal power—began to be considered an indispensable ingredient of any secure settlement.

4

On 22 March in Westminster Hall the peers took their place as judges and Strafford appeared at the bar to answer his accuser, the House of Commons, for life or death. Here in this grim prosecution the contending parties of a divided state met face to face in fear and hatred. If Strafford stood at his life's turning point, the opposition leaders confronted their severest test. In bringing the Lord Lieutenant to trial, they intended to pass judgment on a system of government as well as a man. For them Strafford personified more than any other the injustice and misrule they meant to end. He was the minister at York and Dublin who in the long intermission of parliaments trod down with brutal severity the rights and property of the King's subjects. He was the dark councillor conspiring to erect an absolutist tyranny on the ruins of English freedom. The party managers knew they must affix these stigmata on Strafford and impose exemplary punishment or suffer an irreparable reverse. Failure would undermine their sway in parliament and prepare the ground for a reaction. They could never consider themselves or their cause secure while Strafford lived. His trial represented a crisis in their personal and political fortunes alike.[1]

In formulating the grounds of the impeachment, the legally-minded managers of the prosecution showed how far they could depart from law in almost complete unconsciousness of where they were tending. No one professed a profounder reverence for the law than Pym and his colleagues: the law was not only a religion to them, but a superstition. With praiseworthy effort they excavated the mines of precedent to the depths to prepare their case. Yet that case rested on a principle really revolutionary in its nature. The illegal actions laid to Strafford's charge were declared to constitute treason in that they expressed a fixed determination to subvert the fundamental laws of the realm and therefore the existing form of government as well. This was the gravamen to which all twenty-eight articles of the impeachment were tied. But to conceive treason thus was to base it on the norms of revolutionary justice, not on law. Treason hitherto had been acts against the King's person and authority as defined by

---

[1] The proceedings in Strafford's trial are printed in J. Rushworth, III. Cf. also the account by C. V. Wedgwood, *op. cit.*, which contains references to other sources as well.

statute and by judicial interpretation.[1] Now it was acts against the commonwealth rather than the King, as defined by the House of Commons: including even actions done, as Strafford's were, with the King's command or authorization. On such a view of treason, the King ceased to be the head and protector of the body politic. Not he, but parliament, became the guardian of the law. The supreme crime was not one that struck at the King's person or power, but that undermined the immemorial constitution of the kingdom by attacking its free institutions.[2]

A month before the trial began, Lord Digby, conscious of the legal flaw in the impeachment, urged the House to proceed by bill of attainder instead: this would be the best way, he believed, to remove the scruples the peers might feel as judges that Strafford's offences, however heinous, were not treason.[3] The managers and members rejected his advice. They did not doubt the justice of the accusation, and they desired the solemnity of a judicial condemnation from the upper House that would permit Strafford to be punished without need to have the King's assent, as a bill of attainder required.

But as Digby foresaw, their conception of treason was vulnerable to arguments that Strafford used during his trial with powerful effect. It was hard, the earl pointed out, that a man should be called a traitor for an offence unknown to any statute and now invoked for the first time. His prosecutors could not show a single action of his that was treasonable in itself according to the law. They posed as the law's defenders, but to make out their case, they resorted to an arbitrary construction that placed his treason in the sum and tenor of his deeds rather than in any definite transgression.

The course of Strafford's trial, however, was overshadowed by political exigencies which made even-handed justice impossible. An extremist mood dominated its atmosphere, such as arises when the

---

[1] Cf. G. R. Elton, *The Tudor constitution*, 59–61, for an account of the earlier law of treason.

[2] Precedents for the treason charge against Strafford have been carefully discussed by C. Russell, 'The theory of treason in the trial of Strafford,' *E.H.R.*, LXXX, 314 (1965). Although such precedents existed, the present writer remains convinced that the impeachment involved an appeal to an essentially revolutionary principle. Suggestive observations on the case will also be found in Clayton Roberts, *op. cit.*, ch. 3.

[3] Notestein, *D'Ewes*, 410n., 415–16. Digby was not the only member who saw difficulties. Somewhat earlier, Geoffrey Palmer, one of the lawyers who appeared for the Commons against Strafford, said in reference to the impeachment of Judge Berkeley that the justice's 'offence was not Treason within the 25 Ed. 3 butt whether it was Parliamentary Treason or nott, hee left.' (*ibid.*, 354n.). The phrase is highly significant and illustrates how the parliamentary leaders were asserting a revolutionary doctrine under the guise of law.

opponents of a regime believe that everything they contend for is at stake. Increasingly, a sense of impending violence hovered over the proceedings. Outside parliament the capital's populace stirred with hatred of the Lord Lieutenant. Within, the Commons' members met in daily dread of some intended treachery against them. The Irish army raised by Strafford, of such import in his trial, was still in being: nine thousand men, papists in arms, whom Charles refused to disband despite the House's request.[1] Who knew for what sinister purpose it was reserved? There were fears of Strafford's escape, fears too of intervention from the King's northern army which lay inactive and discontented for want of pay. Suspicions on the latter score were well-founded, for at the beginning of April Pym learned the first details of a plot to march the army to London to overawe the parliament. Its organizers, a group of courtiers and M.P.s holding military commands, undertook their scheme with the King's knowledge and the Queen's encouragement.[2] The party leaders harboured profound distrust of Charles which he did nothing to dissipate. Beset on every side by apprehension, they considered Strafford not only a criminal, but a public enemy whose annihilation was essential to the safety of the state.

Yet with each day the impeachment went on, its outcome seemed more uncertain. The peers did their duty in a judicial spirit, not as partisans, and the Commons' anger rose against them for the latitude —in truth, it was little enough—they allowed Strafford in his defence. The relations between the Houses became badly strained as the trial ran its unprecedented length. The peers, determined to maintain their dignity, would not be the Commons' tool, while the Commons treated their impartiality as an inexcusable indulgence to a traitor.

Strafford behaved under his ordeal with dauntless composure. His mien and reasoning gained palpably upon his judges. The most damaging article was the twenty-third, which charged him with advising the use of the Irish army 'to reduce this kingdom'—a phrase, according to the impeachment, that referred to England. The source of this accusation was the testimony of Secretary Vane, whom the prosecution managers had questioned with other privy councillors in a pre-trial examination. On 5 April Vane was called to give his evidence on Strafford's words in open court. In reply, the earl denied

[1] Notestein, *D'Ewes*, 213. On 14 April the King replied to a request for the Irish army's disbanding with what in effect was a denial, *L.J.*, IV, 216. It was not until the summer of 1641 that he ordered the demobilization of this army; cf. Clarendon, *Rebellion*, III, 252 and *infra*, 257.

[2] Cf. S. R. Gardiner, *History*, IX, 308–18, for an account of the army plot. On 6 April, the House of Commons, fearing danger from the northern army, voted that anyone who ordered it to advance without the consent of both Houses should be accounted an enemy of the state, *C.J.*, II, 116.

ever speaking them or proposing such a thing. The Irish Army, he said, was intended against Scotland, not England. When other councillors were called, none, not even the earl of Northumberland, corroborated Vane's recollection on the crucial point. Thus, as Strafford emphasized, there was but the memory of a single witness to the charge. He countered further with a strong appeal to the sensibility of his judges. They were born, he told them, to great employments. If every opinion a councillor delivered were to be raked over by enemies seeking a treasonous intent, then no noble person of fortune could ever be safe in serving the King.

As the day's proceedings ended, it might well seem that the case against Strafford was in heavy trouble. Yet at this juncture, the opposition leaders became divided themselves on the tactics to be pursued. Despite all difficulties, Pym still hoped for a favourable verdict from the Lords. To protect the younger Vane, he had so far kept secret that he himself had seen and copied the notes of the Council meeting where Strafford was accused of giving his treasonable advice. He now resolved to make public this additional evidence in support of Secretary Vane's testimony. On 10 April he and Sir Henry Vane junior told the House of Commons of their transaction the previous October and Pym read from his own copy the passages relating to the charge in the twenty-third article.[1] Other members, however, weary of the obstacles encountered in the case, probably despairing of the result as well, were already planning to abandon the impeachment for another way. Thus, on the same day that Pym made his sensational disclosure, the oppositionist Sir Arthur Haselrig introduced a bill of attainder against Strafford.[2] After some discussion in which most speakers advocated attainder rather than impeachment, the bill received a first reading.[3]

This was the first political difference to arise among the opposition leaders since the beginning of parliament. To drop the impeachment amounted to a declaration of non-confidence in the peers. It would insult them and impair further the unity of the Houses so necessary to the achievement of reform. These considerations did not weigh with the attainder's proponents. They had seen enough of the Commons' spokesmen appearing before the Lords as pleaders. A legislative declaration of treason would put both Houses on an equal footing; moreover, it would not need to be so strictly subject to the rule of law behind which the traitor sheltered.

---

[1] *C.J.*, II, 118.

[2] Clarendon, *Rebellion*, III, 128, gives Haselrig as the proposer, though he confuses the chronology. It is most unlikely that Halserig would have acted without the support of other oppositionists of like mind.

[3] D'Ewes, *Journal*, B.M. Harl. 164, f. 163b.

It was thoroughly characteristic of Pym's leadership that he was unwilling to endorse a course of action calculated to offend the Lords if he could possibly avoid it.[1] On the 12th, he spoke against a second reading of the attainder bill, urging the House 'to goe the other way because this is the safer to shew that wee & the Lords are reconciled & not severed. . . .' For the moment the House heeded his words; but on the 14th the bill was read a second time.[2] Next day St. John and others vehemently opposed any further pleading before the Lords as prejudicial to the attainder. Both Pym and Hampden, however, as well as Strode and Sir Walter Erle, declared that the House would dishonour itself if it withdrew from the proceedings. The result of the disagreement was a compromise of sorts on the 16th. The members consented to be present in Westminster Hall as a committee of the whole to hear Strafford's counsel argue the issues of law arising from the evidence; nevertheless, they would not permit the managers of the prosecution to reply. If the Lords desired satisfaction on any point, it should be given in a conference of committees of the two Houses.[3] The peers had to acquiesce in this arrangement. In fact, it signified that notwithstanding Pym's and Hampden's persuasions, the House of Commons had definitely abandoned the impeachment.

The attainder was debated in the Commons from the 14th to the 21st. Once the question of procedure was settled, all the party leaders threw themselves into the effort to pass the bill. Everything possible was done to give it the semblance of a judicial verdict whose form alone was altered. The charges in the impeachment were discussed one-by-one in a committee of the whole House which voted them to have been proved and to constitute high treason. Debate revealed that Strafford had made converts. Some members doubted if his acts were treason or tended to subvert the fundamental laws. Others demanded to know what the fundamental laws were. 'I was much amazed,' recorded the indignant D'Ewes, 'to see soe many . . . speak on . . . Straffords side.'[4] The most conspicuous defector was Lord Digby, a manager of the prosecution, who denounced the attainder, even though he had been the first to suggest it. He professed to hate Strafford's tyranny as much as ever, yet he could not in conscience, he declared, vote a death sentence 'upon a Law made a Posteriori.'[5]

---

[1] Miss Wedgwood (*op. cit.*, 357–9) takes no account of the fact that Pym did not favour proceeding by attainder and erroneously supposes that the bill was his idea.　　[2] D'Ewes, Journal, B.M. Harl. 164, f. 165a; *C.J.*, II, 120.
[3] D'Ewes, Journal, B.M. Harl. 163, ff. 47a–48a; *Notes of the proceedings in the Long Parliament . . . by Sir Ralph Verney*, ed. J. Bruce, *Camden society*, XXXI, 1845, 49–50; *C.J.*, II, 122, *L.J.*, IV, 220.
[4] D'Ewes, Journal, B.M. Harl. 163, f. 45a.
[5] Digby's speech, an eloquent utterance, is printed in J. Nalson, *op. cit.*, II, 157–60.

Selden, a long-standing adherent of the Country, also opposed the bill on legal grounds.[1] On 21 April, it passed the Commons in a vote of 204 to 59. Pym was immediately delegated to take it to the Lords. In spite of the large majority, many members deliberately refrained from voting: 'a symptom,' said one of these absentees, 'of no great satisfaction.'[2]

The House of Lords' assent to the attainder was obtained only with the very greatest difficulty. The majority, deeply annoyed by the Commons' refusal to go on with the impeachment, showed its resentment by opposition and delay. Although the peers received the bill on the 21st with a message stressing its urgency, they did not even give it a first reading till the 26th. Three days later both Houses met in Westminster Hall as committees of the whole to hear the Commons justify the legality of the attainder.[3] It was no accident that St. John, the principal advocate of the bill, spoke for the lower House on this occasion. Despite its thick larding of lawyer's citations, his argument stretched the law to make room for its antithesis, reason of state. In a bitter passage, he likened Strafford to a beast of prey, no more entitled to law than foxes or wolves who are killed as they are found.[4] The iron doctrine of a necessity higher than the law was thus publicly enunciated in the most solemn way by a leader of the Long Parliament.[5] It was to reappear in time to haunt its promulgator and to be repeatedly invoked as a justification for every political overturn of the next twenty years.

The advance of a revolution steadily destroys the ground on which moderates try to keep a stand between contending extremes. This was the lot of the peers, who would probably have asserted their independence by rejecting the bill if not for the intensifying pressures on them. Two great fears beset them which all moderates feel in revolutionary times: fear of a 'rightist' reaction, fear of the mutinous people. While they debated the attainder, the air was thick with rumours predicting Strafford's escape and a *coup* against parliament.[6] The Country leaders were convinced that a calamity impended which only Strafford's immediate condemnation could avert. In its agitation, the

---

[1] *Verney notes*, 54.

[2] *C.J.*, II, 125; Sir John Coke, M.P. for Derbyshire, to his father, *H.M.C. Cowper*, II, 279, 283.

[3] *L.J.*, IV, 227. [4] J. Rushworth, III, 702–3.

[5] This was not the first time, however, that an oppositionist used the plea of necessity. On 20 February Pym invoked the same idea in a debate concerning the raising of money to pay the Scots. He declared that the Londoners could be compelled to lend in case of public necessity and that parliament could assume a legislative power to this end. One parliamentary diarist noted that Pym's words were more dangerous to liberty and property than Strafford's; Notestein, *D'Ewes*, 382 and n.

[6] *C.J.*, II, 130; *L.J.*, IV, 230.

House of Commons on 3 May sounded an alarm akin to the famous *la patrie en danger* proclaimed at the end of the next century in revolutionary France. On a proposal from Pym, the members adopted a Protestation vowing to each other before God to defend liberty and religion, the King and the law, against conspiracy and violence.[1] In the next two days the Lords also accepted the Protestation and its circulation was permitted throughout the kingdom. At the same time Pym told the lower House of the plot to disaffect the northern army.[2] His account gave the menacing shapes of the public fever a habitation and a name. Indirectly, it implicated the King and Queen in a conspiracy by some of their own attendants to bring down the army with the aim of intimidating the Houses and liberating Strafford. Under the impression of these developments, the Commons took an extraordinary step. Fearful lest the King dissolve parliament and render it powerless to defend the kingdom, the House ordered a bill drawn up to prohibit the present parliament from being dissolved, adjourned, or prorogued without its own consent. The bill was passed on the 7th and transmitted immediately to the Lords.[3]

No doubt the threat of violence on the King's behalf convinced some of the peers of the necessity to preserve unity with the Commons by passing the attainder. If that were insufficient to persuade them, there was the London populace to reckon with. Thus far the main scene of the revolution had been parliament, but now it poured out on to the streets to incarnate itself for the first time in armed and angry masses. Reports of plots had roused the Londoners to a pitch of excitement and they seethed with impatience at the Lords' recalcitrance. On 3 and 4 May thousands of them carrying swords and staves thronged down to Westminster to demand Strafford's condemnation. Most probably this demonstration was organized by Venn and other citizen oppositionists.[4] Pressing thickly around the arriving noblemen, the crowds clamoured for the earl's execution. Inside the House of Lords the members had to deliberate with the outcries of riotous citizens ringing at the doors.[5]

[1] *C.J.*, II, 132; *Verney notes*, 66–71.
[2] *L.J.*, IV, 234; *C.J.*, II, 134, 135; J. Rushworth, IV, 240. Rushworth dates Pym's report on 3 May, but it was most likely delivered on the 5th; cf. S. R. Gardiner, *History*, IX, 351n. For the army plot, cf. *supra*, 219.
[3] *C.J.*, II, 136, 137.
[4] This may be surmised from Venn's prominence in the presentation of a citizen petition to parliament on 24 April which called for Strafford's punishment. The crowd that assembled on 3 May professed to be seeking an answer to the earlier petition; *C.J.*, II, 125; *L.J.*, IV, 232.
[5] C. H. Firth, *The House of Lords during the civil war*, 86–7; R. Sharpe, *op. cit.*, II, 138–9. The crowds were estimated at five or six to ten thousand. They consisted of shopkeepers, craftsmen, apprentices, and many citizens 'of very good account. . . .'

Before the spectres of reaction and mob violence the peers gave in. On the 4th they intimated to the Commons that they would expedite the attainder if the crowds departed. Four days later, in a House of many absentees, they passed the bill.[1] Because the entries in the Lords' Journal pertaining to the attainder were expunged after the Restoration, the exact vote remains uncertain. Contemporary estimates reckoned it variously as 26 to 19, 35 to 11, and 51 to 9.[2] What is clear is that many noblemen who lacked courage to vote against the attainder still had courage enough not to vote for it. The same day that the upper House condemned Strafford, it also passed the bill against the sitting parliament's dissolution without its own consent.[3] The party leaders in the Commons, aided by the London crowd, thus secured the Lords' assent to the two measures they deemed indispensable to the safety of parliament and their own cause.

Strafford's tragedy was nearly done. Day and night on 8 and 9 May, while threatening multitudes surged around Whitehall, the King in an agony of conscience considered whether to consent to the bill of attainder. Prior to the opening of parliament he had promised to preserve the earl's life and fortune; moreover, honour and gratitude alike bound him to the minister. Yet on the 4th Strafford wrote Charles from the Tower, magnanimously absolving him from all obligation and beseeching the passage of the attainder for the peace of the kingdom.[4] And, in fact, no other course was possible if the King did not wish to provoke civil war.[5] The capital was clearly out of control, even the royal family itself in danger. On the 10th he ratified both Strafford's condemnation and the bill against parliament's dissolution without its own consent. Two days afterward on Tower Hill, before an immense mass of onlookers, the axe prepared by the opposition leaders struck off Strafford's head.

In the momentous confrontation between Strafford and his accusers, it was he rather than they who stood out larger to absorbed contemporaries, as he does still to posterity. He was the greatest tragic figure among the revolution's victims. A man of many flaws, brought low from the summit of power by his arrogance and injustice, he proved himself at the close the equal in spirit of the forces that destroyed him. Yet his triumph in adversity was a purely personal one. Politically, his work was sterile and ended in complete

---

[1] *L.J.*, IV, 233, 240.

[2] Cf. Clarendon, *Rebellion*, III, 196 and n.; C. Russell, *loc. cit.*, 48–50, prints thirteen propositions respecting Strafford's guilt on which the Lords voted affirmatively on 5, 6, and 7 May.   [3] *L.J.*, IV, 241.

[4] Cf. the letter in J. Rushworth, III, 743–4.

[5] Cf. the description in Clarendon, *Rebellion*, III, 197, 202, of 'The rage and fury of the people.'

failure. 'Holder of one position, wrong for years,' he had no legacy to bequeath a revolutionary generation. The men who interposed their will against King Charles I and his two royal sons could receive nothing from Strafford.

The course of Strafford's trial revealed the explosive potencies beneath the surface of the Country's revolution. The germs of a civil war were already present, only held in check for the time by the King's weakness and capitulation. Raging political passions, the intervention of turbulent crowds, a trend towards violence—all ominous pointers that the conflict might easily assume another form. In an ordeal that tried their mettle to the limit, the parliamentary leaders neither wavered nor compromised. They demonstrated that they were no triflers playing at opposition, but shrewd, determined politicians who would have their way.

Nevertheless, to attain their end they subjected the Houses to such pressure that they strained the unity of their parliamentary support. Of the fifty-nine in the House of Commons who voted against the attainder, only four were on parliament's side fifteen months later when the civil war began.[1] It must be assumed that for most of the others, if not all, Strafford's trial was a milestone in their progress towards the King. In the House of Lords, the earl of Southampton, known previously like his father as an adherent of the popular party, dissociated himself from the attack on Strafford, refused to take the Protestation, and thenceforth supported the King. The oppositionist earl of Hertford followed a similar path.[2]

Despite some defections, however, the alliance around the Country in the House of Commons was still intact. Men like Edward Hyde and Lord Falkland, afterwards prominent Royalists, voted for the attainder.[3] The task of reform was only begun, and if members resented the way the parliamentary leaders drove the House, this feeling was offset by their fears of violence from the King. Before' this threat they drew together, judging Strafford's death necessary to parliament's safety.

It was on the King that the proceedings against Strafford bore hardest. Pym's party forced from Charles concessions scarcely compatible with his conception of what it meant to rule. His assent to the

---

[1] Cf. D. Brunton and D. H. Pennington, *op. cit.*, App. VI. The four Parliamentarians who voted against the attainder were John Alford, Robert Scawen, Selden, and Sir Richard Wynn.

[2] *D.N.B.*, *s.v.*, 'Thomas Wriothesley, fourth earl of Southampton;' Clarendon, *Rebellion*, IV, 294, VI, 385.

[3] Hyde's silence on the matter in both the *Rebellion* and the *Life* gives convincing ground to conclude that he voted for the attainder. Firth also thought he did so; cf. *D.N.B.*, *s.v.* On Falkland's vote, cf. *D.N.B.*, *s.v.*, 'Lucius Cary, second viscount Falkland.'

attainder was extorted, not given. The act against parliament's dissolution without its consent was not the redress of a grievance but an aggression upon a long consecrated attribute of regal authority. Faced with the possibility of a *coup*, the Houses ventured to possess themselves of a power never previously claimed by their predecessors. On the other hand, the party managers could declare with reason that they acted from self-defence. Charles obstinately protected the minister whom they branded traitor, while he showed by his encouragement of the army plot that he was ready to sanction the use of force against parliament. Whatever trust they had in his intentions suffered a profound deterioration. Trust, without which reconciliation was impossible and even constitutional reform ineffectual, was the greatest casualty of Strafford's attainder. The earl had laid his head on the block as a peace-offering, but his death made the split between the King and his opponents wider than ever.

5

The storm that struck the King's regime also broke down the barriers to religious innovation. With the meeting of the Long Parliament the Laudian rule collapsed. Its fall put an end to the further possibility of any effective control over the religious life of the people. All at once the rebellious spiritual forces which crown and church had kept in check for many decades found an outlet. Against the desire of parliament itself, England entered an era of religious experimentation unparalleled in its history.

The one point on which nearly all men agreed in 1640 was that the bishops must be paid out for their delinquencies. On 7 November, the speakers who rose for the first time in the Commons to recite the kingdom's woes dwelt with indignation on episcopal usurpations.[1] Not a voice was raised in the prelates' defence. These men found themselves dangerously isolated because of the Anglo-Catholic predominance of recent years. They were pursued in the next months with stinging obloquy, while all about them a clamour of voices proclaimed the hour of emancipation from clerical tyranny.

Among the Commons' earliest actions was to order the release from prison of Prynne and other victims of Laudian persecution.[2] On 28 November thousands of Londoners greeted Prynne and Burton as they arrived in the capital. It was akin, wrote a Puritan witness of the scene, to 'the returne of the captivity from Babilon.'[3] In December

---

[1] Cf. the speeches in J. Rushworth, IV, 21–37. Several are dated the 9th, but D'Ewes's Journal makes clear that they were delivered on the 7th.

[2] *C.J.*, II, 22, 24.

[3] From the diary of Robert Woodford, steward of Northampton, *H.M.C. Ninth report*, pt. II, 499.

the House loosed its thunderbolt against convocation, which had deeply offended because of the canons and oath enacted earlier that year.[1] Resolutions of the 15th and 16th stated that convocation had no power to bind either clergy or laity without assent of parliament and that the canons of 1640 were contrary to law.[2] This declaration, founded on a claim expressed unavailingly in former parliaments, was of far-reaching importance.[3] It extended the principle of lay representation to ecclesiastical legislation; and it tore a gaping breach in the crown's religious supremacy, since hitherto canons had been made with the royal assent alone.[4]

The denunciation of the canons mentioned Laud as 'an Actor in the great Design of the Subversion of the Laws of the Realm, and of the Religion,' i.e., of the Calvinist-Protestant foundation of the national church. This laid the basis for his impeachment on 18 December. The Lords immediately ordered him into custody.[5] He was to remain in prison till his trial and execution four years later. This was still not the end of the canons, however. In April 1641 the lower House was considering a bill to fine the members of convocation of both ecclesiastical provinces, and in August it impeached thirteen bishops for high crimes and misdemeanours in making canons and constitutions ecclesiastical.[6]

Beyond the culpability of individual bishops and the presumption of convocation lay the question of episcopacy itself—whether to try to reform the institution or to abolish it entirely. When parliament opened, London Puritans were already busy circulating a petition in favour of the more radical solution. By mid-November, many names had been secured, but the promoters, on the advice of friendly M.P.s, decided to postpone the petition's delivery until the attack against the bishops had gained momentum.[7] On 11 December it was

[1] Cf. *supra*, 191.

[2] *C.J.*, II, 51, 52; cf. the debate on the powers of convocation in Notestein, *D'Ewes*, 152–7, 160–2.

[3] Cf. J. E. Neale, *Elizabeth I and her parliaments, 1584–1601*, 67, and R. G. Usher, *The reconstruction of the English church*, I, 363–4, II, 116–17. In 1607, the House of Commons passed a bill, subsequently rejected by the Lords, 'to restrain the execution of canons ecclesiastical not confirmed by Parliament'; cf. J. R. Tanner, *Constitutional documents . . . James I*, 230–1.

[4] The House of Lords concurred in these resolutions in June 1641, *L.J.*, IV, 273.

[5] *C.J.*, II, 54.

[6] *Ibid.*, II, 129, 235. J. Rushworth, IV, 235–8, prints some particulars of the bill to fine the members of convocation. It imposed very stiff sums, but seems to have been laid aside.

[7] Edward Bagshawe, the anti-clerical M.P. for Southwark, was shown the petition immediately after his election to the House of Commons. Baillie, one of the Scottish commissioners, saw it in mid-November; B. Hanbury, *op. cit.*, II, 141; R. Baillie, *op. cit.*, I, 274, 275.

brought to the House of Commons. Printed, with a roll of fifteen thousand signatures attached, and accompanied by a crowd of fifteen hundred people, it was presented to the House by the city's oppositionist M.P., Alderman Penington. Only a well-organized group of activists could have planned a demonstration of such size[1].

The petition of the London citizens was the fiercest denunciation of episcopacy to be heard in England since the days of the Disciplinarian movement. Its bold language and comprehensive indictment forced the whole issue of church government squarely into the open. Declaring episcopal rule to be a cause of many evils in both church and state, the petition asked for its abolition 'with all its dependencies, roots and branches. . . .' A long litany of complaints set forth the bishops' misdeeds. They hindered preaching, persecuted good ministers, and suppressed the truth of God; they encouraged their dependents to contemn the nobility and gentry; they propagated Arminian and popish doctrines and fostered the increase of popery and Jesuits; of boundless ambition, they considered their office to be *jure divino* and possessed themselves of temporal dignities; they invaded liberty and property; they drove multitudes of Englishmen to exile; they incited the Scottish war.

Literal truth is not to be found in manifestos. If the Root-and-Branch petition charged the bishops with more than justice allowed, it contained just truth enough to make its accusations plausible. What was significant was that the petitioners accepted these statements. So low had the bishops' reputation fallen that no scandal against them was too extreme to be believed.

The petition displayed one striking omission. Entirely critical in substance, it proposed no alternative to prelacy except the ambiguous formula that 'the government according to God's Word may be . . . placed amongst us.' The means to redress the evils complained of, said the petitioners, they referred 'to the consideration of this Honourable Assembly. . . .'[2]

The Root-and-Branch petition was a blazing star that brought a swarm of satellites in its train: for in the following months petitions on church government came in from all parts of the kingdom—some favouring episcopacy, but many more against. Up and down the counties men promoted subscriptions demanding the hierarchy's overthrow. Members of parliament presented petitions from their constituencies signed by hundreds and thousands.[3] People of every

---

[1] Notestein, *D'Ewes*, 138.

[2] The Root-and-Branch petition is printed in S. R. Gardiner, *Constitutional documents of the Puritan revolution*, 137–44.

[3] Cf., e.g., the petitions submitted on 25 January 1641 by the county members for Hertford, Bedford, Sussex, Surrey, Cheshire, Warwick,

rank were solicited, from noblemen to poor tenants: a Cheshire petition against the bishops, for instance, professed to be signed by more than twelve thousand freeholders and such like, as well as several lords and many knights, esquires, and gentlemen.[1] In their zeal, the bishops' enemies took the hands of ignorant persons who had no idea of what they were endorsing. Very likely fraudulent signatures were not infrequently included.[2]

Yet even allowing for these practices, such a mass outpouring against the church was beyond example. From every quarter the popular anger snapped and bit. In the press, intemperate pamphleteers assailed the hierarchy without restraint. Bishop Hall indignantly appealed to parliament against their violence. '. . . how many furious persons,' he wrote in January 1641, '. . . have burst forth into slanderous libels, bitter pasquins, railing pamphlets . . . wherein they have endeavoured . . . to wound that sacred government, which . . . derives itself from the times of the blessed Apostles. . . .' Three months later he estimated the number of 'late seditious pamphlets' to equal at least one hundred and forty since the beginning of parliament.[3]

At the same time, encouraged by the Commons' grand committee on religion, which created a sub-committee for scandalous ministers, many parishes were complaining against their own clergymen. On 19 December 1640 the sub-committee was made into a separate committee, and during the first months of its existence it received more than eight hundred petitions.[4] Their drift appears in some from Kentish parishes. Petitioners denounced their ministers for being too ceremonial; for preaching against the Scots and Puritans; for burdening men's consciences with superstitious observances; for ridiculing 'sincerity and forwardness in profession, under the names of faction, schisme, and singularity.'[5] In view of this fusillade of criticism, it was no wonder that the county's M.P., Sir Edward Dering, was told by a

---

[1] *C.S.P.D. 1640–41*, 529.

[2] This was acknowledged by Lady Brilliana Harley, who thought only 'such hands should be taken as understand it, and will stand to what they have done' (*Letters of Lady Brilliana Harley*, 113–14). On 18 November 1641, the House of Commons referred to a committee the consideration of irregularities in petitions collected for and against episcopacy, *C.J.*, II, 319.

[3] Joseph Hall, *A humble remonstrance to the high court of parliament*, 1641, *Works*, new ed., 12v., Oxford, 1837, X, 275; *A defence of the humble remonstrance*, 1641, *ibid.*, X, 290.

[4] *C.J.*, II, 54; W. Shaw, *A history of the English Church . . . 1640–1660*, 2v., L., 1900, II, 177.

[5] *Proceedings in Kent*, 148–9, 158–60, 182–3, 192–3, 202–4.

Suffolk, Cambridge, Gloucester, Buckingham, and Norfolk, Notestein, D'Ewes, 282–3.

friend, '. . . the Monstrous Easye receipt of Petitions att the Standing Committees makes Authoritye declyne. . . .'[1]

So sudden a fall of Laud and his clergy made the Puritan mind almost giddy. Surely God's punishment was manifest in this reversal of fortune! And surely the divine favour that accomplished such a mercy to the faithful had fresh dispensations in store! Events nourished an expectation that grew in the church's antagonists with irresistible force. A mood as much as a hope, often inchoate in its yearning, it nevertheless infused religion with a dynamism that buoyed up the entire revolution and swept it on. Its substance was the presentiment of a mighty spiritual rebirth transfiguring the nation into a new Israel. Those whom it inspired felt themselves to be crusaders in a holy cause, their aim not merely the removal of particular evils but the institution of a perpetual sabbath in the land. This glowing hope, the myth of a pious generation, was already voiced at the beginning of parliament when the Rev. Stephen Marshall preached to the House of Commons on 17 November 1640, the first parliamentary fast day, an occasion the more memorable as being also the anniversary of Queen Elizabeth's accession. His sermon exhorted the members that a religious reformation was their supreme task. They were to 'pluck up every plant that God hath not planted. . . . That it may be said of this Parliament . . . as . . . of Josiah, there was never any like him before . . . nor any after him. . . .'[2] Many Puritans came to share Marshall's expectations as the attack upon episcopacy broadened. In the summer of 1641, Milton, deep in controversy against the bishops, exultantly called his time 'an age of ages wherein God is manifestly come downe among us. . . .' 'O perfect, and accomplish thy glorious acts,' he implored the deity, and

When thou hast settled peace in the Church, and righteous judgment in the Kingdome, then shall all thy Saints addresse their voyces of joy . . . standing on the shoare of that red Sea into which our enemies had almost driven us.[3]

Soon after, Lord Brooke gave utterance in a similar vein:

. . . now . . . the Clouds begin to breake away. . . . Now the Sun againe mounteth up in our Horizon. . . . God hath raised up a more glorious Light among these Northerne Iles. . . . Light dilating, and enlarging it

[1] B.M. Stowe MSS. 184, f. 31.

[2] Stephen Marshall, *A sermon preached before the . . . Commons . . . November 17. 1640*, ed. 1645, 3, 40.

[3] John Milton, *Animadversions upon the remonstrants defence*, 1641, *Prose works*, 5v., Bohn ed., L., n.d., III, 72.

selfe, seemeth to become more pure, more Light, more Glorious; and yet it seemes not to be Noone. The Light, still, will, must, cannot but encrease. . . .[1]

The same enlarging vision was reaffirmed by Stephen Marshall when he preached again to the Commons on the eve of the September 1641 recess. Surveying recent developments, he was filled with gratitude:

This one yeer, this wonderful yeer, wherein God hath done more for us . . . then in fourscore years before, breaking so many yokes, giving such hopes and beginnings of a very Jubilee and Resurrection. . . .[2]

Of course, these utopian perspectives were destined to extinction with the years. Many were the would-be builders of the new Jerusalem; but so various were their designs that they could never reconcile their differences. Time would presently show that the opponents of episcopacy agreed only in what they rejected, not in what they would set in the bishops' place. Lord Brooke, killed early in the civil war, did not live to see the total disappointment of his hopes; but Marshall and Milton were to witness the steady fragmentation of religious life and to hear the babel of discord, as the kingdom fell prey to the bitter quarrels of denominational rivals who smote each other mercilessly in press and pulpit.

Yet this result was only to be expected. For how could the newly liberated thrust for reformation be cribb'd and cabin'd inside the canonical definitions of any orthodoxy? The revolution inaugurated the final age of faith among the English people. For the last time the still living spirit of the Protestant Reformation flared up in a fierce resolve to complete the work begun a century ago. Under its invincible pressure, the whole frame of ecclesiastical order gave way. Puritanism, looking forward to a purified national church backed by the state, discovered, however, that it was no longer in sole possession of the field. Within a few months of the opening of parliament, it was joined by a luxuriant growth of separatist bodies whose presence was henceforth fatal to any claim to supremacy by an exclusive state church.

This proliferation was ultimately due to the inspiration of Puritanism itself. For the separatist was a Puritan offspring, sharing the same imperative need for holiness, the same disillusion with the infirmities of the established church. But while the Puritan adhered steadfastly to the ideal of a national church, the separatist broke away, embodying his vision of a purified church order in the sect and congregation

---

[1] Lord Brooke, *A discourse opening the nature of . . . episcopacie*, 1641, ed. 1642, 94–5, 116.　　[2] Stephen Marshall, *A peace-offering to God*, 1641, 40.

determined to live their independent life free of external constraint.[1] From Elizabeth's time on, there were sporadic secessions of this kind —small, persecuted bodies like those formed in the 1580s by Robert Browne, Henry Barrow, and John Greenwood, ardent men bent on reformation 'without tarrying for any.' What separatism represented in essence was the voluntaristic principle of religious association. It was totally opposed to a territorial church embracing the entire nation by compulsion. It would have no part in parish assemblies which mingled the regenerate and the profane in an ungodly hodge-podge. The only earthly church it recognized was the particular group of believers, called and chosen, who joined freely together for worship and discipline. Its polity was therefore irreconcilable not only with bishops and the crown's religious supremacy, but with any Puritan state-enforced ecclesiastical system as well.

Until 1641 separatism was numerically insignificant and without much influence upon religious life. It existed in such obscure bodies as the fissiparous Barrowist churches in England and Holland; in a few anabaptist sects; in the independent congregation which Henry Jacob founded at London in 1616; and in a few other scattered, sometimes ephemeral groups of worshippers, like the conventicles detected at Newington, Surrey in 1632 or at Dover in 1639.[2] Its main centre was London. In 1611 a sectary before the High Commission declared that 'there were yet left six or seven churches in London which had not submitted themselves to the Antichristian rule . . . of Lord byshops. . . .' Nearly twenty years later, the bishop of Exeter told Laud that he knew of eleven congregations of separatists in the capital who met every Sunday in brew houses.[3]

Unlike the Puritan laity, which included a cross-section of the dominant class, separatism was constituted almost wholly of poor

---

[1] For the development and varieties of separatism prior to 1641, cf. C. Burrage, *op. cit.*, I, and W. K. Jordan, *The development of religious toleration in England*, II, 216–314. The separatists and pre-revolutionary congregationalists have been distinguished on the ground that the latter would have retained some degree of communion between their own and other congregations; cf. C. Burrage, *op. cit.*, I, ch. XII. While this was so, congregationalism belonged fundamentally to the separatist phenomenon, both because it abandoned the national church and because it defined the church as a particular body of believers not subject to any superior jurisdiction. The congregationalism of Massachusetts Bay was non-separatist, since there it established a state church; cf. P. Miller, *op. cit.* This was quite exceptional, however, and was never the case in the mother country. Both W. K. Jordan, *The development of religious toleration in England*, II, 219–20, and G. F. Nuttall, the most perceptive modern historian of congregationalism (cf. *Visible saints*, Oxford, 1957, ch. I) treat it as a manifestation of separatist principles. [2] C. Burrage, *op. cit.*, II, 320–2; *C.S.P.D. 1639–40*, 80–3. [3] R. G. Usher, *The rise and fall of the High Commission*, 208; *C.S.P.D. 1631–33*, 74.

and humble folk. A list of sixty-one separatists of Great Yarmouth in 1628 contained such representative occupations as shoemaker, brewer, tailor, carter, gardener, turner, grocer, and servants. Another list from the same town two years later described the richest separatist as a grocer worth £100 at most and heavily in debt; the rest were all poor and those in prison constrained to live 'on the baskett.'[1] To the same inferior strata belonged a group of Londoners arrested at a conventicle in 1638, who gave their trades as clothworker, lastmaker, weaver, and cordwainer.[2] The leader of the Dover conventicle discovered in 1639 was a London mason temporarily employed on some fortifications near the town. Though illiterate, he was a fluent preacher and expounder of Scripture.[3] In Bristol, the separatist group in the 1630s from which the Broadmead Baptist church later evolved, usually met at the house of a glover or a carpenter. The other members included a grocer, a 'writing-schoolmaster,' a farrier, and a victualler. The grocer's widow, Mrs. Kelley, 'was the first woman in this city of Bristol that practised the truth of the Lord, which was then hated and odious, namely separation.'[4]

During the Laudian repression, which fell with equal severity on every species of dissent, the differences between Puritans and separatists were obscured by their common sufferings and common hatred of the ecclesiastical regime. The archbishop's fall, however, altered the situation. As separatism began boldly to assert itself, its divergences from Puritanism became increasingly evident. Its opponents watched its growth in alarm, but could do nothing to check it. From numerous quarters came accounts of the multiplication of sects. A pamphleteer declared that 'the sectaries ... swell now beyond the reach of names and numbers. ...'[5] Nightly conventicles were reported in Norwich, 'as publickely knowne as the sermons in the day time, & ... much more frequented.'[6] A Kentish clergyman complained to Sir Edward Dering about the increase of separatists in the county and their extreme views:

They would have every particular congregation to be independent. ...

[1] P.R.O. S.P. 16/124/81; C. Burrage, *op. cit.*, II, 309–10.
[2] *Ibid.*, II, 323–4.
[3] *C.S.P.D. 1639–40*, 80–3. That the mason was illiterate appears from the fact that he had to make his mark to the report of his examination by the mayor and jurats.
[4] *The records of a church of Christ meeting in Broadmead, Bristol*, ed. E. B. Underhill, *Hanserd Knollys society*, L., 1847.
[5] *A survay of that foolish, seditious ... libell, the Protestation protested*, 1641, cited in B. Hanbury, *op. cit.*, II, 83.
[6] *The Knyvett letters*, ed. B. Schofield, *Norfolk record society*, XX, 1949, 98–9.

They would have the votes about every matter of jurisdiction ... to be drawne up from the whole body of the church ... both men and women. They would have none enter communion but by solemne covenant: Not y^t made in Baptisme, or renewed in the supper of the Lord, but another for reformation after their owne way.[1]

To Sir Robert Harley came a similar address from a Herefordshire clergyman: 'I can assure yow the best ministers complayne in severall countryes how much they suffer ... with that schysme.'[2] D'Ewes noted in his journal in June 1641 that the freedom of preaching by 'mechanicall men' in London redounded to parliament's dishonour, as if while suppressing popery 'wee intended to bring in atheisme & confusion.'[3]

There was a significant meaning to the appearance of this vigorous outgrowth of sects and separatists. Demanding freedom to pursue their spiritual purposes unimpeded, it was they who injected the burning issue of religious toleration into the revolution. Hitherto Puritanism had stood for liberty and reformation against the bishops. The separatists now invoked the identical claim against the Puritans. Already in May 1641, Prynne's fellow martyr, Henry Burton, now become a separatist advocate, was writing:

If a state will set up a National Church ... let not this exclude and bar out the free use of such Congregations ... whereof the spiritual commonwealth of Israel consisteth; over which, Christ, as King, immediately reigneth. ... Let not the conscience of God's people be bound, where Christ hath purchased liberty. ...[4]

Here was a position the Puritan mind found deeply disturbing. 'Is it fitting,' asked the Rev. Thomas Edwards, a *quondam* non-conformist,

that well meaning Christians should be suffered to ... make churches, and ... choose whom they will for Ministers; as some tailor, felt-maker, button-maker. ...

Such a freedom would subvert both state and clergy. Were toleration granted,

the most eminent ministers in this kingdom for parts, grace, and

---

[1] B.M. Stowe MSS. 184, ff. 27–9.

[2] *H.M.C. Portland*, III, 80.

[3] B.M. Harl. 163, f. 276a.

[4] Henry Burton, *The Protestation protested*, 1641, cited in B. Hanbury, *op. cit.*, II, 75. For producing this pamphlet, its printer was committed by the House of Commons, *C.J.*, II, 269–70.

The Country and the Constitutional Revolution

labours will have but little assurance of the continuance of their flocks to them. We see within this nine months though there be no Toleration . . . how are [the separatists] increased and multiplied.[1]

Thus as early as 1641, toleration, the parent of all heresy and schism according to its opposers, was becoming a divisive issue amongst the proponents of reformation. Meanwhile, however, of far greater immediate importance was the question of episcopal church government. For two months following the presentation of the Root-and-Branch petition, the Commons postponed consideration of the matter; this was undoubtedly because the party managers wanted to delay a debate that might provoke strong differences.[2] Towards the end of January 1641 the House received an alternative outline of reform from some hundreds of clergy including leading Puritan divines. Known as the Ministers' Petition, this was equally critical of the bishops, but would have retained them in some form while stripping them of all their secular employments and most of their spiritual jurisdiction.[3] The House had then to decide which of the two petitions to refer to a committee. Over this apparently procedural point, which nevertheless reached to the heart of the church question, the first great ecclesiastical debate occurred on 8 and 9 February.[4]

The ensuing speeches on episcopacy presented the earliest signs of potential division within the broad ranks of the Country and on this account deserve close study.[5] The essential point of difference was not one of conscientious attachment to episcopal church government

[1] Thomas Edwards, *Reasons against independent government of particular congregations, as also against . . . toleration*, 1641, cited in B. Hanbury, *op. cit.*, II, 104, 105.

[2] When the Root-and-Branch petition was presented on 11 December, the response to it in the House revealed germs of discord on the subject. Consideration of it was set for the 17th, but nothing was said of it that day; *C.J.*, II, 49; Notestein, *D'Ewes*, 140. On 13 January 1641, Sir Edward Dering told the House that the petition slept and asked leave to awaken it. Debate was accordingly set for 25 January, but it was then put off again; *Proceedings in Kent*, 27; *C.J.*, II, 67, 73.

[3] *C.J.*, II, 72; Notestein, *D'Ewes*, 277. The Ministers' Petition was presented on 23 January. Among its sponsors were the Revs. Cornelius Burges, Stephen Marshall, and Calybute Downing, *ibid.*, 313. The text has not survived, but its substance has been carefully reconstructed by W. Shaw, *op. cit.*, I, 23–6.

[4] D'Ewes noted in his pedantic way that 'divers mistaking the Question fell unto other long and large disputes,' Notestein, *D'Ewes*, 335. The issue of episcopacy, however, could hardly be separated from that of whether to commit the Root-and-Branch petition, since a favourable vote for the latter also meant that the Commons must at least consider the abolition of bishops. This was just what the petition's opponents wanted to prevent.

[5] The principal speeches are printed in J. Rushworth, IV, 170ff., out of order and sometimes with inaccurate date.

by those favouring its retention. Indeed, the latter vied with the advocates of abolition in the severity of their censure on the prelates and readily admitted the necessity of sharp reform. The crux of disagreement lay elsewhere. In the mass outcry against episcopacy its defenders scented something dangerous in the air: a rising breeze of popular initiative in religion; an attraction to the spirit of innovation; an impulsion towards a church order likely to be less effective than the bishops in buttressing the existing regime of privilege.

Lord Digby, referring to the crowd that brought the London Root-and-Branch petition, declared that it was unfit for a parliament under monarchy to countenance tumultuous assemblies of petitioners: all men of judgment, he added, knew the danger 'when either true, or pretended Stimulation of Conscience hath once given a multitude Agitation.' Sir Benjamin Rudyard asked whether 'a Popular Democratical Government of the Church ... will be ... suitable or acceptable to a Regal Monarchical Government of the State.' Sir John Strangeways stressed the prescriptive right of the bishops as members of the upper House and an estate of the realm. '... if we made a paritie in the church,' he asserted, 'wee must at last come to a paritie in the Commonwealth.' One and all, Lord Falkland and other opponents of the Root-and-Branch petition cautioned against the peril of 'great Mutations in Government,' of the folly of removing, like a scene in a masque, an institution of sixteen hundred years' duration.[1]

It was in their indifference to these considerations that the Root-and-Branch men showed their own political tendency. They disliked episcopacy too much to reckon with the dangers their opponents apprehended. They declined to rebuke the petitioning Londoners who pressed their views on parliament, since citizen action was an instrumentality they could put to use. Oliver Cromwell denied that parity in the church would lead to parity in the commonwealth. Nathaniel Fiennes, the main speaker on the anti-episcopal side, held that monarchy could well stand without bishops. Moreover, in civil government, he pointed out, all jurisdiction under the King was 'Aristocraticall, and placed in many,' as in parliament and county administration. Only in ecclesiastical government did one man in a diocese have full jurisdiction, to the exclusion of others entitled to share the rule of the church. Unless ecclesiastical and civil government were assimilated, he concluded, the former would always try to render the latter as arbitrary and absolute as itself.[2]

Fiennes's speech offered a striking glimpse of a form of ecclesiastical polity very different from episcopacy. At the moment, however,

[1] J. Rushworth, IV, 171, 172, 183, 186; Notestein, *D'Ewes*, 339–40.
[2] J. Rushworth, IV, 174–5, 176, 179; Notestein, *D'Ewes*, 339–40.

the party leaders themselves were not altogether clear how thorough-going a remedy the church required. While not only Fiennes, but Holles as well,[1] advocated abolition, Pym preferred a milder course if possible. Neither his nor Hampden's words in the debate have survived, a pretty sure sign that both said little and avoided inflammatory language. A summary of his remarks reported him to declare that 'he thought it was not the intention of the House to abolish either Episcopacy or the Book of Common Prayer, but to reform both wherein offence was given. . . . And if that could be effected . . . with the concurrence of the King and Lords, they should do a very acceptable work to the people; and such as had not been since the Reformation. . . .'[2] This was wholly in keeping with Pym's methods. He evidently hoped to solve the problem with a minimum of disagreement by measures that would make abolition unnecessary. Nevertheless, if he was more moderate than some of his friends, this was no cause for disagreement. All favoured the commitment of the Root-and-Branch petition both as a threat to hold over the bishops and as an encouragement to their supporters outside parliament. In a test of strength the opposition leaders had the power to work their will. Thus the end of the two-day debate was a vote to commit the Root-and-Branch and all other petitions on church government, with the proviso that the point of episcopacy itself should be reserved for the House's own consideration.[3]

The committee to which the petitions were referred was the 'committee of twenty-four,' a body including Pym and other oppositionist notables. Created on 10 November 1640, various important business had already been delegated to it.[4] It now set about its task with exemplary speed. Adopting the line which Pym had expressed during the church debate as the sense of the House, it reported a series of proposals in March that went unerringly to the core of the laity's grievances against the bishops. These provided that bishops and clergy should be deprived of all secular offices and employments —membership in the House of Lords, the Privy Council, the commission of the peace, the Star Chamber, and other courts. On 1 May a bill to this effect passed the House of Commons without a single negative vote.[5]

[1] D'Ewes noted that Holles spoke against bishops, Notestein, *D'Ewes*, 336.
[2] This was the summary of Edward Bagshawe, M.P. for Southwark; cf. B. Hanbury, *op. cit.*, II, 141–2.
[3] *C.J.*, II, 81. Cf. the notes of opinions in the debate in Notestein, *D'Ewes*, 335–42. Of the associates of the party leaders, Selden alone opposed committing the petition, *ibid.*, 337.
[4] *C.J.*, II, 25. Six members were added to the committee to consider the petitions on church reform, *ibid.*, II, 81.
[5] *Ibid.*, II, 100, 101, 102, 110, 131; D'Ewes, Journal, B.M. Harl. 163, f. 121a.

The Lords' reaction to the bill might have been predicted from the strained relations arising between the Houses as a result of Strafford's trial. Having been coerced into voting the attainder, the upper House was in no mood to alter its constitution at the will of the Commons. The bishops were an estate of the realm: to expel them from parliament, where they had sat for centuries, might be of dangerous consequence in unsettled times.[1] Accordingly, the Lords resolved on 24 May that the bishops should remain in parliament, though offering at the same time to exclude them from other temporal functions. The Commons refused this compromise. On 8 June, after the Houses had failed to reach agreement in a conference, the Lords rejected the bill against the secular employments of the clergy.[2]

Its defeat was a strong check to the policy Pym had prevailed on his more extreme colleagues and followers to adopt. The party managers naturally viewed the episcopate as a solid bloc of votes that would always support the King and oppose measures of church reform coming from the House of Commons. Hence, if bishops were to survive in any form, they must have no power to obstruct, and this required their expulsion from the House of Lords.[3] Hampden himself told Lord Falkland that such was the condition of their continuance.[4]

In the Commons the response to the Lords' resolution of 24 May was to bring into play the threat contained in the Root-and-Branch petition. It took the form of a bill for the abolition of episcopacy drafted by St. John and introduced on the 27th by Sir Edward Dering. Those Puritan intransigents, Cromwell, Haselrig, and the younger Vane, also had a hand in it.[5] As Dering later explained, the measure's purpose 'was to expedite the progresse of another Bill against the secular jurisdiction of the Bishops (at that very time) labouring in the House of Lords. . . .'[6] Having got a first and second reading the same day—the latter by a vote of 139 to 108, it was then referred after acrimonious debate to a committee of the whole House.[7]

---

[1] Cf. the arguments of Viscount Newark, *Two speeches . . . May 21 . . . 24th, 1641.*   [2] *L.J.*, IV, 256, 265, 269.

[3] The Commons' reasons against the bishops' votes stressed their lack of independence and power of obstruction as grounds to expel them from parliament, *C.J.*, II, 167. The same argument was made by Lord Saye in a speech to the House of Lords, W. Cobbett, *Parliamentary history*, 36v., L., 1806–20, II, 810.

[4] Clarendon, *Rebellion*, III, 152.

[5] Clarendon said that St. John drew up the bill, *Rebellion*, III, 156. For the connection with it of Cromwell, Haselrig, and Vane, cf. E. Dering, *A collection of speeches*, 1642, 2.

[6] *Ibid.*, 3.

[7] *C.J.*, II, 159. This reverses the tellers in the vote and must be corrected by D'Ewes, Journal, B.M. Harl. 163, f. 237b.

It did not reappear again until the peers disregarded its warning by their rejection on 8 June of the earlier bill against the secular employments of the clergy.[1] This action was decisive. On the night of the 10th, Pym, Hampden, Sir Robert Harley, and others, meeting privately, concluded that the Root-and-Branch bill against bishops should be moved in the Commons next day. Harley accordingly did so, thereby initiating the debate over episcopacy anew.[2]

The Root-and-Branch bill was considered by the Commons in a committee of the whole from 11 June to early August amidst a welter of other business.[3] The debate brought forth no fresh viewpoints beyond those already voiced the previous February. This time, however, the defenders of episcopacy were seriously embarrassed, since the upper House's action had clouded the prospect of a reform envisaging the bishops' retention. The bill's supporters formed the majority—so much so that in all the votes the House passed relating to it, not a single division occurred. Once more the prudent Rudyard spoke his apprehension at the removal of ancient institutions.[4] The poet, Edmund Waller, who sat for St. Ives, stressed again, as had Lord Digby in February, the danger of abolition to the regime of subordination and privilege.[5] Against such strictures, the younger Vane defended the bill in the accents of the Puritan visionary:

. . . hath not this parliament been called, continued, and preserved . . . by the immediate Finger of God . . . for this work?. . . . Hath not God left [the bishops] to themselves . . . in the evil adminstration of their government, that he might lay them open to us; and lead us . . . by the hand . . . to discern that their rooting up must be our only cure? Let us not then halt any longer between two opinions, but . . . give glory to God, in complying with his Providence. . . .[6]

Now fully committed to the policy of root-and-branch, the Commons' managers secured the enactment of various clauses of the bill against episcopacy in a six-week's procession of votes. These provided that archbishops, bishops, deans and chapters should cease to exist in the church; episcopal lands were to be conveyed to the crown, dean

---

[1] There were several postponements of debate on the Root-and-Branch bill while the Lords' decision was awaited, *C.J.*, II, 159, 165–6.
[2] Cf. *supra*, 202, and *C.J.*, II, 173.
[3] The debates and chronological progress of the bill are described by W. Shaw, *op. cit.*, I, 80–99, who leaves the mistaken impression, however, that its last consideration was on 27 July.
[4] Printed in W. Cobbett, *op. cit.*, II, 833.
[5] E. Waller, *A speech . . . concerning episcopacie*, 1641.
[6] W. Cobbett, *op. cit.*, II, 826.

and chapter lands to feoffees to be devoted to religious uses such as the maintenance of a preaching ministry; all impropriations and advowsons belonging to bishops, deans and chapters, were also to be vested in feoffees. There was thus to be no suspicion that a greedy laity was destroying the bishops in order to gorge itself on ecclesiastical property. Finally, a new scheme of church polity was outlined in a provision that 'such Ecclesiastical Power, as shall be exercised for the Government of the Church, shall be transferred ... into the Hands of Commissioners, to be named in this Act.'[1]

Although various details still lacked to its completion, the Root-and-Branch bill signified the victory of a revolutionary policy in the House of Commons towards the church. Its two notes were the removal of the religious organization from royal control and the subjection of the clergy and ecclesiastical property to parliamentary appointees. Yet even while the members were forging its provisions, the bill was a dead letter. For if the House of Lords had already refused to remove the bishops from parliament, why should it consent to their abolition? Indeed, the peers did not hesitate now to ignore the wishes of the lower House. On 29 July, for instance, they rejected a bill to make the Protestation of the previous May obligatory on all male subjects; they did this to prevent the expulsion from their body of the Catholic noblemen, who could not in conscience have taken the Protestation.[2] Their veto so incensed the lower House that it voted the Protestation, which many in the kingdom had already been subscribing voluntarily, fit to be taken by everyone and then, in a gesture of disrespect for the Lords, ordered its resolution printed.[3] Here was a clear expression of a tendency by the House of Commons towards unilateral action in defiance of the upper House.

In spite of such abrasive incidents, however, the party leaders in the Commons knew that they could not risk a serious quarrel with the Lords just then, for the political situation after Strafford's execution would have made a breach disastrous. The King's behaviour and obscure intentions continued to provoke deep mistrust. Parliament faced the task of disbanding the English and Scottish armies, whose long occupation in the north was becoming an unendurable burden. Moreover, vital measures of constitutional reform were in process which required the cooperation of the two Houses. These circumstances accounted for the otherwise inexplicable fate of the Root-and-Branch bill. Taken up in the Commons for the last time on 3

---

[1] *C.J.*, II, 173, 174, 176, 204, 205.
[2] *L.J.*, IV, 333. The bill, called an act for the security of true religion, passed the Commons on 19 July, *C.J.*, II, 216. The text is in *H.M.C. House of Lords*, XI, *Addenda 1514–1714*, 277–80.
[3] *C.J.*, II, 230.

August, it was then silently laid aside without further consideration.[1] The only possible conclusion is that Pym and his friends had decided the abolition of episcopacy was hopeless and the issue too provocative of disharmony to be pressed further.

Nevertheless, the fundamental antagonism between the Houses persisted. Even after the Root-and-Branch bill was dropped, another outburst of bad feeling occurred at the beginning of September when the two published contradictory orders concerning the performance of divine service. The quarrel was patched up on the eve of the parliamentary recess, as again the need for unity prevailed.[2] It was clear, however, that the pressure coming from the Commons threatened to derange the parity supposed to exist between the Houses. In any disagreement, the peers would insist on their independence and freedom of action; the Commons under its oppositionist leaders would demand the peers' concurrence. If cooperation finally broke down, what solution to the lack of concord could be found? Constitutionally there was none. All that remained was the subjection of the upper to the lower House, in fact if not in law. Should the conflict against the King dissolve the polity to atoms, the Commons' supremacy must fill the void. To such a possible outcome did the differences between the Houses point.

6

During these hectic months of attacks on the Court, alarums and excursions due to fear of plots and violence, controversy over church government, parliament was also busy passing a far-reaching series of reforms through which it hoped to provide future security against misrule. It achieved this in the face of an almost overwhelming mass of business pressing on it from all sides. By force of circumstances the two Houses had become the *de facto* focus of the state. To the Commons in particular all men now looked for redress, for favour, for action of every sort. The members were engulfed in petitions and the host of committees and sub-committees which they had created competed for their time. They had started so many lines of investigation, were occupied with such a variety of matters great and small, that they found their proceedings clogged and disordered by the mountainous weight of their affairs. As early as 8 January 1641 the House took cognizance of the problem, appointing a committee to propose what subjects should be given precedence and what committees

---

[1] *C.J.*, II, 234. On 13 August the House ordered that the bill should be discussed the next Monday, but on that day no mention was made of it, *ibid.*, II, 255.
[2] Cf. the account of this episode in S. R. Gardiner, *History*, X, 14–17.

continued.[1] This committee to lessen committees, as it became known, apparently helped somewhat by its periodic recommendations to accelerate the House's progress. The obstacles it encountered may be gathered from a report made on 28 May by its chairman, Sir John Hotham, who complained that committees for private bills 'tooke away all the companie from committees appointed for publike business soe as the verie committee to lessen committees could not sitt.'[2]

The confused and winding course of parliamentary transactions was unavoidable in view of the breakdown of royal and conciliar authority. Yet notwithstanding, behind the scenes the constructive direction of Pym and his associates was steadily at work. In their role of unofficial leaders they steered parliament as well as they could, preventing the Commons from losing itself in the welter of business and securing the enactment of a broad programme of statutory limitations on royal power. To these Charles was constrained to give his reluctant consent. Politically isolated, lacking influence over the members, responsible for the payment of two armies for which only the Houses could find the money, he had very little choice.

The first constitutional statute was the Triennial Act, passed in February to assure the regularity of parliamentary assemblies. It was introduced by the oppositionist, William Strode, in the form of a bill for annual parliaments. It was then modified in the Commons so as to provide that no longer than three years should elapse between successive parliaments. To secure this end, it established an elaborate procedure for summoning a parliament if the King failed to do so; and it further ordained that the act should be read publicly every year at the assizes and general sessions of the peace.[3]

In May, the act granting the King tonnage and poundage definitely placed this great branch of the revenue under parliament's control. Declaring the King's former exaction of the tax illegal, the preamble stated that impositions on merchandise could only be levied with consent of parliament. The grant was made from 20 May to 15 July, after which it was periodically reenacted for stated intervals. Since Charles I's predecessors had enjoyed tonnage and poundage for life, this was an emphatic assertion of its conditional and parliamentary character.[4]

[1] Notestein, *D'Ewes*, 233; *C.J.*, II, 65. The committee made its first report on the 12th, *ibid.*, II, 66–7.

[2] D'Ewes, Journal, B.M. Harl. 163, f. 241a. On 1 June and 15 July Hotham's committee reported long lists of committees to sit and of work to be done, *C.J.*, II, 162, 212.

[3] 16 Car. I, c. 1, *Statutes of the realm*, V, 54ff.; Notestein, *D'Ewes*, 188n., 196.

[4] 16 Car. I, c. 8, *Statutes of the realm*, V, 104–5; for other limited grants of tonnage and poundage, cf. *ibid.*, V, 114–15, 132–3, 135–7.

Two further statutes deeply circumscribing the crown's authority became law on 5 July. The first stripped the King's Council of the greater part of its judicial jurisdiction so largely expanded in the preceding century. It abolished as contrary to law the Court of Star Chamber and most of the other prerogative tribunals of the King—the Council of the North, the Council in the Marches of Wales, the Court of the Duchy of Lancaster, and the Exchequer Court of the County Palatine of Chester. It also prohibited the King and Council from dealing with any matters touching the property of subjects, which were henceforth to be left to the ordinary courts. As a protection for liberty, it provided as well that persons committed by the King or Council should be entitled to *habeas corpus*; the royal prerogative to commit to prison without showing legal cause, which the judges had upheld in 1627 in the case arising from the forced loan, was thus annulled.[1]

The destruction of the Star Chamber took away one of the most formidable engines of the King's power. The second statute did the same by abolishing the Court of High Commission, the chief agency through which the crown enforced its religious supremacy. It further prohibited any persons exercising ecclesiastical jurisdiction from inflicting fines, prison, or corporal punishment on the King's subjects.[2] Although this legislation left the other church courts still intact, it so denuded them of coercive sanctions that they could neither suppress religious dissent nor even police the moral offences belonging to their charge.

In early August a last group of statutes were passed of only slightly less importance in controlling the royal prerogative. The first annulled the judgment in the ship-money case and pronounced the tax illegal.[3] Another regulated the abuses of the Stannary Courts in their jurisdiction over the tin miners and landlords in Devon and Cornwall.[4] A third, directed to recent exactions under the forest laws, voided all proceedings of the forest courts since 1624 and decreed that no ground should be accounted royal forest unless a court had been held there sixty years before Charles I's accession.[5] A fourth set rigorous limits to the crown's right of purveyance for the royal

---

[1] 16 Car. I, c. 10, *Statutes of the realm*, V, 110–12. St. John proposed that the Star Chamber officials who lost their place should be compensated, and both Houses appointed committees to consider the matter; D'Ewes, Journal, B.M. Harl. 163, f. 382b; *L.J.*, IV, 302, 312; *C.J.*, II, 231.

[2] 16 Car. I, c. 11, *Statutes of the realm*, V, 112–13. The act repealed section VIII of the Elizabethan statute of supremacy, 1 Eliz. c. 1, from which the Court of High Commission derived its legal being.

[3] 16 Car. I, c. 14, *Statutes of the realm*, V, 116–17.

[4] 16 Car. I, c. 15, *ibid.*, V, 117–18.

[5] 16 Car. I, c. 16, *ibid.*, V, 119–20.

household in order to stop extortions which had long been a matter of complaint.[1] The last, dealing with knighthood fines, extinguished still another royal right by ordaining that no person could be compelled to take knighthood or be fined for not doing so.[2]

There are political-constitutional revolutions as well as social ones: for no other description can be given to great alterations of governmental power, even if they should leave the existing order of society untouched. Such was the significance of the statutes of 1641. The effect of a crisis that paralysed the regime, a reflection of invincible public and parliamentary demand, attained under the leadership of an organized opposition, the work of parliament's first ten months meant a historic reversal of the relation between monarchy and subject. It took from the crown almost all the powers which enabled the Tudor rulers to exercise their unrivalled mastery. Although the King would continue to govern, his administration would be subject to new and unprecedented restrictions. No longer could he manifest his authority through administrative-judicial tribunals outside the reach of ordinary law. The being of parliament was placed beyond his will, and henceforth he must consult it regularly. He could acquire no important revenue independent of parliament's consent. The statutes amputated the strongest limbs of the prerogative. They instituted safeguards to protect liberty and property against further invasions by arbitrary power.

Yet great as were these reforms, they no longer sufficed to restore the breakdown in the state. Measures that would have been received with jubilation six months previously were ineffectual by the summer of 1641 to provide a ground of settlement. Even as they were in passage, the Country leaders were pressing fresh demands on the King, searching for guarantees to allay their fears, and gradually gathering the threads of governmental authority into parliament's hands.

It was the King who bore the main responsibility for this. Devoid of any consistent policy, Charles confronted the overturnings of the strife-ridden time in irresolution and uncertainty. Though strong in the consciousness of his regality, he was weak in political judgment and will. He was incapable either of firmly withstanding his opponents or of gaining them to him by genuine compliance. He understood no better than the Queen the true nature of the movement that beat against his throne and lacked all sympathetic sensitivity to the general sense of grievance that called it forth. Unable to identify himself with the feeling of his subjects, he regarded his assent to parliament's bills as something done of his grace for the benefit of

---

[1] 16 Car. I, c. 19, *ibid.*, V, 129–30.
[2] 16 Car. I, c. 20, *ibid.*, V, 131.

others rather than for himself and his kingdom's welfare.[1] The tribulations through which he was passing aggravated his indecision, suggesting to him the most contradictory lines of action. He oscillated between political concessions and the resort to intrigues which might gain him the upper hand over the parliamentary managers. His indulgence in the latter, however, lost him all the credit of the former.

In view of the bitter recollections of the past and the inflamed emotions of the present, it was essential for Charles to show irrefutably that he accepted the constitutional revolution. Yet with the blundering that marked the whole course of his political life, he signally failed to do so. From Strafford's trial on, a continuing crisis of confidence in his intentions undermined all feeling of security as to the permanence of his concessions. This lack of confidence arose from fear that he would try to use violence to restore his position. Pym's revelation of the army plot on 5 May and the ensuing parliamentary investigation of the conspiracy provided convincing reason for distrust.[2] It was doubtless true that Charles's sponsorship of the plot was only half-hearted and that the project of using the army against parliament had little chance of success. But Pym and his friends could not be expected to take that view. If they magnified the dangers of the conspiracy and exploited it to the full against the King, it was because in their circumstances they were bound to place the worst construction on his conduct. They were not impartial judges, but oppositionist politicians who had staked life and fortune against the regime.[3]

---

[1] Charles's speech of assent to the Triennial Bill on 16 February was a characteristic display of his want of political judgment and inability to identify himself with public and parliamentary sentiment. '. . . never Bill passed here . . . of more Favour to the Subjects, than this is. . . . I mention this, to shew unto you . . . the Obligation . . . that you have to me for it. . . . Hitherto you have gone on in that which concerns your selves to amend, and not in those things that nearly concerns the Strength of this Kingdom, neither for the State, nor my own particular. . . . You have taken the Government all in Pieces, and I may say it is almost off the Hinges. . . . this is the greatest Expression of Trust, that before you do anything for me, I do put such a confidence in you.' (J. Rushworth, IV, 188, misdated the 15th).

[2] Cf. *supra*, 219. Committees of both Houses authorized to proceed in secrecy were established to investigate the army plot. The committee of the Commons contained the leading oppositionists; cf. S. R. Gardiner, *History*, IX, 358. For the committee's reports, cf. *Verney notes*, 86–91, 93, 94–9, 110–11.

[3] Clarendon's account of the army plot, like that of Charles's modern apologist, E. Wingfield-Stratford, is vitiated by the assumption that Pym cynically exploited the plot without believing in it. This represents a complete failure to understand how the men in Pym's position regarded the King's activities. There can be no question that they believed in the conspiracy and that Charles's behaviour, and the Queen's even more, justified

Moreover, in the early summer of 1641 Charles aroused new suspicions when he announced that he intended to go to Scotland to attend personally at the approaching meeting of the Scottish parliament. This news caused much disquiet. It was generally thought the King had some hidden purpose in his visit. The peace treaty in negotiation at London between England and Scotland was not yet completed and the armies in the north remained undisbanded. The opposition leaders felt real alarm when they thought of the King passing amid the troops. They further suspected that he hoped to find support in Scotland. This, indeed, appeared to be Charles's idea. He evidently believed that if he granted the demands of the Scottish parliament and distributed liberal favours to the principal Covenanter politicians, he would secure their aid against his English opponents.[1]

The King, in fact, was doing nothing less than play at counter-revolution. No political basis for counter-revolution, however, existed as yet in England. The courtiers who devised the army plot were frivolous *coup d'étatists* representing no one. As for Scotland, it was pure delusion for Charles to imagine that any blandishments of his would induce the leaders of the rebellion to desert their English allies. Both kingdoms still preserved too fresh a memory of their recent grievances. The main effect of Charles's obscure behaviour, therefore, was to aggravate distrust. It repelled moderates and solidified the alliance around the opposition party leaders, while at the same time exciting fears that did not let the revolution come to rest.

To counter the threat of violence and conspiracy, the Houses entered on a quest for guarantees that entailed the assumption of extraordinary powers far exceeding the provisions of the reforming legislation they had in hand. It was the prevalence of this state of mind which resulted in the most innovative statute of the period at the time of the army plot's disclosure. The act against dissolving parliament without its own consent was not the redress of a grievance, but an aggressive encroachment on the sphere of the executive belonging to the crown. Nor was this the only such action on which the Houses ventured because of the public emergency. They also invaded the King's military authority, presuming to issue orders on

---

[1] The despatches of the Venetian ambassador contain numerous allusions to the King's hopes and secret purposes in going to Scotland and the adverse reaction in parliament to his prospective journey, *C.S.P.V. 1640–42*, 153, 171, 177, 193, 205–6.

---

their mistrust; cf. Clarendon, *Rebellion*, III, 218–26; E. Wingfield-Stratford, *King Charles and King Pym*, L., 1949, 114–16.

their own initiative for the movement of ships and trained bands and for the care of castles, arms, and munitions.[1]

These steps were the first in a sequence of usurpations by which parliament in self-defence gradually possessed itself of the powers of governing. On 24 June the Commons adopted ten propositions brought in by Pym, which were presented to the King after obtaining the peers' concurrence.[2] Several of them dealt with immediate issues of security: Charles was asked to bar Catholics from his attendance, to disband the English army, and to delay his Scottish journey until all military forces were demobilized. The other propositions were of wider import, since they cut at the very sinews of the crown's autonomy. The King was 'to take into his Council, and for Managing of the great affairs of the Kingdom, such Officers, and Counsellors, as his People and Parliament may have just Cause to confide in.' A parliamentary superintendence was required as well over the persons attending the Queen and royal children and over the lords lieutenants and their deputies in the counties.[3]

These audacious proposals went far beyond any earlier demands: in effect, they were a claim that the appointment and conduct of ministers should be subject to parliamentary approval. Novel as this was, it suggested itself as an obvious solution to the problem of confidence. Since Charles did not resort voluntarily to a policy of 'bridge appointments,' parliament endeavoured to impose it on him. The King, however, would not submit to be thus bound. Although he consented to disband the army and to defer his journey until 10 August,[4] he made clear that he would not surrender the power to choose his councillors at his discretion.[5] Thus the political impasse remained unresolved.

With Charles's departure impending, parliament hastened to conclude the peace with Scotland. The treaty was formally enacted on 10 August, the day he set out for the north.[6] It conceded the substance of the demands for which the Scots had risen in rebellion, and also provided that parliament should give them a 'friendly assistance' of £300,000 in compensation for their losses.[7] To raise this great sum,

[1] *C.J.*, II, 135, 138.
[2] *Ibid.*, II, 184–5; *L.J.*, IV, 285–7, 290. Pym reported these demands as spokesman for the committee of seven appointed to investigate the army plot.
[3] *C.J.*, II, 185.
[4] *C.J.*, II, 188, 192.
[5] Charles's message to the Houses on 12 July concerning the removal of evil councillors was in effect a denial of their demand to control the appointment of ministers; *L.J.*, IV, 310–11.
[6] *C.J.*, II, 249; *L.J.*, IV, 356.
[7] The treaty is printed in T. Rymer, *Foedera*, XX, 448ff.

of which £80,000 was payable at once, an act had already been passed imposing a poll tax in England.[1] Because the provisions for disbanding the armies could not be fully implemented till the end of the month, the Houses petitioned the King on the 7th to stay two weeks longer.[2] This he refused, for his hopes were now strongly fixed on Scotland. On 14 August he arrived in Edinburgh, having passed through the troops of both nations without incident.

Charles's Scottish journey, in adding to the prevailing insecurity, only invited fresh encroachments on his authority. Besides the anxieties which his activities in Scotland caused at Westminster, his departure left England without any effective government. Into this governmental vacuum parliament stepped. Persuaded of the necessity to provide for the kingdom's safety amidst the dangers arising from the King's absence, the Houses invested themselves with a virtual regency. On 14 August the Commons established a committee of defence to confer with the Lords about military preparedness. To this committee were given powers amounting to a supervision over the entire military and naval establishment of the realm.[3] The Houses further adopted a recommendation from Pym to send commissioners of their own to Scotland to preserve good relations between the two kingdoms.[4] These representatives were little less than parliamentary ambassadors. Six members, all trusted oppositionists, were selected, four from the Commons, two from the Lords. Two of the commissioners were Hampden and Fiennes.[5] Their assignment was proof of the extreme importance the party managers attached to the mission. While their instructions preserved the language of deference to the King, the commissioners' real task was to watch over Charles's doings and counter every move he made. Besides supervising the execution of the peace treaty, which had still to receive the Scottish parliament's ratification, they were to clear the proceedings of the English parliament from any false reports that might raise misunderstandings. They were also to inform the two Houses of all occurrences concerning the welfare of the kingdom.[6]

In deciding how to legalize the appointment and duties of the commissioners, parliament took a long stride towards the acquisition

[1] The poll tax was passed on 3 July; *L.J.*, IV, 298.

[2] *C.J.*, II, 241; *L.J.*, IV, 347.

[3] *C.J.*, II, 257, 258.

[4] *Ibid.*, II, 249.

[5] The others were Sir William Armyne, Sir Philip Stapleton, Lord Howard of Escrick, and the earl of Bedford.

[6] The commissioners' names and instructions are in *C.J.*, II, 265–6. Two earlier versions of these instructions show the commissioners' task even more clearly, *ibid.*, II, 259, 262–3. Pym probably helped draft them, since he reported them to the House.

of a legislative power independent of the crown. The earliest hint of this momentous development occurred on 28 July during a debate in the Commons concerning the effects of the King's approaching departure. D'Ewes, whose deep but uncritical antiquarian erudition was much respected, told the members that 'the two howses may in the absence of the King make ordinances which are of the greatest authoritie next Acts of Parliament. ...'[1] He reverted to the idea again on 16 August in connection with the procedure for authorizing the commissioners. Some members had urged that the Houses could order the Lord Keeper to grant them a commission under the great seal, but this he denied. He proposed an ordinance instead: 'such ordinances of Parliament,' he declared, 'have been of great authoritie in former times. ...'[2] His suggestion was accepted. Four days later the Lords and Commons passed their first ordinance appointing their commissioners to Scotland.[3]

Four more ordinances followed before the recess, including one to confiscate arms belonging to recusants and another prohibiting the King's subjects from taking military service with any foreign prince or state.[4] Doubtless the Houses did not think that in enacting ordinances they were legislating. Yet at the least they were issuing commands in solemn form about matters hitherto reserved exclusively to the crown. These were already incipient acts of sovereignty very near to actual legislation. When the lower House was considering the ordinance to disarm recusants, Selden strongly criticized it, contending that 'it made new lawes, which it could not. ...' To this, Henry Marten, M.P. for Berkshire, one of the very few oppositionists unconcerned about constitutional proprieties, rejoined that 'hee wished wee might account such an Ordinance to be of equall force and power with an Act of Parliament. ...' D'Ewes, however, rebuked this opinion as contrary to law and Magna Charta. An ordinance, he said, 'was merely to binde the members of either howse, but never ... of any force to take from the free subiects of England their goods against their will. ...'; accordingly, if the proposed ordinance contained anything contrary to common or statute law, let it be removed. The House, nevertheless, passed the ordinance as it stood, and so did the Lords after a committee of the Commons stated that it was 'especiallie drawne in pursuit of those Lawes alreadie established. ...'[5]

With the parliamentary recess upon them, the party leaders took

---

[1] D'Ewes, *Journal*, B.M. Harl. 163, f. 416b.
[2] *Ibid.*, B.M. Harl. 164, ff. 32b–33a.
[3] *C.J.*, II, 265–6.
[4] *Ibid.*, II, 277, 285.
[5] D'Ewes, *Journal*, B.M. Harl. 164, ff. 70a, 79a.

steps to continue their direction of affairs while the Houses were dispersed. They did not mean to leave the helm even for a few short weeks at so critical a time. Accordingly, parliament on 9 September created a committee beyond all precedent: a body of forty-seven commoners and seventeen peers to manage business during the recess. This committee was the germ of an executive government and the prototype of the machinery by which the Houses afterwards ruled during the civil war. Its instructions gave it broad authority. It was to supervise the demobilization of the English army then in progress, and to issue directions in the Houses' name to parliament's commissioners in Scotland. This latter power was opposed by several members as too great, but St. John defended it and the Commons passed it without alteration.[1] On information of riots or tumults, the committee was authorized to communicate with sheriffs, J.P.s, and other officials. It could also summon any persons, writings, or records. Its membership included the principal opposition men. Foremost was Pym, who reported on the committee's work to parliament when it reconvened in October. Amongst the rest were St. John, Clotworthy, Strode, the younger Vane, and a goodly number of other party adherents. The representatives of the House of Lords had not the same strong political colouring, though among them were Essex, Warwick, and Mandeville. This was no matter, however, since the committee's work was carried on mainly by Pym and some others of the lower House.[2]

When parliament recessed, the leaders of the Country still retained their ascendancy from the previous November. The political situation, in contrast, had altered considerably. Although a great programme of reforms had been enacted, distrust had nullified its benefits. The King and his opponents stood further from collaboration than ever. Charles refused to confer ministerial power on Pym and his friends, while they in their quest for security were insisting on arrangements he was scarcely likely to grant. Without acknowledging it to themselves or the world, the Houses were groping towards sovereignty. This was the purport of their recent demands and actions, little as they were disposed to recognize the fact. Ten months of unresolved conflict had brought the monarchical constitution to the verge of disintegration, and the opposition party was already forging the elements of a parliamentary governing power to replace the decaying supremacy of the crown.

[1] *Ibid.*, B.M. Harl. 164, ff. 107b–108a.
[2] *C.J.*, II, 288–9, prints the committee's instructions and the names of the members from the Commons; the list of Lords' representatives is in *L.J.*, IV, 395.

The End of the Country

Parliament's six-week recess gave only a momentary respite from the strife of the spring and summer. Nothing but a wisdom far beyond the King's capacity could have found the remedy to moderate the distempers of his sickly, tottering state. Boundless suspicion of Charles on the one side, his keen resentment of his opponents' incessant pressures on the other, were driving the polity towards dissolution.

The Country leaders employed the adjournment to prepare their strategy against the approaching reassembly of the Houses. Pym, who presided at the twice-weekly meetings of the committee appointed for the recess, was then lodging in Chelsea at Lord Mandeville's house.[1] There, as well as at the London residence of the earl of Northumberland and in Kensington at the earl of Holland's house, he and his party associates conferred.[2] Hampden, on mission in Scotland, was kept informed of their counsels through the letters that passed between the committee for the recess in London and parliament's commissioners in Edinburgh.[3]

The King himself was still in Scotland when parliament resumed on 20 October. For English political news, he depended heavily on the letters sent him by Edward Nicholas, Clerk of the Privy Council. Nicholas, a prudent and faithful servant, was not even a member of the Commons, but he did his best to learn all he could of the party managers' plans.[4] He soon warned Charles that they had fresh

[1] The committee for the recess met on Tuesdays and Saturdays in the Exchequer chamber at Westminster. D'Ewes, attending on 12 October, noted Pym in the chair. When Pym afterwards reported to the Commons on the committee's work, he referred to 'my Lodgings at Chelsea. . . .', *C.J.*, II, 288, 290; Coates, *D'Ewes*, 1–2.
[2] Edward Nicholas to the King, J. Evelyn, *Diary*, ed. W. Bray, 4v., L., 1908, IV, 76; *L.J.*, IV, 490; *C.S.P.V. 1640–42*, 215; Clarendon, *Rebellion*, IV, 14.
[3] Nicholas to the King, J. Evelyn, *op. cit.*, IV, 83, and cf. the references to the correspondence between the committee in London and the commissioners in Scotland in Pym's report on 20 October, *C.J.*, II, 289, 290.
[4] On Nicholas, cf. *D.N.B.*, *s.v.* In December 1641 he was knighted and created Secretary of State. J. Forster was mistaken in calling him a member of parliament, *The debates on the Grand Remonstrance*, L., 1860, 285.

demands in store and repeatedly urged the necessity of the King's presence in the capital. '... when ye awe of the Parliament is upon all in generall,' he wrote, '... it is almost impossible for ... your servauntes, to know what to doe or advise. ...'[1] Charles, intent on his Scottish schemes, paid no heed to this advice. He made scarcely any preparations for the reconvening of the Houses, nor did he return to London till the end of November. About the only step he took in anticipation of the end of the recess was that the Queen, who remained in England at Oatlands, told Nicholas to write the bishops and some friendly peers asking their presence when parliament reopened.[2]

The King went to Scotland in the fatuous belief that if he complied with the Covenanters he would gain their aid against his English opponents. His communications to Nicholas hinted obscurely at some design against the parliamentary leaders at Westminster. 'I believe before all be done that they will not have such great cause of joy,' he wrote, and '... some day they may repent of their severitie. ...'[3] From his expressions, it appears pretty plain that he was already revolving in his mind a way to settle scores with the opposition chiefs, which was to issue three months later in his attempt at a counter-revolutionary *coup*.

To the Scots Charles yielded much. He not only ratified the establishment of a Presbyterian state church, but made the even greater surrender of consenting to an act that subjected the royal choice of councillors in Scotland to the advice and approval of the Scottish parliament.[4] This legislation was naturally taken note of in England, and Nicholas shortly informed him that Pym would demand the same power for the English parliament. Charles replied, however, that he would never grant it.[5]

In spite of his concessions, the King failed completely of his purpose in Scotland. The dominant Covenanter party, with the earl of Argyle as its foremost figure, had no motive to separate itself from its English allies, nor did its leaders trust the King to any degree. Doubtless their discussions with the commissioners sent by the English parliament only confirmed their scepticism. Thus they extracted all they could from Charles, while giving nothing in return. The true position was sombrely described by a courtier who accompanied him to Edinburgh: '... his majesties businesses runn in the

---

[1] J. Evelyn, *op. cit.*, IV, 74, 77, 85, 89, 117.

[2] *Ibid.*, IV, 84–5.

[3] *Ibid.*, IV, 78, 79, 81.

[4] This act was passed on 17 September 1641. The first appointment under its provisions was ratified in another act of 15 November, *Acts of the parliament of Scotland*, V, 354–5, 388–9.

[5] J. Evelyn, *op. cit.*, IV, 74, 76, 80.

wonted channell, suttle designes of gaineing the popular opinion and weake executions for the uphowlding of monarkie.'[1] In mid-October, the disclosure of a plot against Argyle inflicted a severe blow on the King's anyway tenuous credit. Probably he possessed only a limited knowledge of the Incident, as the plot was named; but he was aware that some enterprise was afoot and was indiscreet enough to receive Scotsmen into his presence who hated Argyle's ascendancy. Moreover, one of his intimate personal servants was involved. This was sufficient to incite the worst suspicions which the King's enemies both at Edinburgh and London used to his utmost disadvantage.[2] He spent the rest of his sojourn as the helpless witness of his own weakness. The result of all his plans was that Scotland attained a virtual independence of the crown's authority, while the Covenanters consolidated their hold on the kingdom.

Meanwhile, the Country leaders at Westminster had revealed their aims on the reopening of parliament. They had two capital objectives: first, the passage of the previously defeated measure to expel the bishops from the House of Lords; second, the securing of a parliamentary supervision over the selection of the King's ministers. On 21 October, the second day of the sitting, the oppositionist Sir Gilbert Gerrard introduced a new bill against the secular employments of the clergy. It passed on the 23rd against little resistance and was transmitted to the Lords.[3] There it stuck, obstructed, like the former bill, by the dislike of the upper House for any proposal altering its constitution.[4] Thus once more the two Houses were stalemated over a critical issue.

The demand for a parliamentary approval of ministers was presented on the 28th, a revival of Pym's proposition of the previous June.[5] The oppositionist, Robert Goodwin, moved that parliament must have power to remove evil councillors, else 'all wee had done this Parliament would come to nothing, and wee should never be free from danger.' Strode seconded him—in a mostly premeditated speech, noted D'Ewes—contending that 'all wee had done this

---

[1] Endymion Porter to Nicholas, *The Nicholas papers*, ed. G. F. Warner, *Camden society*, XL, 1886, 40.

[2] On the Incident, cf. S. R. Gardiner, *History*, X, 23–7, and further details in C. V. Wedgwood, *The King's peace*, 459–66. The news of the Incident was immediately reported in England, where it did the King much harm, as Nicholas pointed out, J. Evelyn, *op. cit.*, IV, 92–3, 95, 97. A letter from parliament's commissioners to Pym about the Incident was read to the House of Commons on the day it reassembled and was also published as a pamphlet, Coates, *D'Ewes*, 8–9; *C.J.*, II, 290; *L.J.*, IV, 396.

[3] Coates, *D'Ewes*, 21, 30–2; *C.J.*, II, 293; Clarendon, *Rebellion*, IV, 94n.

[4] *L.J.*, IV, 402, 408. On 28 October the Lords deferred consideration of the bill to 10 November, on which day it failed to appear.

[5] Cf. *supra*, 247.

Parliament was nothing unless wee had a negative voice in the placing of the great officers of the King. . . .'[1] This time the proposal met with less agreement than in June. After the passions of the last months, there was evidently a sense of surfeit in the House and a reluctance to be driven at the pace prevailing before the recess. Some members held the legislation already passed to be safeguard enough. Others cautioned strongly against trenching on the King's hereditary rights. Edward Hyde, now in the process of withdrawing his support from the Country, declared that parliament 'had done verie much for the good of the subject' and that 'all particulars weere in a good condition if wee could but preserve them as they weere.' These reactions were danger signals inside the Country alliance. Nevertheless, the opposition leaders continued to sway the House, and the debate resulted in the appointment of a committee to draft a petition to the King about evil counsellors.[2]

It was at this juncture, with parliament not yet sitting two weeks, that the calculations of both the party managers and the King became entwined with an event as incalculable as an eruption or an earthquake, one whose occurrence none foresaw or even imagined, and which helped fan the English political conflict to a consuming heat. On Monday, 1 November, came the report from across the Irish sea of the outbreak of a rebellion in Ireland. The Houses learned the news in an agitated letter from the Irish Privy Council at Dublin. It related that the Catholics of Ulster had risen in a carefully-laid conspiracy, seizing stores of arms and numerous strong places. A rebel attempt to capture Dublin Castle had narrowly failed. The Irish Council feared the spread of the revolt throughout the kingdom. If so, Ireland would be

in the greatest Danger that ever it underwent, considering our Want of Men, Money, and Arms, to enable us to encounter so great Multitudes as they can make . . . against us; the rather because we have pregnant Cause to [think] that the Combination hath taken Force by the incitement of Jesuits, Priests, and Friars.[3]

Thus, the contagion of resistance had now seized the third of the King's realms. That it burst forth with such stupefying surprise was merely proof of English blindness to the true condition of Ireland.[4]

---

[1] Coates, *D'Ewes*, 44, 45.　　　[2] *Ibid.*, 45–7; *C.J.*, II, 297.

[3] The letter was written to the earl of Leicester, Strafford's successor as Lord Lieutenant, who transmitted it to parliament, *L.J.*, IV, 413–14, *C.J.*, II, 300. The King received the news in Edinburgh on 27 October, *The Nicholas papers*, I, 58–9.

[4] All contemporary accounts stressed the unexpectedness of the rebellion; cf. R. Dunlop, *Ireland under the Commonwealth*, 2v., Manchester, 1913, I,

The End of the Country

A subject country, its indigenous population of native Irish and old English ruled by men of alien religion and nationality, Ireland suffered injustices beside which the grievances of England and Scotland paled. During the Anglo-Spanish war of Elizabeth's reign, the Ulster Irish revolted and were only suppressed after a long and terrible struggle. In the sequel, the royal government pursued the policy of promoting large-scale immigration in order to strengthen the English Protestant ascendancy. Since the time of James I it had expropriated vast tracts of Irish land as plantations for alien settlement. The natives were driven off to make way for English and Scotch colonists. Few Irishmen had secure possession of their soil. They lay exposed to the threat of confiscation from the crown on the pretext of defective title, and to the rapacity of English officials who exploited their position unscrupulously for their own enrichment. Catholicism, the religion of the majority of inhabitants, was illegal; and while the King and Strafford had permitted the Irish Catholics some practical toleration for their worship, the prohibition against their faith could be enforced at any time. Under Strafford, Ireland attained a measure of economic prosperity. Moreover, to promote the superior interests of the crown, the Lord Lieutenant also set a curb on the English adventurers and land-jobbers in the Irish administration. But his rigorous rule weighed heavier than that of all his predecessors. His autocratic methods and twisting of the law, his invasion of any right hindering his purpose, his confiscatory measures on the royal behalf, and his arrogant intolerance of the slightest opposition, incurred the mortal hatred of all Ireland, Irish and English alike.

Yet it was not the long-standing oppression in land and religion that precipitated the rebellion, but, rather, two more immediate causes. The first was the diffusion in 1641 of the insubordinate spirit of England and Scotland, which unsettled Ireland as well. The second was Irish Catholic fear of the Long Parliament.

Strafford's impeachment formed an epoch in Irish history. When the members gathered at Westminster in November 1640, the parliament of Ireland was also in session at Dublin. Immediately it joined the attack on the Lord Lieutenant in a remonstrance against his misgovernment which the Irish House of Commons passed on 7 November.[1] From that point on, the force of English authority declined. The

[1] *C.J. Ireland*, I, 279–82. The opposition in the Irish parliament is described by A. Clarke, *The old English in Ireland 1625–42*, Ithaca, 1966, ch. VIII.

---

cxii. The letter of the Irish Privy Council expressed the English wonderment (*L.J.*, IV, 413), as did the history written by Sir John Temple, *The Irish rebellion*, 1646, 16–17. Temple, Leicester's confidant, was in Ireland when the revolt began.

example of English agitation over grievances was not lost upon the Irish. Once free of Strafford's domination, the parliament of Ireland could not be stopped from giving voice to Irish sentiments and claims. These claims, which formed the constitutional background to the rebellion, were incompatible with English supremacy. In effect, they would have placed Ireland in a position similar to Scotland's by ending all subjection to England and retaining only the tie of a common crown. The Irish parliament petitioned the King for 'the taking away of ... national distinctions heretofore in policy observed. ...' It asserted that Ireland should not be bound by legislation enacted in England. It further condemned as a grievance Poynings' Law, the famous Irish statute of 1494, which secured English control over the parliament of Ireland by ordaining that all projected legislation in the latter must first receive the approval of the King's Council in England.[1] Pursuant to these views, the Irish House of Commons solemnly resolved on 26 July 1641 that

The subjects of this his Majesty's Kingdom are a free People, and to be governed only according to the common law of England, and statutes made and established in this Kingdom of Ireland, and according to the lawful customs used in the same.[2]

The irony of the Irish parliament's case was that it appealed to constitutional principles much like those the English opposition proclaimed against Charles I. But the Country leaders at Westminster were completely incapable of sympathy with Irish grievances. Reformers and revolutionaries in the context of English politics, towards Catholic Ireland they were the reverse. They could only see Ireland through the eyes of the Protestant minority of officials and landowners who formed the most durable element of the English ascendancy. They took for granted its dependent status under both the crown and the parliament of England.[3] They could not feel the

[1] *C.S.P. Ireland 1633–47*, 286, 321.

[2] *C.J. Ireland*, I, 501. This resolution was preceded by queries which the Irish Commons adopted in February to assert Irish legislative independence and the liberty of the subject. The queries were defended in June by Patrick Darcy, an M.P., in a speech to the Irish House of Lords; cf. P. Darcy, *An argument*, Dublin, ed. 1746. The resemblance of Darcy's *Argument* and Irish constitutional claims to those of the American colonists before the American revolution has been stressed by C. H. McIlwain, *The American revolution: a constitutional interpretation*, N.Y., 1923, ch. II; cf. also T. Coonan, *The Irish Catholic confederacy and the Puritan revolution*, N.Y., 1954, ch. I and 74–5, 78–9.

[3] In his speech on Strafford's attainder, St. John said, 'The Parliaments of England do bind in Ireland, if Ireland be particularly mentioned. ...'; J. Rushworth, III, 698.

slightest doubt that English security required the subjection of the Irish Catholics, otherwise Ireland, Spain's ally in Elizabeth's time, would become 'a backe doore to open a conquest to England. . . .'[1]

To Irish Catholicism, accordingly, the dominance of the Country-Puritan opposition in the Long Parliament appeared a serious danger. As early as February 1641 the Catholic gentlemen who organized the rebellion began their first hidden preparations, already convinced that the English parliament intended the total extirpation of their religion. Why then, they considered, should not the Irish imitate the Scots, who had secured themselves by a resort to arms?[2]

Indirectly, the King himself abetted their design. He was well aware of Irish fears and in the summer of 1641 he secretly negotiated with some of the chief Irish Catholics to whom he held out the hope of toleration in return for their assistance; possibly he even suggested that they should seize Dublin Castle on his behalf with the help of elements of the Irish army raised by Strafford which was at last being disbanded. If Charles ever made this extremely risky proposal, nothing came of it. Yet by treating with the Irish he unconsciously encouraged the coming revolt and assured that its supporters would not think their purpose displeasing to him.[3] Meanwhile, as the English House of Commons resounded daily with calls for the suppression of papists and the execution of priests, apprehension in Ireland increased. The Irish Catholics became convinced that if ever in control, Pym's party would bind them with iron fetters. Neither their lives, lands, nor religion would be safe, and they would be forced to conform to the Protestant state church on pain of death or banishment. Rumours ran among them too that the Scottish Covenanters would send an army to cut out Catholicism with the sword.

[1] A consideration which members of the English Commons stressed when discussing the danger of Strafford's undisbanded Irish army, Notestein, *D'Ewes*, 229–30.

[2] Cf. Roger More's arguments to persuade Lord Maguire to join the rebellion, *The relation of Lord Maguire. A contemporary history of affairs in Ireland from 1641 to 1652*, ed. J. T. Gilbert, 3v., Dublin, 1879–80, I, pt. 2, 501–2.

[3] Cf. Gardiner's observations and review of the evidence on the King's negotiations with the Irish Catholics, *History*, X, 7n. It is impossible to determine exactly what Charles proposed. The story told in 1650 by the earl of Antrim (printed in R. Cox, *Hibernia Anglicana*, 1689, pt. 2, 206–8) that he suggested the seizure of Dublin Castle must be taken with caution because of its improbabilities, which are mentioned by Cox. Probably the King did not instigate the rebellion, but he did play with the possibility of getting Irish help. This was another of the dangerously imprudent expedients to which he resorted in the hope of restoring his position, and it led to consequences far beyond his anticipations; cf. also R. Dunlop, *op. cit.*, I, cxvi–cxvii.

Herein lay the imperative motive for resistance.[1] Conceiving themselves and their faith to be in direst peril, the despairing Irish rose. The outbreak began in Ulster, where the greatest land confiscations had occurred, and rapidly spread. Before the year's end it was joined by the old English, the lords and gentry of the Pale, the one component of Irish society which, though Catholic, had been strongly disposed to the support of English rule in the earlier century. English power found itself facing the avenging fury of a subject population bent on driving it from Ireland.

The Irish rebellion produced a profound shock in England. Nothing had prepared Englishmen to understand such a defection. Under the stress of the worsening news from beyond the Irish sea in the fall and winter of 1641, the Protestant-Puritan mind became as if possessed with wrath and fear. Its ever-lurking dread of Catholicism, often stirred during the past year, leaped into panic-stricken life. Retaining vivid imaginations of the lurid history of Jesuit treason and the Gunpowder conspiracy, it discovered its most nightmarish fantasies come true in Ireland. It had no conception of the real causes of the revolt, which it attributed exclusively to the malignity of priests. Prone to accept the wildest exaggerations, it was certain that the brutalities and slaughter committed by the Irish meant no less than a deliberate plot to massacre every Protestant man, woman, and child in Ireland.[2]

Before the spectre of treachery and terror in Ireland, the crisis of confidence in England assumed a graver urgency. The opposition leaders knew nothing of the King's communications to the Irish, yet harboured the darkest suspicions. They were persuaded that without secret support from Charles or the Queen the rebellion could not have occurred.[3] This seemed the likelier because only the King could

---

[1] The manifestos of the Irish rebels were unanimous in mentioning fear of the English parliament as a principal cause of the revolt; cf. *The generall remonstrance . . . of the Catholikes of Ireland*, 1641, *The humble remonstrance of the northern Catholicks of Ireland, now in arms*, 1642, and *The true demands of the rebells in Ireland*, 1642. The belief in the coming of a Covenanter army is referred to in *The relation of Lord Maguire, loc. cit.* and by Richard Bellings, the contemporary Irish historian of the Catholic confederation, *History of the Irish confederation*, ed. J. T. Gilbert, 7v., Dublin, 1882–91, I, 15–17.

[2] Lecky's remarks concerning Irish actions may still be accepted; W. E. H. Lecky, *A history of England in the eighteenth century*, 8v., N.Y., ed. 1879, II, 140–85. Although the Irish were guilty of many atrocities, there was no massacre, and contemporary English opinion exaggerated to fantastic proportions the number of victims; cf. also R. Dunlop, *op. cit.*, I, cxvii–cxviii.

[3] Cf. the Venetian ambassador's remarks concerning the party leaders' suspicions, *C.S.P.V. 1640–42*, 241.

take any advantage by it. From the outset the Irish rebels proclaimed themselves his faithful subjects and linked their grievances with his in severe condemnation of the English parliament. Their first manifesto, issued immediately after the start of the revolt, declared that the 'Puritan faction' and the English Commons had invaded the King's prerogative, usurped his authority, and left him naught 'but the bare name of a King.'[1] Believing Charles disposed to tolerate their religion, and having identified their cause with his, the Irish Catholics might easily decide to lend him armed assistance; or, on the other hand, since an army would have to be raised to suppress the rebellion, such a force, if the King controlled it, might well provide him with a sword to destroy his opponents in England.

In these ominous alternatives lay Ireland's tragedy: the Irish struggle could never fuse with the revolution in England nor obtain its help, but, on the contrary, must imperil its very survival. Once more Pym and his friends foresaw the prospect of violence and counter-revolution. To provide against it was now their overriding concern. More than ever they were resolved to render the King harmless by removing all influences but their own from his government; that the sole way to safety lay in investing parliament with the approval and oversight of councillors and thus of every aspect of executive policy.

Within a few days of the news of the rebellion the House of Commons saw the party managers' determination. On 5 November, Pym, reporting for a newly established committee on Irish affairs,[2] submitted a number of propositions which the parliamentary commissioners in Scotland were instructed to present to the King. After these had been accepted, he stood up to offer the members a further motion on his own account. All their efforts to preserve Ireland would be in vain, he said, so long as the King listened to evil counsels. Let them accordingly make a declaration that

howsoever wee had ingaged our selves for the assistance of Ireland yet unles the King would remove his evill counsellors and take such councellors as might be approved by Parliament wee should account our selves absolved from this ingagement.[3]

This proposal to coerce the King with conditions was too audacious to prevail at once, and a debate arose which continued till

---

[1] *The generall remonstrance of the Catholikes of Ireland*, 1641. This must have appeared in London early in November, judging from what looks like a reference to it in the Venetian ambassador's despatch of the 15th, *C.S.P.V. 1640–42*, 240.

[2] A standing committee for Irish affairs was appointed by the House on 2 November, *C.J.*, II, 302.   [3] Coates, *D'Ewes*, 94.

evening without result. Next day Pym submitted his motion again, now as a recommendation of the committee for Irish affairs.[1] Another debate ensued in which once more the House reached no conclusion.[2] Members felt themselves caught in the crux they were to experience repeatedly as the conflict with the crown completed its parliamentary phase and moved ineluctably towards civil war. They had to choose between the rights which the law and precedent gave the King and the severe and novel course dictated by the dangerous situation. On Monday, the 8th, Pym's motion reappeared slightly altered in language but its substance unimpaired. It now professed fidelity and obedience to Charles, yet told him plainly that the Irish rebellion and all the kingdom's evils for many years proceeded from the practices of persons near him in authority and counsel. Unless he would employ such ministers as parliament approved, the declaration continued,

we shall be forced, by Discharge of the Trust which we owe to the State, and to those whom we represent, to resolve upon some such Way of defending Ireland . . . as may concur to the securing of ourselves from . . . mischievous Counsels and Designs . . . and to commend those Aids and Contributions which this great Necessity shall require, to the Custody and Disposing of such Persons of Honour and Fidelity as we have Cause to confide in.[3]

Under the form of a petitionary request this proposal was nearly an ultimatum. It dissociated the King from the state, asserted the paramountcy of parliament's trust to those it represented, and threatened in the name of that trust to assume for parliament a power of command and appointment that did not belong to it. Again a long debate occurred during which the House finally became ready to decide. In the division that followed, Pym's revolutionary article passed by 151 to 110.[4]

This vote disclosed a sizeable movement away from the leadership of the Commons managers. In their search for guarantees, they were demanding endorsement of a step which many members thought both inflammatory and legally impermissible. Even D'Ewes, a pretty

---

[1] Whereas on 5 November Pym introduced his motion from the floor following the report of the committee for Irish affairs, on the 6th he reported it to the House as one of the committee's recommendations. The committee had met the previous evening, and it looks as if Pym had prevailed on it to adopt his proposal; Coates, *D'Ewes*, 94, 95, 99.

[2] *C.J.*, II, 307; Coates, *D'Ewes*, 102.

[3] The text of the declaration appears as nos. 7 and 8 in the instructions to be sent to the parliamentary commissioners in Scotland for presentation to the King, *L.J.*, IV, 431.　　　[4] *C.J.*, II, 307; Coates, *D'Ewes*, 104, 105.

consistent Country adherent, voted negatively, noting in his journal in the cipher reserved for his most private thoughts that the motion was 'of verie dangerous consequence.'[1] The House of Lords also refused to adopt the declaration, despite Pym's vigorous speech at a joint committee urging its necessity. As a consequence the lower House notified the peers that it would send the King the declaration in its own name if they would not concur.[2]

It was evident that parliament's former unanimity in accomplishing the constitutional reforms of previous months could not stand the strain of the opposition leaders' pressure. Beset by reservations, doubts, and downright disaffection, the great Country alliance was cracking. The King, taking note of this, felt his position stronger and was thus less likely to grant additional concessions. He now counted on the obstructiveness of the House of Lords, which he did his best to encourage in his messages from Scotland.[3] Heartened that voices in the Commons championed his right to choose his own councillors, he conveyed his appreciation through Nicholas to Edward Hyde, Lord Falkland, and other upholders of his prerogative.[4] He let it be known that he would never consent to any alteration in the doctrine and government of the church; and several days after the House of Commons passed its second bill against the secular employments of the clergy he created five new bishops. He could not have expressed more bluntly his determination to preserve the episcopal votes in the House of Lords.[5]

There can be little doubt that Pym and his friends fully realized in the first days of November that their hard line was generating resistance in the Commons. They could hardly have failed to consider that they might face a reaction against their sway if they persisted in their demands. Even in the obscurity shrouding their deliberations, it may be surmised that they reviewed the situation and concluded not to recede from their position. Having come so far in their fight, they refused to leave what they had won at the hazard of an unfettered royal executive whose every action they distrusted. Nor could they for a moment overlook Ireland, now the heart of all their anxieties, where any projected counter-revolution possessed a potential military base. The opposition leaders must have agreed to intensify their pressure on the King, resolved to gain their object despite the risk that some of their parliamentary support might split away.

---

[1] *Ibid.*, 105. [2] *L.J.*, IV, 431–2, 438; *C.J.*, II, 315.
[3] J. Evelyn, *op. cit.*, IV, 95.
[4] *Ibid.*, IV, 101. The other M.P.s mentioned by the King were Sir John Strangeways, Edmund Waller, and Sir Robert Holborne.
[5] *Ibid.*, IV, 88, 102. The King told Nicholas that the new bishops should take their seats in parliament as soon as possible.

The means for their purpose lay at hand in a proposal first advanced twelve months before in their consultations at the beginning of the Long Parliament. At that time they intended, according to Mandeville's memoirs, that the House of Commons, 'as the Grand Inquest of the Kingdome' should draw up a remonstrance to the King 'as . . . a faithfull and lively representation . . . of the deplorable Estate of his Kingdome. . . .'; and on 10 November 1640, after motions by St. John and Lord Digby, the House actually named a committee to this end.[1] Although the committee met a few times, the party managers apparently decided to hold the remonstrance in reserve: hence it made no appearance prior to the September recess.[2] But soon after parliament's reassembling they judged the moment had come to bring it forward.[3] On 8 November 1641, accordingly, at the close of the same afternoon that saw the passage of Pym's revolutionary motion on Ireland, the remonstrance was read the first time in the House,[4] to become at once an issue over which the members quarrelled with rising passion until the final vote of 22 November, when the Country alliance broke to pieces.

The *Remonstrance of the state of the kingdom*—later known as the Grand Remonstrance—was the manifesto and apologia alike of the House of Commons and of its steersmen, the leaders of the Country opposition.[5] It was at once an unsparing indictment of the King's reign, a vindication of all parliament had done or yet hoped to do against 'the multiplied evils and corruptions of fifteen years,' and an appeal addressed to the entire political nation. Of its authorship nothing definite can be ascertained. Though containing some expressions that seemingly came straight from Pym,[6] the whole was most

[1] B.M. Add. 15, 567, f. 30v.; Notestein, *D'Ewes*, 27 and n., 532; *C.J.*, II, 25.

[2] The House several times ordered the committee on the remonstrance to meet and bring in its work, e.g., on 28 April, 23 July, and 3 August, *C.J.*, II, 130, 221, 234.

[3] On 25 October the House ordered the remonstrance to be brought in on the 29th, and on the latter day the matter was moved again by the Buckinghamshire oppositionist, Arthur Goodwin. Discussion on it would have begun on 1 November, in accord with Goodwin's motion, had not the news of the Irish rebellion resulted in a week's postponement; *C.J.*, II, 294, 298; Coates, *D'Ewes*, 51.

[4] Coates, *D'Ewes*, 106; cf. also W. Coates, 'Some observations on the "Grand Remonstrance",' *Journal of modern history*, IV, 1 (1932).

[5] I cite the *Remonstrance* from S. R. Gardiner, *Constitutional documents of the Puritan revolution*, 205ff., which reprints the text contained in J. Rushworth, IV, 438ff. Rushworth's and Gardiner's version unaccountably omits almost the entire last page, amounting to nineteen and one-half lines, of the *Remonstrance* as printed in 1641 by authority of the House of Commons. Their numbering of the paragraphs is not always in accord and has no authority in the published text of 1641, but I retain it to facilitate reference.

[6] Cf. the close resemblances between the passage beginning, 'As in all

probably the common product of the small committee of opposition-ist notables to which the House had last given the *Remonstrance* in charge.[1] In spite of its inevitable propagandist tone and aim, it mirrored with perfect fidelity the political mind of the men who long had stood in the front of resistance to Charles's rule and who now felt impelled to circumscribe the King still further in order to preserve the kingdom from impending ruin.

Traced out at length in the *Remonstrance*'s pages was a grim picture of England's decline: the subversion of its liberty and law, the destruction of its traditional principles of government, and the corruption of the power and purity of its Protestant religion. All this it ascribed to a pernicious design of papists abetted by the Arminian clergy and royal councillors who had made the King the unwitting accessory of their nefarious ends. The *Remonstrance* claimed credit for the great benefits conferred by parliament's recent legislation, but pointed out that the forces of treason continued active and powerful. Still infusing their influence upon the King, incessantly plotting against parliament, it was they who kindled the Irish rebellion. Possessed of a party of bishops and Catholic peers in the House of Lords, they misrepresented the House of Commons' purposes as to religion and obstructed its efforts to secure further reforms. Having thus utterly discredited the King's reliability, the *Remonstrance* concluded on the one point its framers deemed needful beyond all others. It called on Charles to entrust the business of government only to persons who had parliament's confidence; in the event of refusal, it threatened to deny him further financial support and to deal with Ireland without his concurrence. It need scarcely be said that the attribution of the woes of Charles's reign to the plots of Romanists and crypto-Romanists was grotesquely mistaken. Yet such indeed was the genuine belief of the *Remonstrance*'s authors. These narrow-minded patriots, prejudiced Puritans, rigid defenders of parliament's

---

[1] The House on 3 August named a much smaller committee to bring in the remonstrance than had been appointed the past November. Except for Sir John Culpepper, all its members were opposition party intimates: Pym, Vane jr., St. John, Strode, Erle, Hampden, and Nathaniel Fiennes. From the task set this committee, it appears that two remonstrances were then contemplated, one on the state of the kingdom, the other on the church; *C.J.*, II, 234, 253. In the draft submitted after the recess, the two were consolidated in a single declaration. Neither Hampden nor Fiennes could have worked on the text presented on 8 November, since they were both still in Scotland, I assume. Hampden, however, was back in the House of Commons by 11 November, Coates, *D'Ewes*, 118. On 16 November, Lord Falkland was added to the committee, *C.J.*, II, 317.

compounded bodies,' (S. R. Gardiner, *Constitutional documents*, 207) and Pym's speech on evil counsellors to the Lords' committee on 13 November 1641, *L.J.*, IV, 431–2.

liberty—in short, these arch-conservative revolutionists—could make no other sense of events, so great was the incomprehension between them and the King. He had done nothing to win their personal sympathy or affection. He neither understood their point of view nor appeared concerned to set their fears at rest. The doubleness of his conduct baffled and dismayed them: the army plot, his Scottish intrigues, the Irish rebellion, all seemed to them aspects of the same ramifying pattern. In the *Remonstrance*, respect for convention restrained them from attacking the King personally or mentioning the Queen. If not for this, they would have laid every grievance at Charles's own door and openly branded Henrietta Maria as the agent-in-chief of the Catholic conspiracy. Instead, they left the matter in the Aesopian obscurity of allusions to the favour and influence enjoyed by Catholics, the non-enforcement of the penal laws, and the reception of a pope's nuncio in England.[1] But precisely because the King himself was untouchable, it seemed all the more essential to the *Remonstrance*'s partisans that parliament for its own security should control the choice of ministers.

On seven separate days between 9 and 22 November the House of Commons discussed the declaration, deleting and amending clauses here and there, but leaving its harsh, strong-spoken substance intact.[2] Finally, on the 22nd the draft was brought in for its fate to be determined, and its proponents and adversaries strove fiercely against each other from noon till after midnight, bent on winning a majority for their side. The members sustained the lengthy debate without intermission, altogether intent on the great argument waged in their midst. The light of the short afternoon faded and candles were brought, as one speaker followed another in the gloom. At last the question was put whether the declaration should pass. The ayes left the chamber, and the party managers learned that they had carried their *Remonstrance* by the slender majority of eleven in a vote of 159 to 148.[3] The division over, one of their side called for the *Remonstrance* to be printed.[4] Immediately a new quarrel flared up despite the late hour. Members who had attacked the declaration all day hotly demanded the right to enter a protest against any vote to print, and were as hotly denied. In the anger of the moment some drew swords: an intimation of the time not many months off when all

[1] Para. 88–94.

[2] The *Remonstrance* was before the Commons on the 9th, 10th, 15th, 16th, 19th, 20th, and 22nd; cf. *C.J.*, II, 309, 311, 316, 317, 320, 321.

[3] Coates, *D'Ewes*, 183–7; *C.J.*, II, 322. D'Ewes left the House about 4 p.m. but later entered into his journal an account of what occurred in his absence. Prof. Coates's editorial notes from other sources piece out D'Ewes's record.

[4] Moved by George Peard, M.P. for Barnstaple, Coates, *D'Ewes*, 186.

England must perforce take up the sword in a controversy become irremediable. A fortunate intervention from Hampden, however, helped to quiet the House's temper. It was then agreed to put aside the question of printing for that night, and as the clock struck two the weary members departed.[1]

A comparison of the vote on the *Remonstrance* with the one taken in April on Strafford's attainder makes instantly clear how far the balance in the House of Commons had shifted. Each of these votes represented a supreme commitment by the opposition leaders from which there was no backing away; on both they staked their parliamentary ascendancy. They had won Strafford's condemnation by 204 to 59; seven months later, in a better-attended House and in one of the biggest dvisions recorded during the Long Parliament, they obtained their victory by a mere majority of eleven.[2] Thus, while they still controlled the Commons, still possessed its sanction for their policy, the alliance they commanded was broken. A whole detachment of their support had abandoned them in a decisive trial of political opinion and parliamentary strength. This large minority now formed the basis of a new party favourable to the King. Rejecting Pym's appeal and warnings, it had made a sharp turn to the right, thereby promising the end of the King's long isolation. Most of its members undoubtedly regretted the breach in the House. They had acted with reluctance, and would still momentarily hesitate and halt on their way. Nevertheless, from the moment of the vote on the *Remonstrance*, their course was set towards the Royalism newly born of the Country alliance's disruption.[3]

---

[1] *Ibid.*, 186–7; *C.J.*, II, 322. Hampden had returned from Scotland by the 11th; cf. *supra*, 263.

[2] In proportion to the number of divisions in the House of Commons, the occasions on which 300 or more members voted was very small. There were only three between the beginning of parliament and the September 1641 recess. These were divisions totalling 325, 320, and 361 on 9 February, 5 March, and 9 June 1641, *C.J.*, II, 81, 97, 171. Two divisions on 22 November preceding the actual vote on the *Remonstrance* numbered 310 and 308, *ibid.*, II, 322. Thus, the vote of 307 on the *Remonstrance* was exceptionally large and shows that members were not deterred by the length of the debate from staying to the end. The last division of the night, however, on a point of detail gave a total of 225, indicating that over 80 members had now left. Some remarks on attendance will be found in V. Snow, 'Attendance trends and absenteeism in the Long Parliament,' *Huntington Library quarterly*, XVIII, 3 (1955).

[3] In the absence of division lists at this period, only a few of the members voting against the *Remonstrance* can be identified by name. It is highly probable, nevertheless, that the minority opposed to the *Remonstrance* comprised pretty nearly the same members who are known to have joined the King subsequently. There were, however, a few exceptions. Sir John Coke, M.P. for Derbyshire, wrote about the vote, 'If you sett Pimme Hollis

What caused this development? The King was still what he had been, and in view of the Irish rebellion the crisis of confidence in his intentions more acute, not less. What, then, prompted the defection that split the Country and led to the gradual emergence from its divided parts of a new political alignment in parliament and the kingdom?

It was the judgment of Gardiner, followed therein by nearly all subsequent historians of the subject since,[1] that the reason lay in the religious differences within the Country. According to him, '. . . if no other question had been at issue than the political one, there would have been no permanent division of parties, and no Civil War. . . .'[2] Gardiner held that those who turned towards Charles were the favourers of episcopacy reacting not against the political line of the Commons managers but against their determination to remodel the church. Hence Pym's motion of 8 November and the sequel of the *Remonstrance* resulted in the

final conversion of the Episcopalian party into a Royalist party. . . . To baffle the Puritans had now become its chief object. For the sake of that it was ready to trust the King, and to take its chance of what the Irish campaign might bring forth.[3]

Noting Charles's resistance to any alteration in the church and the opposition leaders' contrary aim of reformation, Gardiner characterized the situation consequent on the *Remonstrance*'s passage thus:

. . . the struggle which was at hand was not to be waged on mere political grounds. . . . No king, said one party, shall rob us of our religion. No Parliamentary majority, said the other party, shall rob us of our religion. It was this, and this only, which gave to the great struggle its supreme importance.[4]

This view, however, in fact misstates the effect of religious differences in the breach over the *Remonstrance*, and on that account must be emphatically rejected. Doubtless Gardiner conceived it more fittingly ideal that Englishmen should quarrel over religion than on 'mere political grounds.' The reality, nevertheless, was rather differ-

[1] A notable exception is B. H. G. Wormald's study of Clarendon, *op. cit.*
[2] *History*, X, 32.   [3] *Ibid.*, X, 59.   [4] *Ibid.*, X, 78–9.

and Hambdin aside, the best of the House voted against it, as Sr John Culpeper, L^d. Faulkland, Mr Crewe, Sir Robert Pye, Sr John Strangewaies, all the best lawyers, Alderman Somes, Sir Edward Deering, Mr Waller, Sr Ralfe Hopton &c.' (*H.M.C. Cowper*, II, 295). Of this group, Crewe, Pye, and Soame became Parliamentarians.

ent. Severely as the *Remonstrance* criticized the church and bishops, its religious clauses contained nothing revolutionary. In particular, no attempt was made in it to revive the campaign against episcopacy, which the Commons managers abandoned when they dropped the Root-and-Branch bill in the summer.[1] Premissed indeed on the continuance of bishops, it promised further measures to reduce their power and, especially, to abolish their secular employments 'that so the better they might with meekness apply themselves to the discharge of their functions. . . .'[2] In addition, during the preliminary debates on the *Remonstrance* its promoters yielded to the sentiment in the House for deleting all statements derogatory to the prayer book. The document also expressed a vigorous condemnation of sectarianism and a pledge to enforce conformity to the church order established by law.[3] Accordingly, on its religious side the final version of the *Remonstrance* was to a certain extent a compromise. Besides the expulsion of the bishops from parliament, it committed the Commons to three principal reforms: the suppression of superstitious ceremonies, the removal of incompetent clergy, and the provision of a preaching ministry throughout the kingdom.[4] These were about the minimum steps towards the reformation impatiently expected by parliament's Puritan supporters, and came well short of the desires of those who wanted the destruction of episcopacy. Under other circumstances their substance might have been acceptable to many moderate churchmen—persons whom in distinction to the Arminians the *Remonstrance* called 'common Protestants.'[5] But religious questions could no longer be looked at except in their entanglement with the overshadowing political issues posed by the opposition leaders' course.

During the arguments over the *Remonstrance*'s ecclesiastical provisions, the Puritan D'Ewes noted the existence of an 'episcopall partie' in the Commons.[6] His own conduct accordingly demonstrated the weight of political over religious sentiments. Intensely as he disliked bishops and wished for church reform, his reservations towards the *Remonstrance* were stronger still. And so on 22 November, unwilling to take part in the final vote, he quit the House at four in

[1] Cf. *supra*, 240–1.
[2] Para. 183. The clause quoted was opposed but carried in a division of 161–147, *C.J.*, II, 322. Para. 137 is similar to it and also indicated the reform of bishops, not their uprooting.
[3] *C.J.*, II, 317; Coates, *D'Ewes*, 151; para. 184. An attempt to secure the deletion of a statement in para. 189 that the bishops had introduced idolatry was defeated by 124 to 99, *C.J.*, II, 317.
[4] Para. 137, 184, 186.
[5] S. R. Gardiner, *Constitutional documents*, 207.
[6] Coates, *D'Ewes*, 149, 150, 151, 152.

the afternoon because, he wrote, 'there were some particulars in the said declaration which I . . . could not in my conscience assent unto although otherwise my heart and vote went with it in the mayne.'[1]

But what, after all, was this 'episcopall partie' and what did its ecclesiastical conceptions signify? Falkland, Hyde, Sir John Culpepper, and Dering, four prominent voices among those to whom D'Ewes referred, feared less for the church in itself than for the monarchical order which it supported and which was now challenged by the incitements and demands in the *Remonstrance*. In every previous debate on church government before the recess, the defenders of the Anglican establishment had shown the keenest solicitude for the mutual dependence between the ecclesiastical system and the prevailing regime of privilege and subordination. That concern was now of sovereign import to them. In the context of the constitutional innovations and aggressive methods pursued by the Commons managers, religious changes also became dangerous and undesirable. This, rather than intransigent dislike of church reform, defined the nature of the religious question after the Houses reassembled. In May Lord Falkland voted in favour of the first bill against the secular employments of the clergy; in October he voted against the second, having ceased to be in sympathy any longer with the general policy of the opposition leaders.[2] Edward Hyde had always disliked the bill as overturning 'the whole frame and constitution of the kingdom,' but otherwise had actively concurred in the statutes enacted against the prerogative. He was now unqualifiedly hostile to Pym, whose aggression on the crown's legal rights he considered a grave provocation.[3] Sir John Culpepper felt no conscientious attachment to the church, but 'inclined to what was established to avoid the accidents which commonly attend a change.'[4] As for Sir Edward Dering, it was he who introduced the Root-and-Branch bill in May, yet now he was one of the bishops' defenders.[5] Commenting on the disturbed situation and the growth of sectarianism, he warned of the 'wicked sweetnesse of a popular parity,' foresaw the decline of kingship and nobility, and then, he concluded,

All's done. No rather, all's undone, by breaking asunder that well ordered chain of government, which from the chair of Jupiter reacheth

[1] *Ibid.*, 185.
[2] Clarendon, *Rebellion*, III, 151–2, IV, 94n.
[3] *Ibid.*, III, 149–50. Cf. B. H. G. Wormald, *op. cit.*, 3–11, 282–8, for an account of Hyde's 'episcopalianism.' He denies that Hyde separated from the opposition leaders over ecclesiastical issues.
[4] Clarendon, *Life*, 940.
[5] Coates, *D'Ewes*, 151; Sir E. Dering, *A collection of speeches*, 110–11.

down by severall golden links even to the protection of the poorest creature that now lives amongst us.[1]

These were the considerations dominating the alignment on the *Remonstrance*. Its adversaries recognized in it an inflammatory spirit which they believed would set the polity alight. That spirit was apparent in its harsh language and its embittered review of the past; in its revolutionary insistence that parliament should approve ministerial appointments; and finally, in the purpose it was meant to serve. The *Remonstrance* was not a petition to obtain the King's grace, but a device of threat and intimidation. Composed for the general eye, it was intended to mobilize popular passion for the party managers' demands. Hence in the last, decisive debate, Hyde roundly condemned it as destructive to peace, while Culpepper and Dering denounced 'the forme of itt.'[2] 'When I first heard of a Remonstrance,' said Dering, '. . . I did not dream that we should remonstrate downward, tell stories to the people, and talke of the King as of a third person.'[3] 'This [is] a Remonstrance to the people,' Culpepper told the House. 'Remonstrances ought to bee to the king for redresse; this may exasperate. . . . The humours [are] much stirred; and . . . this kingdome much distracted. . . . Wee [are] nott sent to please the people.'[4] Pym met these objections head on. '. . . The honour of the king lies in the saifty of the people,' he replied; '. . . all the plotts and designes [have been] thrust home . . . to the Court, and its time to speake playne English, least posterity shall say that England was lost and noe man durst speak truth. . . . This declaration will binde the peoples hearts to us, when they see how we have been used.'[5]

No compromise was possible over a difference of such magnitude, and the Country split apart.

2

In these altered circumstances the King returned to London on 25 November after his lengthy stay amongst the Scots. Conscious of his access of strength from the recalcitrance of the Lords and the breach in the Commons, he was ready to make an unyielding stand against the further demands of his opponents. His cordial reception by the

[1] *Ibid.*, 165–6. These remarks, written in 1642 as the concluding note to his speeches, were Dering's comment on the state of affairs in the fall and winter of 1641.
[2] Coates, *D'Ewes*, 183n., 184n.
[3] Sir E. Dering, *op. cit.*, 109.
[4] Coates, *D'Ewes*, 184n.
[5] Conflated from the notes of Pym's speech in *ibid.*, 184n. and *Verney notes*, 122–3.

lord mayor and aldermen fortified his firmness. The city's governing body was profuse in its expressions of loyalty and support, and made plain that it looked to him to sustain its authority against any challenge in these insurgent times.[1] The next weeks were to be climacteric. The revolution swayed dangerously, locked between the thrust of the Commons leaders to drive it on and the counter-thrust of the King to halt its advance. Amidst such fiercely contending stresses, it could not remain where it was. Either it must recede to be overwhelmed by a reaction in the royal favour, or it must go forward to invest itself with that supervisory power over the executive which was the core proposition of the *Remonstrance*.

On Pym's side there was no hesitation. Often in the past year he had shown his moderation and desire to achieve a consensus. Now consensus was absent and he stood forth as the advocate of uncompromising, radical measures. But the great parliamentary leader, grey-bearded and in his fifty-eighth year, did not pursue his way as an enthusiast or visionary. Sober and watchful as ever, he held to his course because he recognized no other alternative and was too clear sighted to shrink from accepting the consequences of his own commitments and previous actions.

Three days after the vote on the *Remonstrance*, the party managers demonstrated their continued hold on the Commons. The members who had claimed the right of protestation were sharply rebuked and Geoffrey Palmer, their spokesman, was voted to the Tower.[2] On 1 December the House presented the *Remonstrance* to the King, together with a petition reiterating the necessity of his consent to the bishops' removal from the House of Lords and to the employment in public affairs of persons who possessed parliament's confidence.[3] Although not yet in print, the declaration was known to the Londoners on account of the publicity continually surrounding parliament's doings. A report of it also appeared in the first number of *The heads of severall proceedings in this present parliament*, which came on sale at the end of November, the earliest forerunner of a host of revolutionary newspapers.[4] On 15 December the Commons managers

[1] Cf. *infra*, 285.

[2] *C.J.*, II, 324; Coates, *D'Ewes*, 192–5, 197–9. The divisions taken on 24 and 25 November revealed the alignment in the House. Palmer was committed to the Tower by a vote of 169–128. A motion of the oppositionist, Sir John Hotham, to expel him from membership was defeated, however, by 163–131. The question of protestation in general was definitively settled on 20 December in the House's resolution that no member had the right to protest the action of the majority, whose decision was binding upon all; *C.J.*, II, 350; Coates, *D'Ewes*, 320–3.

[3] *C.J.*, II, 328, 330; S. R. Gardiner, *Constitutional documents*, 202–5. Pym was the petition's main draftsman, Coates, *D'Ewes*, 206n.

[4] Cf. *supra*, 206.

decided to renew their proposal to publish the *Remonstrance*. The motion was put by a couple of oppositionists with the privity of many members, according to D'Ewes. He himself again left the chamber to avoid voting. Although vehemently attacked, the motion was carried by 134 to 83.[1] A few days after the incendiary declaration was blazoned to the world.

It fell upon a disturbed, distempered London amidst an atmosphere close with tension. The capital was on the brink of a revolution in its own internal government,[2] which was foreshadowed by the unruly crowds favourable to the opposition leaders that had been assembling at Westminster. One who witnessed the mob gloomily commented, 'Sects in the body and factions in the head . . . do desperately threaten the dissolution of a well-governed estate.'[3] In the House of Lords the bill against the secular employments of the clergy lay stalled and disregarded. The Commons could do nothing but vainly threaten the peers with unilateral action on the measure, 'this House being the Representative Body of the whole kingdom, and their Lordships being but as particular Persons and coming to Parliament in a particular Capacity. . . .'[4]

This dangerous and innovative doctrine merely helped to strengthen the upper House's obstinacy. The majority of its members in their antagonism to the policy of the Commons were only following the King's lead. From the moment of his return, Charles had decided to make no further concessions. In his first public speech in London, he pledged to maintain the church as it was under Elizabeth and his father.[5] A few days later he pointedly snubbed a recommendation from the Commons that he give offices to the earls of Pembroke and Salisbury as persons who possessed the House's confidence.[6] Finally, in his answer on 23 December to the petition submitted with the *Remonstrance* he gave his verdict conclusively against its demands. The bishops' membership in parliament, he stated, is 'grounded upon the Fundamental Law of the Kingdom, and Constitution of Parliament;' as to the 'Choice of Our Counsellors and Ministers of State. . . . it is the undoubted Right of the Crown of England, to call such Persons to our secret Councils, to publick Employment, and Our particular Service, as We shall think fit. . . .'[7]

---

[1] *C.J.*, II, 344; Coates, *D'Ewes*, 294–5.
[2] Cf. *infra*, 287ff.   [3] *H.M.C. Buccleuch*, I, 287.
[4] *C.J.*, II, 330.   [5] J. Rushworth, IV, 430.
[6] The House recommended Pembroke's appointment as Lord Steward and Salisbury's as Treasurer. On 5 December Charles gave the office of Steward to the duke of Richmond instead; that of Treasurer remained unfilled; *C.J.*, II, 336; G. E. Cokayne, *op. cit.*, X, 832. Cf. the Venetian ambassador's remarks on the episode, *C.S.P.V. 1640–42*, 261.
[7] J. Rushworth, IV, 452–3; *C.J.*, II, 354.

Together with the evident hardening of the King's will appeared signs that he was preparing for a showdown with his opponents. Reports came to the House of Commons that certain of its members would shortly be accused of treason. Charles's partisans were predicting the early end of the opposition's sway and the victory of the 'King's party.'[1] 'The Parliament fly high yet,' wrote one on 9 December, 'but it is conceived it will every day grow more temperate.'[2] Charles now felt strong enough to dismiss the elder Vane, whom he had distrusted ever since Strafford's trial, replacing him as Secretary of State by Edward Nicholas.[3] Repeated rumours spoke of the dismissal of other unfaithful servants and of the forthcoming conferment of ministerial offices on members of parliament hostile to Pym's party.[4] These forecasts were confirmed on 1 January 1642 when the King appointed Lord Falkland as co-Secretary of State and Sir John Culpepper as Chancellor of the Exchequer.[5]

A prey to fears of every sort, the House of Commons was defenceless in the event of violence. Although a guard under the earl of Essex had been posted by parliament at Westminster during the King's absence in Scotland, Charles dismissed it immediately on his return.[6] He meant to keep all military force in the capital at his own disposition and was adamant against the Commons' pleas for its restoration.[7] The party managers naturally placed a sinister interpre-

---

[1] Coates, *D'Ewes*, 212, 213, 215; *C.S.P.D. 1641–43*, 188.   [2] *Ibid.*, 192–3.

[3] *Ibid.*, 193–4. Nicholas had sent the King in Scotland numerous hints of Secretary Vane's disloyalty and communications with the opposition party in England, J. Evelyn, *op. cit.*, IV, 68, 77, 92.

[4] *C.S.P.D. 1641–43*, 192, 201, 211. On the strength of a remark made in a letter by Sir Edward Dering, Gardiner declared that the King first offered the chancellorship of the Exchequer to Pym before appointing Culpepper to the place; *History*, X, 127. J. Forster, *The arrest of the five members*, L., 1860, 48–9, and C. V. Wedgwood, *The King's war*, L., 1958, 55, also accept this story. I know of no other evidence in its favour, however, and reject it as most improbable. At the moment of his alleged offer, Charles was about to launch his long meditated *coup* against Pym's group.

[5] According to Clarendon, Falkland accepted office with the greatest reluctance. One reason was his fear that the world might think he had opposed the dominant party in parliament in order to gain promotion from the King. Both his and Culpepper's preferment aroused the strong disapproval of 'the angry part of the House'; *Rebellion*, IV, 123–5. This would seem sufficient to expose the fallacy of Wormald's suggestion (*Clarendon*, 41) that in the appointment of these former allies of the oppositionists the King now had advisers 'to whom it was difficult to deny confidence. . . .' In fact, because of the tense situation prevailing on the eve of the King's *coup*, the promotion of M.P.s conspicuously separated from Pym could have had no such effect.   [6] Coates, *D'Ewes*, 18n., 70; *L.J.*, IV, 398–9; *C.J.*, II, 325.

[7] *C.J.*, II, 327–8. On 29–30 November, because of the crowds at Westminster, Charles despatched a guard under the earl of Dorset's command with whom the citizens almost came to blows. He then withdrew it, *L.J.*, IV, 455.

tation on his refusal. It served to emphasize the extent of the danger as long as control of armed force rested with the King. The relief of Ireland, the security of parliament, the entire crisis of confidence lay centred in this issue. In consequence the House initiated a fresh aggression on the crown's authority. It was foreshadowed in a motion made by the oppositionist Strode at the end of November that a course be taken to remove the military power from the King. This proposal was the germ of the bill which Sir Arthur Haselrig introduced on 7 December to place command of the kingdom's militia in a general to be named by parliament.[1] In essence, the bill was an application of the principle that ministerial appointments should be subject to parliament's approval. Thus far, however, the House had only advanced this demand by way of petition, and had claimed a right of veto, not of direct nomination. Haselrig's bill went further in proposing by means of statute to invest parliament with complete supervision of the military. Radical as this was, it did not deter the members, and against the clamour of those who urged the militia bill's rejection as an unlawful invasion of the prerogative, a majority voted to receive it.[2] With this decision the House of Commons committed itself to wrest from the King the *ultima ratio* of his monarchical sovereignty.

Charles did not intend to hold to a merely defensive posture against these latest assaults on his crown. Ever since his Scottish journey he had been considering how to master his opponents by a decisive stroke. After his return to London he judged the situation favourable for such an attempt. Whether the plan for the *coup* he had in mind was conceived then, or earlier in Scotland, cannot be determined. Perhaps he had long entertained it in a general way, since it closely resembled Strafford's scheme at the opening of the Long Parliament to get rid of the opposition leaders by accusing them of treason.[3] Possibly he made the decision for its execution because of the urgings of Lord Digby in London: for that brilliant but imprudent gentleman, having deserted the Country during Strafford's attainder, had become Charles's and the Queen's trusted confidant.[4]

---

[1] Coates, *D'Ewes*, 202, 244. The bill also provided that parliament should appoint an admiral.

[2] *C.J.*, II, 334; Coates, *D'Ewes*, 244–8. The vote in favour of receiving the militia bill was 158–125.

[3] Cf. *supra*, 209.

[4] Clarendon attributed the responsibility to Lord Digby, *Rebellion*, IV, 127, 154. His statement, however, that Digby persuaded the King 'to depart from his purpose of doing nothing' (*ibid.*, IV, 146) is unbelievable. Charles's refusal to allow parliament a guard and the rumours that members would be accused of treason were but two of the indications that he was preparing a stroke against his enemies.

The counter-revolution—for this was the King's aim—was to proceed in duly legal form. Pym and several of his near associates were to be charged with treason and placed in confinement; once removed from parliament to face trial, their party supporters would be thoroughly intimidated and their ascendancy at an end. Undoubtedly Charles held himself justified both morally and legally in taking this action. His sense of the rights confided him by God and his royal predecessors was the deepest conviction he possessed. He really did believe the parliamentary managers guilty of treason. If Strafford, his faithful servant, had been condemned to suffer for subverting the law, then so much the more did Pym merit condemnation who in violation of the law was traitorously endeavouring to deprive the King of his regal power.

To effect his aim the King knew that he must cow the London crowd and even suppress it by force if necessary. He therefore acted to secure the Tower, the key to military control of the capital. On 22 December he dismissed the Lieutenant of the Tower, Sir William Balfour, and replaced him with a professional soldier, Col. Lunsford, on whom he felt he could rely.[1] Perhaps Charles imagined that this step, the opening move in his *coup*, would pass unnoticed. Incredible if he thought so! Lunsford, who had served in France and with the royal army in the north, was a swaggerer of notorious reputation.[2] His installation in the Tower at such a time of wrought-up nerves and political fears could not fail to provoke an explosion of suspicion.

The next day, the House of Commons, alarmed by the reports of Lunsford's appointment, asked the Lords to join in remonstrating against it to the King. The upper House refused; it would do nothing to challenge Charles's exercise of his lawful prerogative.[3] The members reacted sharply to this rebuff. On the 24th they gave the militia bill a second reading and resolved that 'This House holds Colonel Lunsford unfit to be ... Lieutenant of the Tower of London; as a Person in whom the Commons of England cannot confide.'[4] They also addressed a stinging declaration to the Lords, in which they condemned the 'Delays and Interruption ... we have received in the House of Peers ... by the great Number of Bishops and Papists, notoriously disaffected to the common Good. ...' They had done their uttermost, they said, to save the commonwealth from ruin; but if Lunsford continued in his charge, we 'hold ourselves bound in

---

[1] *C.S.P.D. 1641–43*, 210; Balfour was to receive £3,000, payable by the Queen's treasurer, for resigning his office in Lunsford's favour.
[2] Cf. *D.N.B.*, *s.v.*
[3] *C.J.*, II, 355; *L.J.*, IV, 487.
[4] *C.J.*, II, 356; the militia bill received a first reading three days earlier, on 21 December, *ibid.*, II, 351.

Conscience to declare and protest, that we are innocent of the Blood which is like to be spilt, and of the Confusion which may overwhelm this State. . . .'[1]

The noblemen received this statement with extreme resentment, which they showed by voting to put off consideration of it for three days to 27 December. A minority of twenty-two opposition lords and their friends, however, entered a vigorous protest against the vote, declaring that the Commons' declaration concerned 'the instant Good and Safety of the King and Kingdom.'[2] Deprived of the peers' cooperation, the lower House then sent a message to the earl of Newport, Constable of the Tower, who was above the Lieutenant in rank, asking him to take immediate custody of the fortress. Newport replied that he could not do so, as on that same day, the 24th, the King had discharged him from his office.[3]

Constitutionally, the House of Commons was at a standstill. Although the thought of acting alone had undoubtedly occurred to its leaders, they did not venture to propose this course; while even with the Lords' support, the House had no legal power to hinder the King's choice of officers. But at this point the London populace took a hand. A revolution against the lord mayor's authority had just begun in the city with the common council election of 21 December.[4] On the 23rd some of the activists in that movement petitioned the Commons against Lunsford's appointment. Another petition with a roll of thirty thousand signatures, which some apprentices delivered, complained of the presence of bishops and Catholic peers in the House of Lords. The apprentices stated their determination 'if need bee to over-match a Royal Coupe.'[5]

Nothing could have been more welcome to the opposition leaders than the spreading agitation in the city. Lacking any means of defence, the Londoners were their sole recourse. Probably the London M.P.s and their citizen friends helped to organize the public reaction. But however it may have been done, it was neither contrived nor artificial. Pym's group enjoyed widespread support in the capital, and popular disapproval of the King's conduct was both broad and deep.

While the Houses stood briefly adjourned over Christmas, London's unrest grew. On Sunday, the 26th, the mayor, Sir Richard Gurney, went to Whitehall to tell the King that if he did not remove Lunsford, the apprentices would attack the Tower. Charles had no

---

[1] *Ibid.*, II, 356–7; *L.J.*, IV, 489.
[2] *L.J.*, IV, 489–90.
[3] *C.J.*, II, 357; *L.J.*, IV, 490.
[4] Cf. *infra*, 288–9.
[5] *C.J.*, II, 354; Coates, *D'Ewes*, 337 and n.; J. Rushworth, IV, 459, 462.

choice but to retreat. That night he dismissed Lunsford and replaced him by Sir John Byron, a man of far better reputation.[1] Nevertheless, the concession came too late to calm the whirlwind his actions had stirred up. During the next three days London was overwhelmed in turmoil that portended a civil war. Rioting crowds crying out against bishops and 'rotten-hearted lords' surged through the neighbourhood of parliament. Fights broke out between citizens and the trained bands summoned by the mayor and the King. A throng of apprentices assaulted Lunsford and some friends in Westminster Hall and were beaten off with swords. A mob attacked Archbishop Williams of York, and, invading Westminster Abbey, tried to pull down the altar and organ. At Whitehall scores of courtiers and ex-officers gathered to defend the King's person.[2] On the 28th a royal proclamation commanded an end to the rioting, but further disorders continued the next day.[3]

The Lords, whose episcopal members were the special object of the mob's anger, had already asked the Commons to join in petitioning the King for a guard and in publishing a declaration against the crowds at Westminster. The lower House replied with a refusal on the 29th. It would have no guard except one approved by parliament and commanded by the earl of Essex—a condition which the peers in their turn refused as invading the King's military authority. The proposed declaration the Commons also rejected, unwilling, noted D'Ewes, 'at this time to discontent the Cittizens of London our surest friends when soe many designes and plotts were daily consulted of against our safetie. . . .'[4]

But even before this reply was received, Lord Digby, who had received a peerage after Strafford's trial, offered an incendiary motion in the House of Lords. Sure that the House of Commons would not rebuke the rioters, he moved that because of the mob's threats parliament was no longer free. He seized here on a possibility that had probably been floating before the King's partisans for some time. Only recently a pamphlet circulating in London had impugned the validity of acts passed during the Scottish occupation in the north.[5] Digby's motion pursued the same purpose and with the riskiest

[1] J. Rushworth, IV, 464; *C.S.P.D. 1641–43*, 216.

[2] Clarendon, *Rebellion*, IV, 111; *C.S.P.D. 1641–43*, 214–18.

[3] J. Rushworth, IV, 466; cf. the Commons' complaints of attacks by ex-officers of the King's army on the citizens at Whitehall, *L.J.*, IV, 496.

[4] *L.J.*, IV, 493, 494, 496; *C.J.*, II, 358–9; Coates, *D'Ewes*, 356.

[5] 'Whether any laws, divine or human, allow subjects to keep an army of Strangers to master their King? Whether statutes enforced upon the King with the awe of an army will be of any force hereafter?', *C.S.P.D. 1641–43*, 113, misdated August. On 18 November the Commons appointed a committee to investigate the origin of this pamphlet, Coates, *D'Ewes*, 165.

implications. If parliament were unfree in December, as he contended, then it had been equally unfree in May when mob intimidation forced the Lords and King to agree to Strafford's attainder and to the act against dissolving parliament without its own consent. The road would be open to infinite questionings and the unsettlement of the very foundations of the constitutional revolution.[1] Although the peers detested the mob, they nevertheless shrank from the vertiginous consequences of Digby's motion, and they resolved by a majority of four 'That this Parliament is at this present a Free Parliament.'[2]

Digby's tactic, however, was immediately renewed by the clerical politician, Archbishop Williams. Formerly bishop of Lincoln, the bustling Williams had returned to public activity in the Long Parliament after many years of royal disfavour and had just been promoted to York. On the 29th he brought the King a protest from twelve bishops declaring that fear of the mob prevented them from attending parliament and pronouncing null all 'Laws, Orders, Votes, Resolutions, and Determinations' passed during their 'forced and violent Absence. . . .' Williams begged the King to send the protest to the upper House, and Charles did so the next morning.[3]

The peers' response, contrary to Charles's expectation, was one of anger and alarm. Placed between the King and the Commons, most wished to support the King, yet condemned this new attempt to invalidate parliament's authority. They promptly transmitted the bishops' statement to the Commons as a matter of 'high and dangerous Consequence . . . entrenching upon the fundamental Privileges and Being of Parliament. . . .' That afternoon the lower House impeached all twelve episcopal signatories for high treason and the Lords ordered them jailed. But at the same time, to express their continued care for the crown's rights, the noblemen denied a further request from the Commons that both Houses petition the King for a guard under the earl of Essex.[4]

As December came to a close, a showdown clearly impended. Fear was general and most of the city's shops were shut. '. . . it is a wonder there is no more blood yet spilt,' a news letter said on the 30th, 'seeing how earnest both sides are. There is no doubt but if the King do not comply with the Commons in all things they desire, a sudden

---

[1] Cf. the observations of a news writer that Digby's motion was a plot 'to make this Parliament no Parliament, and so to overthrow all Acts passed and to cause a dissolution of it for the present. . . .', *C.S.P.D. 1641–43*, 216–17.

[2] *L.J.*, IV, 494, 495; S. R. Gardiner, *History*, X, 120n. The vote was 29–25.

[3] Clarendon, *Rebellion*, IV, 130, 139; *L.J.*, IV, 496–7. The bishop of Peterborough's name is omitted from the list of signers.

[4] *Ibid.*, IV, 497, 498–9; *C.J.*, II, 363–4.

civil war must ensue. . . .'[1] The King felt himself menaced by disorderly mobs whom the Commons encouraged. On their side, the opposition leaders dreaded Charles's intentions. Observing the numbers of demobilized army officers around him at Whitehall, they expected an outbreak of violence at any time.[2] On Friday the 31st, the House of Commons met amidst the keenest apprehensions. The members decided to adjourn until 3 January and meanwhile to sit as a committee of the whole at the London Guildhall, where the strength of the city would surround them. Their last action before adjourning was to send a fresh message to the King reiterating their appeal for a guard under the earl of Essex: 'their [own] Safety,' they declared, 'and the Safety of the whole Kingdom depends upon it, and will not admit of any Delay.'[3]

To this request Charles returned a flat denial, coupled with a solemn assurance that he knew of no violent design against the Commons and would be as careful of the members' security as of his own.[4] His asseverations were worthless: for on Monday, 3 January, when the Houses resumed sitting at Westminster after the weekend adjournment, he launched his blow.[5] That afternoon he ordered the Attorney General, Sir Edward Herbert, to impeach the opposition leaders of high treason and Herbert laid the accusation before the House of Lords. It charged Pym, Hampden, Holles, Strode, Haselrig, and Viscount Mandeville[6] with a formidable list of crimes: they had endeavoured to subvert the fundamental laws and government of the kingdom and to deprive the King of his regal power; they had foully

[1] *C.S.P.D. 1641–43*, 218.

[2] Cf. Pym's statement to the House on 30 December, Coates, *D'Ewes*, 366, and the comments of the Venetian envoy on the situation, *C.S.P.V. 1640–42*, 271.

[3] *C.J.*, II, 365–6; Coates, *D'Ewes*, 373.

[4] J. Rushworth, IV, 471–2. The King's reply was sent to the committee of the whole at the Guildhall on Monday, the 3rd, and was reported to the House in the afternoon when it returned to Westminster, *C.J.*, II, 366; Coates, *D'Ewes*, 375.

[5] Gardiner thought Charles was led to act on hearing that the committee at the Guildhall had resolved to impeach the Queen. The main evidence for this is the story in the Venetian ambassador's despatch of 7 January (S. R. Gardiner, *History*, X, 128; *C.S.P.V. 1640–42*, 275–6). D'Ewes, however, mentions no such plan of the opposition leaders. It is true that he did not attend the committee at the Guildhall; but if the Queen's impeachment had been proposed, he would surely have known of it and referred to it subsequently in connection with the accusation of treason against Pym's group. The story of the proposed attack on the Queen may have been put about by the King's supporters as an excuse after the failure of his *coup*. On 14 January D'Ewes and Sir Hugh Cholmley spoke in the House of false rumours and fears instilled in the King that parliament meant to impeach the Queen, D'Ewes, Journal, B.M. Harl. 162, ff. 325b, 326b.

[6] Referred to in the impeachment by his title of Lord Kimbolton.

aspersed the King in order to alienate his subjects' affections; they had incited the royal army to disobedience and invited a foreign power—the Scots were meant—to invade England; they had attempted to subvert the rights and being of parliament and had raised tumults to force its compliance with their traitorous aims; finally, they had actually levied war against the King.[1]

At last the confrontation between the King and his opponents was at hand! But Charles had seriously miscalculated the effect of his accusation. Beneath the show of constitutional form, the House of Lords, largely Royalist though it now was, smelled something unwholesome and menacing to parliament's life. Hence, instead of commanding the members' arrest, the peers voted to consider whether the charge accorded with law.[2] The Commons in its turn received the news of the impeachment with indignation as a high breach of privilege. Late in the day Charles sent the Sergeant-at-Arms with an order to the Speaker demanding the accused men. The House refused to give them up. The matter, it told the King, required further deliberation as affecting the privilege of parliament and all the commons of England; in the meantime, the five M.P.s would attend daily in readiness to answer a legal charge.[3]

With each passing hour the impeached members remained at liberty the King's *coup* lost some of its impact. Delay was fatal to his enterprise. He therefore decided to go to parliament in person to seize the traitors. The next afternoon, 4 January, Pym and the others were in their places when news came that the King with several hundred armed men was on his way from Whitehall. They were immediately permitted to depart. Leaving the chamber just in time, they were joined by Mandeville and the six fled into the precincts of the city for safety.[4]

A few minutes later Charles arrived at the Commons. Commanding his followers to remain outside, he walked through the standing and uncovered House to the Speaker's chair and there called for the accused men. When it became evident they were gone, he addressed the House in a self-justifying speech. No one, he said, cared more for parliament's privileges than himself. He was determined, however, to have the members, who stood charged with crimes in which a plea of privilege was inadmissible. But he never intended force, and promised 'on the word of a King' to proceed only in a 'legal and fair way.' Having concluded these remarks, he left the chamber amidst cries of 'Privilege, Privilege,' from his auditors. Shortly afterward, too shaken

[1] *L.J.*, IV, 501.
[2] *Ibid.*
[3] Coates, *D'Ewes*, 377; *C.J.*, II, 366–7.
[4] Coates, *D'Ewes*, 381; *Verney notes*, 138.

for further business and feeling that it had missed calamity by a hair, the House adjourned for the day.[1]

This was failure. Charles had lost his quarry, while the armed presence accompanying him belied all his professions of legality. There was no question in anyone's mind that he would have taken the members by force had the House refused to give them up.[2] The next day deepened his reversal. Going into the city in the hope of seizing the accused, he had to pass large crowds which stood by shouting, 'Privilege.' A speech in defence of his proceedings which he delivered to the aldermen and common council was received with strong hostility.[3] On 8 January he issued a proclamation for the apprehension of the accused members. It was to no effect, since no one would execute his order.[4]

Meanwhile, the House of Commons was busy passing judgment on his conduct. Albeit a few voices sought to excuse it, the prevailing sense was one of unqualified condemnation.[5] On the 4th, the House voted the King's warlike coming the day before to be a 'High Breach of the Rights and Privilege of Parliament, and inconsistent with the Liberties and Freedom thereof. . . .' Declaring that it could not remain safely at Westminster, it adjourned until 11 January. In the interval it ordered that a committee of the whole should meet in the city. The Lords followed suit by also adjourning to the same day.[6]

The Commons' committee began sitting at the Guildhall on the 6th.[7] Its main business, naturally, was the legality of the King's proceedings. The impeachment and the order for the members' arrest without the House's consent it pronounced unlawful and a breach of privilege on grounds cogently formulated by D'Ewes. In a charge of treason, he said,

the howse must bee first satisfied with the matter of fact before they part with their members for else all priviledge of Parliament must of necessitie bee destroied for by the same reason that they accuse one of the said members they may accuse 40 or 50 upon imaginarie and false Treasons and soe committ them to custodie. . . .[8]

---

[1] J. Rushworth, IV, 477–8; Coates, *D'Ewes*, 381–4; *Verney notes*, 138–9.
[2] Cf. D'Ewes's comments, Coates, *D'Ewes*, 382–3.
[3] *Ibid.*, 387; J. Rushworth, IV, 479–80; *C.S.P.D. 1641–43*, 242–3.
[4] R. Steele, *op. cit.*, I, 1919. Oddly, the proclamation named only the Commons' members and omitted Mandeville.
[5] Coates, *D'Ewes*, 386.
[6] *C.J.*, II, 368–9; *L.J.*, IV, 504.
[7] The next day the committee sat at the hall of the Grocers Company, where it remained until the House returned to Westminster on the 11th, Coates, *D'Ewes*, 389, 392.
[8] Coates, *D'Ewes*, 389, 391.

The committee then turned to the King's descent upon the Commons. On the 7th it resolved that his coming with soldiers was 'a traiterous designe against the King and Parliament.'[1] The distinction entailed in this resolution between Charles's personal and regal capacity was noteworthy. It meant that he separated himself from his office in acting illegally. As an implied corollary, resistance to him in such a case would be resistance to Charles Stuart, not the King. With this comforting doctrine the men moving down the road to civil war could at necessity resort to arms in good conscience. No rebels, they could proclaim that they defended the King and parliament even as they fired their cannons against Charles's forces.

These votes by the committee amounted to a vindication of the impeached members, who were thereupon invited to return to their parliamentary duties, 'notwithstanding any warrant ... or other matter or accusation against them.'[2] The committee's last important action was to settle the disputed point of a guard for parliament. In the wake of the terror engendered by the King's attempt, it ordered the sheriffs of London to raise a force in the city for parliament's defence. This plain usurpation on the crown's military prerogative was justified by a plea of necessity and was endorsed by both Houses as soon as they reconvened after the adjournment.[3]

The collapse of his scheme to remove the opposition leaders left the King in a situation of humiliating weakness. However he pleaded his good faith, few believed him. His partisans would doubtless have justified the *coup*, had it succeeded; in failure, he incurred only opprobrium. Those moderates who had broken away from the Country in the fall stood momentarily perplexed and vacillating. Now the King, rather than his parliamentary opponents, appeared the aggressor. The House of Lords, too, had been subjected to great provocation by his attempt and accordingly inclined to be somewhat more compliant with the Commons than in recent months.

On 10 January, Pym, Hampden, Holles, Haselrig, and Strode emerged from hiding to attend the committee in the city.[4] Next day, when the Houses met again at Westminster, they returned to parliament in triumph. Huge crowds applauded them on the way, and on the river the mariners and vessels shot salvoes in their honour. The citizen guard raised by the civic authorities was already disposed about the streets and parliament buildings. 'And I saw,' wrote D'Ewes,

upon the topp of the pikes of divers of the Londoners the Protestation[5]

---

[1] Coates, *D'Ewes*, 394. [2] *Verney notes*, 140.
[3] *C.S.P.D. 1641–43*, 247–8; *C.J.*, II, 370; *L.J.*, IV, 504.
[4] Coates, *D'Ewes*, 399.
[5] The pledge to preserve religion, liberty, the rights of parliament and the

*formerlie framed and taken by members of the howse . . . and afterwards
by most of the citizens, hanging like a little square banner. Some had
them also affixed . . . to ther muskets, one had it fastened upon his
breast. . . .*[1]

To be the witness of his own abasement was more than the King
could stomach. He did not wish to remain in London amidst the
immense demonstration for the oppositionist members which, commented the Venetian ambassador, 'strikes to the quick the dignity of
his name and the greatness of his royal fortunes.'[2] Taking a sudden
resolution, he left Whitehall for Hampton Court on 10 January
accompanied by the Queen and royal children.[3] It was the first stage
of a journey that would not see his return to his capital until he came
to face trial and execution there seven years later. He felt no doubt
that the kingdom was on the threshold of rebellion: the defiance of
his treason accusation and the affronts to his authority meant nothing else.[4] Thus it was with the idea of meeting a rebellion that he now
set out to secure a military base and means of war.

3

To London—'The proud, unthankefull, Schismaticall, Rebellious . . .
City of London'[5]—the parliamentary managers owed the defeat of
the King's *coup*. But the intervention that preserved the revolution
was the work of the politically conscious populace, not of the civic
government. Not only did the latter give no sign; it was, in fact,
more decidedly partial to the King in the fall of 1641 than it had
been a year earlier.

A divergence of political sentiment between the magistrates and the
citizenry had existed from the time parliament began. Individually, a
handful of aldermen supported the Country, and had they controlled
the civic corporation they would doubtless have secured its endorsement of Pym's programme. But they did not speak for the court of

[1] J. Rushworth, IV, 484; *C.S.P.V. 1640–42*, 281; *C.S.P.D. 1641–43*, 252;
D'Ewes, Journal, B.M. Harl. 162, f. 318a.
[2] *C.S.P.V. 1640–42*, 281.
[3] *C.S.P.D. 1641–43*, 252.
[4] The Queen told Heenvliet, the agent of the Prince of Orange, on 11
January that 'tout se préparoit à une rebellion,' and that neither she nor the
King 'ne poulvoyent plus endurer ces grandes affrontes . . .'; *Archives . . . de
la maison d'Orange-Nassau*, ed. G. Groen van Prinsterer, 2nd ser., 5v.,
Utrecht, 1858–62, III, 501.
[5] *A letter from Mercurius Civicus to Mercurius Rusticus*, 32.

subject, which the House of Commons adopted in the crisis of Strafford's
attainder; cf. *supra*, 223.

aldermen.[1] As a body, the mayor and his brethren, including most of those senior in service and prestige, were unwilling to associate the official municipality with any action hostile to the crown. Their refusal sprang from a rooted disposition in favour of everything established that was entirely intelligible in such men as these. Belonging to the select stratum of wealthy traders which had provided the city's ruling group for generations, they observed with intense dislike the insubordinate temper rampant among the citizenry. The notion of a tranquillity based on unconditional submission to the authority of the magistrates was all but axiomatic in their mentality; and with them it was not outweighed, as it was with other men of substance in the city, by zeal for religious or political reform. Hence, when the Londoners petitioned against the bishops by the thousands, or when they mobbed the streets in a riotous outcry for Strafford's death and Lunsford's removal from the Tower, they did not receive the slightest sanction from the civic government. Faithful to its tradition of dependence on the crown, the official municipality refrained from all support of the King's opponents in the public controversies of 1641.

Because of this, the main channel of communication between the parliamentary managers and their citizen supporters was London's M.P.s. All four chosen in October 1640 favoured the Country.[2] This outcome was not surprising, since common hall, the electing body, was the most popularly constituted assembly in the municipal government and thus likeliest to reflect general opinion. In May 1641, on the death of Mathew Cradock, John Venn succeeded him as member. The speed of Venn's return—he took his seat in the House of Commons within eight days of Cradock's decease—suggests that the oppositionists desired his presence and perhaps even planned his election.[3] A well-to-do cloth merchant and Puritan, he was to take a considerable part in organizing the citizens' demonstrations and the subsequent revolution against the mayor's authority.

An intimation of that revolution occurred soon after Venn's election in a quarrel between the mayor and commonalty over the choice of the city's sheriffs. The latter together with certain other officials were appointed annually at a common hall in June, and on the usual day, the liverymen, who formed the commonalty under the municipal constitution, assembled for this purpose. According to custom, the mayor was to name one sheriff and common hall the

[1] Cf. the survey of the political outlook of the aldermanic bench in 1640–1 in V. Pearl, *op. cit.*, 113–14.

[2] Cf. *supra*, 146.

[3] Cradock died on 27 May, and the first appearance of Venn's name in the *Journal* was 4 June, M. Keeler, *op. cit.*, 144; *C.J.*, II, 168. I have found no order of the House authorizing an election in London for Cradock's successor.

other. Nevertheless, when Sir Edmund Wright attempted to exercise his prerogative of office, common hall refused to allow it and demanded the power to choose both sheriffs itself. No election could be held. Wright and his aldermanic colleagues then appealed to the King to uphold the mayor's privilege. Charles, perhaps from reluctance to antagonize either side, referred the dispute to the mediation of the House of Lords. The House first commanded the parties to try to settle their difference peaceably amongst themselves. When they proved unable to do so, it decreed that for the coming year the commonalty should choose both sheriffs. It added the hope that one of the two so designated would be the mayor's nominee.[1] Notwithstanding this suggestion, which common hall adopted,[2] the mayor and aldermen protested vehemently against the upper House's judgment. Expressing the fear that the commons of London would throw off the municipal government, they threatened to resign if their authority were not sustained. The peers, however, adhered to their award as best conducive to the city's peace.[3] Their order was entered in the Journal of the common council;[4] furthermore, at the shrievalty election of 1642, the mayor conceded to common hall the appointment of both sheriffs, though with a saving of his prerogative.[5]

Encouraged no doubt by this success, London oppositionists prepared for a fresh contest when common hall met in September 1641 for the annual election of the lord mayor. As in the year before, so again they tried to elect Alderman Soame, one of the city M.P.s. Established usage, however, required that the mayoralty should go to the nominee who was senior alderman. The latter in 1641 was Richard Gurney, a merchant 'well affected & stout' for the King.[6] The defenders of the constitutional *status quo* took care to see that Gurney as legitimate candidate should be victorious. As soon as his name was proposed, the mayor and aldermen pronounced him elected. The presiding sheriff, Clark, the mayor's nominee of the previous summer, then dissolved the meeting, despite indignant calls of 'no election' from Soame's supporters. So to the jubilation of the King's friends, a royal partisan succeeded as mayor, and Nicholas was able to inform Charles of the defeat of the 'Schismaticks' and 'factious party' in the city.[7]

---

[1] *L.J.*, IV, 292, 293, 373.

[2] The two sheriffs appointed were George Garret and George Clark, the latter the mayor's nominee.

[3] *L.J.*, IV, 376–7; *H.M.C. Fourth report*, pt. 1, 99.

[4] 29 September 1641, Journal, 39, f. 230b. A note on the same page states, 'no other officers elected now because of ye difference.'

[5] *Ibid.*, 39, f. 328b.   [6] Nicholas to the King, J. Evelyn, *op. cit.*, IV, 82.

[7] *C.S.P.D. 1641–43* 132: J. Evelyn, *op. cit.*, IV, 82.

The End of the Country

That fall, with political differences more inflamed than ever, the restlessness of London caused the new mayor and his colleagues much anxiety. Disaffection spread abroad against the King undermined their own authority as well. Early in November they complained pointedly to parliament about the condition of the city. Their warrants, they said, were not obeyed, and their government so slighted 'that there is an Equality between the Mayor and the Commons, the Power of the Mayor no more than that of the Commoners of the City.'[1]

Small wonder, then, that when the King returned from Scotland the civic government decided to make the occasion into a resounding manifestation of support. '. . . yor Matie,' Nicholas wrote him, 'was never more welcome to ye better sorte of Londoners than you will now be. . . .'[2] Re-entering the capital on 25 November, Charles received a sumptuous reception.[3] The display of loyalty, however, was more expressive of the official attitude than of the feeling prevalent in the citizen populace. Charles and the magistrates had every reason to turn towards each other at such a time. Addressing the monarch, the recorder begged him

to uphold and countenance that ancient form and frame of Government which hath been long established in the City; that Power and Authority of yours, which you have committed to your Lord Mayor, your true and faithful Subject and Servant, and the fit Reverence and Respect due to the Aldermen his brethren. . . . we shall be thereby the better enabled to serve your Majesty, and constantly to render to you the Fruits of a true Obedience. . . .[4]

Charles on his part took the city's demonstration as strengthening his hand for his approaching dénouement with Pym's group. '. . . now I see,' he said in reply,

that all . . . tumults and disorders have only risen from the meaner sort of people, and that the Affections of the better, and main part of the City, have ever been Loyal to my Person and Government.

He promised to do all in his power to promote London's prosperity and to grant its reasonable demands. As a sign of grace, he knighted the lord mayor and recorder and conferred the same honour a week later on the sheriffs and five aldermen as well.[5]

---

[1] *C.J.*, II, 304; *L.J.*, IV, 420.
[2] J. Evelyn, *op. cit.*, IV, 115.
[3] Cf. the description in *Ovatio Carolina*, 1641.
[4] J. Rushworth, IV, 429–30.   [5] *Ibid.*, IV, 430–1, 434.

To counteract the effect of the King's reception, the city oppositionists got up a petition attesting London's attachment to the House
of Commons. It was delivered to the House on 11 December, a paper
twenty-four yards long containing fifteen thousand names, including
those of several aldermen and of some of the members of the common
council.[1] The petitioners condemned malicious attempts 'to mis-
construe the citizens' loyal entertainment of his Majesty' as 'a
deserting of this honourable assembly. ...' They acknowledged
thankfully the benefits the Commons had done the church and
kingdom, endorsed the bill for the bishops' expulsion from parliament, and asked the House also to take into consideration 'the
abuses that are crept into the ancient government of the City. ...'
They were ready, they said, to hazard their lives against 'all wicked
counsellors and malignant opposers' who try to divide the King from
parliament.[2]

The manner of promoting this petition, which the mayor did his
best to discourage,[3] points to a considerable background of organization. There must have been a network of sympathizers across the
metropolis, since four men from each of London's twenty-six wards
accompanied the petition to the House of Commons.[4] A sight of the
apparatus the city oppositionists built was given by a pamphleteer
who said that they had

*Taverne clubs in each Ward, communicating intelligence to, and from
their table Juncto's, or Sub-Committees sitting in divers private
houses . . . [as] Brownes house a Grocer neare Cheap-side crosse; also a
Drapers house in Watling street[5] . . . to prepare results of each dayes
passages in the City to report to Mr. Pym. . . .[6]*

One of the places where the petition was exhibited for signatures was
the White Lion tavern in Canning Street. In several wards its
sponsors summoned most of the residents of the parish to their
house and exhorted them as Christians and patriots to sign.[7]

The same machinery was set going to call out the London crowds.

[1] Coates, *D'Ewes*, 271.
[2] Text in *C.S.P.D. 1641–43*, 195–6.
[3] Coates, *D'Ewes*, 319–20; *C.J.*, II, 350.
[4] Coates, *D'Ewes*, 271.
[5] This draper was probably Francis Peck, a common council member; cf.
V. Pearl, *op. cit.*, 323, for an account of him.
[6] *Persecutio undecima*, 60. Internal evidence suggests (cf. 4, 34) that the
author of this pamphlet was the Rev. Robert Chestlin, rector of St. Matthew
Friday Street in London, a great hater of the Puritans whose tactics he had
seen at first hand.
[7] *C.S.P.D. 1641–43*, 193, 197.

The End of the Country

Venn, with his connections in the city, was probably the key figure in this. When he passed the word, Pym's supporters flocked in multitudes to Westminster. According to one account, he and the Rev. Cornelius Burges, a great man in the Puritan ministry, 'sent tickets by Porters and Emissaries' to mobilize their 'Mermidons.'[1] On a night at the end of November, Venn was able at short notice to bring down more than a thousand armed citizens to the House of Commons. Mrs. Venn also helped, 'and with great industry solicited many people to go down with their arms. . . .' Following this occurrence, Sir John Strangeways and Edward Kirton accused Venn publicly in the Commons of inciting the crowds to intimidate members, an offence, they said, little less than treason. The House, however, with its majority favourable to Pym, treated the charge as unproved.[2]

Revolution is a stern test not only of political will and strategy, but also of organizational resource. The party that knows how to coordinate its forces, to exploit its followers' zeal to most effect, to harness popular passion to its programme, will always be stronger than an opponent less efficient in these arts. As regards the latter, the London oppositionists were incontestably superior to the King's sympathizers. But between them and the subjection of the capital to their political purpose stood Gurney, the mayor, and his brother aldermen. If the official municipality were to take a different political direction, the authority of its governors, to whom the King looked for aid, had first to be overthrown. In that tense December, amidst increasing disorder and expectation of an approaching dénouement, Pym's citizen allies girded themselves for an attempt to capture the civic government.

The preparations they made are hidden in darkness. Two years later, however, an anonymous tract, *A letter from Mercurius Civicus to Mercurius Rusticus* (1643),[3] gave a circumstantial account of the whole affair which described the oppositionists' tactics:

But because it was impossible to disarme the King, as long as the Lord Major stood firme in his Loyalty, and invested in his power; their maine worke therefore was, first, to pack a Common-Councell of men of their own Faction, and then by advancing the power of their Common-Councell (by the assistance of the House of Commons) above the Lord Majors, to draw the voting of all Queryes, and the Resolution of all

[1] *Persecutio undecima*, 64.
[2] Coates, *D'Ewes*, 214–16; Clarendon, *Rebellion*, IV, 120.
[3] The tract is dated at the end 5 August 1643. It is reprinted in *Somers tracts*, 2nd ed., ed. W. Scott, 13v., L., 1810, IV, 580–98. Its authorship has occasionally been ascribed to the satirist, Samuel Butler, but there is no evidence for this.

*Doubts, or matters under debate, unto the decision of a Major part; and
if any Obstacle lay in their way to these ends, which was not in their
power to remove, presently at a dead lift, Penington or Ven or Vassels
bring an order from the House of Commons, which never failed to
determine all things, for their own Creatures.*[1]

Mercurius Civicus stated nothing more than the truth. The city
oppositionists set out to deprive the mayor of power and win control
of the official municipality; and as the sequel showed, by skilful
organization and adroit manoeuvre, they succeeded.

The revolution in London's government occurred in several stages.
It began on 21 December with the annual election by the wards of
their representatives to the common council. On this occasion the
opposition party made a strenuous effort to secure the return of its
own activists and the defeat of men of adverse view. Evidently some
hard electioneering went on: in Langborne Ward, for instance, the
Puritans were pictured as '. . . infinitely busie at an election of a
Common-Councell man . . . (and from such meetings none of the
Faction would be absent). . . .'[2] Common council members favourable to the King were attacked as corrupt and accused of levying
unequal parish rates which discriminated against the poorer inhabitants.[3] Undoubtedly, the atmosphere in the capital affected the
election. Fear of violence, the Irish scare, alarms from the House of
Commons, had jolted the Londoners out of their workaday routine
and roused them to intense excitement. With a partisanship rare in
municipal politics, it was not difficult, said Mercurius Civicus, for the
'active faction, to instill into their fellow Citizens how much it
Concerned them to make choyce of Godly men (so they miscall
themselves). . . .'[4]

The election resulted in an emphatic reversal for the royal supporters in the city government. Mercurius Civicus declared that 'in most
Wards, the old Common-Councell men were turned out, and new
chosen in, wholy devoted to the Puritan faction. . . .'[5] This was an
exaggeration, but the vote unquestionably made a noticeable alteration in the common council's composition. Out of a total body of
approximately two hundred and fifty, there is evidence for fifty-
seven returns, of which twenty-five were new members.[6] Thus, the

[1] *A letter from Mercurius Civicus*, 14.
[2] *Persecutio undecima*, 59. The author adds that in Langborne Ward with its
three hundred householders, the Puritans could not muster sixty.
[3] Cf. John Bond, *The downfal of old common-counsel-men*, 1641.
[4] *A letter from Mercurius Civicus*, 15.   [5] *Ibid.*, 15.
[6] Cf. the discussion of the election in M. Wren, 'The disputed elections in
London in 1641,' *E.H.R.*, LXIV, 250 (1949) and, more precisely, with a
correction of several of the former's conclusions, in V. Pearl, *op. cit.*, 132–9.

turnover of membership in the common council amounted to at least ten per cent, probably an unprecedented figure for a single election. Amongst the men elected were Owen Rowe, Nathaniel Wright, and William Perkins, militants connected of old with the opposition movement through their membership in the Massachusetts Bay Company. These new councilmen were merchants and tradesmen, masters of shops, great enemies of the bishops, ready to assist the parliamentary leaders by every means. Some occupied a very middling status in the city, as Mercurius Civicus contemptuously recorded: 'Perkins the Taylor, Norminton the Cutler, young beardlesse Coulson the Dyer, Gill the Wine-Cooper, and Jupe the Laten-man in Crooked-Lane. . . .' The richest and most prominent was John Fowke— 'Fowke the Traytor'—a successful merchant whose resistance to Charles I's government had begun in 1627 and continued ever since.[1]

The oppositionists in the common council showed their militancy at once. It was due to them that a petition protesting the King's appointment of Lunsford as Lieutenant of the Tower was submitted on 23 December to the House of Commons in the name of 'divers Common-Council men, and others, of the City of London.'[2] According-ing to custom, however, the new members ought not to have assumed their seats until the Monday after Twelfth Day, 10 January 1642. Nevertheless, they took advantage of the prevailing disorder to attend the common council before time, even those of them whose election was in dispute. The complaints voiced against their intrusion by the defenders of 'the ancient order . . . of the city' were overborne.[3] Thus installed in strength, the oppositionist faction was in a position to affect the official municipality's conduct at the moment of deepest crisis when the King impeached the parliamentary managers.

The next and decisive step in the revolution of the city government occurred on 4 January, the day after the impeachment, and directly in consequence of the King's preparations to seize the accused members at Westminster by force. That morning at the instance of Pym himself, the House of Commons sent three of London's M.P.s with an urgent message to the mayor and common council warning that parliament and the city were in danger.[4] The sequel is revealed in the municipal records. On receipt of the House's message, the common council proceeded to establish a committee of safety to institute measures for the city's defence and security 'in these tymes of feares and daungers. . . .'[5] Six aldermen and twelve councilmen

---

[1] *A letter from Mercurius Civicus*, 15; for an account of Fowke and some of the new oppositionist councilmen, cf. V. Pearl, *op. cit.*, App. II.
[2] C.J., II, 354; J. Rushworth, IV, 459; for this petition, cf. *supra*, 275.
[3] *A letter from Mercurius Civicus*, 16.
[4] C.J., II, 367–8; Coates, *D'Ewes*, 379.   [5] Journal, 40, f. 11.

were appointed to it:[1] three of the former and all of the latter belonged to the opposition faction; the contingent of councilmen, in particular, contained some of the keenest activists in London.[2]

Was the committee of safety a stratagem conceived and prepared for in advance? There is no way of knowing. Real as was the emergency that led to its creation, such a body, standing completely outside the regular machinery of administration, had no precedent in the city. In any case, whether it was an invention of the moment or the product of a well-laid plan, the committee became the instrument by which, with the help of the House of Commons, the London oppositionists made themselves the masters of the municipal government.

The encroachments by the committee of safety started at once. Immediately on its establishment a precept from the lord mayor concerning the security of the wards came forth 'By advise of the Committee assigned by Common Councell assembled this day at the Guildhall.' Other precepts issued subsequently bore such formulae as 'Accordinge to direction of the Committee of late appointed by Act of Common Councell.'[3] The ensuing day, 5 January, was the one on which the King, coming into the city, addressed the mayor, aldermen, and common council in defence of his proceedings against the accused members. The antagonism shown him on this occasion was a suitable prelude to what followed. After his withdrawal the committee of safety brought in a petition strongly condemning his actions. This was adopted and submitted to the King in the name of the mayor, aldermen, and common council.[4] It was noteworthy as the first official declaration of the city government which placed it squarely on the side of Charles's opponents. Another petition followed later in the month supporting the bills to exclude the bishops from parliament and to give the Houses control of the kingdom's militia.[5] Since the mayor, Sir Richard Gurney, and his fellow aldermen could hardly have endorsed these statements, their right to veto the common council's proceedings and to serve as sole spokesmen of the municipality was evidently no longer operative.

From this moment on, the oppositionists steadily expanded their grip. It was by agreement with the committee of safety that on 8 January the Commons' committee sitting in the city directed Lon-

---

[1] *Ibid.* The aldermen: Rainton, Gayer, Garrard, Atkin, Wollaston, Towse. The councilmen: Manwaring, Gibbs, Fowke, Bunce, Peck, S. Warner, Russell, N. Wright, Barkley, Normington, Estwick, Rowe.

[2] The opposition aldermen were Atkins, Wollaston, and Towse; perhaps Gayer should be added. There are biographical sketches of the members of the committee of safety in V. Pearl, *op. cit.*, App. I & II.

[3] Journal, 39, ff. 264, 279b.

[4] Journal, 40, f. 12; cf. the text in J. Rushworth, IV, 480–1.

[5] Journal, 40, f. 18; *L.J.*, IV, 534–5.

don's sheriffs to raise a guard for parliament's defence.[1] The common council did not permit the guard to come under the mayor's authority, but entrusted its command to Philip Skippon, an officer of the Artillery Company who was 'a confiding brother to the Cause.'[2] Two weeks later, pursuant to an order brought down by Venn from the House of Commons, the common council gave its committee of safety full supervision of the London militia.[3] This action delivered up the military resources of the city to Pym's party. A blatant violation of the mayor's prerogative, it exactly paralleled the effort the parliamentary leaders were then making, in fear of a civil war, to strip the King of his authority over the kingdom's armed forces.[4]

Charles's citizen supporters did not let the committee of safety's usurpation of the militia pass without a fight. First, the mayor and aldermen petitioned the House of Lords on 16 February for the restoration of their military jurisdiction which had belonged to them, they said, 'time out of mind. . . .'[5] The House, in which the Royalist peers were by now the weaker party,[6] rejected the petition. Sir Richard Gurney's loyalty, commented Mercurius Civicus, 'was too well knowne, to be admitted, to have any share in that power which was intended to be imployed against the King.'[7]

At the same time, some citizens headed by Sir George Benyon, a rich silk merchant and royal financial official, were busy circulating another petition in favour of the mayor's right over the city militia. Benyon disliked the opposition faction with good reason, as he was one of the 'grave, discreet' councilmen defeated at the recent election.[8] He had said of the House of Commons that its members 'much complained of the King's arbitrary Power; and yet . . . go about an arbitrary Government themselves, which, being Four Hundred, will be more grievous than the other.'[9] On 17 February its sponsors brought the petition to the common council. There it was denied a reading by a vote of ninety to sixty-nine. Although the mayor and most of the aldermen favoured it, their votes were included with the whole instead of counted separately.[10] Mercurius Civicus noted the meaning of this development with indignation:

---

[1] Journal, 40, f. 14.   [2] *Ibid.*, 40, f. 15; *Persecutio undecima*, 56.
[3] Journal, 40, f. 17b.   [4] Cf. *infra*, ch. IX.
[5] *H.M.C. Fifth report*, pt. 1, 8; *L.J.*, IV, 590.
[6] Cf. *infra*, 299.   [7] *A letter from Mercurius Civicus*, 24.
[8] *L.J.*, IV, 683; *A letter from Mercurius Civicus*, 15. In 1631, Benyon became receiver general for Rutland and Northants, *H.M.C. Fourth report*, pt. 1, 97.
[9] *L.J.*, IV, 684.
[10] Journal, 40, ff. 20b–21. The mayor and seven aldermen voted to read the petition, five aldermen voted against. In 1645 John Bellamie cited this vote to support his contention that the aldermanic veto, while never formally abolished, had ceased to hold, *A plea for the commonalty of London*, 11–12.

. . . whereas the Lord Mayor and Aldermen sit apart, from the Commons, and are Covered, when the others are bareheaded, and have a Negative Voice . . . the faction here . . . have cast all into a common huddle, blending the Court of Aldermen with the Commons. And though in outward appearance, they remain two distinct Members of one body, yet, in power, they have made both Levell, Involving the Votes of the Mayor and Aldermen in the major part of the Commons.[1]

Rebuffed by the common council, Benyon and his friends nevertheless persisted with their petition. After soliciting further signatures in shops and at the London Exchange, they presented it to parliament on 24 February. It bore the names of more than two hundred citizens, 'divers of them verie wealthie men,' the House of Commons was told. The petitioners declared that the ordering of the London militia belonged by ancient charter to the mayor and that it was against the freedom of the city to put this power into any other hands.[2]

For Benyon the consequences of his political resistance were ruinous. The Houses, then preparing for possible civil war, considered his conduct far too dangerous to go unpunished and decided to make an example of him. Accordingly, in March the Commons impeached him for his 'false and seditious' petition, as well as for other acts of disaffection against parliament. The Lords, adjudging him guilty, then sentenced him to disenfranchisement, £3,000 fine, and two years' imprisonment.[3] The civic government had already disavowed Benyon's petition with one of its own which, through the victory of the majority principle, was presented—supreme irony—in the name of the mayor, aldermen, and common council.[4] Thus, the oppositionist faction quashed the defiance of the royalist citizens, and Pym could feel sure that London's government was in safe hands if civil war proved unavoidable.

While the conquest of the militia was perhaps the main achievement of the London oppositionists, they annexed the prerogatives of the mayor and aldermen in other regions as well. Constitutionally, the right of summoning a common council pertained to the mayor alone: but on 13 January, an order of the Houses originating with the city's M.P., Alderman Penington, commanded the mayor to convene a common council whenever the committee of safety desired.[5] The

[1] *A letter from Mercurius Civicus*, 21.
[2] *C.J.*, II, 451–2; *L.J.*, IV, 609, 684, 701–2; D'Ewes, Journal, B.M. Harl. 162, f. 402b.
[3] *L.J.*, IV, 683–4. 705.
[4] Cf. the city's petition presented to the Houses on 18 March, *C.J.*, II, 485; *L.J.*, IV, 651.
[5] *C.J.*, II, 376; *L.J.*, IV, 508; D'Ewes, Journal, B.M. Harl. 162, f. 321a.

latter used this usurped power so insolently, declared Mercurius Civicus,

that when they have required Sir Richard Gurney to call a Common-councell, and he hath demanded a reason, they have vouchsafed him no other answer, then this saucy one, that when he came thither he should know.[1]

The common council also charged its committee of safety to investigate disputed returns of councilmen in the recent election, a function hitherto reserved to the mayor and aldermen.[2] On 2 March the committee of safety made its report, which received the common council's approval. Besides ordering a number of new elections, it condemned the practice in certain wards by which small groups of citizens at precinct meetings presumed to elect the members of the common council themselves against the rights of the generality of freemen. Although the precincts might meet to consider suitable persons, the report stated,

yet their power therein extends onely to present the names of such persons to the Wardmote, And that then the said inhabitants of the Ward may in part or in whole approve or reiect that nomination or name others to put in election with them as they finde cause.[3]

Eventually the city oppositionists succeeded in removing Sir Richard Gurney from office altogether. At the end of June, with civil war beginning, the lord mayor attempted to raise forces for the King in London. For this and other Royalist acts, the House of Commons impeached him. His trial followed, in which the militants on the common council and committee of safety testified abundantly against him. On 10 August the House of Lords pronounced him guilty. The unfortunate Gurney was expelled from his mayoralty, pronounced incapable of any future honour, and committed to the Tower.[4] At the peers' order a common hall promptly assembled to name his successor. The choice fell upon Alderman Penington, a man to delight all reformers in church and state.[5] Six weeks later when his interim term expired, Penington was re-elected mayor for the ensuing year.[6]

---

[1] *A letter from Mercurius Civicus*, 21.

[2] Journal, 40, f. 16, order of 19 January 1642.

[3] Journal, 40, f. 21b. The committee of safety's report was published, no doubt, to secure greater publicity; cf. *Articles comprised ... in a report confirmed by Common Councell the second day of March 1641* [1642].

[4] *L.J.*, V, 182, 230–1, 240–1, 246–8, 280.

[5] *Ibid.*, V, 297.

[6] R. Sharpe, *op. cit.*, II, 173.

This signal triumph made the oppositionists' domination of the municipality complete. In seizing power, however, their primary aim was not to liberalize the civic constitution, but to suppress the authority of the Royalist magistrates. If Sir Richard Gurney had shared their political convictions, he would likely have retained his mayoral prerogatives unimpaired. The reforms they introduced, all tending to establish the common council's supremacy, were indeed considerable. Yet they made no attempt to vindicate these innovations by invoking principles of popular government that might have justified their breach of the city's charters and customs. Neither did they try to make their reforms permanent by enacting them into municipal law. The oppositionists' measures all bore an *ad hoc* character; they were the offspring of expediency and emergency and incident to another purpose.

The importance of the revolution in the capital, however, can scarcely be overrated. The oppositionists won power at the moment of showdown between the King and his parliamentary antagonists. Charles counted heavily on the city government's moral and material support for his intended *coup*. He was deprived of both when he needed them most, a loss of incalculable disadvantage. Henceforth, as both sides prepared for the eventuality of war, the official municipality was devoted wholly to Pym's party.

Parliamentarians and Royalists
The Civil War

The King's withdrawal from London on 10 January initiated the final phase of England's ebbing peace. A resort to arms was still avoidable, perhaps, but its dark prospect loomed clearly before every mind. In the House of Commons, D'Ewes reflected the general sense when he spoke of evil auguries and voiced his concern lest the 'misunderstanding betweene us and his Majestie' grow into a flame.[1] Charles's departure was more than a physical remove from the scene of his ignominy and repulse. It signified an act of secession on his part, a bill of divorcement delivered to the Houses and the unfaithful city that had defied and contemned him. He intended not to return until he could do so from a position of strength. Meanwhile, he left his enemies in triumphant occupation at Westminster, loudly acclaimed by the popular voice. From this time he dealt with parliament from afar, their relation increasingly like that of independent states who in a last negotiation stand poised between the alternatives of treaty and the sword.

The situation now, however, did not admit of compromise. Parliament was separated from the King not only by specific differences, but by a mistrust so enveloping that only total acquiescence on his part could dispel it. His attempt against the opposition members was seen as a display of bad faith that justified the exaction of steel-clad guarantees for the sake of future security. His power had to be clipped and contracted to the narrowest limits. Of course, to press him thus meant risking the chance of civil war. Yet Pym and his party felt that their own and the kingdom's safety required nothing less, and very likely calculated that by driving on determinedly they would overbear all opposition as before, and force the King to submit.

Charles, too, suffered from fears. He had heard reports that the Queen would be impeached or separated from him[2]—a story that

---

[1] On 20 January: *Journal*, B.M. Harl. 162, ff. 336a–b.
[2] Cf. the Queen's statement mentioned by the Dutch agent in his despatch of 11 January, *Archives . . . de la maison d'Orange-Nassau*, 2nd ser., III, 502.

perhaps arose amongst his own followers to justify or palliate his attempt against the opposition leaders.[1] Perhaps the account also came to his ears of an intention to depose him in favour of his elder son.[2] On 14 January all these rumours were denounced as false in the Commons, and Pym, as an offer of reassurance, suggested a declaration expressing the House's care for the King's safety and honour.[3] But Charles and Henrietta Maria doubtless put little faith in these professions, since they considered their opponents would stop at nothing to attain their ends.

Charles's immediate thought on quitting London was to get possession of Hull in Yorkshire, where the largest magazine in the kingdom with arms for 16,000 men lay stored. From Hampton Court on 11 January he issued secret orders to the earl of Newcastle, Strafford's former friend, to hasten northward to assume the government of the town.[4] The Houses anticipated the King's purpose, however, and that same day commanded Sir John Hotham, M.P. for Beverly, to secure Hull and not to yield it 'without the King's Authority, signified . . . by the Lords and Commons . . . in Parliament.'[5] The tenor of this instruction indicated plainly that every move towards force on Charles's part was bound to incite the Houses in self-defence to further restrictions on his powers. Several days later they also presumed to direct a general command to the sheriffs and justices of England to suppress assemblies dangerous to the peace.[6] Meanwhile at Hull the position remained undecided, as the mayor would admit neither Newcastle nor Hotham's son, who had come as his father's representative. The Houses dealt with the situation by curtly summoning both the earl and the mayor to explain their conduct.[7] This sufficed to procure obedience, and before the end of January Hotham with three companies of Yorkshire militia was master of the town.[8]

In the face of these resolute measures, Charles made his first conciliatory gesture since the failure of his *coup*. On 20 January he sent the Houses a message lamenting the dangerous state of affairs

---

[1] Cf. *supra*, 278.

[2] Sir John Northcote told the House that this rumour was current, D'Ewes, Journal, B.M. Harl. 162, f. 324b.

[3] *Ibid.*, ff. 325b, 326b.

[4] The order to Newcastle is printed in *L.J.*, IV, 585. The text attests its secrecy as does the King's warrant to Secretary Nicholas not to make a record of it in the Signet Office, *C.S.P.D. 1641–43*, 251.

[5] *L.J.*, IV, 505. Hotham had actually received a patent from the King in 1639 appointing him governor of Hull; cf. *ibid.* and *D.N.B.*, *s.v.*

[6] *L.J.*, IV, 512.

[7] On 20 January: D'Ewes, Journal, B.M. Harl. 162, f. 337b; *L.J.*, IV, 526, 527.

[8] *C.J.*, II, 407; J. Rushworth, IV, 565.

and protesting his desire for an accommodation. Let them submit proposals, he asked, for the maintenance of his regal authority, the establishment of their privileges, the security of true religion, and the settlement of church ceremonies so as to remove all just cause of offence. For his part, he was ready to consider their views and to exceed 'the most indulgent Princes in their Acts of Grace and Favour to their People. . . .'[1]

Although Charles may have been sincere, his mind was not directed entirely towards conciliation. Knowing his weakness while he continued so near London, he sought time to improve his situation, and the Queen informed the Dutch envoy that he would go into Yorkshire to provide himself with means of defence if parliament refused him satisfaction.[2] In any case, however, his offer came too late. The opposition party, convinced that he would try to crush it at the first opportunity, did not look for grace and favour, but for infallible guarantees. The Commons therefore replied to the King's message with a request that he 'raise up . . . a sure Ground of Safety and Confidence' by giving command of the forts and militia to persons recommended by both Houses. The mover of this proposition was Hampden.[3] The peers in their turn refused to adopt it, and the answer accordingly went to the King on 25 January in the name of the Commons alone.[4]

The peers' non-cooperation was merely a further effort on the part of the majority to retain a shred of political independence and to preserve some ground of legality in relation to the King. But to the Commons their actions constituted an intolerable obstruction which must be overcome. Since October the upper House had neglected the bill against the secular employments of the clergy, despite the strong outcry for the bishops' expulsion from parliament;[5] it had obstinately refrained as well from endorsing the demand that the King surrender his authority over the militia. The Commons managers, buoyed up by their recent triumph over Charles, were determined to break the deadlock between the Houses and to force the peers to submit.

In the last week of January the House of Lords was subjected to every form of pressure the oppositionists' supporters could devise. Petitions came in from many counties exhorting the Lords to comply with the Commons lest the kingdom be lost. Petitions to the same effect were submitted by the city governments of Exeter and London. The latter, now fallen under the domination of Pym's allies, declared that the citizens would lend no money for the relief of Ireland till the

---

[1] *L.J.*, IV, 523–4.
[2] *Archives . . . de la maison d'Orange-Nassau*, 2nd ser., IV, 7.
[3] D'Ewes, Journal, B.M. Harl. 162, f. 340b.
[4] *L.J.*, IV, 533; *C.J.*, II, 395–6.   [5] Cf. *supra*, 253.

peers ceased their obstruction; its statement spoke also of the decay of trade and hinted pointedly at an outbreak by the poor if the peers did not promptly pass the bill against the secular employments of the clergy and agree to place the militia in safe hands.[1]

The party leaders shrewdly exploited these importunities to overbear the upper House. At a joint conference on the 25th Pym expressed a note of utmost urgency. In the petitions, he said, 'your Lordships might hear the Voice ... of all England. ... the Agony, Terror, and Perplexity, in which the Kingdom labours, is universal. ...' He intimated plainly that the peers were failing in their duty and appealed for their cooperation lest the Commons 'should be inforced to save the Kingdom alone. ...'[2]

The business slump arising from political unsettlement was used to frighten the Lords with the threat of social insurrection. On 31 January the Commons accepted without a sign of disapproval an inflammatory petition in the name of thousands of London poor warning of the extremities to which want and unemployment might drive them. At the House's bar, the city M.P. Venn introduced the spokesmen for the petitioners. They 'boldlie ... desired to know,' noted D'Ewes, 'who weere the obstructours of our happines.'[3] That evening in a joint conference Holles drove home the point to the Lords. The petition was extraordinary, he acknowledged: 'but now consider the necessity of a multitude, a sleeping lyon, not good to awaken. ...' Rents were unpaid and public distractions had weakened authority. If the worst came, he admonished, the fault would lie with the peers for withholding their cooperation.[4]

Any nobleman who showed his dislike of these pressures exposed himself to risk. The youthful duke of Richmond brought a storm upon himself when he offered a motion that the House of Lords adjourn for six months. His fellow peers compelled him to retract and apologize, but the Commons, thinking the penalty too light, branded Richmond 'one of the malignant Party' and launched an investigation into his use of electoral patronage as Warden of the Cinque Ports.[5] This was as good as to tell the upper House that no defiance of the Commons would be tolerated.

[1] *L.J.*, IV, 534–40, *passim*. Petitions of support also came in to the House of Commons. One from Suffolk on 31 January had over fourteen thousand signatures, D'Ewes, Journal, B.M. Harl. 162, f. 360b.

[2] *L.J.*, IV, 540–3.

[3] D'Ewes, Journal, B.M. Harl. 162, f. 360b; *C.J.*, II, 404. The petition circulated as a printed broadside 'for the use of the Petitioners who are to meet in More Fields and from thence go to the House of Parliament with it in their hands.'; cf. *Catalogue of the Thomason tracts*, I, 67.

[4] *L.J.*, IV, 559; *H.M.C. House of Lords*, n.s., XI, *Addenda, 1514–1714*, 306–7.

[5] *L.J.*, IV, 549–53, 555–6; *C.J.*, II, 400; D'Ewes, Journal, B.M. Harl. 162,

Parliamentarians and Royalists

The House of Lords had no means to counter this campaign. Feeling itself surrounded by hostility and lacking any organized support, it could do nothing but bow to superior strength. On 1 February it accepted the Commons' demand to the King for parliamentary control of the militia; on the 5th it passed the bill expelling the bishops from parliament.[1] The Venetian ambassador ascribed its submission to 'fresh movements among the common people, who openly support the designs of the most seditious. . . .' Another news writer spoke of its 'panic fear of the multitude, who from all the counties come daily in thousands with petitions. . . .'[2]

These votes meant surrender all along the line. They signified the total defeat of the upper House's attempts to take an independent or mediating position between the Commons and the King. The Royalist and more moderate noblemen, no longer hopeful of rendering any service after such a reverse, began to withdraw from parliamentary activity. The peers who favoured the opposition put no obstacles in their way. On 4 February the earl of Southampton, conspicuously loyal to the King, obtained leave to be absent, as did also the earl of Carnarvon.[3] Other noblemen followed their example over the next days and weeks, so that the upper House was left much reduced in numbers. During February the average attendance was forty, compared with about sixty in the previous month. At a call of the House on the 9th, sixty-seven members were recorded absent.[4] It was a body thinned by desertion and disaffection that now confronted the King in union with the House of Commons.

Meanwhile, Charles had given his reply on 29 January to the Commons' petition on the militia. He denied the House's demand, declaring that the military prerogative was an 'inseparable . . . Flower of his Crowne . . . derived unto Him . . . by the fundamentall Lawes of the Kingdome. . . .'[5] His answer was vehemently attacked by

[1] L.J., IV, 558, 564. The Journal does not record the figures in the vote on the bill, but observers gave them as 36–23 in favour; Archives . . . de la maison d'Orange Nassau, 2nd ser., IV, 18; H.M.C. Buccleuch, I, 290.
[2] C.S.P.V. 1640–42, 290; C.S.P.D. 1641–43, 278.
[3] L.J., IV, 562. Southampton returned to the House for a time in March in order to protest against parliament's seizure of the militia power, L.J., IV, 628, 646.
[4] C. H. Firth, The House of Lords during the Civil War, 111 and n.; L.J., IV, 571.   [5] C.J., II, 402; An exact collection, 60–1.

f. 355a. This was not the first time the Commons intervened against the electoral influence of the nobility. In December 1641, because of a 'commendatorie letter' from the earl of Arundel in favour of a candidate in a by-election in his own borough of Arundel, the House passed an order to prohibit such letters by peers as an infringement on the freedom of election; Coates, D'Ewes, 236–7; C.J., II, 337.

299

Holles, Strode, and other oppositionist speakers; and two days later the House responded by passing the militia ordinance, which provided that parliament 'in this Time of so imminent Danger' should exercise authority over the militia through lords lieutenants to be appointed by it in every county.[1] A lone voice, that of Sir Ralph Hopton, M.P. for Wells, pointed out that 'wee could not doe this but by an Act of Parliament. . . .', but to no effect.[2]

The militia ordinance was the most extreme measure that the Commons had thus far sponsored. Yet it represented nothing more than a logical progression from earlier positions. As far back as the previous August the Houses had passed their first ordinance: even then they were reaching towards a legislative power fixed solely in themselves. The party leaders, believing the care of the commonwealth to devolve principally on parliament, had repeatedly used the public emergency to launch encroachments on the executive. For months, moreover, the lower House had been straining to win a parliamentary supervision of the choice of ministers, while latterly the Irish rebellion had led it to challenge the King's military authority both by petition and by bill. If it now took the revolutionary step of preparing to seize control of the militia by the legislative fiat of the Houses alone, it had fully prepared the way for such a development.

To the King's misfortune, the two Houses had finally reached accord just as the thrust of the revolt against his regime was becoming concentrated on the decisive issue of military supremacy. The House of Lords having already consented on 1 February to the Commons' petition for the militia, there was every likelihood that it would also agree to the militia ordinance. On the 7th Charles indicated that he might allow parliament to appoint the militia's commanders for a certain time, on condition that he retained a veto on the persons recommended and was satisfied as to the extent of power they would exercise.[3] This gleam of possible concession did not dissuade the Commons from its course. It went on in the next few days to complete the nomination of lords lieutenants over the militia of the counties and sent their names to the upper House. The persons selected were mainly noblemen believed favourable to the oppositionist side. None was to have more than two English counties under his command, and 'if . . . wee cannot . . . find Lords enough in whom wee may confide,' declared D'Ewes, '. . . wee may . . . take Commoners, men of prime qualitie and faire estates. . . .'[4] For London, the ordering of the militia was confirmed in the city's newly-established committee

[1] D'Ewes, Journal, B.M. Harl. 162, f. 356b (in cipher); *C.J.*, II, 406.
[2] D'Ewes, Journal, B.M. Harl. 162, f. 362b.
[3] *C.J.*, II, 416.
[4] D'Ewes, Journal, B.M. Harl. 162, f. 376b.

of safety. The peers accepted this list of appointments on 12 February; on the 15th they passed the militia ordinance itself.[1] The two Houses in cooperation thus completed the basis for investing themselves under the title of parliament with supremacy over the kingdom's military establishment.

Whether or not the parliamentary leaders would proceed further on their unilateral line now depended on the King. With or against his will they meant to deprive him of his military power. Nevertheless, they still hoped that the threat of the militia ordinance would cause him to submit voluntarily to their demand. Charles had, indeed, already yielded several substantial points while the ordinance was passing through the House of Lords. Not only did he agree to appoint parliament's nominee, Sir John Conyers, as Lieutenant of the Tower; more important still, on the 14th he consented to the bill against the secular employments of the clergy. He also accepted an impressment bill by which he relinquished his prerogative right to conscript men for military service outside their counties without parliament's authorization.[2] After these renunciations, it was less than likely that he would offer anything more to secure an accommodation. Even the bill against the secular employments of the clergy was agreed to by him with the greatest reluctance. He did so only after repeated persuasions from the Queen and Sir John Culpepper, who urged that the removal of the bishops from parliament was the sole way to preserve episcopacy itself, and that if he satisfied the Houses in this he could the more firmly deny them the militia.[3]

Probably the King and Queen decided on these last concessions, however, not so much to draw parliament to a compromise as to spin out the time till they obtained the means of effective resistance. Henrietta Maria was convinced that only the force of arms could reestablish royal authority and she told the Venetian envoy that 'to settle affairs it was necessary to unsettle them first. . . .'[4] With this end in view she and the King were making fresh plans. At the end of January they concluded that she should go to Holland with her daughter, Princess Mary, who had been married the previous year to the son of the Prince of Orange. While abroad, she was to try to procure foreign military assistance for the King. He on his side would betake himself to Yorkshire to rally the loyal gentry and make another attempt to seize Hull or some other stronghold

---

[1] *L.J.*, IV, 577–8, 586.

[2] *L.J.*, IV, 577, 580; 16 Car. I, c.27, c.28, *Statutes of the realm*, V, 138.

[3] Clarendon, *Life*, 942; *Rebellion*, IV, 299–301.

[4] On 10 February, *C.S.P.V. 1640–42*, 295. A little earlier, Charles's nephew, the Elector Palatine, reported that the Queen was against any reconciliation with parliament, since it could only be got on dishonourable conditions, *C.S.P.D. 1641–43*, 276.

from which he could maintain regular communication with the continent.[1]

On 7 February the King, then at Windsor, notified parliament of the Queen's approaching journey.[2] Till she was safely away, he put off his answer to the militia ordinance. Accompanied by him to Dover, Henrietta Maria embarked on the 23rd for Holland where, during the year of her absence, she did everything in her power to sustain her husband's cause. As soon as she was gone, the King set out to execute the measures of resistance he had in mind. On 28 February, just as he was about to start for the north, he delivered his opinion of the militia ordinance. His message, with its tart language and emphatic assertion of his own wishes, offered little hope of his compliance. He was willing to appoint their nominees as lords lieutenants, he informed the Houses, but only if all commissions came from himself and terminated at his discretion. This was the sole arrangement consistent with the authority given him by God and the law for the defence of his people. Further, he would not consent to deprive the mayor and aldermen of London of their rights over the citizen militia. As for any future provisions concerning the militia, they must be effected by statute, not ordinance. Finally, he demanded that anyone who meddled with the militia without authority should be proceeded against by law.[3]

The House of Commons immediately rejected the King's answer in every particular as a denial of parliament's desires. If he persisted in his stand, the members declared, he would hazard the peace and safety of the kingdom; they also warned of the danger to peace if he removed to distant parts and asked him to remain near parliament. D'Ewes, who did not dissent from this intransigence but had no stomach for its risks, entered bleakly in his journal: 'This was soe sadd a dayes work to mee as I withdrew out of the howse . . . the rest of the day. . . .' The Commons' resolutions were promptly carried to the House of Lords, which accepted them without demur.[4]

The opposition party was following a line from which it refused to budge by even a hair's breadth. On 1 March a joint committee brought the King the Houses' resolutions of the previous day along

---

[1] The Queen first told the Dutch agent on 29 January of her intention to go to Holland, *Archives . . . de la maison d'Orange-Nassau*, 2nd ser., IV, 12–13. The plans she and the King made prior to her departure are summarized in a letter she sent him from abroad on 29 September 1642, *Letters of Queen Henrietta Maria*, ed. M. A. E. Green, L., 1857, 112. The entire tenor of her correspondence while away was aimed at stiffening the King's will against any concession to parliament.

[2] *L.J.*, IV, 567. [3] *C.J.*, II, 459–60.

[4] *Ibid.*, II, 460; D'Ewes, Journal, B.M. Harl. 163, ff. 10b–11a; *L.J.*, IV, 619–20.

with a virtual ultimatum: unless he speedily granted their demands, 'they shall be enforced . . . to dispose of the militia by the Authority of both Houses . . . and they resolve to do it accordingly.' Charles, then stopping in Hertfordshire on his way northward, returned an equally unyielding answer. He declined to modify his stand on the militia in any respect, he said, nor did he hold it consistent with his safety or honour to reside near parliament.[1]

This was very nearly the breaking point. With the King's last message before them, the Houses on 2 March voted to put the kingdom in a state of defence by means of the militia ordinance. Consonant to this, they again passed the ordinance on the 5th with the names of their lords lieutenants included. Another vote decreed the nullity of all commissions of lieutenancy issued by the King.[2] These actions breached the inmost citadel of the King's executive authority, yet still the Houses made one more effort to gain his concurrence. At Newmarket on the 9th a joint committee presented him with a declaration expressing the just causes of the Houses' fears and urging that he grant them the security they desired. The appeal was futile, its recriminatory tone more apt to inflame than assuage. '. . . wee might have declared the whole and naked Truth,' noted D'Ewes, 'as well in reverentiall and humble words, as in soe high and asperous termes.'[3] Charles's response was an indignant refusal. He too had grounds for fear, he said; moreover, he had passed all bills for his subjects' ease, granted all that the Houses could reasonably ask; they had done nothing for him in return. To a question from the earl of Pembroke, one of the committee, whether he might not accept the terms of the militia ordinance for a time, he retorted angrily, 'By God, not for an houre; you have askt that of me in this, was never askt of a King. . . .'[4]

The King was nearing York when the Houses on 15 March proclaimed that the militia ordinance 'doth oblige the People, and ought to be obeyed by the fundamental Laws of this Kingdom.' The proposition was reported to the Commons by Pym. Certain members objected to it that only a law with the royal assent could oblige the subject. Nevertheless, it passed without a division, its defenders contending that the militia ordinance was 'warranted by the law of God . . . the law of nature and of necessity. . . .'[5] The King countered with a declaration that any ordinance lacking his consent was

[1] *Ibid.*, IV, 620–2.
[2] *Ibid.*, IV, 622, 625–6, 628.
[3] *Ibid.*, IV, 629–31; D'Ewes, Journal, B.M. Harl. 163, f. 19a.
[4] *L.J.*, IV, 640–1; *An exact collection*, 105.
[5] *C.J.*, II, 479; D'Ewes, Journal, B.M. Harl. 163, f. 33a; *L.J.*, IV, 646. Six noblemen entered their protest against the declaration in the House of Lords.

unlawful and of no force to bind his subjects.[1] To this the Houses replied with the most far-reaching claim ever propounded by the imperious politicians who governed their deliberations. 'When the Lords and Commons in Parliament,' they asserted,

which is the supreme Court of Judicature in the Kingdom, shall declare what the Law of the Land is; to have This not only questioned and controverted, and a Command that it should not be obeyed, is a high Breach of the Privilege of Parliament.

The peers first tried to soften this statement by deleting 'Lords and Commons,' thus tacitly allowing that the crown, too, had a part in parliament. The Commons would have none of the amendment. Even D'Ewes spoke against it, arguing that the disputed proposition meant 'not *ius dare*, but *ius dicere*.' The conceited antiquarian preened himself on the parchment learning that frequently enabled him to furnish his fellow members with a legal excuse for their actions. '... the onlie question now is,' he said, 'whether both howses may not declare what the ancient law is, which I hold stronglie the Howse of Commons [may] doe alone.' The peers acquiesced and on 22 March the two Houses adopted the declaration as their official view.[2]

The split was absolute. The fig leaf of constitutional propriety with which D'Ewes tried to cover the nakedness of the Houses' assumption of legislative power could hardly have deceived anyone. Under the title of parliament the Houses were claiming sovereignty for themselves. All that now remained was for them and the King to prepare to impose their will on each other by whatever means they could.

The King arrived in York on the 19th, hopeful of gathering support about him in the northern counties to withstand a rebellion.[3] At Westminster the Houses were already giving effect to the militia ordinance.[4] In their latest declarations, the irreconcilable antagonists were no longer speaking to, but past, each other. These statements, like their ensuing manifestoes of the spring and summer, were communications to the kingdom and the governing class, appeals from both sides to enlist popular strength for the approaching 'continuation of politics by other means.'

[1] *L.J.*, IV, 647.
[2] *C.J.*, II, 481; *L.J.*, IV, 650, 663; D'Ewes, Journal, B.M. Harl. 163, ff. 37a–b.
[3] The King's itinerary from the Queen's departure to his arrival in York is given in J. Rushworth, IV, 484.
[4] Pym, for instance, moved on 21 March that Sir Edward Hungerford, M.P. for Chippenham, should have 'leave to go into the cuntrie ... where he would be able to doe us much service ... for the settling of the Militia.'; D'Ewes, Journal, B.M. Harl. 163, f. 39b.

As the tide of public differences swept steadily on towards civil war, a massive political realignment occurred in the kingdom. The breakup of the Country, signalized in the past November's vote on the Grand Remonstrance, continued without reversal during the winter and spring of 1641–2. Out of the Country's split, and from its sundered segments, arose the two parties that were shortly to engage each other in blood on the field of battle.

The appearance of the Royalist and Parliamentarian parties marked a fresh stage in the revolution's progress. In no sense did they correspond to the preceding Court-Country division whose conflict dominated Charles's earlier reign and the first period of the Long Parliament's history. The Court, isolated and powerless when parliament assembled, had disintegrated as a political factor. The Country, with public opinion and the governing class largely united in its support, had enacted a far-reaching programme of reforms. But owing to the crisis of confidence in the King, these reforms had failed to end the revolution. The Country leaders embarked on a quest for guarantees that led to ever bolder encroachments on the crown's executive authority. Under their direction parliament was moving steadily, in fact, to take over both the work of government and the legislative power. The unremitting demands of Pym and his associates, their grasping for control of ministerial appointments and the military establishment, their exploitation of the London populace, all strained their public and parliamentary backing to the breaking point. Every politically-conscious person who had acknowledged their ascendancy was compelled to consider whether to accompany the party managers further on a road that was taking England away from its old landmarks and very probably towards armed struggle against its lawful prince.

It was the strength of the oppositionist leaders that they had faced the issue squarely and made their deliberate choice. These men, profoundly conservative as they were at heart, stood ready if necessary to endure the stigma of rebellion and to chance the trials of war rather than leave the King the slightest power to destroy what parliament had won. Many others in the political nation, however, would not consent to follow them in this. Thus, the Country disintegrated, and in the re-groupment of its dismembered elements the Parliamentarian and Royalist parties gradually took shape.

'. . . that which was called the King's party in both Houses,' said one of its foremost adherents,

was made up of persons who were strangers to the Court, of the best

305

fortunes and the best reputation in their several countries, where they were known as having always appeared very zealous in the maintenance of their just rights and opposed as much as in them lay all illegal and grievous impositions.[1]

The author of this description of the newly-emerged Royalism was Edward Hyde, the future historian of the revolution. A Royalist convert himself, his conduct was emblematic of the break of ranks in the governing class that disrupted the Country and gave the King a party. Hyde's personal acquaintance with the King only began in the summer of 1641, when Charles received him in a private interview to acknowledge his parliamentary services on the monarchy's behalf.[2] Already in the process of withdrawing from cooperation with the opposition leaders, his secession became complete during the debate on the Grand Remonstrance.[3] The same political transition was made by his friends, Lord Falkland and Sir John Culpepper, who, like himself, enjoyed some esteem and prominence in the House of Commons. Accordingly, when the King conferred office upon the latter two in January 1642, he offered Hyde promotion as well. Hyde declined it on the ground that he could assist the royal cause better for the time if he remained a private member of parliament. He promised, nevertheless, to send Charles advice and to consult regularly with Falkland and Culpepper about affairs.[4] Henceforward he was effectively in the King's employ notwithstanding his non-official capacity.

His most recent and discerning historian has argued that in thus joining the King Hyde did not change his political position: that what changed was the situation in which Pym pursued a policy incompatible with peace and compromise, while Hyde himself continued to desire a legal settlement based on the statutes passed before the September 1641 recess.[5] This view, however, is a misleading and partial one. In the context of the acute and unbroken crisis of confidence, it was Pym's judgment that there could be no guarantee of permanence for parliament's reforming work nor of the personal safety of the oppositionist leaders without additional securities from the King. The House of Commons' insistence on these securities was, indeed, the practical basis for the formation of the Parliamentarian

[1] Clarendon, *Rebellion*, IV, 94. This statement noting the formation of a Royalist party refers to late January 1642. In a subsequent reference to April and the militia controversy, Clarendon mentions the King's 'own party (for so those began now to be called who preserved their duty and allegiance entire). . . .', *ibid.*, V, 87.
[2] Clarendon, *Life*, 937.   [3] Cf. *supra*, 268.
[4] Clarendon, *Rebellion*, IV, 126; *Life*, 938–9.
[5] Cf. B. H. G. Wormald, *op. cit.*, 13, 17–18, 45–6, 83–4.

party. To diverge from Pym in this, to opt for the King in the contest of wills over the control of ministerial appointments and the militia, meant a change of sides to Royalism. That Hyde acted out of principle need not be denied. Yet the Royalist perspective from which he now saw events, and which afterwards also shaped his *History of the rebellion*, gave him a prejudiced and therefore very inadequate conception of the motives of the Parliamentarian leaders. In particular, it inclined him grossly to underrate the depth and extent of distrust of the King. He treated the crisis of confidence as one of Pym's deliberate contriving, rather than as the authentic consequence of the King's repeated actions. This failing led him into disingenuousness and misrepresentation when he wrote his *History*.[1] Hence, he even explained away the King's attempted *coup d'état* (for which he himself bore no responsibility) as a mere misjudgment, and attributed parliament's breach with the King almost entirely to the artful machinations and unprincipled ambition of Pym's group.[2]

As England's peace expired, it was Hyde who framed the emerging Royalist party's doctrine and therewith enabled the King to assume the unfamiliar role of defender of the legal constitution against the transgressions of the Parliamentarians. He performed this unique service as author of the declarations which the King put forth in answer to parliament's messages. Hyde undertook the task of composing the King's replies at the end of February 1642. As long as he stayed at Westminster, he transmitted the drafts to Charles secretly, who then communicated the result to the Houses as his own. The same ghost-writing arrangement continued when Hyde arrived in York in May to attend Charles in person. With one exception, he was responsible for every important statement of constitutional doctrine which the King published in the wordy war of manifestoes preceding the war of arms—a contribution of inestimable value to the refurbishing and renewal of the monarch's public image.[3]

The policy Hyde advocated for the King in the face of germinating

---

[1] The method and chronology of Clarendon's composition of his *History* have been analysed by C. H. Firth, 'Clarendon's *History of the rebellion*,' 3 pts., *E.H.R.*, XIX, 63–5 (1904). Firth's verdict on Clarendon's account of the coming of the civil war (*ibid.*, pt. 1, 37–8) is severe, but not unfairly so.

[2] The King consulted neither Hyde, Falkland, nor Culpepper before his impeachment of the opposition members. But Hyde, though disapproving the action as ill-advised and unseasonable, believed Pym guilty and considered that the King might have proceeded against the oppositionists more effectively. Charles, he declared, did 'rather what was just than what was expedient. . . .'; *Rebellion*, IV, 149n., 158, 192, 218.

[3] Clarendon, *Life*, 943–4. Before engaging himself to write the King's declarations, Hyde had shown his talent by drafting Charles's reply to the Grand Remonstrance. The only important royal declaration not composed

rebellion was one of non-violence and reliance on the law to preserve his authority. He was

to grant anything that by the law he was obliged to grant, and to deny what by the law was in his own power and which he found inconvenient to consent to, and to oppose and punish any extravagant attempt by the force and power of the law.[1]

How the King was to do this amidst the breakdown of the monarchical constitution and parliament's step-by-step erection of a competing sovereignty Hyde did not explain. In any event, Charles had decided with the Queen on resistance; even then he was in the north to make a further try to secure the arsenal at Hull. Hyde, however, had no knowledge of these counsels when they were first adopted, while later he was plausibly able to represent the King's actions as defensive measures against the seditious conduct of the Houses.[2]

It was therefore to the law that Charles appealed in the declarations Hyde penned on his behalf. These royal utterances contained no recondite theorizing. The sentiments to which they addressed themselves were the long-engrafted ones of honourable loyalty to the crown and deference for established principles. They were directed especially to those men antagonized by parliament's latest demands and the prospect of further unsettlement: persons, as Hyde told the King, 'who have been the severest assertors of the publick liberties, and so besides their duty and loyalty to your person ... value their own interests upon the preservation of your rights.'[3] The themes which the declarations reiterated were the King's innocence of any evil intention towards parliament and the falsity of accusations that he had plotted to destroy its privileges; the many concessions he had made to demonstrate his desire for political reconciliation and the public good; the justifiable reasons he had to fear the popular tumults and seditious language that had driven him from London; above all the King invoked the law—'the Law,' he asserted, '. . .which We always intend shall bee the measure of Our owne power, and expect it shall be the rule of Our Subjects obedience.'[4] Once he quoted shrewdly from a great panegyric on the law which Pym had delivered

[1] Clarendon, *Rebellion*, V, 12.
[2] Hyde recorded that only Culpepper, neither he nor Falkland, knew of the King's design upon Hull, Clarendon, *Life*, 941.
[3] Hyde to the King at York, March 1642, *Clarendon state papers*, II, 138–9.
[4] *An exact collection*, 109.

by him before the civil war was the answer to parliament's Nineteen Propositions (for which cf. *infra*, 318–19), which Falkland and Culpepper wrote, *ibid.*, 937, 953.

a year previously against Strafford and told the Houses to take the words to heart: 'the Law of the Land,' he admonished, 'is the only Rule which preserves the Publick. ... Preserve the Dignity, and Reverence due to that.'[1] From this high ground he denounced the Houses' ordinance power as a subversion of the kingdom's constitution. '... We must declare to all the World,' said the King,

That we are not satisfied, or shall ever allow Our Subjects to be bound by your printed Votes ... or that under pretence of declaring what the Law of the Land is, you shall without us make a new Law, which is plainly the case of the Militia: And what is this but to introduce an Arbitrary way of Government?[2]

Against the legalist arguments of the King, the Houses did not avow any fundamental political or constitutional theory, at least not in explicit terms. Steeped in reverence for the law themselves, the party leaders had no mind to argue the Parliamentarian case on the ground of first principles. Besides, they believed that they were the true defenders of the legal order against arbitrary government, whatever Charles might say, and that practical exigencies existed which amply warranted their programme. Accordingly, the Houses' declarations expressed no awareness or acknowledgment that they were propounding opinions of any novelty. Yet despite this, they implicitly presented the elements of a revolutionary redefinition of the polity, wherein monarchy became no more than the obedient and answerable agency of the community's will expressed through parliament.[3]

The root of Parliamentarian doctrine was the conception of parliament as the organ supremely responsible for the care of the commonwealth—for the preservation of law, liberty, property, and a rightly limited prerogative. Such had been the Country's creed from the beginning. Parliament, of course, included the King: but with the progressive breakdown of the constitution in 1641–2, the Houses claimed the responsibility of parliament for themselves alone. Partly they sought the sanction of law to justify their position. Thus, to refute the King's accusations of illegality they cited both medieval precedents and the 'fundamental law' as grounds for the militia ordinance. '... the two Houses of Parliament,' they said,

... were enabled by their own authority to provide for the repulsing of ... imminent, and evident danger not by any new Law of their own

---

[1] *Ibid.*, 140.   [2] *Ibid.*, 126.

[3] Cf. the discussion of the Houses' views by J. W. Allen, *English political thought*, pt. VI, ch. IV and J. W. Gough, *Fundamental law in English history*, ch. VI.

making as hath been untruly suggested . . . but by the most ancient Law of this Kingdome, even that which is fundamentall and essential to the constitution and subsistance of it.[1]

As these remarks illustrate, the Houses did not admit that their militia ordinance entailed an exercise of legislative power. For the same reason they referred to themselves as a council and as a court—traditional designations of parliament—without ever straightforwardly asserting that they were sovereign. All the same, their reasoning implied no less. For underlying their arguments was the notion that they, as the kingdom's representative body, were entitled to declare the law and to determine public policy in the commonwealth's interest. It was therefore the idea of the Houses as representative—as being, quintessentially, the community itself—that constituted the tacit theoretical basis of the Parliamentarian case.

Repeatedly, the Houses described themselves as 'entrusted' by and for the kingdom. While they allowed that the King also possessed a trust, they pronounced theirs to be superior and controlling. '. . . the Wisedome of this State,' they affirmed, 'hath intrusted the Houses of Parliament with a power to supply what shall be wanting on the part of the Prince. . . .' In their discharge of this trust they proclaimed their judgment binding upon all, the King included: what is 'declared by the Lords and Commons in Parliament needs not the authority of any person . . . to affirme; nor is it in the power of any person . . . to revoke that judgment.'[2]

More than once, indeed, the opinion had been expressed in the Commons that the King possessed no negative voice in legislation. Henry Marten, M.P. for Berkshire, advanced the suggestion that Charles must pass all bills, since his vote 'was included in the Lords votes as the whole Commons of England weere included in ours; because hee elected the Peeres as the Commons did us.'[3] On another occasion, Nathaniel Fiennes said in defence of the militia ordinance that the King was obliged to assent to all measures on which the Houses agreed. It made no difference that D'Ewes replied that the King had always assented to acts—that records would show the kings of England to have rejected more bills than they had passed.[4] The Commons eventually adopted Fiennes's opinion when it voted on 19 May that the King was bound by his coronation oath to pass all bills presented by the Houses for the good of the kingdom.[5]

---

[1] *An exact collection*, 197, 205–6.
[2] Declaration of 19 May 1642, *An exact collection*, 204, 206, 207–8.
[3] D'Ewes, Journal, B.M. Harl. 162, f. 375b. This was on 7 February.
[4] On 1 April, *ibid.*, B.M. Harl. 163, f. 58b.
[5] *C.J.*, II. 580. This was voted in a division of 103–61.

Parliamentarians and Royalists

The Houses thus left the King no shred of independence from themselves. Completely severing his monarchical from his personal capacity, they declared that his politic will, as distinct from his merely personal one, was merged in theirs. Parliament, they informed the King, is

not onely a Court of Judicature . . . to adjudge and determine the Rights and Liberties of the Kingdome . . . but it is likewise a Councell to provide for the necessity, to prevent the imminent dangers, and preserve the . . . safety of the Kingdom, and to declare the King's pleasure in those things as are requisite thereunto, and what they doe herein hath the stampe of Royall authority, although his Majesty . . . do in his own person oppose or interrupt the same; for the Kings Supream . . . and Royal pleasure is exercised and declared in this high Court of Law and Councell after a more eminent and obligatory manner, then it can be by any personall Act or Resolution of his own.[1]

This bifurcation between the office of kingship and its personal incumbent was reminiscent of the rebellious magnates' declaration against Edward II in 1308, wherein they stated that they owed their subjection to the crown rather than to the person of the King.[2] The latter doctrine, however, found no warrant in the law. In the early seventeenth century, indeed, Bacon, Coke, and Ellesmere, the greatest lawyers of the age, all commented on it only to reject it emphatically as inferring 'execrable and detestable consequences.'[3] With the formulation of the same fiction in 1642, the Houses established a justification to annex both the recognized attributes of monarchical supremacy and a legislative power as well which the King had never possessed.

Perhaps the framers of their manifestoes did not perceive that under colour of declaring law they introduced the greatest innovation ever made in England's government. If so, the King at any rate knew better. In a critical review of the Houses' claims, he taxed them with making themselves absolute so as to become the sole disposers

---

[1] *An exact collection*, 304.
[2] Cf. M. McKisack, *The fourteenth century 1307–1399*, Oxford, 1959, 7, 64, and E. Kantorowicz, *The King's two bodies*, Princeton, 1957, 364–6.
[3] F. D. Wormuth, *op. cit.*, 51–2; Bacon, *Works*, XV, 233–5. The views of Bacon, Coke, and Ellesmere were expressed in the great constitutional case of the *post-nati*, 1607. Although English legal thought, as Kantorowicz, *op. cit.*, has shown, was rich in corporational concepts of kingship and made use of the distinction between the King's natural and politic bodies, it did not formulate this doctrine to justify rebellion or to set the crown against the King's person. Bacon said that King and crown could be distinguished but not separated, *Works*, XV, 234.

of all law and public matters by majority vote. He was not wrong. Nor did he exaggerate much in describing the import of the Houses' doctrine as nothing else than a design for

The ruine . . . of Monarchy it Self (Which Wee may justly say, is more than ever was offered in any of Our Predecessours times; for though the Person of the King hath been sometimes unjustly deposed, yet the Regall Power was never before this time stricken at). . . .[1]

3

The clangour of argument in official declarations only mirrored the furious debate which was spreading over the kingdom and eating away its peace. 'I finde all heere full of feares,' said a report from Kent. 'Parents and children, brothers, kindred . . . and deere frends have the seed of difference and division abundantly sowed in them. . . . All is at stake, and the rent is conceived to be so great that it can hardly bee drawne up. . . .'[2] One man praised Pym's 'herroicke courage' and thought parliament's statements enough to 'satisfie any resonable person'; another testified to the persuasive force of the King's views.[3] What mainly undermined Charles's case, however, was that many people did not believe him. There was a numerous body of Englishmen in whose eyes he stood convicted, despite his professions to the contrary, of double-dealing, conspiracy against parliament, complicity in the Irish rebellion. Such persons endorsed parliament's actions and the militia ordinance as measures essential to the security of the commonwealth in an extreme situation. Our invaluable diarist, D'Ewes, held this opinion. The anxious witness of the polity's disintegration, repeatedly pleading with his fellow members for moderation and compromise, he merely stated a widespread belief when, with civil war impending, he told the House of Commons:

. . . I cannot but much wonder what end any man can imagine wee can have in what wee have done of late but the publike good. . . . They must be more uncharitable then Turk or Heathen . . . that shall imagine that soe many persons as the Parliament now consisteth of can bee united in one Act of disloyalty but that what wee have done was of meer necessity and for the preservation of the King and Kingdome.[4]

---

[1] *An exact collection*, 297–8.
[2] *The Oxinden letters 1607–1642*, 272, 306.
[3] *Ibid.*, 271, 307; *Sir Roger Twysden's journal*, ed. L. B. Larking, *Archaeologia Cantiana*, I, 1858, 200.
[4] D'Ewes, Journal, B.M. Harl. 163, f. 121b, 16 May 1642.

Parliamentarians and Royalists

One of the earliest expressions of a popular Royalism was Sir George Benyon's attempt in February 1642 to get up a petition in London against the Houses' claim to dispose of the militia. Benyon was severely punished for his temerity in challenging the Houses' actions.[1] A still more significant outbreak of Royalist sentiment occurred in Kent at the end of March. Although the county and its gentry had been generally favourable to the Country opposition when parliament began, since the autumn of 1641 they were experiencing the same fissiparous process that was dividing all England into hostile camps.[2] Of the two Kent M.P.s, Sir John Culpepper, changing from reformer to Royalist, had entered the King's employment, while Sir Edward Dering had broken his connections with the opposition leaders in the Commons. Early in 1642 Dering published a volume of his parliamentary speeches, thereby so incensing the House that it disabled him from sitting.[3] Parliamentarians considered him to be no better than a turncoat. A pamphlet addressed to him in February 1642 declared:

You have given such a president, that putting my Lord Digbie aside . . . you shall never twice be parallel'd . . . hypocrizing and deluding the expectation of all right honest men . . . as to betray . . . the cause of God, the Church, and the Country . . . forgetting wholly what you were. . . .[4]

Sir Roger Twysden, another Kentishman and friend of Dering, described the progress of his own disillusionment with Pym's party in his autobiography. He too had greeted the Long Parliament as the kingdom's salvation, only to become in time more and more critical of the *ultra vires* tendency of its actions. In this, Twysden, a learned antiquarian who admired England's ancient constitution as the best in the world, was typical of the moderate mentality that carried many gentlemen of his sort into Royalism.[5] '. . . I began to be much troubled,' he related, that 'if wee did change our Task Masters, our burthens would not be lesse. And what was it to me . . . whether the Earl of Strafford or Mr. Pym sate at the helme of government, if their commands carryed equall pressure?' He was completely against the

[1] Cf. *supra*, 291–2.
[2] The best account is now that by A. Everitt, *The community of Kent and the great rebellion, 1640–1660*, Leicester, 1966, which became available too late for me to use.
[3] *C.J.*, II, 411.
[4] [J.P.], *The copie of a letter written unto Sir Edward Dering*, 1642, 4.
[5] Cf. Twysden's *Certaine considerations upon the government of England*, ed. J. M. Kemble, *Camden society*, XLV, 1849, for the exposition of his constitutional views, and the account by J. W. Gough, *op. cit.*, 93–7.

militia ordinance: if the Houses acquired the military power despite the King's denial, 'they had in effect all yᵉ rights of Soveraignity, the people under an absolute arbitrary voting Tyrany. . . .'[1]

The ripening disaffection to parliament signallized in these sentiments manifested itself publicly on 25 March at the Kent assizes. Inspired by Dering, Twysden, and other local notables, a specially empanelled grand jury of justices and gentlemen drew up a Royalist petition to express the county's grievances. Dering himself was the jury's foreman. Addressed to the House of Commons, the petition touched a number of tender points, including the preservation of episcopal church government and the suppression of sects, lay preaching, and seditious sermons. But its sharpest sting was aimed at the militia ordinance which it attacked as arbitrary and illegal. '. . . no Order,' it said, 'in either or both Houses, not grounded on the Laws of the Land, may be enforced on the Subject. . . .'[2]

To attain the widest circulation, the petition's sponsors published it throughout the county and further arranged that a mass meeting should be held at the end of April at Blackheath to carry it to the House of Commons. But the House did not wait for the mutinous spirit in Kent to gather head. It promptly began an investigation into the petition's appearance and summoned Dering, Twysden, and several others as delinquents. For having a copy in his possession, the earl of Bristol was sent to the Tower by the Lords. On 26 April the Commons completed Dering's overthrow when it impeached him for 'high Crimes and Misdemeanors.'[3] Despite these discouragements, some of the petition's supporters delivered it on 30 April to the lower House. Their campaign had lost its impetus, however, and after making a subdued appearance they were patronizingly dismissed by the Speaker as 'young Gentlemen, misled by Some not affected to the Peace of the Kingdom. . . .' By this time, moreover, Parliamentarian sentiment was rapidly organizing itself in the county, so that on 5 May the Houses received a counter-petition of support from Kent containing six thousand signatures and the promise that 'many thousands more intend to subscribe. . . .'[4]

These Kentish episodes were subsidiary to the central conflict which the King and parliament were waging between York and Westminster. Although gestures of negotiation continued, they were overshadowed by invincible animosity which made each side look to

---

[1] *Sir Roger Twysden's journal*, I, 187, 188, 198. Twysden wrote this autobiographical account about 1657, cf. *ibid.*, *Archaeologia Cantiana*, IV, 1861, 195.

[2] *L.J.*, IV, 677–8. The circumstances of the Kentish petition's appearance are given in *ibid.*, V, 17–19 and in *Sir Roger Twysden's journal*, I, 200–13.

[3] *C.J.*, II, 507; *L.J.*, IV, 678, V, 17.

[4] *C.J.*, II, 550, 558; *L.J.*, V, 44.

its own strength. From abroad at the end of March and the beginning of April the Queen sent her husband urgent letters imploring him to occupy Hull without delay. His enemies still counted on his submitting to an accommodation, she wrote, but he was not to think of it: 'it is only trifling and losing time.' Let the Houses see him in action and 'they would speak after another fashion.'[1]

Charles's first view of Yorkshire opinion evidently made him pause. His presence evoked no instant outpouring of political support. Instead, a petition of 5 April drawn up at the county assizes expressed concern at the kingdom's division and begged him to devise expedients to reestablish union with parliament.[2] Meanwhile, as he considered how to secure Hull, he sent the Houses an unexpected proposition on 11 April which became the focus of new fears. In this he stated his intent to go to Ireland to suppress the rebellion and with this object to raise a body of some two thousand men whom he proposed to arm from the arsenal in Hull. In order to remove misunderstandings, he added, he would presently transmit a new bill for the settlement of the militia in a way that would give general satisfaction.[3]

When and how the King conceived this idea does not appear, unless he and the Queen canvassed it as a possibility prior to her departure.[4] Probably he believed that parliament would find it awkward to reject an offer aimed ostensibly at the relief of Ireland. If so it was a further sign of his inferior political judgment and lack of statesmanship, since the Houses would never consent to any scheme that entailed his having an army.

The King's messages naturally aroused speculation as to his real motives. A common opinion held that he wished to go to Ireland to make peace with the rebels on any terms so that he might return to England at the head of an army.[5] This, certainly, was the conjecture of the Parliamentarian leaders. They could imagine no other reason why the King proposed to leave his English realm at so critical a time. Accordingly, the Houses issued a declaration on the 15th rejecting his offer as dangerous and asserting that they would not allow him to levy any soldiers for Ireland.[6]

[1] *Letters of Queen Henrietta Maria,* 59–63.
[2] The petition was offered in the name of gentry, ministers, and freeholders, J. Rushworth, IV, 613.
[3] *L.J.,* IV, 709–10.
[4] Clarendon's explanation of the King's Irish project was that it was a 'stratagem' and a 'counsel . . . very suddenly taken, and communicated to very few, without consideration of the objections that would naturally arise against it. . . .', *Rebellion,* V, 78.
[5] Cf. the despatch of the Venetian envoy, *C.S.P.V. 1642–43,* 46.
[6] *L.J.,* IV, 719–20.

Pym's management of this incident gave proof of how persistently he tried to preserve agreement amongst the Parliamentarian members. It is D'Ewes who permits us a sight of his tactics. In his notes the troubled diarist had begun to refer for the first time to the 'fiery' and 'violent spirits' in the Commons. Thus, when Pym reported the draft of the reply to the King's message, D'Ewes suggested a few softening changes of language, only to be interrupted, he recorded, by 'some indiscreet and violent spirits.' This led him to tell the House to weigh its words well, lest 'wee ... leave the kingdome without all hope or possibilitie of an accomodation betweene his Matie and us. ...' Pym, however,

did with much discretion and modestie approve what I had spoken and comming himselfe to the Clarkes table did amend the said Declaration according to the advice I had given. ...[1]

The modified declaration remained sharp enough, but the episode was characteristic of Pym's methods. Essentially a man of the centre, with nothing in him of the *enragé*, the Parliamentarian chief moderated differences whenever possible. In his role as helmsman, he exerted his leadership to hold together left and right, the more and the less militant, on his own side. In addition, he wished it to be manifest that if peace gave way the fault would be the King's, not parliament's.

This appeared further in the sequel to the King's announcement in his recent message that he would propose a new militia bill. As the Houses were insisting on the legality of the militia ordinance, they might have refused to entertain the King's bill. Instead, the Lords received the bill on 19 April, amended it, and sent it to the Commons the next day. There, Henry Marten, one of D'Ewes's 'violent spirits,' urged its rejection. If the House accepted a bill, he said, 'wee shall condemne our own Act and vilify the ordinance wee had made ... and should seem to give way to the Kings evill counsellors who had ... advized this way of Bill. ...' Good logic, it would appear! Yet no support arose for Marten's view. Clearly, the House's managers were set on avoiding any impression of inflexibility. Then, with Marten alone dissenting, a motion by D'Ewes was carried to read the King's bill a second time and refer it to a committee of the whole.[2]

Despite this treatment, the King's bill had no effect on the course of events. By its provisions Charles offered to share the militia power

---

[1] D'Ewes, Journal, B.M. Harl. 163, f. 75b.
[2] *L.J.*, V, 5; *C.J.*, II, 535; D'Ewes, Journal, B.M. Harl. 163, f. 83b. D'Ewes contended that the militia ordinance was lawful, but that it would be safer to proceed by bill.

with the Houses for one year; during this time he would order the militia subject to their advice while he remained in England, and if he went to Ireland they were to dispose of it alone. In committee, the Commons extended the bill's term to two years and altered it in other particulars as well so as to deprive the King of any part in the militia. The amended bill passed both Houses on 22 April.[1] Six days later Charles denied it his assent, declaring that it excluded him from all power in that 'which God and the Law hath trusted Us solely. . . .'[2] The Houses accordingly proceeded to act on the basis of the militia ordinance. The entire transaction demonstrated that while the Parliamentarian leadership had no doctrinaire commitment to an ordinance, it was immovable in its determination to secure exclusive rule of the militia.

During the consideration of his Irish proposition and militia bill, the King held back from any attempt on Hull. Parliament's dismissal of his offer probably decided him to wait no longer as well as to lay aside further thought of going to Ireland. The Houses of course realized the danger of his proximity to the town. Because of this, they authorized Sir John Hotham to remove its magazine.[3] Before it could be done, the King came before Hull on 23 April with about three hundred men and demanded entrance. Hotham refused, replying that he could not admit the King against parliament's instructions. Again Charles commanded that the gates be thrown open, only to receive the same reply. Thereupon he caused Hotham and those adhering to him to be proclaimed traitors. Withdrawing for the night to Beverly a few miles off, he made a second fruitless attempt the next day to persuade Hull's defenders to open the town. His commands thus set at naught, there was nothing left for him for the time being but to return angrily to York.[4]

The events at Hull brought England's cracked and ailing peace *in articulo mortis*. Hotham's disobedience in parliament's name was proof that rival sovereignties were engaged at its walls. There was certainly no room for both in one realm. In subsequent declarations, the two sides argued acrimoniously over the rights and wrongs of the King's exclusion from Hull. The King as usual took refuge in legal considerations to justify a course of action which really tended

---

[1] *C.J.*, II, 537; *L.J.*, V, 10. The text of the King's militia bill has not survived, but its substance and the amendments made in it can be gathered from the subsequent arguments about it in the King's declaration of 28 April and the Houses' answer of 5 May, *An exact collection*, 158–9, 171–2. Cf. also the Venetian ambassador's description of the bill, *C.S.V.P. 1642–43*, 42.
[2] *An exact collection*, 159.
[3] *L.J.*, V, 4; *C.J.*, II, 533.
[4] Cf. the description of the events at Hull in Sir John Hotham's letter to parliament, *L.J.*, V, 28–9 and in J. Rushworth, IV, 567.

towards force. He affirmed Hull and its magazine to be his own property by the same lawful title that his subjects held their goods. Parliament retorted that the kingdom's towns and forts were not the King's, but a trust to be used by him for the public benefit.[1] Behind these contrary claims stood the stark reality, visible to all, that if the King got Hull he would be in a better position to wage war.

Charles, however, was resolved to take the town and punish the affront he had received there.[2] Over the following weeks he energetically solicited the assistance of the gentry and people of Yorkshire, whom he addressed at large open-air meetings in May and early June. He appealed to the gentry to provide him with a guard on the ground that he had to defend himself when parliament countenanced treason and detained his magazine. The mixed reception of approval and disapproval from the crowds revealed the fractured condition of the county, divided and at odds like all of England.[3] Still, his pleas had some success, so that by the end of May he had formed a troop of Yorkshire gentlemen to which he also added a regiment of about six hundred county militia that appeared in response to his summons.[4]

These were actually the first forces to be raised for civil war. In no other light did the Parliamentarians regard the King's activities at York. Accordingly on 20 May the Houses passed the momentous resolutions that the King, seduced by wicked counsel, intended to levy war on his parliament; that his doing so was 'a breach of the Trust reposed in him by his People' and tended 'to the Dissolution of this Government;' and that all assisting him were 'Traytors, by the fundamental Laws of this Kingdom. . . .' The Commons adopted these votes after strong debate, 'the hotter and more violent spirits prevailing,' according to D'Ewes, 'although there were many negatives. . . .'[5]

While pushing on its war preparations, parliament at the beginning of June drew up a final offer of conditions for an accommodation in the form of nineteen propositions. These, however, did not retrench its earlier demands in the slightest degree. They spelled out more fully, rather, the contemplated subjection of the King to the common-

[1] Cf. the King's declaration of 4 May and parliament's answer of the 26th, *An exact collection*, 163-4, 265-6.
[2] Cf. the Venetian ambassador's description of the King's state of mind, *C.S.V.P. 1642-43*, 53.
[3] The documents relating to these Yorkshire assemblies are printed in J. Rushworth, IV, 615-25.
[4] Clarendon, *Rebellion*, V, 140.
[5] *C.J.*, II, 581; D'Ewes, Journal, B.M. Harl. 163, f. 128b. The phrase, 'seduced by wicked counsel,' was included in the first of these resolutions on Pym's motion.

wealth's representative body. Parliament was to approve the appointment and removal of councillors, ministers, great officers of state, and the chief justices of the common-law courts; foreign alliances and marriage treaties were to be made with its advice; the King was to consent to such a reformation of church government and liturgy as it recommended; he was also to accept the militia ordinance, disband his forces, and grant the custody of forts and castles to persons whom parliament approved; and he was not to hinder the justice of parliament on all delinquents—a direct threat to Charles's closest and most loyal followers.[1]

The Nineteen Propositions defined a surrender, not terms framed to avoid a war. As such the King scornfully rejected them, avowing that they overthrew the law and robbed him of the substance of his regality. He added a sketch of England's traditional balanced constitution to enforce the lesson that neither House was entitled to any share in governing the kingdom.[2] On receipt of this answer, the House of Commons spent some time reviewing the propositions to see how they might be rendered more acceptable. After voting a few modifications, it let the matter drop, being too preoccupied with the imminent trial of arms. There was, in truth, no poultice left to apply against the civil infection epidemic in the kingdom. The Nineteen Propositions remained as the fullest outline of the revolutionary polity which parliament, under the justification of self-defence, was contending for against the King.[3]

Meanwhile, each party was making strong exertions to enlist the militia of the counties on its side. The Parliamentarian lords lieutenants and their deputies acted under the sanction of the Houses' militia ordinance; the Royalist lieutenants invoked the King's authority conveyed to them from June onward in the form of commissions of array, which bid them arm and muster the able-bodied in the counties and suppress all attempts at interference. Each party declared itself to be acting in self-defence; each proclaimed the nullity of the other's orders and the legitimacy of its own.[4]

In this way, people of every rank throughout the realm were put

[1] *C.J.*, II, 599–600.

[2] *An exact collection*, 311ff. The King's answer to the Nineteen Propositions was written by Culpepper and Falkland. Its importance in the evolution of the theory of mixed monarchy and its subsequent uses in controversy are stressed by C. C. Weston, *English constitutional theory and the House of Lords, 1556–1832*, N.Y., 1965, ch. I.

[3] The principal discussions of the propositions occurred on 24, 27, 28 June, and 2 July, *C.J.*, II, 638–9, 642, 643, 648. The Venetian ambassador's despatch of 24 June gave an exaggerated account of the changes the House was willing to make, *C.S.P.V. 1642–43*, 92.

[4] The documents pertaining to the execution of the militia ordinance and the royal commission of array are printed in J. Rushworth, IV, 655ff.

face to face with the contradictory decrees of rival sovereignties. To choose in such a crux was dangerous, yet inescapable. 'For mine own part,' declared the earl of Bristol, one of the last moderates in the House of Lords,

> ... *I cannot find out, under the different Command of the King and Parliament, any such course of Caution and Wariness, by which I can promise to my self Security or Safety.*[1]

It was the common dilemma of the governing class. A Kentish Parliamentarian expressed it similarly:

> ... *my condition beetwixt the commission of Aray and ordinance of Parl: is like his that is between Silla and Carybdis, and nothing butt Omnipotence can bring mee clearely and reputably off. ...*[2]

Brush fires of strife breaking out in many parts of England between the executants of the militia ordinance and the commission of array marked the actual beginning of the civil war. Contemporary writers reckoned that the first casualty fell at Manchester on 15 July when the townsmen were resisting the attempt of the Royalist son of the earl of Derby to implement the commission of array.[3] Prior to this, however, several of the King's supporters had already been slain at Hull.[4] Besides the contention over the militia that erupted in the counties, other martial actions ensued. In mid-June, the earl of Newcastle with troops raised from his own tenants and others, occupied Newcastle and the mouth of the Tyne for the King.[5] Ordnance and munitions also reached Charles from Holland, acquired by the Queen with money from the pawn of crown jewels. Early in June the King in a new move against Hull tried to blockade the town with about twenty-five hundred men, but was repulsed by the defenders and withdrew.[6]

On parliament's side the Houses took these occurrences as the definite initiation of a war. Accordingly on 4 July they appointed a joint committee of safety charged to prepare measures of defence.[7]

---

[1] Speech delivered 20 May 1642, J. Rushworth, IV, 717. The entire address is of great interest. In spite of Bristol's complaint about its publication, it is probably authentic (*L.J.*, V, 87). A few weeks later, Bristol withdrew from parliament and joined the King at York.

[2] *The Oxinden letters 1607–1642*, 312.

[3] J. Rushworth, IV, 680.

[4] Cf. a letter from Hull to the Speaker of the Commons on 13 July, *L.J.*, V 217.   [5] *Ibid.*, V, 170.

[6] *L.J.*, V, 126, 217; J. Rushworth, IV, 600–1, 610–11.

[7] *C.J.*, II, 651; *L.J.*, V, 178.

They followed this with a decision to raise an army of ten thousand volunteers out of London and the neighbouring counties. At the same time, the energetic activity of the earl of Warwick, whom the Houses had named by ordinance to command the fleet, secured the navy under parliament's control.[1] Finally, on 12 July they appointed the earl of Essex as general of parliament's army, and both the peers and the members of the lower House pledged themselves 'to live and die' with Essex in the common cause.[2]

Of these actions, the one of most political importance was the creation of the committee of safety. In this body parliament established a directive organ which gradually undertook many of the functions of a government. The Houses had already made several previous experiments in filling the governmental vacuum left by the disintegration of the King's power. Both the committee of defence and the committee for the recess, formed respectively in August and September the year before, resembled regencies, and the latter, in particular, possessed an extensive competence during its brief term.[3] The committee of safety, following on similar lines, lasted until the end of 1643 and developed into the first true parliamentary executive. With a much smaller membership than the committee for the recess— fifteen compared to sixty-four—it was easier managed and better fitted to cope with the emergencies of war. Ten of the Commons and five noblemen composed it at its inception. Pym, Hampden, Fiennes, Holles, the earl of Essex, and Lord Saye were of the number.[4] The committee began its work at once. It proposed the ordinance of 6 July to recruit two thousand men in and around London for immediate despatch to Hull. It was empowered to issue arms and ammunition as it saw need. To it fell the task of nominating the chief officers of parliament's army.[5] As the war continued, its business grew until it was handling not only army administration and innumerable military problems, but also a considerable part of war finance, the coordination of local defence under Parliamentarian county committees, and even the Houses' first ventures in diplomacy.[6]

4

So did domestic war possess England. Although the King and parliament had yet to form armies, both had accepted the gage of battle

---

[1] *C.J.*, II, 650, 654, 663; *L.J.*, V, 196; *Acts and ordinances of the interregnum*, I, 12.   [2] *C.J.*, II, 668; *L.J.*, V, 206.   [3] Cf. *supra*, 248, 250.
[4] *C.J.*, II, 651; *L.J.*, V, 178. Other members were subsequently added. A full list of the committee's membership until its demise is given by L. Glow, 'The committee of safety,' *E.H.R.*, LXXX, 315 (1965), 313.
[5] *C.J.*, II, 656, 657, 660.
[6] Cf. L. Glow, *op. cit.*, for an account of the committee's history.

and unsheathed their swords. On 9 August at York, Charles proclaimed the earl of Essex and all serving under him to be rebels and traitors. Another proclamation a few days after commanded the King's loyal subjects north of Trent to repair to him in arms at Nottingham.[1] There on 22 August before a company of lords and gentlemen and about two thousand troops, Charles ordered his royal standard erected to signify that he had taken the field. At its top flew a flag with the image of the King's arms and crown and the motto, 'Give Caesar his due.'[2] Parliament, in a manifesto of its reasons for taking arms, had already declared its own altogether different sense of the issue. To the people and the political nation—'those who have sent us hither and intrusted us with all they have, Estates, Liberty, and Life, and that which is the life of their lives, their religion,'—the Houses addressed a solemn monition:

. . . if the King may force this Parliament, they may bid farewell to all Parliaments, from ever receiving good by them; and if Parliaments be lost, they are lost; their Laws are lost, as well those lately made, as in former times, all which will be cut in sunder with the same sword now drawne for the destruction of this Parliament.[3]

Despite this utterance, which was the indubitable conviction of the majority at Westminster, every step towards war made for increased tension within the Parliamentarian party. Although Pym and his confidants doubtless would have preferred peace, they had known the risks of their policy and accepted its consequences without dismay. Men of D'Ewes's sort, on the other hand, having continually reckoned on the King's submission, became timorous and queasy when the opposite happened. But if the worthy diarist longed for peace, neither he nor any other of similar mind in the House of Commons knew how to attain it or had any serious proposals to offer. Reluctantly, yet with a growing sense of inevitability, parliament in the summer of 1642 was drawn to war. All D'Ewes could do as a peace advocate was to voice his scruples and plead for delay, while privately he memorialized his disapproval of the 'fiery spirits.'

Thus, when Edmund Waller moved the House at the end of May to consider means to preserve peace, and Strode attacked the motion as to no purpose, D'Ewes supported Waller.[4] In the midst of their war

[1] *An exact collection*, 503–7, 512–13.
[2] J. Rushworth, IV, 783–4.
[3] *An exact collection*, 496, 2 August 1642.
[4] D'Ewes, Journal, B.M. Harl. 163, f. 135. Waller's motion was carried and included in the instructions given a committee for the defence of the kingdom, *C.J.*, II, 589. The result was the Nineteen Propositions, hardly a platform of accommodation!

preparations, D'Ewes warned his fellow members that the civil conflict might lead to a social revolution:

> ... *all right & propertie, all meum & tuum must cease in a civill warre & wee know not what advantage the meaner sort alsoe may take to divide the spoiles of the rich & noble amongst them, who begin alreadie to alledge, that all being of one mould ther is no reason that some should have soe much & others soe little.*[1]

Because he disliked all measures looking towards arms, he also opposed a proposition on the same occasion that called for parliament's adherents to contribute money, plate, and horses. Nevertheless, it was carried, he noted, 'by those hott earnest men ... with those who commonlie followed them.' This proposition became parliament's first financial ordinance, passed on 9 June.[2]

The next day the House began polling its own members to state what they would give. Some answered with a direct refusal, like the Wiltshire Royalist William Pleydall, who said 'hee had given his No to the propositions & soe desired to be excused.' D'Ewes when named replied that he would declare himself in due time: in his journal, however, he commented that the calling of members in such a way was against the liberty of the House of Commons. As the roll continued, Denzil Holles suggested that members who wished to contribute and conceal their names might do so. The House revealed its state of mind by rejecting this as 'verie derogatorie to the worke. ...'[3]

The size of the Commons' minority representative of a peace tendency is difficult to estimate. It included both the Parliamentarians who felt scruples about an actual war with the King, and the rapidly dwindling number of Royalists who still continued to attend the House. Perhaps the best impression of its extent is obtained from several divisions. On 11 June, for instance, a motion to impeach nine peers who had deserted Westminster for York passed by 109 to 51.[4] Another motion on the 16th directed against the House's absentee members passed by 147 to 91. Most indicative of all was a division on 9 July on the motion to raise an army. It was carried by a vote of 125 to 45. The tellers in favour were Denzil Holles and Sir John Evelyn; the tellers against were the great scholar, John Selden, a peace Parliamentarian, and Sir John Strangeways, a Royalist.[5]

[1] D'Ewes, Journal, B.M. Harl. 163, f. 154b, 8 June 1642.
[2] *Ibid.*, f. 153b; *Acts and ordinances of the interregnum,* I, 6–9.
[3] D'Ewes, Journal, B.M. Harl. 163, ff. 157a (in cipher)–175b.
[4] *C.J.,* II, 620. Edmund Waller was a teller for the negative, Holles and Oliver Cromwell told for the affirmative.
[5] *C.J.,* II, 626, 663. Selden's views appear from glimpses in D'Ewes. On 2

Whatever his reservations, it was out of the question for one of D'Ewes's convictions ever to become a Royalist. But his feet-dragging arguments caused so much irritation that they finally led to a quarrel and the most distressing incident of his parliamentary life. The episode was fully recorded by him in his journal.

On 23 July he came into the House as the members were about to vote a 'long impertinent & dangerous declaration' against the King after but a single reading. Extremely provoked at the 'uniust and violent proceeding,' he attacked the declaration vehemently, only to get into an altercation with Strode, 'a notable prophaner of the Scriptures & a man doubtless void of all truth & pietie.' Shouts for his withdrawal arose which were joined in, he noted bitterly, by 'my formerlie seeming freind Mr Nathaniel Fynes,' and Holles, 'a proud ambitious man. . . .' Although Edmund Waller tried to speak on his behalf, while others caught at his cloak to restrain him, he had to leave the chamber. He was then recalled by Speaker Lenthall and ordered to acknowledge his fault. D'Ewes did so, yet without offering any real retraction, whereupon 'that firebrand Strode' denounced his apology as insufficient. He finally got off through the intervention of Fiennes, who 'did verie noblie expresse himself . . . that I had spoken enough to satisfie the Howse. . . .'

In his private communings D'Ewes poured out his grief and resentment at his treatment by the party leaders with whom 'I had alwaies concurred . . . & oftentimes helde up ther cause ever since the beginning of the Parliament except . . . ther last four months violent preparations for a civill warre.' He wished posterity to know

that when those furious spirits in the Howse of Commons weere iritated with my freedome of expression that had for about several months . . . resisted (& often alsoe alone without being seconded by anie who weere most of them overawed . . .) ther bitter and irreverentiall language towards his Matie, & ther . . . hott preparations for a civill warre, they took this frivolous & uniust occasion to call in question what I said at this time. . . .

Concluding his account, the mortified diarist declared:

This horrible ingratitude for all my services . . . made me resolve to leave off further writing & speaking in the Howse & to come as

---

July, in a discussion of the Nineteen Propositions, he advised the House in vain against insisting on exclusive control of the militia and urged that means be found to accommodate differences with the King, D'Ewes, Journal, B.M. Harl. 163, f. 254b. It will be recalled that Selden also voted against Strafford's attainder.

seldom amongst them as I could seeing libertie of speech was taken away. . . .[1]

Fortunately, D'Ewes loved parliament too well to stick to his resolution. In the days immediately following, however, he attended less diligently, believing members were no longer free to speak their minds. An entry in his journal on 10 August, commenting on the thinness of the House, expressed his attitude at the time:

. . . the hott fierie spirits having begunn a civill warre carried all things now as they listed soe as men made no great hast to the Howse, neither did many at all assemble.[2]

If the imminence of war brought out doubts and scruples in members of the Commons, the same was no less true amongst the peers. The Parliamentarian Lord Paget, for instance, having been appointed lord lieutenant of Buckinghamshire by the Houses, was actively engaged during May in executing the militia ordinance. Then, wrote one of his deputies, he 'began to boggle, and was unfixed in his resolutions.' The publication in June of the royal commission of array made him change allegiances. A letter he sent the House of Lords *en route* to York announced his turnabout. While acknowledging his former zeal for reformation, Paget declared that he could not in conscience take arms against the King. 'I . . . am now on my Way to his Majesty, where I will throw myself down at His feet, and die a loyal Subject.'[3]

The most prominent of aristocratic vacillators was William Cecil, earl of Salisbury. The heir of a great political family which owed everything to the monarchy, Captain of the Gentlemen Pensioners at the Court, Salisbury had nonetheless joined the Court's opponents. Probably he was actuated in this by personal resentment. In 1635 the King denied him the great and profitable office of Master of the Wards, to which he held the reversion and which both his father and grandfather had occupied before him. The captaincy of the Gentlemen Pensioners was given him in compensation, but the loss must have rankled.[4] In August 1641 the House of Commons as a mark of

---

[1] D'Ewes, Journal, B.M. Harl. 163, ff. 291b–292b. The declaration to which D'Ewes excepted so strongly was parliament's statement of justification for taking arms, published 2 August, *An exact collection*, 491ff. One of his criticisms was that the declaration borrowed some of its arguments from a pamphlet, Henry Parker's *Observations upon some of his majesties late answers and expresses*, 1642.　[2] D'Ewes, Journal, B.M. Harl. 164, f. 260b.
[3] B. Whitelocke, *op. cit.*, I, 169–71; *L.J.*, V, 152.
[4] Cf. *H.M.C. Denbigh*, 8; *C.S.P.D. 1634–35*, 529–30; G. E. Aylmer, *The King's servants*, 114–17.

favour asked the King to create him Treasurer, a request which Charles, of course, refused. A little later, Salisbury was also one of the noblemen who supported the policy of the opposition leaders on the militia.[1] Thus, there was no little surprise in parliament when the earl suddenly turned up in York with the King at the end of May. A number of other lords summoned by Charles did the same, and after the Houses had vainly ordered their return to Westminster, the Commons impeached nine of them on 16 June as an example.[2] Salisbury, however, was spared this disgrace through the intercession of his Parliamentarian son-in-law, the earl of Northumberland. The latter believed the erring peer to be redeemable and began at once to try to woo him back to parliament.

As soon as Salisbury's departure became known, Northumberland wrote him in mingled reproach and persuasion:

Your Lo:ps going away in that manner was very unexpected to divers of your freinds, and I do not know how it will be possible in the way of justice to divide your Lop: from the other Lords that are faultie in the like kind; we have hitherto been very moderate in censuring this contempt, for we have only cited your Lop: and the rest to appeare against a certaine day. The opinion wch the world conceaves of this action is the greatest punishment we shall or can inflict upon your Lop: for this offence. The only way to redeeme what you have lost is . . . to returne hither again wth all convenient speede. . . .[3]

A week later, on 7 June, Northumberland wrote again. '. . . our house,' he informed Salisbury,

was more sensible of your leaving them then they were of the rest as lesse expecting it from your Lop: then from almost any of the other Lords; it were not answerable to the respect I have ever confessed unto your Lop: . . . what I conceave to be the true state of your condition, if you do not something to redeeme the good opinion of the Parl:. . . . If I can prevaile I will perswade wth some of my freinds that we may not proceede to hastely against those Lords that are gone from us, so as we may still have it in our powers to shew favor unto those that shall deserve well of the Parlament.[4]

---

[1] *L.J.*, IV, 355, 533.

[2] *L.J.*, V, 141. The impeached peers were the earls of Northampton, Devonshire, Dover, and Monmouth, and lords Howard of Charlton, Rich, Grey of Ruthyn, Coventry, and Capel. The constitutional foundation of the impeachment was that the duty imposed by the writ of summons to attend parliament took precedence over a personal letter from the King commanding attendance at York.

[3] Cecil MSS., v. 131, f. 176 (31 May).   [4] *Ibid.*, ff. 177–8.

Parliamentarians and Royalists

Obviously the Parliamentarian leaders attached the highest importance to having a good presence of eminent noblemen on their side when they were appealing to the nation for support in arms. To them it was worth overlooking Salisbury's aberration if they could obtain his further adherence. Hence, when he still remained at York, Northumberland wrote him on 14 June that 'if your Lop: will speedily returne I dare confidently say that you shall not suffer any kind of censure from our house for what is past. . . .' To reinforce these blandishments, he expatiated to Salisbury in a further letter on the excellent success of parliament's financial ordinance:

The monyes and plate are brought in faster upon our late propositions for the peace and safetie of the kingdom than the treasurers that are appointed can receave it.[1]

These baits sufficed to lure the absent nobleman from York. On 20 June Northumberland was able to inform the House of Lords that Salisbury was at his Hertfordshire residence in readiness to attend parliament. The House immediately vacated a previous order citing him as a delinquent and sent him a cordial invitation to 'come . . . and sit in his Place as a Peer. . . .'[2] The earl's vagrant escapade was at an end. It was his last. He remained a Parliamentarian, and so did his two sons, both of whom had been returned to the House of Commons in 1640 from family boroughs.[3]

One further ray, however, illumines the political calculations of men of Salisbury's sort at this juncture. It comes from a friendly letter—the last relating to the affair—sent him from York after his departure by the Royalist earl of Dorset, who begged him to work for moderation. '. . . this fatall fire once kindeled,' said Dorset,

who knowes how to quench the flames, or where . . . the conflagration may extend. I doe not apprehend yr Lshp. well tempered disposition, can bee induced to ad fewell to the fire: men only . . . of desperat fames or fortunes, cann promise themselves any ammelioration of condition, by such broken and distracted ways. Those thatt inioy such a portion of honor, and such a proportion of estate as (by Gods blessing) you doe, cannot butt really mourn the desperate face of the times. . . . Good my Lo . . . keepe the more violent spirits from passinge the Rubicon, Lett them att London put nothing in execution that may give probable

[1] *Ibid.*, ff. 179, 180.
[2] *L.J.*, V, 151.
[3] Salisbury's heir, Viscount Cranborne, sat for Hertford and his younger son, Robert Cecil, for Old Sarum, both subject to the earl's patronage; cf. M. Keeler, *The Long Parliament*, 51, 71.

ground of feare. . . . Lett many as will despayre: I am one of those, that beleeve [in] an easy and safe way to leade us all [past] this darke and inextricable labyrinth. Lett not feare prevayle above hope, nor reflect on past errors. . . . I am confident, such a beginninge is halfe way to an end. . . .[1]

Delusive hopes! England was swiftly catching fire. To put out the flames, even to contain them, was evidently beyond the power of either the partisans at Westminster or the loyal men at York. Parliament's quest for security against the King, the King's repulsion of parliament's aggression, was ending in the still greater insecurity, the still greater aggression, of a civil war. Weapons to wound and kill were to give the decision, as the sword began to write with its point a scarlet scroll unwound through years.

[1] Cecil MSS., v. 131, ff. 182–3.

Conclusion

By one of those singular correspondences that figuratively declare the passing of things, the day Charles I erected his standard at Nottingham was the same 22 August on which his victorious ancestor, Henry VII, won the crown at Bosworth field. The Spirit of the Pities and Spirits Sinister and Ironic, those phantom intelligences shaped by the poet, must have presided at such a coincidence.[1] From the war of York and Lancaster to the war of King and parliament a very long history ran. Yet in a real sense, what began in 1485 was ending in 1642. The Stuart line derived its English title by descent from Henry VII; and through the labours of the first Tudor and his dynasty, it also received a secure inheritance of the realm's subjection to monarchical authority. Charles I would have had to look back from Nottingham more than seventy years before he could descry an army of Englishmen on foot against their sovereign. The quickly vanquished northern rebellion of 1569–70 was the last of its kind.[2] Tudor order prevailed, so that at the close of Queen Elizabeth's reign the Speaker of the Commons in 1601 could eulogize the monarch for 'the happy and quiet and most sweet and comfortable peace, which, under your most happy and blessed government, we have long enjoyed. . . .'[3] But during 1640–2, a revolution liquidated the regime transmitted from the Tudors. An era of kingship expired with the war between Charles I and the Long Parliament.

What was the precipitating cause of the civil war? Despite the prevalence of religious passions at that time, it was not religion. Religion did, indeed, strongly influence the composition of the

---

[1] Cf. Thomas Hardy, *The dynasts. An epic drama of the war with Napoleon.*
[2] The Essex rebellion of 1601 may be overlooked. It was no more than a small riot in London which was immediately quashed.
[3] Cited in J. E. Neale, *Queen Elizabeth I and her parliaments 1584–1601*, 424. Cf. also Bacon's comment on the Elizabethan peace: 'One rebellion there hath been only, but such a one as was repressed within the space of seven weeks, and did not waste the realm so much as by the destruction or depopulation of one poor town,'. *Certain observations upon a libel*, 1592, *Works*, VIII, 157.

parties, but the war itself began over a political-constitutional question. To the Parliamentarians, it was that the King must give securities for what the revolution had already enacted by submitting to the Houses' advice and relinquishing to them the substance of his executive authority; and with these practical demands, embodied in the Nineteen Propositions, the Parliamentarians united a constitutional doctrine that made the Houses the supreme trustee of the commonwealth's safety, invested them with a legislative power as of right, and required the King to conduct himself as the responsible agent of the kingdom's representative body. To preserve, as they believed, popular and parliamentary liberty, the Parliamentarians arrived at the historic decision, a complete reversal of the teaching of English divines and theorists for over a century, that forcible resistance was justifiable.

To the Royalists, the question was the same, only seen from the antithetical angle. It was one of loyalty to the monarchy and the King's person, of acceptance of Charles's previous concessions as sufficient for future security, and of the necessity to withstand an invasion of royal right that subverted the kingdom's constitution and opened the door to change without foreseeable limit; and with this practical opposition to Parliamentarian demands, the Royalists united a doctrine that condemned resistance as sinful and proclaimed the law as the supreme arbiter which had given the kings of England the authority the Houses were illegally challenging.

The role of religion, as the predominant mental and emotional interest of Englishmen, was to dispose them towards one side or the other. Here Puritanism and the other varieties of dissent naturally had a powerful effect. Almost inevitably, anyone who wanted prelacy down and ceremonies abolished, or who desired the reform of liturgy and prayer book, or who cared greatly about a preaching ministry, was likely to be a Parliamentarian. Somewhat more tenuously, perhaps, one can say the same of those with a fanatic and unreasoning hatred of Catholicism, or whose devotion to a rigid, censorious moralism made them unforgiving of the frivolities of a court. On the other hand, affection for the national church as established, solicitude to keep up the bishops as a bulwark against innovation, inclined the possessors of such sentiments towards Royalism for obvious reasons. As for the minority of English Catholics of every degree and condition, they supported the King nearly universally, since only from him and his victory could they expect any lenity towards their faith.

Beyond these considerations, there was no religious issue representing the formulated views of the parties which was set forth at the commencement of the war. That the King would maintain the

authority of bishops, and at most consent to some alteration in ceremonies, was clear. That greater change than this must come from parliament was equally clear. The Houses themselves, however, had not yet adopted any model of reform. In the Grand Remonstrance, the House of Commons had promised a further reformation and declared its wish to refer for advice to a general synod of divines. In April 1642 the two Houses repeated this pledge, affirming in a joint resolution that they intended 'a due and necessary Reformation' of church government and liturgy, and 'for the better effecting thereof, speedily to have Consultation with godly and learned Divines. . . .'[1] Here the matter stood at the outset of the war. Although the nomination by the Houses of members to a national synod began promptly,[2] that body itself, which became the Westminster Assembly, did not meet until July of the following year.

2

Two general features characterized the revolution from its inception to the early part of the civil war. The first was that the revolution occurred and developed into an armed conflict not because of a class struggle, but in consequence of a revolt within the governing class against the crown. The second, resulting directly from the first, was that the revolution in its initial stages was not at war with the prevailing form of society, of which the leaders of both parties were equally the beneficiaries. In taking a final view we may consider these in turn, and notice also the factors which threatened to drive the revolution onward in a more radical direction.

We have already seen how the conflict between the Court and the Country, overshadowing the political scene in the years preceding 1640, was the polarity in which the revolution had its beginning. That conflict expressed the opposition to the royal government of a part of the governing class, and in 1640–1, far the larger part, around which a great body of favouring popular sentiment also stood. The Country's victory completed the first stage of the revolution and left its memorial in the constitutional statutes passed during the spring and summer of 1641. Then ensued the Country's disruption. Its alliance of parliamentary support broke up, a disaffection against its leaders in the House of Commons set in throughout the kingdom, and a new Royalism gradually came into existence. As the revolution moved into its second stage, the earlier opposition of the Court and the Country was superseded by that of Royalist and Parliamentarian. Under the aegis of these two parties the civil war began.

The war at its outset represented a reorientation of judgment and

[1] *C.J.*, II, 515; *L.J.*, IV, 706. [2] On 20 April 1642; *C.J.*, II, 635.

calculation within the kingdom's established elite. Naturally, each party needed and sought for mass support, but the struggle on both sides was initiated and directed by the sort of privileged persons who had previously governed the English people under the crown. No specifiable set of social or economic characteristics differentiated the leadership of one party from the other. On the contrary, Englishmen started to slay one another at the bidding or suasion of their accustomed governors; and one has to add that the Parliamentarian cause could never have possessed legitimacy in English eyes for a single moment, had it not included numerous representatives of the titular aristocracy and the gentry.

The clearest indication of the nature of the leading strata of the parties comes from the division within parliament itself. In the House of Commons the Parliamentarian members totalled about three hundred and two, the Royalists about two hundred and thirty-six; the stand of a tiny residual handful is undetermined.[1] Between these no significant contrast appeared as regarded status, wealth, or occupation. The gentry naturally dominated in the parties as they did in the House and kingdom; greater and lesser gentry, gentry of 'old' and of 'new' families, were not on different sides; the Houses' seventy-odd lawyers and fifty-odd merchants were also present substantially in both. The only observable distinctions were that the Royalists tended on average to be ten years younger than the Parliamentarian members and to originate more frequently from families with a parliamentary record.[2]

Like the Commons, the House of Lords was also divided, so that the titular aristocracy was prominent in both parties. Perhaps thirty peers became Parliamentarians, perhaps fifty to sixty became Royalists; a remaining (approximate) thirty took no part in affairs because of age, infirmity, or absence from England.[3] Although the Royalist

[1] The figures are those of Brunton and Pennington, *op. cit.*, App. I, table I. Keeler's figures (*op. cit.*, 12) are close: three hundred and ten Parliamentarians, two hundred and twenty-six Royalists.

[2] These are the conclusions of Brunton and Pennington, *op. cit.*, 19–20. The data collected by Keeler are substantially in accord. I have remained unconvinced by Christopher Hill's criticisms of Brunton's and Pennington's findings; cf. his *Puritanism and revolution*, 14–17. The number of lawyers and merchants in the House of Commons is taken from Brunton and Pennington, *op. cit.*, 5, 53, and from Keeler, *op. cit.*, 21.

[3] Exact figures are impossible. Those above come from C. H. Firth, *The House of Lords during the civil war*, 74, 115. Firth gives the total peerage in November 1640 as one hundred and twenty-four and then estimates that half were Royalist, a quarter Parliamentarian, and another quarter nonparticipant. New creations by the King in 1641, of which there were seven (cf. L. Stone, *The crisis of the aristocracy 1558–1641*, App. III), are thus not included. Also, several of the peers of 1640 were dead by 1642.

noblemen thus preponderated, there was again no pattern of socially relevant traits which they shared to the exclusion of their Parliamentarian opponents. Pre-Tudor, Tudor, and Stuart creations appeared on both sides, as did great wealth. The earl of Northumberland, a magnate whose peerage was one of the oldest and most illustrious, was a Parliamentarian. So were the earls of Pembroke, Salisbury, and Holland, all converts from the Court after 1640. On the other hand, the Royalists contained such oppositionist converts as the marquis of Hertford,[1] the earl of Southampton, and lords Paget and Spencer. If Lord Robartes, whose father bought a peerage from the profits of wool, tin, and money-lending, became a Parliamentarian, lords Craven and Campden, whose peerages also derived from commerce and money-lending in the preceding generation, became Royalists.

A nice balancing of personal interest and political-religious conviction doubtless determined the alignment of the peers. In the long run, however, the progress of the revolution brought the nobility nothing but misfortune as an order. The Royalists, going down to defeat, suffered fines, sequestration or confiscation of estates, and sometimes exile. The Parliamentarian lords, in spite of parliament's victory, saw their influence steadily decline amidst the increasing disunion and fragmentation of their party until in 1649 the new-born republic abolished the House of Lords altogether. These developments were not foreseen, of course, when the war began. At that moment the Parliamentarian noblemen were indispensable to their party. Exemplifying more than other men the currently cherished principles of aristocratic honour and pride of birth, they brought it great political prestige. Moreover, even if only a minority of the peerage, they *were* the House of Lords whilst they attended Westminster. Without their concurrence no ordinances could pass: and these ordinances were effective law in all the districts the Houses controlled. On the military side, the earl of Essex's appointment as general also helped the Parliamentarians greatly because of his personal popularity and his social distinction. Perhaps Clarendon exaggerated only a little when he later wrote that 'it had been utterly impossible for the two Houses . . . to have raised an army then if the earl of Essex had not consented to be general of that army.'[2]

The division of families and generations, of which there were numerous instances, gave further proof of the essential social identity between the upper layers of the warring parties. Lord Feilding, another convert from the Court, where all his family connections lay, became a Parliamentarian commander, to his mother's sorrow; his

---

[1] The oppositionist earl of Hertford was created a marquis in June 1640.
[2] *Rebellion*, V, 33; cf. a similar remark, *ibid.*, V, 116n.

Royalist father, the earl of Denbigh, died of wounds fighting for the King in 1643.[1] The earl of Leicester, after becoming Lord Lieutenant of Ireland in 1641, was distrusted by both parties and refused to serve parliament in executing the militia ordinance in Kent; by contrast, his son and heir, Lord Lisle, a member of the Commons, was a faithful Parliamentarian.[2] The earl of Northumberland took parliament's side, but his younger brother, the courtier Henry Percy, took the King's.[3] The earl of Peterborough raised a regiment for parliament and served under the earl of Essex as general of the ordnance. His son, succeeding to the title in 1643, was a Royalist.[4] In the Holles family, the first earl of Clare, who died before the Long Parliament, supported the Country. His older son, the second earl, though wavering somewhat between the parties, was praised by Clarendon as firmly attached to the principles of monarchy and the King's person. His younger son, Denzil Holles, was, of course, one of the foremost oppositionists and Parliamentarians in the House of Commons. Still another relation, a cousin, Gervase Holles, who also sat in the Commons, was expelled as a Royalist in August 1642.[5]

A pattern of split allegiances was seen as well in some other families with recent oppositionist traditions. Notwithstanding that the earl of Warwick was a Country peer and a zealous Parliamentarian, his son, Lord Rich, knight of the shire for Essex, joined the King's party.[6] The earl of Bedford before his death in 1641 belonged to the Country and was Pym's friend and patron. His son, the fifth earl, began as a Parliamentarian but then went over to the Royalists in 1643. A younger son, John Russell, who represented the family borough of Tavistock, also became a Royalist.[7] The M.P.s Edward

---

[1] *D.N.B.*, *s.v.*, 'Basil Feilding second Earl of Denbigh,' 'William Feilding first Earl of Denbigh.' Lord Feilding was summoned to the House of Lords in his father's lifetime. He was the duke of Buckingham's nephew and his first wife was Lord Treasurer Portland's daughter. In 1634 the King appointed him ambassador to Venice. His mother's letters of grief and remonstrance to him are printed in Cecilia Countess of Denbigh, *Royalist father and Roundhead son*, L., 1915, ch. VIII.

[2] *L.J.*, V, 227; R. W. Blencowe, *Sydney papers*, L., 1825, xxi; *D.N.B.*, *s.v.*, 'Philip Sidney third Earl of Leicester.'

[3] *D.N.B.*, *s.v.*, 'Henry Percy Lord Percy of Alnwick.'

[4] *The letter-book of John Viscount Mordaunt 1658–1660*, ed. M. Coate, *Camden society*, 3rd ser., LXIX, 1945, x.

[5] *D.N.B.*, *s.v.*, 'John Holles first Earl of Clare,' and 'John Holles second Earl of Clare'; Clarendon, *Rebellion*, VII, 153; M. Keeler, *op. cit.*, *s.v.*, 'Gervase Holles.'

[6] *D.N.B.*, *s.v.*, 'Robert Rich second Earl of Warwick.' In 1641 Lord Rich was summoned by the King to the House of Lords.

[7] *Ibid.*, *s.v.*, 'William Russell first Duke of Bedford'; M. Keeler, *op. cit.*, *s.v.*, 'William Lord Russell' and 'John Russell.' Lord Russell, M.P. for Tavistock

Phelips and Samuel Sandys, both offspring of men who had won great reputation as oppositionists in earlier Stuart parliaments, broke with family tradition to become Royalists. Sir Edward Alford, another M.P. of like political antecedents, did the same.[1]

Royal officials found themselves equally disunited by the civil war. Instead of rallying to the regime that employed them, a not inconsiderable minority became Parliamentarians. The probable reason for this lay in the character of office itself. Since offices (as we have previously stressed) tended at that period to be treated primarily as private property and only secondarily as the exercise of a public function by entrustment from the King, office-holders did not necessarily feel themselves committed to the royal party. There was, furthermore, little of a bureaucratic ethos prevailing in the crown's service; in fact, men belonging to the administrative elite were much more likely to be actuated by the range of interests and convictions that swayed the higher orders as a whole than by considerations of a purely professional nature. On the other hand, the Parliamentarian leaders, despite their condemnation of the apparatus of prerogative rule, had no quarrel with the state's machinery as such. They proposed neither to destroy nor to reconstruct it—objectives, indeed, completely foreign to the perspective of these at-bottom conservative revolutionists.

The administrative elite accordingly gave allegiance to both parties without any distinction referrable to determining social or economic criteria. Most plainly was this the case in the House of Commons where, of some forty-odd royal office-holders, seventeen became Parliamentarians and twenty-two Royalists (the few others were apparently neutrals).[2] Belonging to the former were such men as the Treasurer of the Household and former Secretary of State, Sir Henry Vane senior; his son, Sir Henry the younger, made Treasurer of the Navy in 1639 through his father's influence; Sir Benjamin Rudyard,

---

[1] M. Keeler, *op. cit., s.v.*

[2] G. E. Aylmer, *The King's servants*, Table 46. This work contains the best and fullest discussion of the political stand of officials; cf. ch. VI, 'Office and politics.' Aylmer gives the total number of officials in the Commons as forty-five. I have preferred his figures to those in M. Keeler, *op. cit.*, Table 5, which reckons the total of officials at twenty-seven, of whom about half were Royalists, ten Parliamentarians, and two neutrals. The two sets of figures are not strictly comparable, however, as they do not use identical criteria for office-holders. Keeler has also counted as Parliamentarians several officials who were supporters of the Country but died before the civil war. I have myself, with the aid of the biographies in her book, counted eighteen officials in the Commons who were Parliamentarians in the civil war.

---

until his succession to the earldom, was followed as the borough's representative by his brother, John.

Surveyor of the Court of Wards; Sir Richard Wynn, Treasurer and Receiver-General to the Queen; Sir Robert Pye, Auditor of the Exchequer; Sir Henry Mildmay, Master of the Jewel House; Sir John Trevor, Auditor of the Duchy of Lancaster; Cornelius Holland, Comptroller of the Prince of Wales's Household; and Dr. Thomas Eden, Master in Chancery.[1] Parliamentarian office-holders were scattered through most branches of the royal government. Heavily outnumbered in the Household departments, they were less so in the Exchequer and the offices under the secretaries of State, while in the Court of Wards and the Duchy of Lancaster they actually slightly exceeded the Royalists.[2]

3

What has been said of the groups mentioned thus far was true as well of the overall character of the parties as civil war engulfed the kingdom. Royalist and Parliamentarian did not correspond to a structural differentiation in English society nor were they the vehicle of contradictory class or economic interests. Both reflected, rather, the schism within the aristocratic order and the general political nation, so that 'every county,' a Parliamentarian memoirist wrote, 'had the civil war, more or less, within itself.'[3]

To be sure, Clarendon's *History of the rebellion* has been instanced as containing the opinion that the war was one of classes. He 'makes no bones,' it has been stated, 'about describing the line-up . . . as a class division.'[4] This interpretation of Clarendon's view, however, rests on a misconception. The great Royalist historian did not picture the body politic as formed of antagonistic classes, but as an ordered hierarchy of status and deference. 'Gentleman,' 'person of honour' and of 'quality'—such was the mode of social categorization that came naturally to his mind. His conception of 'interest,' being altogether conditioned by the postulates of a status order, referred to the influence and dependency at the disposal of the aristocracy. So, he wrote in characteristic fashion, the marquis of Hertford was sent by the King to raise forces in the west because there 'his interest and reputation was greater than any man's'; and with Hertford went 'the lord Seymour . . . the lord Pawlett, Hopton, Stowell . . . and some other gentlemen of the prime quality and interest in the western

[1] Cf. these men in M. Keeler, *op. cit., s.v.* and references to them also in G. E. Aylmer, *op. cit., passim.*
[2] Cf. G. E. Aylmer, *op. cit.,* Table 49, a survey of the allegiance of two hundred officials.
[3] L. Hutchinson, *Memoirs of the life of Colonel Hutchinson,* ed. C. H. Firth, 2v., L., 1885, I, 163.
[4] Christopher Hill, *Puritanism and revolution,* 204.

parts ... who were like to ... be followed by as many men, as any such number of gentlemen in England could be.'[1]

In Clarendon's eyes, the civil war was a defection from order, hence an 'apostasy,' 'confusion,' and 'rebellion,' prompted by ambition, pride, and folly.[2] He liked to represent the Parliamentarians as waging war on gentlemen—'those of quality ... loyally inclined.'[3] He spoke of the 'license of the common people ... against the nobility and gentry (under the style of *cavaliers*)'; dwelt with relish on the disloyalty of the 'great towns and corporations, where, besides the natural malignity, the factious lecturers, and emissaries from the Parliament, had poisoned the affections'; and stressed the Parliamentarianism of the Somerset clothiers, 'people of an inferior degree' who having got fortunes and estates by 'thriving arts,' were angry because not esteemed as gentlemen.[4]

In thus conveying the impression that the Parliamentarians' resistance was an outbreak of social insubordination, Clarendon was guilty of gross misrepresentation. The civil war in its beginning was no revolt of the inferior orders; and although the struggle against the King had in it both the possibility and likelihood of radicalization (a point to which we shall presently return), a development of that sort was merely in germ in 1642 and altogether opposite to the aims and purposes of the Parliamentarian party leaders.

The core of fact in Clarendon's scandalized observations was that the gentry in all probability were more strongly for the King, the inferior trading and burgher element more strongly for parliament. In this most contemporary writers tended to agree.[5] The disproportions, however, did not amount to a distinction of orders, since there were nevertheless plenty of Parliamentarian gentry of all gradations of wealth and eminence, as well as many Royalist citizens and merchants of the prosperous, magisterial type.

---

[1] Clarendon, *Rebellion*, V, 443. Cf. *ibid.*, V, 445, where we are told of the Royalist earl of Cumberland, 'a man of great honour and integrity,' who was not of an active or martial temper, so that he was unlikely 'to oblige any to be firmly ... his friends or to pursue his interests'; moreover, the earl's family fortune was diminished and he 'could not live with that lustre, nor draw so great a dependence upon him, as his ancestors had done.'

[2] *Ibid.*, I, 1, 2.

[3] *Ibid.*, V, 385.

[4] *Ibid.*, VI, 36, V, 385, VI, 5; cf. the remark about Leeds, Halifax, and Bradford, 'three very populous and rich towns, (which depending wholly upon clothiers naturally maligned the gentry)' and were thus at parliament's disposition; *ibid.*, VI, 261.

[5] Besides the remarks of Clarendon already cited, cf., e.g., *Reliquiae Baxterianae*, I, 30–1; T. May, *The history of the parliament ... which began November the third MDCXL*, L., ed. 1812, Bk. II, ch. VI; Sir P. Warwick, *Memoires*, 1701, 215–18.

In the Royalist county of Nottingham, for instance, the Parliamentarian gentry, though including a couple of distinguished families, were a small minority at the beginning of the war.[1] In Cornwall, the gentry are reckoned to have been about equally divided between the parties.[2] In Yorkshire, some two hundred and thirty-odd gentry families have been counted as Royalist, about one hundred as Parliamentarian, with still others split or changing sides.[3] In Cheshire also the gentry of Royalist persuasion outnumbered the Parliamentarians by about one-third.[4] In the eastern counties, on the other hand, the Parliamentarian gentry decidedly predominated. Suffolk was fairly typical of this great Parliamentarian region in that the principal adherents of the party belonged to landed families whose members had governed the county continuously for half a century as justices and deputy lieutenants.[5]

Not infrequently the most noticeable trait distinguishing the gentry of one party from the other was religion. There was, for example, a high proportion of Catholic gentry among the Yorkshire Royalists.[6] The like was true in Lancashire and also in Staffordshire, where apart from this, it has been said, no clear line of social status, economic interest, or family connection separated Royalist from Parliamentarian.[7] These were parts of England where Catholicisim had survived the most tenaciously in all ranks of society. By the same token, the Parliamentarianism of the eastern gentry was associated with the prevalence of Puritanism in such counties as Essex, Norfolk, Suffolk, Lincoln, and Cambridge, long the strongholds of non-conformity and dissent.[8]

As regards the citizen and trading element, while it was probably true that most of its members were strongly Parliamentarian, every town, nevertheless, had its quota of Royalist notables, and certain

---

[1] A. C. Wood, *Nottinghamshire in the civil war*, Oxford, 1937, 33–4.

[2] M. Coate, *Cornwall in the great civil war*, L., 1934, 31, 32.

[3] J. T. Cliffe, *The Yorkshire gentry on the eve of the civil war*, summary of Ph.D. thesis in *Bulletin of the Institute of Historical Research*, XXXIV, 89 (1961), 108.

[4] Cf. R. N. Dore, *The civil wars in Cheshire*, Chester, 1966, 15–16.

[5] *Suffolk and the great rebellion*, 22.

[6] J. T. Cliffe, *op. cit.*, The Catholicism of the Yorkshire gentry also appears from the lists in *Yorkshire Royalist composition papers*, ed. J. W. Clay, *Yorkshire archeological society*, XV, XVIII, XX, 1893–6.

[7] E. Broxap, *The great civil war in Lancashire*, Manchester, 1910, 3; B. Blackwood, *Social and religious aspects of the history of Lancashire 1635–1655* (Oxford B. Litt. thesis), 1956, ch. I; A. Martindale, *Life . . . by himself*, 40, for the statement that Lancashire coastal parishes were 'almost wholly papist, especially as to the gentry. . . .'; *The committee at Stafford 1643–1645*, ed. D. H. Pennington and I. A. Roots, Manchester, 1957, xvii.

[8] *Suffolk and the great rebellion*, 12, 18.

centres held out determinedly for the King. In Lancashire, for example, Manchester was Parliamentarian, but Wigan, which had opposed ship money more than any town in the county, and Preston, were Royalist.[1] Decidedly Royalist too was the city of Chester where 'many Aldermen, Sheriffs ... and common Council-men' were accused by the Houses of being 'violent Fomenters of these unnatural Wars against the Parliament. ...'[2] Newcastle was the greatest of Royalist municipalities.[3] The town corporation announced its loyalty to the King at the outset of the war, helped him with advances of money, and conferred honorary citizenship upon the Royalist commander, the earl of Newcastle. For these offences the House of Commons cited the mayor, Sir Nicholas Cole, and a number of prominent citizens as delinquents.[4] The following year the Newcastle Merchant Adventurers voted the King a loan, and the Company of Hostmen laid an impost on coal to pay the upkeep of the Royalist garrison.[5] In 1644, when the town was under siege by parliament's forces, the mayor and common council continued to proclaim their defiance of the Houses and their loyalty to the King.[6]

Of Parliamentarian cities, London was by all odds foremost, but as has been seen, it contained a good deal of Royalist sentiment in the richer and magisterial sector of the citizenry. Clarendon did not fail to boast of this, in spite of his scathing and snobbish comments on the 'factious humour which possessed most corporations, and the pride of their wealth. ...' The Parliamentarians' strength in London, he remarked, 'consisted of the rabble of the people, far the greatest part of the substantial and wealthy citizens being not of their party. ...'[7] Norwich was another Parliamentarian city that harboured a minority of Royalists in its ruling families.[8] This was also the case in Bristol where the notables of both parties possessed an identical history of office in the civic government and the Society of Merchant Venturers.[9] Bristol's first M.P.s to the Long Parliament, Humphrey Hooke and Richard Long, became Royalists. This was perhaps less remarkable than the fact that on their expulsion from the House of

[1] F. Walker, *Historical geography of southwest Lancashire*, 87–96.
[2] *Acts and ordinances of the interregnum*, I, 876; cf. R. N. Dore, *op. cit.*, 18.
[3] J. U. Nef, *The rise of the British coal industry*, II, 290.
[4] J. Brand, *op. cit.*, II, 461; *C.J.*, II, 774 (20 September 1642).
[5] *Extracts from the records of the Merchant Adventurers of Newcastle*, 133–4; *Extracts from the records of the Company of Hostmen of Newcastle*, 80.
[6] Cf. their declaration in *Reprints of rare tracts*, ed. M. A. Richardson, 4v., Newcastle, 1845–9, I.
[7] *Rebellion*, VI, 271, V, 319.
[8] F. Blomefield, *op. cit.*, III, 383–5; B. Allen, *op. cit.*, 235–6, 250–3.
[9] Cf. the biographical notices of Bristol merchants in *The deposition books of Bristol*, v. I, 1643–7, ed. H. E. Nott, *Bristol record society*, VI, 1935, App. I and P. McGrath (ed.), *op. cit.*, xxvi–xxviii.

Commons, their successors as Bristol's members, John Glanville, the recorder, and John Taylor, the mayor, were also Royalists. The two latter were disabled to sit in 1644.[1] During 1643 while Bristol was occupied by a parliamentary garrison, a number of citizens conspired unsuccessfully to open the city to the King. There were over seventy in the plot, their occupations being such as merchant, soapmaker, cutler, trunkmaker, hatter, vintner, hornmaker, plumber, carpenter, brewer, and mercer—virtually a microcosm of the urban economy.[2]

Whatever side merchants, retailers, and townsmen in general joined, it is altogether doubtful in any case that economic interest was the primary determinant of their party sympathies. The citizen element formed a municipal and provincial, not a national, *bourgeoisie*. Its members possessed neither common material interests nor any consciousness of being a class. Indeed, where commercial or economic considerations apparently influenced party attachment most, the greatest capitalists, such as the customs farmers or some of the members of the East India Company, were as likely as not to be Royalists because of their dependence on trading and financial privileges from the King.[3] A further significant, but separate, factor was the popular opposition which appeared after 1640 in certain towns to the oligarchic power of municipal governing bodies. This unquestionably engendered a disposition towards Royalism, by way of reaction, amongst the magistrates and other citizens of the urban governing class who saw a connection between the preservation of their own authority and the King's.

4

The mood and attitudes prevalent in the early period of the war clearly reflected its character as a division of the political nation and the dominant class. The conflict was unaccompanied by general enthusiasm, and even in enmity the kingdom's governors were rarely actuated by crusading passion for a reckoning. The notes of the time —of 1642–3—were persistent hope of an accommodation and reluctance to see differences carried to an extremity that would render settlement impossible. In the House of Commons sat a body of peace Parliamentarians composed of men like D'Ewes with whose sentiments Pym had to reckon while he laboured to create the machinery

[1] D. Brunton and D. H. Pennington, *op. cit.*, 61; J. Latimer, *The annals of Bristol in the seventeenth century*, 156–7.
[2] *The copy of a letter sent from Bristol*, 1643, 7–8.
[3] Cf. *supra*, 132–5; the editor of the East India Company's records has commented on the Royalism in the company and in London's merchant community, *A calendar of the court minutes of the East India Company 1640–1643*, ed. E. B. Sainsbury, Oxford, 1909, xxiv–xxv.

to sustain a war.[1] Nor was Pym himself, as a centrist leader and a master of expediencies, at all opposed to peace, provided only it could be got on secure conditions. 'Distrust,' however, as the veteran diplomat, Sir Thomas Roe, declared, was 'the great impediment.'[2]

The spectacle of violence which fellow subjects practised on each other evoked distress and sorrow. Noting the first engagement of the war, the old earl of Cork, one of the foremost victims of Strafford's Irish rule, wrote in his diary:

The 23 of October, 1642, the lamentable (and ever to be, by all treu english hearts, lamentable) battaile at Edgehill . . . was fought between the English; His sacred Maty being in person in the head of his Armye, and the earle of Essex, generall of the Army of Parliament. . . . God graunt it may be the last battaile that ever may be fought between our own nation.[3]

Although they felt themselves in the grip of fatality, partisans nevertheless sought to preserve some amity towards their opponents. Sir William Waller, parliament's commander in the west, wrote in June 1643 to his Royalist counterpart, Sir Ralph Hopton:

. . . hostility itself cannot violate my friendship to your person, but I must be true to the cause wherein I serve. . . . that great God who is the searcher of my heart, knows with what a sad sense I go upon this service and with what a perfect hatred I detest this war without an enemy. . . . We are both upon the stage and must act the parts . . . assigned us in this tragedy; let us do it in a way of honour and without personal animosities.[4]

Of like tenor were the sentiments which the Yorkshire Parliamentarian, Sir Hugh Cholmley, tendered the House of Commons:

. . . nothing can divert me from serving the Parliament with all fidelity . . . yet . . . it grieves my heart to see how these calamities increase and how I am forced to draw my sword . . . against . . . many near friends and allies some of which I know both to be well affected in religion and lovers of their liberties. And therefore I most humbly beseech the House

[1] On Pym's war leadership, cf. J. H. Hexter, *The reign of King Pym*, ch. II–III and L. Glow, 'Pym and parliament: the methods of moderation,' *Journal of modern history*, XXXVI, 4 (1964).
[2] J. Webb, *Memorials of the civil war in Herefordshire*, 2v., L., 1879, II, 357–8.
[3] *Lismore papers*, 1st ser., V, 216.
[4] *H.M.C. Duke of Somerset*, 65 (June 1643).

that they will be pleased to lay hold of all occasions that may produce an accomodation between King and Parliament. . . .[1]

Such feelings were doubtless the cause of the belief often expressed by moderates on both sides that England would suffer if either party triumphed completely. '. . . to see hys Maty come in an absolute Conqueror,' wrote the Royalist Sir Roger Twysden, '. . . I was never Cavalier enough to wish. . . .'[2] Lord Savile, another Royalist who had come over from the Country, declared that he 'would not have the King trample on the Parliament, nor the Parliament lessen him so much as to make a way for the people to rule us all.'[3] Sir Thomas Hutchinson, the Parliamentarian M.P. for Nottinghamshire, was described by his daughter-in-law as 'infinitely desirous' that differences should rather be 'composed by accomodation, than ended by conquest. . . .'[4] And according to John Hotham, who had helped to preserve Hull for the Houses,

. . . no man that hath any reasonable share in the commonwealth can desire that either side should be absolute conquerors, for it will be then as it was betwixt Caesar and Pompey, whosoever had the better the Roman liberty was to have the worse.[5]

In contrast to these opinions was the conviction of the Parliamentarian earl of Warwick that the war must be waged vigorously. He told his son-in-law, Lord Mandeville, when the latter was about to set out with Essex's army against the King in September 1642:

I am glad to hear the army is to march, I pray stand well upon your garde both military and politike, for you will never gett the like oportunity if you slip this. . . . and loose not your business with civiltys and compliment. Give the cavaliers an inch they will take an ell, doe the worke thourowly. . . .[6]

Warwick's view, however, was not the typical one, nor was Mandeville as a military commander the man to act on it; for as was to become clear two years later in his quarrel with Oliver Cromwell,

[1] *H.M.C. Portland*, I, 90 (January 1643). Cholmley, M.P. for Scarborough, became a Royalist in 1643; cf. *D.N.B.*, *s.v.*
[2] *Sir Roger Twysden's journal*, III, 151.
[3] *Camden miscellany*, VIII, 1883, 6.
[4] L. Hutchinson, *Memoirs of Colonel Hutchinson*, I, 167–8.
[5] *H.M.C. Portland*, I, 87. The two Hothams, father and son, went over to the King in 1643 and were executed for treason for attempting to betray Hull to the Royalists.
[6] P.R.O. Manchester MSS., 30/15/no. 506.

Conclusion

Mandeville adhered consistently to the belief that the civil war were better ended 'by an accomodation' than 'by the sword.'[1]

One further aspect of the early period of the war, possibly most revealing of all, was the tendency of entire districts to try to preserve neutrality and keep the conflict from their midst. The Yorkshire gentry led the way at the end of September 1642 when the principal personages of both parties in the county subscribed a treaty of pacification and non-assistance to either side. The draftsmen of the agreement were the two knights of the shire, the Parliamentarian Lord Fairfax and the Royalist Henry Belasyse. Next month the Lancashire gentry followed suit. These attempts at neutrality were immediately quashed by the Houses, which condemned the Yorkshire treaty as void of authority and as benefiting only the Royalists to the danger and prejudice of the kingdom.[2]

Despite parliament's disapproval, manifestation of neutralism persisted. The Staffordshire justices and grand jury issued a declaration decrying violence, and in Nottinghamshire the gentry of both parties engaged unsuccessfully in negotiations for a truce.[3] On 8 November at Bristol, the mayor, aldermen, and common council passed a resolution that they were all 'in love and amity one with another, and do desire a friendly association . . . in all mutual accomodation.' With this went an agreement to petition the King and parliament for a reconciliation.[4]

In December a treaty of pacification was also effected in Cheshire between the King's commissioners of array and the Houses' deputy lieutenants. It ordained a cessation of arms except 'ytt bee to resist force, broughte into this Countie,' and included a provision that the representatives of both parties should petition the King and parliament 'for puttinge an end to the great distracions and misery fallen upon this kingdom, by making a speedy peace.' The Houses repudiated the Cheshire agreement, and it was also denounced in a Parliamentarian pamphlet as giving comfort to the Royalists. 'What peace then is this?', asked the author of *Neutrality condemned*:

Unnatural peace, whilst the body of the Kingdome is in danger, so to provide for one member as totally to neglect the rest. . . . Uncharitable peace, to looke on, and not to afford your helping hand to stay the

---

[1] *D.N.B.*, *s.v.*, 'Edward Montagu second Earl of Manchester.' Mandeville succeeded to his father's earldom in November 1642.
[2] Clarendon, *Rebellion*, VI, 257–9; *The Farington papers*, ed. S. M. ffarington, *Chetham society*, XXXIX, 1856, 80–5; *L.J.*, V, 385–6.
[3] *The committee at Stafford*, xx; L. Hutchinson, *op. cit.*, I, App. VI.
[4] J. Latimer, *Annals of Bristol in the seventeenth century*, 160–1.

downfall of a tottering Kingdome, which may be the sooner ruined by your security. ...[1]

These expressions of neutralism did not proceed from an absence of political conviction or party sympathy. They testified merely to the superior strength of local attachments and, even more, to the pre-occupation of communities with keeping plunder and violence from their doors. It was the extent of such feelings that induced the King and parliament to open peace negotiations in February 1643 at Oxford. The treaty failed, however, and the war went on, nullifying all neutralist tendencies. Yet these latter still continued to break forth sporadically: in Devon and Cornwall in 1643, in Sussex in 1644, and most conspicuously of all, in 1645 in Somerset and Dorset, where the 'club-men' organized themselves in a wide movement to defend their neighbourhoods against the military depredations of both parties.[2]

5

Where, then, in this war begun and directed by the governing class did the potentialities for radicalization lie? Whence arose the pressures that afterward challenged (though unsuccessfully) the reign of inequality and privilege? What soil engendered such growths as the Leveller movement which during the later '40s strove for a democratic liberty altogether beyond the Parliamentarianism of 1642?

The answers are not far to seek. The seeds of radicalism, sown broadcast and ready to bring forth their progeny, lay in the revolution's subversion of authority and in the hopes and passions it released; in the liberal-populist element of Parliamentarian doctrine, easily susceptible of development and adaptation to purposes unthought-of by the framers of the Houses' declarations; finally, in the inflammation of multitudes as the result of the economic dislocation, the hardship and suffering, inflicted by the war.

In 1642, alongside the neutralist reactions which the quarrel evoked, there were also expressions on the Parliamentarian side of a

---

[1] T. Malbon, *Memorials of the civil war in Cheshire and Lancashire*, ed. J. Hall, *Lancashire and Cheshire record society*, XIX, 1889, 3–34; *C.J.*, II, 916–17; *L.J.*, V, 533; *Tracts relating to the civil war in Cheshire*, ed. J. Atkinson, *Chetham society*, n.s., LXV, 1909, 80.

[2] For Devon and Cornwall neutralism, cf. Clarendon, *Rebellion*, VI, 254–5 and *H.M.C. Portland*, I, 101–2; for Sussex neutralism, cf. Sir William Waller's statement, *Military memoir of Colonel John Birch*, ed. T. W. Webb, *Camden society*, n.s., VI, 1873, 217; for the club-men, cf. Clarendon, *Rebellion*, IX, 50; J. Sprigge, *Anglia rediviva*, 1647, Pt. II, ch. I, III, and H. G. Tibbutt, *The life and letters of Sir Lewis Dyve, Bedfordshire historical record society*, XXVIII, 1948, 68–9.

different spirit of keenest militancy. Welling up from the depths of Puritan faith, it invested the conflict with a burning urgency and summoned Englishmen to warfare against the wicked ungodly. It was religion, affirmed the Puritan Richard Baxter, 'that filled up the Parliaments armies, and put the Resolution and Valour into their Soldiers. . . .'[1] Many saw the crisis between King and parliament as religion's hour of decision. '. . . the vulgar mind,' said Sir Edward Dering, is 'now fond with imaginary hopes. What will the issue be, when hopes grow still on hopes? and one aime still riseth upon another . . . I cannot divine.'[2]

The note of commitment thundered from the Puritan pulpit. At St. Margaret's in Westminster, where the members of the Commons held a solemn fast service monthly, the elite of the Puritan ministry preached fortifying sermons to the congregation of England's elders.[3] In *Meroz cursed*, a discourse so celebrated that he afterwards delivered it sixty times to different auditories, the Rev. Stephen Marshall denounced the wrath of heaven on neutrals. God acknowledges no 'Neuters,' said Marshall, and

curses all them who come not out to helpe him, as well as those who come to fight against him. And our Saviour at the last day will as well denounce go ye cursed *against them. . . . In this case it is a certaine rule . . . he that is not with me, is against me.*[4]

Another preacher bid the House's members,

by the many Petitions you have had from men, by the solemne Protestations you have made to God . . . by the dependence the Protestant cause abroad hath upon you,

to stand by their holy undertaking.[5] Marshall exhorted his eminent hearers:

. . . go ye on, ye Nobles and Worthies. . . . look and presse to the work which yet remaines: Get the resolution of Zisca that brave Bohemian

---

[1] *Reliquiae Baxterianae*, I, 31.

[2] E. Dering, *A collection of speeches*, 166.

[3] The sermons preached to the House are discussed by E. Kirby, 'Sermons before the Commons 1640–42,' *American historical review*, XLIV, 3 (1939) and H. R. Trevor-Roper, 'The fast sermons of the Long Parliament,' *Essays in British history presented to Sir Keith Feiling*, ed. H. R. Trevor-Roper, L., 1964.

[4] Stephen Marshall, *Meroz cursed*, February 1642, 22–3; *D.N.B.*, *s.v.*, 'Stephen Marshall.'

[5] Thomas Hill, *The trade of truth advanced*, July 1642, 22–3.

Captain, who not only was willing to fight while he lived, but bequeathed his skin when he died, to bee made a drum head for the service of the warre.[1]

Such sermons, delivered with civil war in prospect, were incitements to the godly. They testified to the ferment of hope and ardour that agitated the 'Thundring Legions of praying Christians' amidst the dissolution of the polity.[2]

The most vivid statement of the perspectives which the war opened for the Puritan mind was the Rev. John Goodwin's *Anti-cavalierisme*. Published in October 1642, it was a plea for armed resistance to the King, its title alone indicative of the passions the war was generating. Goodwin, a London minister who was to become one of the foremost pamphleteers of the revolutionary era, addressed himself primarily to the citizens of the capital. With unmeasured rhetoric he urged a fight to the death against the 'bloody' and 'butcherly' Royalists and painted the danger to lives, liberty, and religion from the 'Cavaliers' and their papist confederates. The Parliamentarian cause, to his view, represented a heroic struggle of deliverance from long prevailing spiritual and political tyranny. Men's judgments and conscience had been abased 'by doctrines and tenents, excessively advancing the power of superiours, over inferiours, and binding Iron yokes ... upon those that were in subjection. ...' Now, however, anti-Christ's downfall was drawing near and God had revealed to his servants 'the just and full extent of the lawfull liberties of those that live in subiection.' Moreover, it was to be the Christians 'of ordinary ranke and qualitie' who would have 'the principall hand, in executing the judgements of God upon the Whore.' But the issue extended far beyond England. Bleeding Ireland, the brethren in the plantations of America, all the saints in the churches of other kingdoms, were equally concerned in the outcome. Pious men were to see the cause, Goodwin said, as

a great and solemne invitation from God himselfe unto you, to do greater things for the world, at least for the Christian world, than ever you did unto this day; or then ever you are like to do ... yea then any particular Christian State ever did, or is like to doe, while the world stands.[3]

Goodwin's exultant vision of world emancipation undoubtedly went well beyond the outlook of the mass of zealous men and women

[1] *Meroz cursed*, 52–3.
[2] Thomas Hill, *The trade of truth advanced*, Dedication.
[3] John Goodwin, *Anti-cavalierisme*, 2–3, 30–1, 49–51.

who filled the congregations of the Puritan clergy. It was strikingly symptomatic, however, of the driving energies which the war was bringing into play as an offset to neutralism. At the same time, the breakdown of the monarchical constitution was also accompanied by a political debate of unprecedented intensity. The kingdom, according to Thomas Hobbes, whose own masterpiece, *De cive*, appeared in 1642, 'was boiling hot with questions concerning the right of dominion, and the obedience due from subjects, the true forerunners of an approaching war.'[1] The press teemed with writings that probed boldly into fundamentals. Besides the declarations of the King and parliament, which themselves became subjects of controversy, a great publicistic literature dealing with politics appeared. The free-ranging discussion laid open the issues of the war to common eyes and encouraged the vulgar to weigh the claims of the parties in the scale of their own reason.

A few hints can be given about the circulation of these publications. The House of Commons took care to provide for the widest dissemination of its own declarations. It ordered in June 1642 that they should be printed in runs of nine thousand copies, sealed up in packets, and distributed throughout the counties to sheriffs, high constables, and down to the petty constables or tithing men of the hundreds. All who received packets were to give receipts and each declaration was to be publicly read to the people of the town or parish within seven days of its arrival.[2]

A speech by Sir Edward Dering which was printed in January 1642 sold over forty-five hundred copies: 'never any thing sold like that,' boasted its author.[3] Productions of the London press went by post or carrier to other parts of the realm. By this means a gentleman in distant Devonshire was able to obtain the current pamphlets from his relations in the capital.[4] A minister in Suffolk bought the London news sheets, making frequent entries from them in his diary. In August 1642 he noted that the differences between the King and parliament 'are extant in multitudes of bookes and papers (unto which God in mercy put an end!). ...'[5] Later in the '40s, the diary of a Yorkshire yeoman of Parliamentarian sympathies recorded a quite exceptional range of purchase and reading of controversial writings, both religious and political.[6] In London, pamphlets were sold not

---

[1] T. Hobbes, *De cive*, Preface to English translation, *English works*, II, xx. The English edition was published in 1651.
[2] *C.J.*, II, 609, 616.   [3] *Proceedings in Kent*, xliii.
[4] *Trevelyan papers*, ed. W. C. Trevelyan and C. E. Trevelyan, *Camden society*, CV, 1872, pt. III, 209, 216, 223.
[5] *Diary of John Rous*, 121.
[6] *Diurnall of Capt. Adam Eyre*, ed. H. J. Morehouse, *Yorkshire diaries*, *Surtees society*, LXV, 1875, 23, 24, 57.

only by the booksellers, but also by hawkers in the streets.[1] The first parliamentary ordinance to regulate printing, passed in June 1643 (against which Milton wrote *Areopagitica*, his plea for liberty of the press), mentioned the many persons that

have taken upon them to set up sundry private Printing Presses in corners, and to print, vend, publish, and disperse books, pamphlets, and papers, in such multitudes, that no industry could be sufficient to discover or bring to punish all the several abounding Delinquents.[2]

Of the political tracts of 1642, the one that attracted the greatest notice was the Parliamentarian Henry Parker's *Observations upon some of his Majesties late Answers and Expresses*. It was published in July, went through two editions, and besides provoking a swarm of Royalist replies, had the distinction of being denounced in a royal declaration as an attack upon the crown and monarchy itself.[3] According to Richard Baxter, it was the 'principal Writing' on the Houses' side and 'very much prevailed. . . .'[4] Parker's hard, audacious reasoning cut through the ambiguities and quibbles which served to muffle the assertion of sovereignty in the Houses' own manifestoes. He preferred to make out the Parliamentarian case on the basis of fundamental principles. Sovereignty rightly belongs to parliament, he held, and the King must submit his will because parliament is in essence the community itself. With this went a doctrine tracing the origin of power to the people and deriving political society from 'Pactions' and the 'common consent and agreement' of men. He also declared that 'the Charter of nature intitles all Subjects . . . to safetie by its supreame law'; and further, that 'there bee . . . tacite trusts and reservations in all publike commands, though of the most absolute nature, that can be supposed. . . .'[5]

Writing at the beginning of the civil war, Parker had no motive to consider the remoter implications of his and the Houses' principles. But could not their arguments be appropriated to other ends? If power is a trust from the people, then parliament must be as accoun-

---

[1] Cf. an order of October 1643 by the London common council to suppress the hawkers of pamphlets, Journal, 40, 78b.

[2] *Acts and ordinances of the interregnum*, I, 184.

[3] *An exact collection*, 470.

[4] *Reliquiae Baxterianae*, I, 41.

[5] Henry Parker, *Observations upon some of his majesties late answers and expresses*, 2nd ed., 1642, 34, 1–2, 4. An account of Parker's political ideas is given in J. W. Allen, *English political thought*, 426–35, W. K. Jordan, *Men of substance*, Chicago, 1944, 140–77, and M. Judson, 'Henry Parker and the theory of parliamentary sovereignty,' *Essays . . . in honor of Charles Howard McIlwain*, Cambridge, 1936.

table as the King. A Royalist critic of Parker put the plain consequence in its bearing on the electoral franchise:

*The Commons Vote in right of their electors whom they represent; at
least nine parts of the Kingdome neither doe nor may Vote in their
election ... all that have not 40.s. per annum free-hold Land, whic h
... cannot be above a tenth part. ... Tell me good Sir ... power being
(you say) nothing else but that might and vigour which a society of men
contains in it selfe, why should ... the major part, be over mastred,
and concluded by the Votes of those that are deputed by a minor
number of the people?*[1]

Just here was the point! Parliamentarian theory offered easy
ingress to demands for democratic change in the name of much the
same principles the Houses and their defenders employed against
Charles I. The startling effects of this development would discover
themselves before long. One, for instance, whom the Parliamentarian
argument persuaded was John Lilburne, religious sectarian and
recent victim of Archbishop Laud's repression. In 1642 Lilburne,
according to his own account, was convinced by the reasonings in the
Houses' declarations and writings such as Parker's *Observations* to
take up arms 'in judgment and conscience against the King. . . .'[2] He
was presently to become, by a more extended application of these
same reasonings aided by an admixture of other ideas, the organizer-
in-chief of the Leveller movement and an irrepressible agitator for
political justice against parliament itself.

The emergence of a party of radical opposition from among the
Parliamentarian rank and file was only possible, however, because of
the mass hardship of these years of unsettlement. The civil war
began amidst slump and stagnation. Political breakdown destroyed
confidence and did severe injury to trade. A pamphleteer wrote in
1641 that 'the decay of trade is in everybody's mouth from the sheep-
shearer to the merchant, and even a weak statist, without Galileo's
prospective glass, may see both our wealth and safety therewith
declining.'[3] The textile industry plunged into another depression, after
only barely recovering from the prolonged slump of the '20s. From
many parts came the clothiers' threnody that they could find no vent
for their cloth, that stocks lay dead on their hands. Widespread

---

[1] Sir John Spelman, *A view of a printed book*, 1643, cited in *Complete prose
works of John Milton*, v. II, ed. E. Sirluck, New Haven, 1964, 28–9.
[2] John Lilburne, *The legall fundamentall liberties of the people of England*,
1649, 22–3. Lilburne quoted Parker's *Observations* copiously in *Innocency
and truth justified*, 1646.
[3] Cited in B.E. Supple, *op. cit.*, 129.

unemployment set in. A description of the Essex industry in 1642 spoke of the 'poor men, artificers, as weavers, combers and the like, appertaining to the trade of clothworking ... brought (many of them) to beg their bread, and the rest to live upon the parish charge.'[1]

Hard conditions lasted through the whole of the '40s. Money was scarce, credit difficult to obtain. Excise and other taxes created heavy burdens. The necessities of life reached prices beyond living memory. '. . . things are at that rate,' an Essex clergyman noted in the fall of 1647, 'as never was in our dayes. . . .' And a few months later: 'This time was a sad deare time for poore people, onely their worke beyond expectacion continued plentiful and cheape. . . .'[2] Impoverished tenants were unable to pay their rents. A pamphleteer at the end of the '40s thus described the plight of poor tenants on northern estates:

I have seen multitudes of poor people go bare-footed and bare-legged and scarce a ragge of clothes to cover their nakednesse, or having any bread, or any kind of food to put into their bellies, to keep them from starving. And ask the poor people, whose land they lived in? or who was their Landlord? they would tell us, that it was either the Earl of Northumberland or the Lord Grey. . . .'[3]

The war, too, caused great destruction of property, while plunder and free-quarter added to the widespread misery.[4]

There was no novelty, of course, in poverty and bad times. What *was* in the highest degree novel was the formation of a popular movement that appealed to the victims of the time's oppressions and organized them for independent political action. This was the significance of the Leveller party. The backbone of the party were the small and middle sort of people: shopkeepers, craftsmen, a scattering of agricultural freeholders and tenants, religious sectarians, soldiers of parliament's army, sufferers from excise, monopolies, and debt. They belonged mainly to the inferior strata whose conditions of life had been severely depressed by the war. Already imbued with Parliamentarian doctrines, they responded readily to the agitation of the Levellers. And the party's leaders, taking up their miscellaneous grievances, incorporated them into a programme demanding

[1] *Ibid.*, 12.

[2] *The diary of the Rev. Ralph Josselin 1616–1683*, ed. E. Hockliffe, *Camden society*, 3rd ser., XV, 1908, 45, 46.

[3] Francis Freeman, *Light vanquishing darkness*, 1650, 55–6.

[4] Cf. the account of the depressed conditions of the 1640s in B. Supple, *op. cit.*, 125–31; W. R. Scott, *op. cit.*, I, ch. XII; E. Lipson, *The economic history of England*, III, 315–17; and M. James, *Social problems and policy during the Puritan revolution*, L., 1930, ch. II.

Conclusion

redress through far-reaching political and economic reform. Thus it came about for the first time that a large number of Englishmen strove for a democratic polity and began to talk of natural rights, the liberty of the people, and the establishment of the powers and limits of government by the consent of the governed.

These radical principles pervaded the air of the later '40s. They were asserted against the rich, against privilege and inequality, against parliament itself. '. . . who are the oppressors, but the Nobility and Gentry,' said a Leveller writer, 'and who are the oppressed, is not the Yeoman, the Farmer, the Tradesman, the Labourer . . . ?'[1] When the small masters of the Weavers Company contended for their rights in the gild, they based their case on the natural equality of men and the creation of 'jurisdictive power . . . by a compact and agreement. . . .'[2] More momentous still was the Levellers' call for a parliament chosen by democratic suffrage, a position which one of its advocates justified in permanently memorable words:

. . . I think that the poorest he that is in England hath a life to live, as the greatest he; and therefore . . . I think it's clear, that every man that is to live under a government ought first by his own consent to put himself under that government; and I do think that the poorest man in England is not at all bound in a strict sense to that government that he hath not had a voice to put himself under. . . .[3]

All this is another story, beyond the scope of the present work. But it serves to illustrate the continuity of political development over the 1640s and to show how Leveller democracy and popular opposition to entrenched privilege grew directly from the earlier stages of England's revolution.

[1] Laurence Clarkson, *A general charge*, 1647, 11.
[2] Cf. G. Unwin, *Industrial organization in the sixteenth and seventeenth centuries*, Oxford, 1904, 205.
[3] Col. Rainsborough's words in October 1647 at the Putney debates; cf. A. S. P. Woodhouse, *Puritanism and liberty*, L., 1938, 53.

Index

Index

Petty, Sir William, 24
Phelips, Edward, 335
Phelips, Sir Edward, 79, 82, 86, 87
Philip IV, 1, 4
Pindar, Sir Paul, 133, 135
Pleydall, William, 323
Ponet, John, 195
Portugal, 1, 2
Prerogative, doctrine of, 84–5
Press (*see also* Newspapers)
  secret printing, 193; freedom, 203–6; pamphlet circulation, 347–8
Preston, 339
Preston, John, 63, 65, 66, 174, 176
Protest of twelve bishops, 277
Protestation, 223
Providence Island Company, 101, 103
Prynne, William, 192, 193, 194, 226
Public opinion
  1620s, 106–8; 1641–2, 203–6, 228–9, 258, 347
Puritanism
  and Elizabethan parliaments, 76–7; in the peerage, 93–6; term 'brother', 107; and London oppositionists, 141–3; Newcastle, 150; Norwich, 153–4; definition, 157–8; and separatism, 158–9; evolution of, 159–63; ministers retain hold in the church, 163–70; laity in the governing class, 101, 170–181; ecclesiastical patronage, 177–81; laity in the inferior order, 181–5; and social structure, 185–7; conflict with Arminianism, 188–92; and the Country, 191–2; repression of, 192–5; and right of resistance, 195–7; and church reform 1641–2, 226–41; and civil war, 330, 345–7
Pye, Sir Robert, 210, 266, 336
Pym, John
  and political terminology, 39; enters parliament, 80; and

1628 parliament, 82; and fundamental law, 83–4; and privilege of parliament, 86; and earl of Bedford, 95; holds office, 97; and Buckingham's impeachment, 98; and elections to the Long Parliament, 100; and Providence Island Company, 101, 103; and Puritanism, 102; and Scottish Rebellion, 104–5; leader of Long Parliament, 200–1, 202; committee against Strafford, 203; speech on grievances, 207; and Sir Henry Vane junior, 208–9; and office, 214, 215, 216, 272; and army plot, 219; and Strafford's trial, 220–1; policy on church reform, 237, 238, 239, 241; distrusts King, 247, 248; committee for the recess, 250; 251, demands parliamentary control of councillors, 259–60; and Grand Remonstrance, 262–3, 263, 269, 270–1; accused of treason, 278; appeals for peers' cooperation, 298; and Parliamentarian party, 306–7, 316, 341; committee of safety, 321

Rainton, Nicholas, 140, 290
Ranke, L. von, 5
Rebellion (*see also* Revolution), 13, 15, 111, 115–16, 187, 329
Representation, idea of, 86–7
Resistance, right of, 111–12, 144–5, 195–7
Revolution
  mid-seventeenth century, 1, 2–5; American, 5; English, 5–8, 13, 331; 'great revolutions of the West', 5; French, 5, 9, 11–13; Marx on, 7–8, 11–12; 'bourgeois', 7–8, 120; concept and terminology, 10–18; Russian, 6,

363

Perez Zagorin

Perez Zagorin, Professor of History at the University
of Rochester, was born in Chicago in 1920. He was
previously Professor of History at McGill University,
and he has lectured at Oxford, Manchester, the University of Toronto, the University of Pittsburgh, and
Johns Hopkins. A leading historian of English sixteenth-
and seventeenth-century history and of the early modern period in the United States, Professor Zagorin is
the author of *A History of Political Thought in the
English Revolution* (1954).

DATE DUE

ABOUT THE AUTHOR

JOHN MUELLER is Professor of Political Science at the University of Rochester. His previous books include *War, Presidents, and Public Opinion, Retreat from Doomsday: The Obsolescence of Major War,* and *Quiet Cataclysm: Reflections on the Recent Transformation of World Politics.* He is a regular contributor to numerous academic journals and has written editorial page columns in the *New York Times,* the *Wall Street Journal,* and the *Los Angeles Times.* Outside the field of political science, Mueller has written the prize-winning *Astaire Dancing: The Musical Films* (Knopf) and cowritten *A Foggy Day,* a musical presented at the Shaw Festival in Ontario.